Deviant Behavior

A TEXT-READER IN
THE SOCIOLOGY OF DEVIANCE

FIFTH EDITION

Delos H. Kelly

CALIFORNIA STATE UNIVERSITY, LOS ANGELES

ST. MARTIN'S PRESS
NEW YORK

To Jane, Brett Alan, Erin Lynn, and Alison Michele

Editor: Sabra Scribner
Manager, publishing services: Emily Berleth
Project editor, publishing services: Kalea Chapman
Project management: Taylor Fawns, Publication Services
Production supervisor: Joe Ford
Art director: Lucy Krikorian
Cover design: Rod Hernandez
Cover art: Ed Butler

Library of Congress Catalog Card Number: 94-74758

Manufactured in the United States of America.
09876
fedcba

For information, write:
St. Martin's Press, Inc.
175 Fifth Avenue
New York, NY 10010

ISBN: 0-312-11941-0

ACKNOWLEDGMENTS

Acknowledgments and copyrights are continued at the back of the book on pages 659–660, which constitute an extension of the copyright page.

It is a violation of the law to reproduce these selections by any means whatsoever without the written permission of the copyright holder.

Jack P. Gibbs, "Conceptions of Deviant Behavior: The Old and the New," *Pacific Sociological Review*, pp. 9–11 (Spring, 1966). Reprinted by permission of JAI Press.

Howard S. Becker, "Moral Entrepreneurs: The Creation and Enforcement of Deviant Categories," reprinted by permission of The Free Press, a Division of Simon & Schuster. From *Outsiders*, by Howard S. Becker. Copyright © 1963 by The Free Press.

Steven Spitzer, "The Production of Deviance in Capitalist Society," Copyright © 1975 by the Society for the Study of Social Problems. Reprinted from Social Problems, vol. 22, no. 5, June 1975, pp. 641–646, by permission of the University of California Press Journals.

Peter Conrad, "The Discovery of Hyperkinesis: Notes on the Medicalization of Deviant Behavior," Copyright © 1975 by the Society for the Study of Social Problems. Reprinted from *Social Problems*, vol. 23, no. 1, October 1975, pp. 12–21, by permission of the University of California Press Journals.

Emile Durkheim, "The Normal and the Pathological," reprinted by permission of The Free Press, a Division of Macmillan, Inc. From *The Rules of Sociological Method*, by Emile Durkheim, translated by Sarah A. Solvey and John H. Mueller. Edited by George E. G. Catlin. Copyright © 1938 by George E. G. Catlin; copyright renewed 1966 by Sarah A. Solvey, John H. Mueller, and George E. G. Catlin.

Kai T. Erikson, "On the Sociology of Deviance," reprinted with the permission of Simon & Schuster from the Macmillan College Division title *Wayward Puritans*, by Kai T. Erikson. Copyright © 1966 by Macmillan Publishing Company.

Thorsten Sellin, "The Conflict of Conduct Norms," reprinted from *Culture Conflict and Crime*, a report of the Subcommittee on Delinquency of the Committee on Personality and Culture, *Social Science Research Council Bulletin 41* (New York, 1938).

Contents

Part 3 / Becoming Deviant   215

Part 4 / The Production of Institutional Careers and Identities   297

Entering and Learning Deviant Cultures and Practices:
The Building of Deviant Careers and Identities

Deviant Careers and Identities:
Some Additional Forms and Shapes—Peers,
Gangs, and Organizations

Managing Deviant Careers and Identities

Part 6 / Changing Deviance   585

Introduction
Deviant Conceptions and Categories
and Their Transformation

*Deviant Actors:
Attempts at Exiting and Recovery*

Deviant Organizations, Decision Makers, and Structures

Preface

Some anthologies dealing with the subject of deviance emphasize the ways in which society responds to deviant behavior. Others, by examining why certain individuals violate the social norm, focus on the motivational element. A few trace the evolution of deviant categories. *Deviant Behavior* has been designed to integrate and balance these concerns in a single volume—to explore, through carefully selected readings, the ramifications of deviance for the individual (the *actor*) and for society.

Part 1 considers the ways society defines deviance and the deviant. Of particular interest is the role that specific individuals—especially those who hold political power or who serve as enforcers of the law—play in the labeling of actors and acts as deviant. It will become clear to the reader that no individual and no behavior is inherently deviant; it is society's perception of an actor or an act as deviant that affixes the label. Deviance, in other words, is in the eye of the beholder.

Why does socially prohibited behavior occur—and persist—despite society's efforts to eliminate or discourage it? How can we make sense of deviance? Sociologists approach these questions from a number of different theoretical perspectives. Part 2 presents readings by major theorists representing the most important of these perspectives. The introduction to the section furnishes students with the theoretical framework upon which to build an understanding and an appreciation of these key thinkers. This section contains several empirical pieces that underscore the important relationship that must exist between theory and deviance research. The writings also illustrate how researchers go about their work.

Part 3 follows the beginning *career* of the social deviant in a private domain; it traces the steps by which he or she becomes identified by society as a deviant. It depicts, for example, how a relative attempts to cope with increasingly bizarre or violent behavior of a family member. Frequently, attempts to manage or control the deviant at home fail, and the family turns to institutions and agencies of social control for help.

Once deviants have been institutionalized, their career is determined, to a great extent, by their experiences within the institution. Part 4 explores the workings of several people-processing and people-changing facilities—ranging from the courts to the mental hospital—to examine how such structures deal with clients and how clients, in turn, may adapt their behavior and their personal identities to their surroundings.

For certain types of deviance, institutional controls are far less significant than the traditions and norms of deviant subcultures. Part 5 examines the ways in which such structures shape the career of the male prostitute, the drug dealer, the female prostitute, and others.

Part 6 analyzes the processes by which deviant categories, actors, and structures can be altered or transformed. The first selection offers contemporary accounts of how selected deviant conceptions and categories have undergone significant changes. Clearly, if the underlying content of the prevailing images changes, then so, too, must the picture of deviance change. Thus activities that may have been seen as "deviant" at one time may now be perceived as "acceptable" or even "normal" by various audiences. The next two readings describe various personal and institutional barriers that confront those who desire to move from a deviant to a nondeviant status—in particular, society's reluctance to accept as "normal" anyone who has borne the stigma of deviance. The remaining piece outlines specific ways in which deviant organizations, decision makers, and structures could be controlled, sanctioned, or even rehabilitated.

Overall, then, this book explores the establishment and maintenance of deviant categories; the motivations behind deviant behavior; the identification as deviant of individuals and of particular segments of society, by formal and informal means; the effects of institutionalization upon the deviant; and the efforts of deviants to eradicate the label society has placed upon them. Analysis is also given to the ways in which deviant categories and structures can be altered.

I would like to thank many people for their help in preparing the fifth edition of this book, particularly my editors, Sabra Scribner and Elizabeth Bast. Decisions about adding and deleting material from edition to edition are always made with apprehension. It is difficult to presume to make the right choices for both the people you hope will give your book a fresh examination and the people who have been loyal and contented users of previous editions. Suggestions from the following individuals helped make my deliberations considerably easier: Tammy Anderson, Central Michigan University; Douglas Degher, Northern Arizona University; Julia Hall, Drexel University; Jack D. Harris, Hobart and William Smith Colleges; Joseph Harry, Northern Illinois University; Christopher Hunter, Grinnell College; Neil King, University of California—Santa Barbara; Joanne Nagel, University of Kansas; Susan Silbey, Wellesley College; and Joseph Tropea, George Washington University.

Delos H. Kelly

Deviant Behavior

A TEXT-READER IN
THE SOCIOLOGY OF DEVIANCE

FIFTH EDITION

General Introduction

We all carry in our minds images of deviance and the deviant. To some, deviants are murderers and rapists. Others would include in the list prostitutes, child molesters, wife beaters, and homosexuals. With regard to the motivations behind deviant behavior, some of us would place the blame on the family, while others would emphasize genetic or social factors, especially poverty.

CREATING DEVIANCE

Regardless of what kinds of behavior we consider deviant or what factors we believe cause deviance, we must recognize that deviance *and* the deviant emerge out of a continuous process of interaction among people. For deviance to become a public fact, however, several conditions need to be satisfied: (1) some deviant category (e.g., mores and laws) must exist; (2) a person must be viewed as violating the category; and (3) someone must attempt to enforce this violation of the category. If the individuals demanding enforcement are successful in their efforts to label the violator, the social deviant has been created.

The Creation of Deviant Categories

As far as deviant categories are concerned, relatively little attention has been focused on their evolution. Formal and informal codes of conduct are generally accepted as "givens," and investigators concentrate on the examination of *why* the categories are violated and *how* they are enforced. An approach of this kind is inadequate, however, particularly in view of the fact that new categories are continually evolving and old ones are being modified. Obviously, as the definitions or categories of deviance change, the picture of deviance must also be altered. The changing content of the laws governing cocaine provides an example. If there are no penalties for possessing and using cocaine, one cannot be formally charged and processed for doing so.

In studying deviance, then, a central question needs to be raised: How (and why) do *acts* become defined as deviant?[1] Providing answers to this question requires an examination of how deviance is defined, how the definitions are maintained, and how violators of the definitions are processed and treated. This entails a historical and ongoing analysis of those legislative and political processes that affect the evolution, modification, and

1

enforcement of deviant categories. Central focus must be placed on those who possess the power and resources not only to define deviance but also to apply a label of deviance to a violator and to make the label stick. These processes are highlighted in Part 1 and will be evident in the discussion of the "radical-conflict theory" in Part 2.

Reactions to Violators of Deviant Categories

In terms of the *actor*, an equally important question can be asked: How (and why) do violators of various types of deviant categories (mores, laws, and regulations) become labeled as deviant? Answering this question requires an examination of the interaction occurring between an *actor* and an *audience*. A simple paradigm (Figure 1) can illustrate how the deviant is reacted to and thus socially created. This paradigm can be applied to most of the selections in this volume.

The Interactional Paradigm: A young man (the social *actor*) is seen selling or snorting cocaine (the *act*, a violation of a deviant category) by a police officer (a social *audience*, an enforcer of the deviant category) and is arrested. The youth's deviation thus becomes a matter of public record, and a deviant career is initiated—a career that may be solidified and perpetuated by legal and institutional processing. Another officer, however, might ignore the offense. In the first case, then, the violator is initially labeled as a "deviant," whereas in the second he is not. Figure 1 indicates that audience response not only is critical, but depends on several factors. The example also helps to underscore the fact that there is nothing inherently deviant about any act or actor—their meanings are derived from the interpretations *others* place on them. Hence the notion is put forth that "deviance lies in the eyes of the beholder." This example can be extended by considering the fourth element of the paradigm: *third parties*, or witnesses. Specifically, a young man may be observed selling or snorting cocaine by a peer, and the peer may choose to ignore the offense. Another peer, however, may not only

Figure 1 / Interactional Paradigm

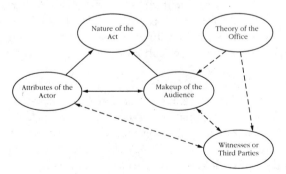

consider the act illegal or deviant but may decide to do something about it. The peer lacks the power to arrest; he can, however, bring in third parties in an effort to create a shared attitude toward the cocaine user—namely, that is he a "criminal" or "deviant." The peer may turn to other peers, and they may decide to call the police and have the user arrested. If this happens, the person's "deviance" becomes a public fact.

Thus, the label "deviant" is a status conferred on a person by an observer or observers. Although an understanding of this process requires an examination of the way the four basic elements of the paradigm interact with one another, such an examination is not sufficient. An awareness of the *theory of the office* that a particular agent or audience operates out of is also necessary, especially if the occupant of the office is an agent of social control. The preceding example, as well as the "organizational paradigm" highlighted in Figure 2, can be used to illustrate this requirement. This paradigm represents a refinement of the "interactional paradigm" described in Figure 1. Here I am focusing on the audience, particularly in terms of how an institution expects certain outcomes on the part of its agents. This paradigm will be generally applied throughout this volume.

The Organizational Paradigm: Although it might be assumed that the police officer in our examples operates on the basis of his or her own initiative, this is frequently far from the truth. The officer, like any institutional or bureaucratic agent concerned with the processing (through the courts) or rehabilitating (in correctional facilities) of clients, is guided and generally constrained by a theory of the office, or "working ideology." The officer, through informal (contacts with other officers) and formal (police academies) socialization experiences, learns how to identify and classify deviants or suspected deviants. These institutional, or "diagnostic," stereotypes (Scheff, 1966) constitute a basic ingredient of a department's official perspective. The officer, for example, learns how to recognize the "typical"

Figure 2 / Organizational Paradigm

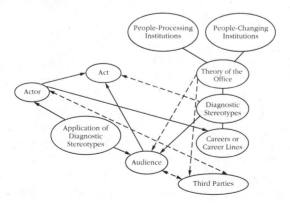

case of child molestation, runaway, or rape. These "normal crimes" (Sudnow, 1965), or "social type designations," not only help the officer make sense out of events; they also provide criteria upon which a suspect can be initially identified, classified, and then selected out to play the role of the deviant.

An institution's stereotypes are basic to the *rate production process*—the creation of a body of institutional statistics. If, for example, a police chief feels that homosexual behavior is morally wrong or criminal, not only will this one individual's conception become embedded within the theory of the office, but the officers will be required to zero in on such activity. This response will produce a set of crime statistics exhibiting an unusually high arrest rate for homosexual exchanges. Similarly, if a police chief formally or informally communicates to his department personnel that African-Americans, Hispanics, Native Americans, and other minorities constitute the "real" deviants, delinquents, and criminals, such people will be disproportionately selected out to play the role of the deviant—that is, they will become more vulnerable to institutional processing. This, too, will produce a set of statistics reflecting a heavy concentration of these individuals. The statistics can, in turn, serve as justification for heavy and continued surveillance in areas containing such groups. Examples of this phenomenon abound.

If we are to approach an understanding of what causes deviance, and particularly of the ways in which institutional careers arise and are perpetuated, then we need initially to analyze and dissect the existing structure of the institutions of social control. To obtain an understanding of how institutions operate requires, as suggested by Figure 2, sensitization to several basic organizational elements and processes: (1) the institution's theory of the office, (2) the content of the institutional stereotypes embedded within the theory of the office and used to identify clients for typing and processing, (3) the existing careers or career lines (and associated role expectations) into which the identified clients are placed, (4) the socialization of institutional agents and their application of diagnostic stereotypes to clients, and (5) the effects of institutional typing and processing, from the perspectives of both the client and the institution.

UNDERSTANDING DEVIANCE

In the discussion of the creation of deviance it was argued that some deviant category must exist, a person must be viewed as violating the category, and someone must make a demand for enforcement. Thus far, too, the focus has been upon the evolution and change of deviant categories, as well as on the interactional aspects—how and why violators of categories may be reacted to. Missing from this analysis, however, is a concern for the motivational aspects—the reasons why people may violate deviant categories.

This concern has been generally ignored by the labeling or interactionist proponents. Their main interest revolves around examining audience reactions and the impact of those reactions on people. Implicit in such a stand is the idea that the reasons for behavior are relatively unimportant. If, however, we are to approach a more complete understanding of deviance from a dynamic perspective, attention must also be given to motivation. Such a view provides us with an opportunity continually to analyze how behavior and labels interact with each other.

Violations of Deviant Categories

Traditionally, writers have concentrated on trying to explain why people may violate various types of deviant categories. Some have spent their time trying to explain group or structural rates of deviance, and others have concentrated on those processes by which individuals learn culture and traditions. These efforts have produced many schools of thought, each with its own set of assumptions. The "anomie" theorists, for example, argue that blocked opportunity can produce a tendency or strain toward deviation. The "conflict" theorists, by contrast, contend that the powerless may consciously violate the laws formulated by the powerful. Understanding deviance, then, requires that we investigate those reasons why people may violate deviant categories and by their violations bring upon themselves a particular labeling. The selections in Part 2 offer some representative attempts to explore this question.

BECOMING DEVIANT

With regard to the process of becoming deviant, an initial distinction can be made between *private* and *public* settings. A husband may violate a particular set of expectations by acting strangely. The wife may try to make sense out of such behavior by rationalizing it away or neutralizing it. She may argue to herself and others that her husband has experienced some personal setbacks and that the peculiar behavior will pass. At this stage the wife is trying to develop a counterdefinition of the situation, and she is also refusing to impute a deviant label to her spouse. The husband's behavior may grow increasingly violent, though, to the point where the wife finds it necessary to bring in agents of social control. She may call the police (third parties) or ultimately have her husband committed to a mental institution. If this should happen, not only have the wife's tolerance limits been exceeded but her attempts at various strategies of *accommodation* (e.g., neutralization or rationalization) have failed. The husband may then be typed as, for example, a schizophrenic and processed in accordance with the establishment's expectations of what the schizophrenic career should entail. The patient is expected, thereafter, to live up to his institutional role—to accept the label and act accordingly. The case of McMurphy in *One Flew Over the Cuckoo's Nest* (Kesey, 1962) describes what may happen when a patient protests against his assigned label. Because McMurphy rejects the "sick role," he becomes embroiled in a running battle with Big Nurse, the institution's agent. In our example, a similar situation may evolve with respect to the husband's response: he may repudiate the institutional tag, he may try to ignore it, or he may accept it. His response, like the responses of observers, is frequently difficult to predict.

In private settings, attempts may be made to regulate and control behavior, and these efforts may be successful. However, once third parties or social-control agents (e.g., the police or psychiatrists) are called in, the individual is frequently on his or her way to becoming an institutional deviant—that is, the organizational paradigm becomes operative, not only from the institution's viewpoint but from the actor's perspective. In particular, if a mental institution is involved, the client becomes viewed as a "mental patient"; this label becomes the patient's *master status* (Becker, 1963), and people will then often react to the person on the basis of the label rather than regarding him or her as sane or "normal." The changing of one's status, or the *status degradation ceremony* (Garfinkel, 1956), also affects the views others have of the "deviant" (one's public identity), as well as how the actor views himself or herself (one's personal identity). The change frequently affects the person's self-esteem (how one views self, positively or negatively, relative to others on selected criteria).

INSTITUTIONAL AND NONINSTITUTIONAL CAREERS

An important distinction should be made between *institutional* and *noninstitutional* careers. A noninstitutional career is one that a person pursues primarily as a matter of choice. The individual takes an active role in structuring and presenting a specific image of self to others. The bookie, gambler, con artist, nudist, skid row alcoholic, and homosexual provide examples. Such individuals generally progress through some semblance of a career: once they gain entry or exposure, they begin to learn the existing culture and traditions. The bookie, for instance, may start out as a runner, "learn the ropes," and then move into other phases of the bookmaking operation. Similarly, the skid row alcoholic who wants to become an accepted member of the "bottle-gang culture" will become familiar with the norms prevalent among the skid row inhabitants, particularly norms that relate to the procurement and consumption of alcohol. Violations of the normative code frequently cause a person to be excluded from the group (Rubington, 1973). As with the sanctioning of "deviants" by "nondeviants," the "labeled deviants" have ways of punishing those who deviate from their own code.

Institutional careers, by contrast, involve those in which the individual plays a relatively passive role. Here, the career is initiated and perpetuated by some socializing or social-control institution; this process was briefly noted in the discussion of how one becomes deviant. The careers of the "school misfit," mental patient, delinquent, and criminal are of this type. The major difference between institutional careers and noninstitutional careers concerns the role of the actor, particularly in the matter of choice and in the means of gaining entry. Once the institutional career begins, though, the mental patient, like the skid row alcoholic, is expected to learn and act in accordance with the existing subculture and its traditions.

Institutional and noninstitutional careers are not mutually exclusive. Frequently, a degree of overlap exists between the two. The skid row alcoholic, for example, may be arrested and sent to an alcoholic ward, where his or her behavior becomes subject to institutional or bureaucratic control. Similarly, the prostitute may be arrested and taken to jail. In both instances the activities become a matter of institutional knowledge and record. A secret homosexual, by contrast, may never directly experience the effects of institutional processing.

The Effects of Institutional and Noninstitutional Careers

The distinction between institutional and noninstitutional careers provides a backdrop against which a person's reactions can be assessed. How, for example, is a person likely to respond to institutional typing and processing as a deviant? Will he or she reject or accept the institutional label? Answering these questions requires a consideration of how the "status degradation ceremony" affects an actor's personal and public identity. If the deviant rejects the label, a discrepancy (or *identity crisis*) occurs between one's personal and public identities—that is, between one's view of self as normal and the institution's view of one as a deviant. Obviously, unless some personal gain can be realized, such as the enhancement of one's prestige or status in the eyes of others, most persons will reject a deviant label imputed to them. Maintaining an image of self that is at odds with the institution's image is not without its costs, though, and eventually the individual may come to accept the label and bring his or her behavior into line with institutional expectations. Lemert (1951) argues that *acceptance of the label* is a critical step on the way to secondary or *career* deviance. Not only do some individuals change their view of self—for instance, from that of "normal" to that of "schizophrenic"—but they often change their mode of dress, mannerisms, and circle of acquaintances. Acceptance of the label, it should be noted, is an important precondition to being certified as "sane" or "rehabilitated" by institutions.

Involvement in noninstitutional careers or activities affects both the participants and other members of society. The covert gay or lesbian teacher, for example, engages in sexual activity that some would consider deviant, and a discrepancy may evolve between her personal and public identities. Privately she may view herself as gay and a normal female, but publicly she is viewed and responded to as a heterosexual teacher. As with the institutional deviant, however, an identity crisis may arise. She may decide to "come out" and admit her sexual preference to others. Such a strategy is not without its costs. She may be ostracized by her family, friends, and acquaintances; and, more than likely, she will be either discriminated against on her job or perhaps fired. In view of these possibilities, she may decide to keep her sexual preference hidden and become involved in a gay subculture. Such involvement can provide her with a degree of social support, as well as appropriate rationalizations to legitimize her way of life. Still, she (and other noninstitutional deviants) is aware not only that she is engaging in potentially discrediting behavior but also that she must operate in a society in which many hostile elements remain.

CHANGING DEVIANCE

Identity problems do not cease when one leaves an institution or decides to "go straight." Public or known ex-deviants, whether of the institutional or noninstitutional variety, continue to be viewed as deviants. What Simmons (1969) calls a "lingering of traces" quite frequently occurs, especially among those who carry an institutionally bestowed label. Institutions, it has been pointed out, are most efficient in assigning deviant labels; they are notoriously inefficient when it comes to removing labels and their associated stigma (Goffman, 1963). Former deviants must continue to bear the brunt of the label—with the result that their behavioral patterns are much less likely to change.

The probability of rehabilitating someone who does not view his or her activity or career as deviant is poor. Many noninstitutional deviants—such as prostitutes, gamblers, and homosexuals—feel little need to "repent"; they believe that the pressures they face and the difficulties they experience result from the intolerance of society. In fact, many of these individuals feel strongly that it is society that should be rehabilitated. On the other hand, some noninstitutional deviants—as well as some institutional deviants, such as mental patients, criminals, and delinquents—may try to transform their "deviant" identity. If they do, they can expect to encounter certain barriers. Job applications, for example, frequently require prospective employees to list any arrests, convictions, or periods of institutionalization—circumstances that can bar entry into many occupations. Such roadblocks can produce feelings of frustration and inferiority. What many ex-deviants soon realize is that even if they change, they will still be effectively discriminated against because of past activities or involvement with stigmatizing institutions. They also learn very quickly that the social and political establishment is virtually unchanging—that the burden of change falls upon *them*.

SUMMARY AND ORGANIZATION OF THIS VOLUME

This book explores the subject of deviance in a number of ways—by focusing in turn on society, on the individual, and on institutions of control and rehabilitation. Part 1 describes how deviant categories evolve and how people who violate these categories become defined as social deviants. Part 2 analyzes why people may elect to violate deviant categories—violations that can initiate the defining or labeling process. Part 3 deals with the deviant career, particularly as it arises in private, noninstitutional settings. Part 4 describes how careers may become initiated and perpetuated by institutions, while Part 5 examines the rise and furtherance of noninstitutional careers. Finally, Part 6 discusses how conceptions, careers, and organizational structures may be altered. Throughout, a major focus is on the impact that involvement in institutional as well as noninstitutional activities and careers has upon actors, audiences, and third parties.

Note

1. For an excellent discussion of questions such as these, see particularly Ronald L. Akers, "Problems in the Sociology of Deviance: Social Definitions and Behavior." *Social Forces*, 46 (June 1968), 455–465.

References

Becker, Howard S. *Outsiders: Studies in the Sociology of Deviance*. New York: Free Press, 1963.

Garfinkel, Harold. "Conditions of Successful Degradation Ceremonies." *American Journal of Sociology*, 61 (March 1956), 420–424.

Goffman, Erving. *Stigma: Notes on the Management of Spoiled Identity*. Englewood Cliffs, N.J.: Prentice Hall, 1963.

——— "The Moral Career of the Mental Patient," *Psychiatry*, 22 (1959), 123–142.

Kesey, Ken. *One Flew Over the Cuckoo's Nest*. New York: Viking, 1962.

Lemert, Edwin. *Social Pathology*. New York: McGraw-Hill, 1951.

Rubington, Earl. "Variations in Bottle-Gang Controls." In Earl Rubington and Martin S. Weinberg, eds., *Deviance: The Interactionist Perspective*. New York: Macmillan, 1973.

Scheff, Thomas J. "Typification in the Diagnostic Practices of Rehabilitation Agencies." In Marvin B. Sussman, ed., *Sociology and Rehabilitation*. Washington, D.C.: American Sociological Association, 1966.

Simmons, J. L. *Deviants*. Berkeley: Glendessary, 1969.

Sudnow, David. "Normal Crimes: Sociological Features of the Penal Code," *Social Problems*, 12 (Winter 1965), 255–270.

Part 1 / Creating Deviance

As noted in the general introduction, approaching an understanding of deviance requires an examination of several interrelated factors. An initial concern involves the way in which the subject matter is to be approached, viewed, and subsequently defined. Does the theorist or researcher, for example, conceptualize and define deviance and the deviant in individual terms, or does he or she invoke some type of structural view? Similarly, is there something inherently deviant about certain acts or actors, or do their meanings derive from the interpretations and reactions of others? If the latter, then not only should the student of deviance be aware that a specific image is being advanced (i.e., the notion that deviance and the deviants are social constructs), but he or she must also recognize the need to examine the evolution of deviant categories and the ways in which violators of the categories may be perceived and responded to. As noted earlier, for deviance to become a social fact, a person must be viewed as violating some deviant category and thereafter be labeled as deviant by a social observer.

The initial two selections in this part introduce, in a general way, the major conceptual and definitional issues in the field of deviance. Some important tools are also introduced. The selections that follow offer illustrations of how the concepts are utilized. In addition, more systematic attention is given to the basic processes involved in the construction of the social deviant: (1) the creation of deviant categories and (2) the reactions to violators of deviant categories.

CONCEPTIONS, ENTREPRENEURS, AND POWER

The idea that deviant categories can be viewed as social constructs represents a particular image of deviance. Such a view also suggests the possibility of competing conceptions. Jack P. Gibbs, in "Conceptions of Deviant Behavior: The Old and the New," acknowledges these points but stresses that the traditional conceptions continue to dominate. How one comes to "think about" a specific phenomenon influences the definitions that are developed, as well as the theory or explanation that may result. For example, in the area of deviance, do we locate pathological or deviant-producing

11

stimuli within the actor or do we look elsewhere, perhaps to society in general? Gibbs maintains that the former viewpoint is favored in the fields of crime and deviance. Historically, the dominant conception has been one of individual pathology. Gibbs then proceeds to compare what he terms the "older conceptions" (e.g., the idea that deviants or criminals possess some *internal* trait that distinguishes them from nondeviants) with the "new conception" (i.e., the view that the essential characteristic of a deviant or deviant act is *external* to the actor and the act). This new perspective emphasizes the *character of the reaction* that a specific act or actor may elicit. If the responses are of a certain kind, deviance comes into being. Gibbs then offers several criticisms of the new conception. Is, for example, this perspective intended to be a substantive theory of deviant behavior, or is it primarily a definitional/conceptual treatment of it? Even if the perspective is viewed as an explanatory framework, Gibbs maintains that several questions have not been answered adequately. "Why," for example, "is the act in question considered deviant and/or criminal in some societies but not in others?"

The Gibbs piece sensitizes one to the fact that the underlying images and conceptions of deviance have changed, and it also helps to highlight the manner in which social observers—either individually or collectively—ascribe meaning to the actions of others. Thus, deviance is very much a product of initiative on the part of observers. Logically, then, the reactors and decision makers must become the object of direct study. What, for example, can we say about the content of their conceptions and belief systems? The selection by Howard S. Becker, "Moral Entrepreneurs: The Creation and Enforcement of Deviant Categories," adds some refinements to these issues. Becker also provides an excellent general overview of how deviant categories, particularly rules, evolve. Central to his analysis is the role of *moral entrepreneurs*, whom he categorizes into *rule creators* and *rule enforcers*. Rule creators are individuals who see some "evil" in society and feel that the evil can be corrected only by legislating against it. Frequently their efforts result in the passage of a new law—that is, the creation of a new deviant category. Becker offers several interesting examples that describe this legislative-political phenomenon. He argues that a successful crusade will not only result in "the creation of a new set of rules" but will often give rise to "a new set of enforcement agencies and officials." It becomes the function of these officials to enforce the new rules. Becker concludes his analysis by offering several comments relating to rule enforcers. He contends, for example, that enforcers are concerned primarily with enforcing the law and not its contents; they are also interested in justifying their own position in the organization, as well as in gaining respect from their clients. Many of these same phenomena can be observed in several other selections, especially those that deal with institutional incarceration and deviance.

THE PRODUCTION OF DEVIANT CATEGORIES AND ACTORS

Quite clearly, in cases where the moral entrepreneurs and their crusades succeed, society is often confronted with a new deviant category and a corresponding enforcement or social-control apparatus. Becker's general discussion of the dynamics behind the passage of various laws (e.g., the Eighteenth Amendment and sexual psychopath laws) offers illustrations of this. Steven Spitzer, in "The Production of Deviance in Capitalist Society," offers another account of how deviant categories and populations are created.

A basic thesis of Spitzer is the argument that most traditional theories of deviance, given their preoccupation with the dramatic and predatory forms of social behavior, have neglected to focus on how deviance and deviant populations are constructed socially. He argues that instead of accepting prevailing definitions as givens, one must become aware of the processes by which deviance is "subjectively constructed" and the way in which deviants are "objectively handled," as well as the "structural bases of behavior and characteristics which come to official attention." Spitzer goes on to provide an insightful account of deviance production and control in capitalist societies. Most insightful, and particularly relevant to Part 4 of this book, is his discussion of not only how "problem populations" are produced by the state but how these populations, once constructed, are transformed into deviants and become the objects of official social control. Spitzer cites several factors that influence the rate at which problem populations are transformed into deviants. For example, increasingly large and threatening problem populations are more likely to be controlled through some type of deviance processing.

Spitzer concludes by discussing two rather distinct groups that evolve as a result of social control efforts: the *social junk* and the *social dynamite*. Social junk is relatively costly (e.g., the aged, the mentally ill, the handicapped), yet not especially threatening to the established order. Social dynamite, however, is more threatening as it possesses the potential to call into question such factors as domination and the current mode of production. Spitzer notes further that the social dynamite, given its more youthful, alienated, and politically volatile nature, is more apt to be controlled through a rapid deployment of control resources; this often results in eventual processing through the legal system. The social junk, by contrast, is more likely to be handled by some agency of the welfare state.

Peter Conrad, in "The Discovery of Hyperkinesis: Notes on the Medicalization of Deviant Behavior," provides another historical account of how conceptions of behavior can change. His initial comments are given to the ways in which selected forms of behavior (e.g., alcoholism and drug addiction) become defined as a medical problem or illness and how, thereafter, the medical profession is mandated or licensed to provide the appropriate treatment. Conrad's focus is given to hyperkinesis, particularly its discovery. In his analysis, he describes the various *clinical* (e.g., the effects of amphetamine drugs on children's behavior) and *social* (e.g., the pharmaceutical revolution and associated government action) factors that gave rise to the creation of this new medical diagnostic category. He then moves to a discussion of how deviant behavior on the part of children became conceptualized as a medical problem, as well as why this happened. Conrad concludes with a discussion of some of the important implications that flow from the medicalization of deviant behavior. For example, the medical profession "has not only a monopoly on anything that can be conceptualized as illness," but also the power to define deviant behavior as a medical problem, so that certain procedures can be done that otherwise would not be allowed (e.g., cutting on the body). Moreover, society has a tendency to individualize social problems. Instead of looking to defects of social systems for causes and solutions, we look within the individuals or, instead of analyzing the social situation that affects a perceived difficult child, we prescribe a stimulant medication. Such a treatment strategy, Conrad asserts, deflects our attention away from the real possibility that the family or classroom situation may be the problem. This tendency to characterize problems in individual, clinical, or medical terms will be given additional attention in Part 6, especially those selections dealing with the rehabilitation of social structures.

The selections by Spitzer and Conrad illustrate how, as a result of changing perceptions, behavior may not only become increasingly defined as deviant but may also become criminalized or medicalized. When this occurs, we can speak of the creation of deviant, criminal, or medical categories. And once the categories are in place, we can begin to analyze how others react to the violators of the categories. Many of the selections in Part 4 and Part 5 offer specific illustrations of how actors may be responded to.

1 / Conceptions of Deviant Behavior: The Old and the New

JACK P. GIBBS

The ultimate end of substantive theory in any science is the formulation of empirical relations among classes of phenomena, e.g., X varies directly with Y, X is present if and only if Y is present. However, unless such propositions are arrived at by crude induction of sheer intuition, there is a crucial step before the formulation of a relational statement. This step can be described as the way the investigator comes to perceive or "think about" the phenomena under consideration. Another way to put it is the development of a "conception."

There is no clear-cut distinction between, on the one hand, a conception of a class of phenomena and, on the other, formal definitions and substantive theory. Since a conception emphasizes the predominant feature of a phenomenon, it is not entirely divorced from a definition of it; but the former is not identical with the latter. Thus, for example, the notion of exploitation looms large in the Marxian conception of relations among social classes; but exploitation is or may be only one feature of class relations, and it does not serve as a formal definition of them. Further, in certain fields, particularly the social sciences, a conception often not only precedes but also gives rise to operational definitions. As the case in point, if an operational definition of social class relies on the use of "reputational technique," the investigator's conception of social class is in all probability non-Marxian.

What has been said of the distinction between definitions and conceptions holds also for the relation between the latter and substantive theory. A conception may generate a particular theory, but it is not identical with it. For one thing, a conception contains definitional elements and is therefore partially tautological, which means that in itself a conception is never a clear-cut empirical proposition. Apart from its tautological character, a conception is too general to constitute a testable idea. Nonetheless, a conception may generate substantive theory, and it is certainly true that theories reflect conceptions. Durkheim's work is a classic illustration. His theory on suicide clearly reflects his view of society and social life generally.

In a field without consensus as to operational definitions and little in the way of systematic substantive theory, conceptions necessarily occupy

15

a central position. This condition prevails in most of the social sciences. There, what purport to be definitions of classes of phenomena are typically general and inconsistent to the point of lacking empirical applicability (certainly in the operational sense of the word). Moreover, what passes for a substantive theory in the social sciences is more often than not actually a loosely formulated conception. These observations are not intended to deride the social sciences for lack of progress. All fields probably go through a "conceptions" stage; it is only more apparent in some than in others.

Of the social sciences, there is perhaps no better clear-cut illustration of the importance of conceptions than in the field identified as criminology and the study of deviant behavior. As we shall see, the history of the field can be described best in terms of changing conceptions of crime, criminals, deviants, and deviation. But the purpose of this paper is not an historical account of major trends in the field. If it is true that conceptions give rise to formal definitions and substantive theory, then a critical appraisal of conceptions is important in its own right. This is all the more true in the case of criminology and the study of deviant behavior, where conceptions are frequently confused with substantive theories, and the latter so clearly reflect the former.

OLDER CONCEPTIONS

In recent years there has been a significant change in the prevailing conception of deviant behavior and deviants. Prior to what is designated here as the "new perspective," it commonly was assumed that there is something inherent in deviants which distinguishes them from non-deviants.[1] Thus, from Lombroso to Sheldon, criminals were viewed as biologically distinctive in one way or another.[2] The inadequacies of this conception are now obvious. After decades of research, no biological characteristic which distinguishes criminals has been discovered, and this generalization applies even to particular types of criminals (e.g., murderers, bigamists, etc.). Consequently, few theorists now even toy with the notion that all criminals are atavistic, mentally defective, constitutionally inferior. But the rejection of the biological conception of crime stems from more than research findings. Even casual observation and mild logic cast doubt on the idea. Since legislators are not geneticists, it is difficult to see how they can pass laws in such a way as to create "born criminals." Equally important, since most if not all "normal" persons have violated a law at one time or another,[3] the assertion that criminals are so by heredity now appears most questionable.

Although the biological conception generally has been rejected, what is here designated as the analytic conception of criminal acts largely has escaped criticism. Rather than view criminal acts as nothing more or less than behavior contrary to legal norms, the acts are construed as somehow injurious to society. The shift from the biological to the analytical conception is thus from the actors to the characteristics of their acts, with the idea being that some acts are inherently "criminal" or at least that criminal acts share intrinsic characteristics in common.

The analytical conception is certainly more defensible than the biological view, but it is by no means free of criticism. Above all, the "injurious" quality of some deviant acts is by no means conspicuous, as witness Durkheim's observation:

> . . . there are many acts which have been and still are regarded as criminal without in themselves being harmful to society. What social danger is there in touching a tabooed object, an impure animal or man, in letting the sacred fire die down, in eating certain meats, in failure to make the traditional sacrifice over the grave of parents, in not exactly pronouncing the ritual formula, in not celebrating holidays, etc.?[4]

Only a radical functionalism would interpret the acts noted by Durkheim as literally injuring society in any reasonable sense of the word. The crucial point is that, far from actually injuring society or sharing some intrinsic feature in common, acts may be criminal or deviant because and only because they are proscribed legally and/or socially. The proscription may be irrational in that members of the society cannot explain it, but it is real nonetheless. Similarly, a law may be "arbitrary" in that it is imposed by a powerful minority and, as a consequence, lacks popular support and is actively opposed. But if the law is consistently enforced (i.e., sanctions are imposed regularly on violators), it is difficult to see how it is not "real."

The fact that laws may appear to be irrational and arbitrary has prompted attempts to define crime independently of legal criteria, i.e., analytically. The first step in this direction was Garofalo's concept of natural crime— acts which violate prevailing sentiments of pity and probity.[5] Garofalo's endeavor accomplished very little. Just as there is probably no act which is contrary to law universally, it is equally true that no act violates sentiments of pity and probity in all societies. In other words, cultural relativity defeats any attempt to compile a list of acts which are crimes universally. Also, it is hard to see why the violation of a rigorously enforced traffic regulation is not a crime even though unrelated to sentiments of pity and probity. If it is not a crime, what is it?

The search for an analytic identification of crime continued in Sellin's proposal to abandon legal criteria altogether in preference for "conduct norms."[6] The rationale for the proposal is simple. Because laws vary and may be "arbitrary" in any one society, a purely legal definition of crime is not suited for scientific study. But Sellin's observations on the arbitrariness of laws apply in much the same way to conduct norms. Just as the content of criminal law varies from one society to the next and from time to time, so does the content of extra-legal norms. Further, the latter may be just as arbitrary as criminal laws. Even in a highly urbanized society such as the United States, there is evidently no rationale or utilitarian reason for all of the norms pertaining to mode of dress. True, there may be much greater conformity to conduct norms than to some laws, but the degree of conformity is hardly an adequate criterion of the "reality" of norms, legal or extra-legal. If any credence whatever can be placed in the Kinsey report, sexual taboos may be violated frequently and yet remain as taboos. As a case in point, even if adultery is now common in the United States, it is significant that the participants typically attempt to conceal their acts. In brief, just as laws may be violated frequently and are "unreal" in that sense, the same applies to some conduct norms; but in neither case do they cease to be norms. They would cease to be norms if and only if one defines deviation in terms of statistical regularities in behavior, but not even Sellin would subscribe to the notion that normative phenomena can or should be defined in statistical terms.

In summary, however capricious and irrational legal and extra-legal norms may appear to be, the inescapable conclusion is that some acts are criminal or deviant for the very simple reason that they are proscribed.

THE NEW CONCEPTION

Whereas both the pathological and the analytical conceptions of deviation assume that some intrinsic feature characterizes deviants and/or deviant acts, an emerging perspective in sociology flatly rejects any such assumption. Indeed, as witness the following statements by Kitsuse, Becker, and Erikson, exactly the opposite position is taken.

Kitsuse: Forms of behavior *per se* do not differentiate deviants from non-deviants; it is the responses of the conventional and conforming members of the society who identify and interpret behavior as defiant which sociologically transform persons into deviants.[7]

Erikson: From a sociological standpoint, deviance can be defined as conduct which is generally thought to require the attention of social control agencies— that is, conduct about which "something should be done." Deviance is not a property *inherent in* certain forms of behavior; it is a property *conferred upon* these forms by the audiences which directly or indirectly witness them. Sociologically, then, the critical variable in the study of deviance is the social *audience* rather than individual *person*, since it is the audience which eventually decides whether or not any given action or actions will become a visible case of deviation.[8]

Becker: From this point of view, deviance is *not* a quality of the act a person commits, but rather a consequence of the application by others of rules and sanctions to an "offender." The deviant is one to whom that label has successfully been applied; deviant behavior is behavior that people so label.[9]

The common assertion in the above statements is that acts can be identified as deviant or criminal only by reference to the character of reaction to them by the public or by the official agents of a politically organized society. Put simply, if the reaction is of a certain kind, then and only then is the act deviant. The crucial point is that the essential feature of a defiant or deviant act is *external* to the actor and the act. Further, even if the act or actors share some feature in common other than social reactions to them, the feature neither defines nor completely explains deviation. To take the extreme case, even if Lombroso had been correct in his assertion that criminals are biologically distinctive, the biological factor neither identifies the criminal nor explains criminality. Purely biological variables may explain why some persons commit certain acts, but they do not explain why the acts are crimes. Consequently, since criminal law is spatially and temporally relative, it is impossible to distinguish criminals from noncriminals (assuming that the latter do exist, which is questionable) in terms of biological characteristics. To illustrate, if act X is a crime in society A but not a crime in society B, it follows that, even assuming Lombroso to have been correct, the anatomical features which distinguish the criminal in society A may characterize the noncriminal in society B. In both societies some persons may be genetically predisposed to commit act X, but the act is a crime in one society and not in the other. Accordingly, the generalization that all persons with certain anatomical features are criminals would be, in this instance, false. True, one may assert that the "born criminal" is predisposed to violate the laws of his own society, but this assumes either that "the genes" know what the law is or that the members of the legislature are geneticists (i.e., they deliberately enact laws in such a way that the "born criminal" will violate them). Either assumption taxes credulity.

The new perspective of deviant behavior contradicts not only the biological but also the analytical conception. Whereas the latter seeks to find something intrinsic in deviant or, more specifically, criminal acts, the new conception denies any such characterization. True, the acts share a common denominator—they are identified by the character of reaction to them—but this does not mean that the acts are "injurious" to society or that they are in any way inherently abnormal. The new conception eschews the notion that some acts are deviant or criminal in all societies. For that matter, the reaction which identifies a deviant act may not be the same from one society or social group to the next. In general, then, the new conception of deviant behavior is relativistic in the extreme.

* * *

Notes

1. Throughout this paper crime is treated as a sub-class of deviant behavior. Particular issues may be discussed with reference to crime, but on the whole the observations apply to deviant behavior generally.

2. Although not essential to the argument, it is perhaps significant that the alleged biological differentiae of criminals have been consistently viewed as "pathological" in one sense or another.

3. See Edwin H. Sutherland and Donald R. Cressey, *Principles of Criminology*, 6th ed., Chicago: J.B. Lippincott, 1960, p. 39.

4. Emile Durkheim, *The Division of Labor in Society*, trans. George Simpson, Glencoe, Illinois: The Free Press, 1949, p. 72.

5. Raffaele Garofalo, *Criminology*, Boston: Little, Brown, & Co., 1914, Chapter I.

6. Thorsten Sellin, *Culture Conflict and Crime*, New York: Social Science Research Council, Bulletin 41, 1938.

7. John I. Kitsuse, "Societal Reaction to Deviant Behavior: Problems of Theory and Method," *Social Problems*, 9 (Winter, 1962), p. 253.

8. Kai T. Erikson, "Notes on the Sociology of Deviance," *Social Problems*, 9 (Spring, 1962), p. 308.

9. Howard S. Becker, *Outsiders*, New York: The Free Press of Glencoe, 1963, p. 9.

2 / Moral Entrepreneurs: The Creation and Enforcement of Deviant Categories

HOWARD S. BECKER

RULE CREATORS

The prototype of the rule creator, but not the only variety as we shall see, is the crusading reformer. He is interested in the content of rules. The existing rules do not satisfy him because there is some evil which profoundly disturbs him. He feels that nothing can be right in the world until rules are made to correct it. He operates with an absolute ethic; what he sees is truly and totally evil with no qualification. Any means is justified to do away with it. The crusader is fervent and righteous, often self-righteous.

It is appropriate to think of reformers as crusaders because they typically believe that their mission is a holy one. The prohibitionist serves as an excellent example, as does the person who wants to suppress vice and sexual delinquency or the person who wants to do away with gambling.

These examples suggest that the moral crusader is a meddling busybody, interested in forcing his own morals on others. But this is a one-sided view. Many moral crusades have strong humanitarian overtones. The crusader is not only interested in seeing to it that other people do what he thinks [is] right. He believes that if they do what is right it will be good for them. Or he may feel that his reform will prevent certain kinds of exploitation of one person by another. Prohibitionists felt that they were not simply forcing their morals on others, but attempting to provide the conditions for a better way of life for people prevented by drink from realizing a truly good life. Abolitionists were not simply trying to prevent slave owners from doing the wrong thing; they were trying to help slaves achieve a better life. Because of the importance of the humanitarian motive, moral crusaders (despite their relatively single-minded devotion to their particular cause) often lend their support to other humanitarian crusades. Joseph Gusfield has pointed out that:

> The American temperance movement during the 19th century was a part of a general effort toward the improvement of the worth of the human being through improved morality as well as economic conditions. The mixture of the religious,

21

the equalitarian, and the humanitarian was an outstanding facet of the moral reformism of many movements. Temperance supporters formed a large segment of movements such as sabbatarianism, abolition, woman's rights, agrarianism, and humanitarian attempts to improve the lot of the poor.…

In its auxiliary interests the WCTU revealed a great concern for the improvement of the welfare of the lower classes. It was active in campaigns to secure penal reform, to shorten working hours and raise wages for workers, and to abolish child labor and in a number of other humanitarian and equalitarian activities. In the 1880's the WCTU worked to bring about legislation for the protection of working girls against the exploitation by men.[1]

As Gusfield says,[2] "Moral reformism of this type suggests the approach of a dominant class toward those less favorably situated in the economic and social structure." Moral crusaders typically want to help those beneath them to achieve a better status. That those beneath them do not always like the means proposed for their salvation is another matter. But this fact—that moral crusades are typically dominated by those in the upper levels of the social structure—means that they add to the power they derive from the legitimacy of their moral position, the power they derive from their superior position in society.

Naturally, many moral crusades draw support from people whose motives are less pure than those of the crusader. Thus, some industrialists supported Prohibition because they felt it would provide them with a more manageable labor force.[3] Similarly, it is sometimes rumored that Nevada gambling interests support the opposition to attempts to legalize gambling in California because it would cut so heavily into their business, which depends in substantial measure on the population of Southern California.[4]

The moral crusader, however, is more concerned with ends than with means. When it comes to drawing up specific rules (typically in the form of legislation to be proposed to a state legislature or the Federal Congress), he frequently relies on the advice of experts. Lawyers, expert in the drawing of acceptable legislation, often play this role. Government bureaus in whose jurisdiction the problem falls may also have the necessary expertise, as did the Federal Bureau of Narcotics in the case of the marihuana problem.

As psychiatric ideology, however, becomes increasingly acceptable, a new expert has appeared—the psychiatrist. Sutherland, in his discussion of the natural history of sexual psychopath laws, pointed to the psychiatrist's influence.[5] He suggests the following as the conditions under which the sexual psychopath law, which provides that a person "who is diagnosed as a sexual psychopath may be confined for an indefinite period in a state hospital for the insane,"[6] will be passed.

First, these laws are customarily enacted after a state of fear has been aroused in a community by a few serious sex crimes committed in quick succession. This is illustrated in Indiana, where a law was passed following three or four sexual attacks in Indianapolis, with murder in two. Heads of families bought guns and watch dogs, and the supply of locks and chains in the hardware stores of the city was completely exhausted....

A second element in the process of developing sexual psychopath laws is the agitated activity of the community in connection with the fear. The attention of the community is focused on sex crimes, and people in the most varied situations envisage dangers and see the need of and possibility for their control....

The third phase in the development of those sexual psychopath laws has been the appointment of a committee. The committee gathers the many conflicting recommendations of persons and groups of persons, attempts to determine "facts," studies procedures in other states, and makes recommendations, which generally include bills for the legislature. Although the general fear usually subsides within a few days, a committee has the formal duty of following through until positive action is taken. Terror which does not result in a committee is much less likely to result in a law.[7]

In the case of sexual psychopath laws, there usually is no government agency charged with dealing in a specialized way with sexual deviations. Therefore, when the need for expert advice in drawing up legislation arises, people frequently turn to the professional group most closely associated with such problems:

In some states, at the committee stage of the development of a sexual psychopath law, psychiatrists have played an important part. The psychiatrists, more than any others, have been the interest group back of the laws. A committee of psychiatrists and neurologists in Chicago wrote the bill which became the sexual psychopath law of Illinois; the bill was sponsored by the Chicago Bar Association and by the state's attorney of Cook County and was enacted with little opposition in the next session of the State Legislature. In Minnesota all the members of the governor's committee except one were psychiatrists. In Wisconsin the Milwaukee Neuropsychiatric Society shared in pressing the Milwaukee Crime Commission for the enactment of a law. In Indiana the attorney-general's committee received from the American Psychiatric Association copies of all the sexual psychopath laws which had been enacted in other states.[8]

The influence of psychiatrists in other realms of the criminal law has increased in recent years.

In any case, what is important about this example is not that psychiatrists are becoming increasingly influential, but that the moral crusader, at some point in the development of his crusade, often requires the services of a professional who can draw up the appropriate rules in an appropriate form. The crusader himself is often not concerned with such details. Enough for him that the main point has been won; he leaves its implementation to others.

By leaving the drafting of the specific rule in the hands of others, the crusader opens the door for many unforeseen influences. For those who draft legislation for crusaders have their own interests, which may affect the legislation they prepare. It is likely that the sexual psychopath laws drawn by psychiatrists contain many features never intended by the citizens who spearheaded the drives to "do something about sex crimes," features which do however reflect the professional interests of organized psychiatry.

*   *   *

RULE ENFORCERS

The most obvious consequence of a successful crusade is the creation of a new set of rules. With the creation of a new set of rules we often find that a new set of enforcement agencies and officials is established. Sometimes, of course, existing agencies take over the administration of the new rule, but more frequently a new set of rule enforcers is created. The passage of the Harrison Act presaged the creation of the Federal Narcotics Bureau, just as the passage of the Eighteenth Amendment led to the creation of police agencies charged with enforcing the Prohibition Laws.

With the establishment of organizations of rule enforcers, the crusade becomes institutionalized. What started out as a drive to convince the world of the moral necessity of a new rule finally becomes an organization devoted to the enforcement of the rule. Just as radical political movements turn into organized political parties and lusty evangelical sects become staid religious denominations, the final outcome of the moral crusade is a police force. To understand, therefore, how the rules creating a new class of outsiders are applied to particular people we must understand the motives and interests of police, the rule enforcers.

Although some policemen undoubtedly have a kind of crusading interest in stamping out evil, it is probably much more typical for the policeman to have a certain detached and objective view of his job. He is not so much concerned with the content of any particular rule as he is with the fact that it is his job to enforce the rule. When the rules are changed, he punishes what was once acceptable behavior just as he ceases to punish behavior that has been made legitimate by a change in the rules. The enforcer, then, may not be interested in the content of the rule as such, but only in the fact that the existence of the rule provides him with a job, a profession, and a *raison d'être*.

Since the enforcement of certain rules provides justification for his way of life, the enforcer has two interests which condition his enforcement activity: first, he must justify the existence of his position and, second, he must win the respect of those he deals with.

These interests are not peculiar to rule enforcers. Members of all occupations feel the need to justify their work and win the respect of others. Musicians would like to do this but have difficulty finding ways of successfully impressing their worth on customers. Janitors fail to win their tenants' respect, but develop an ideology which stresses the quasi-professional responsibility they have to keep confidential the intimate knowledge of tenants they acquire in the course of their work.[9] Physicians, lawyers, and other professionals, more successful in winning the respect of clients, develop elaborate mechanisms for maintaining a properly respectful relationship.

In justifying the existence of his position, the rule enforcer faces a double problem. On the one hand, he must demonstrate to others that the problem still exists: the rules he is supposed to enforce have some point, because infractions occur. On the other hand, he must show that his attempts at enforcement are effective and worthwhile, that the evil he is supposed to deal with is in fact being dealt with adequately. Therefore, enforcement organizations, particularly when they are seeking funds, typically oscillate between two kinds of claims. First, they say that by reason of their efforts the problem they deal with is approaching solution. But, in the same breath, they say the problem is perhaps worse than ever (though through no fault of their own) and requires renewed and increased effort to keep it under control. Enforcement officials can be more vehement than anyone else in their insistence that the problem they are supposed to deal with is still with us, in fact is more with us than ever before. In making these claims, enforcement officials provide good reason for continuing the existence of the position they occupy.

We may also note that enforcement officials and agencies are inclined to take a pessimistic view of human nature. If they do not actually believe in original sin, they at least like to dwell on the difficulties in getting people to abide by rules, on the characteristics of human nature that lead people toward evil. They are skeptical of attempts to reform rule-breakers.

The skeptical and pessimistic outlook of the rule enforcer, of course, is reinforced by his daily experience. He sees, as he goes about his work, the evidence that the problem is still with us. He sees the people who continually repeat offenses, thus definitely branding themselves in his eyes as outsiders. Yet it is not too great a stretch of the imagination to suppose that one of the underlying reasons for the enforcer's pessimism about human nature and the possibilities of reform is that fact that if human nature were per-fectible and people could be permanently reformed, his job would come to an end.

In the same way, a rule enforcer is likely to believe that it is necessary for the people he deals with to respect him. If they do not, it will be very difficult to do his job; his feeling of security in his work will be lost. Therefore, a good deal of enforcement activity is devoted not to the actual enforcement of rules, but to coercing respect from the people the enforcer deals with. This means that one may be labeled as deviant not because he has actually broken a rule, but because he has shown disrespect to the enforcer of the rule.

Westley's study of policemen in a small industrial city furnishes a good example of this phenomenon. In his interview, he asked policemen, "When do you think a policeman is justified in roughing a man up?" He found that "at least 37% of the men believed that it was legitimate to use violence to coerce respect."[10] He gives some illuminating quotations from his interviews:

> Well, there are cases. For example, when you stop a fellow for a routine questioning, say a wise guy, and he starts talking back to you and telling you you are no good and that sort of thing. You know you can take a man in on a disorderly conduct charge, but you can practically never make it stick. So what you do in a case like that is to egg the guy on until he makes a remark where you can justifiably slap him and, then, if he fights back, you can call it resisting arrest.

> Well, a prisoner deserves to be hit when he goes to the point where he tries to put you below him.

> You've gotta get rough when a man's language becomes very bad, when he is trying to make a fool of you in front of everybody else. I think most policemen try to treat people in a nice way, but usually you have to talk pretty rough. That's the only way to set a man down, to make him show a little respect.[11]

What Westley describes is the use of an illegal means of coercing respect from others. Clearly, when a rule enforcer has the option of enforcing a rule or not, the difference in what he does may be caused by the attitude of the offender toward him. If the offender is properly respectful, the enforcer may smooth the situation over. If the offender is disrespectful, then sanctions may be visited on him. Westley has shown that this differential tends to operate in the case of traffic offenses, where the policeman's discretion is perhaps at a maximum.[12] But it probably operates in other areas as well.

Ordinarily, the rule enforcer has a great deal of discretion in many areas, if only because his resources are not sufficient to cope with the volume of rule-breaking he is supposed to deal with. This means that he cannot tackle everything at once and to this extent must temporize with evil. He cannot do the whole job and knows it. He takes his time, on the assumption that the problems he deals with will be around for a long while. He establishes priorities, dealing with things in their turn, handling the most pressing problems immediately and leaving others for later. His attitude toward his work, in short, is professional. He lacks the naive moral fervor characteristic of the rule creator.

If the enforcer is not going to tackle every case he knows of at once, he must have a basis for deciding when to enforce the rule, which persons committing which acts to label as deviant. One criterion for selecting people is the "fix." Some people have sufficient political influence or know-how to be able to ward off attempts at enforcement, if not at the time of apprehension then at a later stage in the process. Very often, this function is professionalized; someone performs the job on a full-time basis, available to anyone who wants to hire him. A professional thief described fixers this way:

> There is in every large city a regular fixer for professional thieves. He has no agents and does not solicit and seldom takes any case except that of a professional thief,

just as they seldom go to anyone except him. This centralized and monopolistic system of fixing for professional thieves is found in practically all of the large cities and many of the small ones.[13]

Since it is mainly professional thieves who know about the fixer and his operations, the consequence of this criterion for selecting people to apply the rules to is that amateurs tend to be caught, convicted, and labeled deviant much more frequently than professionals. As the professional thief notes:

> You can tell by the way the case is handled in court when the fix is in. When the copper is not very certain he has the right man, or the testimony of the copper and the complainant does not agree, or the prosecutor goes easy on the defendant, or the judge is arrogant in his decisions, you can always be sure that someone has got the work in. This does not happen in many cases of theft, for there is one case of a professional to twenty-five or thirty amateurs who know nothing about the fix. These amateurs get the hard end of the deal every time. The coppers bawl out about the thieves, no one holds up his testimony, the judge delivers an oration, and all of them get credit for stopping a crime wave. When the professional hears the case immediately preceding his own, he will think, "He should have got ninety years. It's the damn amateurs who cause all the heat in the stores." Or else he thinks, "Isn't it a damn shame for that copper to send that kid away for a pair of hose, and in a few minutes he will agree to a small fine for me for stealing a fur coat?" But if the coppers did not send the amateurs away to strengthen their records of convictions, they could not sandwich in the professionals whom they turn loose.[14]

Enforcers of rules, since they have no stake in the content of particular rules themselves, often develop their own private evaluation of the importance of various kinds of rules and infractions of them. This set of priorities may differ considerably from those held by the general public. For instance, drug users typically believe (and a few policemen have personally confirmed it to me) that police do not consider the use of marihuana to be as important a problem or as dangerous a practice as the use of opiate drugs. Police base this conclusion on the fact that, in their experience, opiate users commit other crimes (such as theft or prostitution) in order to get drugs, while marihuana users do not.

Enforcers then, responding to the pressures of their own work situation, enforce rules and create outsiders in a selective way. Whether a person who commits a deviant act is in fact labeled a deviant depends on many things extraneous to his actual behavior: whether the enforcement official feels that at this time he must make some show of doing his job in order to justify his position, whether the misbehaver shows proper deference to the enforcer, whether the "fix" has been put in, and where the kind of act he has committed stands on the enforcer's list of priorities.

The professional enforcer's lack of fervor and routine approach to dealing with evil may get him into trouble with the rule creator. The rule creator, as we have said, is concerned with the content of the rules that interest him. He sees them as the means by which evil can be stamped out. He does not understand the enforcer's long-range approach to the same problems and cannot see why all the evil that is apparent cannot be stamped out at once.

When the person interested in the content of a rule realizes or has called to his attention the fact that enforcers are dealing selectively with the evil that concerns him, his righteous wrath may be aroused. The professional is denounced for viewing the evil too lightly, for failing to do his duty. The moral entrepreneur, at whose instance the rule was made, arises again to say that the outcome of the last crusade has not been satisfactory or that the gains once made have been whittled away and lost.

Notes

1. Joseph R. Gusfield, "Social Structure and Moral Reform: A Study of the Woman's Christian Temperance Union," *American Journal of Sociology*, LXI (November, 1955), 223.

2. *Ibid.*

3. See Raymond G. McCarthy, editor, *Drinking and Intoxication* (New Haven and New York: Yale Center of Alcohol Studies and The Free Press of Glencoe, 1959), pp. 395–396.

4. This is suggested in Oscar Lewis, *Sagebrush Casinos: The Story of Legal Gambling in Nevada* (New York: Doubleday and Co., 1953), pp. 223–234.

5. Edwin H. Sutherland, "The Diffusion of Sexual Psychopath Laws," *American Journal of Sociology*, LVI (September, 1950), 142–148.

6. *Ibid.*, pp. 142.

7. *Ibid.*, pp. 143–145.

8. *Ibid.*, pp. 145–146.

9. See Ray Gold, "Janitors Versus Tenants: A Status-Income Dilemma," *American Journal of Sociology*, LVII (March, 1952), 486–493.

10. William A. Westley, "Violence and the Police," *American Journal of Sociology*, LIX (July, 1953), 39.

11. *Ibid.*

12. See William A. Westley, "The Police: A Sociological Study of Law, Custom, and Morality" (unpublished Ph.D. dissertation, University of Chicago, Department of Sociology, 1951).

13. Edwin H. Sutherland (editor), *The Professional Thief* (Chicago: University of Chicago Press, 1937), pp. 87–88.

14. *Ibid.*, pp. 91–92.

3 / The Production of Deviance in Capitalist Society

STEVEN SPITZER

* * *

The concept of deviance production offers a starting point for the analysis of both deviance and control. But for such a construct to serve as a critical tool it must be grounded in a historical and structural investigation of society. For Marx, the crucial unit of analysis is the mode of production that dominates a given historical period. If we are to have a Marxian theory of deviance, therefore, deviance production must be understood in relationship to specific forms of socio-economic organization. In our society, productive activity is organized capitalistically, and it is ultimately defined by "the process that transforms on the one hand, the social means of subsistence and of production into capital, on the other hand the immediate producers into wage labourers" (Marx, 1967:714).

There are two features of the capitalist mode of production important for purposes of this discussion. First, as a mode of production it forms the foundation or infrastructure of our society. This means that the starting point of our analysis must be an understanding of the economic organization of capitalist societies and the impact of that organization on all aspects of social life. But the capitalist mode of production is an important starting point in another sense. It contains contradictions which reflect the internal tendencies of capitalism. These contradictions are important because they explain the changing character of the capitalist system and the nature of its impact on social, political, and intellectual activity. The formulation of a Marxist perspective on deviance requires the interpretation of the process through which the contradictions of capitalism are expressed. In particular, the theory must illustrate the relationship between specific contradictions, the problems of capitalist development, and the production of a deviant class.

The superstructure of society emerges from and reflects the ongoing development of economic forces (the infrastructure). In class societies this superstructure preserves the hegemony of the ruling class through a system of class controls. These controls, which are institutionalized in the family, church, private associations, media, schools, and the state, provide a mechanism for coping with the contradictions and achieving the aims of capitalist development.

Among the most important functions served by the superstructure in capitalist societies is the regulation and management of problem populations. Because deviance processing is only one of the methods available for social control, these groups supply raw material for deviance production, but are by no means synonymous with deviant populations. Problem populations tend to share a number of social characteristics, but most important among these is the fact that their behavior, personal qualities, and/or position threaten the *social relations of production* in capitalist societies. In other words, populations become generally eligible for management as deviant when they disturb, hinder, or call into question any of the following:

1. capitalist modes of appropriating the product of human labor (e.g. when the poor "steal" from the rich)

2. the social conditions under which capitalist production takes place (e.g. those who refuse or are unable to perform wage labor)

3. patterns of distribution and consumption in capitalist society (e.g. those who use drugs for escape and transcendence rather than sociability and adjustment)

4. the process of socialization for productive and non-productive roles (e.g. youth who refuse to be schooled or those who deny the validity of "family life")[1]

5. the ideology which supports the functioning of capitalist society (e.g. proponents of alternative forms of social organization)

Although problem populations are defined in terms of the threat and costs that they present to the social relations of production in capitalist societies, these populations are far from isomorphic with a revolutionary class. It is certainly true that some members of the problem population may under specific circumstances possess revolutionary potential. But this potential can only be realized if the problematic group is located in a position of functional indispensability within the capitalist system. Historically, capitalist societies have been quite successful in transforming those who are problematic and indispensable (the protorevolutionary class) into groups who are either problematic and dispensable (candidates for deviance processing), or indispensable but not problematic (supporters of the capitalist order). On the other hand, simply because a group is manageable does not mean that it ceases to be a problem for the capitalist class. Even though dispensable problem populations cannot overturn the capitalist system, they can represent a significant impediment to its maintenance and growth. It is in this sense that they become eligible for management as deviants.

Problem populations are created in two ways—either directly through the expression of fundamental contradictions in the capitalist mode of production or indirectly through disturbances in the system of class rule. An example of the first process is found in Marx's analysis of the "relative surplus-population."

Writing on the "General Law of Capitalist Accumulation" Marx explains how increased social redundance is inherent in the development of the capitalist mode of production:

> With the extension of the scale of production, and the mass of the labourers set in motion, with the greater breadth and fullness of all sources of wealth, there is also an extension of the scale on which greater attraction of labourers by capital is accompanied by their greater repulsion. . . . The labouring population therefore produces, along with the accumulation of capital produced by it, the means by which itself is made relatively superfluous, . . . and it does this to an always increasing extent (Marx, 1967:631).

In its most limited sense the production of a relative surplus-population involves the creation of a class which is economically redundant. But insofar as the conditions of economic existence determine social existence, this process helps explain the emergence of groups who become both threatening and vulnerable at the same time. The marginal status of these populations reduces their stake in the maintenance of the system while their powerlessness and dispensability renders them increasingly susceptible to the mechanisms of official control.

The paradox surrounding the production of the relative surplus-population is that this population is both useful and menacing to the accumulation of capital. Marx describes how the relative surplus-population "forms a disposable industrial army, that belongs to capital quite as absolutely as if the latter had bred it at its own cost," and how this army "creates, for the changing needs of the self-expansion of capital, a mass of human material always ready for exploitation" (Marx, 1967:632).

On the other hand, it is apparent that an excessive increase in what Marx called the "lowest sediment" of the relative surplus-population might seriously impair the growth of capital. The social expenses and threat to social harmony created by a large and economically stagnant surplus-population could jeopardize the preconditions for accumulation by undermining the ideology of equality so essential to the legitimation of production relations in bourgeois democracies, diverting revenues away from capital investment toward control and support operations, and providing a basis for political organization of the dispossessed.[2] To the extent that the relative surplus-population confronts the capitalist class as a threat to the social relations of production, it reflects an important contradiction in modern capitalist societies: a surplus-population is a necessary product of and condition for the accumulation of wealth on a capitalist basis, but it also creates a form of social expense which must be neutralized or controlled if production relations and conditions for increased accumulation are to remain unimpaired.

Problem populations are also generated through contradictions which develop in the system of class rule. The institutions which make up the superstructure of capitalist society originate and are maintained to guarantee the interests of the capitalist class. Yet these institutions necessarily reproduce, rather than resolve, the contradictions of the capitalist order. In a dialectical fashion, arrangements which arise in order to buttress capitalism are transformed into their opposite—structures for the cultivation of internal threats. An instructive example of this process is found in the emergence and transformation of educational institutions in the United States.

The introduction of mass education in the United States can be traced to the developing needs of corporate capitalism (cf. Karier, 1973; Cohen and Lazerson, 1972; Bowles and Gintis, 1972; Spring, 1972). Compulsory education provided a means of training, testing and sorting, and assimilating wage-laborers, as well as withholding certain populations from the labor market. The system was also intended to preserve the values of bourgeois society and operate as an "inexpensive form of police" (Spring, 1973:31). However, as Gintis (1973) and Bowles (1973) have suggested, the internal contradictions of schooling can lead to effects opposite of those intended. For the poor, early schooling can make explicit the oppressiveness and alienating character of capitalist institutions, while higher education can instill critical abilities which lead students to "bite the hand that feeds them." In both cases educational institutions create troublesome populations (i.e. dropouts and student radicals) and contribute to the very problems they were designed to solve.

After understanding how and why specific groups become generally bothersome in capitalist society, it is necessary to investigate the conditions under which these groups are transformed into proper objects for social control. In other words, we must ask what distinguishes the generally problematic from the specifically deviant. The rate at which problem populations are converted into deviants will reflect the relationship between these populations and the control system. This rate is likely to be influenced by the:

(1) *Extensiveness and Intensity of State Controls.* Deviance processing (as opposed to other control measures) is more likely to occur when problem management is monopolized by the state. As state controls are applied more generally, the proportion of official deviants will increase.

(2) *Size and Level of Threat Presented by the Problem Population.* The larger and more threatening the problem population, the greater the likelihood that this population will have to be controlled through deviance processing rather than other methods. As the threat created by these populations exceeds the capacities of informal restraints, their management requires a broadening of the reaction system and an increasing centralization and coordination of control activities.

(3) *Level of Organization of the Problem Population.* When and if problem populations are able to organize and develop limited amounts of political power, deviance processing becomes increasingly less effective as a tool for social control. The attribution of deviant status is most likely to occur when a group is relatively impotent and atomized.

(4) *Effectiveness of Control Structures Organized through Civil Society.* The greater the effectiveness of the organs of civil society (i.e. the family, church, media, schools, sports) in solving the problems of class control,

the less the likelihood that deviance processing (a more explicitly political process) will be employed.

(5) *Availability and Effectiveness of Alternative Types of Official Processing.* In some cases the state will be able effectively to incorporate certain segments of the problem population into specially created "pro-social" roles. In the modern era, for example, conscription and public works projects (Piven and Cloward, 1971) helped neutralize the problems posed by troublesome populations without creating new or expanding old deviant categories.

(6) *Availability and Effectiveness of Parallel Control Structures.* In many instances the state can transfer its costs of deviance production by supporting or at least tolerating the activities of independent control networks which operate in its interests. For example, when the state is denied or is reluctant to assert a monopoly over the use of force, it is frequently willing to encourage vigilante organizations and private police in the suppression of problem populations. Similarly, the state is often benefited by the policies and practices of organized crime, insofar as these activities help pacify, contain, and enforce order among potentially disruptive groups (Schelling, 1967).

(7) *Utility of Problem Populations.* While problem populations are defined in terms of their threat and costs to capitalist relations of production, they are not threatening in every respect. They can be supportive economically (as part of a surplus labor pool or dual labor market), politically (as evidence of the need for state intervention), and ideologically (as scapegoats for rising discontent). In other words, under certain conditions capitalist societies derive benefits from maintaining a number of visible and uncontrolled "troublemakers" in their midst. Such populations are distinguished by the fact that while they remain generally bothersome, the costs that they inflict are most immediately absorbed by other members of the problem population. Policies evolve, not so much to eliminate or actively suppress these groups, but to deflect their threat away from targets which are sacred to the capitalist class. Victimization is permitted and even encouraged, as long as the victims are members of an expendable class.

Two more or less discrete groupings are established through the operations of official control. These groups are a product of different operating assumptions and administrative orientations toward the deviant population. On the one hand, there is *social junk* which, from the point of view of the dominant class, is a costly yet relatively harmless burden to society. The discreditability of social junk resides in the failure, inability, or refusal of this group to participate in the roles supportive of capitalist society. Social junk is most likely to come to official attention when informal resources have been exhausted or when the magnitude of the problem becomes significant enough to create a basis for "public concern." Since the threat presented by social junk is passive, growing out of its inability to compete and its withdrawal from the prevailing social order, controls are usually designed to regulate and contain rather than eliminate and suppress the problem. Clear-cut examples of social junk in modern capitalist societies might include the officially administered aged, handicapped, mentally ill, and mentally retarded.

In contrast to social junk, there is a category that can be roughly described as *social dynamite*. The essential quality of deviance managed as social dynamite is its potential actively to call into question established relationships, especially relations of production and domination. Generally, therefore, social dynamite tends to be more youthful, alienated, and politically volatile than social junk. The control of social dynamite is usually premised on an assumption that the problem is acute in nature, requiring a rapid and focused expenditure of control resources. This is in contrast to the handling of social junk frequently based on a belief that the problem is chronic and best controlled through broad reactive rather than intensive and selective measures. Correspondingly, social dynamite is normally processed through the legal system with its capacity for active intervention, while social junk is frequently (but not always)[3] administered by the agencies and agents of the therapeutic and welfare state.

Many varieties of deviant populations are alternatively or simultaneously dealt with as either social junk and/or social dynamite. The welfare poor, homosexuals, alcoholics, and "problem children" are among the categories reflecting the equivocal nature of the control process and its dependence on the political, economic, and ideological priorities of deviance production. The changing nature of these priorities and their implications for the future may be best understood by examining some of the tendencies of modern capitalist systems.

*   *   *

Notes

1. To the extent that a group (e.g. homosexuals) blatantly and systematically challenges the validity of the bourgeois family it is likely to become part of the problem population. The family is essential to capitalist society as a unit for consumption, socialization, and the reproduction of the socially necessary labor force (cf. Frankford and Snitow, 1972; Secombe, 1973; Zaretsky, 1973).

2. O'Connor (1973) discusses this problem in terms of the crisis faced by the capitalist state in maintaining conditions for profitable accumulation and social harmony.

3. It has been estimated, for instance, that one-third of all arrests in America are for the offense of public drunkenness. Most of these apparently involve "sick" and destitute "skid row alcoholics" (Morris and Hawkins, 1969).

References

Baran, Paul, and Paul M. Sweezy. 1966. Monopoly Capital. New York: Monthly Review Press.

Becker, Howard S. 1967. "Whose side are we on?" Social Problems 14(Winter): 239–247.

Becker, Howard S., and Irving Louis Horowitz. 1972. "Radical politics and sociological research: Observations on methodology and ideology." American Journal of Sociology 78(July): 48–66.

Blauner, Robert. 1969. "Internal colonialism and ghetto revolt." Social Problems 16(Spring): 393–408.

Bowles, Samuel. 1973. "Contradictions in United States higher education." Pp. 165–199 in James H. Weaver (ed.), Modern Political Economy: Radical versus Orthodox Approaches. Boston: Allyn and Bacon.

Bowles, Samuel, and Herbert Gintis. 1972. "I.Q. in the U.S. class structure." Social Policy 3(November/December): 65–96.

Bureau of Prisons. 1972. National Prisoner Statistics. Prisoners in State and Federal Institutions for Adult Felons. Washington, D.C.: Bureau of Prisons.

Cohen, David K., and Marvin Lazerson. 1972. "Education and the corporate order."Socialist Revolution (March/April): 48–72.

Foucault, Michel. 1965. Madness and Civilization. New York: Random House.

Frankford, Evelyn, and Ann Snitow. 1972. "The trap of domesticity: Notes on the family." Socialist Revolution (July/August): 83–94.

Gintis, Herbert. 1973. "Alienation and power." Pp. 431–465 in James H. Weaver (ed.), Modern Political Economy: Radical versus Orthodox Approaches. Boston: Allyn and Bacon.

Gorz, Andre. 1970. "Capitalist relations of production and the socially necessary labor force." Pp. 155–171 in Arthur Lothstein (ed.), All We Are Saying. . . . New York: G. P. Putnam.

Gross, Bertram M. 1970. "Friendly fascism: A model for America." Social Policy (November/December): 44–52.

Helmer, John, and Thomas Vietorisz. 1973. "Drug use, the labor market and class conflict." Paper presented at Annual Meeting of the American Sociological Association.

Karier, Clarence J. 1973. "Business values and the educational state." Pp. 6–29 in Clarence J. Karier, Paul Violas, and Joel Spring (eds.), Roots of Crisis: American Education in the Twentieth Century. Chicago: Rand McNally.

Liazos, Alexander. 1972. "The poverty of the sociology of deviance: Nuts, sluts and preverts." Social Problems 20(Summer): 103–120.

Mandel, Ernest. 1968. Marxist Economic Theory (Volume I). New York: Monthly Review Press.

Marcuse, Herbert. 1964. One-Dimensional Man. Boston: Beacon Press.

Marx, Karl. 1964. Class Struggles in France, 1848–1850. New York: International Publishers; 1967. Capital (Volume I). New York: International Publishers.

Matza, David. 1969. Becoming Deviant. Englewood Cliffs, N.J.: Prentice Hall.

McIntosh, Mary. 1973. "The growth of racketeering." Economy and Society (February): 35–69.

Morris, Norval, and Gordon Hawkins. 1969. The Honest Politician's Guide to Crime Control. Chicago: University of Chicago Press.

Musto, David F. 1973. The American Disease: Origins of Narcotic Control. New Haven: Yale University Press.

National Institute of Mental Health. 1970. Trends in Resident Patients—State and County Mental Hospitals 1950–1968. Biometry Branch, Office of Program Planning and Evaluation. Rockville, Maryland: National Institute of Mental Health.

O'Connor, James. 1973. The Fiscal Crisis of the State. New York: St. Martin's Press.

Piven, Frances, and Richard A. Cloward. 1971. Regulating the Poor: The Functions of Public Welfare. New York: Random House.

Rimlinger, Gaston V. 1961. "Social security, incentives, and controls in the U.S. and U.S.S.R." Comparative Studies in Society and History 4(November): 104–124; 1966. "Welfare policy and economic development: A comparative historical perspective." Journal of Economic History (December): 556–571.

Schelling, Thomas. 1967. "Economics and criminal enterprise." Public Interest (Spring): 61–78.

Secombe, Wally. 1973. "The housewife and her labour under capitalism." New Left Review (January–February): 3–24.

Spring, Joel. 1972. Education and the Rise of the Corporate State. Boston: Beacon Press; 1973. "Education as a form of social control." Pp. 30–39 in Clarence J. Karier, Paul Violas, and Joel Spring (eds.), Roots of Crisis: American Education in the Twentieth Century. Chicago: Rand McNally.

Turk, Austin T. 1969. Criminality and Legal Order. Chicago: Rand McNally.

Zaretsky, Eli. 1973. "Capitalism, the family and personal life: Parts 1 & 2." Socialist Revolution (January–April/May–June): 69–126, 19–70.

4 / The Discovery of Hyperkinesis: Notes on the Medicalization of Deviant Behavior

PETER CONRAD

INTRODUCTION

The increasing medicalization of deviant behavior and the medical institution's role as an agent of social control has gained considerable notice (Freidson, 1970; Pitts, 1968; Kittrie, 1971; Zola, 1972). By medicalization we mean defining behavior as a medical problem or illness and mandating or licensing the medical profession to provide some type of treatment for it. Examples include alcoholism, drug addiction and treating violence as a genetic or brain disorder. This redefinition is not a new function of the medical institution: psychiatry and public health have always been concerned with social behavior and have traditionally functioned as agents of social control (Foucault, 1965; Szasz, 1970; Rosen, 1972)....

This paper describes how certain forms of behavior in children have become defined as a medical problem and how medicine has become a major agent for their social control since the discovery of hyperkinesis. By discovery we mean both origin of the diagnosis and treatment for this disorder; and discovery of children who exhibit this behavior. The first section analyzes the discovery of hyperkinesis and why it suddenly became popular in the 1960's. The second section will discuss the medicalization of deviant behavior and its ramifications.

THE MEDICAL DIAGNOSIS OF HYPERKINESIS

Hyperkinesis is a relatively recent phenomenon as a medical diagnostic category. Only in the past two decades has it been available as a recognized diagnostic category and only in the last decade has it received widespread notice and medical popularity. However, the roots of the diagnosis and treatment of this clinical entity are found earlier.

Hyperkinesis is also known as Minimal Brain Dysfunction, Hyperactive Syndrome, Hyperkinetic Disorder of Childhood, and by several other diagnostic categories. Although the symptoms and the presumed etiology vary, in general the behaviors are quite similar and greatly overlap.[1] Typical symptom patterns for diagnosing the disorder include: extreme excess of motor activity (hyperactivity); very short attention span (the child flits from activity to activity); restlessness; fidgetiness; often wildly oscillating mood swings (he's fine one day, a terror the next); clumsiness; aggressive-like behavior; impulsivity; in school he cannot sit still, cannot comply with rules, has low frustration level; frequently there may be sleeping problems and acquisition of speech may be delayed (Stewart et al., 1966, 1970; Wender, 1971). Most of the symptoms for the disorder are deviant behaviors.[2] It is six times as prevalent among boys as among girls. We use the term hyperkinesis to represent all the diagnostic categories of this disorder.

THE DISCOVERY OF HYPERKINESIS

It is useful to divide the analysis into what might be considered *clinical factors* directly related to the diagnosis and treatment of hyperkinesis and *social factors* that set the context for the emergence of the new diagnostic category.

Clinical Factors

Bradley (1937) observed that amphetamine drugs had a spectacular effect in altering the behavior of school children who exhibited behavior disorders or learning disabilities. Fifteen of the thirty children he treated actually became more subdued in their behavior. Bradley termed the effect of this medication paradoxical, since he expected that amphetamines would stimulate children as they stimulated adults. After the medication was discontinued the children's behavior returned to premedication level.

A scattering of reports in the medical literature on the utility of stimulant medications for "childhood behavior disorders" appeared in the next two decades. The next significant contribution was the work of Strauss and his associates (Strauss and Lehtinen, 1947) who found certain behavior (including hyperkinesis behaviors) in postencephalitic children suffering from what they called minimal brain injury (damage). This was the first time these behaviors were attributed to the new organic distinction of minimal brain damage.

This disorder still remained unnamed or else it was called a variety of names (usually just "childhood behavior disorder"). It did not appear as a specific diagnostic category until Laufer, et al. (1957) described it as the "hyperkinetic impulse disorder" in 1957. Upon finding "the salient characteristics of the behavior pattern . . . are strikingly similar to those with clear cut organic causation" these researchers described a disorder with no clear-cut history or evidence for organicity (Laufer, et al., 1957).

In 1966 a task force sponsored by the U.S. Public Health Service and the National Association for Crippled Children and Adults attempted to clarify the ambiguity and confusion in terminology and symptomology in diagnosing children's behavior and learning disorders. From over three dozen diagnoses, they agreed on the term "minimal brain dysfunction" as an overriding diagnosis that would include hyperkinesis and other disorders (Clements, 1966). Since this time M.B.D. has been the primary formal diagnosis or label.

In the middle 1950's a new drug, Ritalin, was synthesized, that has many qualities of amphetamines without some of their more undesirable side effects. In 1961 this drug was approved by the F.D.A. for use with children. Since this time there has been much research published on the use of Ritalin in the treatment of childhood behavior disorders. This medication became the "treatment of choice" for treating children with hyperkinesis.

Since the early sixties, more research appeared on the etiology, diagnosis and treatment of hyperkinesis (cf. DeLong, 1972; Grinspoon and Singer, 1973; Cole, 1975)—as much as three-quarters concerned with drug treatment of the disorder. There had been increasing publicity of the disorder in the mass media as well. The *Reader's Guide to Periodical Literature* had no articles on hyperkinesis before 1967, one each in 1968 and 1969, and a total of forty for 1970 through 1974 (a mean of eight per year).

Now hyperkinesis has become the most common child psychiatric problem (Gross and Wilson, 1974:142); special pediatric clinics have been established to treat hyperkinetic children, and substantial federal funds have been invested in etiological and treatment research. Outside the medical profession, teachers have developed a working clinical knowledge of hyperkinesis' symptoms and treatment (cf. Robin and Bosco, 1973); articles appear regularly in mass circulation magazines and newspapers so that parents often come to clinics with knowledge of this diagnosis. Hyperkinesis is no longer the relatively esoteric diagnostic category it may have been twenty years ago; it is now a well-known clinical disorder.

Social Factors

The social factors affecting the discovery of hyperkinesis can be divided into two areas: (1) The Pharmaceutical Revolution; (2) Government Action.

(1) The Pharmaceutical Revolution. Since the 1930's the pharmaceutical industry has been synthesizing and manufacturing a large number of psychoactive drugs, contributing to a virtual revolution in drug making and drug taking in America (Silverman and Lee, 1974).

Psychoactive drugs are agents that affect the central nervous system. Benzedrine, Ritalin, and Dexedrine are all synthesized psychoactive stimulants which were indicated for narcolepsy, appetite control (as "diet pills"), mild depression, fatigue, and more recently hyperkinetic children.

Until the early sixties there was little or no promotion and advertisement of any of these medications for use with childhood disorders.[3] Then two major pharmaceutical firms (Smith, Kline and French, manufacturer of Dexedrine, and CIBA, manufacturer of Ritalin) began to advertise in medical journals and through direct mailing and efforts of the "detail men." Most of this advertising of the pharmaceutical treatment of hyperkinesis was directed to the medical sphere; but some of the promotion was targeted for the educational sector also (Hentoff, 1972). This promotion was probably significant in disseminating information concerning the diagnosis and treatment of this newly discovered disorder.[4] Since 1955 the use of psychoactive medications (especially phenothiazines) for the treatment of persons who are mentally ill, along with the concurrent dramatic decline in inpatient populations, has made psychopharmacology an integral part of treatment for mental disorders. It has also undoubtedly increased the confidence in the medical profession for the pharmaceutical approach to mental and behavioral problems.

(2) Government Action.   Since the publication of the U.S.P.H.S. report on M.B.D. there have been at least two significant governmental reports on treating school children with stimulant medications for behavior disorders. Both of these came as a response to the national publicity created by the *Washington Post* report (1970) that five to 10 percent of the 62,000 grammar school children in Omaha, Nebraska were being treated with "behavior modification drugs to improve deportment and increase learning potential" (quoted in Grinspoon and Singer, 1973). Although the figures were later found to be a little exaggerated, it nevertheless spurred a Congressional investigation (U.S. Government Printing Office, 1970) and a conference sponsored by the Office of Child Development (1971) on the use of stimulant drugs in the treatment of behaviorally disturbed school children.

The Congressional Subcommittee on Privacy chaired by Congressman Cornelius E. Gallagher held hearings on the issue of prescribing drugs for hyperactive school children. In general, the committee showed great concern over the facility in which the medication was prescribed; more specifically that some children at least were receiving drugs from general practitioners whose primary diagnosis was based on teachers' and parents' reports that the child was doing poorly in school. There was also a concern with the absence of follow-up studies on the long-term effects of treatment.

The H.E.W. committee was a rather hastily convened group of professionals (a majority were M.D.'s) many of whom already had commitments to drug treatment for children's behavior problems. They recommended that only M.D.'s make the diagnosis and prescribe treatment, that the pharmaceutical companies promote the treatment of the disorder only through medical channels, that parents should not be coerced to accept any particular treatment and that long-term follow-up research should be done. This report served as blue ribbon approval for treating hyperkinesis with psychoactive medications.

DISCUSSION

We will focus discussion on three issues: How children's deviant behavior became conceptualized as a medical problem; why this occurred when it did; and what are some of the implications of the medicalization of deviant behavior.

How does deviant behavior become conceptualized as a medical problem? We assume that before the discovery of hyperkinesis this type of deviance was seen as disruptive, disobedient, rebellious, anti-social or deviant behavior. Perhaps the label "emotionally disturbed" was sometimes used, when it was in vogue in the early sixties, and the child was usually managed in the context of the family or the school or in extreme cases, the child guidance clinic. How then did this constellation of deviant behaviors become a medical disorder?

The treatment was available long before the disorder treated was clearly conceptualized. It was twenty years after Bradley's discovery of the "paradoxical effect" of stimulants on certain deviant children that Laufer named the disorder and described its characteristic symptoms. Only in the late fifties were both the diagnostic label and the pharmaceutical treatment available. The pharmaceutical revolution in mental health and the increased interest in child psychiatry provided a favorable background for the dissemination of knowledge about this new disorder. The latter probably made the medical profession more likely to consider behavior problems in children as within their clinical jurisdiction.

There were agents outside the medical profession itself that were significant in "promoting" hyperkinesis as a disorder within the medical framework. These agents might be conceptualized in Becker's terms as "moral entrepreneurs," those who crusade for creation and enforcement of the rules (Becker, 1963).[5] In this case the moral entrepreneurs were the pharmaceutical companies and the Association for Children with Learning Disabilities.

The pharmaceutical companies spent considerable time and money promoting stimulant medications for this new disorder. From the middle 1960's on, medical journals and the free "throwaway" magazines contained elaborate advertising for Ritalin and Dexedrine. These ads explained the utility of treating hyperkinesis and urged the physician to diagnose and treat hyperkinetic children. The ads run from one to six pages. For example, a two-page ad in 1971 stated:

MBD...MEDICAL MYTH OR DIAGNOSABLE DISEASE ENTITY What medical practitioner has not, at one time or another, been called upon to examine an impulsive, excitable hyperkinetic child? A child with difficulty in concentrating. Easily frustrated. Unusually aggressive. A classroom rebel. In the absence of any organic pathology, the conduct of such children was, until a few short years ago, usually dismissed as...spunkiness, or evidence of youthful vitality. But it is now evident that in many of these children the hyperkinetic syndrome exists as a distinct medical entity. This syndrome is readily diagnosed through patient histories, neurologic signs, and psychometric testing—has been classified by an expert panel convened by the United States Department of Health, Education and Welfare as Minimal Brain Dysfunction, MBD.

The pharmaceutical firms also supplied sophisticated packets of "diagnostic and treatment" information on hyperkinesis to physicians, paid for professional conferences on the subject, and supported research in the identification and treatment of the disorder. Clearly these corporations had a vested interest in the labeling and treatment of hyperkinesis; CIBA had $13 million profit from Ritalin alone in 1971, which was 15 percent of the total gross profits (Charles, 1971; Hentoff, 1972).

The other moral entrepreneur, less powerful than the pharmaceutical companies, but nevertheless influential, is the Association for Children with Learning Disabilities. Although their focus is not specifically on hyperkinetic children, they do include it in their conception of Learning Disabilities along with aphasia, reading problems like dyslexia and perceptual motor problems. Founded in the early 1950's by parents and professionals, it has functioned much as the National Association for Mental Health does for mental illness: promoting conferences, sponsoring legislation, providing social support. One of the main functions has been to disseminate information concerning this relatively new area in education, Learning Disabilities. While the organization does have a more educational than medical perspective, most of the literature indicates that for hyperkinesis members have adopted the medical model and the medical approach to the problem. They have sensitized teachers and schools to the conception of hyperkinesis as a medical problem.

The medical model of hyperactive behavior has become very well accepted in our society. Physicians find treatment relatively simple and the results sometimes spectacular. Hyperkinesis minimizes parents' guilt by emphasizing "it's not their fault, it's an organic problem" and allows for nonpunitive management or control of deviance. Medication often makes a child less disruptive in the classroom and sometimes aids a child in learning. Children often like their "magic pills" which make their behavior more socially acceptable and they probably benefit from a reduced stigma also.

THE MEDICALIZATION
OF DEVIANT BEHAVIOR

Pitts has commented that "medicalization is one of the most effective means of social control and that it is destined to become the main mode of *formal* social control" (1971:391). Kittrie (1971) has termed it "the coming of the therapeutic state."

Medicalization of mental illness dates at least from the seventeenth century (Foucault, 1965; Szasz, 1970). Even slaves who ran away were once considered to be suffering from the disease *drapedomania* (Chorover, 1973). In recent years alcoholism, violence, and drug addiction as well as hyperactive behavior in children have all become defined as medical problems, both in etiology or explanation of the behavior and the means of social control or treatment.

There are many reasons why this medicalization has occurred. Much scientific research, especially in pharmacology and genetics, has become technologically more sophisticated, and found more subtle correlates with human behavior. Sometimes these findings (as in the case of XYY chromosomes and violence) become etiological explanations for deviance. Pharmacological technology that makes new discoveries affecting behavior (e.g., antabuse, methadone and stimulants) are used as treatment for deviance. In part this application is encouraged by the prestige of the medical profession and its attachment to science. As Freidson notes, the medical profession has first claim to jurisdiction over anything that deals with the functioning of the body and especially anything that can be labeled illness (1970:251). Advances in genetics, pharmacology and "psychosurgery" also may advance medicine's jurisdiction over deviant behavior.

Second, the application of pharmacological technology is related to the humanitarian trend in the conception and control of deviant behavior. Alcoholism is no longer sin or even moral weakness, it is now a disease. Alcoholics are no longer arrested in many places for "public drunkenness," they are now somehow "treated," even if it is only to be dried out. Hyperactive children are now considered to have an illness rather than to be disruptive, disobedient, overactive problem children. They are not as likely to be the "bad boy" of the classroom; they are children with a medical disorder. Clearly there are some real humanitarian benefits to be gained by such a medical conceptualization of deviant behavior. There is less condemnation of the deviants (they have an illness, it is not their fault) and perhaps less social stigma. In some cases, even the medical treatment itself is more humanitarian social control than the criminal justice system.

There is, however, another side to the medicalization of deviant behavior. The four aspects of this side of the issue include (1) the problem of expert control; (2) medical social control; (3) the individualization of social problems; and (4) the "depoliticization" of deviant behavior.

1. *The problem of expert control.* The medical profession is a profession of experts; they have a monopoly on anything that can be conceptualized as illness. Because of the way the medical profession is organized and the mandate it has from society, decisions related to medical diagnoses and treatment are virtually controlled by medical professionals.

Some conditions that enter the medical domain are not *ipso facto* medical problems, especially deviant behavior, whether alcoholism, hyperactivity or drug addiction. By defining a problem as medical it is removed from the public realm where there can be discussion by ordinary people and put on a plane where only medical people can discuss it. As Reynolds states,

> The increasing acceptance, especially among the more educated segments of our populace, of technical solutions—solutions administered by disinterested politically and morally neutral experts—results in the withdrawal of more and more areas of human experience from the realm of public discussion. For when drunkenness, juvenile delinquency, sub par performance and extreme political beliefs are seen as symptoms of an underlying illness or biological defect the merits and drawbacks of such behavior or beliefs need not be evaluated (1973:200–221).

The public may have their own conceptions of deviant behavior but that of the experts is usually dominant.

2. *Medical social control.* Defining deviant behavior as a medical problem allows certain things to be done that could not otherwise be considered; for example, the body may be cut open or psychoactive medications may be given. This treatment can be a form of social control.

In regard to drug treatment Lennard points out: "Psychoactive drugs, especially those legally prescribed, tend to restrain individuals from behavior and experience that are not complementary to the requirements of the dominant value system" (1971:57). These forms of medical social control presume a prior definition of deviance as a medical problem. Psychosurgery on an individual prone to violent outbursts requires a diagnosis that there was something wrong with his brain or nervous system. Similarly, prescribing drugs to restless, overactive and disruptive school children requires a diagnosis of hyperkinesis. These forms of social control, what Chorover (1973) has called "psychotechnology," are very powerful and often very efficient means of controlling deviance. These relatively new and increasingly popular forms of social control could not be utilized without the medicalization of deviant behavior. As is suggested from the discovery of hyperkinesis, if a mechanism of medical social control seems useful, then the deviant behavior it modifies will develop a medical label or diagnosis. No overt malevolence on the part of the medical profession is implied: rather it is part of a complex process, of which the medical profession is only a part. The larger process might be called the individualization of social problems.

3. *The individualization of social problems.* The medicalization of deviant behavior is part of a larger phenomenon that is prevalent in our society, the individualization of social problems. We tend to look for causes and solutions to complex social problems in the individual rather than in the

social system. This view resembles Ryan's (1971) notion of "blaming the victim"; seeing the causes of the problem in individuals rather than in the society where they live. We then seek to change the "victim" rather than the society. The medical perspective of diagnosing an illness in an individual lends itself to the individualization of social problems. Rather than seeing certain deviant behaviors as symptomatic of problems in the social system, the medical perspective focuses on the individual diagnosing and treating the illness, generally ignoring the social situation.

Hyperkinesis serves as a good example. Both the school and the parents are concerned with the child's behavior; the child is very difficult at home and disruptive in school. No punishments or rewards seem consistently to work in modifying the behavior; and both parents and school are at their wits' end. A medical evaluation is suggested. The diagnoses of hyperkinetic behavior leads to prescribing stimulant medications. The child's behavior seems to become more socially acceptable, reducing problems in school and at home.

But there is an alternate perspective. By focusing on the symptoms and defining them as hyperkinesis we ignore the possibility that behavior is not an illness but an adaption to a social situation. It diverts our attention from the family or school and from seriously entertaining the idea that the "problem" could be in the structure of the social system. And by giving medications we are essentially supporting the existing systems and do not allow this behavior to be a factor of change in the system.

4. *The depoliticization of deviant behavior.* Depoliticization of deviant behavior is a result of both the process of medicalization and individualization of social problems. To our western world, probably one of the clearest examples of such a depoliticization of deviant behavior occurred when political dissenters in the Soviet Union were declared mentally ill and confined in mental hospitals (cf. Conrad, 1972). This strategy served to neutralize the meaning of political protest and dissent, rendering it the ravings of mad persons.

The medicalization of deviant behavior depoliticizes deviance in the same manner. By defining the overactive, restless and disruptive child as hyperkinetic we ignore the meaning of behavior in the context of the social system. If we focused our analysis on the school system we might see the child's behavior as symptomatic of some "disorder" in the school or classroom situation, rather than symptomatic of an individual neurological disorder.

CONCLUSION

I have discussed the social ramifications of the medicalization of deviant behavior, using hyperkinesis as the example. A number of consequences of this medicalization have been outlined, including the depoliticization of deviant behavior, decision-making power of experts, and the role of medicine as an agent of social control. In the last analysis medical social control may be the central issue, as in this role medicine becomes a *de facto* agent of the *status quo*. The medical profession may not have entirely sought this role, but its members have been, in general, disturbingly unconcerned and unquestioning in their acceptance of it. With the increasing medical knowledge and technology it is likely that more deviant behavior will be medicalized and medicine's social control function will expand.

Notes

1. The U.S.P.H.S. report (Clements, 1966) included 38 terms that were used to describe or distinguish the conditions that it labeled Minimal Brain Dysfunction. Although the literature attempts to differentiate M.B.D., hyperkinesis, hyperactive syndrome, and several other diagnostic labels, it is our belief that in practice they are almost interchangeable.

2. For a fuller discussion of the construction of the diagnosis of hyperkinesis, see Conrad (1976), especially Chapter 6.

3. The American Medical Association's change in policy in accepting more pharmaceutical advertising in the late fifties may have been important. Probably the F.D.A. approval of the use of Ritalin for children in 1961 was more significant. Until 1970, Ritalin was advertised for treatment of "functional behavior problems in children." Since then, because of an F.D.A. order, it has only been promoted for treatment of M.B.D.

4. The drug industry spends fully 25 percent of its budget on promotion and advertising. See Coleman et al. (1966) for the role of the detail men and how physicians rely upon them for information.

5. Freidson also notes the medical professional role as moral entrepreneur in this process also:

> The profession does treat the illnesses laymen take to it, but it also seeks to discover illness of which the laymen may not even be aware. One of the greatest ambitions of the physician is to discover and describe a "new" disease or syndrome... (1970:252).

References

Becker, Howard S. 1963. *Outsiders: Studies in the Sociology of Deviance.* New York: Free Press.

Bradley, Charles. 1937. "The Behavior of Children Receiving Benzedrine." *American Journal of Psychiatry,* 94 (March): 577–585.

Charles, Alan. 1971. "The Case of Ritalin." *New Republic,* 23 (October): 17–19.

Chorover, Stephen L. 1973. "Big Brother and Psychotechnology." *Psychology Today* (October): 43–54.

Clements, Samuel D. 1966. "Task Force I: Minimal Brain Dysfunction in Children." National Institute of Neurological Diseases and Blindness, Monograph no. 3. Washington, D.C.: U.S. Department of Health, Education and Welfare.

Cole, Sherwood. 1975. "Hyperactive Children: The Use of Stimulant Drugs Evaluated." *American Journal of Orthopsychiatry,* 45 (January): 28–37.

Coleman, James, Elihu Katz, and Herbert Menzel. 1966. *Medical Innovation.* Indianapolis: Bobbs-Merrill.

Conrad, Peter. 1972. "Ideological Deviance: An Analysis of the Soviet Use of Mental Hospitals for Political Dissenters." Unpublished manuscript.

Conrad, Peter. 1976. *Identifying Hyperactive Children: A Study in the Medicalization of Deviant Behavior.* Lexington, Mass.: D.C. Heath and Co.

DeLong, Arthur R. 1972. "What Have We Learned from Psychoactive Drugs Research with Hyperactives?" *American Journal of Diseases in Children*, 123 (February): 177–180.

Foucault, Michel. 1965. *Madness and Civilization*. New York: Pantheon.

Freidson, Eliot. 1970. *Profession of Medicine: A Study of the Sociology of Applied Knowledge*. New York: Dodd, Mead.

Grinspoon, Lester and Susan Singer. 1973. "Amphetamines in the Treatment of Hyperactive Children." *Harvard Educational Review*, 43 (November): 515–555.

Gross, Mortimer B. and William E. Wilson. 1974. *Minimal Brain Dysfunction*. New York: Brunner Mazel.

Hentoff, Nat. 1972. "Drug Pushing in the Schools: The Professionals." *The Village Voice*, 22 (May): 21–23.

Kittrie, Nicholas. 1971. *The Right to Be Different*. Baltimore: Johns Hopkins Press.

Laufer, M. W., Denhoff, E., and Solomons, G. 1957. "Hyperkinetic Impulse Disorder in Children's Behavior Problems." *Psychosomatic Medicine*, 19 (January): 38–49.

Lennard, Henry L. and Associates. 1971. *Mystification and Drug Misuse*. New York: Harper and Row.

Office of Child Development. 1971. "Report of the Conference on the Use of Stimulant Drugs in Treatment of Behaviorally Disturbed Children." Washington, D.C.: Office of Child Development, Department of Health, Education and Welfare, January 11–12.

Pitts, Jesse. 1968. "Social Control: The Concept." In David Sills (ed.), *International Encyclopedia of the Social Sciences*. Vol. 14. New York: Macmillan.

Reynolds, Janice M. 1973. "The Medical Institution." In Larry T. Reynolds and James M. Henslin, *American Society: A Critical Analysis*. New York: David McKay.

Robin, Stanley S. and James J. Bosco. 1973. "Ritalin for School Children: The Teacher's Perspective." *Journal of School Health*, 47 (December): 624–628.

Rosen, George. 1972. "The Evolution of Social Medicine." In Howard E. Freeman, Sol Levine, and Leo Reeder, *Handbook of Medical Sociology*. Englewood Cliffs, N.J.: Prentice-Hall.

Ryan, William. 1970. *Blaming the Victim*. New York: Vintage.

Silverman, Milton and Philip R. Lee. 1974. *Pills, Profits and Politics*. Berkeley: University of California Press.

Sroufe, L. Alan and Mark Stewart. 1973. "Treating Problem Children with Stimulant Drugs." *New England Journal of Medicine*, 289 (August 23): 407–421.

Stewart, Mark A. 1970. "Hyperactive Children." *Scientific American*, 222 (April): 794–798.

Stewart, Mark A., A. Ferris, N. P. Pitts, and A. G. Craig. 1966. "The Hyperactive Child Syndrome." *American Journal of Orthopsychiatry*, 36 (October): 861–867.

Strauss, A. A. and L. E. Lehtinen. 1947. *Psychopathology and Education of the Brain-Injured Child*. Vol. 1. New York: Grune and Stratton.

U.S. Government Printing Office. 1970. "Federal Involvement in the Use of Behavior Modification Drugs on Grammar School Children of the Right to Privacy Inquiry: Hearing Before a Subcommittee of the Committee on Government Operations." Washington, D.C.: 91st Congress, 2nd session (September 29).

Wender, Paul. 1971. *Minimal Brain Dysfunction in Children*. New York: John Wiley and Sons.

Zola, Irving. 1972. "Medicine as an Institution of Social Control." *Sociological Review*, 20 (November): 487–504.

Part 2 / Understanding Deviance: Theories and Perspectives

In Part 1 I introduced a specific concern for the ways in which deviant categories arise, as well as the ways in which violators of existing categories may be reacted to. Missing from this introduction was a concern for *why* actors may exhibit behavior in violation of established norms, rules, regulations, and laws—violations that may cause them to be initially labeled as deviants. I have argued previously that if we are to approach a more complete understanding of deviance in terms of social processes, we must not only analyze the creation of deviant categories and the reactions to violators of categories; we must also examine the motivations for deviance. The selections in this part represent some of the major attempts to accomplish this goal.

Explanations of the motivations for deviance have taken various forms. Some observers would place the blame on a defective family structure or arrested personality adjustment; others would emphasize such conditions as poverty or racism; and there are proponents of the thesis that individuals are born deviant. It should be recognized, however, that no single factor can adequately explain why actors commit deviant acts. For example, findings in the area of delinquency research generally conclude that a combination of family, school, and peer variables is the most likely source of motivations for youth crime and deviance.

The actual attempts at understanding or explaining motivations for deviancy can, for our purposes, be roughly grouped into seven categories: (1) functionalist, (2) culture conflict, (3) cultural transmission, (4) opportunity, (5) radical-conflict, (6) control, and (7) interactionist. Of these particular approaches, it should be noted that functionalism, culture conflict, control theory, and opportunity are basically structural. Some structuralists seek to explain why crime and deviance exist in the social system, whereas others analyze societal-structural conditions that seem to produce pressures toward deviation. The cultural transmission view is concerned primarily with how, through social-psychological-symbolic processes, actors learn existing cultures and traditions. The radical-conflict theorists, by contrast, investigate how the powerful influence the creation of deviant categories and point out the frequent application of such categories to the less powerful. Finally, the interactionists analyze the labeling ceremony and its impact on individuals. Although each of these approaches explicitly emphasizes certain underlying themes, concepts, or processes, there is frequently an implied or direct overlap among the various models. Such linkages are evident in the subsequent discussions of each model.

THE FUNCTIONALIST PERSPECTIVE

Social scientists who use a functionalist model contend that deviance is an integral part of any social system and that such behavior satisfies some societal need. In terms of sociological analysis, advocates of this model maintain that deviance serves the important function of demarcating and maintaining current boundaries of acceptable behavior. These particular conceptions are embedded in Emile Durkheim's work.

In his statement "The Normal and the Pathological," Durkheim argues that crime not only inheres in all societies but also serves a useful function for the collective conscience, particularly in maintaining the social system. And although forms and definitions of criminal and deviant behavior (i.e., the *collective types* or deviant categories) may vary from society to society, such behaviors do provide members with a basis for punishing violators of the prevailing normative codes. Punishment serves as an important reminder to others that certain behaviors are acceptable while others are not. Thus, achievement of an understanding of deviance and its categories requires an examination of the prevailing definitions of conformity.

In "On the Sociology of Deviance," Kai T. Erikson argues that behavior that may be acceptable within a family setting may not be perceived as such by the larger community. Furthermore, conduct that may be viewed unfavorably by the community may actually go unnoticed in other parts of the culture. In varying situations, then, different standards are used to assess whether or not an actor's behavior exceeds a social unit's "tolerance limits." If it does, the violator may be sanctioned negatively. In a sense, a community or social unit is concerned with the maintenance of its boundaries. Erikson argues that interactions occurring between a potential deviant and a community's official agents play an especially important role in "locating and publicizing the group's outer edges." Such confrontations are not without their individual and structural ramifications, however. Not only may a social actor be selected out, formally processed, and cast into a new status (e.g., that of a criminal), but if the violator is a member of a deviant group, the confrontation and resultant sanctioning may operate in such a way as to actually enhance an actor's esteem in the eyes of his or her peers, as well as to solidify and make more obvious the underlying structure, identity, and character of the group. Erikson goes on to offer some interesting observations. For example, he comments on the fact that even though selected institutions have been created to combat deviance, they, like many deviant groups, often operate in such a way as to encourage, promote, and perpetuate it.

It should be noted that Erikson, given his primary focus on the maintenance and operation of normative systems, is not concerned specifically with explaining why actors engage in activities that may cause them to be labeled as deviants by others. The next perspective, however, considers the question of motivation more directly; in doing so, it enters the realm of social-psychological, or interactional, processes, particularly those aspects involved with the inculcation of values and traditions within members of society.

THE CULTURE CONFLICT PERSPECTIVE

A basic premise underlying this perspective is the notion that, because socializing influences and experiences vary a great deal, people are frequently confronted with conflicting definitions of a situation. Furthermore, if they act in accordance with their own values, they may be defined as deviants by those who are operating from a different set of values.

These ideas are elaborated upon by Thorsten Sellin. In "The Conflict of Conduct Norms," he argues that actors are members of numerous groups and are, therefore, exposed to many different sets of conduct norms and values. Among those who migrate from one society to another, the sense of cultural conflict may be particularly severe. Migrants frequently find themselves constrained and regulated by a new and unfamiliar set of values. Sellin cites, as an example, the case in which a father kills the seducer of his daughter. In Sicily, killing a seducer is acceptable; in the United States it is considered murder. A lack of consensus with respect to existing norms, then, may not only give rise to cultural conflicts of various types but may also result in the application of deviant labels to those who violate deviant categories.

J. Mark Watson, in "Outlaw Motorcyclists: An Outgrowth of Lower Class Cultural Concerns," provides another illustration of the culture conflict model. Watson focuses on outlaw motorcyclists—a subculture that he studied as a participant-observer over a period of three years. He begins by describing the biker subculture and the associated outlaw lifestyle. Of interest are the ways in which the outlaw bikers view the world and themselves. They tend to see the world as "hostile, weak, and effeminate" while viewing themselves as "outsiders." Watson concludes with an analysis of how the biker subculture, in its operation, compares with a typology of "focal concerns" (e.g., the emphasis that is placed on "trouble," "toughness," "smartness," and "excitement") developed by Walter Miller. For example, trouble is more than a major theme; it serves important functions for the group (e.g., it provides an opportunity for demonstrating masculinity and helps to enforce group solidarity). The selection gives an excellent feel for how a particular subculture operates in a larger, dominant culture—a culture that possesses the power and resources to tag people as "outsiders."

CULTURAL TRANSMISSION THEORY

A central tenet underlying the cultural transmission model is the idea that one learns cultural traditions and values through symbolic communication with others. Two of the more famous representatives of this position are Gresham M. Sykes and David Matza.

In "Techniques of Neutralization: A Theory of Delinquency," Sykes and Matza argue that juveniles do not really reject middle-class values. Rather, because the existing normative structure has a certain flexibility, actors can "bend" the laws to fit their needs. Also basic to this thesis is the idea that when actors contemplate the commission of a delinquent or criminal act, they must come to grips with any immediate or potential threats to their identity. Developing an effective system of "neutralization" or rationalization is one way of accomplishing this. Sykes and Matza assert, moreover, that this attitude of self-justification is operative during and after the commission of an offense as well. The writers make the additional point that we all use rationalizations, whether we are involved in deviant activities or not.

Diana Scully and Joseph Marolla, in "Convicted Rapists' Vocabulary of Motive: Excuses and Justifications," focus on rape. Their basic assumption is that, contrary to many of the individualistic notions that are advanced to explain it (e.g., rapists are propelled by "irresistible impulses" or "diseased minds"), rape is behavior that is learned in interaction with others. And similar to the Sykes-Matza position, a portion of this learning entails acquiring those attitudes, motives, and actions that are conducive to the sexual assault of women. The researchers, in their interviews with 114 convicted rapists, offer evidence in support of this thesis. They observe that their sample can be divided into two basic categories of rapists: the admitters and the deniers. The "deniers" attempt to justify their rapes by casting aspersions on the victim; in doing so, they often invoke selected cultural stereotypes (e.g., women are seductresses, women really mean "yes" when they say "no," nice girls don't get raped, and the like). The "admitters," by contrast, regard their behavior as wrong, not justifiable, and frequently blame themselves instead of the victim; they use various appeals to excuse their rapes (e.g., drugs, alcohol, emotional problems, and so on).

Several of the articles discussed thus far (e.g., the one by Sykes and Matza) have been concerned rather directly with the way in which socialization processes may bring about behavior that can be labeled as deviant. However, with one notable exception (Watson's theory), none of these writers has systematically examined the conditions that may lead to an exploration of nonconformist adaptations. The next perspective offers a more specific attempt to do so.

OPPORTUNITY THEORY

Those who subscribe to opportunity theory are concerned primarily with the social conditions that may produce a strain toward deviation. Of particular focus is the way actors posture themselves relative to the existing social structure. Robert K. Merton's article, "Social Structure and Anomie," represents what many consider the classic study, within anomie, or opportunity, theory, of the emergence of deviant behavior.

Basic to Merton's explanation is the contention that any society can be characterized in terms of its structure, particularly its goals and its means. A well-integrated society, he reasons, displays a balance between these elements. In such a society, when people want to obtain societal goals, they will use the appropriate institutionalized means for doing so. American society, according to Merton, does not maintain this sort of balance. It is a society in which emphasis is placed almost exclusively on the achievement of goals—regardless of the methods used to attain them. Those affected the most by the imbalance are the *lower classes*. Most members of the lower classes accept the American dream of attaining success; when they attempt to realize their goals through legitimate means, however, they find themselves blocked, mainly because they do not possess the necessary resources. They may substitute other means—for instance, stealing or robbing. Merton refers to these individuals as "innovators." He argues, further, that when there is a disjunction between goals and means, the result may be cultural chaos, or *anomie*. In this situation, the predictability and regulation of behavior become tenuous.

John M. Hagedorn, in "Homeboys, Dope Fiends, Legits, and New Jacks," offers an empirical account that has some relationship to opportunity theory, particularly those aspects that describe how subcultures may arise. The study also challenges some long-standing beliefs about the nature of gang involvement. The specific research questions addressed are two: (1) What happens as gang members age, and (2) are adult gang members typically the same kinds of people, or do gangs exhibit varying types? Hagedorn draws upon data obtained primarily from interviews with 101 members of some 18 gangs. He notes initially that, although more gang members appear to be working today, their overall involvement in the labor market is quite low. Perhaps most insightful and revealing is the fourfold typology of male adult gang membership that emerges from his data: (1) the *legits*, members who had left the gang; (2) the *homeboys*, members who worked alternatively at conventional jobs and drug sales; (3) the *dope fiends*, members who were addicted and participated in drug sales to maintain their source of drugs; and (4) the *new jacks*, members who pursued the drug game as a career. Hagedorn observes that mobility among the categories did occur. For example, some homeboys became legits, while others adopted the new jack role. Hagedorn continues his analysis by examining how his data compare with some of the major gang theories and studies that have been advanced, several of which are part of the anomie, or opportunity, tradition. He notes, for example, that the new jacks seem to mirror Cloward and Ohlin's conception of the criminal subculture, and most particularly their argument that not only must illegitimate opportunity structures exist but the novice must also learn the necessary skills associated with criminal activity; these contingencies seem to apply to the new jacks. Specifically, the existing cocaine economy and the large market for drugs provide the opportunities whereby the new jacks can, through a process of tutelage (i.e., given the opportunity to perform and learn the skills associated with various roles in the drug profession), become entrenched firmly within the drug world. In a sense, they become career deviants. Hagedorn concludes, in part, that although Cloward and Ohlin's opportunity theory seems to have some explanatory utility, it needs to be recast in light of the societal changes that have occurred over the past three decades.

Although several of the statements thus far have offered hypotheses as to why deviance exists in a social system—and why actors commit deviant acts—none has provided an overall framework that can be used to understand how deviant categories arise, why they are violated, and how they are enforced. (The major exception is Becker's general statement in Part 1.) The next perspective addresses these concerns in a more systematic, integrated manner.

RADICAL-CONFLICT THEORY

Radical-conflict theorists study groups, particularly the ways in which their interests and needs influence the definitions, laws, and policies that evolve. Jeffrey H. Reiman, in "A Radical Perspective on Crime," offers a contemporary statement on the conflict model. He maintains that laws and the associated criminal justice system operate in such a manner as to support the established social and economic order. Concentrating on the individual wrongdoer, Reiman argues, is a particularly effective way of attaining this end. By blaming the individual, the criminal justice system simultaneously diverts our attention away from the possible evils of the social order and acquits society of any criminality or injustice. Further, Reiman argues that various types of social arrangements actually sustain and benefit from the perpetuation of the ideology of individual failure or blame. Reiman uses portions of Cloward and Ohlin's theory to buttress his case. For example, even though people are encouraged to succeed, many do fail, and especially those from the lower classes. As Reiman puts it:

" . . . many are called but few are chosen." Involvement in criminal activities does offer an outlet for those experiencing failure and frustration. Thus, not only is society structured in such a way as to actually produce crime, but those who "reap the benefits of the competition for success" (i.e., those who enjoy a high standard of living) do not have to pay for the costs of this competition. The bill is paid by the poor. In fact, the affluent, Reiman argues, deny that they benefit from an economic system that produces a high degree of suffering and frustration for the poor.

This bias against the poor is manifested in other ways. Reiman speaks specifically of the bonuses associated with such a bias. For example, an image is conveyed that the real threat to a decent society comes from the poor. Another important bonus for the powerful is that the bias generates persistent hostility toward the poor. Reiman then notes some of the indignities that the poor suffer at the hands of the welfare system and its agents. Aid, instead of being viewed as an act of justice, is perceived as an act of charity. Many of these points, I might add, will be elaborated on in Part 6, particularly in my discussion of the need to rehabilitate institutions and social systems.

William J. Chambliss, in "A Sociological Analysis of the Law of Vagrancy," provides an interesting account of how selected vagrancy laws came into being. He focuses initially on those social conditions that produced the first full-fledged vagrancy law. This statute, passed in England in 1349, was a partial outgrowth of the Black Death that struck in 1348. Probably the most significant economic effect produced by this pestilence was the decimation of the labor force. At least 50 percent of the population died at a time when the English economy was dependent on a cheap source of labor. Even prior to the Black Death, obtaining an adequate supply of cheap labor was becoming a problem. It was in conditions such as these that the first vagrancy laws emerged. Chambliss maintains that the statutes were actually designed for one express purpose: to force laborers to accept employment under conditions favorable to the landowners. The laws also effectively curtailed the geographical mobility of laborers. In time, such curtailment was no longer necessary. However, the statutes were not eliminated or negated; rather, they underwent some notable alterations. For example, a modification passed in England in 1530 shifted society's focus from laborers to criminals. Chambliss ends by presenting a general discussion of vagrancy laws in the United States—many of which are adoptions of English laws.

CONTROL THEORY

A central feature of control theory is the view that various levels and types of societal commitment, when coupled with other factors, are often important precursors to the commission of deviant acts. Travis Hirschi offers a well-known statement of this position.

In "A Control Theory of Delinquency," he notes that control theorists assume that delinquency will result when an actor's bond to society is weakened or broken. He then proceeds to discuss and analyze the various elements that comprise the bond of society, particularly as they relate to the question of motivation. For example, the "commitment" element refers to the idea that most people invest a great deal of time and energy in conventional lines of activity (e.g., educational and occupational pursuits). When deviant behavior is contemplated, the risks of such deviation must be considered. The guiding assumption is that involvement in deviance or crime would jeopardize one's investments. Hirschi concludes with a section on "belief," another major element of the bond to society. The underlying premise is that society is characterized by a common value system. If this is correct—and if, further, one retains some type of allegiance to established values—then a basic question presents itself: "Why does a man violate the rules in which he believes?" Hirschi, in his attempt to answer this question, rejects the view that an actor must rationalize or neutralize his or her behavior. Hirschi prefers, instead, the notion that the weakness of one's beliefs can be used to explain motivation. When a person's belief in the validity of norms is weakened, the probability of delinquency and deviance increases.

Neal Shover and David Honaker, in "The Socially Bounded Decision Making of Persistent Property Offenders," offer another variant of this position. The researchers are concerned specifically with analyzing the criminal decision-making processes used by persistent property offenders. A central focus, then, becomes the matter of *choice*. Do, for example, prior offenders, in their pursuit of financial or criminal gain, actually "discount or ignore the formal risks of crime?" Shover and Honaker attempt to shed some light on this concern. They offer interview data obtained from 60 career criminals—all of whom had been out of prison at least seven months. The subjects were asked to recount the crimes they had committed subsequent to their release, as well as how the decision was made to commit the crime. Of concern were their assessments of the potential risks and awards associated with the commission of an illegal act. Some interesting findings emerged. For example, the majority gave little thought to the possibility of arrest or subsequent incarceration. The researchers go on to argue that it is useful to examine the decision-making process of offenders within the context of their lifestyle. A central characteristic of this process is referred to as the *life as party* syndrome—a lifestyle that in addition to promoting the notion of "good times," exhibits little concern for those commitments that go beyond one's present social setting. Shover and Honaker conclude by discussing various implications of their results. Risk perceptions, it is suggested, should be analyzed in terms of the various situations or contexts that affect people.

The last perspective to be considered in this section—the interactionist view—is not specifically concerned with the evolution or violation of deviant categories. Rather, this model explores the ways in which people who violate deviant categories (for whatever reasons) are responded to by formal and informal agents of social control. In this respect, definitional and interactional processes are given central focus. As explicated and refined by the interactional and organizational paradigms in the general introduction, this perspective is applied systematically throughout the remainder of this volume.

THE INTERACTIONIST, SOCIETAL REACTIONS, OR LABELING PERSPECTIVE

Individuals who subscribe to the interactionist, or labeling, school examine those social and psychological, or interactional, processes that take place among actors, audiences, and third parties, particularly in terms of their impact on the personal and social-public identity of the actor. The production of a range of deviant careers and identities is also given focus. The main concern, then, is definitional processes and products, and their effects.

Howard S. Becker has explored the concept of *career,* the major orienting focus of this volume, in some depth. He also introduces some important analytical distinctions. In "Career Deviance," he argues that public labeling is generally the most crucial step in building a long-term deviant career. Not only does being branded a deviant affect one's continued social participation, but it frequently produces notable changes in the actor's self-image. The most drastic change, however, seems to occur with respect to the actor's public identity—that is, how others view him or her. Suddenly, in the eyes of others he or she has become a different person; this new status can be effectively referred to as a *master status.* In offering an important distinction between master and subordinate statuses, Becker argues that master statuses assume a certain priority and appear to override most other status considerations.

The status of a deviant is one such status. In relating to a deviant, people will frequently respond to the label and not to the individual. Treatment of an actor in this fashion—as if he or she is generally deviant and not specifically deviant—can serve as a self-fulfilling prophecy whereby attempts are made to mold the actor into the image others have of him or her. Deliberate attempts may be made, for example, to exclude the deviant from any meaningful social intercourse. The actor may respond negatively to such treatment, and, over time, exclusion and its associated reactions can actually give rise to more deviance. The treatment situation, Becker claims, is especially likely to produce such a result. Many of these processes will become even more evident in my discussion of the initiation and perpetuation of deviant careers, particularly those careers that are subject to institutional processing (Part 4). Actor response to labeling is given further analysis in the next selection.

In "Anorexia Nervosa and Bulimia: The Development of Deviant Identities," Penelope A. McLorg and Diane E. Taub, in keeping with the societal reactions, or labeling, tradition, provide data on how an anorexic or bulimic identity develops. The researchers draw heavily upon Lemert's distinction between *primary* and *secondary* deviance. The primary deviant, it is reasoned, is a person who may engage in norm violation or acts of deviance, yet not view himself or herself as deviant. The secondary, or career, deviant, by contrast, not only assumes a new status and associated roles (i.e., moves from a nondeviant to a deviant status) but also accepts the corresponding identity (i.e., comes to view self as a deviant, both in terms of personal and public identity). In the case of the beginning career of the anorexic, the initial experience or behavior elicits positive responses and compliments from significant others. Terms such as "sleek," "good looking," and "fashionable" may be used to characterize the woman. When emaciation is approached, however, family members begin to show increasing concern about the anorexic's compulsive exercising, preoccupation with food preparation, and ritualistic eating patterns. For the bulimic, others also begin to question how, given the large intake of food, she can stay slim. This type of heightened awareness of eating behavior leads to the labeling of respondents as an anorexic or bulimic. How the affected anorexics react to the label is often problematic. McLorg and Taub report that some reject the label and argue that they are only being "ultra-healthy." Others accept the label and admit that their lives are being disrupted by the eating disorder. The binge/purgers, by contrast, are more apt to admit they are bulimic and that their weight is "abnormal." Ultimately, not only did many of the respondents assume the status as an anorexic or bulimic but, in terms of secondary or career deviance, they also exhibited the corresponding identity. These changes in status, identity, and role expectations brought about additional and frequently negative reactions from others. McLorg and Taub cite the case where the "school's brain" became relabeled as the "school's anorexic." Others were labeled as "starving waifs" or "pigs." These observations, it can be noted, offer additional insight into Becker's comments about what it means to be perceived as occupying a deviant or master status. Quite clearly, the evidence suggests that some people tend to respond to the new status and its range of negative labels and not to the individual.

5 / The Normal and the Pathological

EMILE DURKHEIM

Crime is present not only in the majority of societies of one particular species but in all societies of all types. There is no society that is not confronted with the problem of criminality. Its form changes; the acts thus characterized are not the same everywhere; but, everywhere and always, there have been men who have behaved in such a way as to draw upon themselves penal repression. If, in proportion as societies pass from the lower to the higher types, the rate of criminality, i.e., the relation between the yearly number of crimes and the population, tended to decline, it might be believed that crime, while still normal, is tending to lose this character of normality. But we have no reason to believe that such a regression is substantiated. Many facts would seem rather to indicate a movement in the opposite direction. From the beginning of the [nineteenth] century, statistics enable us to follow the course of criminality. It has everywhere increased. In France the increase is nearly 300 per cent. There is, then, no phenomenon that presents more indisputably all the symptoms of normality, since it appears closely connected with the conditions of all collective life. To make of crime a form of social morbidity would be to admit that morbidity is not something accidental, but, on the contrary, that in certain cases it grows out of the fundamental constitution of the living organism; it would result in wiping out all distinction between the physiological and the pathological. No doubt it is possible that crime itself will have abnormal forms, as, for example, when its rate is unusually high. This excess is, indeed, undoubtedly morbid in nature. What is normal, simply, is the existence of criminality, provided that it attains and does not exceed, for each social type, a certain level, which it is perhaps not impossible to fix in conformity with the preceding rules.[1]

Here we are, then, in the presence of a conclusion in appearance quite paradoxical. Let us make no mistake. To classify crime among the phenomena of normal sociology is not to say merely that it is an inevitable, although regrettable phenomenon, due to the incorrigible wickedness of men; it is to affirm that it is a factor in public health, an integral part of all healthy societies. This result is, at first glance, surprising enough to have puzzled even ourselves for a long time. Once this first surprise has been overcome, however, it is not difficult to find reasons explaining this normality and at the same time confirming it.

In the first place crime is normal because a society exempt from it is utterly impossible. Crime, we have shown elsewhere, consists of an act that offends certain very strong collective sentiments. In a society in which criminal acts are no longer committed, the sentiments they offend would have to be found without exception in all individual consciousnesses, and they must be found to exist with the same degree as sentiments contrary to them. Assuming that this condition could actually be realized, crime would not thereby disappear; it would only change its form, for the very cause which would thus dry up the sources of criminality would immediately open up new ones.

Indeed, for the collective sentiments which are protected by the penal law of a people at a specified moment of its history to take possession of the public conscience or for them to acquire a stronger hold where they have an insufficient grip, they must acquire an intensity greater than that which they had hitherto had. The community as a whole must experience them more vividly, for it can acquire from no other source the greater force necessary to control these individuals who formerly were the most refractory. For murderers to disappear, the horror of bloodshed must become greater in those social strata from which murderers are recruited; but, first it must become greater throughout the entire society. Moreover, the very absence of crime would directly contribute to produce this horror; because any sentiment seems much more respectable when it is always and uniformly respected.

One easily overlooks the consideration that these strong states of the common consciousness cannot be thus reinforced without reinforcing at the same time the more feeble states, whose violation previously gave birth to mere infraction of convention—since the weaker ones are only the prolongation, the attenuated form, of the stronger. Thus robbery and simple bad taste injure the same single altruistic sentiment, the respect for that which is another's. However, this same sentiment is less grievously offended by bad taste than by robbery; and since, in addition, the average consciousness has not sufficient intensity to react keenly to the bad taste, it is treated with greater tolerance. That is why the person guilty of bad taste is merely blamed, whereas the thief is punished. But, if this sentiment grows stronger, to the point of silencing in all consciousnesses the inclination which disposes man to steal, he will become more sensitive to the offenses which, until then, touched him but lightly. He will react against them, then, with more energy; they will be the object of greater opprobrium, which will transform certain of them from the simple moral faults that they were and give them the quality of crimes. For example, improper contracts, or contracts improperly executed, which only incur public blame or civil damages, will become offenses in law.

Imagine a society of saints, a perfect cloister of exemplary individuals. Crimes, properly so called, will there be unknown; but faults which appear venial to the layman will create there the same scandal that the ordinary offense does in ordinary consciousnesses. If, then, this society has the power to judge and punish, it will define these acts as criminal and will treat them as such. For the same reason, the perfect and upright man judges his smallest failings with a severity that the majority reserve for acts more truly in the nature of an offense. Formerly, acts of violence against persons were more frequent than they are today, because respect for individual dignity was less strong. As this has increased, these crimes have become more rare; and also, many acts violating this sentiment have been introduced into the penal law which were not included there in primitive times.[2]

In order to exhaust all the hypotheses logically possible, it will perhaps be asked why this unanimity does not extend to all collective sentiments without exception. Why should not even the most feeble sentiment gather enough energy to prevent all dissent? The moral consciousness of the society would be present in its entirety in all the individuals, with a vitality sufficient to prevent all acts offending it—the purely conventional faults as well as the crimes. But a uniformity so universal and absolute is utterly impossible; for the immediate physical milieu in which each one of us is placed, the hereditary antecedents, and the social influences vary from one individual to the next, and consequently diversify consciousnesses. It is impossible for all to be alike, if only because each one has his own organism and that these organisms occupy different areas in space. That is why, even among the lower peoples, where individual originality is very little developed, it nevertheless does exist.

Thus, since there cannot be a society in which the individuals do not differ more or less from the collective type, it is also inevitable that, among these divergences, there are some with a criminal character. What confers this character upon them is not the intrinsic quality of a given act but that definition which the collective conscience lends them. If the collective conscience is stronger, if it has enough authority practically to suppress these divergences, it will also be more sensitive, more exacting; and, reacting against the slightest deviations with the energy it otherwise displays only against more considerable infractions, it will attribute to them the same gravity as formerly to crimes. In other words, it will designate them as criminal.

Crime is, then, necessary; it is bound up with fundamental conditions of all social life, and by that very fact it is useful, because these conditions of which it is part are themselves indispensable to the normal evolution of morality and law.

Indeed, it is no longer possible today to dispute the fact that law and morality vary from one social type to the next, nor that they change within the same type if the conditions of life are modified. But, in order that these transformations may be possible, the collective sentiments at the basis of morality must not be hostile to change, and consequently must have but moderate energy. If they were too strong, they would no longer be plastic. Every pattern is an obstacle to new patterns, to the extent that the first pattern is inflexible. The better a structure is articulated, the more it offers a healthy resistance to all modification; and this is equally true of functional, as of anatomical, organization. If there were no crimes, this condition could not have been fulfilled; for such a hypothesis presupposes that collective sentiments have arrived at a degree of intensity unexampled in history. Nothing is good indefinitely and to an unlimited extent. The authority which the moral conscience enjoys must not be excessive; otherwise no one would dare criticize it, and it would too easily congeal into an immutable form. To make progress, individual originality must be able to express itself. In order that the originality of the idealist whose dreams transcend his century may find expression, it is necessary that the originality of the criminal, who is below the level of his time, shall also be possible. One does not occur without the other.

Nor is this all. Aside from this indirect utility, it happens that crime itself plays a useful role in this evolution. Crime implies not only that the way remains open to necessary changes but that in certain cases it directly prepares these changes. Where crime exists, collective sentiments are sufficiently flexible to take on a new form, and crime sometimes helps to determine the form they will take. How many times, indeed, it is only an anticipation of future morality—a step toward what will be! According to Athenian law, Socrates was a criminal, and his condemnation was no more than just. However, his crime, namely, the independence of his thought, rendered a service not only to humanity but to his country. It served to prepare a new morality and faith which the Athenians needed, since the traditions by which they had lived until then were no longer in harmony with the current conditions of life. Nor is the case of Socrates unique; it is reproduced periodically in history. It would never have been possible to establish the freedom of thought we now enjoy if the regulations prohibiting it had not been violated before being solemnly abrogated. At that time, however, the violation was a crime, since it was an offense against sentiments still very keen in the average conscience. And yet this crime was useful as a prelude to reforms which daily became more necessary. Liberal philosophy had as its precursors the heretics of all kinds who were justly punished by secular authorities during the entire course of the Middle Ages and until the eve of modern times.

From this point of view the fundamental facts of criminality present themselves to us in an entirely new light. Contrary to current ideas, the criminal no longer seems a totally unsociable being, a sort of parasitic element, a strange and unassimilable body, introduced into the midst of society.[3] On the contrary, he plays a definite role in social life. Crime, for its part, must no longer be conceived as an evil that cannot be too much suppressed. There is no occasion for self-congratulation when the crime rate drops noticeably below the average level, for we may be certain that this apparent progress is associated with some social disorder. Thus, the number of assault cases never falls so low as in times of want.[4] With the drop in the crime rate, and as a reaction to it, comes a revision, or the need of a revision in the theory of punishment. If, indeed, crime is a disease, its punishment is its remedy and cannot be otherwise conceived; thus, all the discussions it arouses bear on the point of determining what the punishment must be in order to fulfil this role of remedy. If crime is not pathological at all, the object of punishment cannot be to cure it, and its true function must be sought elsewhere.

Notes

1. From the fact that crime is a phenomenon of normal sociology, it does not follow that the criminal is an individual normally constituted from the biological and psychological points of view. The two questions are independent of each other. This independence will be better understood when we have shown, later on, the difference between psychological and sociological facts.

2. Calumny, insults, slander, fraud, etc.

3. We have ourselves committed the error of speaking thus of the criminal, because of a failure to apply our rule (*Division du travail social,* pp. 395–96).

4. Although crime is a fact of normal sociology, it does not follow that we must not abhor it. Pain itself has nothing desirable about it; the individual dislikes it as society does crime, and yet it is a function of normal physiology. Not only is it necessarily derived from the very constitution of every living organism, but it plays a useful role in life, for which reason it cannot be replaced. It would, then, be a singular distortion of our thought to present it as an apology for crime. We would not even think of protesting against such an interpretation, did we not know to what strange accusations and misunderstandings one exposes oneself when one undertakes to study moral facts objectively and to speak of them in a different language from that of the layman.

6 / On the Sociology of Deviance

KAI T. ERIKSON

Human actors are sorted into various kinds of collectivity, ranging from relatively small units such as the nuclear family to relatively large ones such as a nation or culture. One of the most stubborn difficulties in the study of deviation is that the problem is defined differently at each one of these levels: behavior that is considered unseemly within the context of a single family may be entirely acceptable to the community in general, while behavior that attracts severe censure from the members of the community may go altogether unnoticed elsewhere in the culture. People in society, then, must learn to deal separately with deviance at each one of these levels and to distinguish among them in his own daily activity. A man may disinherit his son for conduct that violates old family traditions or ostracize a neighbor for conduct that violates some local custom, but he is not expected to employ either of these standards when he serves as a juror in a court of law. In each of the three situations he is required to use a different set of criteria to decide whether or not the behavior in question exceeds tolerable limits.

In the next few pages we shall be talking about deviant behavior in social units called "communities," but the use of this term does not mean that the argument applies only at that level of organization. In theory, at least, the argument being made here should fit all kinds of human collectivity—families as well as whole cultures, small groups as well as nations—and the term "community" is only being used in this context because it seems particularly convenient.[1]

The people of a community spend most of their lives in close contact with one another, sharing a common sphere of experience which makes them feel that they belong to a special "kind" and live in a special "place." In the formal language of sociology, this means that communities are boundary maintaining: each has a specific territory in the world as a whole, not only in the sense that it occupies a defined region of geographical space but also in the sense that it takes over a particular niche in what might be called cultural space and develops its own "ethos" or "way" within that compass. Both of these dimensions of group space, the geographical and the cultural, set the community apart as a special place and provide an important point of reference for its members.

64

When one describes any system as boundary maintaining, one is saying that it controls the fluctuation of its consistent parts so that the whole retains a limited range of activity, a given pattern of constancy and stability, within the larger environment. A human community can be said to maintain boundaries, then, in the sense that its members tend to confine themselves to a particular radius of activity and to regard any conduct which drifts outside that radius as somehow inappropriate or immoral. Thus the group retains a kind of cultural integrity, a voluntary restriction on its own potential for expansion, beyond that which is strictly required for accommodation to the environment. Human behavior can vary over an enormous range, but each community draws a symbolic set of parentheses around a certain segment of that range and limits its own activities within that narrower zone. These parentheses, so to speak, are the community's boundaries.

Now people who live together in communities cannot relate to one another in any coherent way or even acquire a sense of their own stature as group members unless they learn something about the boundaries of the territory they occupy in social space, if only because they need to sense what lies beyond the margins of the group before they can appreciate the special quality of the experience which takes place within it. Yet how do people learn about the boundaries of their community? And how do they convey this information to the generations which replace them?

To begin with, the only material found in a society for marking boundaries is the behavior of its members—or rather, the networks of interaction which link these members together in regular social relations. And the interactions which do the most effective job of locating and publicizing the group's outer edges would seem to be those which take place between deviant persons on the one side and official agents of the community on the other. The deviant is a person whose activities have moved outside the margins of the group, and when the community calls him to account for that vagrancy it is making a statement about the nature and placement of its boundaries. It is declaring how much variability and diversity can be tolerated within the group before it begins to lose its distinctive shape, its unique identity. Now there may be other moments in the life of the group which perform a similar service: wars, for instance, can publicize a group's boundaries by drawing attention to the line separating the group from an adversary, and certain kinds of religious ritual, dance ceremony, and other traditional pageantry can dramatize the difference between "we" and "they" by portraying a symbolic encounter between the two. But on the whole, members of a community inform one another about the placement of their boundaries by participating in the confrontations which occur when persons who venture out to the edges of the group are met by policing agents whose special business it is to guard the cultural integrity of the community. Whether these confrontations take the form of criminal trials, excommunication hearings, courts-martial, or even psychiatric case conferences, they act as boundary-maintaining devices in the sense that they demonstrate to whatever audience is concerned where the line is drawn between behavior that belongs in the special universe of the group and behavior that does not. In general, this kind of information is not easily relayed by the straightforward use of language. Most readers of this paragraph, for instance, have a fairly clear idea of the line separating theft from more legitimate forms of commerce, but few of them have ever seen a published statute describing these differences. More likely than not, our information on the subject has been drawn from publicized instances in which the relevant laws were applied—and for that matter, the law itself is largely a collection of past cases and decisions, a synthesis of the various confrontations which have occurred in the life of the legal order.

It may be important to note in this connection that confrontations between deviant offenders and the agents of control have always attracted a good deal of public attention. In our own past, the trial and punishment of offenders were staged in the market place and afforded the crowd a chance to participate in a direct, active way. Today, of course, we no longer parade deviants in the town square or expose them to the carnival atmosphere of a Tyburn, but it is interesting that the "reform" which brought about this change in penal practice coincided almost exactly with the development of newspapers as a medium of mass information. Perhaps this is no more than an accident of history, but it is nonetheless true that newspapers (and now radio and television) offer much the same kind of entertainment as public hangings or a Sunday visit to the local gaol. A considerable portion of what we call "news" is devoted to reports about deviant behavior and its consequences, and it is no simple matter to explain why these items should be considered newsworthy or why they should command the extraordinary attention they do. Perhaps they appeal to a number of psychological perversities among the mass audience, as commentators have suggested, but at the same time they constitute one of our main sources of information about the normative outlines of society. In a figurative sense, at least, morality and immorality meet at the public scaffold, and it is during this meeting that the line between them is drawn.

Boundaries are never a fixed property of any community. They are always shifting as the people of the group find new ways to define the outer limits of their universe, new ways to position themselves on the larger cultural map. Sometimes changes occur within the structure of the group which require its members to make a new survey of their territory—a change of leadership, a shift of mood. Sometimes changes occur in the surrounding environment, altering the background against which the people of the group have measured their own uniqueness. And always, new generations are moving in to take their turn guarding old institutions and need to be informed about the contours of the world they are inheriting. Thus single encounters between the deviant and his community are only fragments of an ongoing social process. Like an article of common law, boundaries remain a meaningful point of reference only so long as they are repeatedly tested by persons on the fringes of the group and repeatedly defended by persons chosen to represent the group's inner morality. Each time the community moves to censure some act of deviation, then, and convenes a formal ceremony to deal with the responsible offender, it sharpens the authority of the violated norm and restates where the boundaries of the group are located.

For these reasons, deviant behavior is not a simple kind of leakage which occurs when the machinery of society is in poor working order, but may be, in controlled quantities, an important condition for preserving the stability of social life. Deviant forms of behavior, by marking the outer edges of group life, give the inner structure its special character and thus supply the framework within which the people of the group develop an orderly sense of their own cultural identity. Perhaps this is what Aldous Huxley had in mind when he wrote:

> Now tidiness is undeniably good—but a good of which it is easily possible to have too much and at too high a price.... The good life can only be lived in a society in which tidiness is preached and practised, but not too fanatically, and where efficiency is always haloed, as it were, by a tolerated margin of mess.[2]

This raises a delicate theoretical issue. If we grant that human groups often derive benefit from deviant behavior, can we then assume that they are organized in such a way as to promote this resource? Can we assume, in other words, that forces operate in the social structure to recruit offenders and to commit them to long periods of service in the deviant ranks? This is not a question which can be answered with our present store of empirical data, but one observation can be made which gives the question an interesting perspective—namely, that deviant forms of conduct often seem to derive nourishment from the very agencies devised to inhibit them. Indeed, the agencies built by society for preventing deviance are often so poorly equipped for the task that we might well ask why this is regarded as their "real" function in the first place.

It is by now a thoroughly familiar argument that many of the institutions designed to discourage deviant behavior actually operate in such a way as to perpetuate it. For one thing, prisons, hospitals, and other similar agencies provide aid and shelter to large numbers of deviant persons, sometimes giving them a certain advantage in the competition for social resources. But beyond this, such institutions gather marginal people into tightly segregated groups, give them an opportunity to teach one another the skills and attitudes of a deviant career, and even provoke them into using these skills by reinforcing their sense of alienation from the rest of society.[3] Nor is this observation a modern one:

> The misery suffered in gaols is not half their evil; they are filled with every sort of corruption that poverty and wickedness can generate; with all the shameless and profligate enormities that can be produced by the impudence of ignominy, the range of want, and the malignity of dispair. In a prison the check of the public

eye is removed; and the power of the law is spent. There are few fears, there are no blushes. The lewd inflame the more modest; the audacious harden the timid. Everyone fortifies himself as he can against his own remaining sensibility; endeavoring to practise on others the arts that are practised on himself; and to gain the applause of his worst associates by imitating their manners.[4]

These lines, written almost two centuries ago, are a harsh indictment of prisons, but many of the conditions they describe continue to be reported in even the most modern studies of prison life. Looking at the matter from a long-range historical perspective, it is fair to conclude that prisons have done a conspicuously poor job of reforming the convicts placed in their custody; but the very consistency of this failure may have a peculiar logic of its own. Perhaps we find it difficult to change the worst of our penal practices because we *expect* the prison to harden the inmate's commitment to deviant forms of behavior and draw him more deeply into the deviant ranks. On the whole, we are a people who do not really expect deviants to change very much as they are processed through the control agencies we provide for them, and we are often reluctant to devote much of the community's resources to the job of rehabilitation. In this sense, the prison which graduates long rows of accomplished criminals (or, for that matter, the state asylum which stores its most severe cases away in some back ward) may do serious violence to the aims of its founders; but it does very little violence to the expectations of the population it serves.

These expectations, moreover, are found in every corner of society and constitute an important part of the climate in which we deal with deviant forms of behavior.

To begin with, the community's decision to bring deviant sanctions against one of its members is not a simple act of censure. It is an intricate rite of transition, at once moving the individual out of his ordinary place in society and transferring him into a special deviant position.[5] The ceremonies which mark this change of status, generally, have a number of related phases. They supply a formal stage on which the deviant and his community can confront one another (as in the criminal trial); they make an announcement about the nature of his deviancy (a verdict or diagnosis, for example); and they place him in a particular role which is thought to neutralize the harmful effects of his misconduct (like the role of prisoner or patient). These commitment ceremonies tend to be occasions of wide public interest and ordinarily take place in a highly dramatic setting.[6] Perhaps the most obvious example of a commitment ceremony is the criminal trial, with its elaborate formality and exaggerated ritual, but more modest equivalents can be found wherever procedures are set up to judge whether or not someone is legitimately deviant.

Now an important feature of these ceremonies in our own culture is that they are almost irreversible. Most provisional roles conferred by society— those of the student or conscripted soldier, for example—include some kind of terminal ceremony to mark the individual's movement back out of the role once its temporary advantages have been exhausted. But the roles allotted the deviant seldom make allowance for this type of passage. He is ushered into the deviant position by a decisive and often dramatic ceremony, yet is retired from it with scarcely a word of public notice. And as a result, the deviant often returns home with no proper license to resume a normal life in the community. Nothing has happened to cancel out the stigmas imposed upon him by earlier commitment ceremonies; nothing has happened to revoke the verdict or diagnosis pronounced upon him at that time. It should not be surprising, then, that the people of the community are apt to greet the returning deviant with a considerable degree of apprehension and distrust, for in a very real sense they are not at all sure who he is.

A circularity is thus set into motion which has all the earmarks of a "self-fulfilling prophesy," to use Merton's fine phrase. On the one hand, it seems quite obvious that the community's apprehensions help reduce whatever chances the deviant might otherwise have had for a successful return home. Yet at the same time, everyday experience seems to show that these suspicions are wholly reasonable, for it is a well-known and highly publicized fact that many if not most ex-convicts return to crime after leaving prison and that large numbers of mental patients require further treatment after an initial hospitalization. The common feeling that deviant persons never really change, then, may derive from a faulty premise; but the feeling is expressed so frequently and with such conviction that it eventually creates the facts which later "prove" it to be correct. If the returning deviant encounters this circularity often enough, it is quite understandable that he, too, may begin to wonder whether he has fully graduated from the deviant role, and he may respond to the uncertainty by resuming some kind of deviant activity. In many respects, this may be the only way for the individual and his community to agree what kind of person he is.

Moreover this prophesy is found in the official policies of even the most responsible agencies of control. Police departments could not operate with any real effectiveness if they did not regard ex-convicts as a ready pool of suspects to be tapped in the event of trouble, and psychiatric clinics could not do a successful job in the community if they were not always alert to the possibility of former patients suffering relapses. Thus the prophesy gains currency at many levels within the social order, not only in the poorly informed attitudes of the community at large, but in the best informed theories of most control agencies as well.

In one form or another this problem has been recognized in the West for many hundreds of years, and this simple fact has a curious implication. For if our culture has supported a steady flow of deviation throughout long periods of historical change, the rules which apply to any kind of evolutionary thinking would suggest that strong forces must be at work to keep the flow intact—and this because it contributes in some important way to the survival of the culture as a whole. This does not furnish us with sufficient warrant to declare that deviance is "functional" (in any of the many senses of that term), but it should certainly make us wary of the assumption so often made in sociological circles that any well-structured society is somehow designed to prevent deviant behavior from occurring.[7]

It might be then argued that we need new metaphors to carry our thinking about deviance onto a different plane. On the whole, American sociologists have devoted most of their attention to those forces in society which seem to assert a centralizing influence on human behavior, gathering people together into tight clusters called "groups" and bringing them under the jurisdiction of governing principles called "norms" or "standards." The questions which sociologists have traditionally asked of their data, then, are addressed to the uniformities rather than the divergencies of social life: how is it that people learn to think in similar ways, to accept the same group moralities, to move by the same rhythms of behavior, to see life with the same eyes? How is it, in short, that cultures accomplish the incredible alchemy of making unity out of diversity, harmony out of conflict, order out of confusion? Somehow we often act as if the differences between people can be taken for granted, being too natural to require comment, but that the symmetry which human groups manage to achieve must be explained by referring to the molding influence of the social structure.

But variety, too, is a product of the social structure. It is certainly remarkable that members of a culture come to look so much alike; but it is also remarkable that out of all this sameness a people can develop a complex division of labor, move off into diverging career lines, scatter across the surface of the territory they share in common, and create so many differences of temper, ideology, fashion, and mood. Perhaps we can conclude, then, that two separate yet often competing currents are found in any society: those forces which promote a high degree of conformity among the people of the community so that they know what to expect from one another, and those forces which encourage a certain degree of diversity so that people can be deployed across the range of group space to survey its potential, measure its capacity, and, in the case of those we call deviants, patrol its boundaries. In such a scheme, the deviant would appear as a natural product of group differentiation. He is not a bit of debris spun out by faulty social machinery, but a relevant figure in the community's overall division of labor.

Notes

1. In fact, the first statement of the general notion presented here was concerned with the study of small groups. See Robert A. Dentler and Kai T. Erikson, "The Functions of Deviance in Groups," *Social Problems*, VII (Fall 1959), pp. 98–107.

2. Aldous Huxley, *Prisons: The "Carceri" Etchings by Piranesi* (London: The Trianon Press, 1949), p. 13.

3. For a good description of this process in the modern prison, see Gresham Sykes, *The Society of Captives* (Princeton, N.J.: Princeton University Press, 1958). For discussions of similar problems in two different kinds of mental hospital, see Erving Goffman, *Asylums* (New York: Bobbs-Merrill, 1962) and Kai T. Erikson, "Patient Role and Social Uncertainty: A Dilemma of the Mentally Ill," *Psychiatry*, XX (August 1957), pp. 263–274.

4. Written by "a celebrated" but not otherwise identified author (perhaps Henry Fielding) and quoted in John Howard, *The State of the Prisons*, London, 1777 (London: J. M. Dent and Sons, 1929), p. 10.

5. The classic description of this process as it applies to the medical patient is found in Talcott Parsons, *The Social System* (Glencoe, Ill.: The Free Press, 1951).

6. See Harold Garfinkel, "Successful Degradation Ceremonies," *American Journal of Sociology*, LXI (January 1956), pp. 420–424.

7. Albert K. Cohen, for example, speaking for a dominant strain in sociological thinking, takes the question quite for granted: "It would seem that the control of deviant behavior is, by definition, a culture goal." See "The Study of Social Disorganization and Deviant Behavior" in Merton, et al., *Sociology Today* (New York: Basic Books, 1959), p. 465.

7 / The Conflict of Conduct Norms

THORSTEN SELLIN

CULTURE CONFLICTS AS CONFLICTS OF CULTURAL CODES

...There are social groups on the surface of the earth which possess complexes of conduct norms which, due to differences in the mode of life and the social values evolved by these groups, appear to set them apart from other groups in many or most respects. We may expect conflicts of norms when the rural dweller moves to the city, but we assume that he has absorbed the basic norms of the culture which comprises both town and country. How much greater is not the conflict likely to be when Orient and Occident meet, or when the Corsican mountaineer is transplanted to the lower East Side of New York. Conflicts of cultures are inevitable when the norms of one cultural or subcultural area migrate to or come in contact with those of another.

Conflicts between the norms of divergent cultural codes may arise

1. when these codes clash on the border of contiguous culture areas;

2. when, as may be the case with legal norms, the law of one cultural group is extended to cover the territory of another; or

3. when members of one cultural group migrate to another.[1]

Speck, for instance, notes that "where the bands popularly known as Montagnais have come more and more into contact with Whites, their reputation has fallen lower among the traders who have known them through commercial relationships within that period. The accusation is made that they have become less honest in connection with their debts, less trustworthy with property, less truthful, and more inclined to alcoholism and sexual freedom as contacts with the frontier towns have become easier for them. Richard White reports in 1933 unusual instances of Naskapi breaking into traders' store houses."[2]

Similar illustrations abound in the works of the cultural anthropologists. We need only to recall the effect on the American Indian of the culture conflicts induced by our policy of acculturation by guile and force. In this instance, it was not merely contact with the white man's culture, his religion, his business methods, and his liquor, which weakened the tribal mores. In addition, the Indian became subject to the white man's law and this brought conflicts as well, as has always been the case when legal norms have been imposed upon a group previously ignorant of them. Maunier[3] in discussing the diffusion of French law in Algeria, recently stated: "In introducing the *Code Penal* in our colonies, as we do, we transform into offenses the ancient usages of the inhabitants which their customs permitted or imposed. Thus, among the Khabyles of Algeria, the killing of adulterous wives is ritual murder committed by the father or brother of the wife and not by her husband, as elsewhere. The woman having been sold by her family to her husband's family, the honor of her relatives is soiled by her infidelity. Her father or brother has the right and the duty to kill her in order to cleanse by her blood the honor of her relatives. Murder in revenge is also a duty, from family to family, in case of murder of or even in case of insults to a relative: the vendetta, called the *rekba* in Khabylina, is imposed by the law of honor. But these are crimes in French law! Murder for revenge, being premeditated and planned, is assassination, punishable by death! . . . What happens, then, often when our authorities pursue the criminal, guilty of an offense against public safety as well as against morality: public enemy of the French order, but who has acted in accord with a respected custom? The witnesses of the assassination, who are his relatives, or neighbors, fail to lay charges against the assassin; when they are questioned, they pretend to know nothing; and the pursuit is therefore useless. A French magistrate has been able to speak of the conspiracy of silence among the Algerians; a conspiracy aiming to preserve traditions, always followed and obeyed, against their violation by our power. This is the tragic aspect of the conflict of laws. A recent decree forbids the husband among the Khabyles to profit arbitrarily by the power given him according to this law to repudiate his wife, demanding that her new husband pay an exorbitant price for her—this is the custom of the *lefdi*. Earlier, one who married a repudiated wife paid nothing to the former husband. It appears that the first who tried to avail himself of the new law was killed for violating the old custom. The abolition of the ancient law does not always occur without protest or opposition. That which is a crime was a duty; and the order which we cause to reign is sometimes established to the detriment of 'superstition'; it is the gods and the spirits, it is believed, that would punish any one who fails to revenge his honor."

When Soviet law was extended to Siberia, similar effects were observed. Anossow[4] and Wirschubski[5] both relate that women among the Siberian tribes, who, in obedience to the law, laid aside their veils, were killed by their relatives for violating one of the most sacred norms of their tribes.

We have noted that culture conflicts are the natural outgrowth of processes of social differentiation, which produce an infinity of social groupings, each with its own definitions of life situations, its own interpretations of social relationships, its own ignorance or misunderstanding of the social values of other groups. The transformation of a culture from a homogeneous and well-integrated type to a heterogeneous and disintegrated type is therefore accompanied by an increase of conflict situations. Conversely, the operation of integrating processes will reduce the number of conflict situations. Such conflicts within a changing culture may be distinguished from those created when different cultural systems come in contact with one another, regardless of the character or stage of development of these systems. In either case, the conduct of members of a group involved in the conflict of codes will in some respects be judged abnormal by the other group.

THE STUDY OF CULTURE CONFLICTS

In the study of culture conflicts, some scholars have been concerned with the effect of such conflicts on the conduct of specific persons, an approach which is naturally preferred by psychologists and psychiatrists and by sociologists who have used the life history technique. These scholars view the conflict as internal. Wirth[6] states categorically that a culture "conflict can be said to be a factor in delinquency only if the individual feels it or acts as if it were present." Culture conflict is mental conflict, but the character of this conflict is viewed differently by the various disciplines which use this term. Freudian psychiatrists[7] regard it as a struggle between deeply rooted biological urges which demand expression and the culturally created rules which give rise to inhibitive mechanisms which thwart this expression and drive them below the conscious level of the mind, whence they rise either by ruse in some socially acceptable disguise, as abnormal conduct when the inhibiting mechanism breaks down, or as neuroses when it works too well. The sociologist, on the other hand, thinks of mental conflict as being primarily the clash between antagonistic conduct norms incorporated in personality. "Mental conflict in the person," says Burgess in discussing the case presented by Shaw in *The Jack-Roller*, "may always be explained in terms of the conflict of divergent cultures."[8]

If this view is accepted, sociological research on culture conflict and its relationships to abnormal conduct would have to be strictly limited to a study of the personality of cultural hybrids. Significant studies could be conducted only by the life-history case technique applied to persons in whom the conflict is internalized, appropriate control groups being utilized, of course....

The absence of mental conflict, in the sociological sense, may, however, be well studied in terms of culture conflict. An example may make this clear. A few years ago a Sicilian father in New Jersey killed the sixteen-year-old seducer of his daughter, expressing surprise at his arrest since he had merely defended his family honor in a traditional way. In this case a mental conflict in the sociological sense did not exist. The conflict was external and occurred between cultural codes or norms. We may assume that where such conflicts occur violations of norms will arise merely because persons who have absorbed the norms of one cultural group or area migrate to another and that such conflict will continue so long as the acculturation process has not been completed.... Only then may the violations be regarded in terms of mental conflict.

If culture conflict may be regarded as sometimes personalized, or mental, and sometimes as occurring entirely in an impersonal way solely as a conflict of group codes, it is obvious that research should not be confined to the investigation of mental conflicts and that contrary to Wirth's categorical statement that it is impossible to demonstrate the existence of a culture conflict "objectively... by a comparison between two cultural codes"[9] this procedure has not only a definite function, but may be carried out by researchers employing techniques which are familiar to the sociologist.

The emphasis on the life history technique has grown out of the assumption that "the experiences of one person at the same time reveals the life activities of his group" and that "habit in the individual is an expression of custom in society."[10] This is undoubtedly one valid approach. Through it we may hope to discover generalizations of a scientific nature by studying persons who (1) have drawn their norms of conduct from a variety of groups with conflicting norms, or (2) who possess norms drawn from a group whose code is in conflict with that of the group which judges the conduct. In the former case alone can we speak of mental or internal culture conflict; in the latter, the conflict is external.

If the conduct norms of a group are, with reference to a given life situation, inconsistent, or if two groups possess inconsistent norms, we may assume that the members of these various groups will individually reflect such group attitudes. Paraphrasing Burgess, the experiences of a group will reveal the life activities of its members. While these norms can, no doubt, be best established by a study of a sufficient number of representative group members, they may for some groups at least be fixed with sufficient certainty to serve research purposes by a study of the social institutions, the administration of justice, the novel, the drama, the press, and other expressions of group attitudes. The identification of the groups in question having been made, it might be possible to determine to what extent such conflicts are reflected in the conduct of their members. Comparative studies based on the violation rates of the members of such groups, the trends of such rates, etc., would dominate this approach to the problem.

In conclusion, then, culture conflict may be studied either as mental conflict or as a conflict of cultural codes. The criminologist will naturally tend to concentrate on such conflicts between legal and nonlegal conduct norms. The concept of conflict fails to give him more than a general framework of reference for research. In practice, it has, however, become nearly synonymous with conflicts between the norms of cultural systems or areas. Most researches which have employed it have been done on immigrant or race groups in the United States, perhaps due to the ease with which such groups may be identified, the existence of more statistical data recognizing such groupings, and the conspicuous differences between some immigrant norms and our norms.

Notes

1. This is unfortunately not the whole story, for with the rapid growth of impersonal communication, the written (press, literature) and the spoken word (radio, talkie), knowledge concerning divergent conduct norms no longer grows solely out of direct personal contact with their carriers. And out of such conflicts grow some violations of custom and of law which would not have occurred without them.

2. Speck, Frank G. "Ethical Attributes of the Labrador Indians." *American Anthropologist.* N. S. 35:559–94. October–December 1933. P. 559.

3. Maunier, René. "La diffusion du droit français en Algérie." Harvard Tercentenary Publications, *Independence, Convergence, and Borrowing in Institutions, Thought, and Art.* Cambridge: Harvard University Press. 1937. Pp. 84–85.

4. Anossow, J. J. "Die volkstümlichen Verbrechen im Strafkodex der USSR." *Monatsschrift für Kriminalpsychologie und Strafrechtsreform.* 24:534–37. September 1933.

5. Wirschubski, Gregor. "Der Schutz der Sittlichkeit im Sowjetstrafrecht." *Zeitschrift für die gesamte Strafrechtswissenschaft.* 51:317–28. 1931.

6. Wirth, Louis. "Culture Conflict and Misconduct." *Social Forces.* 9:484–92. June 1931. P. 490. Cf. Allport, Floyd H. "Culture Conflict versus the Individual as Factors in Delinquency." *Ibid.* Pp. 493–97.

7. White, William A. *Crimes and Criminals.* New York: Farrar & Rinehart. 1933. Healy, William. *Mental Conflict and Misconduct.* Boston: Little, Brown & Co. 1917. Alexander, Franz and Healy, William. *Roots of Crime.* New York: Alfred A. Knopf. 1935.

8. Burgess, Ernest W. in Clifford R. Shaw's *The Jack-Roller.* Chicago: University of Chicago Press. 1930. Pp. 184–197, p. 186.

9. Wirth, Louis. *Op. cit.* P. 490. It should be noted that Wirth also states that culture should be studied "on the objective side" and that "the sociologist is not primarily interested in personality but in culture."

10. Burgess, Ernest W. *Op. cit.* P. 186.

8 / Outlaw Motorcyclists: An Outgrowth of Lower Class Cultural Concerns

J. MARK WATSON

INTRODUCTION

Walter Miller's (1958) typology of focal concerns of lower class culture as a generating milieu for gang delinquency is by most standards a classic in explaining gang behavior among juvenile males. Its general heuristic value is here demonstrated by the striking parallel between this value system and that of adult outlaw motorcyclists.

The reader may remember Miller's general schema, which concerned the strain between the value system of youthful lower class males and the dominant, middle class value system of those in a position to define delinquent behavior. Miller, by describing these values (he used the term "focal concerns"), anticipated conflict theory, without directly pointing out the conflicting values of the middle class definers of delinquent behavior. Although there have been some disagreements surrounding details of Miller's description of the functioning of adolescent gangs, the basic focal concerns described in the typology have been relatively free of criticism as to their validity in describing the values of young lower class males. Some questions have been raised about the degree to which these values actually are in contrast with those of middle class adolescents, however (see, for example, Gordon et al., 1963). Because the typology itself is contained in the discussion of biker values, it will not be discussed separately here.

METHODOLOGY

The findings of the paper are based on my 3 years of participant observation in the subculture of outlaw motorcyclists. Although I am not a member of any outlaw clubs, I am or have been acquainted with members and officers of various clubs, as well as more loosely organized groups of motorcyclists for 10 years. I am myself a motorcycle enthusiast, which facilitated a natural entry into the biker scene. I both build and ride bikes and gained direct access to local biker groups by frequenting places where bikers congregate to work on their bikes. Building a bike gave me legitimation and access to local biker groups and eventually led to contact with other bikers, including outlaws. Groups observed varied from what could be classified as clubs to loose-knit groups of associated motorcyclists. Four groups were studied in depth. Two small local groups in middle Tennessee were subjects of direct participation. Here they are given the fictional names of the Brothers and the Good Old Boys. In addition, one regional group from North Carolina, given the fictional name of Bar Hoppers, was studied through interviews with club officers and members. One national-level group, one of the largest groups of outlaw motorcyclists, was extensively observed and interviewed, primarily at regional and national events. This group is given the fictional name of the Convicts. Additional information was also gathered by attempting to interview at regional and national events members and officers of a wide range of clubs. This was easily done by simply looking at club "colors" (patches) and seeking out members of clubs that were not already represented in the study. This technique was used primarily to check for the representativeness of behavior, values, beliefs, and other characteristics observed in in-depth studies of the four clubs mentioned above. Another source of validation of conclusions was extensive use of biker literature such as magazines and books by or about bikers.

Data were collected by means of interviews conducted from January 1977 to March 1980. Interviews were informally administered in the sense that no formal interview schedule was used. Instead, bikers were queried in the context of what would pass for normal conversation. Extensive observations of behavior were made while directly participating in the activities of the groups, everyday events such as hanging out and from building bikes to "runs," (trips), swap meets, and cult events, such as speed week at Daytona Beach, Florida, and the National Motorcycle Drag Championships at Bowling Green, Kentucky. Such events led to contact with bikers from all over the United States, inasmuch as these events attract a national sample of dedicated bikers, including the whole range of types from simple enthusiasts to true outlaws. Notes and impressions were taken at night and/or after the events. Groups and individuals were generally not aware that they were being studied, although I made no attempt to hide my intentions. Some bikers who came to know me were curious about a university professor participating in such activities and accordingly were told that a study was being conducted. This honesty was prompted by fear of being suspected of being a narcotics agent. Such self-revelation was rarely necessary as the author affected the clothing and jargon of bikers and was accepted as such. Frequent invitations to engage in outrageous and illegal behavior (e.g., drug use and purchase of stolen parts) that would not be extended to outsiders were taken as a form of symbolic acceptance. My demeanor and extensive association with lower class gangs in adolescence combined with the type of mechanical skills necessary to build bikes mentioned earlier may have contributed to an ability to blend in. Reactions to self-revelation, when necessary, generally ranged from amazement to amusement. I suspect that, as is true with the general population, most bikers had no idea what a sociologist was, but the presence of a professor in their midst was taken as a sort of legitimation for the group.

Observations and conclusions were cross-checked on an ongoing basis with a group of five biker informants whom I knew well, including members of the Brothers, Good Old Boys, and the Convicts who lived in the mid-Tennessee area. Informants were selected on the basis of several criteria. First, informants had to know and be known well enough by me to establish a trusting relationship. This limited informants to local bikers found in my area of residence. As mentioned above, outlaw motorcyclists are not particularly trusting, and this obstacle had to be overcome. Second, informants had to be articulate enough to communicate such concepts as values. Most bikers are not particularly articulate, so this criterion eliminated many members of local groups whom I knew well. Third, informants had to have extensive experience in biker subculture. Consequently, informants were limited to bikers who had traveled and lived in a wide geographic area and had experience wider than that represented by the mid-South region. Consequently, informants were generally older than the typical biker population, varying in age from the early 30s to the mid-40s. Three of the informants were former or current owners of custom motorcycle shops that catered to biker clientele. All were what might be defined as career bikers. Finally, all informants had to possess enough objectivity about the biker lifestyle to be willing to read and comment on the author's conclusions. Many of these conclusions, though valid and objective, one hopes, are not particularly flattering to participants in the outlaw motorcyclists subculture. One informant was lost because of obvious antagonism generated by some conclusions. In addition, conversations with hundreds of unsuspecting bikers were held in order to ascertain the generalizability of observations. The latter technique involved appearing to be ignorant or confused and simply asking for a definition of the situation, for example, "What's happening?" or, "What are they doing?" or even venturing an evaluation such as, "That's stupid; Why do they do that?" all in order to elicit a response from an observer of some act. It must be kept in mind that research conducted with this kind of deviant subculture can be dangerous. Because many outlaws do not welcome scrutiny and carefully avoid those whom they feel may not be trusted, which includes most nonbikers, I remained as unobtrusive as possible. Consequently, the methodology was adapted to the setting. Generally, I felt my presence was accepted. Throughout the study I sensed no change in the cyclists' behavior over time by my presence. This acceptance can be symbolized by my receiving a nickname (Doc) and eventually being defined as an expert in a certain type of obsolete motorcycle (the Harley-Davidson 45-cubic-inch side-valve model). I assumed the role of an inside outsider.

THE BIKER SUBCULTURE

We may locate outlaw bikers in the general spectrum of bikers as the most "outrageous" (their own term, a favorite modifier indicating something distinctively appealing to their own jaded sense of values) on the continuum of bikers, which extends from housewives on mopeds to clubs that actually engage in illegal behavior with a fair degree of frequency, thus the term "outlaws" (Thompson, 1967:9). Outlaws generally adopt certain symbols and lead a lifestyle that is clearly defined and highly visible to other bikers. Symbols include extensive tattooing, beard, dirty jeans, earrings, so-called stroker caps and quasi-military pins attached, engineer's boots, and cut-off jackets with club emblems, called "colors," sewn on the back. Weapons, particularly buck knives and guns of any sort, and chains (motorcycle or other types) are favorite symbols as well (Easyriders, February, 1977:28, 29, 55). By far the most important symbol, however, is the Harley-Davidson V-twin motorcycle.[1] It should be kept in mind that many other motorcyclists affect these symbols, although they are by no means outlaws. Outlaws almost always belong to clubs, whereas many motorcyclists who do not belong to the clubs use them as reference groups and attempt to imitate some aspects of their behavior. These symbols and the basic lifestyle are generalizable to a wide range of bikers and may even be found among British and European bikers, with the exception of the Harley-Davidson motorcycle (Choppers, April 1980:12).

OUTLAW LIFESTYLE

For the outlaw, his lifestyle takes on many of the characteristics of dedication to a religious sect (Watson, 1979). This lifestyle is in many respects a lower class variation of bohemian, "dropout" subcultures. Such similarities include frequent unemployment and disdain for cleanliness, orderliness, and other concerns of conventional culture. For example, I have observed bikes being built and stored in living rooms or kitchens, two non-essential rooms in the subculture. This is apparently a common practice. Parts may be stored in an oil bath in the bathtub, also a nonessential device. The biker and other bohemian subcultures may appear similar on the basis of casual observations, but some outlaw biker values are strikingly different from the beatnik or hippy subcultures of the 1950s and 1960s. Other bohemian subcultures emphasized humanistic values, whereas the outlaw bikers' values emphasize male dominance, violence, force, and racism (Easyriders, October 1977:15). Although individual freedom and choice are also emphasized, the clubs actually suppress individual freedom, while using the value to defend their lifestyle from outsiders. For example, when the Convicts take a club trip called a "run," all members must participate. Those whose bikes are "down" for repairs are fined and must find a ride in a truck with the women. Many club rules require members to follow orders as prescribed by club decisions upon threat of violence and expulsion. Club rules generally include a constitution and bylaws that are surprisingly elaborate and sophisticated for groups of this nature. Many club members express pride in their written regulations. It seems likely that the basic format is borrowed from that developed by the Hell's Angels (Thompson, 1967:72). Most club decisions are made in a democratic way, but minority rights are not respected. Once such a decision is made, it is imperative to all members, with risk of physical retribution for failure to conform. Typical rules include care of colors, which are to never touch the ground or be washed. They are treated essentially as a flag. Other rules mentioned above and below have to do with following group decisions without dissent and such requirements as defending club honor through unanimous participation in avenging affronts to other clubs' members. Club rules may be enforced by self-appointed committees or by formally designated sergeants at arms or enforcers. One informant expressed it this way: "They'll take your bike, your old lady, and stomp the shit out of you if you make 'em look bad." This particular expression related to some prospective "probate" members and their failure to live up to club rules requiring violent reactions to challenges to club honor. The observation came from a retired club member when I queried him about an almost surreal conflict over the wearing of a club symbol by a nonmember.

Use of mind-altering drugs is another area of overlap between biker and bohemian subcultures. Outlaw bikers will take or drink almost anything to alter their consciousness (Easyriders, May 1978:24, 25). The groups studied regularly used "uppers," "downers," and marijuana but rarely used hallucinogens. One informant explained that the latter "fuck you up so you can't ride, so we don't use it much." Apparently, one can ride on uppers, downers, or when drunk but not when hallucinating. Curiously enough, the most commonly used drug is alcohol taken in the rather mild form of beer (though in great quantity). Where there are outlaw bikers one will usually find drugs, but one will almost always find beer.

Outsider status, the use of drugs, and the seeking of cheap rent result in frequent overlap between outlaw bikers and other bohemian types, in both territory and interpersonal relations. The bikers usually tolerate the other bohemians, because the latter share an interest in and serve as a source of supply of, or customers for, drugs. Bikers, however, view them with contempt because they are not masculine enough. Hippies, dopers, and fairies are similar types as far as bikers are concerned. Masculinity as a dominant value is expressed in many ways, including toughness and a general concern with looking mean, dirty, and "outrageous." When asked about a peripheral member of a local group, one informant replied, "He's a hippy, but he don't ride. We put up with him because he has good dope. I feel sorry for him because he's just a fucked-up puke."

Some other biker-associated values include racism, concern with Nazism, and in-group superiority. "Righteousness" is achieved through adherence to these values. One celebrity member of the Brothers had been convicted of killing a young black man in a street confrontation. He is reported to have jumped bail and lived with a Nazi couple in South America, where he worked as a ranch hand. This particular member spoke some German and frequently spouted racist and Nazi doctrine. A typical righteous outlaw belongs to a club, rides an American-made motorcycle, is a white male, displays the subculture's symbols, hates most if not all nonwhites and Japanese motorcycles, works irregularly at best, dresses at all times in dirty jeans, cut-off denim jacket, and engineer's boots, drinks beer, takes whichever drugs are available, and treats women as objects of contempt.

OUTLAW BIKER WORLD VIEW AND SELF-CONCEPT

The outlaw biker generally views the world as hostile, weak, and effeminate. Perhaps this view is a realistic reaction to a working-class socialization experience. However, the reaction contains certain elements of a self-fulfilling prophecy. Looking dirty, mean, and generally undesirable may be a way of frightening others into leaving one alone, although, in many senses such an appearance arouses anger, hostility, and related emotions in the observer and results in the persecution that such qualities are intended to protect one from.

Bikers tend to see the world in terms of here and now. They are not especially hostile toward most social institutions such as family, government, and education. Most of the local group members had finished high school and had been employed from time to time, and some had been college students. Some were veterans, and nearly all had been married more than once. Few had been successful in these endeavors, however. They are generally not capable of establishing the temporal commitments necessary for relating to such institutions. For example, marriages and similar relationships rarely last more than a few years, and education requires concentrated effort over a time span that they are generally not willing or in many cases not capable of exerting. Most of them drift from one job to another or have no job at all. Simply keeping up with where the informants were living proved to be a challenge. I frequently had a call from a local biker relating that he was "on his way over" only to find that he did not arrive at all or arrived hours or days later. I have been on runs that were to depart in the early morning and that did not in fact depart until hours later. The biker's sense of time and commitment to it is not only lower class, but more typical of preliterate societies. The result is frequent clashes with bureaucratically organized institutions, such as government and economy, which are oriented toward impulse control, commitment, and punctuality, and failure in organizations that require long-term commitments or interpersonal relations, such as family and education.

A similar view of regulation causes frequent conflicts. Bikers are not basically violent but are impulsive. Regulations that conflict with their impulses are ignored. Attempts to enforce such regulations (generally by law enforcement officers) are viewed not as legal regulation but as unreasonable demands (harassment). Of course, this impulsiveness can be destructive and self-defeating. I have seen bikers destroy engines they spent hundreds of dollars on by simply overreving them. I have also seen doors, jukeboxes, bike gas tanks, and other items destroyed in an impulsive moment—sometimes in rage, sometimes in humor, or out of boredom. Bikers demand freedom to follow these impulses, which often involve behavior defined by the observer as outrageous. Occasionally bikers reinforce this conception by conforming to the stereotype and deliberately shocking more conventional people, especially if they feel their social space is being invaded. An illustrative incidence occurred in 1978 at the National Championship Drag Races, an event for motorcycles in Bowling Green, Kentucky. An area of a local amusement park was designated "for bikers only." This area was clearly marked with large signs. Occasionally local citizens and outraged tourists insisted on driving through to see the scene. Bikers had begun "partying" and engaging in heavy drinking, drug use, and generally impulsive behavior, including frequent male and female nudity, which occasioned some notice but no shock to other bikers. However, when outsiders drove through, they were deliberately exposed to substantial nudity and what were no doubt interpreted as obscene and disgusting displays by those viewing them. The result was that the city of Bowling Green declined future events of that nature. The races have been held elsewhere in subsequent years.

Outlaw bikers generally view themselves as outsiders. I have on occasion invited local bikers to settings that would place them in contact with members of the middle class. Their frequent response is that they would "not fit in" or would "feel out of place." Basically, they seem to feel that they cannot compete with what sociologists define as the middle class although I have never heard the term used by bikers. Outlaws see themselves as losers, as symbolized by tatoos, patches, and even their humor, which portrays them as ignorant. "One percenter" is a favorite patch, referring to its wearers as the most deviant fraction of the biker fraternity. In effect, the world that they create for themselves is an attempt to suspend the rules of competition that they cannot win by and create a world where one does not compete but simply exists (Montgomery, 1976, 1979). Pretense and self-importance are ways to lose acceptance quickly in such a situation. One does not compete with or "put down" a fellow biker, for he is a "brother."

It is not that bikers are uniformly hostile toward the outside world; they are indifferent toward, somewhat threatened by, and contemptuous of it.

MILLER'S FOCAL CONCERNS AS EXPRESSED IN OUTLAW BIKER CULTURE

Trouble

Trouble is a major theme of the outlaw biker culture as illustrated by the very use of the term "outlaw." The term refers to one who demonstrates his distinctiveness (righteousness) by engaging in outrageous and even illegal behavior. Trouble seems to serve several purposes in this subculture. First, flirting with trouble is a way of demonstrating masculinity—trouble is a traditionally male prerogative. Trouble also enforces group solidarity through emphasizing the outsider status of the outlaw, a status that can be sustained only by the formation of counterculture. Given the outlaw biker's world view and impulsiveness, trouble comes without conscious effort. Trouble may come over drug use, stolen bikes or parts, possession of firearms, or something as simple as public drunkenness. Some of the local bikers whom I knew well had prison records for manslaughter (defined as self-defense by the subjects), receiving stolen property, drug possession, statutory rape, and assault on an officer. All saw these sentences as unjust and claimed that the behavior was justifiable or that they were victims of a case of overzealous regulation of everyday activities or deliberate police harassment.

Trouble used to take the form of violence between biker clubs and groups (Easyriders, April 1977:13, 41). Most of this activity was generated by issues of club honor involving the stealing of women or perceived wrongs by members of other clubs. The general motivation for this activity seemed to be an opportunity to demonstrate toughness (see below). The only open conflict that I saw was an incident, mentioned earlier, between the Brothers and the Convicts over the right of the other groups to wear a one percenter badge as part of their club colors. In recent years most groups have abandoned the practice of interclub violence and emphasize instead the conflict between group members and police. An issue that is a current example of this conflict and that therefore serves this unifying purpose is the mandatory helmet laws in many states and the related attempts of the federal Department of Transportation to regulate modification by owners of motorcycles (Supercycle, May 1979:4, 14–15, 66).

Organized reaction to trouble in the sense of attempts to regulate motorcycles and motorcyclists is probably as close to political awareness and class consciousness as bikers come. Outlaw types, however, generally have little to do with these activities, partly because they view them as hopeless and partly because they correctly perceive their support and presence at such activities as unwelcome and poor public relations.

Toughness

In addition to trouble, toughness is at the heart of the biker emphasis on masculinity and outrageousness. To be tough is to experience trouble without showing signs of weakness. Therefore, the objective of trouble is to demonstrate the masculine form of toughness. Bikers have contempt for such comforts as automobiles or even devices that increase biking comfort or safety such as eye protection, helmets, windshields, farings or even frames with spring rear suspension (a so-called hardtail is the preferred frame). Bikers wear denim or leather, but the sleeves are generally removed to show contempt for the danger of "road rash," abrasions caused by contact with the road surface at speed, which protective material can prevent. Part of toughness is the prohibition against expressing love for women and children in any but a possessive way. Women are viewed with contempt and are regarded as a necessary nuisance (generally referred to as "cunts," "whores," or "sluts"), as are children ("rug rats"). Curiously, bikers seem to attract an adequate supply of women despite the poor treatment they receive from them in such a situation. One informant expressed his contempt for women in this way, "Hell, if I could find a man with a pussy, I wouldn't fuck with women. I don't like 'em. They're nothing but trouble." When asked about the female's motivation for participation in the subculture, one (male) informant stated simply "they're looking for excitement." The women attracted to such a scene are predictably tough and hard-bitten themselves. Not all are unattractive, but most display signs of premature aging typical of lower class and deviant lifestyles. All work to keep up their mate and his motorcycle. I must admit that my interviews with biker women were limited lest my intentions be misinterpreted. I could have hired some of them under sexual pretenses, as many may be bought, but ethical and financial considerations precluded this alternative. My general impression is that these women generally come from lower class families in which the status of the female is not remarkably different from that they currently enjoy. Being a biker's "old lady" offers excitement and opportunities to engage in exhibitionist and outlandish behavior that in their view contrasts favorably with the lives of their mothers. Many are mothers of illegitimate children before they resort to bikers and may view themselves as fallen women who have little to lose in terms of respectability. Most seem to have fairly low self-concepts, which are compatible with their status as bikers' old ladies.

Of course, the large, heavy motorcycles bikers ride are symbolic of their toughness as well. Not everyone can ride such a machine because of its sheer weight. Many models are "kick start," and require some strength and skill just to start. A certain amount of recklessness is also used to express toughness. To quote Bruce Springsteen: "It's a death trap, a suicide rap" (Springsteen, 1975), and the ability to ride it, wreck it, and survive demonstrates toughness in a very dramatic way. An example of my experience in this regard may be illuminating. Although I had ridden motorcycles for years, I became aware of the local biker group while building my first Harley-Davidson. Full acceptance by this group was not extended until my first and potentially fatal accident, however. Indeed, local bikers who had only vaguely known me offered the gift of parts and assistance in reconstructing my bike and began to refer to me by a new nickname, "Doc." I sensed and was extended a new degree of acceptance after demonstrating my "toughness" by surviving the accident. Toughness, in this sense, is a combination of stupidity and misfortune, and hardly relates to any personal virtue.

Smartness

On this characteristic, biker values seem to diverge from general lower class values as described by Miller. The term "dumb biker" is frequently used as a self-description. Given the choice of avoiding, outsmarting, or confronting an opponent, the biker seems to prefer avoidance or confrontation. Confrontation gives him the opportunity to demonstrate toughness by generating trouble. Avoidance is not highly valued, but no one can survive all the trouble he could generate, and the stakes are frequently the highest—life itself or at least loss of freedom. The appearance of toughness and outlandishness mentioned above make confrontation a relatively infrequent occurrence, as few outsiders will challenge a group of outlaw bikers unless the issue is of great significance. Smartness, then, does not seem to be an emphasized biker value or characteristic. Gambling on outsmarting an opponent is for low stakes such as those faced by the adolescents Miller studied.

Excitement

One of the striking things about the outlaw lifestyle is its extremes. Bikers hang out at chopper (motorcycle) shops, clubhouses, or bars during the day, except when they are in prison or jail, which is not uncommon. Places frequented by bikers are generally located in lower class neighborhoods. A clubhouse, for example, is generally a rented house which serves as a headquarters, party location, and place for members to "crash" when they lack more personal accommodations. They are not unlike a lower class version of a fraternity house. Outlaws tend to designate bars as their own. This involves taking over bars to the exclusion of their usual lower or working-class clientele. Such designations are frequently short-lived as the bars may be closed as a public nuisance or the proprietor may go out of business for economic or personal reasons as a result of the takeover. I know of at least one such bar that was burned by local people to rid the neighborhood of the nuisance. Its owner relocated the business some 40 miles away.

Local bikers who worked generally had unskilled and semi-skilled jobs, which are dull in themselves. Examples include laborers, factory workers, construction workers, and hospital orderlies. Many do not work regularly, being supported by their women.[2] In any case, most of their daylight hours are spent in a deadly dull environment, where the most excitement may be a mechanical problem with a bike. Escape from this dull lifestyle is dramatic in its excesses. Drugs, alcohol, and orgiastic parties are one form of escape. Other escapes include the run or simply riding the bikes for which the subculture is named. Frequently both forms of escape are combined, and such events as the Daytona and Sturgis runs are remarkable, comparing favorably to Mardi Gras as orgiastic events. Living on the edge of trouble, appearing outlandish, fierce, and tough, itself yields a form of self-destructive excitement, especially when it can be used to outrage others. Unlike the situation that Miller studied, excitement and trouble rarely seem to center around women, as their status among bikers is even lower than in the lower class in general. I have never seen a conflict over a woman among bikers and am struck by the casual manner in which they move from one biker to another. The exchange of women seems to be the male's prerogative, and women appear to be traded or given away as casually as pocket knives are exchanged among old men. I have on occasion been offered the use of a female for the duration of a run. This offer was always made by the male and was made in the same manner that one might offer the use of a tool to a neighbor. (I have never been offered the loan of a bike, however.) The low regard for women combined with the traditional biker's emphasis on brotherhood seem to minimize conflicts over women. Those conflicts that do occur over women seem to occur between clubs and are a matter of club honor rather than jealousy or grief over the loss of a relationship.

Fate

Because bikers do not emphasize smartness to the extent that Miller perceived it among the lower class, the role of fate in explaining failure to succeed is somewhat different for them. In Miller's analysis fate was a rationalization used when one was outsmarted. The biker's attitude toward fate goes much deeper and could be described as figuratively and literally fatalistic. The theme of death is central to their literature and art.[3] A biker who becomes economically successful or who is too legitimate is suspect. He is no longer one of them. He has succeeded in the outside and in a sense has sold out. His success alone shows his failure to subscribe to the basic values that they hold. He is similar to a rich Indian—no longer an Indian but a white man with red skin. Members of local groups, the Brothers and the Good Old Boys, came and went. Membership fluctuated. Few members resigned because of personal difficulty. However, many former members were still around. The single characteristic that they all shared was economic success. Although these former members tended to be older than the typical member, many current members were as old or older. Success in small businesses were typical. Some former members had been promoted to lower management positions in local factories and related businesses, apparently were no longer comfortable in their former club roles, and so resigned. Some kept their bikes, others exchanged them for more respectable touring bikes, and others sold their bikes. In any case, although some maintained limited social contact and others participated in occasional weekend runs, their success appeared to make them no longer full participants in group activities and resulted ultimately in their formal resignation from the clubs. Bikers basically see themselves as losers and affect clothing, housing, and other symbols of the embittered and dangerous loser. They apparently no longer dream the unrealistic adolescent dreams of the "big break." Prison and death are seen as natural concomitants of the biker lifestyle. Fate is the grim reaper that so often appears in biker art.

Autonomy

Autonomy in the form of freedom is central to the outlaw biker expressed philosophy and in this respect closely parallels the lower class themes outlined by Miller. A studied insistence that they be left alone by harassing law enforcement agencies and overregulating bureaucrats is a common theme in biker literature and personal expressions. The motorcycle itself is an individual thing, begrudgingly including an extra seat for an "old lady" or "down" brother. Ironically, the outlaw biker lifestyle is so antisocial vis-à-vis the wider society that it cannot be pursued individually. A lone outlaw knows he is a target, an extremely visible and vulnerable one. Therefore, for purposes of self-protection, the true outlaw belongs to a club and rarely makes a long trip without the company of several brothers.

Outlaw clubs are themselves both authoritarian and democratic. Members may vote on issues or at least select officers,[4] but club policy and rules are absolute and may be enforced with violence (Choppers, March 1978: 36–39). Antisocial behavior associated with the outlaw lifestyle itself frequently results in loss of autonomy. Most prisons of any size not only contain a substantial biker population but may contain local (prison) chapters of some of the larger clubs (Life, August 1979:80–81). Easyriders, a biker magazine, regularly contains sections for pen pals and other requests from brothers in prison (Easyriders, October 1977:16–19, 70). So, although autonomy in the form of the right to be different is pursued with a vengeance, the ferocity with which it is pursued ensures its frequent loss.

Miller noted an ambivalent attitude among lower class adolescents toward authority: they both resented it and sought situations in which it was forced on them. The structure of outlaw clubs and the frequent incarceration that is a result of their lifestyle would seem to be products of a similar ambivalence. Another loss of autonomy that Miller noted among lower class gangs was a dependence on females that caused dissonance and was responsible for lower class denigration of female status. Outlaws take the whole process a step further, however. Many of their women engage in prostitution, topless waitressing, or menial, traditionally female labor. Some outlaws live off the income of several women and in this sense are dependent on them but only in the sense that a pimp is dependent on his string of girls. From their point of view, the females see themselves as protected by and dependent on the male rather than the other way around.

CONCLUSION

Miller's typology of lower class focal concerns appears to be a valid model for analyzing outlaw biker cultures, just as it was for analyzing some forces behind juvenile gang delinquency. Although there are some differences in values and their expression, the differences are basically those occurring by the transferring of the values from street-wise adolescents to adult males. Both groups could be described as lower class, but my experiences with bikers indicate a working-class family background with downward mobility. A surprising proportion of the bikers interviewed indicated respectable working-class or lower middle-class occupations for their fathers. Examples included postal worker, forestry and lumber contractor, route sales business owner, and real estate agency owner. They are definitely not products of multigenerational poverty. I would classify them as nonrespectable working-class marginals.

The study is presented primarily as an ethnographic description of a difficult and sometimes dangerous subculture to study, which when viewed from the outside appears as a disorganized group of deviants but when studied carefully with some insider's insights is seen to have a coherent and reasonably consistent value system and a lifestyle based on that value system.

Notes

1. A favorite T-shirt observed at cult events is one saying, "If you ain't a Harley rider, you ain't shit!"

2. Outlaw bikers sometimes support themselves by dealing in drugs, bootleg liquor, and prostitution of their women.

3. Of the fiction in the entire 1977 issue of Easyriders, 40% of the articles concerned themselves with death.

4. Officer selection may be based on many processes, some of which would hardly be recognized as democratic by those outside the subculture. Leaders are popularly selected, however. Physical prowess may be the basis of selection, for example.

References

Choppers
 1978 "Club profile: Northern Indiana Invaders M/C." (March):36–39.
Choppers
 1980 "Mailbag." (April):12.
Easyriders
 1977 "Gun nut report." (February):28, 29, 55.
Easyriders
 1977 "Gang wars are a thing of the past." (April):13, 41.
Easyriders
 1977 "Man is the ruler of woman." (October):15.
Easyriders
 1977 "Jammin in the joint." (October):16–19, 70 (Also "Mail call").
Easyriders
 1978 "The straight dope on Quaaludes." (May):24–25.
Gordon, Robert A., Short, Jr., James F., Cartwright, Desmond, and Strodtbeck, Fred
 1963 "Values and gang delinquency." American Journal of Sociology 69:109–128.
Life
 1979 "Prison without stripes." (August):80–81.
Miller, Walter B.
 1958 "Lower class culture as a generating milieu for gang delinquency." Journal of Social Issues 14:5–19.
Montgomery, Randall
 1976 "The outlaw motorcycle subculture." Canadian Journal of Criminology and Corrections 18.
Montgomery, Randall
 1979 "The outlaw motorcycle subculture II." Canadian Journal of Criminology and Corrections 19.
Springsteen, Bruce
 1975 "Born to run." Columbia Records.
Supercycle
 1979 "On reserve." (May):4, 14–15, 66.
Thompson, Hunter
 1967 Hell's Angels: A strange and terrible saga. New York: Random House.
Watson, John M.
 1979 "Righteousness on two wheels: Bikers as a secular sect." Unpublished paper read at the Southwestern Social Science Association, March 1979.

9 / Techniques of Neutralization: A Theory of Delinquency

GRESHAM M. SYKES
DAVID MATZA

As Morris Cohen once said, one of the most fascinating problems about human behavior is why men violate the laws in which they believe. This is the problem that confronts us when we attempt to explain why delinquency occurs despite a greater or lesser commitment to the usages of conformity. A basic clue is offered by the fact that social rules or norms calling for valued behavior seldom if ever take the form of categorical imperatives. Rather, values or norms appear as *qualified* guides for action, limited in their applicability in terms of time, place, persons, and social circumstances. The moral injunction against killing, for example, does not apply to the enemy during combat in time of war, although a captured enemy comes once again under the prohibition. Similarly, the taking and distributing of scarce goods in a time of acute social need is felt by many to be right, although under other circumstances private property is held inviolable. The normative system of a society, then, is marked by what Williams has termed *flexibility*; it does not consist of a body of rules held to be binding under all conditions.[1]

This flexibility is, in fact, an integral part of the criminal law in that measures for "defenses to crimes" are provided in pleas such as non-age, necessity, insanity, drunkenness, compulsion, self-defense, and so on. The individual can avoid moral culpability for his criminal action—and thus avoid the negative sanctions of society—if he can prove that criminal intent was lacking. *It is our argument that much delinquency is based on what is essentially an unrecognized extension of defenses to crimes, in the form of justifications for deviance that are seen as valid by the delinquent but not by the legal system or society at large.*

These justifications are commonly described as rationalizations. They are viewed as following deviant behavior and as protecting the individual from self-blame and the blame of others after the act. But there is also reason to believe that they precede deviant behavior and make deviant behavior possible. It is this possibility that Sutherland mentioned only in passing and that other writers have failed to exploit from the viewpoint of sociological

91

theory. Disapproval flowing from internalized norms and conforming others in the social environment is neutralized, turned back, or deflected in advance. Social controls that serve to check or inhibit deviant motivational patterns are rendered inoperative, and the individual is freed to engage in delinquency without serious damage to his self-image. In this sense, the delinquent both has his cake and eats it too, for he remains committed to the dominant normative system and yet so qualifies its imperatives that violations are "acceptable" if not "right." Thus the delinquent represents not a radical opposition to law-abiding society but something more like an apologetic failure, often more sinned against than sinning in his own eyes. We call these justifications of deviant behavior techniques of neutralization; and we believe these techniques make up a crucial component of Sutherland's "definitions favorable to the violation of law." It is by learning these techniques that the juvenile becomes delinquent, rather than by learning moral imperatives, values, or attitudes standing in direct contradiction to those of the dominant society. In analyzing these techniques, we have found it convenient to divide them into five major types.

THE DENIAL OF RESPONSIBILITY

Insofar as the delinquent can define himself as lacking responsibility for his deviant actions, the disapproval of self or others is sharply reduced in effectiveness as a restraining influence. As Justice Holmes has said, even a dog distinguishes between being stumbled over and being kicked, and modern society is no less careful to draw a line between injuries that are unintentional, i.e., where responsibility is lacking, and those that are intentional. As a technique of neutralization, however, the denial of responsibility extends much further than the claim that deviant acts are an "accident" or some similar negation of personal accountability. It may also be asserted that delinquent acts are due to forces outside of the individual and beyond his control such as unloving parents, bad companions, or a slum neighborhood. In effect, the delinquent approaches a "billiard ball" conception of himself in which he sees himself as helplessly propelled into new situations. From a psychodynamic viewpoint, this orientation toward one's own actions may represent a profound alienation from self, but it is important to stress the fact that interpretations of responsibility are cultural constructs and not merely idiosyncratic beliefs. The similarity between this mode of justifying illegal behavior assumed by the delinquent and the implications of a "sociological" frame of reference or a "humane" jurisprudence is readily apparent.[2] It is not the validity of this orientation that concerns us here, but its function of deflecting blame attached to violations of social norms and its relative independence of a particular personality structure.[3] By learning to view himself as more acted upon than acting, the delinquent prepares the way for deviance from the dominant normative system without the necessity of a frontal assault on the norms themselves.

THE DENIAL OF INJURY

A second major technique of neutralization centers on the injury or harm involved in the delinquent act. The criminal law has long made a distinction between crimes which are *mala in se* and *mala prohibita*—that is, between acts that are wrong in themselves and acts that are illegal but not immoral—and the delinquent can make the same kind of distinction in evaluating the wrongfulness of his behavior. For the delinquent, however, wrongfulness may turn on the question of whether or not anyone has clearly been hurt by his deviance, and this matter is open to a variety of interpretations. Vandalism, for example, may be defined by the delinquent simply as "mischief"—after all, it may be claimed, the persons whose property has been destroyed can well afford it. Similarly, auto theft may be viewed as "borrowing," and gang fighting may be seen as a private quarrel, an agreed upon duel between two willing parties, and thus of no concern to the community at large. We are not suggesting that this technique of neutralization, labeled the denial of injury, involves an explicit dialectic. Rather, we are arguing that the delinquent frequently, and in a hazy fashion, feels that his behavior does not really cause any great harm despite the fact that it runs counter to law. Just as the link between the individual and his acts may be broken by the denial of responsibility, so may the link between acts and their consequences be broken by the denial of injury. Since society sometimes agrees with the delinquent, e.g., in matters such as truancy, "pranks," and so on, it merely reaffirms the idea that the delinquent's neutralization of social controls by means of qualifying the norms is an extension of common practice rather than a gesture of complete opposition.

THE DENIAL OF THE VICTIM

Even if the delinquent accepts the responsibility for his deviant actions and is willing to admit that his deviant actions involve an injury or hurt, the moral indignation of self and others may be neutralized by an insistence that the injury is not wrong in light of the circumstances. The injury, it may be claimed, is not really an injury; rather, it is a form of rightful retaliation or punishment. By a subtle alchemy the delinquent moves himself into the position of an avenger and the victim is transformed into a wrong-doer. Assaults on homosexuals or suspected homosexuals, attacks on members of minority groups who are said to have gotten "out of place," vandalism as revenge on an unfair teacher or school official, thefts from a "crooked" store owner—all may be hurts inflicted on a transgressor, in the eyes of the delinquent. As Orwell has pointed out, the type of criminal admired by the general public has probably changed over the course of years and Raffles no longer serves as a hero;[4] but Robin Hood, and his latter-day derivatives such as the tough detective seeking justice outside the law, still capture the popular imagination, and the delinquent may view his acts as part of a similar role.

To deny the existence of the victim, then, by transforming him into a person deserving injury is an extreme form of a phenomenon we have mentioned before, namely, the delinquent's recognition of appropriate and inappropriate targets for his delinquent acts. In addition, however, the existence of the victim may be denied for the delinquent, in a somewhat different sense, by the circumstances of the delinquent act itself. Insofar as the victim is physically absent, unknown, or a vague abstraction (as is often the case in delinquent acts committed against property), the awareness of the victim's existence is weakened. Internalized norms and anticipations of the reactions of others must somehow be activated if they are to serve as guides for behavior; and it is possible that a diminished awareness of the victim plays an important part of determining whether or not this process is set in motion.

THE CONDEMNATION OF THE CONDEMNERS

A fourth technique of neutralization would appear to involve a condemnation of the condemners or, as McCorkle and Korn have phrased it, a rejection of the rejectors.[5] The delinquent shifts the focus of attention from his own deviant acts to the motives and behavior of those who disapprove of his violations. His condemners, he may claim, are hypocrites, deviants in disguise, or impelled by personal spite. This orientation toward the conforming world may be of particular importance when it hardens into a bitter cynicism directed against those assigned the task of enforcing or expressing the norms of the dominant society. Police, it may be said, are corrupt, stupid, and brutal. Teachers always show favoritism and parents always "take it out" on their children. By a slight extension, the rewards of conformity—such as material success—become a matter of pull or luck, thus decreasing still further the stature of those who stand on the side of the law-abiding. The validity of this jaundiced viewpoint is not so important as its function in turning back or deflecting the negative sanctions attached to violations of the norms. The delinquent, in effect, has changed the subject of the conversation in the dialogue between his own deviant impulses and the reactions of others; and by attacking others, the wrongfulness of his own behavior is more easily repressed or lost to view.

THE APPEAL TO HIGHER LOYALTIES

Fifth, and last, internal and external social controls may be neutralized by sacrificing the demands of the larger society for the demands of the smaller social groups to which the delinquent belongs, such as the sibling pair, the gang, or the friendship clique. It is important to note that the delinquent does not necessarily repudiate the imperatives of the dominant normative system, despite his failure to follow them. Rather, the delinquent may see himself as caught up in a dilemma that must be resolved, unfortunately, at the cost of violating the law. One aspect of this situation has been studied by Stouffer and Toby in their research on the conflict between particularistic and universalistic demands, between the claims of friendship and general social obligations, and their results suggest that "it is possible to classify people according to a predisposition to select one or the other horn of a dilemma in role conflict."[6] For our purposes, however, the most important point is that deviation from certain norms may occur not because the norms are rejected but because others' norms, held to be more pressing or involving a higher loyalty, are accorded precedence. Indeed, it is the fact that both sets of norms are believed in that gives meaning to our concepts of dilemma and role conflict.

The conflict between the claims of friendship and the claims of law, or a similar dilemma, has of course long been recognized by the social scientist (and the novelist) as a common human problem. If the juvenile delinquent frequently resolves his dilemma by insisting that he must "always help a buddy" or "never squeal on a friend," even when it throws him into serious difficulties with the dominant social order, his choice remains familiar to the supposedly law-abiding. The delinquent is unusual, perhaps, in the extent to which he is able to see the fact that he acts in behalf of the smaller social groups to which he belongs as a justification for violations of society's norms, but it is a matter of degree rather than of kind.

"I didn't mean it." "I didn't really hurt anybody." "They had it coming to them." "Everybody's picking on me." "I didn't do it for myself." These slogans or their variants, we hypothesize, prepare the juvenile for delinquent acts. These "definitions of the situation" represent tangential or glancing blows at the dominant normative system rather than the creation of an opposing ideology; and they are extensions of patterns of thought prevalent in society rather than something created *de novo*.

Techniques of neutralization may not be powerful enough to fully shield the individual from the force of his own internalized values and the reactions of conforming others, for as we have pointed out, juvenile delinquents often appear to suffer from feelings of guilt and shame when called into account for their deviant behavior. And some delinquents may be so isolated from the world of conformity that techniques of neutralization need not be called into play. Nonetheless, we would argue that techniques of neutralization are critical in lessening the effectiveness of social controls and that they lie behind a large share of delinquent behavior. Empirical research in this area is scattered and fragmentary at the present time, but the work of Redl,[7] Cressey,[8] and others has supplied a body of significant data that has done much to clarify the theoretical issues and enlarge the fund of supporting evidence. Two lines of investigation seem to be critical at this stage. First, there is need for more knowledge concerning the differential distribution of techniques of neutralization, as operative patterns of thought, by age, sex, social class, ethnic group, etc. On a priori grounds it might be assumed that these justifications for deviance will be more readily seized by segments of society for whom a discrepancy between common social ideals and social practice is most apparent. It is also possible, however, that the habit of "bending" the dominant normative system—if not "breaking" it—cuts across our cruder social categories and is to be traced primarily to patterns of social interaction within the familial circle. Second, there is need for a greater understanding of the internal structure of techniques of neutralization, as a system of beliefs and attitudes, and its relationship to various types of delinquent behavior. Certain techniques of neutralization would appear to be better adapted to particular deviant acts than to others, as we have suggested, for example, in the case of offenses against property and the denial of the victim. But the issue remains far from clear and stands in need of more information.

In any case, techniques of neutralization appear to offer a promising line of research in enlarging and systematizing the theoretical grasp of juvenile delinquency. As more information is uncovered concerning techniques of neutralization, their origins, and their consequences, both juvenile delinquency in particular and deviation from normative systems in general may be illuminated.

Notes

1. Cf. Robin Williams, Jr., *American Society*, New York: Knopf, 1951, p. 28.

2. A number of observers have wryly noted that many delinquents seem to show a surprising awareness of sociological and psychological explanations for their behavior and are quick to point out the causal role of their poor environment.

3. It is possible, of course, that certain personality structures can accept some techniques of neutralization more readily than others, but this question remains largely unexplored.

4. George Orwell, *Dickens, Dali, and Others*, New York: Reynal, 1946.

5. Lloyd W. McCorkle and Richard Korn, "Resocialization Within Walls," *The Annals of the American Academy of Political and Social Science*, 293 (May, 1954), pp. 88–98.

6. See Samuel A. Stouffer and Jackson Toby, "Role Conflict and Personality," in *Toward a General Theory of Action*, edited by Talcott Parsons and Edward A. Shils, Cambridge, Mass.: Harvard University Press, 1951, p. 494.

7. See Fritz Redl and David Wineman, *Children Who Hate*, Glencoe, Ill.: The Free Press, 1956.

8. See D. R. Cressey, *Other People's Money*, Glencoe, Ill.: The Free Press, 1953.

10 / Convicted Rapists' Vocabulary of Motive: Excuses and Justifications

DIANA SCULLY
JOSEPH MAROLLA

  Psychiatry has dominated the literature on rapists since "irresistible impulse" (Glueck, 1925:323) and "disease of the mind" (Glueck, 1925:243) were introduced as the causes of rape. Research has been based on small samples of men, frequently the clinicians' own patient population. Not surprisingly, the medical model has predominated: rape is viewed as an individualistic, idiosyncratic symptom of a disordered personality. That is, rape is assumed to be a psychopathologic problem and individual rapists are assumed to be "sick." However, advocates of this model have been unable to isolate a typical or even predictable pattern of symptoms that are causally linked to rape. Additionally, research has demonstrated that fewer than 5 percent of rapists were psychotic at the time of their rape (Abel *et al.*, 1980).

We view rape as behavior learned socially through interaction with others; convicted rapists have learned the attitudes and actions consistent with sexual aggression against women. Learning also includes the acquisition of culturally derived vocabularies of motive, which can be used to diminish responsibility and to negotiate a non-deviant identity.

Sociologists have long noted that people can, and do, commit acts they define as wrong and, having done so, engage various techniques to disavow deviance and present themselves as normal. Through the concept of "vocabulary of motive," Mills (1940:904) was among the first to shed light on this seemingly perplexing contradiction. Wrong-doers attempt to reinterpret their actions through the use of a linguistic device by which norm breaking conduct is socially interpreted. That is, anticipating the negative consequences of their behavior, wrong-doers attempt to present the act in terms that are both culturally appropriate and acceptable.

Following Mills, a number of sociologists have focused on the types of techniques employed by actors in problematic situations (Hall and Hewitt, 1970; Hewitt and Hall, 1973; Hewitt and Stokes, 1975; Sykes and Matza, 1957). Scott and Lyman (1968) describe excuses and justifications, linguistic "accounts" that explain and remove culpability for an untoward act after it has been committed. *Excuses* admit the act was bad or inappropriate but deny full responsibility, often through appeals to accident, or biological drive, or through scapegoating. In contrast, *justifications* accept responsibility for the act but deny that it was wrong—that is, they show in this situation the act was appropriate. *Accounts* are socially approved vocabularies that neutralize an act or its consequences and are always a manifestation of an underlying negotiation of identity.

Stokes and Hewitt (1976:837) use the term "aligning actions" to refer to those tactics and techniques used by actors when some feature of a situation is problematic. Stated simply, the concept refers to an actor's attempt, through various means, to bring his or her conduct into alignment with culture. Culture in this sense is conceptualized as a "set of cognitive constraints—objects—to which people must relate as they form lines of conduct" (1976:837), and includes physical constraints, expectations and definitions of others, and personal biography. Carrying out aligning actions implies both awareness of those elements of normative culture that are applicable to the deviant act and, in addition, an actual effort to bring the act into line with this awareness. The result is that deviant behavior is legitimized.

This paper presents an analysis of interviews we conducted with a sample of 114 convicted, incarcerated rapists. We use the concept of accounts (Scott and Lyman, 1968) as a tool to organize and analyze the vocabularies of motive which this group of rapists used to explain themselves and their actions. An analysis of their accounts demonstrates how it was possible for 83 percent (n = 114)[1] of these convicted rapists to view themselves as non-rapists.

When rapists' accounts are examined, a typology emerges that consists of admitters and deniers. Admitters (n = 47) acknowledged that they had forced sexual acts on their victims and defined the behavior as rape. In contrast, deniers[2] either eschewed sexual contact or all association with the victim (n = 35),[3] or admitted to sexual acts but did not define their behavior as rape (n = 32).

The remainder of this paper is divided into two sections. In the first, we discuss the accounts which the rapists used to justify their behavior. In the second, we discuss those accounts which attempted to excuse the rape. By and large, the deniers used justifications while the admitters used excuses. In some cases, both groups relied on the same themes, stereotypes, and images: some admitters, like most deniers, claimed that women enjoyed being raped. Some deniers excused their behavior by referring to alcohol or drug use, although they did so quite differently than admitters. Through these narrative accounts, we explore convicted rapists' own perceptions of their crimes.

METHODS AND VALIDITY

From September, 1980, through September, 1981, we interviewed 114 male convicted rapists who were incarcerated in seven maximum or medium security prisons in the Commonwealth of Virginia. All of the rapists had been convicted of the rape or attempted rape (n = 8) of an adult woman, although a few had teenage victims as well. Men convicted of incest, statutory rape, or sodomy of a male were omitted from the sample.

Twelve percent of the rapists had been convicted of more than one rape or attempted rape, 39 percent also had convictions for burglary or robbery, 29 percent for abduction, 25 percent for sodomy, and 11 percent for first or second degree murder. Eighty-two percent had a previous criminal history but only 23 percent had records for previous sex offenses. Their sentences for rape and accompanying crimes ranged from 10 years to an accumulation by one man of seven life sentences plus 380 years; 43 percent of the rapists were serving from 10 to 30 years and 22 percent were serving at least one life term. Forty-six percent of the rapists were white and 54 percent were black. Their ages ranged from 18 to 60 years; 88 percent were between 18 and 35 years. Forty-two percent were either married or cohabitating at the time of their offense. Only 20 percent had a high school education or better, and 85 percent came from working-class backgrounds. Despite the popular belief that rape is due to a personality disorder, only 26 percent of these rapists had any history of emotional problems. When the rapists in this study were compared to a statistical profile of felons in all Virginia prisons, prepared by the Virginia Department of Corrections, rapists who volunteered for this research were disproportionately white, somewhat better educated, and younger than the average inmate.

All participants in this study were volunteers. We sent a letter to every inmate (n = 3500) at each of the seven prisons. The letters introduced us as professors at a local university, described our research as a study of men's attitudes toward sexual behavior and women, outlined our procedures for ensuring confidentiality, and solicited volunteers from all criminal cate-gories. Using one follow-up letter, approximately 25 percent of all inmates, including rapists, indicated their willingness to be interviewed by mailing an information sheet to us at the university. From this pool of volunteers, we constructed a sample of rapists based on age, education, race, severity of current offenses, and previous criminal records. Obviously, the sample was not random and thus may not be representative of all rapists.

Each of the authors—one woman and one man—interviewed half of the rapists. Both authors were able to establish rapport and obtain information. However, the rapists volunteered more about their feelings and emotions to the female author and her interviews lasted longer.

All rapists were given an 89-page interview, which included a general background, psychological, criminal, and sexual history, attitude scales, and 30 pages of open-ended questions intended to explore their perceptions of their crimes, their victims, and theirselves. Because a voice print is an absolute source of identification, we did not use tape recorders. All interviews were hand recorded. With some practice, we found it was possible to record much of the interview verbatim. While hand recording inevitably resulted in some lost data, it did have the advantage of eliciting more confidence and candor in the men.

Interviews with the rapists lasted from three hours to seven hours; the average was about four-and-one-half hours. Most of the rapists were reluctant to end the interview. Once rapport had been established, the men wanted to talk, even though it sometimes meant, for example, missing a meal.

Because of the reputation prison inmates have for "conning," validity was a special concern in our research. Although the purpose of the research was to obtain the men's own perceptions of their acts, it was also necessary to establish the extent to which these perceptions deviated from other descriptions of their crimes. To establish validity, we used the same technique others have used in prison research: comparing factual information, including details of the crime, obtained in the interview with pre-sentence reports on file at the prisons (Athens, 1977; Luckenbill, 1977; Queen's Bench Foundation, 1976). Pre-sentence reports, written by a court worker at the time of conviction, usually include general background information, a psychological evaluation, the offender's version of the details of the crime, and the victim's or police's version of the details of the crime. Using these records allowed us to clarify two important issues: first, the amount of change that had occurred in rapists' accounts from pre-sentencing to the time when we interviewed them; and, second, the amount of discrepancy between rapists' accounts, as told to us, and the victims' and/or police versions of the crime, contained in the pre-sentence reports.

The time between pre-sentence reports and our interviews (in effect, the amount of time rapists had spent in prison before we interviewed them) ranged from less than one year to 20 years; the average was three years. Yet despite this time lapse, there were no significant changes in the way rapists explained their crimes, with the exception of 18 men who had denied their crimes at their trials but admitted them to us. There were no cases of men who admitted their crime at their trial but denied them when talking to us.

However, there were major differences between the accounts we heard of the crimes from rapists and the police's and victim's versions. Admitters (including deniers turned admitters) told us essentially the same story as the police and victim versions. However, the admitters subtly understated the force they had used and, though they used words such as *violent* to describe their acts, they also omitted reference to the more brutal aspects of their crime.

In contrast, deniers' interview accounts differed significantly from victim and police versions. According to the pre-sentence reports, 11 of the 32 deniers had been acquainted with their victim. But an additional four deniers told us they had been acquainted with their victims. In the pre-sentence reports, police or victim versions of the crime described seven rapes in which the victim had been hitchhiking or was picked up in a bar; but deniers told us this was true of 20 victims. Weapons were present in 21 of the 32 rapes according to the pre-sentence reports, yet only nine men acknowledged the presence of a weapon and only two of the nine admitted they had used it to threaten or intimidate their victim. Finally, in at least seven of the rapes, the victim had been seriously injured,[4] but only three men admitted injury. In

Table 1 / Comparison of Admitter's and Denier's Crimes Police/Victim Versions in Pre-Sentence Reports

Characteristics	Percent Admitters $n = 47$	Percent Deniers $n = 32$
White Assailant	57	41
Black Assailant	43	59
Group Rape	23	13
Multiple Rapes	43	34
Assailant a Stranger	72	66
Controversial Situation	06	22
Weapon and/or Injury Present (includes victim murdered)	74	69

two of the three cases, the victim had been murdered; in these cases the men denied the rape but not the murder. Indeed, deniers constructed accounts for us which, by implicating the victim, made their own conduct appear to have been more appropriate. They never used words such as *violent*, choosing instead to emphasize the sexual component of their behavior.

It should be noted that we investigated the possibility that deniers claimed their behavior was not criminal because, in contrast to admitters, their crimes resembled what research has found the public define as a controversial rape, that is, victim an acquaintance, no injury or weapon, victim picked up hitchhiking or in a bar (Burt, 1980; Burt and Albin, 1981; Williams, 1979). However, as Table 1 indicates, the crimes committed by deniers were only slightly more likely to involve these elements.

This contrast between pre-sentence reports and interviews suggest several significant factors related to interview content validity. First, when asked to explain their behavior, our sample of convicted rapists (except deniers turned admitters) responded with accounts that had changed surprisingly little since their trials. Second, admitters' interview accounts were basically the same as others' versions of their crimes, while deniers systematically put more blame on the victims.

JUSTIFYING RAPE

Deniers attempted to justify their behavior by presenting the victim in a light that made her appear culpable, regardless of their own actions. Five themes run through attempts to justify their rapes: (1) women as seductresses; (2) women mean "yes" when they say "no"; (3) most women eventually relax and enjoy it; (4) nice girls don't get raped; and (5) guilty of a minor wrongdoing.

1) Women as Seductresses

Men who rape need not search far for cultural language which supports the premise that women provoke or are responsible for rape. In addition to common cultural stereotypes, the fields of psychiatry and criminology (particularly the subfield of victimology) have traditionally provided justifications for rape, often by portraying raped women as the victims of their own seduction (Albin, 1977; Marolla and Scully, 1979). For example, Hollander (1924:130) argues:

> Considering the amount of illicit intercourse, rape of women is very rare indeed. Flirtation and provocative conduct, i.e., tacit (if not actual) consent is generally the prelude to intercourse.

Since women are supposed to be coy about their sexual availability, refusal to comply with a man's sexual demands lacks meaning and rape appears normal. The fact that violence and, often, a weapon are used to accomplish the rape is not considered. As an example, Abrahamsen (1960:61) writes:

> The conscious or unconscious biological or psychological attraction between man and woman does not exist only on the part of the offender toward the woman but, also, on her part toward him, which in many instances may, to some extent, be the impetus for his sexual attack. Often a woman [sic] unconsciously wishes to be taken by force—consider the theft of the bride in Peer Gynt.

Like Peer Gynt, the deniers we interviewed tried to demonstrate that their victims were willing and, in some cases, enthusiastic participants. In these accounts, the rape became more dependent upon the victim's behavior than upon their own actions.

Thirty-one percent (n = 10) of the deniers presented an extreme view of the victim. Not only willing, she was the aggressor, a seductress who lured them, unsuspecting, into sexual action. Typical was a denier convicted of his first rape and accompanying crimes of burglary, sodomy, and abduction. According to the pre-sentence reports, he had broken into the victim's house and raped her at knife point. While he admitted to the breaking and entry, which he claimed was for altruistic purposes ("to pay for the prenatal care of a friend's girlfriend"), he also argued that when the victim discovered him, he had tried to leave but she had asked him to stay. Telling him that she cheated on her husband, she had voluntarily removed her clothes and seduced him. She was, according to him, an exemplary sex partner who "enjoyed it very much and asked for oral sex.[5] Can I have it now?" he reported her as saying. He claimed they had spent hours in bed, after which the victim had told him he was good looking and asked to see him again. "Who would believe I'd meet a fellow like this?" he reported her as saying.

In addition to this extreme group, 25 percent (n = 8) of the deniers said the victim was willing and had made some sexual advances. An additional 9 percent (n = 3) said the victim was willing to have sex for money or drugs. In two of these three cases, the victim had been either an acquaintance or picked up, which the rapists said led them to expect sex.

2) Women Mean "Yes" When They Say "No"

Thirty-four percent (n = 11) of the deniers described their victim as unwilling, at least initially, indicating either that she had resisted or that she had said no. Despite this, and even though (according to pre-sentence reports) a weapon had been present in 64 percent (n = 7) of these 11 cases, the rapists justified their behavior by arguing that either the victim had not resisted enough or that her "no" had really meant "yes." For example, one denier who was serving time for a previous rape was subsequently convicted of attempting to rape a prison hospital nurse. He insisted he had actually completed the second rape, and said of his victim: "She semi-struggled but deep down inside I think she felt it was a fantasy come true." The nurse, according to him, had asked a question about his conviction for rape, which he interpreted as teasing. "It was like she was saying, 'rape me.' " Further, he stated that she had helped him along with oral sex and "from her actions, she was enjoying it." In another case, a 34-year-old man convicted of abducting and raping a 15-year-old teenager at knife point as she walked on the beach, claimed it was a pickup. This rapist said women like to be overpowered before sex, but to dominate after it begins.

> A man's body is like a coke bottle, shake it up, put your thumb over the opening and feel the tension. When you take a woman out, woo her, then she says "no, I'm a nice girl," you have to use force. All men do this. She said "no" but it was a societal no, she wanted to be coaxed. All women say "no" when they mean "yes" but its a societal no, so they won't have to feel responsible later.

Claims that the victim didn't resist or, if she did, didn't resist enough, were also used by 24 percent (n = 11) of admitters to explain why, during the incident, they believed the victim was willing and that they were not raping. These rapists didn't redefine their acts until some time after the crime. For example, an admitter who used a bayonet to threaten his victim, an employee of the store he had been robbing, stated:

> At the time I didn't think it was rape. I just asked her nicely and she didn't resist. I never considered prison. I just felt like I had met a friend. It took about five years of reading and going to school to change my mind about whether it was rape. I became familiar with the subtlety of violence. But at the time, I believed that as long as I didn't hurt anyone it wasn't wrong. At the time, I didn't think I would go to prison. I thought I would beat it.

Another typical case involved a gang rape in which the victim was abducted at knife point as she walked home about midnight. According to two of the rapists, both of whom were interviewed, at the time they had thought the victim had willingly accepted a ride from the third rapist (who was not interviewed). They claimed the victim didn't resist and one reported her as saying she would do anything if they would take her home. In this rapist's view, "She acted like she enjoyed it, but maybe she was just acting. She wasn't crying, she was engaging in it." He reported that she had been friendly to the rapist who abducted her and, claiming not to have a home phone, she gave him her office number—a tactic eventually used to catch the three. In retrospect, this young man had decided, "She was scared and just relaxed and enjoyed it to avoid getting hurt." Note, however, that while he had redefined the act as rape, he continued to believe she enjoyed it.

Men who claimed to have been unaware that they were raping viewed sexual aggression as a man's prerogative at the time of the rape. Thus they regarded their act as little more than a minor wrongdoing even though most possessed or used a weapon. As long as the victim survived without major physical injury, from their perspective, a rape had not taken place. Indeed, even U.S. courts have often taken the position that physical injury is a necessary ingredient for a rape conviction.

3) Most Women Eventually Relax and Enjoy It

Many of the rapists expected us to accept the image, drawn from cultural stereotype, that once the rape began, the victim relaxed and enjoyed it.[6] Indeed, 69 percent (n = 22) of deniers justified their behavior by claiming not only that the victim was willing, but also that she enjoyed herself, in some cases to an immense degree. Several men suggested that they had fulfilled their victims' dreams. Additionally, while most admitters used adjectives such as "dirty," "humiliated," and "disgusted," to describe how they thought rape made women feel, 20 percent (n = 9) believed that their victim enjoyed herself. For example, one denier had posed as a salesman to gain entry to his victim's house. But he claimed he had had a previous sexual relationship with the victim, that she agreed to have sex for drugs, and that the opportunity to have sex with him produced "a glow, because she was really into oral stuff and fascinated by the idea of sex with a black man. She felt satisfied, fulfilled, wanted me to stay, but I didn't want her." In another case, a denier who had broken into his victim's house but who insisted the victim was his lover and let him in voluntarily, declared "She felt good, kept kissing me and wanted me to stay the night. She felt proud after sex with me." And another denier, who had hid in his victim's closet and later attacked her while she slept, argued that while she was scared at first, "once we got into it, she was ok." He continued to believe he hadn't committed rape because "she enjoyed it and it was like she consented."

4) Nice Girls Don't Get Raped

The belief that "nice girls don't get raped" affects perception of fault. The victim's reputation, as well as characteristics or behavior which violate normative sex role expectations, are perceived as contributing to the commission of the crime. For example, Nelson and Amir (1975) defined hitchhike rape as a victim-precipitated offense.

In our study, 69 percent (n = 22) of deniers and 22 percent (n = 10) of admitters referred to their victims' sexual reputation, thereby evoking the stereotype that "nice girls don't get raped." They claimed that the victim was known to have been a prostitute, or a "loose" woman, or to have had a lot of affairs, or to have given birth to a child out of wedlock. For example, a denier who claimed he had picked up his victim while she was hitchhiking stated, "To be honest, we [his family] knew she was a damn whore and whether she screwed one or 50 guys didn't matter." According to pre-sentence reports this victim didn't know her attacker and he abducted her at knife point from the street. In another case, a denier who claimed to have known his victim by reputation stated:

> If you wanted drugs or a quick piece of ass, she would do it. In court she said she was a virgin, but I could tell during sex [rape] that she was very experienced.

When other types of discrediting biographical information were added to these sexual slurs, a total of 78 percent (n = 25) of the deniers used the victim's reputation to substantiate their accounts. Most frequently, they referred to the victim's emotional state or drug use. For example, one denier claimed his victim had been known to be loose and, additionally, had turned state's evidence against her husband to put him in prison and save herself from a burglary conviction. Further, he asserted that she had met her current boyfriend, who was himself in and out of prison, in a drug rehabilitation center where they were both clients.

Evoking the stereotype that women provoke rape by the way they dress, a description of the victim as seductively attired appeared in the accounts of 22 percent (n = 7) of deniers and 17 percent (n = 8) of admitters. Typically, these descriptions were used to substantiate their claims about the victim's reputation. Some men went to extremes to paint a tarnished picture of the victim, describing her as dressed in tight black clothes and without a bra; in one case, the victim was portrayed as sexually provocative in dress and carriage. Not only did she wear short skirts, but she was observed to "spread her legs while getting out of cars." Not all of the men attempted to assassinate their victim's reputation with equal vengeance. Numerous times they made subtle and offhand remarks like, "She was a waitress and you know how they are."

The intent of these discrediting statements is clear. Deniers argued that the woman was a "legitimate" victim who got what she deserved. For example, one denier stated that all of his victims had been prostitutes; pre-sentence reports indicated they were not. Several times during his interview, he referred to them as "dirty sluts," and argued "anything I did to them was justified." Deniers also claimed their victim had wrongly accused them and was the type of woman who would perjure herself in court.

5) Only a Minor Wrongdoing

The majority of deniers did not claim to be completely innocent and they also accepted some accountability for their actions. Only 16 percent (n = 5) of deniers argued that they were totally free of blame. Instead, the majority of deniers pleaded guilty to a lesser charge. That is, they obfuscated the rape by pleading guilty to a less serious, more acceptable charge. They accepted being over-sexed, accused of poor judgment or trickery, even some violence, or guilty of adultery or contributing to the delinquency of a minor, charges that are hardly the equivalent of rape.

Typical of this reasoning is a denier who met his victim in a bar when the bartender asked him if he would try to repair her stalled car. After attempting unsuccessfully, he claimed the victim drank with him and later accepted a ride. Out riding, he pulled into a deserted area "to see how my luck would go." When the victim resisted his advances, he beat her and he stated:

> I did something stupid. I pulled a knife on her and I hit her as hard as I would hit a man. But I shouldn't be in prison for what I did. I shouldn't have all this time [sentence] for going to bed with a broad.

This rapist continued to believe that while the knife was wrong, his sexual behavior was justified.

In another case, the denier claimed he picked up his under-age victim at a party and that she voluntarily went with him to a motel. According to pre-sentence reports, the victim had been abducted at knife point from a party. He explained:

> After I paid for a motel, she would have to have sex but I wouldn't use a weapon. I would have explained I spent money and, if she still said no, I would have forced her. If it had happened that way, it would have been rape to some people but not to my way of thinking. I've done that kind of thing before. I'm guilty of sex and contributing to the delinquency of a minor, but not rape.

In sum, deniers argued that, while their behavior may not have been completely proper, it should not have been considered rape. To accomplish this, they attempted to discredit and blame the victim while presenting their own actions as justified in the context. Not surprisingly, none of the deniers thought of himself as a rapist. A minority of the admitters attempted to lessen the impact of their crime by claiming the victim enjoyed being raped. But despite this similarity, the nature and tone of admitters' and deniers' accounts were essentially different.

EXCUSING RAPE

In stark contrast to deniers, admitters regarded their behavior as morally wrong and beyond justification. They blamed themselves rather than the victim, although some continued to cling to the belief that the victim had contributed to the crime somewhat, for example, by not resisting enough.

Several of the admitters expressed the view that rape was an act of such moral outrage that it was unforgivable. Several admitters broke into tears at intervals during their interviews. A typical sentiment was,

> I equate rape with someone throwing you up against a wall and tearing your liver and guts out of you.... Rape is worse than murder... and I'm disgusting.

Another young admitter frequently referred to himself as repulsive and confided:

> I'm in here for rape and in my own mind, its the most disgusting crime, sickening. When people see me and know, I get sick.

Admitters tried to explain their crime in a way that allowed them to retain a semblance of moral integrity. Thus, in contrast to deniers' justifications, admitters used excuses to explain how they were compelled to rape. These excuses appealed to the existence of forces outside of the rapists' control. Through the use of excuses, they attempted to demonstrate that either intent was absent or responsibility was diminished. This allowed them to admit rape while reducing the threat to their identity as a moral person. Excuses also permitted them to view their behavior as idiosyncratic rather than typical and, thus, to believe they were not "really" rapists. Three themes run through these accounts: (1) the use of alcohol and drugs; (2) emotional problems; and (3) nice guy image.

1) The Use of Alcohol and Drugs

A number of studies have noted a high incidence of alcohol and drug consumption by convicted rapists prior to their crime (Groth, 1979; Queen's Bench Foundation, 1976). However, more recent research has tentatively concluded that the connection between substance use and crime is not as direct as previously thought (Ladouceur, 1983). Another facet of alcohol and drug use mentioned in the literature is its utility in disavowing deviance. McCaghy (1968) found that child molesters used alcohol as a technique for neutralizing their deviant identity. Marolla and Scully (1979), in a review of psychiatric literature, demonstrated how alcohol consumption is applied differently as a vocabulary of motive. Rapists can use alcohol both as an excuse for their behavior and to discredit the victim and make her more responsible. We found the former common among admitters and the latter common among deniers.

Alcohol and/or drugs were mentioned in the accounts of 77 percent (n = 30) of admitters and 84 percent (n = 21) of deniers and both groups were equally likely to have acknowledged consuming a substance—admitters, 77 percent (n = 30); deniers, 72 percent (n = 18). However, admitters said they had been affected by the substance; if not the cause of their behavior, it was at least a contributing factor. For example, an admitter who estimated his consumption to have been eight beers and four "hits of acid" reported:

> Straight, I don't have the guts to rape. I could fight a man but not that. To say, "I'm going to do it to a woman," knowing it will scare and hurt her, takes guts or you have to be sick.

Another admitter believed that his alcohol and drug use,

> ... brought out what was already there but in such intensity it was uncontrollable. Feelings of being dominant, powerful, using someone for my own gratification, all rose to the surface.

In contrast, deniers' justifications required that they not be substantially impaired. To say that they had been drunk or high would cast doubt on their ability to control themselves or to remember events as they actually happened. Consistent with this, when we asked if the alcohol and/or drugs had had an effect on their behavior, 69 percent (n = 27) of admitters, but only 40 percent (n = 10) of deniers, said they had been affected.

Even more interesting were references to the victim's alcohol and/or drug use. Since admitters had already relieved themselves of responsibility through claims of being drunk or high, they had nothing to gain from the assertion that the victim had used or been affected by alcohol and/or drugs. On the other hand, it was very much in the interest of deniers to declare that their victim had been intoxicated or high: that fact lessened her credibility and made her more responsible for the act. Reflecting these observations, 72 percent (n = 18) of deniers and 26 percent (n = 10) of admitters maintained that alcohol or drugs had been consumed by the victim. Further, while 56 percent (n = 14) of deniers declared she had been affected by this use, only 15 percent (n = 6) of admitters made a similar claim. Typically, deniers argued that the alcohol and drugs had sexually aroused their victim or rendered her out of control. For example, one denier

Table 2 / Rapists' Accounts of Own and Victims' Alcohol and/or Drug (A/D) Use and Effect

	Admitters n = 39 %	Deniers n = 25 %
Neither Self nor Victim Used A/D	23	16
Self Used A/D	77	72
Of Self Used, no Victim Use	51	12
Self Affected by A/D	69	40
Of Self Affected, no Victim Use or Affect	54	24
Self A/D Users who were Affected	90	56
Victim Used A/D	26	72
Of Victim Used, no Self Use	0	0
Victim Affected by A/D	15	56
Of Victim Affected, no Self Use or Affect	0	40
Victim A/D Users who were Affected	60	78
Both Self and Victim Used and Affected by A/D	15	16

insisted that his victim had become hysterical from drugs, not from being raped, and it was because of the drugs that she had reported him to the police. In addition, 40 percent (n = 10) of deniers argued that while the victim had been drunk or high, they themselves either hadn't ingested or weren't affected by alcohol and/or drugs. None of the admitters made this claim. In fact, in all of the 15 percent (n = 6) of cases where an admitter said the victim was drunk or high, he also admitted to being similarly affected.

These data strongly suggest that whatever role alcohol and drugs play in sexual and other types of violent crime, rapists have learned the advantage to be gained from using alcohol and drugs as an account. Our sample was aware that their victim would be discredited and their own behavior excused or justified by referring to alcohol and/or drugs.

2) Emotional Problems

Admitters frequently attributed their acts to emotional problems. Forty percent (n = 19) of admitters said they believe an emotional problem had been at the root of their rape behavior, and 33 percent (n = 15) specifically related the problem to an unhappy, unstable childhood or a marital-domestic situation. Still others claimed to have been in a general state of unease. For example, one admitter said that at the time of the rape he had been depressed, feeling he couldn't do anything right, and that something had been missing from his life. But he also added, "being a rapist is not part of my personality." Even admitters who could locate no source for an emotional problem evoked the popular image of rapists as the product of disordered personalities to argue they also must have problems:

> The fact that I'm a rapist makes me different. Rapists aren't all there. They have problems. It was wrong so there must be a reason why I did it. I must have a problem.

Our data do indicate that a precipitating event, involving an upsetting problem of everyday living, appeared in the accounts of 80 percent (n = 38) of admitters and 25 percent (n = 8) of deniers. Of those experiencing a precipitating event, including deniers, 76 percent (n = 35) involved a wife or girlfriend. Over and over, these men described themselves as having been in a rage because of an incident involving a woman with whom they believed they were in love.

Frequently, the upsetting event was related to a rigid and unrealistic double standard for sexual conduct and virtue which they applied to "their" woman but which they didn't expect from men, didn't apply to themselves, and, obviously, didn't honor in other women. To discover that the "pedestal" didn't apply to their wife or girlfriend sent them into a fury. One especially articulate and typical admitter described his feeling as follows.

After serving a short prison term for auto theft, he married his "childhood sweetheart" and secured a well-paying job. Between his job and the volunteer work he was doing with an ex-offender group, he was spending long hours away from home, a situation that had bothered his wife. In response to her request, he gave up his volunteer work, though it was clearly meaningful to him. Then, one day, he discovered his wife with her former boyfriend "and my life fell apart." During the next several days, he said his anger had made him withdraw into himself and, after three days of drinking in a motel room, he abducted and raped a stranger. He stated:

> My parents have been married for many years and I had high expectations about marriage. I put my wife on a pedestal. When I walked in on her, I felt like my life had been destroyed, it was such a shock. I was bitter and angry about the fact that I hadn't done anything to my wife for cheating. I didn't want to hurt her [victim], only to scare and degrade her.

It is clear that many admitters, and a minority of deniers, were under stress at the time of their rapes. However, their problems were ordinary— the types of upsetting events that everyone experiences at some point in life. The overwhelming majority of the men were not clinically defined as mentally ill in court-ordered psychiatric examinations prior to their trials. Indeed, our sample is consistent with Abel *et al.* (1980) who found fewer than 5 percent of rapists were psychotic at the time of their offense.

As with alcohol and drug intoxication, a claim of emotional problems works differently depending upon whether the behavior in question is being justified or excused. It would have been counter-productive for deniers to have claimed to have had emotional problems at the time of the rape. Admitters used psychological explanations to portray themselves as having been temporarily "sick" at the time of the rape. Sick people are usually blamed for neither the cause of their illness nor for acts committed while in that state of diminished capacity. Thus, adopting the sick role removed responsibility by excusing the behavior as having been beyond the ability of the individual to control. Since the rapists were not "themselves," the rape was idiosyncratic rather than typical behavior. Admitters asserted a non-deviant identity despite their self-proclaimed disgust with what they had done. Although admitters were willing to assume the sick role, they did not view their problem as a chronic condition, nor did they believe themselves to be insane or permanently impaired. Said one admitter, who believed that he needed psychological counseling: "I have a mental disorder, but I'm not crazy." Instead, admitters viewed their "problem" as mild, transient, and curable. Indeed, part of the appeal of this excuse was that not only did it relieve responsibility, but, as with alcohol and drug addiction, it allowed the rapist to "recover." Thus, at the time of their interviews, only 31 percent (n = 14) of admitters indicated that "being a rapist" was part of their self-concept. Twenty-eight percent (n = 13) of admitters stated they had never thought of themselves as rapists, 8 percent (n = 4) said they were unsure, and 33 percent (n = 16) asserted they had been a rapist at one time but now were recovered. A multiple "exrapist," who believed his "problem" was due to "something buried in my subconscious" that was triggered when his girlfriend broke up with him, expressed a typical opinion:

> I was a rapist, but not now. I've grown up, had to live with it. I've hit the bottom of the well and it can't get worse. I feel born again to deal with my problems.

3) Nice Guy Image

Admitters attempted to further neutralize their crime and negotiate a non-rapist identity by painting an image of themselves as a "nice guy." Admitters projected the image of someone who had made a serious mistake but, in every other respect, was a decent person. Fifty-seven percent (n = 27) expressed regret and sorrow for their victim indicating that they wished there were a way to apologize for or amend their behavior. For example, a participant in a rape-murder, who insisted his partner did the murder, confided, "I wish there was something I could do besides saying 'I'm sorry, I'm sorry.' I live with it 24 hours a day and, sometimes, I wake up crying in the middle of the night because of it."

Schlenker and Darby (1981) explain the significance of apologies beyond the obvious expression of regret. An apology allows a person to admit guilt while at the same time seeking a pardon by signalling that the event should not be considered a fair representation of what the person is really like. An apology separates the bad self from the good self, and promises more acceptable behavior in the future. When apologizing, an individual is attempting to say: "I have repented and should be forgiven," thus making it appear that no further rehabilitation is required.

The "nice guy" statements of the admitters reflected an attempt to communicate a message consistent with Schlenker's and Darby's analysis of apologies. It was an attempt to convey that rape was not a representation of their "true" self. For example,

> It's different from anything else I've ever done. I feel more guilt about this. It's not consistent with me. When I talk about it, it's like being assaulted myself. I don't know why I did it, but once I started, I got into it. Armed robbery was a way of life for me, but not rape. I feel like I wasn't being myself.

Admitters also used "nice guy" statements to register their moral opposition to violence and harming women, even though, in some cases, they had seriously injured their victims. Such was the case of an admitter convicted of a gang rape:

> I'm against hurting women. She should have resisted. None of us were the type of person that would use force on a woman. I never positioned myself on a woman unless she showed an interest in me. They would play to me, not me to them. My weakness is to follow. I never would have stopped, let alone pick her up without

the others. I never would have let anyone beat her. I never bothered women who didn't want sex; never had a problem with sex or getting it. I loved her—like all women.

Finally, a number of admitters attempted to improve their self-image by demonstrating that, while they had raped, it could have been worse if they had not been a "nice guy." For example, one admitter professed to being especially gentle with his victim after she told him she had just had a baby. Others claimed to have given the victim money to get home or make a phone call, or to have made sure the victim's children were not in the room. A multiple rapist, whose pattern was to break in and attack sleeping victims in their homes, stated:

> I never beat any of my victims and I told them I wouldn't hurt them if they cooperated. I'm a professional thief. But I never robbed the women I raped because I felt so bad about what I had already done to them.

Even a young man, who raped his five victims at gun point and then stabbed them to death, attempted to improve his image by stating:

> Physically they enjoyed the sex [rape]. Once they got involved, it would be difficult to resist. I was always gentle and kind until I started to kill them. And the killing was always sudden, so they wouldn't know it was coming.

SUMMARY AND CONCLUSIONS

Convicted rapists' accounts of their crimes include both excuses and justifications. Those who deny what they did was rape justify their actions; those who admit it was rape attempt to excuse it or themselves. This study does not address why some men admit while others deny, but future research might address this question. This paper does provide insight on how men who are sexually aggressive or violent construct reality, describing the different strategies of admitters and deniers.

Admitters expressed the belief that rape was morally reprehensible. But they explained themselves and their acts by appealing to forces beyond their control, forces which reduced their capacity to act rationally and thus compelled them to rape. Two types of excuses predominated: alcohol/drug intoxication and emotional problems. Admitters used these excuses to negotiate a moral identity for themselves by viewing rape as idiosyncratic rather than typical behavior. This allowed them to reconceptualize themselves as recovered or "exrapists," someone who had made a serious mistake which did not represent their "true" self.

In contrast, deniers' accounts indicate that these men raped because their value system provided no compelling reason not to do so. When sex is viewed as a male entitlement, rape is no longer seen as criminal. However, the deniers had been convicted of rape, and like the admitters, they attempted to negotiate an identity. Through justifications, they constructed a "controversial" rape and attempted to demonstrate how their behavior, even if not quite right, was appropriate in the situation. Their denials, drawn from common cultural rape stereotypes, took two forms, both of which ultimately denied the existence of a victim.

The first form of denial was buttressed by the cultural view of men as sexually masterful and women as coy but seductive. Injury was denied by portraying the victim as willing, even enthusiastic, or as politely resistant at first but eventually yielding to "relax and enjoy it." In these accounts, force appeared merely as a seductive technique. Rape was disclaimed: rather than harm the woman, the rapist had fulfilled her dreams. In the second form of denial, the victim was portrayed as the type of woman who "got what she deserved." Through attacks on the victim's sexual reputation and, to a lesser degree, her emotional state, deniers attempted to demonstrate that since the victim wasn't a "nice girl," they were not rapists. Consistent with both forms of denial was the self-interested use of alcohol and drugs as a justification. Thus, in contrast to admitters, who accentuated their own use as an excuse, deniers emphasized the victim's consumption in an effort to both discredit her and make her appear more responsible for the rape. It is important to remember that deniers did not invent these justifications. Rather, they reflect a belief system which has historically victimized women by promulgating the myth that women both enjoy and are responsible for their own rape.

While admitters and deniers present an essentially contrasting view of men who rape, there were some shared characteristics. Justifications particularly, but also excuses, are buttressed by the cultural view of women as sexual commodities, dehumanized and devoid of autonomy and dignity. In this sense, the sexual objectification of women must be understood as an important factor contributing to an environment that trivializes, neutralizes, and, perhaps, facilitates rape.

Finally, we must comment on the consequences of allowing one perspective to dominate thought on a social problem. Rape, like any complex continuum of behavior, has multiple causes and is influenced by a number of social factors. Yet, dominated by psychiatry and the medical model, the underlying assumption that rapists are "sick" has pervaded research. Although methodologically unsound, conclusions have been based almost exclusively on small clinical populations of rapists—that extreme group of rapists who seek counseling in prison and are the most likely to exhibit psychopathology. From this small, atypical group of men, psychiatric findings have been generalized to all men who rape. Our research, however, based on volunteers from the entire prison population, indicates that some rapists, like deniers, viewed and understood their behavior from a popular cultural perspective. This strongly suggests that cultural perspectives, and not an idiosyncratic illness, motivated their behavior. Indeed, we can argue that the psychiatric perspective has contributed to the vocabulary of motive that rapists use to excuse and justify their behavior (Scully and Marolla, 1984).

Efforts to arrive at a general explanation for rape have been retarded by the narrow focus of the medical model and the preoccupation with clinical populations. The continued reduction of such complex behavior to a singular cause hinders, rather than enhances, our understanding of rape.

Notes

This research was supported by a grant (R01 MH33013) from the National Center For the Prevention and Control of Rape, National Institute of Mental Health. The authors thank the Virginia Department of Corrections for their cooperation and assistance in this research. Correspondence to: Department of Sociology and Anthropology, Virginia Commonwealth University, 312 Shafer Court, Richmond, VA 23284.

1. These numbers include pretest interviews. When the analysis involves either questions that were not asked in the pretest or that were changed, they are excluded and thus the number changes.

2. There is, of course, the possibility that some of these men really were innocent of rape. However, while the U.S. criminal justice system is not without flaw, we assume that it is highly unlikely that this many men could have been unjustly convicted of rape, especially since rape is a crime with traditionally low conviction rates. Instead, for purposes of this research, we assume that these men were guilty as charged and that their attempt to maintain an image of non-rapist springs from some psychologically or sociologically interpretable mechanism.

3. Because of their outright denial, interviews with this group of rapists did not contain the data being analyzed here and, consequently, they are not included in this paper.

4. It was sometimes difficult to determine the full extent of victim injury from the pre-sentence reports. Consequently, it is doubtful that this number accurately reflects the degree of injuries sustained by victims.

5. It is worth noting that a number of deniers specifically mentioned the victim's alleged interest in oral sex. Since our interview questions about sexual history indicated that the rapists themselves found oral sex marginally acceptable, the frequent mention is probably another attempt to discredit the victim. However, since a tape recorder could not be used for the interviews and the importance of these claims didn't emerge until the data was being coded and analyzed, it is possible that it was mentioned even more frequently but not recorded.

6. Research shows clearly that women do not enjoy rape. Holmstrom and Burgess (1978) asked 93 adult rape victims, "How did it feel sexually?" Not one said they enjoyed it. Further, the trauma of rape is so great that it disrupts sexual functioning (both frequency and satisfaction) for the overwhelming majority of victims, at least during the period immediately following the rape and, in fewer cases, for an extended period of time (Burgess and Holmstrom, 1979; Feldman-Summers et al., 1979). In addition, a number of studies have shown that rape victims experience adverse consequences prompting some to move, change jobs, or drop out of school (Burgess and Holmstrom, 1974; Kilpatrick et al., 1979; Ruch et al., 1980; Shore, 1979).

References

Abel, Gene, Judith Becker, and Linda Skinner
1980 "Aggressive behavior and sex." Psychiatric Clinics of North America 3(2):133–151.
Abrahamsen, David
1960 The Psychology of Crime. New York: John Wiley.
Albin, Rochelle
1977 "Psychological studies of rape." Signs 3(2):423–435.

Athens, Lonnie
  1977 "Violent crimes: A symbolic interactionist study." Symbolic Interaction 1(1):56–71.
Burgess, Ann Wolbert, and Lynda Lytle Holmstrom
  1974 Rape: Victims of Crisis. Bowie: Robert J. Brady.
  1979 "Rape: Sexual disruption and recovery." American Journal of Orthopsychiatry 49(4):648–657.
Burt, Martha
  1980 "Cultural myths and supports for rape." Journal of Personality and Social Psychology 38(2):217–230.
Burt, Martha, and Rochelle Albin
  1981 "Rape myths, rape definitions, and probability of conviction." Journal of Applied Psychology 11(3):212–230.
Feldman-Summers, Shirley, Patricia E. Gordon, and Jeanette R. Meagher
  1979 "The impact of rape on sexual satisfaction." Journal of Abnormal Psychology 88(1):101–105.
Glueck, Sheldon
  1925 Mental Disorders and the Criminal Law. New York: Little Brown.
Groth, Nicholas A.
  1979 Men Who Rape. New York: Plenum Press.
Hall, Peter M., and John P. Hewitt
  1970 "The quasi-theory of communication and the management of dissent." Social Problems 18(1):17–27.
Hewitt, John P., and Peter M. Hall
  1973 "Social problems, problematic situations, and quasi-theories." American Journal of Sociology 38(3):367–374.
Hewitt, John P., and Randall Stokes
  1975 "Disclaimers." American Sociological Review 40(1):1–11.
Hollander, Bernard
  1924 The Psychology of Misconduct, Vice, and Crime. New York: Macmillan.
Holmstrom, Lynda Lytle, and Ann Wolbert Burgess
  1978 "Sexual behavior of assailant and victim during rape." Paper presented at the annual meetings of the American Sociological Association, San Francisco, September 2–8.
Kilpatrick, Dean G., Lois Veronen, and Patricia A. Resnick
  1979 "The aftermath of rape: Recent empirical findings." American Journal of Orthopsychiatry 49(4):658–669.
Ladouceur, Patricia
  1983 "The relative impact of drugs and alcohol on serious felons." Paper presented at the annual meetings of the American Society of Criminology, Denver, November 9–12.
Luckenbill, David
  1977 "Criminal homicide as a situated transaction." Social Problems 25(2):176–187.
McCaghy, Charles
  1968 "Drinking and deviance disavowal: The case of child molesters." Social Problems 16(1):43–49.
Marolla, Joseph, and Diana Scully
  1979 "Rape and psychiatric vocabularies of motive." Pp. 301–318 in Edith

S. Gomberg and Violet Franks (eds.), Gender and Disordered Behavior: Sex Differences in Psychopathology. New York: Brunner/Mazel.

Mills, C. Wright
1940 "Situated actions and vocabularies of motive." American Sociological Review 5(6):904–913.

Nelson, Steve, and Menachem Amir
1975 "The hitchhike victim of rape: A research report." Pp. 47–65 in Israel Drapkin and Emilio Viano (eds.), Victimology: A New Focus. Lexington, KY: Lexington Books.

Queen's Bench Foundation
1976 Rape; Prevention and Resistance. San Francisco: Queen's Bench Foundation.

Ruch, Libby O., Susan Meyers Chandler, and Richard A. Harter
1980 "Life change and rape impact." Journal of Health and Social Behavior 21(3):248–260.

Schlenker, Barry R., and Bruce W. Darby
1981 "The use of apologies in social predicaments." Social Psychology Quarterly 44(3):271–278.

Scott, Marvin, and Stanford Lyman
1968 "Accounts." American Sociological Review 33(1):46–62.

Scully, Diana, and Joseph Marolla
1984 "Rape and psychiatric vocabularies of motive: Alternative perspectives." In Ann Wolbert Burgess (ed.), Handbook on Rape and Sexual Assault. New York: Garland Publishing.

Shore, Barbara K.
1979 "An examination of critical process and outcome factors in rape." Rockville, MD: National Institute of Mental Health.

Stokes, Randall, and John P. Hewitt
1976 "Aligning actions." American Sociological Review 41(5):837–849.

Sykes, Gresham M., and David Matza
1957 "Techniques of neutralization." American Sociological Review 22(6): 664–670.

Williams, Joyce
1979 "Sex role stereotypes, women's liberation, and rape: A cross-cultural analysis of attitude." Sociological Symposium 25 (Winter):61–97.

11 / Social Structure and Anomie

ROBERT K. MERTON

There persists a notable tendency in sociological theory to attribute the malfunctioning of social structure primarily to those of man's imperious biological drives which are not adequately restrained by social control. In this view, the social order is solely a device for "impulse management" and the "social processing" of tensions. These impulses which break through social control, be it noted, are held to be biologically derived. Nonconformity is assumed to be rooted in original nature.[1] Conformity is by implication the result of a utilitarian calculus or unreasoned conditioning. This point of view, whatever its other deficiencies, clearly begs one question. It provides no basis for determining the nonbiological conditions which induce deviations from prescribed patterns of conduct. In this paper, it will be suggested that certain phases of social structure generate the circumstances in which infringement of social codes constitutes a "normal" response.[2]

The conceptual scheme to be outlined is designed to provide a coherent, systematic approach to the study of socio-cultural sources of deviate behavior. Our primary aim lies in discovering how some social structures *exert a definite pressure* upon certain persons in the society to engage in nonconformist rather than conformist conduct. The many ramifications of the scheme cannot all be discussed; the problems mentioned outnumber those explicitly treated.

Among the elements of social and cultural structure, two are important for our purposes. These are analytically separable although they merge imperceptibly in concrete situations. The first consists of culturally defined goals, purposes, and interests. It comprises a frame of aspirational reference. These goals are more or less integrated and involve varying degrees of prestige and sentiment. They constitute a basic, but not the exclusive, component of what Linton aptly has called "designs for group living." Some of these cultural aspirations are related to the original drives of man, but they are not determined by them. The second phase of the social structure defines, regulates, and controls the acceptable modes of achieving these goals. Every social group invariably couples its scale of desired ends with moral or institutional regulation of permissible and required procedures for attaining these ends. These regulatory norms and moral imperatives do not necessarily coincide with technical or efficiency norms. Many procedures which from the standpoint of *particular individuals* would be most efficient in securing desired values, e.g., illicit oil-stock schemes, theft, fraud, are ruled out of the institutional area of permitted conduct. The choice of expedients is limited by the institutional norms.

To say that these two elements, culture goals and institutional norms, operate jointly is not to say that the ranges of alternative behaviors and aims bear some constant relation to one another. The emphasis upon certain goals may vary independently of the degree of emphasis upon institutional means. There may develop a disproportionate, at times, a virtually exclusive, stress upon the value of specific goals, involving relatively slight concern with the institutionally appropriate modes of attaining these goals. The limiting case in this direction is reached when the range of alternative procedures is limited only by technical rather than institutional considerations. Any and all devices which promise attainment of the all important goal would be permitted in this hypothetical polar case.[3] This constitutes one type of cultural malintegration. A second polar type is found in groups where activities originally conceived as instrumental are transmuted into ends in themselves. The original purposes are forgotten, and ritualistic adherence to institutionally prescribed conduct becomes virtually obsessive.[4] Stability is largely ensured while change is flouted. The range of alternative behaviors is severely limited. There develops a tradition-bound, sacred society characterized by neophobia. The occupational psychosis of the bureaucrat may be cited as a case in point. Finally, there are the intermediate types of groups where a balance between culture goals and institutional means is maintained. These are the significantly integrated and relatively stable, though changing, groups.

An effective equilibrium between the two phases of the social structure is maintained as long as satisfactions accrue to individuals who conform to both constraints, viz., satisfactions from the achievement of the goals and satisfactions emerging directly from the institutionally canalized modes of striving to attain these ends. Success, in such equilibrated cases, is twofold. Success is reckoned in terms of the product and in terms of the process, in terms of the outcome and in terms of activities. Continuing satisfactions must derive from sheer *participation* in a competitive order as well as from eclipsing one's competitors if the order itself is to be sustained. The occasional sacrifices involved in institutionalized conduct must be compensated by socialized rewards. The distribution of statuses and roles through competition must be so organized that positive incentives for conformity to roles and adherence to status obligations are provided *for every position* within the distributive order. Aberrant conduct, therefore, may be viewed as a symptom of dissociation between culturally defined aspirations and socially structured means.

Of the types of groups which result from the independent variation of the two phases of the social structure, we shall be primarily concerned with the first, namely, that involving a disproportionate accent on goals.

This statement must be recast in a proper perspective. In no group is there an absence of regulatory codes governing conduct, yet groups do vary in the degree to which these folkways, mores, and institutional controls are effectively integrated with the more diffuse goals which are part of the culture matrix. Emotional convictions may cluster about the complex of socially acclaimed ends, meanwhile shifting their support from the culturally defined implementation of these ends. As we shall see, certain aspects of the social structure may generate countermores and antisocial behavior precisely because of differential emphases on goals and regulations. In the extreme case, the latter may be so vitiated by the goal-emphasis that the range of behavior is limited only by considerations of technical expediency. The sole significant question then becomes, which available means is most efficient in netting the socially approved value?[5] The technically most feasible procedure, whether legitimate or not, is preferred to the institutionally prescribed conduct. As this process continues, the integration of the society becomes tenuous and anomie ensues.

Thus, in competitive athletics, when the aim of victory is shorn of its institutional trappings and success in contests becomes construed as "winning the game" rather than "winning through circumscribed modes of activity," a premium is implicitly set upon the use of illegitimate but technically efficient means. The star of the opposing football team is surreptitiously slugged; the wrestler furtively incapacitates his opponent through ingenious but illicit techniques; university alumni covertly subsidize "students" whose talents are largely confined to the athletic field. The emphasis on the goal has so attenuated the satisfactions deriving from sheer participation in the competitive activity that these satisfactions are virtually confined to a successful outcome. Through the same process, tension generated by the desire to win in a poker game is relieved by successfully dealing oneself four aces, or, when the cult of success has become completely dominant, by sagaciously shuffling the cards in a game of solitaire. The faint twinge of uneasiness in the last instance and the surreptitious nature of public delicts indicate clearly that the institutional rules of the game are *known* to those who evade them, but that the emotional supports of these rules are largely vitiated by cultural exaggeration of the success-goal.[6] They are microcosmic images of the social macrocosm.

Of course, this process is not restricted to the realm of sport. The process whereby exaltation of the end generates a *literal demoralization*, i.e., a deinstitutionalization, of the means is one which characterizes many[7] groups in which the two phases of the social structure are not highly integrated. The extreme emphasis upon the accumulation of wealth as a symbol of success[8] in our own society militates against the completely effective control of institutionally regulated modes of acquiring a fortune.[9] Fraud, corruption, vice, crime, in short, the entire catalogue of proscribed behavior, becomes increasingly common when the emphasis on the *culturally induced* success-goal becomes divorced from a coordinated institutional emphasis.

This observation is of crucial theoretical importance in examining the doctrine that antisocial behavior most frequently derives from biological drives breaking through the restraints imposed by society. The difference is one between a strictly utilitarian interpretation which conceives man's ends as random and an analysis which finds these ends deriving from the basic values of the culture.[10]

Our analysis can scarcely stop at this juncture. We must turn to other aspects of the social structure if we are to deal with the social genesis of the varying rates and types of deviate behavior characteristic of different societies. Thus far, we have sketched three ideal types of social orders constituted by distinctive patterns of relations between culture ends and means. Turning from these types of *culture patterning*, we find five logically possible, alternative modes of adjustment or adaptation *by individuals* within the culture-bearing society or group.[11] These are schematically presented in the following table, where (+) signifies "acceptance," (−) signifies "elimination," and (±) signifies "rejection and substitution of new goals and standards."

	Culture Goals	Institutionalized Means
I. Conformity	+	+
II. Innovation	+	−
III. Ritualism	−	+
IV. Retreatism	−	−
V. Rebellion[12]	±	±

Our discussion of the relation between these alternative responses and other phases of the social structure must be prefaced by the observation that persons may shift from one alternative to another as they engage in different social activities. These categories refer to role adjustments in specific situations, not to personality *in toto*. To treat the development of this process in various spheres of conduct would introduce a complexity unmanageable within the confines of this paper. For this reason, we shall be concerned primarily with economic activity in the broad sense, "the production, exchange, distribution, and consumption of goods and services" in our competitive society, wherein wealth has taken on a highly symbolic cast. Our task is to search out some of the factors which exert pressure upon individuals to engage in certain of these logically possible alternative responses. This choice, as we shall see, is far from random.

In every society, Adaptation I (conformity to both culture goals and means) is the most common and widely diffused. Were this not so, the stability and continuity of the society could not be maintained. The mesh of expectancies which constitutes every social order is sustained by the modal behavior of its members falling within the first category. Conventional role behavior oriented toward the basic values of the group is the rule rather than the exception. It is this fact alone which permits us to speak of a human aggregate as comprising a group or society.

Conversely, Adaptation IV (rejection of goals and means) is the least common. Persons who "adjust" (or maladjust) in this fashion are, strictly speaking, *in* the society but not *of* it. Sociologically, these constitute the true "aliens." Not sharing the common frame of orientation, they can be included within the societal population merely in a fictional sense. In this category are *some* of the activities of psychotics, psychoneurotics, chronic autists, pariahs, outcasts, vagrants, vagabonds, tramps, chronic drunkards, and drug addicts.[13] These have relinquished, in certain spheres of activity, the culturally defined goals, involving complete aim-inhibition in the polar case, and their adjustments are not in accord with institutional norms. This is not to say that in some cases the source of their behavioral adjustments is not in part the very social structure which they have in effect repudiated nor that their very existence within a social area does not constitute a problem for the socialized population.

This mode of "adjustment" occurs, as far as structural sources are concerned, when both the culture goals and institutionalized procedures have been assimilated thoroughly by the individual and imbued with affect and high positive value, but where those institutionalized procedures which promise a measure of successful attainment of the goals are not available to the individual. In such instances, there results a two-fold mental conflict insofar as the moral obligation for adopting institutional means conflicts with the pressure to resort to illegitimate means (which may attain the goal) and inasmuch as the individual is shut off from means which are both legitimate *and* effective. The competitive order is maintained, but the frustrated and handicapped individual who cannot cope with this order drops out. Defeatism, quietism, and resignation are manifested in escape mechanisms which ultimately lead the individual to "escape" from the requirements of the society. It is an expedient which arises from continued failure to attain the goal by legitimate measures and from an inability to adopt the illegitimate route because of internalized prohibitions and institutionalized compulsives, *during which process the supreme value of the success-goal has as yet not been renounced.* The conflict is resolved by eliminating *both* precipitating elements, the goals and means. The escape is complete, the conflict is eliminated, and the individual is associated.

Be it noted that where frustration derives from the inaccessibility of effective institutional means for attaining economic or any other type of highly valued "success," that Adaptations II, III, and V (innovation, ritualism, and rebellion) are also possible. The result will be determined by the particular personality, and thus, the *particular* cultural background, involved. Inadequate socialization will result in the innovation response whereby the conflict and frustration are eliminated by relinquishing the institutional means and retaining the success-aspiration; an extreme assimilation of institutional demands will lead to ritualism wherein the goal is dropped as beyond one's reach but conformity to the mores persists; and rebellion occurs when emancipation from the reigning standards, due to frustration or to marginalist perspectives, leads to the attempt to introduce a "new social order."

Our major concern is with the illegitimacy adjustment. This involves the use of conventionally proscribed but frequently effective means of attaining at least the simulacrum of culturally defined success—wealth, power, and the like. As we have seen, this adjustment occurs when the individual has assimilated the cultural emphasis on success without equally internalizing the morally prescribed norms governing means for its attainment. The question arises, Which phases of our social structure predispose toward this mode of adjustment? We may examine a concrete instance, effectively analyzed by Lohman,[14] which provides a clue to the answer. Lohman has shown that specialized areas of vice in the near north side of Chicago constitute a "normal" response to a situation where the cultural emphasis upon pecuniary success has been absorbed, but where there is little access to conventional and legitimate means for attaining such success. The conventional occupational opportunities of persons in this area are almost completely limited to manual labor. Given our cultural stigmatization of manual labor, and its correlate, the prestige of white collar work, it is clear that the result is a strain toward innovational practices. The limitation of opportunity to unskilled labor and the resultant low income cannot compete *in terms of conventional standards of achievement* with the high income from organized vice.

For our purposes, this situation involves two important features. First, such antisocial behavior is in a sense "called forth" by certain conventional values of the culture *and* by the class structure involving differential access to the approved opportunities for legitimate, prestige-bearing pursuit of the culture goals. The lack of high integration between the means-and-end elements of the cultural pattern and the particular class structure combine to favor a heightened frequency of antisocial conduct in such groups. The second consideration is of equal significance. Recourse to the first of the alternative responses, legitimate effort, is limited by the fact that actual advance toward desired success-symbols through conventional channels is, despite our persisting open-class ideology,[15] relatively rare and difficult for those handicapped by little formal education and few economic resources. The dominant pressure of group standards of success is, therefore, on the gradual attenuation of legitimate, but by and large ineffective, strivings and the increasing use of illegitimate, but more or less effective, expedients of vice and crime. The cultural demands made on persons in this situation are incompatible. On the one hand, they are asked to orient their conduct toward the prospect of accumulating wealth and on the other, they are largely denied effective opportunities to do so institutionally. The consequences of such structural inconsistency are psychopathological personality, and/or antisocial conduct, and/or revolutionary activities. The equilibrium between culturally designated means and ends becomes highly unstable with the progressive emphasis on attaining the prestige-laden ends by any means whatsoever. Within this context, Capone represents the triumph of amoral intelligence over morally prescribed "failure," when the channels of vertical mobility are closed or narrowed[16] *in a society which places a high premium on economic affluence and social ascent for* all *its members.*[17]

This last qualification is of primary importance. It suggests that other phases of the social structure besides the extreme emphasis on pecuniary success must be considered if we are to understand the social sources of antisocial behavior. A high frequency of deviate behavior is not generated simply by "lack of opportunity" or by this exaggerated pecuniary emphasis. A comparatively rigidified class structure, a feudalistic or caste order, may limit such opportunities far beyond the point which obtains in our society today. It is only when a system of cultural values extols, virtually above all else, certain *common* symbols of success *for the population at large* while its social structure rigorously restricts or completely eliminates access to approved modes of acquiring these symbols *for a considerable part of the same population* that antisocial behavior ensues on a considerable scale. In other words, our egalitarian ideology denies by implication the existence of noncompeting groups and individuals in the pursuit of pecuniary success. The same body of success-symbols is held to be desirable for all. These goals are held to *transcend class lines*, not to be bounded by them, yet the actual social organization is such that there exist class differentials in the accessibility of these *common* success-symbols. Frustration and thwarted aspiration lead to the search for avenues of escape from a culturally induced intolerable situation; or unrelieved ambition may eventuate in illicit attempts to acquire the dominant values.[18] The American stress on pecuniary success and ambitiousness for all thus invites exaggerated anxieties, hostilities, neuroses, and antisocial behavior.

This theoretical analysis may go far toward explaining the varying correlations between crime and poverty.[19] Poverty is not an isolated variable. It is one in a complex of interdependent social and cultural variables. When viewed in such a context, it represents quite different states of affairs. Poverty as such, and consequent limitation of opportunity, are not sufficient to induce a conspicuously high rate of criminal behavior. Even the often mentioned "poverty in the midst of plenty" will not necessarily lead to this result. Only insofar as poverty and associated disadvantages in competition for the culture values approved for *all* members of the society are linked with the assimilation of a cultural emphasis on monetary accumulation as a symbol of success is antisocial conduct a "normal" outcome. Thus, poverty is less highly correlated with crime in southeastern Europe than in the United States. The possibilities of vertical mobility in these European areas would seem to be fewer than in this country, so that neither poverty *per se* nor its association with limited opportunity is sufficient to account for the varying correlations. It is only when the full configuration is considered, poverty, limited opportunity, and a commonly shared system of success-symbols, that we can explain the higher association between poverty and crime in our society than in others where rigidified class structure is coupled with *differential class symbols of achievement.*

In societies such as our own, then, the pressure of prestige-bearing success tends to eliminate the effective social constraint over means employed to this end. "The-end-justifies-the-means" doctrine becomes a guiding tenet for action when the cultural structure unduly exalts the end and the social organization unduly limits possible recourse to approved means. Otherwise put, this notion and associated behavior reflect a lack of cultural coordination. In international relations, the effects of this lack of integration are notoriously apparent. An emphasis upon national power is not readily coordinated with an inept organization of legitimate, i.e., internationally defined and accepted, means for attaining this goal. The result is a tendency toward the abrogation of international law, treaties become scraps of paper, "undeclared warfare" serves as a technical evasion, the bombing of civilian populations is rationalized,[20] just as the same societal situation induces the same sway of illegitimacy among individuals.

The social order we have described necessarily produces this "strain toward dissolution." The pressure of such an order is upon outdoing one's competitors. The choice of means within the ambit of institutional control will persist as long as the sentiments supporting a competitive system, i.e., deriving from the possibility of outranking competitors and hence enjoying the favorable response of others, are distributed throughout the entire system of activities and are not confined merely to the final result. A stable social structure demands a balanced distribution of affect among its various segments. When there occurs a shift of emphasis from the satisfactions deriving from competition itself to almost exclusive concern with successful competition, the resultant stress leads to the breakdown of the regulatory structure.[21] With the resulting attenuation of the institutional imperatives, there occurs an approximation of the situation erroneously held by utilitarians to be typical of society generally wherein calculations of advantage and fear of punishment are the sole regulating agencies. In such situations, as Hobbes observed, force and fraud come to constitute the sole virtues in view of their relative efficiency in attaining goals—which were for him, of course, not culturally derived.

It should be apparent that the foregoing discussion is not pitched on a moralistic plane. Whatever the sentiments of the writer or reader concerning the ethical desirability of coordinating the means-and-goals phases of the social structure, one must agree that lack of such coordination leads to anomie. Insofar as one of the most general functions of social organization is to provide a basis for calculability and regularity of behavior, it is increasingly limited in effectiveness as these elements of the structure become dissociated. At the extreme, predictability virtually disappears and what may be properly termed cultural chaos or anomie intervenes.

This statement, being brief, is also incomplete. It has not included an exhaustive treatment of the various structural elements which predispose toward one rather than another of the alternative responses open to individuals; it has neglected, but not denied the relevance of, the factors determining the specific incidence of these responses; it has not enumerated the various concrete responses which are constituted by combinations of specific values of the analytical variables; it has omitted, or included only by implication, any consideration of the social functions performed by illicit responses; it has not tested the full explanatory power of the analytical scheme by examining a large number of group variations in the frequency of deviate and conformist behavior; it has not adequately dealt with rebellious conduct which seeks to refashion the social framework radically; it has not examined the relevance of cultural conflict for an analysis of culture-goal and institutional-means malintegration. It is suggested that these and related problems may be profitably analyzed by this scheme.

Notes

1. E.g., Ernest Jones, *Social Aspects of Psychoanalysis*, 28, London, 1924. If the Freudian notion is a variety of the "original sin" dogma, then the interpretation advanced in this paper may be called the doctrine of "socially derived sin."

2. "Normal" in the sense of a culturally oriented, if not approved, response. This statement does not deny the relevance of biological and personality differences which may be significantly involved in the *incidence* of deviate conduct. Our focus of interest is the social and cultural matrix; hence we abstract from other factors. It is in this sense, I take it, that James S. Plant speaks of the "normal reaction of normal people to abnormal conditions." See his *Personality and the Cultural Pattern*, 248, New York, 1937.

3. Contemporary American culture has been said to tend in this direction. See André Siegfried, *America Comes of Age*, 26–37, New York, 1927. The alleged extreme(?) emphasis on the goals of monetary success and material prosperity leads to dominant concern with technological and social instruments designed to produce the desired result, inasmuch as institutional controls become of secondary importance. In such a situation, innovation flourishes as the *range of means* employed is broadened. In a sense, then, there occurs the paradoxical emergence of "materialists" from an "idealistic" orientation. Cf. Durkheim's analysis of the cultural conditions which predispose toward crime and innovation, both of which are aimed toward efficiency, not moral norms. Durkheim was one of the first to see that "contrairement aux idées courantes le criminel n'apparait plus comme un être radicalement insociable, comme une sorte d'elément parasitaire, de corps étranger et inassimilable, introduit au sein de la société; c'est un agent régulier de la vie sociale." See *Les Règles de la Méthode Sociologique*, 86–89, Paris, 1927.

4. Such ritualism may be associated with a mythology which rationalizes these actions so that they appear to retain their status as means, but the dominant pressure is in the direction of strict ritualistic conformity, irrespective of such rationalizations. In this sense, ritual has proceeded farthest when such rationalizations are not even called forth.

5. In this connection, one may see the relevance of Elton Mayo's paraphrase of the title of Tawney's well-known book. "Actually the problem *is not that of the sickness of an acquisitive society; it is that of the acquisitiveness of a sick society.*" *Human Problems of an Industrial Civilization*, 153, New York, 1933. Mayo deals with the process through which wealth comes to be a symbol of social achievement. He sees this as arising from a state of anomie. We are considering the unintegrated monetary-success goal as an element in producing anomie. A complete analysis would involve both phases of this system of interdependent variables.

6. It is unlikely that interiorized norms are completely eliminated. Whatever residuum persists will induce personality tensions and conflict. The process involves a certain degree of ambivalence. A manifest rejection of the institutional norms is coupled with some latent retention of their emotional correlates. "Guilt feelings," "sense of sin," "pangs of conscience" are obvious manifestations of this unrelieved tension; symbolic adherence to the nominally repudiated values or rationalizations constitute a more subtle variety of tensional release.

7. "Many," and not all, unintegrated groups, for the reason already mentioned. In groups where the primary emphasis shifts to institutional means, i.e., when the range of alternatives is very limited, the outcome is a type of ritualism rather than anomie.

8. Money has several peculiarities which render it particularly apt to become a symbol of prestige divorced from institutional controls. As Simmel emphasized, money is highly abstract and impersonal. However acquired, through fraud or institutionally, it can be used to purchase the same goods and services. The anonymity of metropolitan culture, in conjunction with this peculiarity of money, permits wealth, the sources of which may be unknown to the community in which the plutocrat lives, to serve as a symbol of status.

9. The emphasis upon wealth as a success-symbol is possibly reflected in the use of the term "fortune" to refer to a stock of accumulated wealth. This meaning becomes common in the late sixteenth century (Spenser and Shakespeare). A similar usage of the Latin *fortuna* comes into prominence during the first century B.C. Both these periods were marked by the rise to prestige and power of the "bourgeoisie."

10. See Kingsley Davis, "Mental Hygiene and the Class Structure," *Psychiatry*, 1928, 1:esp. 62–63; Talcott Parsons, *The Structure of Social Action*, 59–60, New York, 1937.

11. This is a level intermediate between the two planes distinguished by Edward Sapir; namely, culture patterns and personal habit systems. See his "Contribution of Psychiatry to an Understanding of Behavior in Society," *Amer. J. Sociol.*, 1937, 42:862–870.

12. This fifth alternative is on a plane clearly different from that of the others. It represents a *transitional* response which seeks to *institutionalize* new procedures oriented toward revamped cultural goals shared by the members of the society. It thus involves efforts to *change* the existing structure rather than to perform accommodative actions *within* this structure, and introduces additional problems with which we are not at the moment concerned.

13. Obviously, this is an elliptical statement. These individuals may maintain some orientation to the values of their particular differentiated groupings within the larger society or, in part, of the conventional society itself. Insofar as they do so, their conduct cannot be classified in the "passive rejection" category (IV). Nels Anderson's description of the behavior and attitudes of the bum, for example, can readily be recast in terms of our analytical scheme. See *The Hobo*, 93–98, *et passim*, Chicago, 1923.

14. Joseph D. Lohman, "The Participant Observer in Community Studies," *Amer. Sociol. Rev.*, 1937, 2:890–898.

15. The shifting historical role of this ideology is a profitable subject for exploration. The "office-boy-to-president" stereotype was once in approximate accord with the facts. Such vertical mobility was probably more common then than now, when the class structure is more rigid. (See the following note.) The ideology largely persists, however, possibly because it still performs a useful function for maintaining the *status quo*. For insofar as it is accepted by the "masses," it constitutes a useful sop for those who might rebel against the entire structure, were this consoling hope removed. This ideology now serves to lessen the probability of Adaptation V. In short, the role of this notion has changed from that of an approximately valid empirical theorem to that of an ideology, in Mannheim's sense.

16. There is a growing body of evidence, though none of it is clearly conclusive, to the effect that our class structure is becoming rigidified and that vertical mobility is declining. Taussig and Joslyn found that American business leaders are being *increasingly* recruited from the upper ranks of our society. The Lynds have also found a "diminished chance to get ahead" for the working classes in Middletown. Manifestly, these objective changes are not alone significant; the individual's subjective evaluation of the situation is a major determinant of the response. The extent to which this change in opportunity for social mobility has been recognized by the least advantaged classes is still conjectural, although the Lynds present some suggestive materials. The writer suggests that a case in point is the increasing frequency of cartoons which observe in a tragi-comic vein that "my old man says everybody can't be President. He says if ya can get three days a week steady on W.P.A. work ya ain't doin' so bad either." See F. W. Taussig and C. S. Joslyn, *American Business Leaders*, New York, 1932; R. S. and H. M. Lynd, *Middletown in Transition*, 67 ff., chap. 12, New York, 1937.

17. The role of the Negro in this respect is of considerable theoretical interest. Certain elements of the Negro population have assimilated the dominant caste's values of pecuniary success and social advancement, but they also recognize that social ascent is at present restricted to their own caste almost exclusively. The pressures upon the Negro which would otherwise derive from the structural inconsistencies we have noticed are hence not identical with those upon lower class whites. See Kingsley Davis, *op. cit.*, 63; John Dollard, *Caste and Class in a Southern Town*, 66 ff., New Haven, 1936; Donald Young, *American Minority Peoples*, 581, New York, 1932.

18. The psychical coordinates of these processes have been partly established by the experimental evidence concerning *Anspruchsniveaus* and levels of performance. See Kurt Lewin, *Vorsatz, Willie and Bedurfnis*, Berlin, 1926; N. F. Hoppe, "Erfolg und Misserfolg," *Psychol. Forschung*, 1930, 14:1–63; Jerome D. Frank, "Individual Differences in Certain Aspects of the Level of Aspiration," *Amer. J. Psychol.*, 1935, 47:119–128.

19. Standard criminology texts summarize the data in this field. Our scheme of analysis may serve to resolve some of the theoretical contradictions which P. A. Sorokin indicates. For example, "not everywhere nor always do the poor show a greater proportion of crime... many poorer countries have had less crime than the richer countries.... The [economic] improvement in the second half of the nineteenth century, and the beginning of the twentieth, has not been followed by a decrease of crime." See his *Contemporary Sociological Theories*, 560–561, New York, 1928. The crucial point is, however, that poverty has varying social significance in different social structures, as we shall see. Hence, one would not expect a linear correlation between crime and poverty.

20. See M. W. Royse, *Aerial Bombardment and the International Regulation of War*, New York, 1928.

21. Since our primary concern is with the socio-cultural aspects of this problem, the psychological correlates have been only implicitly considered. See Karen Horney, *The Neurotic Personality of Our Time*, New York, 1937, for a psychological discussion of this process.

12 / Homeboys, Dope Fiends, Legits, and New Jacks

JOHN M. HAGEDORN

This paper addresses issues that are controversial in both social science and public policy. First, what happens to gang members as they age? Do most gang members graduate from gangbanging to drug sales, as popular stereotypes might suggest? Is drug dealing so lucrative that adult gang members eschew work and become committed to the drug economy? Have changes in economic conditions produced underclass gangs so deviant and so detached from the labor market that the only effective policies are more police and more prisons?

Second, and related to these questions, are male adult gang members basically similar kinds of people, or are gangs made up of different types? Might some gang members be more conventional, and others less so? What are the implications of this "continuum of conventionality" within drug-dealing gangs for public policy? Data from a Milwaukee study on gangs and drug dealing shed some light on these issues.

GANG MEMBERS, DRUGS, AND WORK

An underlying question is whether the drug economy provides sufficient incentives to keep gang members away from legal work. If drug sales offer highly profitable opportunities for all who are willing to take the risks, we might expect many adult gang members to be committed firmly to the drug economy. On the other hand, if drug dealing entails many risks and produces few success stories, gang members might be expected to have a more variable relationship to illicit drug sales. In that case we could look at variation within the gang to explain different behaviors.

The research literature contains few empirical studies on the pull of the drug economy away from licit work. On the more general level, Carl Taylor (1990:120) asserts that "when drug distribution becomes the employer, $3.65 or $8.65 can't compare with drug business income." Martin Sanchez Jankowski (1991:101), in his study of gangs in three cities, found an "entrepreneurial spirit" to be the "driving force in the world view and behavior of gang members." This "entrepreneurial spirit" pushes gang members to make rational decisions to engage in drug sales. Jerome Skolnick (1990) and his students argue that gangs are centrally involved with profitable mid-level drug distribution, although these findings have been challenged by researchers (Klein and Maxson, 1993; Waldorf, 1993).

Others have found that gang involvement in drug sales varies substantially (see Cummings and Monte, 1993; Huff, 1990). Klein et al. (1991) remind us that not all gangs are involved with drug sales, a point that is often overlooked in the discussion of an invariant gang/drug nexus. Among those who sell drugs, actual income varies. Fagan (1991) points out that earnings from drug dealing in two Manhattan neighborhoods ranged from about $1,000 to nearly $5,000 per month. Although most drug sellers had little involvement with the formal economy, 25% of Fagan's dealers also worked in conventional jobs, and most reported both illegal *and* legal income for each month. This finding suggests that incentives from drug sales were not always sufficient to make dealing a full-time job.

Similarly, a Rand Corporation study (MacCoun and Reuter, 1992:485) found that the typical Washington, D.C. small dealer made about $300 per month and the typical big dealer $3,700, with an average of about $1,300. Sullivan (1989) found illicit economic activities in Brooklyn to be a youthful enterprise, quickly outgrown when "real" jobs offered themselves. The seriousness of criminal activity varied with the intactness of networks providing access to legitimate work. Most of Williams's (1989) New York "cocaine kids" matured out of the drug business as they became young adults and their drug-dealing clique broke up. Padilla's (1992:162) "Diamonds" became "disillusioned" with the empty promises of street-level dealing and aspired to legitimate jobs.

These few studies suggest substantial variation in the degree and duration of gang involvement in drug dealing. The drug economy is not an un-questionably profitable opportunity for gang members; rather, its promise appears to be more ambiguous. If that conclusion is valid, research must examine both the actual amounts of money earned by adult gang drug dealers *and* variation within the gang to understand gang involvement in drug dealing. We have a few studies on how much money gang members make from selling drugs, but hardly any contemporary data on different types of gang members.

VARIATION WITHIN THE GANG

Some research has portrayed gang members as relatively invariant. Walter Miller (1969) viewed gang delinquents as representative of a lower-class cultural milieu; his six "focal concerns" are persistent and distinctive features of the entire American "lower class." Similarly, Jankowski (1991:26–28) said that male gang members were one-dimensional "tough nuts," defiant individuals with a rational "social Darwinist worldview" who displayed defiant individualism "more generally" than other people in low-income communities.

Other research, however, has suggested that gang members vary, particularly on their orientation toward conventionality. Whyte (1943) classified his Cornerville street corner men as either "college boys" or "corner boys," depending on their aspirations. Cloward and Ohlin (1960:95), applying Merton's (1957) earlier typology, categorized lower-class youths in four cells of a matrix, depending on their aspirations and "criteria for success." Many of their delinquents repudiated the legitimacy of conventional society and resorted to innovative solutions to attain success goals. Cloward and Ohlin took issue with Cohen (1955) and Matza (1964), whose delinquents were internally conflicted but, as a group, imputed legitimacy to the norms of the larger society.

Some more recent researchers also have found variation in conventionality within gangs. Klein (1971), echoing Thrasher (1927), differentiated between "core" and "fringe" members, a distinction that policy makers often use today as meaning more or less deviant. In the same view, Taylor (1990:8–9) saw gang members as "corporates," "scavengers," "emulators," "auxiliaries," or "adjuncts," mainly on the basis of their distance from gang membership. Fagan (1990:206), like Matza and Cohen, found that "conventional values may coexist with deviant behaviors for gang delinquents and other inner city youth." MacLeod (1987:124) observed surprising variation between ethnic groups. The white "hallway hangers" believed "stagnation at the bottom of the occupational structure to be almost inevitable" and were rebellious delinquents, whereas the African American "brothers" reacted to similar conditions by aspiring to middle-class status.

Joan Moore is one of the few researchers who have looked carefully at differentiation within gangs. In her early work (1978), she discovered both square and deviant career models among East Los Angeles gang members. In an impressive restudy (1991) she found that most adult gang members were working conventional jobs, but those who had been active in the gang in recent years had more difficulty finding employment as job networks collapsed. Many veteran gang members had been addicted to heroin for years, but by the 1990s few were dealing drugs to support themselves. Moore found that both male and female Chicano gang members could be categorized as "tecatos," "cholos," or "squares," a typology similar to those suggested for the nongang poor by Anderson (1978, 1990) and Hannerz (1969).

If gang members in fact vary on orientation to conventionality, and if the drug economy itself offers only an ambiguous lure, jobs and other programs that strengthen "social capital" (Coleman, 1988) might be effective means of integrating many adult gang members into the community (see Sampson and Laub, 1993). On the other hand, if adult gang members are look-alike criminals who are dazzled by the prospect of vast profits in the drug trade, jobs and social programs would have little effect, and our present incarceration strategy may be appropriate.

This paper provides quantitative and qualitative data on the conventional orientations of young adult gang members in Milwaukee. First we report on the licit work and illicit drug-dealing patterns of adult gang members. Then we offer a typology, drawn from Milwaukee data, that demonstrates a "continuum of conventionality" between core members of drug-dealing gangs. In conclusion, we discuss research and public policy consequences of the study.

RESEARCH METHODS AND SOURCES OF DATA

The interpretations presented here draw on observation and extensive fieldwork conducted over a number of years, specifically from two funded interview studies, in 1987 and in 1992. During the early 1980s I directed the first gang diversion program in the city and became acquainted with many leaders and other founders of Milwaukee's gangs. I have maintained a privileged relationship with many of these individuals.

In the 1987 study, we interviewed 47 members of 19 Milwaukee male and female gangs (Hagedorn, 1988). These "founders" were the core gang members who were present when their gangs took names. Founders are likely to be representative of hard-core gang members, not of peripheral members or "wannabes." As time has passed, the gang founders' exploits have been passed down, and younger Milwaukee gang members have looked up to them as street "role models." Our research design does not enable us to conclude how fully our sample represents subsequent groups of adult gang members.

As part of our current study, we conducted lengthy audiotaped interviews with 101 founding members of 18 gangs in the city; 90 were male and 11 female. Sixty percent were African American, 37% Latino, and 3% white. Their median age was 26 years, with 75% between 23 and 30. Twenty-three respondents also had been interviewed in the 1987 study; 78 were interviewed here for the first time. Members from two gangs interviewed in the earlier study could not be located. Each respondent was paid $50.

The interview picks up the lives of the founding members since 1987, when we conducted our original study, and asks them to recount their careers in the drug business, to discuss their pursuit of conventional employment, and to reflect on their personal lives. The respondents also were asked to describe the current status of their fellow gang members. In the 1987 study, we collected rosters of all members of each gang whose founders we interviewed. In the current study, we asked each respondent to double check the roster of his or her gang to make sure it was accurate. In both studies, we asked respondents to tell us whether the other members were still alive, had graduated from high school, were currently locked up, or were working. In the 1992 study, we also asked whether each of the founding members was selling or using dope (in our data "dope" means cocaine), had some other hustle, or was on the run, among other questions.

To understand more clearly the variation between and within the gangs, we interviewed nearly the entire rosters of three gangs and about half (64 of 152) of the original founding members from eight male gangs in three different types of neighborhoods. In each of these gangs, we interviewed some who still were involved with both the gang and the dope game and some who no longer were involved. This paper reports on data on all of the 90 males we interviewed and on their accounts of the present circumstances of 236 founders of 14 male gangs.

The interviews in this most recent study were conducted in late 1992 and early 1993.[1] As in the original study, the research follows an inductive and collaborative model (see Moore, 1978), in which gang members cooperate with the academic staff to focus the research design, construct interview schedules, conduct interviews, and interpret the findings.

FINDINGS: DRUG DEALING AND WORK

As expected, gang members appear to be working more today than five years ago, but participation in the formal labor market remains quite low (see Table 1).[2]

These low levels of labor market participation apply to more than gang members. A recent Milwaukee study revealed that in 1990, 51% of jobs held by *all* African American males age 20 to 24, slightly younger than our study population, lasted less than six weeks. The average *annual* income in retail trade, where most subjects held jobs, was $2,023; for jobs in service, $1,697; in education, $3,084 (Rose et al., 1992). African American young

Table 1 / 1992 Status of Male Gang Founders, 236 Founding Members of 14 Male Groups

Predominant Activity/Status	African American	White	Latino	Total
Work: Part-Time or Full-Time	22.2%	68.8%	27.6%	30.5%
Hustling: Nearly All Selling Cocaine	50.4	15.4	56.3	47.9
Deceased	7.7	6.3	5.7	6.8
Whereabouts Unknown	19.7	9.4	10.3	14.8
Total N = 100%	N = 117	N = 32	N = 87	N = 236

NOTE: Column percentages may not equal 100% because of rounding.

adults as a whole (and probably nongang Latinos) clearly were not working regularly and were not earning a living wage.

Selling cocaine seems to have filled the employment void. In 1987 only a few gang members dealt drugs, mainly marijuana. Within African American gangs, at least, cocaine dealing was not prevalent. By 1992, however, cocaine had become a major factor in Milwaukee's informal economy, evolving into widespread curbside sales and numerous drug houses (see Hamid, 1992). Of the 236 fellow gang founders, 72% reportedly had sold cocaine at some time in the last five years.[3]

That involvement has not been steady, however. We collected detailed data on the length of involvement in the drug economy and the amount of money made by those we interviewed. We asked our respondents to indicate how they had supported themselves in each month of the past three years, and then asked how much money they made in both legal and illegal employment. For most respondents, selling cocaine was an on-again, off-again proposition. About half (35) of those who had sold cocaine sold in no more than 12 months out of the past 36; only 12% (9) sold in more than 24 of the past 36 months. Latinos sold for slightly longer periods than African Americans, 17.7 months to 13.1 months ($p = .07$).

When gang members did sell dope, they made widely varying amounts of money. About one-third of those who sold reported that they made no more than they would have earned if they worked for minimum wage. Another one-third made the equivalent of $13 to $25 an hour. Only three of the 73 sellers ever made "crazy money," or more than $10,000 per month, at any time during their drug-selling careers. Mean monthly income from drug sales was approximately $2,400, or about $15 per hour for full-time work. By contrast, mean monthly income for legal work was only $677; Latinos made more than African Americans ($797 per month to $604 per month, $p = .08$; table not shown). The *maximum* amount of money earned monthly by any gang member from legal income was $2,400, the *mean* for gang drug sales (see Table 2).[4]

Qualitative data from our interviews support the view that for some respondents, the dope game indeed lives up to its stereotype. One dealer credibly reported income from his three drug houses at about $50,000 per month for several months in 1989. Another told how he felt about making so much money:

Q: Did you ever make crazy money?
R#220: Yeah...one time my hands had turned green from all that money, I couldn't wash it off, man, I loved it. Oh man, look at this...just holding all that money in my hand turned my hands green from just counting all that money. Sometimes I'd sit back and just count it maybe three, four times, for the hell of it.

Even for big dealers, however, that money didn't last. Some "players" were "rolling" for several years, but most took a fall within a year or so. As with Padilla's Diamonds, disappointments with the drug trade seemed to exceed its promise for most gang members. Prison and jail time frequently interrupted their lives. More than three-quarters of all gang founders on our rosters had spent some time in jail in the past five years, as had two-thirds of our respondents. Even so, our respondents had worked a mean of 14.5 months out of the last 36 in legitimate jobs, had worked 14.5 months selling dope, and had spent the remaining seven months in jail. Twenty-five percent of our respondents had worked legitimate jobs at least 24 of the past 36 months.

Yet an anomaly confronted us as we analyzed our data on work. As might be expected, nine out of 10 of those who were not working at the time of our interview had sold dope in the past three years. We also found, however, that three-quarters of those who *were* working in 1992 had sold dope as well within the previous five years (see Table 3).

These findings lend themselves to alternative explanations. It may be that three-quarters of those who were working had sold cocaine in the past, but had stopped and were getting their lives together. A second interpretation is that full-time employment is nothing more than an income supplement or "front" for continuation in the drug game. Some gang founders indeed fit into one or the other of these categories.

A third interpretation evolved as we received reports from our staff and respondents about the current status of their fellow gang members. A few days after an interview with "Roger," one of our staff members would report that "Roger" was no longer working for a temporary agency, as he had reported, but was "back in the dope game." The next week "Roger" might call us from jail. A week or so later, we would learn that he was

Table 2 / Mean Monthly Income from Drug Dealing: 1989–1991, 87 African American and Latino Respondents

Average Monthly Income from Drug Sales	African American	Latino[a]	Total
Never sold	15.8%	23.3%	18.4%
Less Than $1,000 Monthly (Equivalent to Less Than $6/Hour)	28.1	30.0	28.7
Between $1,000 and $2,000 Monthly (Equivalent to $7–$12/Hour)	28.1	6.7	20.7
Between $2,000 and $4,000 Monthly (Equivalent to $13–$25/Hour)	25.3	33.3	28.7
More Than $10,000 Monthly	1.8	6.7	3.4
Total N = 100%	N = 57	N = 30	N = 87

[a] Three whites were excluded from the analysis. One white founder never sold, and the other two made less than $2,000 monthly.

NOTE: Column percentages may not equal 100% because of rounding.

Table 3 / 1992 Work Status by Involvement in Cocaine Sales, 220 Surviving Founding Members of 14 Male Gangs

Sold Dope Last Five Years?	Working Now	Not Working Now[a]	Work Status Unknown	Totals
Have Sold Dope	75.0%	91.2%	40.0%	77.7%
Have Not Sold Dope	16.7	5.3	2.9	8.6
Unknown	8.3	3.5	57.1	13.6
Total N = 100%	N = 72	N = 113	N = 35	N = 220

[a] Includes selling cocaine, being "on the run," being locked up, and being involved in other street hustles.

out on bail, his "lady" had put pressure on him, and he was now working full-time in construction with his brother-in-law. Our offices were flooded with similar reports about dozens of people on our rosters. Working and selling drugs were both part of the difficult, topsy-turvy lives led by our respondents. Elliot Liebow's (1967:219) colorful description of the confused lives on Tally's Corner also fits our data: "Traffic is heavy in all directions."

These vicissitudes became too complicated for us to track, so we "froze" the status of founders on our rosters at the time of the last and most reliable interview. Some of our founders seemed to be committed to the dope business and a few had "gone legit," but most of those we were trying to track appeared to be on an economic merry-go-round, with continual movement in and out of the secondary labor market. Although their average income from drug sales far surpassed their income from legal employment, most Milwaukee male gang members apparently kept trying to find licit work.

To help explain this movement in and out of the formal labor market, we created a typology of adult gang members, using constant comparisons (Strauss, 1987). This categorization has some similarities to earlier typologies, but it differs in that it intends to account for the different orientations of gang members in an era of decreased legitimate economic opportunities and increased drug-related, illicit opportunities.

A TYPOLOGY OF MALE ADULT GANG MEMBERS

We developed four ideal types on a continuum of conventional behaviors and values: (1) those few who had gone *legit*, or had matured out of the gang; (2) *homeboys*, a majority of both African American and Latino adult gang members, who alternately worked conventional jobs and took various roles in drug sales; (3) *dope fiends,* who were addicted to cocaine and participated in the dope business as a way to maintain access to the drug; and (4) *new jacks,* who regarded the dope game as a career.

Some gang members, we found, moved over time between categories, some had characteristics of more than one category, and others straddled the boundaries (see Hannerz, 1969:57). Thus a few homeboys were in the process of becoming legit, many moved into and out of cocaine addiction, and others gave up and adopted a new jack orientation. Some new jacks returned to conventional life; others received long prison terms or became addicted to dope. Our categories are not discrete, but our typology seemed to fit the population of gang members we were researching. Our "member checks" (Lincoln and Guba, 1985:314–316) of the constructs with gang members validated these categories for male gang members.

Legits

Legits were those young men who had walked away from the gang. They were working or may have gone on to school. Legits had not been involved in the dope game at all, or not for at least five years. They did not use cocaine heavily, though some may have done so in the past. Some had moved out of the old neighborhood; others, like our project staff, stayed to help out or "give back" to the community. These are prime examples of Whyte's "college boys" or Cloward and Ohlin's Type I, oriented to economic gain and class mobility. The following quote is an example of a young African American man who "went legit" and is now working and going to college.

Q: Looking back over the past five years, what major changes took place in your life—things that happened that really made things different for you?

R#105: I had got into a relationship with my girl, that's one thing. I just knew I couldn't be out on the streets trying to hustle all the time. That's what changed me, I just got a sense of responsibility.

Today's underclass gangs appear to be fundamentally different from those in Thrasher's or Cloward and Ohlin's time, when most gang members "matured out" of the gang. Of the 236 Milwaukee male founders, only 12 (5.1%) could be categorized as having matured out: that is, they were working full time *and* had not sold cocaine in the past five years. When these data are disaggregated by race, the reality of the situation becomes even clearer. We could verify only two of 117 African Americans and one of 87 Latino male gang founders who were currently working and had not sold dope in the past five years. One-third of the white members fell into this category.[5]

Few African American and Latino gang founders, however, were resigned to a life of crime, jail, and violence. After a period of rebellion and living the fast life, the majority of gang founders, or "homeboys," wanted to settle down and go legit, but the path proved to be very difficult.

Homeboys

"Homeboys" were the majority of all adult gang members. They were not firmly committed to the drug economy, especially after the early thrill of fast money and "easy women" wore off. They had reached an age, the mid-twenties, when criminal offenses normally decline (Gottfredson and Hirschi, 1990). Most of these men were unskilled, lacked education, and had had largely negative experiences in the secondary labor market. Some homeboys were committed more strongly to the streets, others to a more conventional life. Most had used cocaine, some heavily at times, but their use was largely in conjunction with selling from a house or corner with their gang "homies." Most homeboys either were married or had a "steady" lady. They also had strong feelings of loyalty to their fellow gang members.

Here, two different homeboys explain how they had changed, and how hard that change was:

Q: Looking back over the past five years, what major changes took place in your life—things that happened that really made things different for you?

R#211: The things that we went through wasn't worth it, and I had a family, you know, and kids, and I had to think about them first, and the thing with the drug game was, that money was quick, easy, and fast, and it went like that, the more money you make the more popular you was. You know, as I see it now it wasn't worth it because the time that I done in penitentiaries I lost my sanity. To me it feels like I lost a part of my kids, because, you know, I know they still care, and they know I'm daddy, but I just lost out. Somebody else won and I lost.

Q: Is she with somebody else now?

R#211: Yeah. She hung in there about four or five months after I went to jail.

Q: It must have been tough for her to be alone with all those kids.

R#211: Yeah.

Q: What kind of person are you?

R#217: Mad. I'm a mad young man. I'm a poor young man. I'm a good person to my kids and stuff, and given the opportunity to have something nice and stop working for this petty-ass money I would try to change a lot of things....

        ...I feel I'm the type of person that given the opportunity to try to have something legit, I will take it, but I'm not going to go by the slow way, taking no four, five years working at no chicken job and trying to get up to a manager just to start making six, seven dollars. And then get fired when I come in high or drunk or something. Or miss a day or something because I got high smoking weed, drinking beer, and the next day come in and get fired; then I'm back in where I started from. So I'm just a cool person, and if I'm given the opportunity and if I can get a job making nine, ten dollars an hour, I'd let everything go; I'd just sit back and work my job and go home. That kind of money I can live with. But I'm not going to settle for no three, four dollars an hour, know what I'm saying?

Homeboys present a more confused theoretical picture than legits. Cloward and Ohlin's Type III delinquents were rebels, who had a "sense of injustice" or felt "unjust deprivation" at a failed system (1960:117). Their gang delinquency is a collective solution to the failure of institutional arrangements. They reject traditional societal norms; other, success-oriented illegitimate norms replace conventionality.

Others have questioned whether gang members' basic outlook actually rejects conventionality. Matza (1964) viewed delinquents' rationalizations of their conduct as evidence of techniques meant to "neutralize" deeply held conventional beliefs. Cohen (1955:129–137) regarded delinquency as a nonutilitarian "reaction formation" to middle-class standards, though middle-class morality lingers, repressed and unacknowledged. What appears to be gang "pathological" behavior, Cohen points out, is the result of the delinquent's striving to attain core values of "the American way of life." Short and Strodtbeck (1965), testing various gang theories, found that white and African American gang members, and lower- and middle-class youths, had similar conventional values.

Our homeboys are older versions of Cohen's and Matza's delinquents, and are even more similar to Short and Strodtbeck's study subjects. Milwaukee homeboys shared three basic characteristics: (1) They worked regularly at legitimate jobs, although they ventured into the drug economy when they believed it was necessary for survival. (2) They had very conventional aspirations; their core values centered on finding a secure place in the American way of life. (3) They had some surprisingly conventional ethical beliefs about the immorality of drug dealing. To a man, they justified their own involvement in drug sales by very Matza-like techniques of "neutralization."

Homeboys are defined by their in-and-out involvement in the legal and illegal economies. Recall that about half of our male respondents had sold drugs no more than 12 of the past 36 months. More than one-third never served any time in jail. Nearly 60% had worked legitimate jobs at least 12 months of the last 36, with a mean of 14.5 months. Homeboys' work patterns thus differed both from those of legits, who worked solely legal jobs, and new jacks who considered dope dealing a career.

To which goal did homeboys aspire, being big-time dope dealers or holding a legitimate job? Rather than having any expectations of staying in the dope game, homeboys aspired to settling down, getting married, and living at least a watered-down version of the American dream. Like Padilla's (1992:157) Diamonds, they strongly desired to "go legit." Although they may have enjoyed the fast life for a while, it soon went stale. Listen to this homeboy, the one who lost his lady when he went to jail:

Q: Five years from now, what would you want to be doing?
R#211: Five years from now? I want to have a steady job, I want to have been working that job for about five years, and just with a family somewhere.
Q: Do you think that's gonna come true?

R#211: Yeah, that's basically what I'm working on. I mean, this bullshit is over now, I'm twenty-five, I've played games long enough, it don't benefit nobody. If you fuck yourself away, all you gonna be is fucked, I see it now.

Others had more hopeful or wilder dreams, but a more sobering outlook on the future. The other homeboy, who said he wouldn't settle for three or four dollars an hour, speaks as follows:

Q: Five years from now, what would you want to be doing?
R#217: Owning my own business. And rich. A billionaire.
Q: What do you realistically expect you'll be doing in five years?
R#217: Probably working at McDonald's. That's the truth.

Homeboys' aspirations were divided between finding a steady full-time job and setting up their own business. Their strivings pertained less to being for or against "middle-class status" than to finding a practical, legitimate occupation that could support them (see Short and Strodtbeck, 1965). Many homeboys believed that using skills learned in selling drugs to set up a small business would give them a better chance at a decent life than trying to succeed as an employee.

Most important, homeboys "grew up" and were taking a realistic look at their life chances. This homeboy spoke for most:

Q: Looking back over the past five years, what major changes have taken place in your life—things that made a difference about where you are now?
R#220: I don't know, maybe maturity.... Just seeing life in a different perspective ... realizing that from sixteen to twenty-three, man, just shot past. And just realizing that it did, shucks, you just realizing how quick it zoomed past me. And it really just passed me up without really having any enjoyment of a teenager. And hell, before I know it I'm going to hit thirty or forty, and I ain't going to have nothing to stand on. I don't want that shit. Because I see a lot of brothers out here now, that's forty-three, forty-four and ain't got shit. They's still standing out on the corner trying to make a hustle. Doing this, no family, no stable home and nothing. I don't want that shit.... I don't give a fuck about getting rich or nothing, but I want a comfortable life, a decent woman, a family to come home to. I mean, everybody needs somebody to care for. This ain't where it's at.

Finally, homeboys were characterized by their ethical views about selling dope. As a group, they believed dope selling was "unmoral"—wrong, but necessary for survival. Homeboys' values were conventional, but in keeping with Matza's findings, they justified their conduct by neutralizing their violation of norms. Homeboys believed that economic necessity was the overriding reason why they could not live up to their values (see Liebow, 1967:214). They were the epitome of ambivalence, ardently believing that dope selling was both wrong and absolutely necessary. One longtime dealer expressed this contradiction:

Q: Do you consider it wrong or immoral to sell dope?
R#129:   Um-hum, very wrong.
Q: Why?
R#129:   Why, because it's killing people.
Q: Well how come you do it?
R#129:   It's also a money maker.
Q: Well how do you balance those things out? I mean, here you're doing
           something that you think is wrong, making money. How does that make
           you feel when you're doing it, or don't you think about it when you're
           doing it?
R#129:   Once you get a (dollar) bill, once you look at, I say this a lot, once you
           look at those dead white men [*presidents' pictures on currency*], you care
           about nothing else, you don't care about nothing else. Once you see those
           famous dead white men. That's it.
Q: Do you ever feel bad about selling drugs, doing something that was
           wrong?
R#129:   How do I feel? Well a lady will come in and sell all the food stamps, all of
           them. When they're sold, what are the kids gonna eat? They can't eat the
           dope cause she's gonna go smoke that up, or do whatever with it. And
           then you feel like "wrong." But then, in the back of your mind, man, you
           just got a hundred dollars worth of food stamps for thirty dollars worth
           of dope, and you can sell them at the store for seven dollars on ten, so
           you got seventy coming. So you get seventy dollars for thirty dollars. It is
           not wrong to do this. It is not wrong to do this!

Homeboys also refused to sell to pregnant women or to juveniles. Contrary to Jankowski's (1991:102) assertion that in gangs "there is no ethical
code that regulates business ventures," Milwaukee homeboys had some
strong moral feelings about how they carried out their business:

R#109:   I won't sell to no little kids. And, ah, if he gonna get it, he gonna get it
           from someone else besides me. I won't sell to no pregnant woman. If she
           gonna kill her baby, I want to sleep not knowing that I had anything to
           do with it. Ah, for anybody else, hey, it's their life, you choose your life
           how you want.
Q: But how come—I want to challenge you. You know if kids are coming
           or a pregnant woman's coming, you know they're going to get it some-
           where else, right? Someone else will make their money on it; why not
           you?
R#109:   'Cause the difference is I'll be able to sleep without a guilty conscience.

Homeboys were young adults living on the edge. On the one hand, like
most Americans, they had relatively conservative views on social issues and
wanted to settle down with a job, a wife, and children. On the other hand,
they were afraid they would never succeed, and that long stays in prison
would close doors and lock them out of a conventional life. They did not
want to continue to live on the streets, but they feared that hustling might
be the only way to survive.[6]

Dope Fiends

Dope fiends are gang members who are addicted to cocaine. Thirty-eight percent of all African American founders were using cocaine at the time of our interview, as were 55% of Latinos and 53% of whites. African Americans used cocaine at lower rates than white gang members, but went to jail twice as often. The main focus in a dope fiend's life is getting the drug. Asked what they regretted most about their life, dope fiends invariably said "drug use," whereas most homeboys said "dropping out of school."

Most Milwaukee gang dope fiends, or daily users of cocaine, smoked it as "rocks." More casual users, or reformed dope fiends, if they used cocaine at all, snorted it or sprinkled it on marijuana (called a "primo") to enhance the high. Injection was rare among African Americans but more common among Latinos. About one-quarter of those we interviewed, however, abstained totally from use of cocaine. A majority of the gang members on our rosters had used cocaine since its use escalated in Milwaukee in the late 1980s.

Of 110 gang founders who were reported to be currently using cocaine, 37% were reported to be using "heavily" (every day, in our data), 44% "moderately" (several times per week), and 19% "lightly" (sporadically). More than 70% of all founders on our rosters who were not locked up were currently using cocaine to some extent. More than one-third of our male respondents considered themselves, at some time in their lives, to be "heavy" cocaine users.

More than one-quarter of our respondents had used cocaine for seven years or more, roughly the total amount of time cocaine has dominated the illegal drug market in Milwaukee. Latinos had used cocaine slightly longer than African Americans, for a mean of 75 months compared with 65. Cocaine use followed a steady pattern in our respondents' lives; most homeboys had used cocaine as part of their day-to-day life, especially while in the dope business.

Dope fiends were quite unlike Cloward and Ohlin's "double failures," gang members who used drugs as part of a "retreatist subculture." Milwaukee dope fiends participated regularly in conventional labor markets. Of the 110 founders who were reported as currently using cocaine, slightly more were working legitimate jobs than were not working. Most dope fiends worked at some time in their homies' dope houses or were fronted an ounce or an "eightball" (3.5 grams) of cocaine to sell. Unlike Anderson's "wineheads," gang dope fiends were not predominantly "has-beens" and did not "lack the ability and motivation to hustle" (Anderson, 1978:96–97). Milwaukee cocaine users, like heroin users (Johnson et al., 1985; Moore, 1978; Preble and Casey, 1969), played an active role in the drug-selling business.

Rather than spending their income from drug dealing on family, clothes, or women, dope fiends smoked up their profits. Eventually many stole dope belonging to the boss or "dopeman" and got into trouble. At times their dope use made them so erratic that they were no longer trusted and were forced to leave the neighborhood. Often, however, the gang members who were selling took them back and fronted them cocaine to sell to put them back on their feet. Many had experienced problems in violating the cardinal rule, "Don't get high on your own supply," as in this typical story:

R#131:   ...if you ain't the type that's a user, yeah, you'll make fabulous money but if you was the type that sells it and uses it and do it at the same time, you know, you get restless. Sometimes you get used to taking your own drugs.... I'll just use the profits and just do it...and then the next day if I get something again, I'd just take the money to pay up and keep the profits .... You sell a couple of hundred and you do a hundred. That's how I was doing it.

Cocaine use was a regular part of the lives of most Milwaukee gang members engaged in the drug economy. More than half of our respondents had never attended a treatment program; more than half of those who had been in treatment went through court-ordered programs. Few of our respondents stopped use by going to a treatment program. Even heavy cocaine use was an "on-again, off-again" situation in which most gang members alternately quit by themselves and started use again (Waldorf et al., 1991).

Alcohol use among dope fiends and homeboys (particularly 40-ounce bottles of Olde English 800 ale) appears to be even more of a problem than cocaine use. Like homeboys, however, most dope fiends aspired to have a family, to hold a steady job, and to find some peace. The wild life of the dope game had played itself out; the main problem was how to quit using.[7]

New Jacks

Whereas homeboys had a tentative relationship with conventional labor markets and held some strong moral beliefs, new jacks had chosen the dope game as a career. They were often loners, strong individualists like Jankowski's (1991) gang members, who cared little about group norms. Frequently they posed as the embodiment of media stereotypes. About one-quarter of our interview respondents could be described as new jacks: they had done nothing in the last 36 months except hustle or spend time in jail.

In some ways, new jacks mirror the criminal subculture described by Cloward and Ohlin. If a criminal subculture is to develop, Cloward and Ohlin argued, opportunities to learn a criminal career must be present, and close ties to conventional markets or customers must exist. This situation distinguishes the criminal from the violent and the retreatist subcultures. The emergence of the cocaine economy and a large market for illegal drugs provided precisely such an opportunity structure for this generation of gang members. New jacks are those who took advantage of the opportunities, and who, at least for the present, have committed themselves to a career in the dope game.

Q: Do you consider it wrong or immoral to sell dope?

R#203: I think it's right because can't no motherfucker live your life but you.

Q: Why?

R#203: Why? I'll put it this way . . . I love selling dope. I know there's other niggers out here love the money just like I do. And ain't no motherfucker gonna stop a nigger from selling dope . . . I'd sell to my own mother if she had the money.

New jacks, like other gang cocaine dealers, lived up to media stereotypes of the "drug dealer" role and often were emulated by impressionable youths. Some new jacks were homeboys from Milwaukee's original neighborhood gangs, who had given up their conventional dreams; others were members of gangs that were formed solely for drug dealing (see Klein and Maxson, 1993). A founder of one new jack gang described the scene as his gang set up shop in Milwaukee. Note the strong mimicking of media stereotypes:

R#126: . . . it was crime and drug problems before we even came into the scene. It was just controlled by somebody else. We just came on with a whole new attitude, outlook, at the whole situation. It's like, have you ever seen the movie *New Jack City*, about the kid in New York? You see, they was already there. We just came out with a better idea, you know what I'm saying?

New jacks rejected the homeboys' moral outlook. Many were raised by families with long traditions of hustling or a generation of gang affiliations, and had few hopes of a conventional future. They are the voice of the desperate ghetto dweller, those who live in Carl Taylor's (1990-36) "third culture" made up of "underclass and urban gang members who exhibit signs of moral erosion and anarchy" or propagators of Bourgois's (1990:631) "culture of terror." New jacks fit the media stereotype of all gang members, even though they represent fewer than 25% of Milwaukee's adult gang members.

DISCUSSION: GANGS, THE UNDERCLASS, AND PUBLIC POLICY

Our study was conducted in one aging postindustrial city, with a population of 600,000. How much can be generalized from our findings can be determined only by researchers in other cities, looking at our categories and determining whether they are useful. Cloward and Ohlin's opportunity theory is a workable general theoretical framework, but more case studies are needed in order to recast their theory to reflect three decades of economic and social changes. We present our typology to encourage others to observe variation within and between gangs, and to assist in the creation of new taxonomies and new theory.

Our paper raises several empirical questions for researchers: Are the behavior patterns of the founding gang members in our sample representative of adult gang members in other cities? In larger cities, are most gang members now new jacks who have long given up the hope of a conventional life, or are most still homeboys? Are there "homeboy" gangs and "new jack" gangs, following the "street gang/drug gang" notion of Klein and Maxson (1993)? If so, what distinguishes one from the other? Does gang members' orientation to conventionality vary by ethnicity or by region? How does it change over time? Can this typology help account for variation in rates of violence between gang members? Can female gang members be typed in the same way as males?

Our data also support the life course perspective of Sampson and Laub (1993:255), who ask whether present criminal justice policies "are producing unintended criminogenic effects." Milwaukee gang members are like the persistent, serious offenders in the Gluecks' data (Glueck and Glueck, 1950). The key to their future lies in building social capital that comes from steady employment and a supportive relationship, without the constant threat of incarceration (Sampson and Laub, 1993:162–168). Homeboys largely had a wife or a steady lady, were unhappily enduring "the silent, subtle humiliations" of the secondary labor market (Bourgois, 1990:629), and lived in dread of prison. Incarceration for drug charges undercut their efforts to find steady work and led them almost inevitably back to the drug economy.

Long and mandatory prison terms for use and intent to sell cocaine lump those who are committed to the drug economy with those who are using or are selling in order to survive. Our prisons are filled disproportionately with minority drug offenders (Blumstein, 1993) like our homeboys, who in essence are being punished for the "crime" of not accepting poverty or of being addicted to cocaine. Our data suggest that jobs, more accessible drug treatment, alternative sentences, or even decriminalization of nonviolent drug offenses would be better approaches than the iron fist of the war on drugs (see Hagedorn, 1991; Reinarman and Levine, 1990; Spergel and Curry, 1990).

Finally, our typology raises ethical questions for researchers. Wilson (1987:8) called the underclass "collectively different" from the poor of the past, and many studies focus on underclass deviance. Our study found that some underclass gang members had embraced the drug economy and had forsaken conventionality, but we also found that the *majority* of adult gang members are still struggling to hold onto a conventional orientation to life.

Hannerz (1969:36) commented more than two decades ago that dichotomizing community residents into "respectables" and "disrespectables" "seems often to emerge from social science writing about poor black people or the lower classes in general." Social science that emphasizes differences within poor communities, without noting commonalities, is one-sided and often distorts and demonizes underclass life.

Our data emphasize that there is no Great Wall separating the underclass from the rest of the central-city poor and working class. Social research should not build one either. Researchers who describe violent and criminal gang actions without also addressing gang members' orientation to conventionality do a disservice to the public, to policy makers, and to social science.

Notes

1. This study was funded by NIDA Grant R01 DA 07218. The funding agency bears no responsibility for data or interpretations presented here.

2. Rosters of gangs in 1992 were refined and new gangs were added; thus it was difficult to make comparisons with 1987 rosters. In 1987, with N = 225, 20% of white male gang members, 10% of Latinos, and 27% of African Americans were working.

3. Selling cocaine is not only a gang-related phenomenon. Half of those who were reported as no longer involved with the gang also had sold cocaine within the last five years.

4. We asked respondents to report on the number of months they worked legitimate jobs, worked selling dope, and were in prison. We then asked them to tell us the average amount of money they made in those months working or selling dope. Hourly estimates are based on the monthly average divided by 160 hours. Most respondents reported that they worked selling dope "24/7", meaning full time.

5. About 15% of the founders whereabouts were not known by our informants, but "unknown" status was no guarantee that the missing member had gone legit. One founder of an African American gang was reported to us in a pretest as having "dropped from sight," but later we learned that he had been a victim of one of serial killer Jeffrey Dahmer's grisly murders. Others, with whom our respondents no longer have contact, may be heavy cocaine users who left the gang and the neighborhood because they were no longer trustworthy.

6. Homeboys varied as well. Some were entrepreneurs or players; typically they were the "dopemen" who started a "dopehouse" where other gang members could work. Others worked only sporadically in dopehouses as a supplement to legitimate work or during unemployment. Finally, some, often cocaine users, worked most of the time at the dopehouse and only sporadically at legitimate jobs. Although homeboys also varied over time in their aspirations to conventionality, as a group they believed that the lack of jobs and the prison time were testing their commitment to conventional values. We found no significant differences between Latino and African American homeboys.

7. It is too early to tell how many persons will succeed at freeing themselves from cocaine use. Ansley Hamid (1992) found that by the 1990s, most New York crack users were in their thirties and poor; their heavy drug involvement had ruined their chances for conventional careers.

References

Anderson, Elijah
    1978 A Place on the Corner. Chicago: University of Chicago Press.
    1990 Streetwise: Race, Class, and Change in an Urban Community. Chicago: University of Chicago Press.
Blumstein, Alfred
    1993 Making rationality relevant. Criminology 31:1–16.
Bourgois, Phillippe
    1990 In search of Horatio Alger: culture and ideology in the crack economy. Contemporary Drug Problems 16:619–649.
Cloward, Richard and Lloyd Ohlin
    1960 Delinquency and Opportunity. Glencoe, Ill.: Free Press.
Cohen, Albert
    1955 Delinquent Boys. Glencoe, Ill.: Free Press.

Coleman, James S.
  1988 Social capital in the creation of human capital. American Journal of Sociology 94:S95-S120.
Cummings, Scott and Daniel J. Monte
  1993 Gangs. Albany: State University of New York Press.
Fagan, Jeffrey
  1990 Social processes of delinquency and drug use among urban gangs. In C. Ronald Huff (ed.), Gangs in America. Newbury Park: Sage.
  1991 Drug selling and licit income in distressed neighborhoods: The economic lives of street-level drug users and dealers. In Adele V. Harrell and George E. Peterson (eds.), Drugs, Crime, and Social Isolation. Washington: Urban Institute Press.
Glueck, Sheldon and Eleanor Glueck
  1950 Unraveling Juvenile Delinquency. New York: Commonwealth Fund.
Gottfredson, Michael and Travis Hirschi
  1990 A General Theory of Crime. Stanford: Stanford University Press.
Hagedorn, John M.
  1988 People and Folks: Gangs, Crime, and the Underclass in a Rustbelt City. Chicago: Lakeview.
  1991 Gangs, neighborhoods, and public policy. Social Problems 38:529-542.
Hamid, Ansley
  1992 The developmental cycle of a drug epidemic: the cocaine smoking epidemic of 1981-1991. Journal of Psychoactive Drugs 24:337-348.
Hannerz, Ulf
  1969 Soulside: Inquiries into Ghetto Culture and Community. New York: Columbia University Press.
Huff, C. Ronald
  1990 Gangs in America. Newbury Park: Sage.
Jankowski, Martin Sanchez
  1991 Islands in the Street: Gangs and American Urban Society. Berkeley: University of California Press.
Johnson, Bruce D., Terry Williams, Kojo Dei, and Harry Sanahria
  1985 Taking Care of Business: The Economics of Crime by Heroin Abusers. Lexington, Mass.: Heath.
Klein, Malcolm W.
  1971 Street Gangs and Street Workers. Englewood Cliffs, N.J.: Prentice Hall.
  1992 The new street gang...or is it? Contemporary Sociology 21:80-82.
Klein, Malcolm W. and Cheryl L Maxson
  1993 Gangs and cocaine trafficking. In Craig Uchida and Doris Mackenzie (eds.), Drugs and the Criminal Justice System. Newbury Park: Sage.
Klein, Malcolm W., Cheryl L. Maxson, and Lea C. Cunningham
  1991 Crack, street gangs, and violence. Criminology 29:623-650.
Liebow, Elliot
  1967 Tally's Corner. Boston: Little, Brown.
Lincoln, Yvonna S. and Egon G. Guba
  1985 Naturalistic Inquiry. Beverly Hills: Sage.
MacCoun, Robert and Peter Reuter
  1992 Are the wages of sin $30 an hour? Economic aspects of street-level drug dealing. Crime and Delinquency 38:477-491.

MacLeod, Jay
1987 Ain't No Makin' It: Leveled Aspirations in a Low-Income Neighborhood. Boulder: Westview.
Matza, David
1964 Delinquency and Drift. New York: Wiley.
Merton, Robert K.
1957 Social Theory and Social Structure. 1968. New York: Free Press.
Miller, Walter B.
1969 Lower class culture as a generating milieu of gang delinquency. Journal of Social Issues 14:5–19.
Moore, Joan W.
1978 Homeboys: Gangs, Drugs, and Prison in the Barrios of Los Angeles. Philadelphia: Temple University Press.
1991 Going Down to the Barrio: Homeboys and Homegirls in Change. Philadelphia: Temple University Press.
Padilla, Felix
1992 The Gang as an American Enterprise. New Brunswick: Rutgers University Press.
Preble, Edward and John H. Casey
1969 Taking care of business: The heroin user's life on the street. International Journal of the Addictions 4:1–24.
Reinarman, Craig and Harry G. Levine
1990 Crack in context: politics and media in the making of a drug scare. Contemporary Drug Problems 16:535–577.
Rose, Harold M., Ronald S. Edari, Lois M. Quinn, and John Pawasrat
1992 The Labor Market Experience of Young African American Men from Low-Income Families in Wisconsin. Milwaukee: University of Wisconsin–Milwaukee Employment and Training Institute.
Sampson, Robert J. and John H. Laub
1993 Crime in the Making: Pathways and Turning Points through Life. Cambridge: Harvard University Press.
Short, James F. and Fred L. Strodtbeck
1965 Group Process and Gang Delinquency. Chicago: University of Chicago Press.
Skolnick, Jerome H.
1990 The social structure of street drug dealing. American Journal of Police 9:1–41.
Spergel, Irving A. and G. David Curry
1990 Strategies and perceived agency effectiveness in dealing with the youth gang problem. In C. Ronald Huff (ed.), Gangs in America. Beverly Hills: Sage.
Strauss, Anselm L.
1987 Qualitative Analysis for Social Scientists. Cambridge: Cambridge University Press.
Sullivan, Mercer L.
1989 Getting Paid: Youth Crime and Work in the Inner City. Ithaca: Cornell University Press.
Taylor, Carl
1990 Dangerous Society. East Lansing: Michigan State University Press.

Thrasher, Frederick
  1927 The Gang. 1963. Chicago: University of Chicago Press.
Waldorf, Dan
  1993 Final Report of the Crack Sales, Gangs, and Violence Study: NIDA Grant 5#R01DA06486. Alameda: Institute for Scientific Analysis.
Waldorf, Dan, Craig Reinarman, and Sheigla Murphy
  1991 Cocaine Changes: The Experience of Using and Quitting. Philadelphia: Temple University Press.
Whyte, William Foote
  1943 Street Corner Society. Chicago: University of Chicago Press.
Williams, Terry
  1989 The Cocaine Kids. Reading, Mass.: Addison-Wesley.
Wilson, William Julius
  1987 The Truly Disadvantaged. Chicago: University of Chicago.

13 / A Radical Perspective on Crime

JEFFREY H. REIMAN

THE IMPLICIT IDEOLOGY OF CRIMINAL JUSTICE

Every criminal justice system conveys a subtle, yet powerful message in support of established institutions. It does this for two interconnected reasons.

First, because it concentrates on *individual* wrongdoers. This means that *it diverts our attention away from our institutions, away from consideration of whether our institutions themselves are wrong or unjust or indeed "criminal."*

Second, because the criminal law is put forth as the *minimum neutral ground rules* for any social living. We are taught that no society can exist without rules against theft and violence, and thus the criminal law is put forth as politically neutral, as the minimum requirements of *any* society, as the minimum obligations that any individual owes his fellows to make social life of any decent sort possible. Thus, it not only diverts our attention away from the possible injustice of our social institutions, but *the criminal law bestows upon those institutions the mantle of its own neutrality.* Since the criminal law protects the established institutions (e.g., the prevailing economic arrangements are protected by laws against theft, etc.), attacks on those established institutions become equivalent to violations of the minimum requirements for any social life at all. In effect, *the criminal law enshrines the established institutions as equivalent to the minimum requirements for any decent social existence—and it brands the individual who attacks those institutions as one who has declared war on all organized society and who must therefore be met with the weapons of war.*

This is the powerful magic of criminal justice. By virtue of its focus on *individual* criminals, it diverts us from the evils of the *social* order. By virtue of its presumed neutrality, it transforms the established social (and economic) order from being merely *one* form of society open to critical comparison with others into *the* conditions of *any* social order and thus immune from criticism. Let us look more closely at this process.

What is the effect of focusing on individual guilt? Not only does this divert our attention from the possible evils in our institutions, but it puts forth half the problem of justice as if it were the *whole* problem. To focus on

149

individual guilt is to ask whether or not the individual citizen has fulfilled his obligations to his fellow citizens. *It is to look away from the issue of whether his fellow citizens have fulfilled their obligations to him.*

To look only at individual responsibility is to look away from social responsibility. To look only at individual criminality is to close one's eyes to social injustice and to close one's ears to the question of whether our social institutions have exploited or violated the individual. *Justice is a two-way street—but criminal justice is a one-way street.*

Individuals owe obligations to their fellow citizens because their fellow citizens owe obligations to them. Criminal justice focuses on the first and looks away from the second. *Thus, by focusing on individual responsibility for crime, the criminal justice system literally acquits the existing social order of any charge of injustice!*

This is an extremely important bit of ideological alchemy. It stems from the fact [that] the same act can be criminal or not, unjust or just, depending on the conditions in which it takes place. Killing someone is ordinarily a crime. But if it is in self-defense or to stop a deadly crime, it is not. Taking property by force is usually a crime. But if the taking is just retrieving what has been stolen, then no crime has been committed. Acts of violence are ordinarily crimes. But if the violence is provoked by the threat of violence or by oppressive conditions, then, like the Boston Tea Party, what might ordinarily be called criminal is celebrated as just. This means that when we call an act a crime *we are also making an implicit judgment about the conditions in response to which it takes place.* When we call an act a crime, we are saying that the conditions in which it occurs are not themselves criminal or deadly or oppressive or so unjust as to make an extreme response reasonable or justified, that is, to make such a response non-criminal.

This means that when the system holds an individual responsible for a crime, *it is implicitly conveying the message that the social conditions in which the crime occurred are not responsible for the crime,* that they are not so unjust as to make a violent response to them excusable. The criminal justice system conveys as much by what it does not do as by what it does. By holding the individual responsible, *it literally acquits the society of criminality or injustice.*

Judges are prone to hold that an individual's responsibility for a violent crime is diminished if it was provoked by something that might lead a "reasonable man" to respond violently and that criminal responsibility is eliminated if the act was in response to conditions so intolerable that any "reasonable man" would have been likely to respond in the same way. In this vein, the law acquits those who kill or injure in self-defense and treats lightly those who commit a crime when confronted with extreme provocation. The law treats leniently the man who kills his wife's lover and the woman who kills her brutal husband, even when neither has acted directly in self-defense. By this logic, when we hold an individual completely responsible for a crime, we are saying that the conditions in which it occurred are such that a "reasonable man" should find them tolerable. In other words, by focusing on individual responsibility for crimes, *the criminal justice system broadcasts the message that the social order itself is reasonable and not intolerably unjust.*

Thus the criminal justice system serves to focus moral condemnation on individuals and to deflect it away from the social order that may have either violated the individual's rights or dignity or literally pushed him or her to the brink of crime. This not only serves to carry the message that our social institutions are not in need of fundamental questioning, but it further suggests that the justice of our institutions is obvious, not to be doubted. Indeed, since it is deviations from these institutions that are crimes, the established institutions become the implicit standard of justice from which criminal deviations are measured.

This leads to the second way in which a criminal justice system always conveys an implicit ideology. It arises from the presumption that the criminal law is nothing but the politically neutral minimum requirements of any decent social life. What is the consequence of this?

Obviously, as already suggested, this presumption transforms the prevailing social order into justice incarnate and all violations of the prevailing order into injustice incarnate. This process is so obvious that it may be easily missed.

Consider, for example, the law against theft. It does indeed seem to be one of the minimum requirements of social living. As long as there is scarcity, any society—capitalist or socialist—will need rules preventing individuals from taking what does not belong to them. But the law against theft is more: it is a law against stealing what individuals *presently* own. *Such a law has the effect of making present property relations a part of the criminal law.*

Since stealing is a violation of the law, this means that present property relations become the implicit standard of justice against which criminal deviations are measured. Since criminal law is thought of as the minimum requirements of any social life, this means that present property relations become equivalent to the minimum requirements of *any* social life. And the criminal who would alter the present property relations becomes nothing less than someone who is declaring war on all organized society. The question of whether this "war" is provoked by the injustice or brutality of the society is swept aside. Indeed, this suggests yet another way in which the criminal justice system conveys an ideological message in support of the established society.

Not only does the criminal justice system acquit the social order of any charge of injustice, it specifically cloaks the society's own crime-producing tendencies. I have already observed that by blaming the individual for a crime, the society is acquitted of the charge of injustice. I would like to go further now and argue that by blaming the individual for a crime, the society is acquitted of the charge of complicity in that crime! This is a point worth developing, since many observers have maintained that modern competitive societies such as our own have structural features that tend to generate crime. Thus, holding the individual responsible for his or her crime serves the function of taking the rest of society off the hook for their role in sustaining and benefiting from social arrangements that produce crime. Let us take a brief detour to look more closely at this process.

Cloward and Ohlin argue in their book *Delinquency and Opportunity*[1] that much crime is the result of the discrepancy between social goals and the legitimate opportunities available for achieving them. Simply put, in our society everyone is encouraged to be a success, but the avenues to success are open only to some. The conventional wisdom of our free enterprise democracy is that anyone can be a success if he or she has the talent and the ambition. Thus, if one is not a success, it is because of their own shortcomings: laziness or lack of ability or both. On the other hand, opportunities to achieve success are not equally open to all. Access to the best schools and the best jobs is effectively closed to all but a few of the poor and begins to open wider only as one goes up the economic ladder. The result is that many are called but few are chosen. And many who have taken the bait and accepted the belief in the importance of success and the belief that achieving success is a result of individual ability must cope with the feelings of frustration and failure that result when they find the avenues to success closed. Cloward and Ohlin argue that one method of coping with these stresses is to develop alternative avenues to success. Crime is such an alternative. Crime is a means by which people who believe in the American dream pursue it when they find the traditional routes barred. Indeed, it is plain to see that the goals pursued by most criminals are as American as apple pie. I suspect that one of the reasons that American moviegoers enjoy gangster films—movies in which gangsters such as Al Capone, Bonnie and Clyde, or Butch Cassidy and the Sundance Kid are the heroes, as distinct from police and detective films whose heroes are defenders of the law—is that even where they deplore the hero's methods, they identify with his or her notion of success, since it is theirs as well, and respect the courage and cunning displayed in achieving that success.

It is important to note that the discrepancy between success goals and legitimate opportunities in America is not an aberration. It is a structural feature of modern competitive industrialized society, a feature from which many benefits flow. Cloward and Ohlin write that

> ...a crucial problem in the industrial world...is to locate and train the most talented persons in every generation, irrespective of the vicissitudes of birth, to occupy technical work roles.... Since we cannot know in advance who can best fulfill the requirements of the various occupational roles, the matter is presumably settled through the process of competition. But how can men throughout the social order be motivated to participate in this competition? ...
>
> One of the ways in which the industrial society attempts to solve this problem is by defining success-goals as potentially accessible to all, regardless of race, creed, or socioeconomic position.[2]

But since these universal goals are urged to encourage a competition to weed out the best, there are necessarily fewer openings than seekers. And since those who achieve success are in a particularly good position to exploit their success to make access for their own children easier, the competition is rigged to work in favor of the middle and upper classes. As a result, "many lower-class persons . . . are the victims of a contradiction between the goals toward which they have been led to orient themselves and socially structured means of striving for these goals."[3]

> [The poor] experience desperation born of the certainty that their position in the economic structure is relatively fixed and immutable—a desperation made all the more poignant by their exposure to a cultural ideology in which failure to orient oneself upward is regarded as a moral defect and failure to become mobile as proof of it.[4]

The outcome is predictable. "Under these conditions, there is an acute pressure to depart from institutional norms and to adopt illegitimate alternatives."[5]

In brief, this means that the very way in which our society is structured to draw out the talents and energies that go into producing our high standard of living has a costly side effect: it produces crime. But by holding individuals responsible for this crime, those who enjoy that high standard of living can have their cake and eat it. They can reap the benefits of the competition for success and escape the responsibility of paying for the costs of that competition. By holding the poor crook legally and morally guilty, the rest of society not only passes the costs of competition on to the poor, but they effectively deny that they (the affluent) are the beneficiaries of an economic system that exacts such a high toll in frustration and suffering.

Willem Bonger, the Dutch Marxist criminologist, maintained that competitive capitalism produces egotistic motives and undermines compassion for the misfortunes of others and thus makes human beings literally *more capable of crime*—more capable of preying on their fellows without moral inhibition or remorse—than earlier cultures that emphasized cooperation rather than competition.[6] Here again, the criminal justice system relieves those who benefit from the American economic system of the costs of that system. By holding criminals morally and individually responsible for their crimes, we can forget that the motives that lead to crime—the drive for success at any cost, linked with the beliefs that success means outdoing others and that violence is an acceptable way of achieving one's goals—are the same motives that powered the drive across the American continent and that continue to fuel the engine of America's prosperity.

David Gordon, a contemporary political economist, maintains "that nearly all crimes in capitalist societies represent perfectly *rational* responses to the structure of institutions upon which capitalist societies are based."[7] That is, like Bonger, Gordon believes that capitalism tends to provoke crime in all economic strata. This is so because most crime is motivated by a desire for property or money and is an understandable way of coping with the pressures of inequality, competition, and insecurity, all of which are essential ingredients of capitalism. Capitalism depends, Gordon writes,

> ...on basically competitive forms of social and economic interaction and upon substantial inequalities in the allocation of social resources. Without inequalities, it would be much more difficult to induce workers to work in alienating environments. Without competition and a competitive ideology, workers might not be inclined to struggle to improve their relative income and status in society by working harder. Finally, although rights of property are protected, capitalist societies do not guarantee economic security to most of their individual members. Individuals must fend for themselves, finding the best available opportunities to provide for themselves and their families.... Driven by the fear of economic insecurity and by a competitive desire to gain some of the goods unequally distributed throughout the society, many individuals will eventually become "criminals."[8]

To the extent that a society makes crime a reasonable alternative for a large number of its members from all classes, that society is itself not very reasonably or humanely organized and bears some degree of responsibility for the crime it encourages. Since the criminal law is put forth as the minimum requirements that can be expected of any "reasonable man," its enforcement amounts to a denial of the real nature of the social order to which Gordon and the others point. Here again, by blaming the individual criminal, the criminal justice system serves implicitly but dramatically to acquit the society of its criminality.

THE BONUS OF BIAS

We turn now to consideration of the additional ideological bonus that is derived from the criminal justice system's bias against the poor. This bonus is a product of the association of crime and poverty in the popular mind. This association, the merging of the "criminal classes" and the "lower classes" into the "dangerous classes," was not invented in America. The word "villain" is derived from the Latin *villanus*, which means a farm servant. And the term "villein" was used in feudal England to refer to a serf who farmed the land of a great lord and who was literally owned by that lord.[9] In this respect, our present criminal justice system is heir to a long and hallowed tradition.

The value of this association was already seen when we explored the "average citizen's" concept of the Typical Criminal and the Typical Crime. It is quite obvious that throughout the great mass of middle America, far more fear and hostility are directed toward the predatory acts of the poor than the rich. Compare the fate of politicians in recent history who call for tax reform, income redistribution, prosecution of corporate crime, and any sort of regulation of business that would make it better serve American social goals with that of politicians who erect their platform on a call for "law and order," more police, less limits on police power, and stiffer prison sentences for criminals—and consider this in light of what we have already seen about the real dangers posed by corporate crime and business-as-usual.

In view of all that has been said already, it seems clear that Americans have been systematically deceived as to what are the greatest dangers to their lives, limbs and possessions. The very persistence with which the system functions to apprehend and punish poor crooks and ignore or slap on the wrist equally or more dangerous individuals is testimony to the sticking power of this deception. That Americans continue to tolerate the gentle treatment meted out to white-collar criminals, corporate price fixers, industrial polluters, and political-influence peddlers, while voting in droves to lock up more poor people faster and longer, indicates the degree to which they harbor illusions as to who most threatens them. It is perhaps also part of the explanation for the continued dismal failure of class-based politics in America. American workers rarely seem able to forget their differences and unite to defend their shared interests against the rich whose wealth they produce. Ethnic divisions serve this divisive function well, but undoubtedly the vivid portrayal of the poor—and, of course, the blacks—as hovering birds of prey waiting for the opportunity to snatch away the workers' meager gains serves also to deflect opposition away from the upper class. A politician who promises to keep their communities free of blacks and their prisons full of them can get their votes even if the major portion of his or her policies amount to continuation of favored treatment of the rich at their expense. Surely this is a minor miracle of mind control.

The most important "bonus" derived from the identification of crime and poverty is that it paints the picture that the threat to decent middle Americans comes from those below them on the economic ladder, not those above. For this to happen the system must not only identify crime and poverty, but *it must also fail to reduce crime so that it remains a real threat.* By doing this, it deflects the fear and discontent of middle Americans, and their possible opposition, away from the wealthy. The two politicians who most clearly gave voice to the discontent of middle Americans in the post-World War II period were George Wallace and Spiro Agnew. Is it any accident that their politics were extremely conservative and their anger reserved for the poor (the welfare chiselers) and the criminal (the targets of law and order)?

There are other bonuses as well. For instance, if the criminal justice system functions to send out a message that bestows legitimacy on present property relations, the dramatic impact is mightily enhanced if the violator of the present arrangements is propertyless. In other words, the crimes of the well-to-do "redistribute" property among the haves. In that sense, they do not pose a symbolic challenge to the larger system in which some have much and many have little or nothing. If the criminal threat can be portrayed as coming from the poor, then the punishment of the poor criminal becomes a morality play in which the sanctity of legitimacy of the system in which some have plenty and others have little or nothing is dramatically affirmed. It matters little who the poor criminals really rip off. What counts is that middle Americans come to fear that those poor criminals are out to steal what they own.

There is yet another and, I believe, still more important bonus for the powerful in America, produced by the identification of crime and poverty. It might be thought that the identification of crime and poverty would produce sympathy for the criminals. My suspicion is that it produces or at least reinforces the reverse: *hostility toward the poor.*

Indeed, there is little evidence that Americans are very sympathetic to criminals or poor people. I have already pointed to the fact that very few Americans believe poverty to be a cause of crime. Other surveys find that most Americans believe that police should be tougher than they are now in dealing with crime (83 percent of those questioned in a 1972 survey); that courts do not deal harshly enough with criminals (75 percent of those questioned in a 1969 survey); that a majority of Americans would like to see the death penalty for convicted murderers (57 percent of those questioned in November 1972); and that most would be more likely to vote for a candidate who advocated tougher sentences for law-breakers (83 percent of those questioned in a 1972 survey).[10] Indeed, the experience of Watergate seems to suggest that sympathy for criminals begins to flower only when we approach the higher reaches of the ladder of wealth and power. For some poor ghetto youth who robs a liquor store, five years in the slammer is our idea of tempering justice with mercy. When a handful of public officials try to walk off with the U.S. Constitution, a few months in a minimum security prison will suffice. If the public official is high enough, resignation from office and public disgrace tempered with a $60,000-a-year pension is punishment enough.

My view is that since the criminal justice system—in fact and fiction— deals with *individual legal* and *moral* guilt, the association of crime with poverty does not mitigate the image of individual moral responsibility for crime, the image that crime is the result of an individual's poor character. My suspicion is that it does the reverse: it generates the association of poverty and individual moral failing and thus *the belief that poverty itself is a sign of poor or weak character.* The clearest evidence that Americans hold this belief is to be found in the fact that attempts to aid the poor are regarded as acts of charity rather than as acts of justice. Our welfare system has all the demeaning attributes of an institution designed to give handouts to the undeserving and none of the dignity of an institution designed to make good on our responsibilities to our fellow human beings. If we acknowledged the degree to which our economic and social institutions themselves breed poverty, we would have to recognize our own responsibilities toward the poor. If we can convince ourselves that the poor are poor because of their own shortcomings, particularly moral shortcomings like incontinence or indolence, then we need acknowledge no such responsibility to the poor. Indeed, we can go further and pat ourselves on the back for our generosity and handing out the little that we do, and of course, we can make our recipients go through all the indignities that mark them as the undeserving objects of our benevolence. By and large, this has been the way in which Americans have dealt with their poor.[11] It is a way that enables us to avoid asking the question of why the richest nation in the world continues to produce massive poverty. It is my view that this conception of the poor is subtly conveyed by the way our criminal justice system functions.

Obviously, no ideological message could be more supportive of the present social and economic order than this. It suggests that poverty is a sign of individual failing, not a symptom of social or economic injustice. It tells us loud and clear that massive poverty in the midst of abundance is not a sign pointing toward the need for fundamental changes in our social and economic institutions. It suggests that the poor are poor because they deserve to be poor, or at least because they lack the strength of character to overcome poverty. When the poor are seen to be poor in character, then economic poverty coincides with moral poverty and the economic order coincides with the moral order—as if a divine hand guided its workings, capitalism leads to everyone getting what they morally deserve!

If this association takes root, then when the poor individual is found guilty of a crime, the criminal justice system acquits the society of its responsibility not only for the crime *but for poverty as well.*

With this, the ideological message of criminal justice is complete. The poor rather than the rich are seen as the enemies of the mass of decent middle Americans. Our social and economic institutions are held to be responsible for neither crime nor poverty and thus are in need of no fundamental questioning or reform. The poor are poor because they are poor of character. The economic order and the moral order are one. And to the extent that this message sinks in, the wealthy can rest easily—even if they cannot sleep the sleep of the just.

Thus, we can understand why the criminal justice system creates the image of crime as the work of the poor and fails to stem it so that the threat of crime remains real and credible. The result is ideological alchemy of the highest order. The poor are seen as the real threat to decent society. The ultimate sanctions of criminal justice dramatically sanctify the present social and economic order, and *the poverty of criminals makes poverty itself an individual moral crime!*

Such are the ideological fruits of a losing war against crime whose distorted image is reflected in the criminal justice carnival mirror and widely broadcast to reach the minds and imaginations of America.

Notes

1. Richard A. Cloward and Lloyd E. Ohlin, *Delinquency and Opportunity: A Theory of Delinquent Gangs* (New York: The Free Press, 1960), esp. pp. 77–107.

2. Ibid., p. 81.

3. Ibid., p. 105.

4. Ibid., p. 107.

5. Ibid., p. 105.

6. Willem Bonger, *Criminality and Economic Conditions*, abridged and with an introduction by Austin T. Turk (Bloomington, Indiana: Indiana University Press, 1969), pp. 7–12, 40–47. Willem Adriaan Bonger was born in Holland in 1876 and died by his own hand in 1940 rather than submit to the Nazis. His *Criminalité et conditions économiques* first appeared in 1905. It was translated into English and published in the United States in 1916. Ibid., pp. 3–4.

7. David M. Gordon, "Capitalism, Class and Crime in America," *Crime and Delinquency* (April 1972), p. 174.

8. Ibid., p. 174.

9. William and Mary Morris, *Dictionary of Word and Phrase Origins*, II (New York: Harper & Row, 1967), p. 282.

10. *Sourcebook*, pp. 203, 204, 223, 207; see also p. 177.

11. Historical documentation of this can be found in David J. Rothman, *The Discovery of the Asylum: Social Order and Disorder in the New Republic* (Boston: Little, Brown, 1971); and in Frances Fox Piven and Richard A. Cloward, *Regulating the Poor: The Functions of Public Welfare* (New York: Pantheon, 1971), which carries the analysis up to the present.

14 / A Sociological Analysis of the Law of Vagrancy

WILLIAM J. CHAMBLISS

With the outstanding exception of Jerome Hall's analysis of theft[1] there has been a severe shortage of sociologically relevant analyses of the relationship between particular laws and the social setting in which these laws emerge, are interpreted, and take form. The paucity of such studies is somewhat surprising in view of widespread agreement that such studies are not only desirable but absolutely essential to the development of a mature sociology of law.[2] A fruitful method of establishing the direction and pattern of this mutual influence is to systematically analyze particular legal categories, to observe the changes which take place in the categories and to explain how these changes are themselves related to and stimulate changes in the society. This chapter is an attempt to provide such an analysis of the law of vagrancy in Anglo-American Law.

LEGAL INNOVATION: THE EMERGENCE OF THE LAW OF VAGRANCY IN ENGLAND

There is general agreement among legal scholars that the first full fledged vagrancy statute was passed in England in 1349. As is generally the case with legislative innovations, however, this statute was preceded by earlier laws which established a climate favorable to such change. The most significant forerunner to the 1349 vagrancy statute was in 1274 when it was provided:

> Because that abbies and houses of religion have been overcharged and sore grieved, by the resort of great men and other, so that their goods have not been sufficient for themselves, whereby they have been greatly hindered and impoverished, that they cannot maintain themselves, nor such charity as they have been accustomed to do; it is provided, that none shall come to eat or lodge in any house of religion, or any other's foundation than of his own, at the costs of the house, unless he be required by the governor of the house before his coming hither.[3]

Unlike the vagrancy statutes this statute does not intend to curtail the movement of persons from one place to another, but is solely designed to provide the religious houses with some financial relief from the burden of providing food and shelter to travelers.

The philosophy that the religious houses were to give alms to the poor and to the sick and feeble was, however, to undergo drastic change in the next fifty years. The result of this changed attitude was the establishment of the first vagrancy statute in 1349 which made it a crime to give alms to any who were unemployed while being of sound mind and body. To wit:

> Because that many valiant beggars, as long as they may live of begging, do refuse to labour, giving themselves to idleness and vice, and sometimes to theft and other abominations; it is ordained, that none, upon pain of imprisonment shall, under the colour of pity or alms, give anything to such which may labour, or presume to favour them towards their desires; so that thereby they may be compelled to labour for their necessary living.[4]

It was further provided by this statute that:

> ...every man and woman, of what condition he be, free or bond, able in body, and within the age of threescore years, not living in merchandize nor exercising any craft, nor having of his own whereon to live, nor proper land whereon to occupy himself, and not serving any other, if he in convenient service (his estate considered) be required to serve, shall be bounded to serve him which shall him require.... And if any refuse, he shall on conviction by two true men, ... be commited to gaol till he find surety to serve.
>
> And if any workman or servant, of what estate or condition he be, retained in any man's service, do depart from the said service without reasonable cause or license, before the term agreed on, he shall have pain of imprisonment.[5]

There was also in this statute the stipulation that the workers should receive a standard wage. In 1351 this statute was strengthened by the stipulation:

> And none shall go out of the town where he dwelled in winter, to serve the summer, if he may serve in the same town.[6]

By 34 Ed. 3 (1360) the punishment for these acts became imprisonment for fifteen days and if they "do not justify themselves by the end of that time, to be sent to gaol till they do."

A change in official policy so drastic as this did not, of course, occur simply as a matter of whim. The vagrancy statutes emerged as a result of changes in other parts of the social structure. The prime-mover for this legislative innovation was the Black Death which struck England about 1348. Among the many disastrous consequences this had upon the social structure was the fact that it decimated the labor force. It is estimated that by the time the pestilence had run its course at least fifty per cent of the population of England had died from the plague. This decimation of the labor force would necessitate rather drastic innovations in any society but its impact was heightened in England where, at this time, the economy was highly dependent upon a steady supply of cheap labor.

Even before the pestilence, however, the availability of an adequate supply of cheap labor was becoming a problem for the landowners. The crusades and various wars had made money necessary to the lords and, as a result, the lord frequently agreed to sell the serfs their freedom in order to obtain the needed funds. The serfs, for their part, were desirous of obtaining their freedom (by "fair means" or "foul") because the larger towns which were becoming more industrialized during this period could offer the serf greater personal freedom as well as a higher standard of living. This process is nicely summarized by Bradshaw:

> By the middle of the 14th century the outward uniformity of the manorial system had become in practice considerably varied . . . for the peasant had begun to drift to the towns and it was unlikely that the old village life in its unpleasant aspects should not be resented. Moreover the constant wars against France and Scotland were fought mainly with mercenaries after Henry III's time and most villages contributed to the new armies. The bolder serfs either joined the armies or fled to the towns, and even in the villages the free men who held by villein tenure were as eager to commute their services as the serfs were to escape. Only the amount of "free" labor available enabled the lord to work his demesne in many places.[7]

And he says regarding the effect of the Black Death:

> . . . in 1348 the Black Death reached England and the vast mortality that ensued destroyed that reserve to labor which alone had made the manorial system even nominally possible.[8]

The immediate result of these events was of course no surprise: Wages for the "free" man rose considerably and this increased, on the one hand, the landowner's problems and, on the other hand, the plight of the unfree tenant. For although wages increased for the personally free laborers, it of course did not necessarily add to the standard of living of the serf, if anything it made his position worse because the landowner would be hard pressed to pay for the personally free labor which he needed and would thus find it more and more difficult to maintain the standard of living for the serf which he had heretofore supplied. Thus the serf had no alternative but flight if he chose to better his position. Furthermore, flight generally meant both freedom and better conditions since the possibility of work in the new weaving industry was great and the chance of being caught small.[9]

It was under these conditions that we find the first vagrancy statutes emerging. There is little question but that these statutes were designed for one express purpose: to force laborers (whether personally free or unfree) to accept employment at a low wage in order to insure the landowner an adequate supply of labor at a price he could afford to pay. Caleb Foote concurs with this interpretation when he notes:

> The anti-migratory policy behind vagrancy legislation began as an essential complement of the wage stabilization legislation which accompanied the breakup of feudalism and the depopulation caused by the Black Death. By the Statutes

of Labourers in 1349–1351, every able-bodied person without other means of support was required to work for wages fixed at the level preceding the Black Death; it was unlawful to accept any more, or to refuse an offer to work, or to flee from one country to another to avoid offers of work or to seek higher wages, or go give alms to able-bodied beggars who refused to work.[10]

In short, as Foote says in another place, this was "an attempt to make the vagrancy statutes a substitute for serfdom."[11] This same conclusion is equally apparent from the wording of the statute where it is stated:

> Because great part of the people, and especially of workmen and servants, late died in pestilence; many seeing the necessity of masters, and great scarcity of servants, will not serve without excessive wages, and some rather willing to beg in idleness than by labour to get their living: it is ordained, that every man and woman, of what condition he be, free or bond, able in body and within the age of threescore years, not living in merchandize, (etc.) be required to serve....

The innovation in the law, then, was a direct result of the aforementioned changes which had occurred in the social setting. In this case these changes were located for the most part in the economic institution of the society. The vagrancy laws were designed to alleviate a condition defined by the lawmakers as undesirable. The solution was to attempt to force a reversal, as it were, of a social process which was well underway; that is, to curtail mobility of laborers in such a way that labor would not become a commodity for which the landowners would have to compete.

Statutory Dormancy: A Legal Vestige

In time, of course, the curtailment of the geographical mobility of laborers was no longer requisite. One might well expect that when the function served by the statute was no longer an important one for society, the statutes would be eliminated from the law. In fact, this has not occurred. The vagrancy statutes have remained in effect since 1349. Furthermore, as we shall see in some detail later, they were taken over by the colonies and have remained in effect in the United States as well.

The substance of the vagrancy statutes changed very little for some time after the first ones in 1349–1351 although there was a tendency to make punishments more harsh than originally. For example, in 1360 it was provided that violators of the statute should be imprisoned for fifteen days,[12] and in 1388 the punishment was to put the offender in the stocks and to keep him there until "he find surety to return to his service."[13] That there was still, at this time, the intention of providing the landowner with labor is apparent from the fact that this statute provides:

> ...and he or she which use to labour at the plough and cart, or other labour and service of husbandry, till they be of the age of 12 years, from thenceforth shall abide at the same labour without being put to any mistery or handicraft: and any covenant of apprenticeship to the contrary shall be void.[14]

The next alteration in the statutes occurs in 1495 and is restricted to an increase in punishment. Here it is provided that vagrants shall be "set in stocks, there to remain by the space of three days and three nights, and there to have none other sustenance but bread and water; and after the said three days and nights, to be had out and set at large, and then to be commanded to void the town."[15]

The tendency to increase the severity of punishment during this period seems to be the result of a general tendency to make finer distinctions in the criminal law. During this period the vagrancy statutes appear to have been fairly inconsequential in either their effect as a control mechanism or as a generally enforced statute.[16] The processes of social change in the culture generally and the trend away from serfdom and into a "free" economy obviated the utility of these statutes. The result was not unexpected. The judiciary did not apply the law and the legislators did not take it upon themselves to change the law. In short, we have here a period of dormancy in which the statute is neither applied nor altered significantly.

A SHIFT IN FOCAL CONCERN

Following the squelching of the Peasant's Revolt in 1381, the services of the serfs to the lord " ... tended to become less and less exacted, although in certain forms they lingered on till the seventeenth century. ... By the sixteenth century few knew there were any bondmen in England ... and in 1575 Queen Elizabeth listened to the prayers of almost the last serfs in England ... and granted them manumission."[17]

In view of this change we would expect corresponding changes in the vagrancy laws. Beginning with the lessening of punishment in the statute of 1503 we find these changes. However, instead of remaining dormant (or becoming more so) or being negated altogether, the vagrancy statutes experienced a shift in focal concern. With this shift the statutes served a new and equally important function for the social order or England. The first statute which indicates this change was in 1530. In this statute (22 H. 8. c. 12 1530) it was stated:

> If any person, being whole and mighty in body, and able to labour, be taken in begging, or be vagrant and can give no reckoning how he lawfully gets his living; ... and all other idle persons going about, some of them using divers and subtil crafty and unlawful games and plays, and some of them feigning themselves to have knowledge of ... crafty sciences ... shall be punished as provided.

What is most significant about this statute is the shift from an earlier concern with laborers to a concern with *criminal* activities. To be sure, the stipulation of persons "being whole and mighty in body, and able to labour, be taken in begging, or be vagrant" sounds very much like the concerns of the earlier statutes. Some important differences are apparent however when the rest of the statute includes those who "...can give no reckoning how he lawfully gets his living"; "some of them using divers and subtil crafty and unlawful games and plays." This is the first statute which specifically focuses upon these kinds of criteria for adjudging someone a vagrant.

It is significant that in this statute the severity of punishment is increased so as to be greater not only than provided by the 1503 statute but the punishment is more severe than that which had been provided by *any* of the pre-1503 statutes as well. For someone who is merely idle and gives no reckoning of how he makes his living the offender shall be:

> ...had to the next market town, or other place where they [the constables] shall think most convenient, and there to be tied to the end of a cart naked, and to be beaten with whips throughout the same market town or other place, till his body be bloody by reason of such whipping.[18]

But, for those who use "divers and subtil crafty and unlawful games and plays," etc., the punishment is "...whipping at two days together in manner aforesaid."[19] For the second offense, such persons are:

> ...scourged two days, and the third day to be put upon the pillory from nine of the clock till eleven before noon of the same day and to have one of his ears cut off.[20]

And if he offend the third time "...to have like punishment with whipping, standing on the pillory and to have his other ear cut off."

This statute (1) makes a distinction between types of offenders and applies the more severe punishment to those who are clearly engaged in "criminal" activities, (2) mentions a specific concern with categories of "unlawful" behavior, and (3) applies a type of punishment (cutting off the ear) which is generally reserved for offenders who are defined as likely to be a fairly serious criminal.

Only five years later we find for the first time that the punishment of death is applied to the crime of vagrancy. We also note a change in terminology in the statute:

> and if any ruffians...after having been once apprehended...shall wander, loiter, or idle use themselves and play the vagabonds...shall be eftfoons not only whipped again, but shall have the gristle of his right ear clean cut off. And if he shall again offend, he shall be committed to gaol till the next sessions; and being their convicted upon indictment, he shall have judgements to suffer pains and execution of death, as a felon, as an enemy of the commonwealth.[21]

It is significant that the statute now makes persons who repeat the crime of vagrancy a felon. During this period then, the focal concern of the vagrancy statutes becomes a concern for the control of felons and is no longer primarily concerned with the movement of laborers.

These statutory changes were a direct response to changes taking place in England's social structure during this period. We have already pointed out that feudalism was decaying rapidly. Concomitant with the breakup of feudalism was an increased emphasis upon commerce and industry. The commercial emphasis in England at the turn of the sixteenth century is of particular importance in the development of vagrancy laws. With commercialism came considerable traffic bearing valuable items. Where there were 169 important merchants in the middle of the fourteenth century there were 3,000 merchants engaged in foreign trade alone at the beginning of the sixteenth century.[22] England became highly dependent upon commerce for its economic support. Italians conducted a great deal of the commerce in England during this early period and were held in low repute by the populace. As a result, they were subject to attacks by citizens and, more important, were frequently robbed of their goods while transporting them. "The general insecurity of the times made any transportation hazardous. The special risks to which the alien merchant was subjected gave rise to the royal practice of issuing formally executed covenants of safe conduct through the realm."[23]

Such a situation not only called for the enforcement of existing laws but also called for the creation of new laws which would facilitate the control of persons preying upon merchants transporting goods. The vagrancy statutes were revived in order to fulfill just such a purpose. Persons who had committed no serious felony but who were suspected of being capable of doing so could be apprehended and incapacitated through the application of vagrancy laws once these laws were refocused so as to include "...any ruffians...[who] shall wander, loiter, or idle use themselves and play the vagabond...."[24]

The new focal concern is continued in 1 Ed. 6. c. 3 (1547) and in fact is made more general so as to include:

> Whoever man or woman, being not lame, impotent, or so aged or diseased that he or she cannot work, not having whereon to live, shall be lurking in any house, or loitering or idle wandering by the highway side, or in streets, cities, towns, or villages, not applying themselves to some honest labour, and so continuing for three days; or running away from their work; every such person shall be taken for a vagabond. And...upon conviction of two witnesses...the same loiterer (shall) be marked with a hot iron in the breast with the letter V, and adjudged him to the person bringing him, to be his slave for two years....

Should the vagabond run away, upon conviction, he was to be branded by a hot iron with the letter S on the forehead and to be thenceforth declared a slave forever. And in 1571 there is modification of the punishment to be inflicted, whereby the offender is to be "branded on the chest with the letter V" (for vagabond). And, if he is convicted the second time, the brand is to be made on the forehead. It is worth noting here that this method of punishment, which first appeared in 1530 and is repeated here with somewhat more force, is also an indication of a change in the type of person to whom the law is intended to apply. For it is likely that nothing so permanent as branding would be applied to someone who was wandering but looking for work, or at worst merely idle and not particularly dangerous *per se.* On the other hand, it could well be applied to someone who was likely to be engaged in other criminal activities in connection with being "vagrant."

By 1571 in the statute of 14 Ed. c. 5 the shift in focal concern is fully developed:

> All rogues, vagabonds, and sturdy beggers shall...be committed to the common gaol...he shall be grievously whipped, and burnt thro' the gristle of the right ear with a hot iron of the compass of an inch about....And for the second offense, he shall be adjudged a felon, unless some person will take him for two years in to his service. And for the third offense, he shall be adjudged guilty of felony without benefit of clergy.

And there is included a long list of persons who fall within the statute: "proctors, procurators, idle persons going about using subtil, crafty and unlawful games or plays; and some of them feigning themselves to have knowledge of...absurd sciences...and all fencers, bearwards, common players in interludes, and minstrels...all juglers, pedlars, tinkers, petty chapmen...and all counterfeiters of licenses, passports and users of the same." The major significance of this statute is that it includes all the previously defined offenders and adds some more. Significantly, those added are more clearly criminal types, counterfeiters, for example. It is also significant that there is the following qualification of this statute: "Provided also, that this act shall not extend to cookers, or harvest folks, that travel for harvest work, corn or hay."

That the changes in this statute were seen as significant is indicated by the following statement which appears in the statute:

> And whereas by reason of this act, the common gaols of every shire are like to be greatly pestered with more number of prisoners than heretofore hath been, for that the said vagabonds and other lewd persons before recited shall upon their apprehension be committed to the said gaols; it is enacted....[25]

And a provision is made for giving more money for maintaining the gaols. This seems to add credence to the notion that this statute was seen as being significantly more general than those previously.

It is also of importance to note that this is the first time the term *rogue* has been used to refer to persons included in the vagrancy statutes. It seems, *a priori,* that a "rogue" is a different social type than is a "vagrant" or a "vagabond"; the latter terms implying something more equivalent to the idea of a "tramp" whereas the former (rogue) seems to imply a more disorderly and potentially dangerous person.

The emphasis upon the criminalistic aspect of vagrants continues in Chapter 17 of the same statute:

> Whereas divers *licentious* persons wander up and down in all parts of the realm, to countenance their *wicked behavior;* and do continually assemble themselves

armed in the highways, and elsewhere in troops, *to the great terror* of her majesty's true subjects, *the impeachment of her laws,* and the disturbance of the peace and tranquility of the realm; and whereas many outrages are daily committed by these dissolute persons, and more are likely to ensure if speedy remedy be not provided. (Italics added.)

With minor variations (e.g., offering a reward for the capture of a vagrant) the statutes remained essentially of this nature until 1743. In 1743 there was once more an expansion of the types of persons included such that "all persons going about as patent gatherers, or gatherers of alms, under pretense of loss by fire or other casualty; or going about as collectors for prisons, gaols, or hospitals; all persons playing or betting at any unlawful games; and all persons who run away and leave their wives or children ... all persons wandering abroad, and lodging in alehouses, barns, outhouses, or in the open air, not giving good account of themselves," were types of offenders added to those already included.

By 1743 the vagrancy statutes had apparently been sufficiently reconstructed by the shifts of concern so as to be once more a useful instrument in the creation of social solidarity. This function has apparently continued down to the present day in England and the changes from 1743 to present have been all in the direction of clarifying or expanding the categories covered but little has been introduced to change either the meaning or the impact of this branch of the law.

We can summarize this shift in focal concern by quoting from Halsbury. He has noted that in the vagrancy statutes:

> ... elaborate provision is made for the relief and incidental control of destitute wayfarers. These latter, however, form but a small portion of the offenders aimed at by what are known as the Vagrancy Laws, ... many offenders who are in no ordinary sense of the word vagrants, have been brought under the laws relating to vagrancy, and the great number of the offenses coming within the operation of these laws have little or no relation to the subject of poor relief, but are more properly directed towards the prevention of crime, the preservation of good order, and the promotion of social economy.[26]

Before leaving this section it is perhaps pertinent to make a qualifying remark. We have emphasized throughout this section how the vagrancy statutes underwent a shift in focal concern as the social setting changed. The shift in focal concern is not meant to imply that the later focus of the statutes represents a completely new law. It will be recalled that even in the first vagrancy statute there was reference to those who "do refuse labor, giving themselves to idleness and vice and sometimes to theft and other abominations." Thus the possibility of criminal activities resulting from persons who refuse to labor was recognized even in the earliest statute. The fact remains, however, that the major emphasis in this statute and in the statutes which followed the first one was always upon the "refusal to labor" or "begging." The "criminalistic" aspect of such persons was relatively unimportant. Later, as we have shown, the criminalistic potential becomes of paramount importance. The thread runs back to the earliest statute but the reason for the statutes' existence as well as the focal concern of the statutes is quite different in 1743 than it was in 1349.

VAGRANCY LAWS IN THE UNITED STATES

In general, the vagrancy laws of England, as they stood in the middle eighteenth century, were simply adopted by the states. There were some exceptions to this general trend. For example, Maryland restricted the application of vagrancy laws to "free" Negroes. In addition, for *all* states the vagrancy laws were even more explicitly concerned with the control of criminals and undesirables than had been the case in England. New York, for example, explicitly defines prostitutes as being a category of vagrants during this period. These exceptions do not, however, change the general picture significantly and it is quite appropriate to consider the U.S. vagrancy laws as following from England's of the middle eighteenth century with relatively minor changes. The control of criminals and undesirables was the *raison d'être* of the vagrancy laws in the U.S. This is as true today as it was in 1750. As Caleb Foote's analysis of the application of vagrancy statutes in the Philadelphia court shows, these laws are presently applied indiscriminately to persons considered a "nuisance." Foote suggests that "...the chief significance of this branch of the criminal law lies in its quantitative impact and administration usefulness."[27] Thus it appears that in America the trend begun in England in the sixteenth, seventeenth and eighteenth centuries has been carried to its logical extreme and the laws are now used principally as a mechanism for "clearing the streets" of the derelicts who inhabit the "skid rows" and "Bowerys" of our large urban areas.

Since the 1800's there has been an abundant source of prospects to which the vagrancy laws have been applied. These have been primarily those persons deemed by the police and the courts to be either actively involved in criminal activities or at least peripherally involved. In this context, then, the statutes have changed very little. The functions served by the statutes in England of the late eighteenth century are still being served today in both England and the United States. The locale has changed somewhat and it appears that the present day application of vagrancy statutes is focused upon the arrest and confinement of the "down and outers" who inhabit certain sections of our larger cities but the impact has remained constant. The lack of change in the vagrancy statutes, then, can be seen as a reflection of the society's perception of a continuing need to control some of its "suspicious" or "undesirable" members.[28]

A word of caution is in order lest we leave the impression that this administrative purpose is the sole function of vagrancy laws in the U.S.

today. Although it is our contention that this is generally true it is worth remembering that during certain periods of our recent history, and to some extent today, these laws have also been used to control the movement of workers. This was particularly the case during the depression years and California is of course infamous for its use of vagrancy laws to restrict the admission of migrants from other states.[29] The vagrancy statutes, because of their history, still contain germs within them which make such effects possible. Their main purpose, however, is clearly no longer the control of laborers but rather the control of the undesirable, the criminal and the "nuisance."

DISCUSSION

The foregoing analysis of the vagrancy laws has demonstrated that these laws were a legislative innovation which reflected the socially perceived necessity of providing an abundance of cheap labor to landowners during a period when serfdom was breaking down and when the pool of available labor was depleted. With the eventual breakup of feudalism the need for such laws eventually disappeared and the increased dependence of the economy upon industry and commerce rendered the former use of the vagrancy statutes unnecessary. As a result, for a substantial period the vagrancy statutes were dormant, undergoing only minor changes and, presumably, being applied infrequently. Finally, the vagrancy laws were subjected to considerable alteration through a shift in the focal concern of the statutes. Whereas in their inception the laws focused upon the "idle" and "those refusing to labor" after the turn of the sixteenth century the emphasis came to be upon "rogues," "vagabonds," and others who were suspected of being engaged in criminal activities. During this period the focus was particularly upon "road men" who preyed upon citizens who transported goods from one place to another. The increased importance of commerce to England during this period made it necessary that some protection be given persons engaged in this enterprise and the vagrancy statutes provided one source for such protection by refocusing the acts to be included under the statutes.

Comparing the results of this analysis with the findings of Hall's study of theft we see a good deal of correspondence. Of major importance is the fact that both analyses demonstrate the truth of Hall's assertion that "The functioning of courts is significantly related to concomitant cultural needs, and this applies to the law of procedure as well as to substantive law."[30]

Our analysis of the vagrancy laws also indicates that when changed social conditions create a perceived need for legal changes, these alterations will be effected through the revision and refocusing of existing statutes. This process was demonstrated in Hall's analysis of theft as well as in our analysis of vagrancy. In the case of vagrancy the laws were dormant when the focal concern of the laws was shifted so as to provide control over potential criminals. In the case of theft the laws were re-interpreted (interestingly, by the courts and not by the legislature) so as to include persons who were transporting goods for a merchant but who absconded with the contents of the packages transported.

It also seems probable that when the social conditions change and previously useful laws are no longer useful there will be long periods when these laws will remain dormant. It is less likely that they will be officially negated. During this period of dormancy it is the judiciary which has principal responsibility for *not* applying the statutes. It is possible that one finds statutes being negated only when the judiciary stubbornly applies laws which do not have substantial public support. An example of such laws in contemporary times would be the "Blue Laws." Most states still have laws prohibiting the sale of retail goods on Sunday yet these laws are rarely applied. The laws are very likely to remain but to be dormant unless a recalcitrant judge or a vocal minority of the population insists that the laws be applied. When this happens we can anticipate that the statutes will be negated.[31] Should there arise a perceived need to curtail retail selling under some special circumstances, then it is likely that these laws will undergo a shift in focal concern much like the shift which characterized the vagrancy laws. Lacking such application the laws will simply remain dormant except for rare instances where they will be negated.

This analysis of the vagrancy statutes (and Hall's analysis of theft as well) has demonstrated the importance of "vested interest" groups in the emergence and/or alteration of laws. The vagrancy laws emerged in order to provide the powerful landowners with a ready supply of cheap labor. When this was no longer seen as necessary and particularly when the landowners were no longer dependent upon cheap labor nor were they a powerful interest group in the society the laws became dormant. Finally a new interest group emerged and was seen as being of great importance to the society and the laws were then altered so as to afford some protection to this group. These findings are thus in agreement with Weber's contention that "status groups" determine the content of the law.[32] The findings are inconsistent, on the other hand, with the perception of the law as simply a reflection of "public opinion" as is sometimes found in the literature.[33] We should be cautious in concluding, however, that either of these positions is necessarily correct. The careful analysis of other laws, and especially of laws which do not focus so specifically upon the "criminal," are necessary before this question can be finally answered.

In conclusion, it is hoped that future analyses of changes within the legal structure will be able to benefit from this study by virtue of (1) the data provided and (2) the utilization of a set of concepts (innovation, dormancy, concern and negation) which have proved useful in the analysis of the vagrancy law. Such analyses should provide us with more substantial grounds for rejecting or accepting as generally valid the description of some of the processes which appear to characterize changes in the legal system.

Notes

1. Hall, J., *Theft, Law and Society* (Bobbs-Merrill, 1939). See also, Alfred R. Lindesmith, "Federal Law and Drug Addiction," *Social Problems*, Vol. 7, No. 1, 1959, p. 48.

2. See, for examples, Rose, A., "Some Suggestions for Research in the Sociology of Law," *Social Problems*, Vol. 9, No. 3, 1962, pp. 281–283, and Geis, G., "Sociology, Criminology, and Criminal Law," *Social Problems*, Vol. 7, No. 1, 1959, pp. 40–47. For a more complete listing of most of the statutes dealt with in this report the reader is referred to Burn, *The History of the Poor Laws*. Citations of English statutes should be read as follows: 3 Ed. 1. c. 1. refers to the third act of Edward the first, chapter one, etc.

3. 3 Ed. 1. c. 1.

4. 35 Ed. 1. c. 1.

5. 23 Ed. 3.

6. 25 Ed. 3 (1351).

7. Bradshaw, F., *A Social History of England*, p. 54.

8. *Ibid.*

9. *Ibid.*, p. 57.

10. Foote, C., "Vagrancy Type Law and Its Administration," *Univ. of Pennsylvania Law Review* (104), 1056, p. 615.

11. *Ibid.*

12. 34 Ed. 3 (1360).

13. 12 R. 2 (1388).

14. *Ibid.*

15. 11 H. & C. 2 (1495).

16. As evidenced for this note the expectation that "...the common gaols of every shire are likely to be greatly pestered with more numbers of prisoners than heretofore..." when the statutes were changed by the statute of 14 Ed. c. 5 (1571).

17. Bradshaw, *op. cit.*, p. 61.

18. 22 H. 8. c. 12 (1530).

19. *Ibid.*

20. *Ibid.*

21. 27 H. 8. c. 25 (1535).

22. Hall, *op. cit.*, p. 21.

23. *Ibid.*, p. 23.

24. 27 H. 8. c. 25 (1535).

25. 14 E., c. 5. (1571).

26. Earl of Halsbury, *The Laws of England* (Butterworth & Co., Bell Yard, Temple Bar, 1912), pp. 606–607.

27. Foote, *op. cit.*, p. 613. Also see in this connection, Irwin Deutscher; "The Petty Offender," *Federal Probation*, XIX, June, 1955.

28. It is on this point that the vagrancy statutes have been subject to criticism. See for example, Lacey, Forrest W., "Vagrancy and Other Crimes of Personal Condition," *Harvard Law Review* (66), p. 1203.

29. *Edwards v. California*, 314 S. 160 (1941).

30. Hall, *op. cit.*, p. XII.

31. Negation, in this instance, is most likely to come about by the repeal of the statute. More generally, however, negation may occur in several ways including the declaration of a statute as unconstitutional. This later mechanism has been used even for laws which have been "on the books" for long periods of time. Repeal is probably the most common, although not the only, procedure by which a law is negated.

32. Rheinstein, M., *Max Weber on Law in Economy and Society* (Harvard University Press, 1954).

33. Friedman, N., *Law in a Changing Society* (Berkeley and Los Angeles: University of California Press, 1959).

15 / A Control Theory of Delinquency

TRAVIS HIRSCHI

Control theories assume that delinquent acts result when an individual's bond to society is weak or broken. Since these theories embrace two highly complex concepts, the *bond* of the individual to *society,* it is not surprising that they have at one time or another formed the basis of explanations of most forms of aberrant or unusual behavior. It is also not surprising that control theories have described the elements of the bond to society in many ways, and that they have focused on a variety of units as the point of control. . . .

ELEMENTS OF THE BOND

Attachment

In explaining conforming behavior, sociologists justly emphasize sensitivity to the opinion of others.[1] Unfortunately, . . . they tend to suggest that man *is* sensitive to the opinion of others and thus exclude sensitivity from their explanations of deviant behavior. In explaining deviant behavior, psychologists, in contrast, emphasize insensitivity to the opinion of others.[2] Unfortunately, they too tend to ignore variation, and, in addition, they tend to tie sensitivity inextricably to other variables, to make it part of a syndrome or "type," and thus seriously to reduce its value as an explanatory concept. The psychopath is characterized only in part by "deficient attachment to or affection for others, a failure to respond to the ordinary motivations founded in respect or regard for one's fellow";[3] he is also characterized by such things as "excessive aggressiveness," "lack of superego control," and "an infantile level of response."[4] Unfortunately, too, the behavior that psychopathy is used to explain often becomes part of the *definition* of psychopathy. As a result, in Barbara Wootton's words: "[The psychopath] is . . . *par excellence,* and without shame or qualification, the model of the circular process by which mental abnormality is inferred from anti-social behavior while anti-social behavior is explained by mental abnormality."[5]

The problems of diagnosis, tautology, and name-calling are avoided if the dimensions of psychopathy are treated as causally and therefore problematically interrelated, rather than as logically and therefore necessarily

172

bound to each other. In fact, it can be argued that all of the characteristics attributed to the psychopath follow from, are effects of, his lack of attachment to others. To say that to lack attachment to others is to be free from moral restraints is to use lack of attachment to explain the guiltlessness of the psychopath, the fact that he apparently has no conscience or superego. In this view, lack of attachment to others is not merely a symptom of psychopathy, it *is* psychopathy; lack of conscience is just another way of saying the same thing; and the violation of norms is (or may be) a consequence.

For that matter, given that man is an animal, "impulsivity" and "aggressiveness" can also be seen as natural consequences of freedom from moral restraints. However, since the view of man as endowed with natural propensities and capacities like other animals is peculiarly unpalatable to sociologists, we need not fall back on such a view to explain the amoral man's aggressiveness.[6] The process of becoming alienated from others often involves or is based on active interpersonal conflict. Such conflict could easily supply a reservoir of *socially derived* hostility sufficient to account for the aggressiveness of those whose attachments to others have been weakened.

Durkheim said it many years ago: "We are moral beings to the extent that we are social beings."[7] This may be interpreted to mean that we are moral beings to the extent that we have "internalized the norms" of society. But what does it mean to say that a person has internalized the norms of society? The norms of society are by definition shared by the members of society. To violate a norm is, therefore, to act contrary to the wishes and expectations of other people. If a person does not care about the wishes and expectations of other people—that is, if he is insensitive to the opinion of others—then he is to that extent not bound by the norms. He is free to deviate.

The essence of internalization of norms, conscience, or superego thus lies in the attachment of the individual to others.[8] This view has several advantages over the concept of internalization. For one, explanations of deviant behavior based on attachment do not beg the question, since the extent to which a person is attached to others can be measured independently of his deviant behavior. Furthermore, change or variation in behavior is explainable in a way that it is not when notions of internalization or superego are used. For example, the divorced man is more likely after divorce to commit a number of deviant acts, such as suicide or forgery. If we explain these acts by reference to the superego (or internal control), we are forced to say that the man "lost his conscience" when he got a divorce; and, of course, if he remarries, we have to conclude that he gets his conscience back.

This dimension of the bond to conventional society is encountered in most social control-oriented research and theory. F. Ivan Nye's "internal control" and "indirect control" refer to the same element, although we avoid the problem of explaining changes over time by locating the "conscience" in the bond to others rather than making it part of the personality.[9] Attachment to others is just one aspect of Albert J. Reiss's "personal controls"; we avoid his problems of tautological empirical *observations* by making the relationship between attachment and delinquency problematic rather than definitional.[10] Finally, Scott Briar and Irving Piliavin's "commitment" or "stake in conformity" subsumes attachment, as their discussion illustrates, although the terms they use are more closely associated with the next element to be discussed.[11]

Commitment

"Of all passions, that which inclineth men least to break the laws, is fear. Nay, excepting some generous natures, it is the only thing, when there is the appearance of profit or pleasure by breaking the laws, that makes men keep them."[12] Few would deny that men on occasion obey the rules simply from fear of the consequences. This rational component in conformity we label commitment. What does it mean to say that a person is committed to conformity? In Howard S. Becker's formulation it means the following:

> First, the individual is in a position in which his decision with regard to some particular line of action has consequences for other interests and activities not necessarily [directly] related to it. Second, he has placed himself in that position by his own prior actions. A third element is present though so obvious as not to be apparent; the committed person must be aware [of these other interests] and must recognize that his decision in this case will have ramifications beyond it.[13]

The idea, then, is that the person invests time, energy, himself, in a certain line of activity—say, getting an education, building up a business, acquiring a reputation for virtue. When or whenever he considers deviant behavior, he must consider the costs of this deviant behavior, the risk he runs of losing the investment he has made in conventional behavior.

If attachment to others is the sociological counterpart of the superego or conscience, commitment is the counterpart of the ego or common sense. To the person committed to conventional lines of action, risking one to ten years in prison for a ten-dollar holdup is stupidity, because to the committed person the costs and risks obviously exceed ten dollars in value. (To the psychoanalyst, such an act exhibits failure to be governed by the "reality-principle.") In the sociological control theory, it can be and is generally assumed that the decision to commit a criminal act may well be rationally determined—that the actor's decision was not irrational given the risks and costs he faces. Of course, as Becker points out, if the actor is capable of in some sense calculating the costs of a line of action, he is also capable of calculational errors: ignorance and error return, in the control theory, as possible explanations of deviant behavior.

The concept of commitment assumes that the organization of society is such that the interest of most persons would be endangered if they were to engage in criminal acts. Most people, simply by the process of living in an organized society, acquire goods, reputations, prospects that they do not want to risk losing. These accumulations are society's insurance that they will abide by the rules. Many hypotheses about the antecedents of delinquent behavior are based on this premise. For example, Arthur L. Stinchcombe's hypothesis that "high school rebellion...occurs when future status is not clearly related to present performance"[14] suggests that one is committed to conformity not only by what one has but also by what one hoped to obtain. Thus "ambition" and/or "aspiration" play an important role in producing conformity. The person becomes committed to a conventional line of action, and he is therefore committed to conformity.

Most lines of action in a society are of course conventional. The clearest examples are educational and occupational careers. Actions thought to jeopardize one's chances in these areas are presumably avoided. Interestingly enough, even nonconventional commitments may operate to produce conventional conformity. We are told, at least, that boys aspiring to careers in the rackets or professional thievery are judged by their "honesty" and "reliability"—traits traditionally in demand among seekers of office boys.[15]

Involvement

Many persons undoubtedly owe a life of virtue to a lack of opportunity to do otherwise. Time and energy are inherently limited: "Not that I would not, if I could, be both handsome and fat and well dressed, and a great athlete, and make a million a year, be a wit, a bon vivant, and a lady killer, as well as a philosopher, a philanthropist, a statesman, warrior, and African explorer, as well as a 'tone-poet' and saint. But the thing is simply impossible."[16] The things that William James here says he would like to be or do are all, I suppose, within the realm of conventionality, but if he were to include illicit actions he would still have to eliminate some of them as simply impossible.

Involvement or engrossment in conventional activities is thus often part of a control theory. The assumption, widely shared, is that a person may be simply too busy doing conventional things to find time to engage in deviant behavior. The person involved in conventional activities is tied to appointments, deadlines, working hours, plans, and the like, so the opportunity to commit deviant acts rarely arises. To the extent that he is engrossed in conventional activities, he cannot even think about deviant acts, let alone act out his inclinations.[17]

This line of reasoning is responsible for the stress placed on recreational facilities in many programs to reduce delinquency, for much of the concern with the high school dropout, and for the idea that boys should be drafted into the army to keep them out of trouble. So obvious and persuasive is the idea that involvement in conventional activities is a major deterrent to delinquency that it was accepted even by Sutherland: "In the general area of juvenile delinquency it is probable that the most significant difference between juveniles who engage in delinquency and those who do not is that the latter are provided abundant opportunities of a conventional type for satisfying their recreational interests, while the former lack those opportunities or facilities."[18]

The view that "idle hands are the devil's workshop" has received more sophisticated treatment in recent sociological writings on delinquency. David Matza and Gresham M. Sykes, for example, suggest that delinquents have the values of a leisure class, the same values ascribed by Veblen to *the* leisure class: a search for kicks, disdain of work, a desire for the big score, and acceptance of aggressive toughness as proof of masculinity.[19] Matza and Sykes explain delinquency by reference to this system of values, but they note that adolescents at all class levels are "to some extent" members of a leisure class, that they "move in a limbo between earlier parental domination and future integration with the social structure through the bonds of work and marriage."[20] In the end, then, the leisure of the adolescent produces a set of values, which, in turn, leads to delinquency.

Belief

Unlike the cultural deviance theory, the control theory assumes the existence of a common value system within the society or group whose norms are being violated. If the deviant is committed to a value system different from that of conventional society, there is, within the context of the theory, nothing to explain. The question is, "Why does a man violate the rules in which he believes?" It is not, "Why do men differ in their beliefs about what constitutes good and desirable conduct?" The person is assumed to have been socialized (perhaps imperfectly) into the group whose rules he is violating; deviance is not a question of one group imposing its rules on the members of another group. In other words, we not only assume the deviant *has* believed the rules, we assume he believes the rules even as he violates them.

How can a person believe it is wrong to steal at the same time he is stealing? In the strain theory, this is not a difficult problem. (In fact, ... the strain theory was devised specifically to deal with this question.) The motivation to deviance adduced by the strain theorist is so strong that we can well understand the deviant act even assuming the deviator believes strongly that it is wrong.[21] However, given the control theory's assumptions about motivation, if both the deviant and the nondeviant believe the deviant act is wrong, how do we account for the fact that one commits it and the other does not?

Control theories have taken two approaches to this problem. In one approach, beliefs are treated as mere words that mean little or nothing if the other forms of control are missing. "Semantic dementia," the dissociation between rational faculties and emotional control which is said to be characteristic of the psychopath, illustrates this way of handling the problem.[22] In short, beliefs, at least insofar as they are expressed in words, drop out of the picture; since they do not differentiate between deviants and nondeviants, they are in the same class as "language" or any other characteristic common to all members of the group. Since they represent no real obstacle to the commission of delinquent acts, nothing need be said about how they are handled by those committing such acts. The control theories that do not mention beliefs (or values), and many do not, may be assumed to take this approach to the problem.

The second approach argues that the deviant rationalizes his behavior so that he can at once violate the rule and maintain his belief in it. Donald R. Cressey had advanced this argument with respect to embezzlement,[23] and Sykes and Matza have advanced it with respect to delinquency.[24] In both Cressey's and Sykes and Matza's treatments, these rationalizations (Cressey calls them "verbalizations," Sykes and Matza term them "techniques of neutralization") occur prior to the commission of the deviant act. If the neutralization is successful, the person is free to commit the act(s) in question. Both in Cressey and in Sykes and Matza, the strain that prompts the effort at neutralization also provides the motive force that results in the subsequent deviant act. Their theories are thus, in this sense, strain theories. Neutralization is difficult to handle within the context of a theory that adheres closely to control theory assumptions, because in the control theory there is no special motivational force to account for the neutralization. This difficulty is especially noticeable in Matza's later treatment of this topic, where the motivational component, the "will to delinquency," appears *after* the moral vacuum has been created by the techniques of neutralization.[25] The question thus becomes: Why neutralize?

In attempting to solve a strain-theory problem with control-theory tools, the control theorist is thus led into a trap. He cannot answer the crucial question. The concept of neutralization assumes the existence of moral obstacles to the commission of deviant acts. In order plausibly to account for a deviant act, it is necessary to generate motivation to deviance that is at least equivalent in force to the resistance provided by these moral obstacles. However, if the moral obstacles are removed, neutralization and special motivation are no longer required. We therefore follow the implicit logic of control theory and remove these moral obstacles by hypothesis. Many persons do not have an attitude of respect toward the rules of society; many persons feel no moral obligation to conform regardless of personal advantage. Insofar as the values and beliefs of these persons are consistent with their feelings, and there should be a tendency toward consistency, neutralization is unnecessary; it has already occurred.

Does this merely push the question back a step and at the same time produce conflict with the assumption of a common value system? I think not. In the first place, we do not assume, as does Cressey, that neutralization occurs in order to make a specific criminal act possible.[26] We do not assume, as do Sykes and Matza, that neutralization occurs to make many delinquent acts possible. We do not assume, in other words, that the person constructs a system of rationalizations in order to justify commission of acts he *wants* to commit. We assume, in contrast, that the beliefs that free a man to commit deviant acts are *unmotivated* in the sense that he does not construct or adopt them in order to facilitate the attainment of illicit ends. In the second place, we do not assume, as does Matza, that "delinquents concur in the conventional assessment of delinquency."[27] We assume, in contrast, that there is *variation* in the extent to which people believe they should obey the rules of society, and, furthermore, that the less a person believes he should obey the rules, the more likely he is to violate them.[28]

In chronological order, then, a person's beliefs in the moral validity of norms are, for no teleological reason, weakened. The probability that he will commit delinquent acts is therefore increased. When and if he commits a delinquent act, we may justifiably use the weakness of his beliefs in explaining it, but no special motivation is required to explain either the weakness of his beliefs or, perhaps, his delinquent act.

The keystone of this argument is of course the assumption that there is variation in belief in the moral validity of social rules. This assumption is amenable to direct empirical test and can thus survive at least until its first confrontation with data. For the present, we must return to the idea of a common value system with which this section was begun.

The idea of a common (or perhaps better, a single) value system is consistent with the fact, or presumption, of variation in the strength of moral beliefs. We have not suggested that delinquency is based on beliefs counter to conventional morality; we have not suggested that delinquents do not believe delinquent acts are wrong. They may well believe these acts are wrong, but the meaning and efficacy of such beliefs are contingent on other beliefs and, indeed, on the strength of other ties to the conventional order.[29]

Notes

1. Books have been written on the increasing importance of interpersonal sensitivity in modern life. According to this view, controls from within have become less important than controls from without in *producing* conformity. Whether or not this observation is true as a description of historical trends, it is true that interpersonal sensitivity has become more important in *explaining* conformity. Although logically it should also have become more important in explaining nonconformity, the opposite has been the case, once again showing that Cohen's observation that an explanation of conformity should be an explanation of deviance cannot be translated as "an explanation of conformity has to be an explanation of deviance." For the view that interpersonal sensitivity currently plays a greater role than formerly in producing conformity, see William J. Goode, "Norm Commitment and Conformity to Role-Status Obligations," *American Journal of Sociology*, LXVI (1960), 246–258. And, of course, also see David Riesman, Nathan Glazer, and Rouel Denney, *The Lonely Crowd* (Garden City, New York: Doubleday, 1950), especially Part I.

2. The literature on psychopathy is voluminous. See William McCord and Joan McCord, *The Psychopath* (Princeton: D. Van Nostrand, 1964).

3. John M. Martin and Joseph P. Fitzpatrick, *Delinquent Behavior* (New York: Random House, 1964), p. 130.

4. *Ibid.* For additional properties of the psychopath, see McCord and McCord, *The Psychopath,* pp. 1–22.

5. Barbara Wootton, *Social Science and Social Pathology* (New York: Macmillan, 1959), p. 250.

6. "The logical untenability [of the position that there are forces in man 'resistant to socialization'] was ably demonstrated by Parsons over 30 years ago, and it is widely recognized that the position is empirically unsound because it assumes [!] some universal biological drive system distinctly separate from socialization and social context—a basic and intransigent human nature" (Judith Blake and Kingsley Davis, "Norms, Values, and Sanctions," *Handbook of Modern Sociology,* ed. Robert E. L. Faris [Chicago: Rand McNally, 1964], p. 471).

7. Emile Durkheim, *Moral Education,* trans. Everett K. Wilson and Herman Schnurer (New York: The Free Press, 1961), p. 64.

8. Although attachment alone does not exhaust the meaning of internalization, attachments and beliefs combined would appear to leave only a small residue of "internal control" not susceptible in principle to direct measurement.

9. F. Ivan Nye, *Family Relationships and Delinquent Behavior* (New York: Wiley, 1958), pp. 5–7.

10. Albert J. Reiss, Jr., "Delinquency as the Failure of Personal and Social Controls," *American Sociological Review,* XVI (1951), 196–207. For example, "Our observations show...that delinquent recidivists are less often persons with mature ego ideals or non-delinquent social roles" (p. 204).

11. Scott Briar and Irving Piliavin, "Delinquency, Situational Inducements, and Commitment to Conformity," *Social Problems,* XIII (1965), 41–42. The concept "stake in conformity" was introduced by Jackson Toby in his "Social Disorganization and Stake in Conformity: Complementary Factors in the Predatory Behavior of Hoodlums," *Journal of Criminal Law, Criminology and Police Science,* XLVIII (1957), 12–17. See also his "Hoodlum or Business Man: An American Dilemma," *The Jews,* ed. Marshall Sklare (New York: The Free Press, 1958), pp. 542–550. Throughout the text, I occasionally use "stake in conformity" in speaking in general of the strength of the bond to conventional society. So used, the concept is somewhat broader than is true for either Toby or Briar and Piliavin, where the concept is roughly equivalent to what is here called "commitment."

12. Thomas Hobbes, *Leviathan* (Oxford: Basil Blackwell, 1957), p. 195.

13. Howard S. Becker, "Notes on the Concept of Commitment," *American Journal of Sociology,* LXVI (1960), 35–36.

14. Arthur L. Stinchcombe, *Rebellion in a High School* (Chicago: Quadrangle, 1964), p. 5.

15. Richard A. Cloward and Lloyd E. Ohlin, *Delinquency and Opportunity* (New York: The Free Press, 1960), p. 147, quoting Edwin H. Sutherland, ed., *The Professional Thief* (Chicago: University of Chicago Press, 1937), pp. 211–213.

16. William James, *Psychology* (Cleveland: World Publishing Co., 1948), p. 186.

17. Few activities appear to be so engrossing that they rule out contemplation of alternative lines of behavior, at least if estimates of the amount of time men spend plotting sexual deviations have any validity.

18. *The Sutherland Papers,* ed. Albert K. Cohen et al. (Bloomington: Indiana University Press, 1956), p. 37.

19. David Matza and Gresham M. Sykes, "Juvenile Delinquency and Subterranean Values," *American Sociological Review,* XXVI (1961), 712–719.

20. *Ibid.,* p.718.

21. The starving man stealing the loaf of bread is the image evoked by most strain theories. In this image, the starving man's belief in the wrongness of his act is clearly not something that must be explained away. It can be assumed to be present without causing embarrassment to the explanation.

22. McCord and McCord, *The Psychopath,* pp. 12–15.

23. Donald R. Cressey, *Other People's Money* (New York: The Free Press, 1953).

24. Gresham M. Sykes and David Matza, "Techniques of Neutralization: A Theory of Delinquency," *American Sociological Review,* XXII (1957), 664–670.

25. David Matza, *Delinquency and Drift* (New York: Wiley, 1964), pp. 181–191.

26. In asserting that Cressey's assumption is invalid with respect to delinquency, I do not wish to suggest that it is invalid for the question of embezzlement, where the problem faced by the deviator is fairly specific and he can reasonably be assumed to be an upstanding citizen. (Although even here the fact that the embezzler's nonsharable financial problem often results

from some sort of hanky-panky suggests that "verbalizations" may be less necessary than might otherwise be assumed.)

27. *Delinquency and Drift*, p. 43.

28. This assumption is not, I think, contradicted by the evidence presented by Matza against the existence of a delinquent subculture. In comparing the attitudes and actions of delinquents with the picture painted by delinquent subculture theorists, Matza emphasizes—and perhaps exaggerates—the extent to which delinquents are tied to the conventional order. In implicitly comparing delinquents with a supermoral man, I emphasize—and perhaps exaggerate—the extent to which they are not tied to the conventional order.

29. The position taken here is therefore somewhere between the "semantic dementia" and the "neutralization" positions. Assuming variation, the delinquent is, at the extremes, freer than the neutralization argument assumes. Although the possibility of wide discrepancy between what the delinquent professes and what he practices still exists, it is presumably much rarer than is suggested by studies of articulate "psychopaths."

16 / The Socially Bounded Decision Making of Persistent Property Offenders

NEAL SHOVER
DAVID HONAKER

The 1970s were marked by the eclipse of labeling theory as the dominant individual-level criminological theory and by the reappearance of interest in approaches originally advanced by classical theorists. Economists and cognitive psychologists along with many in the criminological mainstream advanced an interpretation of crime as *choice,* offering models of criminal decision making grounded in the assumption that the decision to commit a criminal act springs from the offender's assessment of its anticipated net utilities (e.g., Becker 1968; Heineke 1978; Carroll 1978; Reynolds 1985). This movement in favor of rational-choice approaches to crime spurred empirical investigation of problems that previously were limited primarily to studies of the death penalty and its impact on the homicide rate.

Early investigations of a rational choice interpretation of crime reported a weak but persistent relationship between the certainty of punishment and rates of serious property crimes (Blumstein, Cohen, and Nagin 1978). It was recognized, however, that an understanding of criminal decision making also requires knowledge about individual perceptions and beliefs about legal threats and other constraints on decision making (e.g., Manski 1978). Investigators moved on two main fronts to meet this need. Some used survey methods to explore differential involvement in minor forms of deviance in samples of restricted age ranges, typically high school and college students (e.g., Waldo and Chiricos 1972). Alternatively they examined the link between risk assessments and criminal participation in samples more representative of the general population (e.g., Tittle 1980). Serious shortcomings of these studies are that most either ignore the potential rewards of crime entirely or they fail to examine its emotional and interpersonal utilities. Still other investigators turned attention to serious criminal offenders and began expanding the narrow existing knowledge base (e.g., Claster 1967), chiefly through the use of cross sectional research designs and survey methods.

For more than a decade now, investigators have studied offenders' attitudes toward legitimate and criminal pursuits, their perceptions of and beliefs about the risks of criminal behavior, and their estimates of the payoffs from conventional and criminal pursuits (e.g., Petersilia et al. 1978; Peterson & Braiker 1980). These studies raise serious questions about the fit between offenders' calculus and a priori assumptions about their utilities and criminal decision making. One investigation of 589 incarcerated property offenders concluded, for example, that the subjects apparently do not utilize "a sensible cost-benefit analysis" when weighing the utilities of crime (Figgie 1988, p. 25). They substantially underestimate the risk of arrest for most crimes, routinely overestimate the monetary benefit they expect, and seem to have "grossly inaccurate perceptions of the costs and benefits associated with property crime" (Figgie 1988, p. 81). Unfortunately, both design and conceptual problems undermine confidence in the findings of this and similar studies. Cross sectional survey methods, for example, are poorly suited for examining dynamic decision-making *processes*. Most such studies also fail to examine offenders' estimates of the likely payoffs from noncriminal alternatives or their non-monetary utilities, such as emotional satisfaction (Katz 1988).

As newer, empirically-based models of criminal decision making have been developed (e.g., Clarke and Cornish 1985; Cornish and Clarke 1986), a growing number of investigators are using ethnographic methods to examine the offender's criminal calculus, often in real or simulated natural settings (e.g., Carrol 1982; Carrol and Weaver 1986). The research reported here continues this line of ethnographic inquiry by using retrospective interviews to examine criminal decision making by serious and persistent property offenders. The focus of our attention is the decision to commit a crime rather than the target-selection decision that has received substantial attention elsewhere (e.g., Scar 1973; Repetto 1974; Maguire 1982; Bennett and Wright 1984a; Rengert and Wasilchick 1985; Cromwell, Olson, and Avary 1991). The first objective is to examine how closely the decision to commit crime conforms to a classical rational choice model in which decisions assumedly are based largely on an assessment of potential returns from alternative courses of action and the risk of legal sanctions. A second objective is to examine the influence of the lifestyle pursued by many persistent property offenders on the salience of their utilities and the risks they assess in criminal decision making.

METHODS AND MATERIALS

The materials for analysis were collected during 1987–1988 as part of a larger study of crime desistance. From the population of all men incarcerated in Tennessee state prisons during 1987 we selected a sample of recidivists with a demonstrated preference for property crimes who were also nearing release from confinement. To select the sample, members of the research team first examined Tennessee Board of Paroles records to identify offenders incarcerated in Tennessee state prisons whose parole was imminent. We then used Department of Corrections records to cull the list of all but those (1) with at least one prior felony confinement, and (2) whose previous or current confinement was for serious property crime. Next the researchers visited prisons, primarily those located in the mid- and eastern areas of the state, and explained the study to and requested research participation from potential subjects. After meeting individually with approximately 75 inmates we reached our sample size objective of 60 subjects. Fifty-eight members of the sample had served at least one prior prison sentence and the remaining two had served one or more jail sentences. They had served time primarily for armed robbery, burglary, or theft. By limiting the sample as outlined we sought to approximate a population of career criminals, a type of offender that has received substantial attention from scholars and policy makers (Petersilia 1980; Blumstein et al. 1988). Subjects ranged from 23 to 70 years of age, with an average age of 34.1 years. In addition to the sample's adult criminal and incarceration profile, 47 percent (n = 28) of the men had also served one or more terms of juvenile confinement. Every member of the sample was interviewed approximately one month prior to release from prison. All data used in the present study, however, were collected in post-release interviews with the men.

Seven to 10 months after their release from prison we successfully traced, contacted, and interviewed 46 of the original sample of 60 men (76.7 percent). (In addition, we established contact with one subject who declined our request for an interview, and with close relatives of another who failed to respond to repeated requests that he contact us.) Semi-structured ethnographic interviews were the principal data-collection technique. The interview included questions about the former prisoners' activities and living arrangements following release, self-report items measuring postrelease criminal participation, and questions about the context of reinvolvement in crime. They were paid $100 for completing the interviews, all of which were audiotape recorded and transcribed for subsequent analysis. Fourteen subjects were in jail or prison again when interviewed, but most were interviewed in their former or newly established home communities.

Part of the interviews produced detailed descriptions of the most recent, easily recalled property crime that each subject had committed in the free world prior to the interview. They described either crimes they had committed prior to incarceration or, for those subjects who were locked up when interviewed, their return to jail or prison. Our objective was to gain through the repeat offender's eyes an understanding of the decision to commit specific criminal acts. We asked our subjects to focus their recollection on how the decision was made, and to provide a detailed account of the potential risks and rewards they assessed while doing so. The result was 40 usable descriptions of crimes and attempted crimes, which included 15 burglaries, 12 armed robberies, 5 grand larcenies, 4 unarmed robberies, 2 auto thefts, 1 series of check forgeries, and 1 case of receiving and concealing stolen property. Transcripts of the interviews were analyzed using *The Ethnograph,* a software package for use on text-based data (Seidel, Kjolseth, and Seymour 1988). Use of this software enabled us to code and to retrieve for analysis segments of interview text.

FINDINGS

Analysis reveals the most striking aspect of the subjects' decision making for the crimes they described is that a majority gave little or no thought to the possibility of arrest and confinement. Of 34 subjects who were asked specifically whether they considered the risk of arrest or who spontaneously indicated whether they did so, 21 (62 percent) said they did not. The comments of two subjects are typical:

Q: Did you think about . . . getting caught?
A: No.
Q: [H]ow did you manage to put that out of your mind?
A: [It] never did come into it.
Q: Never did come into it?
A: Never did, you know. It didn't bother me.

Q: Were you thinking about bad things that might happen to you?
A: None whatsoever.
Q: No?
A: I wasn't worried about getting caught or anything, you know. I was a positive thinker through everything, you know. I didn't have no negative thoughts about it whatsoever.

The 13 remaining subjects (38%) acknowledged they gave some thought to the possibility of arrest but most said they managed to dismiss it easily and to carry through with their plans:

Q: Did you worry much about getting caught? On a scale of one to ten, how would you rank your degree of worry that day?
A: [T]he worry was probably a one. You know what I mean? The worry was probably one. I didn't think about the consequences, you know. I know it's stupidity, but it didn't—that [I] might go to jail, I mean—it crossed my mind but it didn't make much difference.

Q: As you thought about doing that [armed robbery], were there things that you were worried about?
A: Well, the only thing that I was worried about was—. . . getting arrested didn't even cross my mind—just worrying about getting killed is the only thing, you know, getting shot. That's the only thing. . . . But, you know, . . . you'd have to be really crazy not to think about that . . . you could possibly get in trouble. It crossed my mind, but I didn't worry about it all that much.

Some members of our sample said they managed deliberately and consciously to put out of mind all thoughts of possible arrest:

When I went out to steal, I didn't think about the negative things. 'Cause if you think negative, negative things are going to happen. And that's the way I looked at it.... I done it just like it was a job or something. Go out and do it, don't think about getting caught, 'cause that would make you jumpy, edgy, nervous. If you looked like you were doing something wrong, then something wrong is gonna happen to you.... You just, you just put [the thought of arrest] out of your mind, you know.

Q: Did you think about [the possibility of getting caught] very much that night?
A: I didn't think about it that much, you know.... [I]t comes but, you know, you can wipe it away.
Q: How do you wipe it away?
A: You just blank it out. You blank it out.

Another subject said simply that "I try to put that [thought of arrest] the farthest thing from my mind that I can."

Many subjects attribute their ability to ignore or to dismiss all thought of possible arrest to a state of intoxication or drug-altered consciousness:

Q: You didn't think about going to prison?
A: Never did. I guess it was all that alcohol and stuff, and drugs.... The day I pulled that robbery?—no. I was so high I didn't think about nothing.

Another subject told us that he had been drinking the entire day that he committed the crime and, by the time it occurred, he was in "nightlight city."

While it is clear that the formal risks of crime were not considered carefully by most members of the sample, equally striking is the finding that very few thought about or assessed legitimate alternatives before opting to commit a criminal act. Of 22 subjects who were asked specifically whether they had done so, 16 indicated that they gave no thought whatsoever to legitimate alternatives. The six subjects who did either ignored or quickly dismissed them as inapplicable, given their immediate circumstances.

We recognize the methodological shortcomings of the descriptions of criminal decision making and behavior used as data for this study. Since the subjects were questioned in detail only about specific offenses they could remember well, the sample of descriptions may not be representative of the range of crimes they committed. By definition, they are memorable ones. Moreover, the recall period for these crimes ranged from one to 15 years, raising the possibility of errors caused by selective recall. Whether or not this could have produced systematic bias in the data is unknown. We cannot rule out the possibility that past crimes are remembered as being less rational than they actually were at the time of commission. Such a tendency could account in part for our interpretation of the data and our description of their style of decision making. The fact that we limited the sample to recidivists means also that we cannot determine how much their behavior may reflect either innate differences (Gottfredson and Hirschi 1990) or experiential effects, i.e., the effects of past success in committing crime and avoiding arrest (Nagin and Paternoster 1991). It could be argued that the behavior of our subjects, precisely because they had demonstrated a willingness to commit property crimes and had done so in the past, limits the external validity of their reports. Given sample selection criteria and these potential data problems, generalizations beyond the study population must be made with caution.

This said, we believe that the remarkable similarity between our findings and the picture of criminal decision making reported by others who have studied serious property offenders strengthens their credibility significantly. A study of 83 imprisoned burglars revealed that 49 percent did not think about the chances of getting caught for any particular offense during their last period of offending. While 37 percent of them did think about it, most thought there was little or no chance it would happen (Bennett and Wright 1984a, Table A14). Interviews with 113 men convicted of robbery or an offense related to robbery revealed that "over 60 percent... said they had not even thought about getting caught." Another 17 percent said that they had thought about the possibility but "did not believe it to be a problem" (Feeney 1986, p. 59–60). Analysis of prison interviews with 77 robbers and 45 burglars likewise revealed their "general obliviousness toward the consequences [of their crimes] and no thought of being caught" (Walsh 1986, p. 157). In sum, our findings along with the findings from other studies suggest strongly that many serious property offenders seem to be remarkably casual in weighing the formal risks of criminal participation. As one of our subjects put it, "you think about going to prison about like you think about dying, you know." The impact of alcohol and drug use in diminishing concern with possible penalties also has been reported by many others (e.g., Bennett and Wright 1984b; Cromwell, Olson, and Avary 1991).

If the potential legal consequences of crime do not figure prominently in crime commission decision making by persistent thieves, what *do* they think about when choosing to commit crime? Walsh (1980; 1986) shows that typically they focus their thoughts on the money that committing a crime may yield and the good times they expect to have with it when the crime is behind them. Carroll's data (1982) likewise indicate that the amount of gain offenders expect to receive is "the most important dimension" in their decision making, while the certainty of punishment is the least important of the four dimensions on which his subjects assessed crime opportunities. Our findings are consistent with these reports; our subjects said that they focused on the expected gains from their crimes:

> I didn't think about nothing but what I was going to do when I got that money, how I was going to spend it, what I was going to do with it, you know.

> See, you're not thinking about those things [possibility of being arrested]. You're thinking about that big paycheck at the end of thirty to forty-five minutes worth of work.

[A]t the time [that you commit crime], you throw all your instincts out the window.... Because you're just thinking about money, and money only. That's all that's on your mind, because you want that money. And you throw, you block everything off until you get the money.

Although confidence in our findings is bolstered by the number of points on which they are similar to reports by others who have explored crime commission decision making, they do paint a picture of decision making that is different from what is known about the way at least some offenders make target selection decisions. Investigators (e.g., Cromwell, Olson, and Avary 1991) have shown that target decisions approximate simple commonsense conceptions of rational behavior (Shover 1991). A resolution of the problem presented by these contradictory findings is suggested by others (Cromwell, Olson, and Avary 1991) and is also apparent in our data: Criminal participation often results from a *sequence* of experientially and analytically discrete decisions, all of potentially varying degrees of intentional rationality. Thus, once a *motivational* crime commission decision has been made, offenders may move quickly to selecting, or to exploiting, an apparently suitable target. At this stage of the criminal participation process, offenders are preoccupied with the *technical* challenge of avoiding failure at what now is seen as a *practical task*. As one subject put it, "you don't think about getting caught, you think about how in hell you're going to do it *not* to get caught, you know." His comments were echoed by another man: "The only thing you're thinking about is looking and acting and trying *not* to get caught." Last, consider the comments of a third subject: "I wasn't afraid of getting caught, but I was cautious, you know. Like I said, I was thinking only in the way to prevent me from getting caught." Just as bricklayers do not visualize graphically or deliberate over the bodily carnage that could follow from a collapsed scaffold *once there is a job to be done,* many thieves apparently do not dwell at length on the likelihood of arrest or on the pains of imprisonment when proceeding to search out or exploit suitable criminal opportunities.

The accumulated evidence on crime commission decision making by persistent offenders is substantial and persuasive: the rationality they employ is limited or bounded severely (e.g., Carroll 1982; Cromwell, Olson, and Avary 1991). While unsuccessful persistent offenders may calculate potential benefits and costs before committing criminal acts, they apparently do so differently or weigh utilities differently than as sketched in a priori decision-making models. As Walsh (1980, p. 141) suggests, offenders' "definitions of costs and rewards seem to be at variance with society's estimates of them." This does not mean their decision making is *irrational,* but it does point to the difficulties of understanding it and then refining theoretical models of the process. Our objective in the remainder of this paper is an improved understanding of criminal decision making based on analysis of the socially anchored purposes, utilities, and risks of the acts that offenders commit. Put differently, we explore the contextual origins of their bounded rationality.

LIFESTYLE, UTILITIES, AND RISK

It is instructive to examine the decision making of persistent property offenders in context of the lifestyle that is characteristic of many in their ranks: *life as party*. The hallmark of life as party is the enjoyment of "good times" with minimal concern for the obligations and commitments that are external to the person's immediate social setting. It is a lifestyle distinguished in many cases by two repetitively cyclical phases and correspondingly distinctive approaches to crime. When offenders' efforts to maintain the lifestyle (i.e., their party pursuits) are largely successful, crimes are committed in order to sustain circumstances or a pattern of activities they experience as pleasurable. As Walsh (1986, p. 15) puts it, crimes committed under these circumstances are "part of a continuing satisfactory way of life." By contrast, when offenders are less successful at party pursuits, their crimes are committed in order to avoid circumstances experienced as threatening, unpleasant, or precarious. Corresponding to each of these two phases of party pursuits is a distinctive set of utilities and stance toward legal risk.

Life as Party

Survey and ethnographic studies alike show that persistent property offenders spend much of their criminal gains on alcohol and other drugs (Petersilia et al. 1978; Maguire 1982; Gibbs and Shelley 1982; Figgie 1988; Cromwell, Olson, and Avary 1991). The proceeds of their crimes, as Walsh has noted (1986, p. 72), "typically [are] used for personal, non-essential consumption (e.g., 'nights out'), rather than, for example, to be given to family or used for basic needs." Thieves spend much of their leisure hours enjoying good times. Our subjects were no different in this regard. For example,

> I smoked an ounce of pot in a day, a day and a half. Every other day I had to go buy a bag of pot, at the least. And sometimes I've went two or three days in a row.... And there was never a day went by that I didn't [drink] a case, case and a half of beer. And [I] did a 'script of pills every two days.

While much of their money is consumed by the high cost of drugs, a portion may be used for ostentatious enjoyment and display of luxury items and activities that probably would be unattainable on the returns from blue-collar employment:

> [I]t was all just, it was all just a big money thing to me at the time, you know. Really, what it was was impressing everybody, you know. "Here Floyd is, and he's never had nothing in his life, and now look at him: he's driving new cars, and wearing jewelry," you know.

Life as party is enjoyed in the company of others. Typically it includes shared consumption of alcohol or other drugs in bars and lounges, on street corners, or while cruising in automobiles. In these venues, party pursuers celebrate and affirm values of spontaneity, autonomy, independence, and resourcefulness. Spontaneity means that rationality and long-range planning are eschewed in favor of enjoying the moment and permitting the day's activities and pleasures to develop in an unconstrained fashion. This may mean, for example, getting up late, usually after a night of partying, and then setting out to contact and enjoy the company of friends and associates who are known to be predisposed to partying:

> I got up around about eight-thirty that morning. . . .
>
> Q: Eight-thirty? Was that the usual time that you got up?
>
> A: Yeah, if I didn't have a hangover from the night before. . . .
>
> Q: What kind of drugs were you doing then?
>
> A: I was doing. . . Percadans, Dilauds, taking Valiums, drinking. . . . [A]nyway, I got up that morning about eight-thirty, took me a bath, put on some clothes and . . . decided to walk [over to his mother's home]. [T]his particular day, . . . my nephew was over [there]. . . . We was just sitting in the yard and talking and drinking beer, you know. . . . It was me, him, and my sister. We was sitting out there in the yard talking. And this guy that we know, . . . he came up, he pulled up. So my nephew got in the car with him and they left. So, you know, I was sitting there talking to my sister. . . . And then, in the meantime, while we was talking, they come back, about thirty minutes later with a case of beer, some marijuana and everything, . . . and there was another one of my nephews in the car with them. So me, two of my sisters, and two of my nephews, we got in the car with this guy here and we just went riding. So we went to Hadley Park and . . . we stayed out there. There were so many people out there, they were parked on the grass and things, and the vice squad come and run everybody away. So when they done that, we left. . . . So we went back out [toward his mother's home] but instead of going over to my mother's house we went to this little joint [tavern]. Now we're steady drinking and smoking weed all during this day. So when we get there, we park and get out and see a few friends. We [were] talking and getting high, you know, blowing each other a shotgun [sharing marijuana].

Enjoyment of party pursuits in group context is enhanced through the collective emphasis on personal autonomy. Because it is understood by all that participants are free to leave if they no longer enjoy or do not support group activities, the continuing presence of each participant affirms for the remainder the pleasures of the lifestyle. Uncoerced participation thus reinforces the shared assumption that group activities are appropriate and enjoyable. The behavioral result of the emphasis on autonomy is acceptance of or acquiescence in group decisions and activities.

Party pursuits also appeal to offenders because they permit conspicuous display of independence (Persson 1981). This generally means avoidance of the world of routine work and freedom from being "under someone's thumb." It also may include being free to avoid or to escape from restrictive routines:

> I just wanted to be doing something. Instead of being at home, or something like that. I wanted to be running, I wanted to be going to clubs, and picking

up women, and shooting pool. And I liked to go to [a nearby resort community] and just drive around over there. A lot of things like that. . . . I was drinking two pints or more a day. . . . I was doing Valiums and I was doing Demerol. . . . I didn't want to work.

The proper pursuit and enjoyment of life as party is expensive, due largely to the costs of drugs. As one of our subjects remarked: "We was doing a lot of cocaine, so cash didn't last long, you know. If we made $3,000, two thousand of it almost instantly went for cocaine." Some party pursuers must meet other expenses as well if the lifestyle is to be maintained:

> Believe it or not, I was spending [$700] a day.
> Q: On what?
> A: Pot, alcohol, women, gas, motel rooms, food.
> Q: You were living in hotels, motels?
> A: Yeah, a lot of times, I was. I'd take a woman to a motel. I bought a lot of clothes. I used to like to dress pretty nicely, I'd buy suits.

Party pursuits require continuous infusions of money, and no single method of generating funds allows enjoyment of it for more than a few days. Consequently, the emphasis on spontaneity, autonomy, and independence is matched by the importance attached to financial resourcefulness. This is evidenced by the ability to sustain the lifestyle over a period of time. Doing so earns for offenders a measure of respect from peers for their demonstrated ability to "get over." It translates into "self-esteem . . . as a folk hero beating the bureaucratic system of routinized dependence" (Walsh 1986, p. 16). The value of and respect for those who demonstrate resourcefulness means that criminal acts, as a means of sustaining life as party, generally are not condemned by the offender's peers.

The risks of employing criminal solutions to the need for funds are approached blithely but confidently in the same spontaneous and playful manner as are the rewards of life as party. In fact, avoidance of careful and detailed planning is a way of demonstrating possession of valued personal qualities and commitment to the lifestyle. Combined with the twin assumptions that peers have chosen freely and that one should not interfere with their autonomy, avoidance of rational planning finds expression in a reluctance to suggest that peers should weigh carefully the possible consequences of whatever they choose to do. Thus, the interaction that precedes criminal incidents is distinguished by circumspection and the use of linguistic devices that relegate risk and fear to the background of attention. The act of stealing, for example, is referred to obliquely but knowingly as "doing something" or as "making money":

> [After a day of partying,] I [got] to talking about making some money, because I didn't have no money. This guy that we were riding with, he had all the money. . . . So me and him and my nephew, we get together, talking about making some money. This guy tells me, he said, "man, I know where there's a good place at."

Q: Okay, so you suggested you all go somewhere and rob?

A: Yeah, "make some"—well, we called it "making money."

Q: Okay. So, then you and this fellow met up in the bar.... Tell me about the conversation?

A: Well, there wasn't much of a conversation to it, really.... I asked him if he was ready to go, if he wanted to go do something, you know. And he knew what I meant. He wanted to go make some money somehow, any way it took.

To the external observer, inattention to risk at the moment when it would seem most appropriate may seem to border on irrationality. For the offender engaged in party pursuits, however, it is but one aspect of behaviors that are rational in other respects. It opens up opportunities to enjoy life as party and to demonstrate commitment to values shared by peers. Resourcefulness and disdain for conventional rationality affirm individual character and style, both of which are important in the world of party pursuits (Goffman 1967).

Party Pursuits and Eroding Resources

Paradoxically, the pursuit of life as party can be appreciated and enjoyed to the fullest extent only if participants moderate their involvement in it while maintaining identities and routines in the straight world. Doing so maintains "escape value" but it also requires an uncommon measure of discipline and forbearance. The fact is that extended and enthusiastic enjoyment of life as party threatens constantly to deplete irrevocably the resources needed to sustain measured enjoyment of its pleasures. Three aspects of the life-as-party lifestyle can contribute to this end.

First, some offenders become ensnared increasingly by the chemical substances and drug using routines that are common there. In doing so, the meaning of drug consumption changes:

> See, I was doing drugs every day. It just wasn't every other day, it was to the point that, after the first few months doing drugs, I would have to do "X amount" of drugs, say, just for instance, just to feel like I do now. Which is normal.

Once the party pursuer's physical or psychological tolerance increases significantly, drugs are consumed not for the high they once produced but instead to maintain a sense of normality by avoiding sickness or withdrawal.

Second, party pursuits erode legitimate fiscal and social capital. They can not be sustained by legitimate employment and they may in fact undermine both one's ability and inclination to hold a job. Even if offenders are willing to work at the kinds of employment available to them, and evidence suggests that many are not (Cromwell, Olson, and Avary 1991), the time schedules of work and party pursuits conflict. The best times of the day for committing many property crimes are also the times the offender would be at work, and it is nearly impossible to do both consistently and well. For those who pursue life as a party, legitimate employment often is foregone or sacrificed (Rengert and Wasilchick 1985). The absence of income from noncriminal sources reinforces the need to find other sources of money.

Determined pursuit of life as party also may affect participants' relationships with legitimate significant others. Many offenders manage to enjoy the lifestyle successfully only by exploiting the concern and largesse of family and friends. This may take the form of repeated requests for and receipt of personal loans that go unreturned, occasional thefts, or other forms of exploitation:

> I lived well for awhile. I lived well...until I started shooting cocaine real bad, intravenously....[A]nd then everything, you know, went up in smoke, you know. Up my arm. The watches, the rings,...the car, you know. I used to have a girl, man, and her daddy had two horses. I put them in my arm. You know what I mean?...I made her sell them horses. My clothes and all that stuff, a lot of it, they went up in smoke when I started messing with that cocaine.

Eventually, friends and even family members may come to believe that they have been exploited or that continued assistance will only prolong a process that must be terminated. As one subject told us, "Oh, I tried to borrow money, and borrow money and, you know, nobody would loan it to me. Because they knew what I was doing." After first refusing further assistance, acquaintances, friends, and even family members may avoid social contacts with the party pursuer or sever ties altogether. This dialogue occurred between the interviewer and one of our subjects.

> Q: [B]esides doing something wrong, did you think of anything else that you could do to get money?...Borrow it?
> A: No, I'd done run that in the ground. See, you burn that up. That's burned up, right there, borrowing, you know....Once I borrow, you know, I might get $10 from you today and, see, I'll be expecting to be getting $10 tomorrow, if I could. And then, when I see you [and] you see me coming, you say, "no, I don't have none."...[A]s the guys in the penitentiary say, "you absorb all of your remedies," you see. And that's what I did: I burned my remedies up, you know.

Last, when party pursuits are not going well, feelings of shame and self-disgust are not uncommon (Frazier and Meisenhelder 1985). Unsuccessful party pursuers as a result may take steps to reduce these feelings by distancing themselves voluntarily from conventional others:

> Q: You were married to your wife at that time?
> A: Yeah, I was married...
> Q: Where was she living then?
> A: I finally forced her to go home, you know...I made her go home, you know. And it caused an argument, for her to go home to her mother's. I felt like that was the best thing I did for her, you know. She hated me...for it at the time, didn't understand none of it. But, really, I intentionally made her go. I really spared her the misery that we were going to have. And it came. It came in bundles.

When party pursuers sustain severe losses of legitimate income and social resources, regardless of how it occurs, they grow increasingly isolated from conventional significant others. The obvious consequence is that this reduces interpersonal constraints on their behavior.

As their pursuit of life as party increasingly assumes qualities of difficulty and struggle, offenders' utilities and risk perceptions also change. Increasingly, crimes are committed not to enhance or sustain the lifestyle so much as to forestall unpleasant circumstances. Those addicted to alcohol or other drugs, for example, must devote increasing time and energy to the quest for monies to purchase their chemicals of choice. Both their drug consumption and the frequency of their criminal acts increase (Ball et al. 1983; Johnson et al. 1985). For them, as for others, inability to draw on legitimate or low-risk resources may precipitate a crisis. One of our respondents retold how, facing a court appearance on a burglary charge, he needed funds to hire an attorney:

> I needed some money bad or if I didn't, if I went to court the following day, I was going to be locked up. The judge was going to lock me up. Because I didn't have no lawyer. And I had went and talked to several lawyers and they told me . . . they wanted a thousand dollars, that if I couldn't come up with no thousand dollars, they couldn't come to court with me. . . . [S]o I went to my sister. I asked my sister, I said, "look here, what about letting me have seven or eight hundred dollars"—which I knowed she had the money because she . . . had been in a wreck and she had gotten some money out of a suit. And she said, "well, if I give you the money you won't do the right thing with it." And I was telling her, "no, no, I need a lawyer." But I couldn't convince her to let me have the money. So I left. . . . I said, shit, I'm fixin' to go back to jail. . . . [S]o as I left her house and was walking—I was going to catch the bus—the [convenience store] and bus stop was right there by each other. So, I said I'm going to buy me some gum. . . . [A]nd in the process of me buying the chewing gum, I seen two ladies, they was counting money. So I figured sooner or later one of them was going to come out with the money. . . . I waited on them until . . . one came out with the money, and I got it.

Confronted by crisis and preoccupied with relieving immediate distress, the offender eventually may experience and define himself as propelled by forces beyond his control. Behavioral options become dichotomized into those that hold out some possibility of relief, however risky, and those that promise little but continued pain. Legitimate options are few and are seen as unlikely solutions. A criminal act may offer some hope of relief, however temporary. The offender may imbue the criminal option with almost magical prospects for ending or reversing the state of discomfort:

> I said, "well, look at it like this": if I don't do it, then tomorrow morning I've got the same [problems] that I've got right now. I could be hungry. I'm going to want food more. I'm going to want cigarettes more. I'm going to want everything more. [But] if I do it, and if I make it, then I've got all I want.

Acts that once were the result of blithe unconcern with risk can over time come to be based on a personal determination to master or reverse what is experienced as desperately unpleasant circumstances. As a result, inattention to risk in the offender's decision making may give way to the perception that he has *nothing to lose:*

> It...gets to the point that you get into such a desperation. You're not working, you can't work. You're drunk as hell, been that way two or three weeks. You're no good to yourself, and you're no good to anybody else. Self-esteem is gone [and] spiritually, mentally, physically, financially bankrupt. You ain't got nothing to lose.

Desperate to maintain or reestablish a sense of normality, the offender pursues emotional relief with a decision to act decisively, albeit in the face of legal odds recognized as narrowing. By acting boldly and resolutely to make the best of a grim situation, one gains a measure of respect, if not from others, then at least from oneself.

> I think, when you're doing...drugs like I was doing, I don't think you tend to rationalize much at all. I think it's just a decision you make. You don't weigh the consequences, the pros and the cons. You just do it.

> You know, all kinds of things started running through my mind. If I get caught, then there, there I am with another charge. Then I said, well if I don't do something, I'm going to be in jail. And I just said, "I'm going to do it."

The fact that sustained party pursuits often cause offenders to increase the number of offenses they commit and to exploit criminal opportunities that formerly were seen as risky should not be interpreted as meaning they believe they can continue committing crime with impunity. The opposite is true. Many offenders engaged in crimes intended to halt or reverse eroding fortunes are aware that eventually they will be arrested if they continue doing so:

> Q: How did you manage not to think about, you know, that you could go to prison?
> A: Well, you think about it afterwards. You think, "wow, boy, I got away with it again." But you know, sooner or later, the law of averages is gonna catch up with you. You just can't do it [commit crime] forever and ever and ever. And don't think you're not gonna get caught, cause you will.

Bennett and Wright (1984a) likewise show that a majority of persistent offenders endorse the statement that they will be caught "eventually." The cyclical transformation of party pursuits from pleasant and enjoyable to desperate and tenuous is one reason they are able to commit crimes despite awareness of inevitable and potentially severe legal penalties.

The threat posed by possible arrest and imprisonment, however, may not seem severe to some desperate offenders. As compared to their marginal and precarious existence, it may be seen as a form of relief:

> [When he was straight], I'd think about [getting caught]: I could get this, and that [penalties]....[A]nd then I would think, well, I know this is going to

end one day, you know. But, you know, you get so far out there, and get so far off into it that it really don't matter, you know. But you think about that. . . . I knew, eventually, I would get caught, you know. . . . I was off into drugs and I just didn't care if I got caught or not.

When I [got] caught—and they caught me right at the house—it's kind of like, you feel good, because you're glad it's over, you know. I mean, a weight being lifted off your head. And you say, well, I don't have to worry about this shit no more, because they've caught me. And it's over, you know.

In sum, due to offenders' eroding access to legitimately secured funds, their diminishing contact with and support from conventional significant others, and their efforts to maintain drug consumption habits, crimes that once were committed for recreational purposes increasingly become desperate attempts to forestall or reverse uncomfortable or frustrating situations. Pursuing the short term goal of maximizing enjoyment of life, legal threats can appear to the offender either as remote and improbable contingencies when party pursuits fulfill their recreational purposes or as an acceptable risk in the face of continued isolation, penury, and desperation.

We analyzed the descriptions of crime provided by our subjects, and their activities on the day the crime occurred. We focused specifically on: (1) the primary purpose of their crimes, i.e., whether they planned to use the proceeds of crime for pleasure or to cope with unpleasant contingencies, and (2) the extent and subjective meaning of their drug use at the time they decided to commit the crime in question. Based on the analysis, we classified the crimes of 15 subjects as behaviors committed in the enjoyment of life as party and 13 as behaviors committed in order to enhance or restore enjoyment of this lifestyle. The 12 remaining offenders could not be classified because of insufficient information in the crime descriptions or they are isolated criminal acts that do not represent a specific lifestyle. Two subjects, for example, described crimes that were acts of vengeance directed at the property of individuals who had treated them or their relatives improperly. One of the men related how he decided to burglarize a home for reasons of revenge:

I was mad. . . . When I was in the penitentiary, my wife went to his house for a party and he give her a bunch of cocaine. . . . It happened, I think, about a week before I got out. . . . I just had it in my mind what I wanted to do: I wanted to hurt him like I was hurt. . . . I was pretty drunk, when I went by [his home], and I saw there wasn't no car there. So, I just pulled my car in.

The other subject told how an acquaintance had stolen drugs and other possessions from his automobile. In response the subject "staked out the places where he would be for several days before I caught him, at gun point, [and] made him take me to his home, [which] I ransacked, and found some of the narcotics that he had stolen from me." Although neither of these crimes was committed in pursuit of life as party, other crimes committed by both these subjects during their criminal careers did occur as part of that lifestyle. Other investigators have similarly reported that revenge is the dominant motive in a minority of property offenses (e.g., Cromwell, Olson, and Avary 1991, p. 22).

IMPLICATIONS

We have suggested that daily routines characteristic of the partying lifestyle of persistent and unsuccessful offenders may modify both the salience of their various decision utilities and their perceptions of legal risk in the process of their crime commission decisions. This is not to say that these decisions are irrational, only that they do not conform to decision making as sketched by rational choice theories. Our objective was not to falsify the rational choice approach to criminal decision making, for we know of no way this could be accomplished. Whatever it is, moreover, rationality is not a dichotomous variable. Indeed, offenders' target selection decision making appears more rational in the conventional sense than do crime commission decisions.

The lesson here for theories of criminal decision making is that while utilities and risk assessment may be properties of individuals, they are also shaped by the social and personal contexts in which decisions are made. Whether their pursuit of life as party is interpreted theoretically as the product of structural strain, choice, or even happenstance is of limited importance to an understanding of offenders' discrete criminal forays. What is important is that their lifestyle places them in situations that may facilitate important transformations in the utilities of prospective actions. If nothing else, this means that some situations more than others make it possible to discount or ignore risk. We are not the first to call attention to this phenomenon:

> [The] situational nature of sanction properties has escaped the scales and indicators employed in official record and self-report survey research. In this body of research an arrest and a year in prison are generally assumed to have the same meaning for all persons and across all situations. The situational grounding of sanction properties suggests[, however,] that we look beyond official definitions of sanctions and the attitudinal structure of individuals to the properties of situations (Ekland-Olson et al. 1984, p. 174).

Along the same line, the longitudinal survey of adult offenders concludes that decision making "may be conditioned by elements within the immediate situation confronting the individual ... [such that] perceptions of the opportunity, returns, and support for crime within a given situation may influence ... perceptions of risks and the extent to which those risks are discounted" (Piliavin et al. 1986, p. 115). The same interpretation has been suggested by Shover and Thompson (1992) for their failure to find an expected positive relationship between risk estimates and crime desistance among former prison inmates.

In light of the sample and data limitations of this study we cannot and have not argued that the lifestyle we described *generates* or *produces* the characteristic decision-making behaviors of persistent property offenders. The evidence does not permit such interpretive liberties. It does seem reasonable to suggest, however, that the focal concerns and shared perspectives of those who pursue life as party may function to *sustain* offenders' freewheeling, but purposeful, decision-making style. Without question there is a close *correspondence* between the two. Our ability to explain and predict decision making requires that we gain a better understanding of how utilities and risk perceptions are constrained by the properties of situations encountered typically by persons in their daily rounds. In other words, we must learn more about the daily worlds that comprise the immediate contexts of criminal decision-making behavior.

Note

This research was supported by grant #86-IJ-CX-0068 from the U.S. Department of Justice, National Institute of Justice (Principal Investigator: Neal Shover). Points of view or opinions expressed here do not necessarily reflect the official position or policies of the Department of Justice. For their critical comments while the paper was in gestation we are grateful to Derek Cornish and to participants in a March 1991 colloquium at the Centre for Socio-Legal Studies, Wolfson College, University of Oxford. Werner Einstadter, Michael Levi, Mike Maguire, and anonymous reviewers also provided helpful comments.

References

Ball J. C., Shaffer, J. W. and Nurco, D. N. (1983) "The day-to-day criminality of heroin addicts in Baltimore: A study in the continuity of offense rates," *Drug and Alcohol Dependence, 12,* 119–142.

Becker, G. (1968) "Crime and punishment: An economic approach," *Journal of Political Economy, 76,* 169–217.

Bennett, T. and Wright, R. (1984a) *Burglars on Burglary,* Hampshire, U.K.: Gower.

—— (1984b) "The relationship between alcohol use and burglary," *British Journal of Addiction, 79,* 431–437.

Blumstein, A., Cohen, J. and Nagin, D., editors (1978) *Deterrence and Incapacitation: Estimating the Effects of Criminal Sanctions on Crime Rates,* Washington, D.C.: National Academy of Sciences.

Carroll, J. S. (1978) "A psychological approach to deterrence: The evaluation of crime opportunities," *Journal of Personality and Social Psychology, 36,* 1512–1520.

—— (1982) "Committing a crime: The offender's decision," in: J. Konecni and E. B. Ebbesen (Eds.), *The Criminal Justice System: A Social-Psychological Analysis,* San Francisco: W. H. Freeman.

Carroll, J. S. and Weaver, F. (1986) "Shoplifters' perceptions of crime opportunities: A process-tracing study," in: D. B. Cornish and R. V. Clarke (Eds.), *The Reasoning Criminal: Rational Choice Perspectives on Offending,* New York: Springer-Verlag.

Clarke, R. V. and Cornish, D. B. (1985) "Modeling offenders' decisions: A framework for research and policy," in: M. Tonry and N. Morris (Eds.), *Crime and Justice: A Review of Research,* Vol. 4, Chicago: University of Chicago Press.

Claster, D. S. (1967) "Comparison of risk perception between delinquents and nondelinquents," *Journal of Criminal Law, Criminology, and Police Science, 58,* 80–86.

Cornish, D. B. and Clarke, R. V., editors (1986) *The Reasoning Criminal: Rational Choice Perspectives on Offending,* New York: Springer-Verlag.

Cromwell, P. F., Olson, J. N. and Avary, D. W. (1991) *Breaking and Entering: An Ethnographic Analysis of Burglary,* Newbury Park, Calif.: Sage.

Ekland-Olson, S., Lieb, J. and Zurcher, L. (1984) "The paradoxical impact of criminal sanctions: Some microstructural findings," *Law & Society Review, 18,* 159–178.

Feeney, F. (1986) "Robbers as decision-makers," in: D. B. Cornish and R. V. Clarke (Eds.), *The Reasoning Criminal: Rational Choice Perspectives on Offending,* New York: Springer-Verlag.

Figgie International (1988) *The Figgie Report Part VI—The Business of Crime: The Criminal Perspective,* Richmond, Va.: Figgie International, Inc.

Frazier, C. E. and Meisenholder, T. (1985) "Criminality and emotional ambivalence: Exploratory notes on an overlooked dimension," *Qualitative Sociology, 8,* 266–284.

Gibbs, J. J. and Shelley, P. L. (1982) "Life in the fast lane: A retrospective view by commercial thieves," *Journal of Research in Crime and Delinquency, 19,* 299–330.

Goffman, E. (1967) *Interaction Ritual,* Garden City, N.Y.: Anchor.

Gottfredson, M. R. and Hirschi, T. (1990) *A General Theory of Crime,* Stanford, Calif.: Stanford University Press.

Heineke, J. M., editor (1978) *Economic Models of Criminal Behavior,* Amsterdam: North-Holland.

Johnson, B. D., Goldstein, P. J., Preble, E., Schmeidler, J., Lipton, D. D., Spunt, B. and Miller, T. (1985) *Taking Care of Business: The Economics of Crime by Heroin Addicts,* Lexington, Mass.: D.C. Heath.

Katz, J. (1988) *Seductions of Crime,* New York: Basic Books.

Maguire, M. in collaboration with T. Bennett (1982) *Burglary in a Dwelling,* London: Heinemann.

Manski, C. F. (1978) "Prospects for inference on deterrence through empirical analysis of individual criminal behavior," in: A. Blumstein, J. Cohen, and D. Nagin (Eds.), *Deterrence and Incapacitation: Estimating the Effects of Criminal Sanctions on Crime Rates,* Washington, D.C.: National Academy of Sciences.

Nagin, D. S. and Paternoster, R. (1991) "On the relationship of past to future participation in delinquency," *Criminology, 29,* 163–189.

Persson, M. (1981) "Time-perspectives amongst criminals," *Acta Sociologica, 24,* 149–165.

Petersilia, J. (1980) "Criminal career research: A review of recent evidence," in: N. Morris and M. Tonry (Eds.), *Crime and Justice: An Annual Review of Research,* Vol. 2, Chicago: University of Chicago Press.

—— Greenwood, P. W. and Lavin, M. (1978) *Criminal Careers of Habitual Felons,* Washington, D.C.: U.S. Department of Justice, National Institute of Law Enforcement and Criminal Justice.

Peterson, M. A. and Braiker, H. B. (1980) *Doing Crime: A Survey of California Prison Inmates,* Santa Monica, Calif.: Rand Corporation.

Piliavin, I., Gartner, R. and Matsueda, R. (1986) "Crime, deterrence, and rational choice," *American Sociological Review, 51,* 101–119.

Rengert, G. F. and Wasilchick, J. (1985) *Suburban Burglary,* Springfield, Ill.: Charles C. Thomas.

Repetto, T. A. (1974) *Residential Crime,* Cambridge, Mass.: Ballinger.

Reynolds, M. O. (1985) *Crime by Choice: An Economic Analysis,* Dallas: Fisher Institute.

Scarr, H. A. (1973) *Patterns of Burglary* (second edition), Washington, D.C.: U.S. Department of Justice, National Institute of Law Enforcement and Criminal Justice.

Seidel, J. V., Kjolseth, R. and Seymour, E. (1988) *The Ethnograph: A User's Guide* (Version 3.0), Littleton, Col.: Qualis Research Associates.

Shover, N. (1991) "Burglary," in: M. Tonry (Ed.), *Crime and Justice: An Annual Review of Research,* Vol. 14, Chicago: University of Chicago Press.

Shover, N. and Thompson, C. Y. (1992) "Age, differential expectations, and crime desistance," *Criminology, 30,* 89–109.

Tittle, C. R. (1980) *Sanctions and Deviance: The Question of Deterrence,* New York: Praeger.

Waldo, G. P. and Chiricos, T. G. (1972) "Perceived penal sanction and self-reported criminality: A neglected approach to deterrence research," *Social Problems, 19,* 522–540.

Walsh, D. (1980) *Break-Ins: Burglary from Private Houses,* London: Constable.

—— (1986) *Heavy Business,* London: Routledge & Kegan Paul.

17 / Career Deviance

HOWARD S. BECKER

One of the most crucial steps in the process of building a stable pattern of deviant behavior is likely to be the experience of being caught and publicly labeled as a deviant. Whether a person takes this step or not depends not so much on what he does as on what other people do, on whether or not they enforce the rule he has violated.... First of all, even though no one else discovers the nonconformity or enforces the rules against it, the individual who has committed the impropriety may himself act as an enforcer. He may brand himself as deviant because of what he has done and punish himself in one way or another for his behavior. This is not always or necessarily the case, but may occur. Second, there may be cases like those described by psychoanalysts in which the individual really wants to get caught and perpetrates his deviant act in such a way that it is almost sure he will be.

In any case, being caught and branded as deviant has important consequences for one's further social participation and self-image. The most important consequence is a drastic change in the individual's public identity. Committing the improper act and being publicly caught at it place him in a new status. He has been revealed as a different kind of person from the kind he was supposed to be. He is labeled a "fairy," "dope fiend," "nut," or "lunatic," and treated accordingly.

In analyzing the consequences of assuming a deviant identity let us make use of Hughes' distinction between master and auxiliary status traits.[1] Hughes notes that most statuses have one key trait which serves to distinguish those who belong from those who do not. Thus the doctor, whatever else he may be, is a person who has a certificate stating that he has fulfilled certain requirements and is licensed to practice medicine; this is the master trait. As Hughes points out, in our society a doctor is also informally expected to have a number of auxiliary traits: most people expect him to be upper middle class, white, male, and Protestant. When he is not there is a sense that he has in some way failed to fill the bill. Similarly, though skin color is the master status trait determining who is Negro and who is white, Negroes are informally expected to have certain status traits and not to have others; people are surprised and find it anomalous if a Negro turns out to be a doctor or a college professor. People often have the master status trait but lack some of the auxiliary, informally expected characteristics; for example, one may be a doctor but be female or Negro.

200

Hughes deals with this phenomenon in regard to statuses that are well thought of, desired and desirable (noting that one may have the formal qualifications for entry into a status but be denied full entry because of lack of the proper auxiliary traits), but the same process occurs in the case of deviant statuses. Possession of one deviant trait may have a generalized symbolic value, so that people automatically assume that its bearer possesses other undesirable traits allegedly associated with it.

To be labeled a criminal one need only commit a single criminal offense, and this is all the term formally refers to. Yet the word carries a number of connotations specifying auxiliary traits characteristic of anyone bearing the label. A man who has been convicted of housebreaking and thereby labeled criminal is presumed to be a person likely to break into other houses; the police, in rounding up known offenders for investigation after a crime has been committed, operate on this premise. Further, he is considered likely to commit other kinds of crimes as well, because he has shown himself to be a person without "respect for the law." Thus, apprehension for one deviant act exposes a person to the likelihood that he will be regarded as deviant or undesirable in other respects.

There is one other element in Hughes' analysis we can borrow with profit: the distinction between master and subordinate statuses.[2] Some statuses, in our society as in others, override all other statuses and have a certain priority. Race is one of these. Membership in the Negro race, as socially defined, will override most other status considerations in most other situations; the fact that one is a physician or middle-class or female will not protect one from being treated as a Negro first and any of these other things second. The status of deviant (depending on this kind of deviance) is this kind of master status. One receives the status as a result of breaking a rule, and the identification proves to be more important than most others. One will be identified as a deviant first, before other identifications are made. The question is raised: "What kind of person would break such an important rule?" And the answer is given: "One who is different from the rest of us, who cannot or will not act as a moral human being and therefore might break other important rules." The deviant identification becomes the controlling one.

Treating a person as though he were generally rather than specifically deviant produces a self-fulfilling prophecy. It sets in motion several mechanisms which conspire to shape the person in the image people have of him.[3] In the first place, one tends to be cut off, after being identified as deviant, from participation in more conventional groups, even though the specific consequences of the particular deviant activity might never of themselves have caused the isolation had there not also been the public knowledge and reaction to it. For example, being a homosexual may not affect one's ability to do office work, but to be known as a homosexual in an office may make it impossible to continue working there. Similarly, though the effects of opiate drugs may not impair one's working ability, to be known as an addict will probably lead to losing one's job. In such cases, the individual finds it difficult to conform to other rules which he had no intention or desire to break, and perforce finds himself deviant in these areas as well. The homosexual who is deprived of a "respectable" job by the discovery of his deviance may drift into unconventional, marginal occupations where it does not make so much difference. The drug addict finds himself forced into other illegitimate kinds of activity, such as robbery and theft, by the refusal of respectable employers to have him around.

When the deviant is caught, he is treated in accordance with the popular diagnosis of why he is that way, and the treatment itself may likewise produce increasing deviance. The drug addict, popularly considered to be a weak-willed individual who cannot forego the indecent pleasures afforded him by opiates, is treated repressively. He is forbidden to use drugs. Since he cannot get drugs legally, he must get them illegally. This forces the market underground and pushes the price of drugs up far beyond the current legitimate market price into a bracket that few can afford on an ordinary salary. Hence the treatment of the addict's deviance places him in a position where it will probably be necessary to resort to deceit and crime in order to support his habit.[4] The behavior is a consequence of the public reaction to the deviance rather than a consequence of the inherent qualities of the deviant act.

Notes

1. Everett C. Hughes, "Dilemmas and Contradictions of Status," *American Journal of Sociology*, L (March, 1945), 353–359.
2. *Ibid.*
3. See Marsh Ray, "The Cycle of Abstinence and Relapse Among Heroin Addicts," *Social Problems*, 9 (Fall, 1961), 132–140.
4. See *Drug Addiction: Crime or Disease?* Interim and Final Reports of the Joint Committee of the American Bar Association and the American Medical Association on Narcotic Drugs (Bloomington, Indiana: Indiana University Press, 1961).

18 / Anorexia Nervosa and Bulimia: The Development of Deviant Identities

PENELOPE A. McLORG
DIANE E. TAUB

INTRODUCTION

Current appearance norms stipulate thinness for women and muscularity for men; these expectations, like any norms, entail rewards for compliance and negative sanctions for violations. Fear of being overweight—of being visually deviant—has led to a striving for thinness, especially among women. In the extreme, this avoidance of overweight engenders eating disorders, which themselves constitute deviance. Anorexia nervosa, or purposeful starvation, embodies visual as well as behavioral deviation; bulimia, binge-eating followed by vomiting and/or laxative abuse, is primarily behaviorally deviant.

Besides a fear of fatness, anorexics and bulimics exhibit distorted body images. In anorexia nervosa, a 20–25 percent loss of initial body weight occurs, resulting from self-starvation alone or in combination with excessive exercising, occasional binge-eating, vomiting and/or laxative abuse. Bulimia denotes cyclical (daily, weekly, for example) binge-eating followed by vomiting or laxative abuse; weight is normal or close to normal (Humphries et al., 1982). Common physical manifestations of these eating disorders include menstrual cessation or irregularities and electrolyte imbalances; among behavioral traits are depression, obsessions/compulsions, and anxiety (Russell, 1979; Thompson and Schwartz, 1982).

Increasingly prevalent in the past two decades, anorexia nervosa and bulimia have emerged as major health and social problems. Termed an epidemic on college campuses (Brody, as quoted in Schur, 1984:76), bulimia affects 13% of college students (Halmi et al., 1981). Less prevalent, anorexia nervosa was diagnosed in 0.6% of students utilizing a university health center (Stangler and Printz, 1980). However, the overall mortality rate of anorexia nervosa is 6% (Schwartz and Thompson, 1981) to 20% (Humphries et al., 1982); bulimia appears to be less life-threatening (Russell, 1979).

Particularly affecting certain demographic groups, eating disorders are most prevalent among young, white, affluent (upper-middle to upper class) women in modern, industrialized countries (Crisp, 1977; Willi and Grossman, 1983). Combining all of these risk factors (female sex, youth, high socioeconomic status, and residence in an industrialized country), prevalence of anorexia nervosa in upper class English girls' schools is reported at 1 in 100 (Crisp et al., 1976). The age of onset for anorexia nervosa is bimodal at 14.5 and 18 years (Humphries et al., 1982); the most frequent age of onset for bulimia is 18 (Russell, 1979).

Eating disorders have primarily been studied from psychological and medical perspectives.[1] Theories of etiology have generally fallen into three categories: the ego psychological (involving an impaired child-maternal environment); the family systems (implicating enmeshed, rigid families); and the endocrinological (involving a precipitating hormonal defect). Although relatively ignored in previous studies, the sociocultural components of anorexia nervosa and bulimia (the slimness norm and its agents of reinforcement, such as role models) have been postulated as accounting for the recent, dramatic increases in these disorders (Schwartz et al., 1982; Boskind-White, 1985).[2]

Medical and psychological approaches to anorexia nervosa and bulimia obscure the social facets of the disorders and neglect the individuals' own definitions of their situations. Among the social processes involved in the development of an eating disorder is the sequence of conforming behavior, primary deviance, and secondary deviance. Societal reaction is the critical mediator affecting the movement through the deviant career (Becker, 1973). Within a framework of labeling theory, this study focuses on the emergence of anorexic and bulimic identities, as well as on the consequences of being career deviants.

METHODOLOGY

Sampling and Procedures

Most research on eating disorders has utilized clinical subjects or non-clinical respondents completing questionnaires. Such studies can be criticized for simply counting and describing behaviors and/or neglecting the social construction of the disorders. Moreover, the work of clinicians is often limited by therapeutic orientation. Previous research may also have included individuals who were not in therapy on their own volition and who resisted admitting that they had an eating disorder.

Past studies thus disregard the intersubjective meanings respondents attach to their behavior and emphasize researchers' criteria for definition as anorexic or bulimic. In order to supplement these sampling and procedural designs, the present study utilizes participant observation of a group of self-defined anorexics and bulimics.[3] As the individuals had acknowledged their eating disorders, frank discussion and disclosure were facilitated.

Data are derived from a self-help group, BANISH, Bulimics/Anorexics In Self-Help, which met at a university in an urban center of the mid-South. Founded by one of the researchers (D.E.T.), BANISH was advertised in local newspapers as offering a group experience for individuals who were anorexic or bulimic. Despite the local advertisements, the campus location of the meetings may have selectively encouraged university students to attend. Nonetheless, in view of the modal age of onset and socioeconomic status of individuals with eating disorders, college students have been considered target populations (Crisp et al., 1976; Halmi et al., 1981).

The group's weekly two-hour meetings were observed for two years. During the course of this study, thirty individuals attended at least one of the meetings. Attendance at meetings was varied: ten individuals came nearly every Sunday; five attended approximately twice a month; and the remaining fifteen participated once a month or less frequently, often when their eating problems were "more severe" or "bizarre." The modal number of members at meetings was twelve. The diversity in attendance was to be expected in self-help groups of anorexics and bulimics.

> ... most people's involvement will not be forever or even a long time. Most people get the support they need and drop out. Some take the time to help others after they themselves have been helped but even they may withdraw after a time. It is a natural and in many cases *necessary* process (emphasis in original) (American Anorexia/Bulimia Association, 1983).

Modeled after Alcoholics Anonymous, BANISH allowed participants to discuss their backgrounds and experiences with others who empathized. For many members, the group constituted their only source of help; these respondents were reluctant to contact health professionals because of shame, embarrassment, or financial difficulties.

In addition to field notes from group meetings, records of other encounters with all members were maintained. Participants visited the office of one of the researchers (D.E.T.), called both researchers by phone, and invited them to their homes or out for a cup of coffee. Such interaction facilitated genuine communication and mutual trust. Even among the fifteen individuals who did not attend the meetings regularly, contact was maintained with ten members on a monthly basis.

Supplementing field notes were informal interviews with fifteen group members, lasting from two to four hours. Because they appeared to represent more extensive experience with eating disorders, these interviewees were chosen to amplify their comments about the labeling process, made during group meetings. Conducted near the end of the two-year observation period, the interviews focused on what the respondents thought antedated and maintained their eating disorders. In addition, participants described others' reactions to their behaviors as well as their own interpretations of these reactions. To protect the confidentiality of individuals quoted in the study, pseudonyms are employed.

Description of Members

The demographic composite of the sample typifies what has been found in other studies (Fox and James, 1976; Crisp, 1977; Herzog, 1982; Schlesier-Stropp, 1984). Group members' ages ranged from nineteen to thirty-six, with the modal age being twenty-one. The respondents were white, and all but one were female. The sole male and three of the females were anorexic; the remaining females were bulimic.[4]

Primarily composed of college students, the group included four non-students, three of whom had college degrees. Nearly all members derived from upper-middle or lower-upper class households. Eighteen students and two non-students were never-marrieds and uninvolved in serious relationships; two non-students were married (one with two children); two students were divorced (one with two children); and six students were involved in serious relationships. The duration of eating disorders ranged from three to fifteen years.

CONFORMING BEHAVIOR

In the backgrounds of most anorexics and bulimics, dieting figures prominently, beginning in the teen years (Crisp, 1977; Johnson et al., 1982; Lacey et al., 1986). As dieters, these individuals are conformist in their adherence to the cultural norms emphasizing thinness (Garner et al., 1980; Schwartz et al., 1982). In our society, slim bodies are regarded as the most worthy and attractive; overweight is viewed as physically and morally unhealthy— "obscene," "lazy," "slothful," and "gluttonous" (DeJong, 1980; Ritenbaugh, 1982; Schwartz et al., 1982).

Among the agents of socialization promoting the slimness norm is advertising. Female models in newspaper, magazine, and television advertisements are uniformly slender. In addition, product names and slogans exploit the thin orientation; examples include "Ultra Slim Lipstick," "Miller Lite," and "Virginia Slims." While retaining pressures toward thinness, an Ayds commercial attempts a compromise for those wanting to savor food: "Ayds ...so you can taste, chew, and enjoy, while you lose weight." Appealing particularly to women, a nationwide fast-food restaurant chain offers low-calorie selections, so individuals can have a "license to eat." In the latter two examples, the notion of enjoying food is combined with the message to be slim. Food and restaurant advertisements overall convey the pleasures of eating, whereas advertisements for other products, such as fashions and diet aids, reinforce the idea that fatness is undesirable.

Emphasis on being slim affects everyone in our culture, but it influences women especially because of society's traditional emphasis on women's appearance. The slimness norm and its concomitant narrow beauty standards exacerbate the objectification of women (Schur, 1984). Women view themselves as visual entities and recognize that conforming to appearance expectations and "becoming attractive object[s] [are] role obligation[s]" (Laws, as quoted in Schur, 1984:66). Demonstrating the beauty motivation behind dieting, a recent Nielsen survey indicated that of the 56 percent of all women aged 24 to 54 who dieted during the previous year, 76 percent did so for cosmetic, rather than health, reasons (Schwartz et al., 1982). For most female group members, dieting was viewed as a means of gaining attractiveness and appeal to the opposite sex. The male respondent, as well, indicated that "when I was fat, girls didn't look at me, but when I got thinner, I was suddenly popular."

In addition to responding to the specter of obesity, individuals who develop anorexia nervosa and bulimia are conformist in their strong commitment to other conventional norms and goals. They consistently excel at school and work (Russell, 1979; Bruch, 1981; Humphries et al., 1982), maintaining high aspirations in both areas (Theander, 1970; Lacey et al., 1986). Group members generally completed college-preparatory courses in high school, aware from an early age that they would strive for a college degree. Also, in college as well as high school, respondents joined honor societies and academic clubs.

Moreover, pre-anorexics and -bulimics display notable conventionality as "model children" (Humphries et al., 1982:199), "the pride and joy" of their parents (Bruch, 1981:215), accommodating themselves to the wishes of others. Parents of these individuals emphasize conformity and value achievement (Bruch, 1981). Respondents felt that perfect or near-perfect grades were expected of them; however, good grades were not rewarded by parents, because "A's" were common for these children. In addition, their parents suppressed conflicts, to preserve the image of the "all-American family" (Humphries et al., 1982). Group members reported that they seldom, if ever, heard their parents argue or raise their voices.

Also conformist in their affective ties, individuals who develop anorexia nervosa and bulimia are strongly, even excessively, attached to their parents. Respondents' families appeared close-knit, demonstrating palpable emotional ties. Several group members, for example, reported habitually calling home at prescribed times, whether or not they had any news. Such families have been termed "enmeshed" and "overprotective," displaying intense interaction and concern for members' welfare (Minuchin et al., 1978; Selvini-Palazzoli, 1978). These qualities could be viewed as marked conformity to the norm of familial closeness.[5]

Another element of notable conformity in the family milieu of pre-anorexics and -bulimics concerns eating, body weight/shape, and exercising (Kalucy et al., 1977; Humphries et al., 1982). Respondents reported their fathers' preoccupation with exercising and their mothers' engrossment in food preparation. When group members dieted and lost weight, they received an extraordinary amount of approval. Among the family, body size became a matter of "friendly rivalry." One bulimic informant recalled that she, her mother, and her coed sister all strived to wear a size 5, regardless of their heights and body frames. Subsequent to this study, the researchers learned that both the mother and sister had become bulimic.

As pre-anorexics and -bulimics, group members thus exhibited marked conformity to cultural norms of thinness, achievement, compliance, and parental attachment. Their families reinforced their conformity by adherence to norms of family closeness and weight/body shape consciousness.

PRIMARY DEVIANCE

Even with familial encouragement, respondents, like nearly all dieters (Chernin, 1981), failed to maintain their lowered weights. Many cited their lack of willpower to eat only restricted foods. For the emerging anorexics and bulimics, extremes such as purposeful starvation or binging accompanied by vomiting and/or laxative abuse appeared as "obvious solutions" to the problem of retaining weight loss. Associated with these behaviors was a regained feeling of control in lives that had been disrupted by a major crisis. Group members' extreme weight-loss efforts operated as coping mechanisms for entering college, leaving home, or feeling rejected by the opposite sex.

The primary inducement for both eating adaptations was the drive for slimness: with slimness came more self-respect and a feeling of superiority over "unsuccessful dieters." Brian, for example, experienced a "power trip" upon consistent weight loss through starvation. Binges allowed the purging respondents to cope with stress through eating while maintaining a slim appearance. As former strict dieters, Teresa and Jennifer used binging/purging as an alternative to the constant self-denial of starvation. Acknowledging their parents' desires for them to be slim, most respondents still felt it was a conscious choice on their part to continue extreme weight-loss efforts. Being thin became the "most important thing" in their lives—their "greatest ambition."

In explaining the development of an anorexic or bulimic identity, Lemert's (1951; 1967) concept of primary deviance is salient. Primary deviance refers to a transitory period of norm violations which do not affect an individual's self-concept or performance of social roles. Although respondents were exhibiting anorexic or bulimic behavior, they did not consider themselves to be anorexic or bulimic.

At first, anorexics' significant others complimented their weight loss, expounding on their new "sleekness" and "good looks." Branch and Eurman (1980:631) also found anorexics' families and friends describing them as "well-groomed," "neat," "fashionable," and "victorious." Not until the respondents approached emaciation did some parents or friends become concerned and withdraw their praise. Significant others also became increasingly aware of the anorexics' compulsive exercising, preoccupation with food preparation (but not consumption), and ritualistic eating patterns (such as cutting food into minute pieces and eating only certain foods at prescribed times).

For bulimics, friends or family members began to question how the respondents could eat such large amounts of food (often in excess of 10,000 calories a day) and stay slim. Significant others also noticed calluses across the bulimics' hands, which were caused by repeated inducement of vomiting. Several bulimics were "caught in the act," bent over commodes. Generally, friends and family required substantial evidence before believing that the respondents' binging or purging was no longer sporadic.

SECONDARY DEVIANCE

Heightened awareness of group members' eating behavior ultimately led others to label the respondents "anorexic" or "bulimic." Respondents differed in their histories of being labeled and accepting the labels. Generally first termed anorexic by friends, family, or medical personnel, the anorexics initially vigorously denied the label. They felt they were not "anorexic enough," not skinny enough; Robin did not regard herself as having the "skeletal" appearance she associated with anorexia nervosa. These group members found it difficult to differentiate between socially approved modes of weight loss—eating less and exercising more—and the extremes of those behaviors. In fact, many of their activities—cheerleading, modeling, gymnastics, aerobics—reinforced their pursuit of thinness. Like other anorexics, Chris felt she was being "ultra-healthy," with "total control" over her body.

For several respondents, admitting they were anorexic followed the realization that their lives were disrupted by their eating disorder. Anorexics' inflexible eating patterns unsettled family meals and holiday gatherings. Their regimented lifestyle of compulsively scheduled activities—exercising, school, and meals—precluded any spontaneous social interactions. Realization of their adverse behaviors preceded the anorexics' acknowledgment of their subnormal body weight and size.

Contrasting with anorexics, the binge/purgers, when confronted, more readily admitted that they were bulimic and that their means of weight loss was "abnormal." Teresa, for example, knew "very well" that her bulimic behavior was "wrong and unhealthy," although "worth the physical risks." While the bulimics initially maintained that their purging was only a temporary weight-loss method, they eventually realized that their disorder represented a "loss of control." Although these respondents regretted the self-indulgence, "shame," and "wasted time," they acknowledged their growing dependence on binging/purging for weight management and stress regulation.

The application of anorexic or bulimic labels precipitated secondary deviance, wherein group members internalized these identities. Secondary deviance refers to norm violations which are a response to society's labeling: "secondary deviation...becomes a means of social defense, attack or adaptation to the overt and covert problems created by the societal reaction to primary deviance" (Lemert, 1967:17). In contrast to primary deviance, secondary deviance is generally prolonged, alters the individual's self-concept, and affects the performance of his/her social roles.

As secondary deviants, respondents felt that their disorders "gave a purpose" to their lives. Nicole resisted attaining a normal weight because it was not "her"—she accepted her anorexic weight as her "true" weight. For Teresa, bulimia became a "companion"; and Julie felt "every aspect of her life," including time management and social activities, was affected by her bulimia. Group members' eating disorders became the salient element of their self-concepts, so that they related to familiar people and new acquaintances as anorexics or bulimics. For example, respondents regularly compared their body shapes and sizes with those of others. They also became sensitized to comments about their appearance, whether or not the remarks were made by someone aware of their eating disorder.

With their behavior increasingly attuned to their eating disorders, group members exhibited role engulfment (Schur, 1971). Through accepting anorexic or bulimic identities, individuals centered activities around their deviant role, downgrading other social roles. Their obligations as students, family members, and friends became subordinate to their eating and exercising rituals. Socializing, for example, was gradually curtailed because it interfered with compulsive exercising, binging, or purging.

Labeled anorexic or bulimic, respondents were ascribed a new status with a different set of role expectations. Regardless of other positions the individuals occupied, their deviant status, or master status (Hughes, 1958; Becker, 1973), was identified before all others. Among group members, Nicole, who was known as the "school's brain," became known as the "school's anorexic." No longer viewed as conforming model individuals, some respondents were termed "starving waifs" or "pigs."

Because of their identities as deviants, anorexics' and bulimics' interactions with others were altered. Group members' eating habits were scrutinized by friends and family and used as a "catch-all" for everything negative that happened to them. Respondents felt self-conscious around individuals who knew of their disorders; for example, Robin imagined people "watching and whispering" behind her. In addition, group members believed others expected them to "act" anorexic or bulimic. Friends of some anorexic group members never offered them food or drink, assuming continued disinterest on the respondents' part. While being hospitalized, Denise felt she had to prove to others she was not still vomiting, by keeping her bathroom door open. Other bulimics, who lived in dormitories, were hesitant to use the restroom for normal purposes lest several friends be huddling at the door, listening for vomiting. In general, individuals interacted with the respondents largely on the basis of their eating disorder; in doing so, they reinforced anorexic and bulimic behaviors.

Bulimic respondents, whose weight-loss behavior was not generally detectable from their appearance, tried earnestly to hide their bulimia by binging and purging in secret. Their main purpose in concealment was to avoid the negative consequences of being known as a bulimic. For these individuals, bulimia connoted a "cop-out": like "weak anorexics," bulimics pursued thinness but yielded to urges to eat. Respondents felt other people regarded bulimia as "gross" and had little sympathy for the sufferer. To avoid these stigmas or "spoiled identities," the bulimics shrouded their behaviors.

Distinguishing types of stigma, Goffman (1963) describes discredited (visible) stigma and discreditable (invisible) stigmas. Bulimics, whose weight was approximately normal or even slightly elevated, harbored discreditable stigmas. Anorexics, on the other hand, suffered both discreditable and discredited stigmas—the latter due to their emaciated appearance. Certain anorexics were more reconciled than the bulimics to their stigmas: for Brian, the "stigma of anorexia was better than the stigma of being fat." Common to the stigmatized individuals was an inability to interact spontaneously with others. Respondents were constantly on guard against topics of eating and body size.

Both anorexics and bulimics were held responsible by others for their behavior and presumed able to "get out of it if they tried." Many anorexics reported being told to "just eat more," while bulimics were enjoined to simply "stop eating so much." Such appeals were made without regard for the complexities of the problem. Ostracized by certain friends and family members, anorexics and bulimics felt increasingly isolated. For respondents, the self-help group presented a non-threatening forum for discussing their disorders. Here, they found mutual understanding, empathy, and support. Many participants viewed BANISH as a haven from stigmatization by "others."

Group members, as secondary deviants, thus endured negative consequences, such as stigmatization, from being labeled. As they internalized the labels anorexic or bulimic, individuals' self-concepts were significantly influenced. When others interacted with the respondents on the basis of their eating disorders, anorexic or bulimic identities were encouraged. Moreover, group members' efforts to counteract the deviant labels were thwarted by their master statuses.

DISCUSSION

Previous research on eating disorders has dwelt almost exclusively on medical and psychological facets. Although necessary for a comprehensive understanding of anorexia nervosa and bulimia, these approaches neglect the social processes involved. The phenomena of eating disorders transcend concrete disease entities and clinical diagnoses. Multifaceted and complex, anorexia nervosa and bulimia require a holistic research design, in which sociological insights must be included.

A limitation of medical/psychiatric studies, in particular, is researchers' use of a priori criteria in establishing salient variables. Rather than utilizing predetermined standards of inclusion, the present study allows respondents to construct their own reality. Concomitant to this innovative approach to eating disorders is the selection of a sample of self-admitted anorexics and bulimics. Individuals' perceptions of what it means to become anorexic or bulimic are explored. Although based on a small sample, findings can be used to guide researchers in other settings.

With only five to ten percent of reported cases appearing in males (Crisp, 1977; Stangler and Printz, 1980), eating disorders are primarily a women's aberrance. The deviance of anorexia nervosa and bulimia is rooted in the visual objectification of women and attendant slimness norm. Indeed, purposeful starvation and binging/purging reinforce the notion that "a society gets the deviance it deserves" (Schur, 1979:71). As recently noted (Schur, 1984), the sociology of deviance has generally bypassed systematic studies of women's norm violations. Like male deviants, females endure label applications, internalizations, and fulfillments.

The social processes involved in developing anorexic or bulimic identities comprise the sequence of conforming behavior, primary deviance, and secondary deviance. With a background of exceptional adherence to conventional norms, especially the striving for thinness, respondents subsequently exhibit the primary deviance of starving or binging/purging. Societal reaction to these behaviors leads to secondary deviance, wherein respondents' self-concepts and master statuses become anorexic or bulimic. Within this framework of labeling theory, the persistence of eating disorders, as well as the effects of stigmatization, are elucidated.

Although during the course of this research some respondents alleviated their symptoms through psychiatric help or hospital treatment programs, no one was labeled "cured." An anorexic is considered recovered when weight is normal for two years; a bulimic is termed recovered after being symptom-free for one and one-half years (American Anorexia/Bulimia Association Newsletter, 1985). Thus deviance disavowal (Schur, 1971), or efforts after normalization to counteract the deviant labels, remains a topic for future exploration.

Notes

1. Although instructive, an integration of the medical, psychological, and sociocultural perspectives on eating disorders is beyond the scope of this paper.

2. Exceptions to the neglect of sociocultural factors are discussions of sex-role socialization in the development of eating disorders. Anorexics' girlish appearance has been interpreted as a rejection of femininity and womanhood (Orbach, 1979; Bruch, 1981; Orbach, 1985). In contrast, bulimics have been characterized as over-conforming to traditional female sex roles (Boskind-Lodahl, 1976).

3. Although a group experience for self-defined bulimics has been reported (Boskind-Lodahl, 1976), the researcher, from the outset, focused on Gestalt and behaviorist techniques within a feminist orientation.

4. One explanation for fewer anorexics than bulimics in the sample is that, in the general population, anorexics are outnumbered by bulimics at 8 or 10 to 1 (Lawson, as reprinted in American Anorexia/Bulimia Association Newsletter, 1985:1). The proportion of bulimics to anorexics in the sample is 6.5 to 1. In addition, compared to bulimics, anorexics may be less likely to attend a self-help group as they have a greater tendency to deny the existence of an eating problem (Humphries et al., 1982). However, the four anorexics in the present study were among the members who attended the meetings most often.

5. Interactions in the families of anorexics and bulimics might seem deviant in being inordinately close. However, in the larger societal context, the family members epitomize the norms of family cohesiveness. Perhaps unusual in their occurrence, these families are still within the realm of conformity. Humphries and colleagues (1982:202) refer to the "highly enmeshed and protective" family as part of the "idealized family myth."

References

American Anorexia/Bulimia Association. 1983. Correspondence. April.

American Anorexia/Bulimia Association Newsletter. 1985. 8(3).

Becker, Howard S. 1973. *Outsiders.* New York: Free Press.

Boskind-Lodahl, Marlene. 1976. "Cinderella's stepsisters: A feminist perspective on anorexia nervosa and bulimia." *Signs, Journal of Women in Culture and Society* 2:342–56.

Boskind-White, Marlene. 1985. "Bulimarexia: A sociocultural perspective." Pp. 113–26 in S. W. Emmett (ed.), *Theory and Treatment of Anorexia Nervosa and Bulimia: Biomedical, Sociocultural and Psychological Perspectives.* New York: Brunner/Mazel.

Branch, C. H. Hardin, and Linda J. Eurman. 1980. "Social attitudes toward patients with anorexia nervosa." *American Journal of Psychiatry* 137:631–32.

Bruch, Hilde. 1981. "Developmental considerations of anorexia nervosa and obesity." *Canadian Journal of Psychiatry* 26:212–16.

Chernin, Kim. 1981. *The Obsession: Reflections on the Tyranny of Slenderness.* New York: Harper and Row.

Crisp, A. H. 1977. "The prevalence of anorexia nervosa and some of its associations in the general population." *Advances in Psychosomatic Medicine* 9:38–47.

Crisp, A. H., R. L. Palmer, and R. S. Kalucy. 1976. "How common is anorexia nervosa? A prevalence study." *British Journal of Psychiatry* 128:549–54.

DeJong, William. 1980. "The stigma of obesity: The consequences of naive assumptions concerning the causes of physical deviance." *Journal of Health and Social Behavior* 21:75–87.

Fox, K. C. and N. McI. James. 1976. "Anorexia nervosa: A study of 44 strictly defined cases." *New Zealand Medical Journal* 84:309–12.

Garner, David M., Paul E. Garfinkel, Donald Schwartz, and Michael Thompson. 1980. "Cultural expectations of thinness in women." *Psychological Reports* 47: 483–91.

Goffman, Erving. 1963. *Stigma.* Englewood Cliffs, NJ: Prentice-Hall.

Halmi, Katherine A., James R. Falk, and Estelle Schwartz. 1981. "Binge-eating and vomiting: A survey of a college population." *Psychological Medicine* 11:697–706.

Herzog, David B. 1982. "Bulimia: The secretive syndrome." *Psychosomatics* 23: 481–83.

Hughes, Everett C. 1958. *Men and Their Work.* New York: Free Press.

Humphries, Laurie L., Sylvia Wrobel, and H. Thomas Wiegert. 1982. "Anorexia nervosa." *American Family Physician* 26:199–204.

Johnson, Craig L., Marilyn K. Stuckey, Linda D. Lewis, and Donald M. Schwartz. 1982. "Bulimia: A descriptive survey of 316 cases." *International Journal of Eating Disorders* 2(1):3–16.

Kalucy, R. S., A. H. Crisp, and Britta Harding. 1977. "A study of 56 families with anorexia nervosa." *British Journal of Medical Psychology* 50:381–95.

Lacey, Hubert J., Sian Coker, and S. A. Birtchnell. 1986. "Bulimia: Factors associated with its etiology and maintenance." *International Journal of Eating Disorders* 5:475–87.

Lemert, Edwin M. 1951. *Social Pathology*. New York: McGraw-Hill.

———. 1967. *Human Deviance, Social Problems and Social Control*. Englewood Cliffs, NJ: Prentice Hall.

Minuchin, Salvador, Bernice L. Rosman, and Lester Baker. 1978. *Psychosomatic Families: Anorexia Nervosa in Context*. Cambridge, MA: Harvard University Press.

Orbach, Susie. 1979. *Fat is a Feminist Issue*. New York: Berkeley.

———. 1985. "Visibility/invisibility: Social considerations in anorexia nervosa—a feminist perspective." Pp. 127–38 in S. W. Ernmett (ed.), *Theory and Treatment of Anorexia Nervosa and Bulimia: Biomedical, Sociocultural, and Psychological Perspectives*. New York: Brunner/Mazel.

Ritenbaugh, Cheryl. 1982. "Obesity as a culture-bound syndrome." *Culture, Medicine, and Psychiatry* 6:347–61.

Russell, Gerald. 1979. "Bulimia nervosa: An ominous variant of anorexia nervosa." *Psychological Medicine* 9:429–48.

Schlesier-Stropp, Barbara. 1984. "Bulimia: A review of the literature." *Psychological Bulletin* 95:247–57.

Schur, Edwin M. 1971. *Labeling Deviant Behavior*. New York: Harper and Row.

———. 1979. *Interpreting Deviance: A Sociological Introduction*. New York: Harper and Row.

———. 1984. *Labeling Women Deviant: Gender, Stigma, and Social Control*. New York: Random House.

Schwartz, Donald M., and Michael G. Thompson. 1981. "Do anorectics get well? Current research and future needs." *American Journal of Psychiatry* 138:319–23.

Schwartz, Donald M., Michael G. Thompson, and Craig L. Johnson. 1982. "Anorexia nervosa and bulimia: The socio-cultural context." *International Journal of Eating Disorders* 1(3):20–36.

Selvini-Palazzoli, Mara. 1978. *Self-Starvation: From Individual to Family Therapy in the Treatment of Anorexia Nervosa*. New York: Jason Aronson.

Stangler, Ronnie S., and Adolph M. Printz. 1980. "DSM-III: Psychiatric diagnosis in a university population." *American Journal of Psychiatry* 137:937–40.

Theander, Sten. 1970. "Anorexia nervosa." *Acta Psychiatrica Scandinavica Supplement* 214:24–31.

Thompson, Michael G., and Donald M. Schwartz. 1982. "Life adjustment of women with anorexia nervosa and anorexic-like behavior." *International Journal of Eating Disorders* 1(2):47–60.

Willi, Jurg, and Samuel Grossmann. 1983. "Epidemiology of anorexia nervosa in a defined region of Switzerland." *American Journal of Psychiatry* 140:564–67.

Part 3 / Becoming Deviant

PRIVATE DOMAINS, INFORMATION CONTROL, AND ACCOMMODATION

In Part 1, I made some general statements about the way deviant categories arise and the way violators of these categories may be reacted to. In Part 2, I explored some of the major theories and perspectives that serve to explain why actors may commit deviant acts. In this part of the book, I will deal more systematically with reactions that may bring about early stages of deviant careers—careers which may ultimately become subject to institutional control and regulation (Part 4).

In the general introduction, a distinction was made between the initiation of the labeling ceremony in a private domain and initiation in the public domain. I also noted how those engaged in deviant pursuits attempt to manage their behavior and attitudes in such a way as to avoid detection by socially significant "straights," especially formal agents of social control. This avoidance clearly indicates both the existence of some potentially stigmatizing or discreditable feature of their biography and the knowledge that detection is frequently associated with a range of personal and social costs. As an example, the drug pusher runs the risk of being sanctioned by the courts. It is conceivable, of course, that the pusher may never experience any direct contact with the social-control apparatus. In such a case he or she would remain what I have termed a noninstitutional deviant. Still, the pusher is aware of the potentially damaging nature of his or her activities and realizes that if authorities became aware of those activities, that knowledge could be used to initiate some type of institutional career.

In the analysis of strategies for information control and management, it is useful, therefore, to think in terms of actor *and* audience response. The pusher, in an effort to protect his or her self-image and identity cluster, as well as to reduce the odds of being officially designated as a deviant, may employ certain strategies (e.g., denying to self and others that he or she is a pusher). Similarly, those who must deal with actual or potential deviance often invoke various types of coping or accommodative strategies. A wife, for example, may try to accommodate herself to her husband's increasingly violent behavior. If she is successful, the deviance will remain primarily a matter of private knowledge, regulation, and management—although the wife herself may consider her husband to be deviant. If, on the other hand, the wife's accommodative strategies (e.g., attempts at neutralization or rationalization) fail, she may find it necessary to bring in third parties (e.g., social-control agents like the police) to regulate her husband's behavior. Not only have the wife's "tolerance limits" been exceeded in this case, but behavior that had been managed in the private setting now becomes subject to institutional control. And the husband may be typed, processed, and responded to as an involuntary mental patient.

The selections that follow explore some of the ways in which strategies for management and accommodation operate in private settings. The lead article introduces an important analytical distinction concerning public and personal identity, while the remaining pieces illustrate how audiences may not only help in the production of deviant behavior or beginning deviant careers, but also how audiences may respond to deviant or increasingly violent behavior on the part of significant or generalized others. These pieces also provide excellent illustrations of the usefulness of many of the basic concepts and processes introduced in Parts 1 and 2. For example, Ferraro and Johnson, in their analysis of spouse battery, rely very heavily on Sykes and Matza's neutralization techniques (selection 9 in this book). Although some attention is placed on an actor's behavior, it should be emphasized that the primary focus in this part is given to audience response to perceived or actual deviance on the part of others.

Erving Goffman, in "Information Control and Personal Identity: The Discredited and the Discreditable," draws an important distinction between the *discredited* and the *discreditable*. He notes that when there is a discrepancy between an actor's actual social identity and his or her virtual one, it is possible that this information, if it is stigmatizing, will become known to us before we interact with the actor. A stigmatizing feature or, as Goffman prefers, a "spoiled identity," can affect how we actually relate to the stigmatized. We may, for example, recognize a discrediting feature or make no notice of it. The actor is, however, often viewed as a discredited person. When the "known differentness" or stigmatizing feature of an actor's biography is not known, he or she must be viewed, conceptually, as potentially discreditable. This situation, Goffman argues, presents the actor with a dilemma. Does one tell or not tell? Does one lie or not lie? Or, does one release the potentially discrediting and stigmatizing information to selected individuals in specific settings or domains? Goffman reasons that the release of stigmatizing information can produce certain effects. For example, the release of information can help to confirm or round out the image one may have of an actor. At this point, Goffman introduces a useful distinction among *prestige symbols, stigma symbols,* and *disidentifiers.* A prestige symbol (e.g., a wedding band or a badge) often draws attention to a positive aspect of one's identity, while a stigma symbol (e.g., a conviction for rape or child molestation) causes focus on a discrediting or debasing feature of identity. A disidentifier (e.g., an advanced education of a street person) can be a sign that may disrupt or cast doubt on the validity of an actor's virtual identity. Goffman cautions that not only do signs vary in their reliability, but they can be used as a source of information about the identity of others. He cites, as an example, how anyone who associates with a known criminal or person wanted for arrest can be contaminated.

Patricia A. Adler and Peter Adler, in "Tinydopers: A Case Study of Deviant Socialization," focus on the phenomenon of *tinydoping* or, in this case, the practice of marijuana smoking on the part of young children. This activity, the researchers suggest, raises some interesting questions about changing societal mores and and parental socialization. Adler and Adler give specific attention to marijuana-smoking children under the age of nine. Of particular focus is the way in which parents actually influence and socialize their children with respect to the use of marijuana. They present case materials on four children they feel to be typical of other children and adults. After describing various patterns and stages of development, the researchers move to an analysis of how parents instruct their children in the ways of dealing with the outside world. And while the use of marijuana may be open and direct in the privacy of one's own confines, parents are aware that by allowing marijuana use on the part of their young children, they are frequently taking on "an extra social and legal stigma." The motivation for doing so seems to be the desire on the part of the parents to have their children view marijuana smoking in a positive light and not as an evil or unnatural thing. In the words of Adler and Adler, "thus, to destigmatize marijuana they stigmatize themselves in the face of society." The researchers conclude by offering additional insight into the "moral passage" or transformation of marijuana's social and legal status from criminalization to relative legitimization. They demonstrate what is likely to happen when smoking spreads to one of society's sacred groups— children. Adler and Adler present a five-stage of model of social change that they feel captures the diffusion and legitimization of marijuana. For example, during Stage I (the 1940s), the "carriers" or users were what the authors term "stigmatized outgroups" (blacks). By stage II (the 1950s), usage had spread to "ingroup deviants" (e.g., jazz musicians) who identified with stigmatized outgroups. From there, usage spread to such "avant-garde ingroup members" as college students (Stage III, the 1960s), to such "normal ingroup members" as the middle class (Stage IV, the 1970s), and finally to such "sacred groups" as children (Stage V, from 1975 on). Adler and Adler maintain that the spread of deviance to Stage V can produce social revulsion and trigger attempts to ban the behavior by children; this appears to be the case with respect to tinydopers. This analysis of the moral passage of marijuana has direct relevance for the discussion in Part 6 on the transformation of deviant categories.

Joseph W. Schneider and Peter Conrad, in their article "In the Closet with Illness: Epilepsy, Stigma Potential and Information Control," provide an interesting account of how people attempt to manage what they view as discreditable information about themselves. These writers focus on a sample of eighty epileptics, none of whom has a history of long-term institutionalization. The researchers, in their reliance on the metaphor of the closet, initially advance the concept of "stigma potential" to emphasize the fact that epilepsy is a trait that causes one's identity to be discredited. The characterization of the stigma as "potential," they argue, rests on two basic assumptions: (1) that knowledge of the attribute (i.e., epilepsy) be limited to a few people, and (2) that if the trait were to become more widely known, significant changes in self, along with various controls of behavior, might result. Schneider and Conrad cite several examples that underscore the stigma potential of epilepsy (e.g., being discriminated against in the area of employment and being prohibited from marrying in some states). The authors then assert that stigma is not an automatic result of possessing some discreditable trait. Rather, the significance of " 'having' epilepsy is a product of a collective definitional process"—one in which the actor and others participate. A discreditable trait or performance becomes relevant to self only if it is perceived as such by the actor. How might the potentially stigmatized feel that others think about them, and how might others react to disclosure? Schneider and Conrad note that our understanding of an actor's *perception of stigma* is limited. They then discuss various strategies relative to concealment and disclosure (i.e., whether, and under what conditions, one will come out of the closet or not). For example, parental training regarding the stigma of epilepsy is often very important. Not only do parents frequently serve as coaches but, as they do so, the children learn how to deal with the fact that they are potentially discreditable. Other people also teach the importance of concealment. The authors end by discussing the strategies of selective concealment and instrumental telling.

"The Adjustment of the Family to the Crisis of Alcoholism," by Joan K. Jackson, provides an excellent account of how family members, particularly wives, try to adjust to a husband's alcoholism. Jackson's article offers a fruitful examination of how the accommodative process actually works. A wife may at first deny that a drinking problem exists by rationalizing it away, and she may be successful in her attempts. However, it may happen that not only does the drinking become progressively worse, but a family crisis develops. The wife may then decide that there is no real hope for the marriage and leave. Jackson maintains that even though many wives do leave their husbands, they frequently return; their return is often prompted by an increased understanding of alcoholism and by the need to lessen their feelings of guilt at leaving a sick man. When a wife returns, she will attempt to reorganize the family while still relying upon accommodative strategies as necessary.

Kathleen J. Ferraro and John M. Johnson, in "How Women Experience Battering: The Process of Victimization," present some recent evidence on the battering of women. The accounts of 120 battered women provide the major data source. The researchers are concerned specifically with identifying those conditions that keep women locked in abusive relationships. What they discover is that instead of seeking help or escaping, most women initially rationalize the violence that is perpetrated upon them by their husbands. Ferraro and Johnson cite several reasons why battered women resort to rationalization. The main one involves the relative lack of institutional, legal, and cultural supports. Thus, practical and social constraints, when coupled with the factors of commitment and love, prompt the use of rationalizations. Ferraro and Johnson, in extending Sykes and Matza's "techniques of neutralization," develop a six-category typology of rationalizations. Each woman in their study used at least one of these techniques, and some used more than one. In terms of the specific rationalizations, women who invoke "the denial of victimization" technique often blame themselves, thereby neutralizing the spouse's responsibility. Some felt that if they had been more passive or conciliatory, the violence could have been avoided. Rationalizations may be effective for some; however, when battered women cease to rationalize and begin to acknowledge their abuse, the process of feeling victimized begins. The researchers discuss six catalysts that bring about this redefinition of abuse (e.g., a change in the level of abuse, a change in resources, and a change in the visibility of violence). Ferraro and Johnson conclude with a discussion of what they term the emotional career of victimization; they also comment on the aftermath of leaving.

19 / Information Control and Personal Identity: The Discredited and the Discreditable

ERVING GOFFMAN

When there is a discrepancy between an individual's actual social identity and his virtual one, it is possible for this fact to be known to us before we normals contact him, or to be quite evident when he presents himself before us. He is a discredited person, and it is mainly he I have been dealing with until now. As suggested, we are likely to give no open recognition to what is discrediting of him, and while this work of careful disattention is being done, the situation can become tense, uncertain, and ambiguous for all participants, especially the stigmatized one.

The cooperation of a stigmatized person with normals in acting as if his known differentness were irrelevant and not attended to is one main possibility in the life of such a person. However, when his differentness is not immediately apparent, and is not known beforehand (or at least known by him to be known to the others), when in fact his is a discreditable, not a discredited, person, then the second main possibility in his life is to be found. The issue is not that of managing tension generated during social contacts, but rather that of managing information about his failing. To display or not to display; to tell or not to tell; to let on or not to let on; to lie or not to lie; and in each case, to whom, how, when, and where. For example, while the mental patient is in the hospital, and when he is with adult members of his own family, he is faced with being treated tactfully as if he were sane when there is known to be some doubt, even though he may not have any; or he is treated as insane, when he knows this is not just. But for the ex-mental patient the problem can be quite different; it is not that he must face prejudice against himself, but rather that he must face unwitting acceptance of himself by individuals who are prejudiced against persons of the kind he can be revealed to be. Wherever he goes his behavior will falsely confirm for the other that they are in the company of what in effect they demand but may discover they haven't obtained, namely, a mentally untainted person like themselves. By intention or in effect the ex-mental patient conceals information about his real social identity, receiving and accepting treatment based on false suppositions concerning himself. It is this second general issue, the management of undisclosed discrediting information about self, that I am focusing on in these notes, in brief, "passing." The concealment of creditable facts—reverse passing—of course occurs, but is not relevant here.[1]

The information of most relevance in the study of stigma has certain properties. It is information about an individual. It is about his more or less abiding characteristics, as opposed to the moods, feelings, or intents that he might have at a particular moment.[2] The information as well as the sign through which it is conveyed, is reflexive and embodied; that is, it is conveyed by the very person it is about, and conveyed through bodily expression in the immediate presence of those who receive the expression. Information possessing all of these properties I will here call "social." Some signs that convey social information may be frequently and steadily available, and routinely sought and received; these signs may be called "symbols."

The social information conveyed by any particular symbol may merely confirm what other signs tell us about the individual, filling out our image of him in a redundant and unproblematic way. Some lapel buttons, attesting to social club membership, are examples, as are male wedding rings in some contexts. However, the social information conveyed by a symbol can establish a special claim to prestige, honor, or desirable class position—a claim that might not otherwise be presented or, if otherwise presented, then not automatically granted. Such a sign is popularly called a "status symbol," although the term 'prestige symbol" might be more accurate, the former term being more suitably employed when a well-organized social position of some kind is the referent. Prestige symbols can be contrasted to *stigma symbols,* namely, signs which are essentially effective in drawing attention to a debasing identity discrepancy, breaking up what would otherwise be a coherent overall picture, with a consequent reduction in our valuation of the individual. The shaved head of female collaborators in World War II is an example, as is an habitual solecism through which someone affecting middle class manner and dress repeatedly employs a word incorrectly or repeatedly mispronounces it.

In addition to prestige symbols and stigma symbols, one further possibility is to be found, namely, a sign that tends—in fact or hope—to break up an otherwise coherent picture but in this case in a positive direction desired by the actor, not so much establishing a new claim as throwing severe doubt on the validity of the virtual one. I shall refer here to disidentifiers. One example is the "good English" of an educated northern Negro visiting the South[3]; another is the turban and mustache affected by some urban lower class Negroes.[4] A study of illiterates provides another illustration:

> Therefore, when goal orientation is pronounced or imperative and there exists a high probability that definition as illiterate is a bar to the achievement of the goal, the illiterate is likely to try to "pass" as literate.... The popularity in the group studied of windowpane lenses with heavy horn frames ("bop glasses") may be viewed as an attempt to emulate the stereotype of the businessman-teacher-young intellectual and especially the high status jazz musician.[5]

A New York specialist in the arts of vagrancy provides still another illustration:

> After seven-thirty in the evening, in order to read a book in Grand Central or Penn Station, a person either has to wear horn-rimmed glasses or look exceptionally prosperous. Anyone else is apt to come under surveillance. On the other hand, newspaper readers never seem to attract attention and even the seediest vagrant can sit in Grand Central all night without being molested if he continues to read a paper.[6]

Note that in this discussion of prestige symbols, stigma symbols, and disidentifiers, signs have been considered which routinely convey social information. These symbols must be distinguished from fugitive signs that have not been institutionalized as information carriers. When such signs make claims to prestige, one can call them points; when they discredit tacit claims, one can call them slips.

Some signs carrying social information, being present, first of all, for other reasons, have only an overlay of informational function. There are stigma symbols that provide examples: the wrist markings which disclose that an individual has attempted suicide; the arm pock marks of drug addicts; the handcuffed wrists of convicts in transit;[7] or black eyes when worn in public by females, as a writer on prostitution suggests:

> "Outside [the prison where she now is] I'd be in the soup with it. Well, you know how it is: the law sees a chic with a shiner figures she's up to something. Bull figures maybe in the life. Next thing trails her around. Then maybe bang! busted."[8]

Other signs are designed by man solely for the purpose of conveying social information, as in the case of insignia of military rank. It should be added that the significance of the underlay of a sign can become reduced over time, becoming, at the extreme, merely vestigial, even while the informational function of the activity remains constant or increases in importance. Further, a sign that appears to be present for non-informational reasons may sometimes be manufactured with malice aforethought solely because of its informing function, as when dueling scars were carefully planned and inflicted.

Signs conveying social information vary according to whether or not they are congenital, and, if not, whether, once employed, they become a permanent part of the person. (Skin color is congenital; a brand mark or maiming is permanent but not congenital; a convict's head-shave is neither congenital nor permanent.) More important, impermanent signs solely employed to convey social information may or may not be employed against the will of the informant; when they are, they tend to be stigma symbols.[9] Later it will be necessary to consider stigma symbols that are voluntarily employed.

It is possible for signs which mean one thing to one group to mean something else to another group, the same category being designated but differently characterized. For example, the shoulder patches that prison officials require escape-prone prisoners to wear[10] can come to mean one thing to guards, in general negative, while being a mark of pride for the wearer relative to his fellow prisoners. The uniform of an officer may be a matter of pride to some, to be worn on every possible occasion; for other officers, weekends may represent a time when they can exercise their choice and wear mufti, passing as civilians. Similarly, while the obligation to wear the school cap in town may be seen as a privilege by some boys, as will the obligation to wear a uniform on leave by "other ranks," still there will be wearers who feel that the social information conveyed thereby is a means of ensuring control and discipline over them when they are off duty and off the premises.[11] So, too, during the eighteen hundreds in California, the absence of a pigtail (queue) on a Chinese man signified for Occidentals a degree of acculturation, but to fellow-Chinese a question would be raised as to respectability—specifically, whether or not the individual had served a term in prison where cutting off of the queue was obligatory; loss of queue was for a time, then, very strongly resisted.[12]

Signs carrying social information vary of course as to reliability. Distended capillaries on the cheek and nose, sometimes called "venous stigmata" with more aptness than meant, can be and are taken as indicating alcoholic excess. However, teetotalers can exhibit the same symbol for other physiological reasons, thereby giving rise to suspicions about themselves which aren't justified, but with which they must deal nonetheless.

A final point about social information must be raised; it has to do with the informing character of the "with" relationship in our society. To be "with" someone is to arrive at a social occasion in his company, walk with him down a street, be a member of his party in a restaurant, and so forth. The issue is that in certain circumstances the social identity of those an individual is with can be used as a source of information concerning his own social identity, the assumption being that he is what the others are. The extreme, perhaps, is the situation in criminal circles: a person wanted for arrest can legally contaminate anyone he is seen with, subjecting them to arrest on suspicion. (A person for whom there is a warrant is therefore said "to have smallpox," and his criminal disease is said to be "catching.")[13] In any case, an analysis of how people manage the information they convey about themselves will have to consider how they deal with the contingencies of being seen "with" particular others.

Notes

1. For one instance of reverse passing, see "H.E.R. Cules" and "Ghost-Writer and Failure," in P. Toynbee, ed., *Underdogs* (London: Weidenfeld, and Nicolson, 1961), Chap. 2, pp. 30–39. There are many other examples. I knew a physician who was careful to refrain from using external symbols of her status, such as car-license tags, her only evidence of profession being an identification carried in her wallet. When faced with a public accident in which medical service was already being rendered the victim, or in which the victim was past helping, she would, upon examining the victim at a distance from the circle around him, quietly go her way without announcing her competence. In these situations she was what might be called a female impersonator.

2. The difference between mood information and other kinds of information is treated in G. Stone, "Appearance and the Self," in A. Rose, *Human Behavior and Social Processes* (Boston: Houghton Mifflin, 1962), pp. 86–118. See also E. Goffman, *The Presentation of Self in Everyday Life* (New York: Doubleday & Co., Anchor Books, 1959), pp. 24–25.

3. G. J. Fleming, "My Most Humiliating Jim Crow Experience," *Negro Digest* (June 1954), 67–68.

4. B. Wolfe, "Ecstatic in Blackface," *Modern Review,* III (1950), 204.

5. Freeman and Kasenbaum, *op. cit.,* p. 372.

6. E. Love, *Subways Are for Sleeping* (New York: Harcourt, Brace & World, 1957), p. 28.

7. A. Heckstall-Smith, *Eighteen Months* (London: Allan Wingate, 1954), p. 43.

8. T. Rubin, *In the Life* (New York: The Macmillan Company, 1961), p. 69.

9. In his *American Notes,* written on the basis of his 1842 trip, Dickens records in his chapter on slavery some pages of quotations from local newspapers regarding lost and found slaves. The identifications contained in these advertisements provide a full range of identifying signs. First, there are relatively stable features of the body that in context can incidentally provide partial or full positive identification: age, sex, and scarrings (these resulting from shot and knife wounds, from accidents, and from lashings). Self-admitted name is also provided, though usually, of course, only the first name. Finally, stigma symbols are often cited, notably branded initials and cropped ears. These symbols communicate the social identity of slave but, unlike iron bands around the neck or leg, also communicate something more narrow than that, namely, ownership by a particular master. Authorities then had two concerns about an apprehended Negro: whether or not he was a runaway slave, and, if he was, to whom did he belong.

10. See G. Dendrickson and F. Thomas, *The Truth About Dartmoor* (London: Victor Gollancz, 1954), p. 55, and F. Norman, *Bang to Rights* (London: Secker and Warburg, 1958), p. 125. The use of this type of symbol is well presented in E. Kogon, *The Theory and Practice of Hell* (New York: Berkley Publishing Corp., n.d.), pp. 41–42, where he specifies the markings used in concentration camps to identify differentially political prisoners, second offenders, criminals, Jehovah's Witnesses, "shiftless elements," Gypsies, Jews, "race defilers," foreign nationals (according to nation), feeble-minded, and so forth. Slaves on the Roman slave market also were often labeled as to nationality; see M. Gordon, "The Nationality of Slaves Under the Early Roman Empire," in M. I. Finley, ed., *Slavery in Classical Antiquity* (Cambridge: Heffer, 1960), p. 171.

11. T. H. Pear, *Personality, Appearance and Speech* (London: George Allen and Unwin, 1957), p. 58.

12. A. McLeod, *Pigtails and Gold Dust* (Caldwell, Idaho: Caxton Printers, 1947), p. 28. At times religious-historical significance was also attached to wearing this queue; see *ibid.,* p. 204.

13. See D. Maurer, *The Big Con* (New York: Pocket Books, 1949), p. 298.

20 / Tinydopers: A Case Study of Deviant Socialization

PATRICIA A. ADLER
PETER ADLER

Marijuana smoking is now filtering down to our youngest generation; a number of children from 0—8 years old are participating in this practice under the influence and supervision of their parents. This phenomenon, *tinydoping,* raises interesting questions about changes in societal mores and patterns of socialization. We are not concerned here with the desirability or morality of the activity. Instead, we will discuss the phenomenon, elucidating the diverse range of attitudes, stratagems and procedures held and exercised by parents and children.

An examination of the history and cultural evolution of marijuana over the last several decades illuminates the atmosphere in which tinydoping arose. Marijuana use, first located chiefly among jazz musicians and ghetto communities, eventually expanded to "the highly alienated young in flight from families, schools and conventional communities" (Simon and Gagnon, 1968:60. See also Goode, 1970; Carey, 1968; Kaplan, 1971; and Grinspoon, 1971). Blossoming in the mid-1960s, this youth scene formed an estranged and deviant subculture offsetting the dominant culture's work ethic and instrumental success orientation. Society reacted as an angry parent, enforcing legal, social and moral penalties against its rebellious children. Today, however, the pothead subculture has eroded and the population of smokers has broadened to include large numbers of middle-class and establishment-oriented people.

Marijuana, then, may soon take its place with alcohol, its "prohibition" a thing of the past. These two changes can be considered movements of moral passage:

> Movements to redefine behavior may eventuate in a moral passage, a transition of the behavior from one moral status to another.... What is attacked as criminal today may be seen as sick next year and fought over as possibly legitimate by the next generation. (Gusfield, 1967:187. See also Matza, 1969; Kitsuse, 1962; Douglas, 1970; and Becker, 1963 for further discussions of the social creation of deviance.)

Profound metamorphoses testify to this redefinition: frequency and severity of arrest is proportionately down from a decade ago; the stigma of a marijuana-related arrest is no longer as personally and occupationally ostracizing; and the fear that using grass will press the individual into close contact with hardened criminals and cause him to adopt a deviant self-identity or take up criminal ways has also largely passed.

The transformation in marijuana's social and legal status is not intrinsic to its own characteristics or those of mood-altering drugs in general. Rather, it illustrates a process of becoming socially accepted many deviant activities or substances may go through. This research suggests a more generic model of social change, a sequential development characteristic of the diffusion and legitimation of a formerly unconventional practice. Five stages identify the spread of such activities from small isolated outgroups, through increasing levels of mainstream society, and finally to such sacred groups as children.[1] Often, however, as with the case of pornography, the appearance of this quasi-sanctioned conduct among juveniles elicits moral outrage and a social backlash designed to prevent such behavior in the sacred population, while leaving it more open to the remainder of society.

Most treatments of pot smoking in the sociological literature have been historically and subculturally specific (see Carey, 1968; Goode, 1970; Grupp, 1971; Hochman, 1972; Kaplan, 1971; and Simon and Gagnon, 1968), swiftly dated by our rapidly changing society. Only Becker's (1953) work is comparable to our research since it offers a general sequential model of the process for becoming a marijuana user.

The data in this paper show an alternate route to marijuana smoking. Two developments necessitate a modification of Becker's conceptualization. First, there have been many changes in norms, traditions and patterns of use since the time he wrote. Second, the age of this new category of smokers is cause for reformulation. Theories of child development proposed by Mead (1934), Erikson (1968), and Piaget (1948) agree that prior to a certain age children are unable to comprehend subtle transformations and perceptions. As we will see, the full effects and symbolic meanings of marijuana are partially lost to them due to their inability to differentiate between altered states of consciousness and to connect this with the smoking experience. Yet this does not preclude their becoming avid pot users and joining in the smoking group as accepted members.

Socialization practices are the final concern of this research. The existence of tinydoping both illustrates and contradicts several established norms of traditional childrearing. Imitative behavior (see Piaget, 1962), for instance, is integral to tinydoping since the children's desire to copy the actions of parents and other adults is a primary motivation. Boundary maintenance also arises as a consideration: as soon as their offspring can communicate, parents must instruct them in the perception of social borders and the need for guarding group activities as secret. In contrast, refutations of convention include the introduction of mood-altering drugs into the sacred childhood period and, even more unusual, parents and children get high together. This bridges, often to the point of eradication, the inter-generational gap firmly entrenched in most societies. Thus, although parents view their actions as normal, tinydoping must presently be considered as deviant socialization.

METHODS

Collected over the course of 18 months, our data include observations of two dozen youngsters between the ages of birth and eight, and a similar number of parents, aged 21 to 32, all in middle-class households. To obtain a complete image of this practice we talked with parents, kids and other involved observers (the "multiperspectival" approach, Douglas, 1976). Many of our conversations with adults were taped but our discussions with the children took the form of informal, extemporaneous dialogue, since the tape recorder distracts and diverts their attention. Finally, our study is exploratory and suggestive; we make no claim to all-inclusiveness in the cases or categories below.

THE KIDS

The following four individuals, each uniquely interesting, represent many common characteristics of other children and adults we observed.

"Big Ed": The Diaperdoper

Big Ed derives his name from his miniature size. Born three months prematurely, now three years old, he resembles a toy human being. Beneath his near-white wispy hair and toddling diapered bottom, he packs a punch of childish energy. Big Ed's mother and older siblings take care of him although he often sees his father who lives in a neighboring California town. Laxity and permissiveness characterize his upbringing, as he freely roams the neighborhood under his own and other children's supervision. Exposure to marijuana has prevailed since birth and in the last year he advanced from passive inhalation (smoke blown in his direction) to active puffing on joints. Still in the learning stage, most of his power is expended blowing air into the reefer instead of inhaling. He prefers to suck on a "bong" (a specially designed waterpipe), delighting in the gurgling sound the water makes. A breast fed baby, he will go to the bong for oral satisfaction, whether it is filled or not. He does not actively seek joints, but Big Ed never refuses one when offered. After a few puffs, however, he usually winds up with smoke in his eyes and tearfully retreats to a glass of water. Actual marijuana inhalation is minimal; his size renders it potent. Big Ed has not absorbed any social restrictions related to pot use or any awareness of its illegality, but is still too young to make a blooper as his speech is limited.

Stephanie: The Social Smoker

Stephanie is a dreamy four-year old with quite good manners, calm assurance, sweet disposition and a ladylike personality and appearance. Although her brothers are rough and tumble, Stephanie can play with the boys or amuse herself sedately alone or in the company of adults. Attendance at a progressive school for the last two years has developed her natural curiosity and intelligence. Stephanie's mother and father both work, but still find enough recreational time to raise their children with love and care and to engage in frequent marijuana smoking. Accordingly, Stephanie has seen grass since infancy and accepted it as a natural part of life. Unlike the diaperdoper, she has mastered the art of inhalation and can breathe the smoke out through her nose. Never grasping or grubbing for pot, she has advanced from a preference for bongs or pipes and now enjoys joints when offered. She revels in being part of a crowd of smokers and passes the reefer immediately after each puff, never holding it for an unsociable amount of time. Her treasure box contains a handful of roaches (marijuana butts) and seeds (she delights in munching them as snacks) that she keeps as mementos of social occasions with (adult) "friends." After smoking, Stephanie becomes more bubbly and outgoing. Dancing to records, she turns in circles as she jogs from one foot to the other, releasing her body to the rhythm. She then eats everything in sight and falls asleep—roughly the same cycle as adults, but faster.

When interviewed, Stephanie clearly recognized the difference between a cigarette and a joint (both parents use tobacco), defining the effects of the latter as good but still being unsure of what the former did and how the contents of each varied. She also responded with some confusion about social boundaries separating pot users from non-users, speculating that perhaps her grandmother did smoke it but her grandfather certainly did not (neither do). In the words of her father: "She knows not to tell people about it but she just probably wouldn't anyway."

Josh: The Self-gratifier

Everyone in the neighborhood knows Josh. Vociferous and outgoing, at age five he has a decidedly Dennis-the-Menace quality in both looks and personality. Neither timid nor reserved, he boasts to total strangers of his fantastic exploits and talents. Yet behind his bravado swagger lies a seeming insecurity and need for acceptance, coupled with a difficulty in accepting authority, which has led him into squabbles with peers, teachers, siblings and parents.

Josh's home shows the traditional division of labor. His mother stays home to cook and care for the children while his father works long hours. The mother is always calm and tolerant about her youngster's smart-alec ways, but his escapades may provoke an explosive tirade from his father. Yet this male parent is clearly the dominating force in Josh's life. Singling Josh out from his younger sister and brother, the father has chosen him as his successor in the male tradition. The parent had himself begun drinking and smoking cigarettes in his early formative years, commencing pot use as a teenager, and now has a favorable attitude toward the early use of stimulants which he is actively passing on to Josh.

According to his parents, his smoking has had several beneficial effects. Considering Josh a "hyper" child, they claim that it calms him down to a more normal speed, often permitting him to engage in activities which would otherwise be too difficult for his powers of concentration. He also appears to become more sedate and less prone to temper tantrums, sleeping longer and more deeply. But Josh's smoking patterns differ significantly from our last two subjects. He does not enjoy social smoking, preferring for his father to roll him "pinners" (thin joints) to smoke by himself. Unlike many other tinydopers, Josh frequently refuses the offer of a joint saying, "Oh that! I gave up smoking that stuff." At age five he claims to have already quit and gone back several times. His mother backs this assertion as valid; his father brushes it off as merely a ploy to shock and gain attention. Here, the especially close male parent recognizes the behavior as imitative and accepts it as normal. To others, however, it appears strange and suggests surprising sophistication.

Josh's perception of social boundaries is also mature. Only a year older than Stephanie, Josh has made some mistakes but his awareness of the necessity for secrecy is complete; he differentiates those people with whom he may and may not discuss the subject by the experience of actually smoking with them. He knows individuals but cannot yet socially categorize the boundaries. Josh also realizes the contrast between joints and cigarettes down to the marijuana and tobacco they contain. Interestingly, he is aggressively opposed to tobacco while favoring pot use (this may be the result of anti-tobacco cancer propaganda from kindergarten).

Kyra: The Bohemian

A worldly but curiously childlike girl is seven-year-old Kyra. Her wavy brown hair falls to her shoulders and her sun-tanned body testifies to many hours at the beach in winter and summer. Of average height for her age, she dresses with a maturity beyond her years. Friendly and sociable, she has few reservations about what she says to people. Kyra lives with her youthful mother and whatever boyfriend her mother fancies at the moment. Their basic family unit consists of two (mother and daughter), and they have travelled together living a free life all along the West Coast and Hawaii. While Josh's family was male dominated, this is clearly female centered, all of Kyra's close relatives being women. They are a bohemian group, generation after generation following a hip, up-to-the-moment, unshackled lifestyle. The house is often filled with people, but when the visitors clear out, a youthful, thrillseeking mother remains, who raises this daughter by treating her like a sister or friend. This demand on Kyra to behave as an adult may produce some internal strain, but she seems to have grown accustomed to it. Placed in situations others might find awkward, she handles them with precocity. Like her mother, she is being reared for a life of independence and freedom.

Pot smoking is an integral part of this picture. To Kyra it is another symbol for her adulthood; she enjoys it and wants to do it a lot. At seven she is an accomplished smoker; her challenge right now lies in the mastery of rolling joints. Of our four examples, social boundaries are clearest to Kyra. Not only is she aware of the necessary secrecy surrounding pot use, but she is able to socially categorize types of people into marijuana smokers and straights. She may err in her judgment occasionally, but no more so than any adult.

STAGES OF DEVELOPMENT

These four and other cases suggest a continuum of reactions to marijuana that is loosely followed by most tinydopers.

From birth to around 18 months a child's involvement is passive. Most parents keep their infants nearby at all times and if pot is smoked the room becomes filled with potent clouds. At this age just a little marijuana smoke can be very powerful and these infants, the youngest diaperdopers, manifest noticeable effects. The drug usually has a calming influence, putting the infant into a less cranky mood and extending the depth and duration of sleep.

After the first one and a half years, the children are more attuned to what is going on around them: they begin to desire participation in a "monkey see, monkey do" fashion. During the second year, a fascination with paraphernalia generally develops, as they play with it and try to figure it out. Eager to smoke with the adults and older children, they are soon discouraged after a toke (puff) or two. They find smoking difficult and painful (particularly to the eyes and throat)—after all, it is not easy to inhale burning hot air and hold it in your lungs.

But continual practice eventually produces results, and inhalation seems to be achieved somewhere during the third or fourth year. This brings considerable pride and makes the kids feel they have attained semi-adult status. Now they can put the paraphernalia to work. Most tinydopers of this age are wild about "roach clips," itching to put their joints into them as soon as possible after lighting.

Ages four and five bring the first social sense of the nature of pot and who should know about it. This begins as a vague idea, becoming further refined with age and sophistication. Finally, by age seven or eight kids have a clear concept of where the lines can be drawn between those who are and aren't "cool," and can make these distinctions on their own. No child we interviewed, however, could verbalize about any specific effects felt after smoking marijuana. Ironically, although they participate in smoking and actually manifest clear physical symptoms of the effects, tinydopers are rationally and intellectually unaware of how the drug is acting upon them. They are too young to notice a change in their behavior or to make the symbolic leap and associate this transformation with having smoked pot previously. The effects of marijuana must be socially and consensually delineated from non-high sensations for the user to fully appreciate the often subtle perceptual and physiological changes that have occurred. To the youngster the benefits of pot smoking are not at all subtle: he is permitted to imitate his elders by engaging in a social ritual they view as pleasurable and important; the status of adulthood is partially conferred on him by allowing this act; and his desire for acceptance is fulfilled through inclusion in his parents' peer group. This constitutes the major difference in appreciation between the child and adult smoker.

PARENTS' STRATEGIES

The youth of the sixties made some forceful statements through their actions about how they evaluated the Establishment and the conventional American lifestyle. While their political activism has faded, many former members of this group still feel a strong commitment to smoking pot and attach a measure of symbolic significance to it. When they had children the question then arose of how to handle the drug vis-á-vis their offspring. The continuum of responses they developed ranges from total openness and permissiveness to various measures of secrecy.

Smoking Regularly Permitted

Some parents give their children marijuana whenever it is requested. They may wait until the child reaches a certain age, but most parents in this category started their kids on pot from infancy. These parents may be "worried" or "unconcerned."

Worried: Ken and Deedy are moderate pot smokers, getting high a few times a week. Both had been regular users for several years prior to having children. When Deedy was pregnant she absolutely refused to continue her smoking pattern.

> I didn't know what effect it could have on the unborn child. I tried to read and find out, but there's very little written on that. But in the *Playboy* Advisor there was an article: they said we advise you to stay away from all drugs when you're pregnant. That was sort of my proof. I figured they don't bullshit about

these types of things. I sort of said now at least somebody stands behind me because people were saying, "You can get high, it's not going to hurt the baby."

This abstinence satisfied them and once the child was born they resumed getting high as before. Frequently smoking in the same room as the baby, they began to worry about the possible harmful effects this exposure might have on his physical, psychological and mental development. After some discussion, they consulted the family pediatrician, a prominent doctor in the city.

I was really embarrassed, but I said, "Doctor, we get high, we smoke pot, and sometimes the kid's in the room. If he's in the room can this hurt him? I don't want him to be mentally retarded." He said, "Don't worry about it, they're going to be legalizing it any day now—this was three years ago—it's harmless and a great sedative."

This reassured them on two counts: they no longer were fearful in their own minds, and they had a legitimate answer when questioned by their friends.[2]

Ken and Deedy were particularly sensitive about peer reactions:

Some people say, "You let your children get high?!" They really act with disgust. Or they'll say, "Oh you let your kids get high," and then they kind of look at you like, "That's neat, I think." And it's just nice to be able to back it up.

Ken and Deedy were further nonplussed about the problem of teaching their children boundary maintenance. Recognizing the need to prevent their offspring from saying things to the wrong people, they were unsure how to approach this subject properly.

How can you tell a kid, how can you go up to him and say, "Well you want to get high, but don't tell anybody you're doing it"? You can't. We didn't really know how to tell them. You don't want to bring the attention, you don't want to tell your children not to say anything about it because that's a sure way to get them to do it. We just never said anything about it.

They hope this philosophy of openness and permissiveness will forestall the need to limit their children's marijuana consumption. Limits, for them, resemble prohibitions and interdictions against discussing grass: they make transgressions attractive. Both parents believe strongly in presenting marijuana as an everyday occurrence, definitely not as an undercover affair. When asked how they thought this upbringing might affect their kids, Deedy offered a fearful but doubtful speculation that her children might one day reject the drug.

I don't imagine they'd try to abuse it. Maybe they won't even smoke pot when they get older. That's a big possibility. I doubt it, but hopefully they won't be that way. They've got potheads for parents.

Unconcerned: Alan and Anna make use of a variety of stimulants—pot, alcohol, cocaine—to enrich their lives. Considered heavy users, they consume marijuana and alcohol daily. Alan became acquainted with drugs, particularly alcohol, at a very early age and Anna first tried them in her teens. When they decided to have children the question of whether they would permit the youngsters to partake in their mood-altering experiences never arose. Anna didn't curtail her drug intake during pregnancy; her offspring were conceived, formed and weaned on this steady diet. When queried about their motivations, Alan volunteered:

> What the hell! It grows in the ground, it's a weed. I can't see anything wrong with doing anything, inducing any part of it into your body anyway that you possibly could eat it, smoke it, intravenously, or whatever, that it would ever harm you because it grows in the ground. It's a natural thing. It's one of God's treats.

All of their children have been surrounded by marijuana's aromatic vapor since the day they returned from the hospital. Alan and Anna were pleased with the effect pot had on their infants; the relaxed, sleepy and happy qualities achieved after inhaling pot smoke made childrearing an easier task. As the little ones grew older they naturally wanted to share in their parents' activities. Alan viewed this as the children's desire to imitate rather than true enjoyment of any effects:

> Emily used to drink Jack Daniels straight and like it. I don't think it was taste, I think it was more of an acceptance thing because that's what I was drinking. She was also puffing on joints at six months.

This mimicking, coupled with a craving for acceptance, although recognized by Alan in his kids, was not repeated in his own feelings toward friends or relatives. At no time during the course of our interview or acquaintance did he show any concern with what others thought of his behavior; rather, his convictions dominated, and his wife passively followed his lead.

In contrast to the last couple, Alan was not reluctant to address the problem of boundary maintenance. A situation arose when Emily was three, where she was forced to learn rapidly:

> One time we were stopped by the police while driving drunk. I said to Emily—we haven't been smoking marijuana. We all acted quiet and Emily realized there was something going on and she delved into it. I explained that some people are stupid and they'll harm you very badly if you smoke marijuana. To this day I haven't heard her mention it to anyone she hasn't smoked with.

As each new child came along, Alan saw to it that they learned the essential facts of life.

Neither Alan nor Anna saw any moral distinction between marijuana smoking and other, more accepted pastimes. They heartily endorsed marijuana as something to indulge in like "tobacco, alcohol, sex, breathing or anything else that brings pleasure to the senses." Alan and Anna hope their children will continue to smoke grass in their later lives. It has had beneficial effects for them and they believe it can do the same for their kids:

> I smoked marijuana for a long time, stopped and developed two ulcers; and smoked again and the two ulcers went away. It has great medicinal value.

Smoking Occasionally Permitted

In contrast to uninterrupted permissiveness, other parents restrict marijuana use among their children to specific occasions. A plethora of reasons and rationalizations lie behind this behavior, some openly avowed by parents and others not. Several people believe it is okay to let the kids get high as long as it isn't done too often. Many other people do not have any carefully thought-out notion of what they want, tending to make spur-of-the-moment decisions. As a result, they allow occasional but largely undefined smoking in a sporadic and irregular manner. Particular reasons for this inconsistency can be illustrated by three examples from our research:

1. *Conflicts between parents* can confuse the situation. While Stella had always planned to bring her children up with pot, Burt did not like the idea. Consequently, the household rule on this matter varied according to the unpredictable moods of the adults and which parent was in the house.

2. Mike and Gwen had trouble *making up their minds*. At one time they thought it probably couldn't harm the child, only to decide the next day they shouldn't take chances and rescind that decision.

3. Lois and David didn't waver hourly but had *changing ideas over time*. At first they were against it, but then met a group of friends who liked to party and approved of tinydoping. After a few years they moved to a new neighborhood and changed their lifestyle, again prohibiting pot smoking for the kids.

These are just a few of the many situations in which parents allow children an occasional opportunity to smoke grass. They use various criteria to decide when those permissible instances ought to be, most families subscribing to several of the following patterns:

Reward: The child receives pot as a bonus for good behavior in the past, present or future. This may serve as an incentive: "If you're a good boy today, Johnny, I may let you smoke with us tonight," or to celebrate an achievement already completed like "going potty" or reciting the alphabet.

Guilt: Marijuana can be another way of compensating children for what they aren't getting. Historically, parents have tried to buy their kids off or make themselves loved through gifts of money or toys but pot can also be suitable here. This is utilized both by couples with busy schedules who don't have time for the children ("We're going out again tonight so we'll give you this special treat to make it up to you") and by separated parents who are trying to compete with the former spouse for the child's love ("I know Mommy doesn't let you do this but you can do special things when you're with me").

Cuteness: To please themselves parents may occasionally let the children smoke pot because it's cute. Younger children look especially funny because they cannot inhale, yet in their eagerness to be like Mommy and Daddy they make a hilarious effort and still have a good time themselves. Often this will originate as amusement for the parents and then spread to include cuteness in front of friends. Carrying this trend further, friends may roll joints for the little ones or turn them on when the parents are away. This still precludes regular use.

Purposive: Giving marijuana to kids often carries a specific anticipated goal for the parents. The known effects of pot are occasionally desired and actively sought. They may want to calm the child down because of the necessities of a special setting or company. Sleep is another pursued end, as in "Thank you for taking Billy for the night; if he gives you any trouble just let him smoke this and he'll go right to bed." They may also give it to the children medicinally. Users believe marijuana soothes the upset stomach and alleviates the symptoms of the common cold better than any other drug. As a mood elevator, many parents have given pot to alleviate the crankiness young children develop from a general illness, specific pain or injury. One couple used it experimentally as a treatment for hyperactivity (see Josh).

Abstention

Our last category of marijuana-smoking parents contains those who do not permit their children any direct involvement with illegal drugs. This leaves several possible ways to treat the topic of the adults' own involvement with drugs and how open they are about it. Do they let the kids know they smoke pot? Moreover, do they do it in the children's presence?

Overt: The great majority of our subjects openly smoked in front of their children, defining marijuana as an accepted and natural pastime. Even parents who withhold it from their young children hope that the kids will someday grow up to be like themselves. Thus, they smoke pot overtly. These marijuana smokers are divided on the issue of other drugs, such as pills and cocaine.

a. *permissive*—One group considers it acceptable to use any drug in front of the children. Either they believe in what they are doing and consider it right for the kids to observe their actions, or they don't worry about it and just do it.

b. *pragmatic*—A larger, practically oriented group differentiated between "smokable" drugs (pot and hashish) and the others (cocaine and pills), finding it acceptable to let children view consumption of the former group, but not the latter. Rationales varied for this, ranging from safety to morality:

> Well, we have smoked hashish around them but we absolutely never ever do coke in front of them because it's a white powder and if they saw us snorting a white powder there goes the drain cleaner, there goes baby powder. Anything white, they'll try it; and that goes for pills too. The only thing they have free rein of is popping vitamins.

Fred expressed his concern over problems this might engender in the preservation of his children's moral fiber:

> If he sees me snorting coke, how is he going to differentiate that from heroin? He gets all this anti-drug education from school and they tell him that heroin is bad. How can I explain to him that doing coke is okay and it's fun and doesn't hurt you but heroin is something else, so different and bad? How could I teach right from wrong?

c. *capricious*—A third group is irregular in its handling of multiple drug viewing and their offspring. Jon and Linda, for instance, claim that they don't mind smoking before their child but absolutely won't permit other drugs to be used in his presence. Yet in fact they often use almost any intoxicant in front of him, depending on their mood and how high they have already become.

In our observations we have never seen any parent give a child in the tinydoper range any kind of illegal drug other than marijuana and, extremely rarely, hashish. Moreover, the treatment of pot has been above all direct and open: even those parents who don't permit their children to join have rejected the clandestine secrecy of the behind-closed-doors approach. Ironically, however, they must often adopt this strategy toward the outside world; those parents who let it be known that they permit tinydoping frequently take on an extra social and legal stigma. Their motivation for doing so stems from a desire to avoid having the children view pot and their smoking it as evil or unnatural. Thus, to destigmatize marijuana they stigmatize themselves in the face of society.

CONCLUSIONS

Tinydoping, with its combined aspects of understandably innovative social development and surprising challenges to convention, is a fruitful subject for sociological analysis. A review of historical and cultural forces leading to the present offers insight into how and why this phenomenon came to arise. Essentially, we are witnessing the moral passage of marijuana, its transformation from an isolated and taboo drug surrounded by connotations of fear and danger, into an increasingly accepted form of social relaxation, similar to alcohol. The continuing destigmatization of pot fosters an atmosphere in which parents are willing to let their children smoke.

Marijuana's social transition is not an isolated occurrence, however. Many formerly deviant activities have gradually become acceptable forms of behavior. Table 1 presents a general model of social change which outlines the sequential development and spread of a conduct undergoing legitimization.

Particular behaviors which first occur only among relatively small and stigmatized outgroups are frequently picked up by ingroup deviants who identify with the stigmatized outgroup. In an attempt to be cool and avant-garde, larger clusters of ingroup members adopt this deviant practice, often for the sake of nonconformity as well as its own merits. By this time the deviant activity is gaining exposure as well as momentum and may spread to normal ingroup members. The final step is its eventual introduction to sacred groups in the society, such as children.

Becker's (1953) research and theory are pertinent to historical stages I and II. More recently, Carey (1968) and Goode (1970) have depicted stage III. To date, sociologists have not described stage IV and we are the first to portray stage V.

The general value of this model can be further illustrated by showing its application to another deviant activity which has followed a similar progression—pornography. Initially a highly stigmatized practice engaged in by people largely hidden from public view, it slowly became incorporated into a wider cross-section of the population. With the advent of *Playboy*, mainstream media entered the scene, resulting in the present proliferation of sexually-oriented magazines and tabloids. Recently, however, this practice passed into stage V; a violent societal reaction ensued, with moralist groups crusading to hold the sacred period of childhood free from such deviant intrusions.

Table 1 / Sequential Model of Social Change: The Diffusion and Legitimization of Marijuana

Stage		Carriers	
I	1940's	Stigmatized outgroup	Blacks
II	1950's	Ingroup deviants who identify with stigmatized outgroup	Jazz musicians
III	1960's	Avant-garde ingroup members	College students and counterculture
IV	1970's	Normal ingroup members	Middle class
V	1975+	Sacred group	Children

Tinydoping has not become broadly publicly recognized but, as with pornography, the widespread (collective) softening of attitudes has not extended to youngsters. Rather, a backlash effect stemming from conventional morality condemns such "intrusions and violations of childhood" as repulsive. Thus, the spread of deviance to Group V prompts social revulsion and renewed effort to ban the behavior by children while allowing it to adults.

These data also recommend a re-examination of sociological theories about marijuana use. Becker's (1953) theory is in some ways timeless, illuminating a model of the actor which encompasses a dynamic processual development. It proposes an initiation process that precedes bona fide membership in a pot smoking milieu. Minimally, this includes: learning the proper techniques to ensure adequate consumption; perception of the drug's unique effects; association of these effects with the smoking experience; and the conceptualization of these effects as pleasurable. Symbolic *meaning* is crucial to this schema: through a "sequence of social experiences" the individual continually reformulates his attitudes, eventually learning to view marijuana smoking as desirable. The formation of this conception is the key to understanding the motivations and actions of users.

Accepting this model for the adult initiate, the present research has explored an historically novel group (tinydopers), describing a new route to becoming a marijuana user taken by these children. As has been shown, tinydopers are unable to recognize the psychological and physiological effects of pot or to connect them with having smoked. This effectively precludes their following Becker's model which accords full user status to the individual only after he has successfully perceived the effects of the drug and marked them as pleasurable. Our research into child perception relied mostly on observation and inference since, as Piaget (1948) noted, it is nearly impossible to discover this from children; the conceptual categories are too sophisticated for their grasp. That the marijuana affects them is certain: giddy, they laugh, dance and run to the refrigerator, talking excitedly and happily until they suddenly fall asleep. But through observations and conversations before, during and after the intoxicated periods, tinydopers were found to be unaware of any changes in themselves.

Their incomplete development, perceptually, cognitively and interactionally, is the cause of this ignorance. According to the socialization theories of Mead (1934), Erikson (1968), and Piaget (1948), children of eight and under are still psychologically forming, gradually learning to function. Piaget particularly notes definitive cognitive stages, asserting that conservation, transformation and classification are all too advanced for the tinydoper age bracket. According to Mead (see also Adler and Adler, 1979), the essence lies in their lack of mature selves, without which they cannot fully act and interact competently. The ages 8–9 seem to be a decisive turning point as youngsters change in internal psychological composition and become capable of *reflecting* on themselves, both through their own eyes and those of the other. (Mead argues that this is possible only after the child has completed the play, game and generalized other stages and can competently engage in roletaking.) Hence, before that time they cannot genuinely recognize their "normal selves" or differentiate them from their "high selves." Without this perception, the effects of marijuana are held to those created by the parents, who frame the experience with their own intentional and unintentional definitions of the situation. Thus, tinydopers become marijuana users almost unconsciously, based on a decision made by others. Moreover, the social meanings they associate with its use are very different than those experienced by adult initiates.

How does this new practice correspond to conventional modes of child rearing? One traditional procedure we see reaffirmed is imitative behavior (see Piaget, 1962), through which the child learns and matures by copying the actions of significant adult models. Several of the illustrative cases chosen show particularly how directly the youngsters are influenced by their desire to behave and be like older family members and friends. They have two aspirations: wanting to be accorded quasi-adult status and longing for acceptance as members of the social group. Parents have corresponding and natural positive feelings about inculcating meaningful beliefs and values into their offspring. Teaching boundary maintenance is also a necessary adjunct to allowing tinydoping. Marijuana's continued illegality and social unacceptability for juveniles necessitate parents ensuring that information about pot smoking is neither intentionally nor accidentally revealed by youngsters. Children must early learn to differentiate between members of various social groups and to judge who are and are not appropriate to be told. This is difficult because it involves mixing positive and negative connotations of the drug in a complex manner. Valuable parallels for this contradictory socialization can be found in child use of alcohol and tobacco, as well as to families of persecuted religious groups (i.e., Marrano Jews in 15th century Spain, covert Jews in Nazi Germany and possibly Mormons in the 19th century). Members of these enclaves believed that what they were teaching their offspring was fundamentally honorable, but still had to communicate to the younger generation their social ostracization and the need to maintain some barriers of secrecy.

Juxtaposed to those aspects which reproduce regular features of socialization are the contradictory procedures. One such departure is the introduction of mood-altering intoxicants into the sacred childhood period. Tinydoping violates the barriers created by most societies to reserve various types of responsibilities, dangers and special pleasures (such as drugs and sex) for adults only. Yet perhaps the most unusual and unprecedented facet of tinydoping socialization observed is the intergenerational bridging that occurs between parent and child. By introducing youngsters into the adult social group and having them participate as peers, parents permit generational boundaries to become extremely vague, often to the point of nonexistence. Several cases show how children have come to look at parents and other adults as friends. This embodies extreme variance from cultures and situations where parents love and treasure their children yet still treat them unequally.

How then can tinydoping be compared to traditional childrearing practices and habits? Existing indicators suggest both similarity and divergence. The parents in this study consider marijuana a substance they overwhelmingly feel comfortable with, regard as something "natural" (i.e., Alan and Anna), and would like their progeny to be exposed to in a favorable light. To them, tinydoping represents a form of normal socialization within the context of their subcultural value system. From the greater society's perspective, however, the illegality of the behavior, aberration from conventional child rearing norms and uncertain implications for futurity combine to define tinydoping as deviant socialization.

Notes

1. The period of childhood has traditionally been a special time in which developing adults were given special treatment to ensure their growing up to be capable and responsible members of society. Throughout history and in most cultures children have been kept apart from adults and sheltered in protective isolation from certain knowledge and practices (see Aries, 1965).

2. Particularly relevant to these "justifications" is Lyman and Scott's (1968) analysis of accounts, as statements made to relieve one of culpability. Specifically, they can be seen as "denial of injury" (Sykes and Matza, 1957) as they assert the innocuousness of giving marijuana to their child. An "excuse" is further employed, "scapegoating" the doctor as the one really responsible for this aberration. Also, the appeal to science has been made.

References

Adler, Peter and Patricia A. Adler
1979 "Symbolic Interactionism," in Patricia A. Adler, Peter Adler, Jack D. Douglas, Andrea Fontana, C. Robert Freeman and Joseph Kotarba, An Introduction to the Sociologies of Everyday Life, Boston: Allyn and Bacon.
Aries, Phillipe
1965 Centuries of Childhood: A Social History of Family Life, New York: Vintage.
Becker, Howard S.
1953 "Becoming a Marijuana User," American Journal of Sociology, 59, November.
1963 Outsiders, New York: Free Press.
Carey, James T.
1968 The College Drug Scene, Englewood Cliffs: Prentice Hall.
Douglas, Jack D.
1970 "Deviance and Respectability: The Social Construction of Moral Meanings," in Jack D. Douglas (ed.), Deviance and Respectability, New York: Basic Books.
Douglas, Jack D.
1976 Investigative Social Research, Beverly Hills: Sage.
Erikson, Erik
1968 Identity, Youth and Crisis, New York: Norton.
Goode, Erich
1970 The Marijuana Smokers, New York: Basic Books.

Grinspoon, Lester
   1971 Marihuana Reconsidered, Cambridge: Harvard University Press.
Grupp, Stanley E. (ed.)
   1971 Marihuana, Columbus, Ohio: Charles E. Merrill.
Gusfield, Joseph R.
   1967 "Moral Passage: The Symbolic Process in Public Designations of Deviance,"
   Social Problems, 15, II, Fall.
Hochman, Joel S.
   1972 Marijuana and Social Evolution, Englewood Cliffs: Prentice Hall.
Kaplan, John
   1971 Marihuana: The New Prohibition, New York: Pocket.
Kitsuse, John I.
   1962 "Societal Reactions to Deviant Behavior," Social Problems, 9, 3, Winter.
Lyman, Stanford and Marvin B. Scott
   1968 "Accounts," American Sociological Review, 33, 1.
Matza, David
   1969 Becoming Deviant, Englewood Cliffs: Prentice Hall.
Mead, George H.
   1934 Mind, Self and Society, Chicago: The University of Chicago Press.
Piaget, Jean
   1948 The Moral Judgment of the Child, New York: Free Press.
   1962 Play, Dreams and Imitation in Childhood, New York: Norton.
Simon, William and John H. Gagnon
   1968 "Children of the Drug Age," Saturday Review, September 21.
Sykes, Gresham and David Matza
   1957 "Techniques of Neutralization," American Sociological Review, 22,
   December.

21 / In the Closet with Illness: Epilepsy, Stigma Potential and Information Control

JOSEPH W. SCHNEIDER
PETER CONRAD

The metaphor of the closet has been used frequently to discuss how people avoid or pursue "deviant" identities. Formulated originally in the homosexual subculture, to be "in the closet" has meant to be a secret or covert homosexual. Sociologists have adopted the notion of "coming out" of the closet to describe the development of a gay identity, focusing on self-definition and "public" disclosure as important elements of identity formation (Dank, 1971; Humphreys, 1972; Warren, 1974; Ponse, 1976). Kitsuse (1980) recently has extended the concept of coming out to refer to the "social affirmation of the self" for a wide variety of disvalued groups, including feminists, elderly people, blacks, prostitutes, marijuana users, American Nazis, and many others. In arguing against an "oversocialized" view of deviants encouraged by some narrow labeling interpretations, Kitsuse suggests that increasing numbers of disvalued people in American society have "come out" to affirm their identities as legitimate grounds for the dignity, worth and pride they believe is rightfully theirs.

This link between the closet metaphor and the development of identity is premised, however, on the assumption that in "coming out" there is indeed something to come out to; that there are some developed or developing social definitions that provide the core of this new, open and proud self. Certainly in the case of homosexuality, abandoning the closet of secrecy and concealment was facilitated greatly by the availability of a public identity as "gay and proud." But what of those disvalued by some attribute, performance, or legacy for whom there is no alternate new and proud identity? And what of those for whom even the existence of some "old" and "spoiled" identity may be questionable? In such cases where there may be no clear identity to move from or to, the closet metaphor may seem to lack insight and hence be of little use. We believe, however, that this metaphor taps a more fundamental sociological problem that may, but need not, be linked to the formation of identity.

In this paper we argue that the metaphor of the closet, entry into and exit from it, may be used to focus on the more general sociological problem of how people attempt to manage what they see as discreditable information about themselves. We draw on depth interview data from a study of people with epilepsy—a stigmatized illness (see also Schneider and Conrad, 1979). We try to see how people attempt to maintain favorable or at least neutral definitions of self, given a condition for which no "new" readily available supportive identity or subculture yet exists, and which most of the time—except for the occurrence of periodic seizures—is invisible. By extending the metaphor of the closet to describe this situation, we hope both to increase its analytic utility and learn more about how people manage nondeviant yet stigmatized conditions.[1]

Our sample of 80 people is divided roughly equally by sex, ranging in age from 14 to 54. Most of the respondents come from a metropolitan area of the midwest and none have a history of long-term institutionalization for epilepsy. Interviews were conducted over a two and a half year period beginning in mid-1976, and respondents were selected on the basis of availability and willingness to participate. We used a snowball sampling technique, relying on advertisements in local newspapers, invitation letters passed anonymously by common acquaintances, and names obtained from local social agencies, self-help groups, and health workers. No pretense to statistical representativeness is intended nor was it sought. Due to official restrictions and perceived stigma associated with epilepsy, a population listing from which to draw such a sample does not exist. Our intention was to develop a sample from which theoretical insights would emerge (see Glaser and Strauss, 1967).

We will try here to provide an "insider's" view[2] of 1) how people with epilepsy themselves define their condition as undesirable and discreditable, and, hence, grounds for being "in the closet"; and of 2) how they attempt to manage this discreditable information in such a way as to protect their reputations and rights as normal members of society. We first discuss epilepsy as a potentially stigmatized condition, then move to illustrations of how people perceive the stigma of epilepsy and adopt various strategies of concealment and (paradoxically) selective disclosure, all directed toward protecting what they believe to be a threatened self.

THE STIGMA POTENTIAL OF EPILEPSY

We suggest the concept "stigma potential" to emphasize the significance of epilepsy as an attribute discreditable to one's personal identity (cf. Goffman, 1963:157). Description of the stigma as "potential" rests on two assumptions: 1) that knowledge of one's epilepsy be limited to relatively few others, and 2) that if it were to become more widely known, significant redefinition of self, accompanied by various restrictions and regulation of conduct, might well follow. Although Goffman suggests that possession of such discreditable attributes weighs heavily and shamefully on one's own definitions of self, whether others have the same knowledge or not, we prefer to make that an empirical question. Like Goffman's discreditable person, Becker's (1963, 1973) secret or potential deviant recognizes his or her own acts, qualities and characteristics, *and* is aware of certain relevant prohibitions in the larger cultural and social setting. Given this knowledge, the potential deviant is one who concludes that there is at least some probability that disclosure would lead to discrediting and undesirable consequences. Becker is more equivocal on the issue of self-derogation and shame, requiring only that the actor be aware that rules do exist which may be applied and enforced if others become aware of the hidden practice or attribute. Although shame is an important phenomenon, it is not necessary to the rise of information control strategies. It is of both theoretical and practical interest that epilepsy is an attribute that would seem to create precisely this kind of potentially deviant or stigmatized person.

Like leprosy and venereal disease, epilepsy is an illness with an ancient associated stigma. Furthermore, epileptic seizures—which can range from nearly imperceptible "spacing out" to the more common, dramatic and bizarre grand mal convulsions—constitute violations of taken-for-granted expectations about the competence of actors in social settings, and are thus likely candidates for becoming "deviant behaviors." Although physicians have been defining and treating it for centuries (Temkin, 1971), epilepsy has long been associated with disreputability, satanic possession, and evil (Lennox and Lennox, 1960). Nineteenth century medical and psychiatric research, including that of Maudsley and Lombroso, suggested a causal link between epilepsy and violent crime[3] and encouraged myths about the relation of epilepsy, violent behavior and mental illness. This research supported placing epileptics in colonies and later special hospitals, excluding them from jobs, from entering the United States as immigrants, and sometimes even from marrying and having children.

The advent of anticonvulsant medications (e.g., phenobarbital in 1912 and Dilantin in 1938) allowed for greater medical control of seizures, enabling epileptics to live more conventional lives. Modern medical conceptualizations of epilepsy as a seizure disorder produced by "intermittent electrochemical impulses in the brain" (U.S. Dept. HEW-NIH, 1975) are far removed from the earlier morally-tinged interpretations. But historical residues of the deviant status of epilepsy remain central to the condition's current social reality. The stigma potential of epilepsy is well-documented. In a fairly recent review of the literature, Arangio (1975, 1976) found that stigma was still pervasive. It was manifested in various forms of social discrimination: difficulty in obtaining a driver's license; until 1965, prohibitions (in some states) against marrying; discrimination in obtaining employment (e.g., until 1959 epileptics were not hired for federal civil service positions); difficulties in obtaining all types of insurance; laws (in nine states) that permit sterilization of epileptics under some conditions; and laws (in 17 states) that allow for institutionalization of epileptics (Arangio,

1975). Researchers using intermittent Gallup poll data over the 25-year period 1949 to 1974 found a decrease in attitudinal prejudice toward epileptics, although 20 percent of the population in 1974 still maintained that epileptics should not be employed (Caveness et al., 1974).

Such attitudes and official regulations are, of course, not lost on people with epilepsy. A recent nationwide survey found that one quarter of all epileptics do not tell their employers about epilepsy, and half indicated that having epilepsy created problems in getting a job (Perlman, 1977). While these and other "objective" aspects of prejudice and discrimination toward people with epilepsy have been documented, the ways in which such features of the larger cultural and social world are given meaning in people's subjective experience is less accessible and relatively unexplored.

THE PERCEPTION OF STIGMA

Stigma is by no means an automatic result of possessing some discreditable attribute. The significance of "having" epilepsy is a product of a collective definitional process in which the actor's perspective occupies a central place. As suggested earlier, a discreditable attribute or performance becomes relevant to self only if the individual perceives it as discreditable, whether or not such perceptions are actually applied by others to self or simply considered as a relevant "object" in the environment that must be taken into account. The actor has an important part in the construction of the meaning of epilepsy and of illness generally. It is of course logically possible that people otherwise deemed "ill" are unaware of what their conditions mean to the others with whom they interact: for example, a person surprised by sympathetic reactions to his or her disclosure of cancer, or a young "tough" who in polite society wears venereal disease as a badge of sexual prowess.

Most sociological work on stigma assumes that the stigmatized learn the meaning of their attribute or performance primarily through direct exposure to rejection and disapproval from others. Less understood is the place of the *perception of stigma*—of what the putatively stigmatized think others think of them and "their kind" and about how these others might react to disclosure. This brings us back to the situation of Goffman's discreditable actor, but makes actors' definitions central and problematic. Such actor definitions of epilepsy provide the foundation on which the stigma of epilepsy is constructed.

Over and over in our interviews, people with epilepsy told us that they "have" something that others "don't understand," and that this lack of understanding and knowledge of "what epilepsy is" is a fundamental source of what they see as an actual or potentially negative reaction. They believe that what little information others have about epilepsy is probably incorrect and stereotypical, sometimes incorporating elements of madness and evil. Adjectives such as "frightened" and "scared" were used to describe others' views of epilepsy. One woman, whose epilepsy had been diagnosed at middle age and who had lost a teaching job because of seizures at work, said:

> Well, I understand it now and *I'm* not afraid of it. But most people are unless they've experienced it, and so you just don't talk to other people about it, and if you do, never use the word "epilepsy." The word itself, I mean job-ways, insurance-ways... anything, the hang-ups there are on it. There's just too much prejudice so the less said about it the better.

One man compared others' ignorance and fear of epilepsy to similar reactions to leprosy: "The public is so ill educated toward an epileptic. It's like someone with leprosy walking into a room. You see a leper and you run because you're afraid of it." And another woman spoke of epilepsy's "historical implications":

> The fact of having epilepsy. It isn't the seizures. I think they are a very minor part of it. Its implications are so *enormous*. The historical implications of epilepsy are fantastic. I'm lucky to have been born when I was. If I was born at the beginning of this century I would have been discarded... probably locked away somewhere.

In these and similar ways, people recognize that ignorance and fear taint public images of epilepsy. They then take such recognitions into account in their own strategies and decisions about how to control such discrediting information.

Seizures in social situations are an important aspect of this discrediting perception of epilepsy. Seizures might be seen as sociologically akin to such involuntary *faux pas* as breaking wind or belching. Farts or belches, however, are reasonably familiar and normalized in middle-class society, but people with epilepsy believe that others ordinarily consider seizures as beyond the boundaries of undesirable but nevertheless "normal" conduct. One woman suggested seizures are "like having your pants fall down" in public. Another described how she believed others see seizures: "I can't use the word 'horrible,' but they think...it's *ugly*. It is. It's strange. It's something you're not used to seeing." People with epilepsy believe that others see the actual behaviors associated with seizures—including unconsciousness, violent muscle contractions, falling to the ground, or simply being "absent" from the social scene—as objective grounds for a more fundamental, "essential" disreputability. The stigma was described this way by another woman:

> It's one of those fear images; it's something that people don't know about and it has strong negative connotations in people's minds. It's a bad image, something scary, sort of like a beggar; it's dirty, the person falling down and frothing at the mouth and jerking and the bystanders not knowing what to do. It's something that happens in public which isn't "nice."

As these data suggest, aside from the question of shame of self-labeling, people who have epilepsy perceive the social meanings attached to it and to seizures as threats to their status as normal and competent members of society.

COACHES FOR CONCEALMENT: LEARNING TO BE DISCREDITABLE

How do people construct these views of others' perceptions? As we suggested, conventional sociological wisdom has emphasized direct disvaluing treatment by others. While this interactive experience is undoubtedly important to study, our data strongly suggest that people with epilepsy also learn such views from significant and supportive others, particularly from parents. Parental training in the stigma of epilepsy is most clear for people who were diagnosed when they were children, but stigma coaches were also identified by those who were diagnosed when they were adults.[4]

Our data indicate that the more the parents convey a definition of epilepsy as something "bad," and the less willing they are to talk about it with their children, the more likely the child is to see it as something to be concealed. One thirty-four-year-old woman had maintained a strategy of tightly controlled secrecy from the time she was diagnosed as having epilepsy at age fourteen. She recalled her parents' reaction:

> Complete disbelief. You know, "We've never had anything like that in our family." I can remember that was very plainly said, almost like I was something … something was wrong. They did not believe it. In fact, we went to another doctor and then it was confirmed.

These parents proceeded to manage their daughter's epilepsy by a combination of silence and maternal "coaching" on how to conceal it from others. When asked if she told her husband of her epilepsy before they were married, the same woman said:

> I talked to Mom about it. She said, "Don't tell him because some people don't understand. He may not understand. That's not something you talk about." I asked her, "Should I talk to him about passing out?" She said, "Never say 'epilepsy.' It's not something we talk about."

She had learned her "lesson" well and concealed her illness for almost twenty years.

Family silence about epilepsy can itself be a lesson in stigma. One middle-aged woman who was just beginning to "break through" (cf. Davis, 1961) such silence, said that her parents had never told her she had epilepsy: "They just told me I suffered from fainting fits." She had filled this vacuum of silence by concluding that she must be "going mad." Throughout her childhood, and even in her present relationship with her parents, epilepsy had been "brushed under the carpet": "It's not nice to talk about those things." Like sexual variety in the late nineteenth century, epilepsy was obviously something "bad" because it was something "people just didn't (i.e., shouldn't) talk about."

Parents are not the only coaches for secrecy. Close associates, friends, and even professionals sometimes suggest concealment as a strategy for dealing with epilepsy, particularly in circumstances where it is believed to be a disqualifying characteristic. One woman described such advice by a physician-medical examiner who said he "had to" fire her from a teaching job because of her seizures: "He advised me to lie about it. He said, 'If you don't miss work from it and it's not visible to anybody, lie about it.' And I've been doing that since and I've been able to work since."

As the literature on subcultures makes clear, stigmatized people can learn practical survival strategies from others' experience. A supportive subculture surrounding epilepsy is only in its infancy, as is true for most illnesses,[5] but various self-help groups do exist through which people with epilepsy may learn relevant coping skills (see Borman et al., 1980). In the absence of a developed subculture for people like themselves, some people with epilepsy learn the importance of concealment from people with other illnesses. As one woman said of her diabetic husband's experience:

> He didn't know. He hadn't gone through this [or] met other diabetics. He didn't know how to carry out a lie. One of the things that we learned, again from the diabetes, was how [to] lie if they asked for a urine sample. We now have met, through the rap sessions, people who said, "You bring somebody else's urine!" Well, that's a pretty shocking thing to have to do. Yeah, there are times when you gotta lie.

The importance of others as coaches for concealment is clear. Through this "diabetes underground" her husband learned how to lie, then taught it to her.

Some significant others, however, including some parents, adopt strategies of openness, honesty and neutralization. Parents who define their child's epilepsy "just like any other medical problem" and "certainly nothing to be ashamed of" apparently encourage their children to have a much more neutral view and a more open informational control strategy. One successful businessman credited his parents with managing epilepsy so as to minimize it and prevent him from using it as a "crutch" or "excuse":

> The parents of an epileptic child are the key to the whole ball of wax, in recognizing that you have a problem in the family but not to let that control the total actions and whole livelihood and whole future of the family. Accept it and go about doing what has to be done to maintain an even keel.

The themes of "taking epilepsy in stride," not "using" it as a "cop-out" are reminiscent of the cautions against the temptation to use medical excuses which Parsons (1951) analyzed (cf. Waitzkin and Waterman, 1974). They were common to the accounts given to us by people who seemed to portray their epilepsy as "no big thing," partly from concern that such comments might be interpreted by others as requests for "sympathy" and "special treatment." Parents who cautioned against such "special pleading" uses of epilepsy also typically were recalled as having taught their children the values of self-reliance, independence and achievement—as another way of overcoming an emphasis on epilepsy and its significance. Learning that epilepsy need not be a barrier to personal or social acceptance led individuals to be more "out" of than "in" the closet of epilepsy; learning to believe that epilepsy was a shameful flaw encouraged, understandably, the development of just the opposite strategy.

STRATEGIES OF SELECTIVE CONCEALMENT: THE CLOSET OF EPILEPSY HAS A REVOLVING DOOR

Most discussions of the self and the "closet" assume that one can only be in or out, and that being out must follow a period of being in. As we learned more about how people experience epilepsy, we realized that such a view of the closet of epilepsy was much too simple. Sometimes people conceal their epilepsy, sometimes they do not, and the same persons can be both "open" and "closed" during the same period in their lives. In short, both concealment and disclosure proved to be quite complex and selective strategies of information management.

A part of the "wisdom" of the world of epilepsy is that there are some people you can tell about your illness and others you cannot (cf. Goffman, 1963). Even the most secretive (and twelve of our respondents said we were the first people they had told about their epilepsy except for their physician and immediate family) had told at least several other people about their condition. Close friends and family members are perhaps the most clear instance of "safe others," but "people I feel comfortable with" and those who "won't react negatively to epilepsy" are also sometimes told. Such persons are often used to test reactions: "I think the first couple of times I mentioned it was with my very closest friends to sort of test the water and when it wasn't any problem, then I began to feel freer to mention it."

The development of more diffuse disclosure or "coming out" seemed contingent on how these early disclosures went. Just as perceived "positive" results may encourage people to come out more, perceived "negative" consequences from trial disclosures may encourage a return to concealment as the predominant way to control personal and social impacts. As one woman put it:

> I tried to get a driver's license when I was 18 or 19, after I was married. We were living in Mississippi and I put it on [the form] that I was epileptic, only because I was afraid if I pass out and I'm drivin' a car, well, that's dangerous. I took the thing up there and they said, "Epileptics can't—you have to have a doctor's thing." We moved about two months later to California. I got my driver's license and didn't put it down.

Later on she made another attempt at disclosure, this time on an application to live in a college dormitory. After being disqualified from living on campus and then declining a scholarship, she decided that secrecy was the only strategy by which she could minimize the risk of rejection and differential treatment. In retrospect, she concluded: "I don't know if maybe I wasn't testing . . . at the time, you know, well, is it okay? If things had been different, maybe I could have talked about it." When asked if she discussed epilepsy with new people she meets, another woman spoke specifically of this "risk":

> It depends. I still find it hard, but I'm trying to. I have to trust somebody a lot before I'll tell them in terms of a friendship basis. All my close friends know, but in terms of my work, forget it. This is a risk I can't take after the previous experience. I still have great in-built fears about losing a job from it. I'm not ready to put myself at that risk.

An upwardly-mobile young administrator said he lost his driver's license as a result of disclosing his epilepsy. He recalled that experience and what he had "learned" from it: "I started out tryin' to be honest about it and got burned. So I gave up bein' honest about it in that circumstance." Although this man did disclose his epilepsy to a wide variety of others, including his employer, he said he regularly lied about it on driver's license forms.

Such data clearly suggest that people can and do maintain carefully segregated and selective strategies of managing the stigma potential of epilepsy. Some situations were considered considerably more "high risk" than others. In employment, for example, concealment, including lying on initial employment applications, was thought to be the best general strategy. Because they thought there would be reprisals if their employers subsequently learned of their epilepsy, respondents who advocated such concealment typically said they adopted a monitoring or "see how it's going" approach to possible later disclosure. If they saw approval in others' reactions to them during initial contacts, they could attempt disclosure. One young woman who said she had not had a seizure for 19 years and took no medication was still very sensitive about her "past" when applying for a job:

> Well, employers are the only thing I haven't been open with. On an application, I will not write it. If I feel I have a chance for a job and I'm gonna make it, I'll bring it up. But to put it on that application—because employers, they look at it, they see that thing checked; it just gives me a feeling that they don't give you a chance.

Although she said she never had experienced discriminatory treatment in employment, this woman said she usually waits "until I get into that interview and sell myself first. Then I'll come out and say, 'There's one more point. . . .' " Another respondent said he would wait until "I have my foot in the door and they said, 'Hey, he's doing okay' " before disclosing his epilepsy to his employers. People who had tried this strategy of gradual disclosure after employer approval of their work were often surprised that others made so little of their condition. As a result of such experiences they proceeded to redefine some aspects of their own "theories" of others' reactions to epilepsy.

Finally, concealing epilepsy—staying in the closet—was believed important in situations where others might be predisposed to criticize. One woman, who said she was open to friends, commented that she wouldn't want others "in the neighborhood" to know. She explained: "At this point I'm not involved in quarrels. I would think that if I got into a quarrel or feuding situation, it [the epilepsy] would be something that would be used against me." The same view of epilepsy as ammunition for critics was expressed by a man who defined his work as "very political." He thought that if others learned of his epilepsy, they would "add that on as an element of my character that makes [me] undesirable." Sometimes this "closing ranks" against adversaries can even exclude those who otherwise would be told. One woman said that because her brother married a woman "I don't particularly care for," she had decided simply not to tell him of her diagnosis. Her sister-in-law was "the type that would say, you know, 'You're crazy because you have it,' or 'There's something wrong with you.' And she would probably laugh." Even a physician may be seen more as a gatekeeper than an advocate and counselor. One man expressed this theme in many of our interviews quite clearly:

> If he is going to go running to the state and tell the state every time I have a seizure, I don't feel I can be honest with that doctor. He is not keeping his part of the bargain. Everything on my medical records is supposed to be sacred.

Taken together, these data suggest that the process of information management used by people with epilepsy is much more complex than the now-familiar metaphor of being either "in or out of the closet" would lead us to believe. They also indicate that, in strategies of disclosure and concealment of potentially stigmatizing attributes, being out of or in the closet of *epilepsy* may often have much less to do with one's "identity" than with the more practical matter of preventing others from applying limiting and restrictive rules that disqualify one from normal social roles. Epilepsy is something that is hidden at some times and in some places and disclosed quite readily at other times and in other places. Such disclosure and concealment appear contingent upon a complex interaction of one's learned perceptions of the stigma of epilepsy, actual "test" experiences with others before and/or after disclosure, and the nature of the particular relationships involved.

INSTRUMENTAL TELLING: DISCLOSING AS A MANAGEMENT STRATEGY

Information management may include disclosure as well as concealment, even when the information is potentially discreditable. Except for the respondents who adopted rigidly secretive strategies, the people we spoke to said they "usually" or "always" told certain others of their epilepsy under certain circumstances. In this final section we discuss two types of such telling that emerged in our data: telling as "therapy" and "preventive telling." Both involve disclosure but, like concealment, are conscious attempts to mitigate the potentially negative impact of epilepsy on one's self and daily round.

Telling as Therapy

Disclosing feelings of guilt, culpability, and self-derogation can be cathartic, as we know from a variety of social science research. Particularly for those who have concealed what they see as some personal blemish or flaw, such telling can serve a "therapeutic" function for the self by sharing or diffusing the burden of such information. It can free the energy used to control information for other social activities. Such relief, however, requires a properly receptive audience: that is, listeners who are supportive, encouraging, empathetic, and nonjudgmental. Such occasions of telling and hearing cannot only be cathartic, they also can encourage people with epilepsy to define their condition as a nonremarkable and neutral facet of self, perhaps even an "interesting" one, as one man told us. This sort of "telling as therapy" is akin to what Davis (1961) described as the relief associated with breaking through the collectively created and negotiated silence surrounding the physical disabilities of polio victims when they interacted with normals.

Such therapeutic telling seems instrumental primarily in its impact on the actor's self-definition: at the minimum, it simply externalizes what is believed to be significant information about self that has been denied one's intimates and associates. Many of the people we interviewed, in recalling such experiences of "coming out" to select and safe audiences, emphasized the importance of talk as therapy. One woman said of such talking: "It's what's got me together about it [the epilepsy]." And a man recalled how telling friends about epilepsy allowed him to minimize it in his own mind:

I think in talking to them [friends] I would try to convince myself that it didn't have to be terribly important. Now that I think more about it, I was probably just defiant about it: "I ain't gonna let this Goddamned thing get in my way, period."

For a final example, one of the few respondents, who in keeping with her mother's careful coaching had told virtually no one, insightfully suggested how she might use the interview itself as grounds for redefining her epilepsy and self:

It just seems so weird now that I've—because I'm talking to you about it, and I've never talked to anybody about it. It's really not so bad. You know it hasn't affected me that much, but no one wants to talk about it.... [Talking about epilepsy] makes me feel I'm really not so bad off. Just because I can't find answers to those questions, cuz like I think I feel sorry for myself. I can sit around the house and just dream up all these things, you know, why I'm persecuted and [all].

Such selection disclosure to supportive and nonjudgmental others can thus help "banish the ghosts" that flourish in secrecy and isolation. It allows for feedback and the renegotiation of the perception of stigma. Through externalizing what is believed to be a potentially negative feature of self, people with epilepsy *and* their audiences can redefine this attribute as an "ordinary" or "typical" part of themselves (Dingwall, 1976). As we have already indicated, however, this strategy appears to be effective primarily among one's intimates and close friends. When facing strangers or those whose reactions cannot be assumed supportive, such as prospective employers, the motor vehicle bureau, or virtually any bureaucracy's application form, such openness can be set aside quickly.

Preventive Telling

Another kind of instrumental telling we discovered in our data could be called "preventive": disclosure to influence others' actions and/or ideas toward self and toward epileptics in general. One variety of such preventive telling occurs when actors think it probable that others, particularly others with whom they share some routine, will witness their seizures. The grounds cited for such disclosure are that others then "will know what it is" and "won't be scared." By "knowing what it is," respondents mean others define "it"—the epilepsy and seizure—as a *medical* problem, thereby removing blame and responsibility from the actor for the aberrant conduct in question. The actors assume that others should not be "frightened" if they too learn that "it" is a medical problem.

To engage such anticipatory preventive telling is to offer a kind of "medical disclaimer" (cf. Hewitt and Stokes, 1975) intended to influence others' reactions should a seizure occur. By bringing a blameless, beyond-my-control medical interpretation to such potentially discrediting events, people attempt to reduce the risk that more morally disreputable interpretations might be applied by naive others witnessing one's seizures. One young woman recalled that she felt "great" when her parents told her junior high teachers about epilepsy, because "I'd rather have them know than think I was a dummy or something . . . or think I was having . . . you know, *problems*." Reflecting the power of medical excuses (as well as a relative hierarchy of legitimacy among medical excuses), a middle-aged man who described himself as an "alcoholic" told of how he would disclose epilepsy to defuse others' complaints about his drinking:

> I'd say, "I have to drink. It's the only way I can maintain. . . . I have seizures you know" . . . and this kind of thing. People would then feel embarrassed. Or you'd say, "I'm epileptic," then they'd feel embarrassed and say, "Oh, well, gee, we're sorry, that's right. We forgot about that."

Such accounts illustrate the kind of social currency that medical definitions possess in general and in particular with respect to epilepsy. As with all currency, however, its effectiveness as a medium of acceptable exchange rests on its mutual validation by those who give and receive it; what others in fact think of such accounts remains largely unknown.

Beyond providing a medical frame of reference through which others may interpret seizures, such preventive telling may also include specific instructions about what others should do when seizures do occur. Because people with epilepsy believe others are almost totally ignorant of what seizures are, they similarly assume that others have little idea of how to react to seizures. By providing what in effect are directions for others to follow, people who do preventive telling believe they are protecting not only their body but their self. As the young administrator we quoted earlier put it:

> Down the road, I'll usually make a point to tell someone I'm around a lot because I know that it's frightening. So I will, partly for my own purposes, tell them I've got it; if I have one [seizure] that it's nothing to worry about. And don't take me to the hospital even if I ask you to. I always tell people that I work with because I presume I'll be with them for some long period of time. And I may have a seizure and I want them to know what *not* to do, in particular.

Through such telling, people solve some of the problems that a seizure represents for naive others. While these others then have the task of carrying out such instructions—which typically are "do nothing," "make me comfortable," "don't call the ambulance," and "keep me from hurting myself"—the authority, and therefore responsibility, for such reaction rests with the individual giving the instructions.

Disclosure of one's epilepsy may depend also on the anticipation of rejection at some subsequent telling or disclosure occasion. "Coming out" to those who appear to be candidates for "close" relationships is a strategy for minimizing the pain of later rejection. As one man said, "If they're going to leave [because of epilepsy] better it be sooner than later." Another spoke of such telling as a "good way of testing" what kind of friend such persons would be. "Why go through all the trauma of falling in love with someone if they are going to hate your guts once they find out you're an epileptic?"

We discovered that people also disclose their epilepsy when they feel it necessary or important to "educate" others. While this strategy is sometimes mediated and supported through participation in various self-help groups, some individuals initiated it themselves. One young man who became active in a local self-help group described his "rap" on epilepsy as follows:

> It's a good manner, I use it quite a bit. I'll come through and say epilepsy is a condition, not a disease. I can throw out all the statistics. I usually say most people are not in wheelchairs or in bed because of epilepsy, they're walking the streets just like I am and other people. Anything like that to make comparisons, to get a point across.

Another respondent, who believed she had benefited greatly by an early talk with a veteran epileptic, spoke of the importance of such education: "That's why I think it is important to come out of the closet to some extent. Because once people have met an epileptic and found out that it's a *person* with epilepsy, that helps a lot." Exposure to a person who "has epilepsy" but is conventional in all other ways may stimulate others to redefine their image of "epileptics."

CONCLUSION

Illness is an individualizing and privatizing experience. As Parsons (1951) argued, occupants of the sick role are not only dissuaded from "enjoying" the exemptions associated with their state but are segregated and separated from other sick people. When individuals desire to be "normal" and lead conventional lives the potential of stigma is isolating; persons fear disclosure of discreditable information and may limit their contacts or connections with others. As Ponse observes, "The veils of anonymity are often as effective with one's own as with those from whom one wishes to hide. Thus, an unintended consequence of secrecy is that it isolates members from one another" (1976:319). Persons with stigmatized illnesses like epilepsy, and perhaps with other illness as well, are doubly insulated from one another, at least in one very important sense. Because there is no illness subculture they are separate, alone and unconnected with others sharing the same problems (for an unusual exception, see Gussow and Tracey, 1968). And this very desire to lead conventional and stigma-free lives further separates and isolates them from each other. It is not surprising that the vast majority of people with epilepsy we interviewed did not know a single other epileptic.

Returning to our metaphor of the closet, we can now see that the potential of stigma certainly leads some people to create the closet as a secret and safe place. And usually, whether with homosexuality or epilepsy, people are in the closet alone. There are important differences, however. Few people in the closet with epilepsy even have any idea where other closets may be. Because there is usually no supportive subculture (a few recent and important self-help groups are notable exceptions) there is no place for a person with epilepsy to get insider information or to test the possible effects of coming out. Since most people with epilepsy want to be considered conventional people with a medical disorder, there is little motivation to come out and develop an epileptic identity. It is little wonder, then, that the closet of epilepsy has a revolving door.

To summarize: for those who possess some discreditable feature of self, some generally hidden "fact" or quality, the disclosure of which they believe will bring undesired consequences, the attempt to control information is a major strategy. We have described several ways people with epilepsy engage in such management work. Our data have suggested that the idea of being "in the closet" and that of being a "secret deviant" need to be extended to incorporate the complex reality of how people very selectively disclose or withhold discreditable information about themselves. Finally, we have shown how disclosing can serve the same ends as concealing. In addition, we suggest that sociological explorations into the experience of illness may well lend new dimensions to old concepts and give us greater understanding of the ways people manage such discomforting and vulnerable parts of their lives.

References

Anspach, Renee R.
1979 "From stigma to identity politics: Political activism among the physically disabled and former mental patients." Social Science and Medicine 13A:766–73.
Arangio, Anthony J.
1975 Behind the Stigma of Epilepsy. Washington, D.C.: Epilepsy Foundation of America.
1976 "The stigma of epilepsy." American Rehabilitation 2 (September/October): 4–6.
Becker, Howard S.
1963 Outsiders. New York: Macmillan.
1973 "Labeling theory reconsidered." Pp. 177–208 in Howard S. Becker, Outsiders, New York: Free Press.
Borman, Leonard D., James Davies and David Droge
1980 "Self-help groups for persons with epilepsy." In B. Hermann (ed.), A Multidisciplinary Handbook of Epilepsy. Springfield, Ill.: Thomas.
Caveness, W. F., H. Houston Merritt and G. H. Gallup, Jr.
1974 "A survey of public attitudes towards epilepsy in 1974 with an indication of trends over the past twenty-five years." Epilepsia 15:523–36.
Conrad, Peter and Joseph W. Schneider
1980 Deviance and Medicalization: From Badness to Sickness. St. Louis, Missouri: Mosby.
Dank, Barry M.
1971 "Coming out in the gay world." Psychiatry 34 (May): 180–97.
Davis, Fred
1961 "Deviance disavowal: The management of strained interaction by the visibly handicapped." Social Problems 9 (Fall):120–32.
Dingwall, Robert
1976 Aspects of Illness. New York: St. Martin's.
Fabrega, Horacio, Jr.
1972 "The study of disease in relation to culture." Behavioral Science 17: 183–200.
1979 "The ethnography of illness." Social Science and Medicine 13A:565–76.
Freidson, Eliot
1966 "Disability as social deviance." Pp. 71–99 in M. Sussman (ed.), Sociology and Rehabilitation. Washington, D.C.: The American Sociological Association.
1970 Profession of Medicine. New York: Dodd, Mead.
Glaser, Barney G. and Anselm L. Strauss
1967 The Discovery of Grounded Theory. Chicago: Aldine.
Goffman, Erving
1963 Stigma. Englewood Cliffs, N.J.: Prentice Hall.
Gussow, Zachary, and George S. Tracey
1968 "Status, ideology and adaptation to stigmatized illness: A study of leprosy." Human Organization 27 (4):316–25.

Hewitt, John P. and Randall Stokes
1975 "Disclaimers." American Sociological Review 40:1–11.
Humphreys, Laud
1972 Out of the Closets. Englewood Cliffs, N.J.: Prentice Hall.
Idler, Ellen L.
1979 "Definitions of health and illness in medical sociology." Social Science and Medicine 13A:723–31.
Kitsuse, John I.
1980 "Coming out all over: Deviants and the politics of social problems." Social Problems 28:1.
Lennox, Gordon W. and Margaret A. Lennox
1960 Epilepsy and related disorders, Volume I. Boston: Little, Brown.
Mark, Vernon H. and Frank R. Ervin
1970 Violence and the Brain. New York: Harper & Row.
Parsons, Talcott
1951 The Social System. New York: Free Press.
Perlman, Leonard G.
1977 The Person With Epilepsy: Life Style, Needs, Expectations. Chicago: National Epilepsy League.
Ponse, Barbara
1976 "Secrecy in the lesbian world." Urban Life 5 (October): 313–38.
Schneider, Joseph W. and Peter Conrad
1979 "Medical and sociological typologies: The case of epilepsy." Unpublished manuscript, Drake University, Des Moines, Iowa.
Strauss, Anselm L. and Barney G. Glaser
1975 Chronic Illness and the Quality of Life. St. Louis, Missouri: Mosby.
Temkin, Oswei
1971 The Falling Sickness, Second edition. Baltimore, Maryland: Johns Hopkins Press.
U.S. Department of Health Education and Welfare—National Institute of Health
1975 The NINCDS Epilepsy Research Program. Washington, D.C.: U.S. Government Printing Office.
Waitzkin, H. K. and B. Waterman
1974 The Exploitation of Illness in Capitalist Society. Indianapolis: Bobbs-Merrill.
Warren, Carol A. B.
1974 Identity and Community in the Gay World. New York: Wiley.
West, Patrick B.
1979a "Making sense of epilepsy." Pp. 162–69 in D. J. Osborne, M. M. Gruneberg and J. R. Eiser (eds.), Research in Psychology and Medicine, Volume 2. New York: Academic.
1979b "An investigation into the social construction and consequences of the label epilepsy." Sociological Review 27:719–41.

Notes

1. The moral parallel between illness and deviance has been well-recognized in the sociological literature. Parsons (1951) first noted that illness and crime are analytically similar because they both represent threats to effective role performance and are "dysfunctional" for society, calling forth appropriate mechanisms of social control. Freidson (1966, 1970) addressed this moral parallel more directly, by arguing that both illness and deviance are disvalued

and disvaluing attributes variously attached to actors and situations believed to challenge preferred and dominant definitions of appropriate conduct and "health." More recently, Dingwall (1976) has advocated a phenomenological, insider's approach to illness as lived experience. He suggests that illness might be considered deviance (1) to the extent that it involves behavior perceived by others as "out of the ordinary" or unusual, and (2) if sufficient intentionality or willfulness can be attributed to the ill/deviant actor for the conduct in question (see also Conrad and Schneider, 1980). While we stop short of concluding that epilepsy is "deviant," it seems clear from our data that it is stigmatized, at least in the eyes of those who have it.

2. While there is a relative imbalance of sociological "insider" accounts of being deviant, such work is even more rare for the experience of illness. We have few sociological studies of what it is like *to be* sick, to *have* cancer, diabetes, schizophrenia, heart disease, and so on (for exceptions see Davis, 1961; Gussow and Tracey, 1968; Strauss and Glaser, 1975). This may be due in part to the historic dominance of professional medical definitions of health and illness. We agree with Dingwall (1976), Fabrega (1972, 1979), and Idler (1979), that more research is needed into how these and other illnesses are experienced as social phenomena.

3. For a more current version of the argument linking the biophysiology of the brain and violence, see Mark and Ervin (1970).

4. See West's (1979a, b) discussion of 24 British families containing a child with epilepsy and how parents managed negative stereotypes of epilepsy in light of their child's diagnosis.

5. For an interesting discussion of some exceptions, see Anspach's (1979) analysis of the "identity politics" of the physically disabled and former mental patients. As we suggest, the availability of a new and positive identity is crucial to the development of the kind of politics Anspach describes.

22 / The Adjustment of the Family to the Crisis of Alcoholism

JOAN K. JACKSON

...Over a 3-year period, the present investigator has been an active participant in the Alcoholics Anonymous Auxiliary in Seattle. This group is composed partly of women whose husbands are or were members of Alcoholics Anonymous, and partly of women whose husbands are excessive drinkers but have never contacted Alcoholics Anonymous. At a typical meeting one-fifth would be the wives of Alcoholics Anonymous members who have been sober for some time; the husbands of another fifth would have recently joined the fellowship; the remainder would be equally divided between those whose husbands were "on and off" the Alcoholics Anonymous program and those whose husbands had as yet not had any contact with Alcoholics Anonymous.

At least an hour and a half of each formal meeting of this group is taken up with a frank discussion of the current family problems of the members. As in other meetings of Alcoholics Anonymous the questions are posed by describing the situation which gives rise to the problem, and the answers are a narration of the personal experiences of other wives who have had a similar problem, rather than direct advice. Verbatim shorthand notes have been taken of all discussions, at the request of the group, who also make use of the notes for the group's purposes. Informal contact has been maintained with past and present members. In the past 3 years 50 women have been members of this group.

The families represented by these women are at present in many different stages of adjustment and have passed through several stages during the past few years. The continuous contact over a prolonged period permits generalizations about processes and changes in family adjustments.

In addition, in connection with research on hospitalized alcoholics, many of their wives have been interviewed. The interviews with the hospitalized alcoholics, as well as with male members of Alcoholics Anonymous, have also provided information on family interactions. Further information has been derived from another group of wives, not connected with Alcoholics Anonymous, and from probation officers, social workers and court officials.

The following presentation is limited insofar as it deals only with families seeking help for the alcoholism of the husband. Other families are known to have solved the problem through divorce, often without having attempted to help the alcoholic member first. Others never seek help and never separate. There were no marked differences between the two groups seeking help, one through the hospital and one through the A.A. Auxiliary. The wives of hospitalized alcoholics gave a history of the family crisis similar to that given by women in the Auxiliary.

A second limitation is that only the families of male alcoholics are dealt with. It is recognized that the findings cannot be generalized to the families of alcoholic women without further research. Due to differences between men and women in their roles in the family as well as in the pattern of drinking, it would be expected that male and female alcoholics would in some ways have a different effect on family structure and function.

A third limitation is imposed for the sake of clarity and brevity: only the accounts of the wives of their attempts to stabilize their family adjustments will be dealt with. For any complete picture, the view of the alcoholic husband would also have to be included.

It must be emphasized that this paper deals with the definitions of the family situations by the wives, rather than with the actual situation. It has been noted that frequently wife and husband do not agree on what has occurred. The degree to which the definition of the situation by the wife or husband correlates with actual behavior is a question which must be left for further research.

The families represented in this study are from the middle and lower classes. The occupations of the husbands prior to excessive drinking include small business owners, salesmen, business executives, skilled and semiskilled workers. Prior to marriage the wives have been nurses, secretaries, teachers, saleswomen, cooks, or waitresses. The economic status of the childhood families of these husbands and wives ranged from very wealthy to very poor.

Method

From the records of discussions of the Alcoholics Anonymous Auxiliary, the statements of each wife were extracted and arranged in a time sequence. Notes on informal contacts were added at the point in the sequence where they occurred. The interviews with the wives of hospitalized alcoholics were similarly treated. These working records on individual families were then examined for uniformities of behavior and for regularities in changes over time.

The similarities in the process of adjustment to an alcoholic family member are presented here as stages of variable duration. It should be stressed that only the similarities are dealt with. Although the wives have shared the patterns dealt with here, there have been marked differences in the length of time between stages, in the number of stages passed through up to the present time, and in the relative importance to the family constellation of any one type of behavior. For example, all admitted nagging, but the amount of nagging was variable.

When the report of this analysis was completed it was read before a meeting of the Auxiliary with a request for correction of any errors in fact or interpretation. Corrections could be presented either anonymously or publicly from the floor. Only one correction was suggested and has been incorporated. The investigator is convinced that her relationship with the group is such that there would be no reticence about offering corrections. Throughout her contact with this group her role has been that of one who is being taught, very similar to the role of the new member. The overall response of the group to the presentation indicated that the members individually felt that they had been portrayed accurately.

The sense of having similar problems and similar experiences is indicated also in the reactions of new members to the Auxiliary's summarization of the notes of their discussions. Copies of these summaries are given to new members, who commonly state that they find it a relief to see that their problems are far from unique and that there are methods which successfully overcome them.

Statement of the Problem

For purposes of this presentation, the family is seen as involved in a cumulative crisis. All family members behave in a manner which they hope will resolve the crisis and permit a return to stability. Each member's action is influenced by his previous personality structure, by his previous role and status in the family group, and by the history of the crisis and its effects on his personality, roles and status up to that point. Action is also influenced by the past effectiveness of that particular action as a means of social control before and during the crisis. The behavior of family members in each phase of the crisis contributes to the form which the crisis takes in the following stages and sets limits on possible behavior in subsequent stages.

Family members are influenced, in addition, by the cultural definitions of alcoholism as evidence of weakness, inadequacy, or sinfulness; by the cultural prescriptions for the roles of family members; and by the cultural values of family solidarity, sanctity, and self-sufficiency. Alcoholism in the family poses a situation defined by the culture as shameful but for the handling of which there are no prescriptions which are effective or which permit direct action not in conflict with other cultural prescriptions. While in crises such as illness or death the family members can draw on cultural definitions of appropriate behavior for procedures which will terminate the crisis, this is not the case with alcoholism in the family. The cultural view has been that alcoholism is shameful and should not occur. Only recently has any information been offered to guide families in their behavior toward their alcoholic member and, as yet, this information resides more in technical journals than in the media of mass communication. Thus, in facing alcoholism, the family is in an unstructured situation and must find the techniques for handling it through trial and error.

STAGES IN FAMILY ADJUSTMENT
TO AN ALCOHOLIC MEMBER

The Beginning of the Marriage

At the time marriage was considered, the drinking of most of the men was within socially acceptable limits. In a few cases the men were already alcoholics but managed to hide this from their fiancées. They drank only moderately or not at all when on dates and often avoided friends and relatives who might expose their excessive drinking. The relatives and friends who were introduced to the fiancée were those who had hopes that "marriage would straighten him out" and thus said nothing about the drinking. In a small number of cases the men spoke with their fiancées of their alcoholism. The women had no conception of what alcoholism meant, other than that it involved more than the usual frequency of drinking, and they entered the marriage with little more preparation than if they had known nothing about it.

Stage 1.   Incidents of excessive drinking begin and, although they are sporadic, place strains on the husband-wife interaction. In attempts to minimize drinking, problems in marital adjustment not related to the drinking are avoided.

Stage 2.   Social isolation of the family begins as incidents of excessive drinking multiply. The increasing isolation magnifies the importance of family interactions and events. Behavior and thought become drinking-centered. Husband-wife adjustment deteriorates and tension rises. The wife begins to feel self-pity and to lose her self-confidence as her behavior fails to stabilize her husband's drinking. There is an attempt still to maintain the original family structure, which is disrupted anew with each episode of drinking, and as a result the children begin to show emotional disturbance.

Stage 3.   The family gives up attempts to control the drinking and begins to behave in a manner geared to relieve tension rather than achieve long-term ends. The disturbance of the children becomes more marked. There is no longer an attempt to support the alcoholic in his roles as husband and father. The wife begins to worry about her own sanity and about her inability to make decisions or act to change the situation.

Stage 4.   The wife takes over control of the family and the husband is seen as a recalcitrant child. Pity and strong protective feelings largely replace the earlier resentment and hostility. The family becomes more stable and organized in a manner to minimize the disruptive behavior of the husband. The self-confidence of the wife begins to be rebuilt.

Stage 5. The wife separates from her husband if she can resolve the problems and conflicts surrounding this action.

Stage 6. The wife and children reorganize as a family without the husband.

Stage 7. The husband achieves sobriety and the family, which had become organized around an alcoholic husband, reorganizes to include a sober father and experiences problems in reinstating him in his former roles.

Stage 1. Attempts to Deny the Problem

Usually the first experience with drinking as a problem arises in a social situation. The husband drinks in a manner which is inappropriate to the social setting and the expectations of others present. The wife feels embarrassed on the first occasion and humiliated as it occurs more frequently. After several such incidents she and her husband talk over his behavior. The husband either formulates an explanation for the episode and assures her that such behavior will not occur again, or he refuses to discuss it at all. For a time afterward he drinks appropriately and drinking seems to be a problem no longer. The wife looks back on the incidents and feels that she has exaggerated them, feels ashamed of herself for her disloyalty and for her behavior. The husband, in evaluating the incident, feels shame also and vows such episodes will not recur. As a result, both husband and wife attempt to make it up to the other and, for a time, try to play their conceptions of the ideal husband and wife roles, minimizing or avoiding other difficulties which arise in the marriage. They thus create the illusion of a "perfect" marriage.

Eventually another inappropriate drinking episode occurs and the pattern is repeated. The wife worries but takes action only in the situations in which inappropriate drinking occurs, as each long intervening period of acceptable drinking behavior convinces her that a recurrence is unlikely. As time goes on, in attempting to cope with individual episodes, she runs the gamut of possible trial and error behaviors, learning that none is permanently effective.

If she speaks to other people about her husband's drinking, she is usually assured that there is no need for concern, that her husband can control his drinking and that her fears are exaggerated. Some friends possibly admit that his drinking is too heavy and give advice on how they handled similar situations with their husbands. These friends convince her that her problem will be solved as soon as she hits upon the right formula for dealing with her husband's drinking.

During this stage the husband-wife interaction is in no way "abnormal." In a society in which a large proportion of men drink, most wives have at some time had occasion to be concerned, even though only briefly, with an episode of drinking which they considered inappropriate (2). In a society in which the status of the family depends on that of the husband, the wife feels threatened by any behavior on his part which might lower it. Inappropriate drinking is regarded by her as a threat to the family's reputation and standing in the community. The wife attempts to exert control and often finds herself blocked by the sacredness of drinking behavior to men in America. Drinking is a private matter and not any business of the wife's. On the whole, a man reacts to his wife's suggestion that he has not adequately controlled his drinking with resentment, rebelliousness, and a display of emotion which makes rational discussion difficult. The type of husband-wife interaction outlined in this stage has occurred in many American families in which the husband never became an excessive drinker.

Stage 2. Attempts to Eliminate the Problems

Stage 2 begins when the family experiences social isolation because of the husband's drinking. Invitations to the homes of friends become less frequent. When the couple does visit friends, drinks are not served or are limited, thus emphasizing the reason for exclusion from other social activities of the friendship group. Discussions of drinking begin to be sidestepped awkwardly by friends, the wife, and the husband.

By this time the periods of socially acceptable drinking are becoming shorter. The wife, fearing that the full extent of her husband's drinking will become known, begins to withdraw from social participation, hoping to reduce the visibility of his behavior, and thus the threat to family status.

Isolation is further intensified because the family usually acts in accordance with the cultural dictate that it should be self-sufficient and manage to resolve its own problems without recourse to outside aid. Any experiences which they have had with well-meaning outsiders, usually relatives, have tended to strengthen this conviction. The husband has defined such relatives as interfering and the situation has deteriorated rather than improved.

With increasing isolation, the family members begin to lose perspective on their interaction and on their problems. Thrown into closer contact with one another as outside contacts diminish, the behavior of each member assumes exaggerated importance. The drinking behavior becomes the focus of anxiety. Gradually all family difficulties become attributed to it. (For example, the mother who is cross with her children will feel that, if her husband had not been drinking, she would not have been so tense and would not have been angry.) The fear that the full extent of drinking may be discovered mounts steadily; the conceptualization of the consequences of such a discovery becomes increasingly vague and, as a result, more anxiety-provoking. The family feels different from others and alone with its shameful secret.

Attempts to cover up increase. The employer who calls to inquire about the husband's absence from work is given excuses. The wife is afraid to face the consequences of loss of the husband's pay check in addition to her other concerns. Questions from the children are evaded or they are told that their father is ill. The wife lives in terror of the day when the children will be told by others of the nature of the "illness." She is also afraid that the children may describe their father's symptoms to teachers or neighbors. Still feeling that the family must solve its own problems, she keeps her troubles to herself and hesitates to seek outside help. If her husband beats her, she will bear it rather than call in the police. (Indeed, often she has no idea that this is even a possibility.) Her increased isolation has left her without the advice of others as to sources of help in the community. If she knows of them, an agency contact means to her an admission of the complete failure of her family as an independent unit. For the middle-class woman particularly, recourse to social agencies and law enforcement agencies means a terrifying admission of loss of status.

During this stage, husband and wife are drawing further apart. Each feels resentful of the behavior of the other. When this resentment is expressed, further drinking occurs. When it is not, tension mounts and the next drinking episode is that much more destructive of family relationships. The reasons for drinking are explored frantically. Both husband and wife feel that if only they could discover the reason, all members of the family could gear their behavior to making drinking unnecessary. The discussions become increasingly unproductive, as it is the husband's growing conviction that his wife does not and cannot understand him.

On her part, the wife begins to feel that she is a failure, that she has been unable to fulfill the major cultural obligations of a wife to meet her husband's needs. With her increasing isolation, her sense of worth derives almost entirely from her roles as wife and mother. Each failure to help her husband gnaws away at her sense of adequacy as a person.

Periods of sobriety or socially acceptable drinking still occur. These periods keep the wife from making a permanent or stable adjustment. During them her husband, in his guilt, treats her like a queen. His behavior renews her hope and rekindles positive feelings toward him. Her sense of worth is bolstered temporarily and she grasps desperately at her husband's reassurance that she is really a fine person and not a failure and an unlovable shrew. The periods of sobriety also keep her family from facing the inability of the husband to control his drinking. The inaccuracies of the cultural stereotype of the alcoholic—particularly that he is in a constant state of inebriation—also contribute to the family's rejection of the idea of alcoholism, as the husband seems to demonstrate from time to time that he can control his drinking.

Family efforts to control the husband become desperate. There are no culturally prescribed behavior patterns for handling such a situation and the family is forced to evolve its own techniques. Many different types of behavior are tried but none brings consistent results; there seems to be no way of predicting the consequences of any action that may be taken. All attempts to stabilize or structure the situation to permit consistent behavior fail. Threats of leaving, hiding his liquor away, emptying the bottles down the drain, curtailing his money, are tried in rapid succession, but none is effective. Less punitive methods, as discussing the situation when he is sober, babying him during hangovers, and trying to drink with him to keep him at home, are attempted and fail. All behavior becomes oriented around the drinking, and the thought of family members becomes obsessive on this subject. As no action seems to be successful in achieving its goal, the wife persists in trial-and-error behavior with mounting frustration. Long-term goals recede into the background and become secondary to just keeping the husband from drinking today.

There is still an attempt to maintain the illusion of husband-wife-children roles. When father is sober, the children are expected to give him respect and obedience. The wife also defers to him in his role as head of the household. Each drinking event thus disrupts family functioning anew. The children begin to show emotional disturbances as a result of the inconsistencies of parental behavior. During periods when the husband is drinking the wife tries to shield them from the knowledge and effects of his behavior, at the same time drawing them closer to herself and deriving emotional support from them. In sober periods, the father tries to regain their favor. Due to experiencing directly only pleasant interactions with their father, considerable affection is often felt for him by the children. This affection becomes increasingly difficult for the isolated wife to tolerate, and an additional source of conflict. She feels that she needs and deserves the love and support of her children and, at the same time, she feels it important to maintain the children's picture of their father. She counts on the husband's affection for the children to motivate a cessation of drinking as he comes to realize the effects of his behavior on them.

In this stage, self-pity begins to be felt by the wife, if it has not entered previously. It continues in various degrees throughout the succeeding stages. In an attempt to handle her deepening sense of inadequacy, the wife often tries to convince herself that she is right and her husband wrong, and this also continues through the following stages. At this point the wife often resembles what Whalen (1) describes as "The Sufferer."

Stage 3. Disorganization

The wife begins to adopt a "What's the use?" attitude and to accept her husband's drinking as a problem likely to be permanent. Attempts to understand one another become less frequent. Sober periods still engender hope, but hope qualified by skepticism; they bring about a lessening of anxiety and this is defined as happiness.

By this time some customary patterns of husband-wife-children interaction have evolved. Techniques which have had some effectiveness in controlling the husband in the past or in relieving pent-up frustration are used by the wife. She nags, berates or retreats into silence. Husband and wife are both on the alert, the wife watching for increasing irritability and restlessness which mean a recurrence of drinking, and the husband for veiled aspersions on his behavior or character.

The children are increasingly torn in their loyalties as they become tools in the struggle between mother and father. If the children are at an age of comprehension, they have usually learned the true nature of their family situation, either from outsiders or from their mother, who has given up attempts to bolster her husband's position as father. The children are often bewildered but questioning their parents brings no satisfactory answers as the parents themselves do not understand what is happening. Some children become terrified; some have increasing behavior problems within and outside the home; others seem on the surface to accept the situation calmly.[1]

During periods of the husband's drinking, the hostility, resentment and frustrations felt by the couple is allowed expression. Both may resort to violence—the wife in self-defense or because she can find no other outlet for her feelings. In those cases in which the wife retaliates to violence in kind, she feels a mixture of relief and intense shame at having deviated so far from what she conceives to be "the behavior of a normal woman."

When the wife looks at her present behavior, she worries about her "normality." In comparing the person she was in the early years of her marriage with the person she has become, she is frightened. She finds herself nagging and unable to control herself. She resolves to stand up to her husband when he is belligerent but instead finds herself cringing in terror and then despises herself for her lack of courage. If she retaliates with violence, she is filled with self-loathing at behaving in an "unwomanly" manner. She finds herself compulsively searching for bottles, knowing full well that finding them will change nothing, and is worried because she engages in such senseless behavior. She worries about her inability to take constructive action of any kind. She is confused about where her loyalty lies, whether with her husband or her children. She feels she is a failure as a wife, mother and person. She believes she should be strong in the face of adversity and instead feels herself weak.

The wife begins to feel herself avoiding sexual contact with her husband when he has been drinking. Sex under these circumstances, she feels, is sex for its own sake rather than an indication of affection for her. Her husband's lack of consideration of her needs to be satisfied leaves her feeling frustrated. The lack of sexual responsiveness reflects her emotional withdrawal from him in other areas of family life. Her husband, on his part, feels frustrated and rejected; he accuses her of frigidity and this adds to her concern about her adequacy as a woman.[2]

By this time the opening wedge has been inserted into the self-sufficiency of the family. The husband has often been in difficulty with the police and the wife has learned that police protection is available. An emergency has occurred in which the seeking of outside help was the only possible action to take; subsequent calls for aid from outsiders do not require the same degree of urgency before they can be undertaken. However, guilt and a lessening of self-respect and self-confidence accompany this method of resolving emergencies. The husband intensifies these feelings by speaking of the interference of outsiders, or of his night in jail.

In Stage 3 all is chaos. Few problems are met constructively. The husband and wife both feel trapped in an intolerable, unstructured situation which offers no way out. The wife's self-assurance is almost completely gone. She is afraid to take action and afraid to let things remain as they are. Fear is one of the major characteristics of this stage: fear of violence, fear of personality damage to the children, fear for her own sanity, fear that relatives will interfere, and fear that they will not help in an emergency. Added to this, the family feels alone in the world and helpless. The problems, and the behavior of family members in attempting to cope with them, seem so shameful that help from others is unthinkable. They feel that attempts to get help would meet only with rebuff, and that communication of the situation will engender disgust.

At this point the clinical picture which the wife presents is very similar to what Whalen (1) has described as "The Waverer."

Stage 4. Attempts to Reorganize in Spite of the Problems

Stage 4 begins when a crisis occurs which necessitates that action be taken. There may be no money or food in the house; the husband may have been violent to the children; or life on the level of Stage 3 may have become intolerable. At this point some wives leave, thus entering directly into Stage 5.

The wife who passes through Stage 4 usually begins to ease her husband out of his family roles. She assumes husband and father roles. This involves strengthening her role as mother and putting aside her role as wife. She becomes the manager of the home, the discipliner of the children, the decision-maker; she becomes somewhat like Whalen's (1) "Controller." She either ignores her husband as much as possible or treats him as her most recalcitrant child. Techniques are worked out for getting control of his pay check, if there still is one, and money is doled out to her husband on the condition of his good behavior. When he drinks, she threatens to leave him, locks him out of the house, refuses to pay his taxi bills, leaves him in jail overnight rather than pay his bail. Where her obligations to her husband conflict with those to her children, she decides in favor of the latter. As she views her husband increasingly as a child, pity and a sense of being desperately needed by him enter. Her inconsistent behavior toward him, deriving from the lack of predictability inherent in the situation up to now, becomes reinforced by her mixed feelings toward him.

In this stage the husband often tries to set his will against hers in decisions about the children. If the children have been permitted to stay with a friend overnight, he may threaten to create a scene unless they return immediately. He may make almost desperate efforts to gain their affection and respect, his behavior ranging from getting them up in the middle of the night to fondle them to giving them stiff lectures on children's obligations to fathers. Sometimes he will attempt to align the males of the family with him against the females. He may openly express resentment of the children and become belligerent toward them physically or verbally.

Much of the husband's behavior can be conceptualized as resulting from an increasing awareness of his isolation from the other members of the family and their steady withdrawal of respect and affection. It seems to be a desperate effort to regain what he has lost, but without any clear idea of how this can be accomplished—an effort to change a situation in which everyone is seen as against him; and, in reality, this is becoming more and more true. As the wife has taken over control of the family with some degree of success, he feels, and becomes, less and less necessary to the ongoing activity of the family. There are fewer and fewer roles left for him to play. He becomes aware that members of the family enjoy each other's company without him. When he is home he tries to enter this circle of warmth or to smash it. Either way he isolates himself further. He finds that the children discuss with the mother how to manage him and he sees the children acting on the basis of their mother's idea of him. The children refuse to pay attention to his demands: they talk back to him in the same way that they talk back to one another, adding pressure on him to assume the role of just another child. All this leaves him frustrated and, as a result, often aggressive or increasingly absent from home.

The children, on the whole, become more settled in their behavior as the wife takes over the family responsibilities. Decisions are made by her and upheld in the face of their father's attempts to interfere. Participation in activities outside the home is encouraged. Their patterns of interaction with their father are supported by the mother. Whereas in earlier stages the children often felt that there were causal connections between their actions and their father's drinking, they now accept his unpredictability. "Well," says a 6-year-old, "I'll just have to get used to it. I have a drunken father."

The family is more stabilized in one way but in other ways insecurities are multiplied. Pay checks are received less and less regularly. The violence or withdrawal of the father increases. When he is away the wife worries about automobile accidents or injury in fights, which become more and more probable as time passes. The husband may begin to be seriously ill from time to time; his behavior may become quite bizarre. Both of these signs of increasing illness arouse anxiety in the family.

During this stage hopes may rise high for father's "reform" when he begins to verbalize wishes to stop drinking, admits off and on his inability to stop, and sounds desperate for doing something about his drinking. Now may begin the trek to sanitariums for the middle-class alcoholic, to doctors, or to Alcoholics Anonymous. Where just the promise to stop drinking has failed to revive hope, sobriety through outside agencies has the ability to rekindle it brightly. There is the feeling that at last he is "taking really constructive action." In failure the discouragement is deeper. Here another wedge has been inserted into the self-sufficiency of the family.

By this time the wedges are many. The wife, finding she has managed to bring some semblance of order and stability to her family, while not exactly becoming a self-assured person, has regained some sense of worth which grows a little with each crisis she meets successfully. In addition, the very fact of taking action to stabilize the situation brings relief. On some occasion she may be able to approach social agencies for financial help, often during a period when the husband has temporarily deserted or is incarcerated. She may have gone to the family court; she may have consulted a lawyer about getting a restraining order when the husband was in a particularly belligerent state. She has begun to learn her way around among the many agencies which offer help.

Often she has had a talk with an Alcoholics Anonymous member and has begun to look into what is known about alcoholism. If she has attended a few Alcoholics Anonymous meetings, her sense of shame has been greatly alleviated as she finds so many others in the same boat. Her hopes rise as she meets alcoholics who have stopped drinking, and she feels relieved at being able to discuss her problems openly for the first time with an audience which understands fully. She begins to gain perspective on her problem and learns that she herself is involved in what happens to her husband, and that she must change. She exchanges techniques of management with other wives and receives their support in her decisions.

She learns that her husband is ill rather than merely "ornery," and this often serves to quell for the time being thoughts about leaving him which have begun to germinate as she has gained more self-confidence. She learns that help is available but also that her efforts to push him into help are unavailing. She is not only supported in her recently evolved behavior of thinking first of her family, but now this course also emerges from the realm of the unconceptualized and is set in an accepted rationale. She feels more secure in having a reason and a certainty that the group accepts her as "doing the right thing." When she reports deviations from what the group thinks is the "right way," her reasons are understood; she receives solid support, but there is also pressure on her to alter her behavior again toward the acceptable. Blaming and self-pity are actively discouraged. In group discussions she still admits to such feelings but learns to recognize them as they arise and to go beyond them to more productive thinking.

How much her altered behavior changes the family situation is uncertain, but it helps her and gives her security from which to venture forth to further actions of a consistent and constructive type, constructive at least from the point of view of keeping her family on as even a keel as possible in the face of the disruptive influence of the husband. With new friends whom she can use as a sounding board for plans, and with her growing acquaintance with the alternatives and possible patterns of behavior, her thinking ceases to be circular and unproductive. Her anxiety about her own sanity is alleviated as she is reassured by others that they have experienced the same concern and that the remedy is to get her own life and her family under better control. As she accomplishes this, the difference in her feelings about herself convinces her that this is so.

Whether or not she has had a contact with wives of Alcoholics Anonymous members or other wives who have been through a similar experience and have emerged successfully, the very fact of taking hold of her situation and gradually making it more manageable adds to her self-confidence. As her husband is less and less able to care for himself or his family, she begins to feel that he needs her and that without her he would be destroyed. Such a feeling makes it difficult for her to think of leaving him. His almost complete social isolation at this point and his cries for help reinforce this conviction of being needed.

The drinking behavior is no longer hidden. Others obviously know about it, and this becomes accepted by the wife and children. Already isolated and insulated against possible rejection, the wife is often surprised to find that she has exaggerated her fears of what would happen were the situation known. However, the unpredictability of her husband's behavior makes her reluctant to form social relationships which could be violently disrupted or to involve others in the possible consequences of his behavior.

Stage 5. Efforts to Escape the Problems

Stage 5 may be the terminal one for the marriage. In this stage the wife separates from her husband. Sometimes the marriage is re-established after a period of sobriety, when it appears certain that the husband will not drink again. If he does revert to drinking, the marriage is sometimes finally terminated but with less emotional stress than the first time. If the husband deserts, being no longer able to tolerate his lack of status in his family, Stage 6 may be entered abruptly.

The events precipitating the decision to terminate the marriage may be near-catastrophic, as when there is an attempt by the husband to kill the wife or children, or they may appear trivial to outsiders, being only the last straw to an accumulation of years.

The problems in coming to the decision to terminate the marriage cannot be underestimated. Some of these problems derive from emotional conflicts; some are related to very practical circumstances in the situation; some are precipitated by the conflicting advice of outsiders. With several children dependent on her, the wife must decide whether the present situation is more detrimental to them than future situations she can see arising if she should leave her husband. The question of where the money to live on will come from must be thought out. If she can get a job, will there be enough to provide for child care also while she is away from home? Should the children, who have already experienced such an unsettled life, be separated from her to be cared for by others? If the family still owns its own home, how can she retain control of it? If she leaves, where can she go? What can be done to tide the family over until her first earnings come in? How can she ensure her husband's continued absence from the home and thus be certain of the safety of individuals and property in her absence? These are only a small sample of the practical issues that must be dealt with in trying to think her way through to a decision to terminate the marriage.

Other pressures act on her to impede the decision-making process. "If he would only stay drunk till I carry out what I intend to do," is a frequent statement. When the husband realizes that his wife really means to leave, he frequently sobers up, watches his behavior in the home, plays on her latent and sometimes conscious feelings of her responsibility for the situation, stresses his need for her and that without her he is lost, tears away at any confidence she has that she will be able to manage by herself, and threatens her and the children with injury or with his own suicide if he carries out her intention.

The children, in the meantime, are pulling and pushing on her emotions. They think she is "spineless" to stay but unfair to father's chances for ultimate recovery if she leaves. Relatives, who were earlier alienated in her attempts to shield her family but now know of the situation, do not believe in its full ramifications. They often feel she is exaggerating and persuade her to stay with him. Especially is this true in the case of the "solitary drinker." His drinking has been so well concealed that the relatives have no way of knowing the true nature of the situation. Other relatives, afraid that they will be called on for support, exert pressure to keep the marriage intact and the husband thereby responsible for debts. Relatives who feel she should leave him overplay their hands by berating the husband in such a manner as to evoke her defense of him. This makes conscious the positive aspects of her relationship with him, causing her to waver in her decision. If she consults organized agencies, she often gets conflicting advice. The agencies concerned with the well-being of the family may counsel leaving; those concerned with rehabilitating the husband may press her to stay. In addition, help from public organizations almost always involves delay and is frequently not forthcoming at the point where she needs it most.

The wife must come to terms with her own mixed feelings about her husband, her marriage and herself before she can decide on such a step as breaking up the marriage. She must give up hope that she can be of any help to her husband. She must command enough self-confidence, after years of having it eroded, to be able to face an unknown future and leave the security of an unpalatable but familiar past and present. She must accept that she has failed in her marriage, not an easy thing to do after having devoted years to stopping up the cracks in the family structure as they appeared. Breaking up the marriage involves a complete alteration in the life goals toward which all her behavior has been oriented. It is hard for her to rid herself of the feeling that she married him and he is her responsibility. Having thought and planned for so long on a day-to-day basis, it is difficult to plan for a long-term future.

Her taking over the family raises her self-confidence but failure to carry through on decisions undermines the new gains that she has made. Vacillation in her decisions tends to exasperate the agencies trying to help her, and she begins to feel that help from them may not be forthcoming if she finally decides to leave.

Some events, however, help her to arrive at a decision. During the absences of her husband she has seen how manageable life can be and how smoothly her family can run. She finds that life goes on without him. The wife who is working comes to feel that "my husband is a luxury I can no longer afford." After a few short-term separations in which she tries out her wings successfully, leaving comes to look more possible. Another step on the path to leaving is the acceptance of the idea that, although she cannot help her husband, she can help her family. She often reaches a state of such emotional isolation from her husband that his behavior no longer disturbs her emotionally but is only something annoying which upsets daily routines and plans.

Stage 6. Reorganization of Part of the Family

The wife is without her husband and must reorganize her family on this basis. Substantially the process is similar to that in other divorced families, but with some additions. The divorce rarely cuts her relationships to her husband. Unless she and her family disappear, her husband may make attempts to come back. When drunk, he may endanger her job by calls at her place of work. He may attempt violence against members of the family, or he may contact the children and work to gain their loyalty so that pressure is put on the mother to accept him again. Looking back on her marriage, she forgets the full impact of the problem situation on her and on the children and feels more warmly toward her husband, and these feelings can still be manipulated by him. The wide circulation of information on alcoholism as an illness engenders guilt about having deserted a sick man. Gradually, however, the family becomes reorganized.

Stage 7. Recovery and Reorganization of the Whole Family

Stage 7 is entered if the husband achieves sobriety, whether or not separation has preceded. It was pointed out that in earlier stages most of the problems in the marriage were attributed to the alcoholism of the husband, and thus problems in adjustment not related directly to the drinking were unrecognized and unmet. Also, the "sober personality" of the husband was thought of as the "real" personality, with a resulting lack of recognition of other factors involved in his sober behavior, such as remorse and guilt over his actions, leading him to act to the best of his ability like "the ideal husband" when sober. Irritation or other signs of growing tension were viewed as indicators of further drinking, and hence the problems giving rise to them were walked around gingerly rather than faced and resolved. Lack of conflict and lack of drinking were defined as indicating a perfect adjustment. For the wife and husband facing a sober marriage after many years of an alcoholic marriage, the expectations of what marriage without alcoholism will be are unrealistically idealistic, and the reality of marriage almost inevitably brings disillusionments. The expectation that all would go well and that all problems be resolved with the cessation of the husband's drinking cannot be met and this threatens the marriage from time to time.

The beginning of sobriety for the husband does not bring too great hope to the family at first. They have been through this before but are willing to help him along and stand by him in the new attempt. As the length of sobriety increases, so do the hopes for its permanence and efforts to be of help. The wife at first finds it difficult to think more than in terms of today, waking each morning with fear of what the day will bring and sighing with relief at the end of each sober day.

With the continuation of sobriety, many problems begin to crop up. Mother has for years managed the family, and now father again wishes to be reinstated in his former roles. Usually the first role reestablished is that of breadwinner, and the economic problems of the family begin to be alleviated as debts are gradually paid and there is enough left over for current needs. With the resumption of this role, the husband feels that the family should also accept him at least as a partner in the management of the family. Even if the wife is willing to hand over some of the control of the children, for example, the children often are not able to accept this change easily. Their mother has been both parents for so long that it takes time to get used to the idea of consulting their father on problems and asking for his decisions. Often the father tries too hard to manage this change overnight, and the very pressure put on the children toward this end defeats him. In addition, he is unable to meet many of the demands the children make on him because he has never really become acquainted with them or learned to understand them and is lacking in much necessary background knowledge of their lives.

The wife, who finds it difficult to conceive of her husband as permanently sober, feels an unwillingness to let control slip from her hands. At the same time she realizes that reinstatement of her husband in his family roles is necessary to his sobriety. She also realizes that the closer his involvement in the family the greater the probability of his remaining sober. Yet she remembers events in the past in which his failure to handle his responsibilities was catastrophic to the family. Used to avoiding anything which might upset him, the wife often hesitates to discuss problems openly. At times, if she is successful in helping him to regain his roles as father, she feels resentful of his intrusion into territory which she has come to regard as hers. If he makes errors in judgment which affect the family adversely, her former feelings of being his superior may come to the fore and affect her interaction with him. If the children begin to turn to him, she may feel a resurgence of self-pity at being left out and find herself attempting to swing the children back toward herself. Above all, however, she finds herself feeling resentful that some other agency achieved what she and the children could not.

Often the husband makes demands for obedience, for consideration and for pampering which members of the family feel unable to meet. He may become rather euphoric as his sobriety continues and feel superior for a time.

Gradually, however, the drinking problem sinks into the past and marital adjustment at some level is achieved. Even when this has occurred, the drinking problem crops up occasionally, as when the time comes for a decision about whether the children should be permitted to drink. The mother at such times becomes anxious, sees in the child traits which remind her of her husband, worries whether these are the traits which mean future alcoholism. At parties, at first, she is watchful and concerned about whether her husband will take a drink or not. Relatives and friends may, in a party mood, make the husband the center of attention by emphasizing his nondrinking. They may unwittingly cast aspersions on his character by trying to convince him that he can now "drink like a man." Some relatives and friends have gone so far as secretly to "spike" a nonalcoholic drink and then cry "bottoms up!" without realizing the risk of reactivating patterns from the past.

If sobriety has come through Alcoholics Anonymous, the husband frequently throws himself so wholeheartedly into A.A. activities that his wife sees little of him and feels neglected. As she worries less about his drinking, she may press him to cut down on these activities. That this is dangerous, since A.A. activity is correlated with success in Alcoholics Anonymous, has been shown by Lahey (4). Also, the wife discovers that, though she has a sober husband, she is by no means free of alcoholics. In his Twelfth Step work, he may keep the house filled with men he is helping. In the past her husband has avoided self-searching; and now he may become excessively introspective, and it may be difficult for her to deal with this.

If the husband becomes sober through Alcoholics Anonymous and the wife participates actively in groups open to her, the thoughts of what is happening to her, to her husband and to her family will be verbalized and interpreted within the framework of the Alcoholics Anonymous philosophy and the situation will probably be more tolerable and more easily worked out.

SUGGESTIONS FOR FURTHER RESEARCH

The above presentation has roughly delineated sequences and characteristics of family adjustment to an alcoholic husband. A more detailed delineation of the stages is required. The extent to which these findings, based on families seeking help, can be generalized to other families of alcoholics needs to be determined, and differences between these families and others specified. Consideration should be given to the question of correspondence between the wife's definition of the situation and that which actually occurs.

Further research is needed on the factors which determine the rate of transition through the stages, and on the factors which retard such a transition, sometimes to the extent that the family seems to remain in the same stage almost permanently. In the group studied, the majority passed from one stage to the next but took different lengths of time to make the transition. Those wives whose husbands have been sober a long time had all passed through all the stages. None of the long-term members remained in the same stage throughout the time that the group was under study.

Other problems which require clarification are: (a) What are the factors within families which facilitate a return to sobriety or hamper it? (b) What variations in family behavior are determined by social class? (c) What problems are specific to the different types of drinking patterns of the husband—for example, the periodic drinker, the steady drinker, the solitary drinker, the sociable drinker, the drinker who becomes belligerent, and the drinker who remains calm? There are indications in the data gathered in the present study that such specific problems arise.

SUMMARY

The onset of alcoholism in a family member has been viewed as precipitating a cumulative crisis for the family. Seven critical stages have been delineated. Each stage affects the form which the following one will take. The family finds itself in an unstructured situation which is undefined by the culture. Thus it is forced to evolve techniques of adjustment by trial and error. The unpredictability of the situation, added to its lack of structure, engenders anxiety in family members which gives rise to personality difficulties. Factors in the culture, in the environment, and within the family situation prolong the crisis and deter the working out of permanent adjustment patterns. With the arrest of the alcoholism, the crisis enters its final stage. The family attempts to reorganize to include the ex-alcoholic and makes adjustments to the changes which have occurred in him.

It has been suggested that the clinical picture presented by the wife to helping agencies is not only indicative of a type of basic personality structure but also of the stage in family adjustment to an alcoholic. That the wives of alcoholics represent a rather limited number of personality types can be interpreted in two ways, which are not mutually exclusive.

(a) That women with certain personality attributes tend to select alcoholics or potential alcoholics as husbands in order to satisfy unconscious personality needs;

(b) That women undergoing similar experiences of stress, within similarly unstructured situations, defined by the culture and reacted to by members of the society in such a manner as to place limits on the range of possible behavior, will emerge from this experience showing many similar neurotic personality traits. As the situation evolves some of these personality traits will also change. Changes have been observed in the women studied which correlate with altered family interaction patterns. This hypothesis is supported also by observations on the behavior of individuals in other unstructured situations, in situations involving conflicting goals and loyalties, and in situations in which they were isolated from supporting group interaction. It is congruent also with the theory of reactions to increased and decreased stress.

Notes

1. Some effects of alcoholism of the father on children have been discussed by Newell (3).

2. It is of interest here that marriage counselors and students of marital adjustment are of the opinion that unhappy marriage results in poor sexual adjustment more often than poor sexual adjustment leads to unhappy marriage. If this proves to be true, it would be expected that most wives of alcoholics would find sex distasteful while their husbands are drinking. The wives of the inactive alcoholics report that their sexual adjustments with their husbands are currently satisfactory; many of those whose husbands are still drinking state that they enjoyed sexual relationships before the alcoholism was established.

References

1. Whalen, T. Wives of alcoholics: four types observed in a family service agency. Quart. J. Stud. Alc. 14:632–641, 1953.

2. Club and Educational Bureaus of Newsweek. Is alcoholism everyone's problem? Platform, N.Y., p. 3, Jan. 1950.

3. Newell, N. Alcoholism and the father-image. Quart. J. Stud. Alc. 11:92–96, 1950.

4. Lahey, W. W. A comparison of social and personal factors identified with selected members of Alcoholics Anonymous. Master's Thesis; University of Southern California; 1950.

23 / How Women Experience Battering: The Process of Victimization

KATHLEEN J. FERRARO
JOHN M. JOHNSON

On several occasions since 1850, feminists in Britain and the United States have initiated campaigns to end the battering of women by husbands and lovers, but have received little sympathy or support from the public (Dobash and Dobash, 1979). Sociologists systematically ignored the existence of violence against women until 1971, when journal articles and conferences devoted to the topic of domestic violence began to appear (Gelles, 1974; O'Brien, 1971; Steinmetz and Straus, 1974). Through the efforts of grass-roots activists and academics, battering has been recognized as a widespread social problem (Tierney, 1982). In 1975 a random survey of U.S. families found that 3.8 percent of women experienced severe violence in their marriage (Strauss *et al.,* 1980). The National Crime Survey of 1976 found that one-fourth of all assaults against women who had ever been married were committed by their husbands or ex-husbands (Gacquin, 1978). Shelters providing services to battered women in the United States have not been able to keep pace with requests for assistance (Colorado Association for Aid to Battered Women, 1978; Ferraro, 1981a; Roberts, 1981; Women's Advocates, 1980).

Although the existence of violence against women is now publicly acknowledged, the experience of being battered is poorly understood. Research aimed at discovering the incidence and related social variables has been based on an operational definition of battering which focuses on the violent act. The Conflict Tactic Scales (CTS) developed by Straus (1979), for example, is based on the techniques used to resolve family conflicts. The Violence Scale of the CTS ranks eight violent behaviors, ranging in severity from throwing something at the other person to using a knife or gun (Straus, 1979). The scale is not designed to explore the context of violent actions, or their meanings for the victim or perpetrator. With notable exceptions (Dobash and Dobash, 1979), the bulk of sociological research on battered women has focused on quantifiable variables (Gelles, 1974, 1976; O'Brien, 1971; Steinmetz, 1978; Straus, 1978).

279

Interviews with battered women make it apparent that the experience of violence inflicted by a husband or lover is shocking and confusing. Battering is rarely perceived as an unambiguous assault demanding immediate action to ensure future safety. In fact, battered women often remain in violent relationships for years (Pagelow, 1981).

Why do battered women stay in abusive relationships? Some observers answer facilely that they must like it. The masochism thesis was the predominant response of psychiatrists writing about battering in the 1960s (Saul, 1972; Snell *et al.*, 1964). More sympathetic studies of the problem have revealed the difficulties of disentangling oneself from a violent relationship (Hilberman, 1980; Martin, 1976; Walker, 1979). These studies point to the social and cultural expectations of women and their status within the nuclear family as reasons for the reluctance of battered women to flee the relationship. The socialization of women emphasizes the primary value of being a good wife and mother, at the expense of personal achievement in other spheres of life. The patriarchal ordering of society assigns a secondary status to women, and provides men with ultimate authority, both within and outside the family unit. Economic conditions contribute to the dependency of women on men; in 1978 U.S. women earned, on the average, 58 percent of what men earned (U.S. Department of Labor, 1980). In sum, the position of women in U.S. society makes it extremely difficult for them to reject the authority of men and develop independent lives free of marital violence (Dobash and Dobash, 1979; Pagelow, 1981).

Material and cultural conditions are the background in which personal interpretations of events are developed. Women who depend on their husbands for practical support also depend on them as sources of self-esteem, emotional support, and continuity. This paper looks at how women make sense of their victimization within the context of these dependencies. Without dismissing the importance of the macro forces of gender politics, we focus on inter- and intrapersonal responses to violence. We first describe six techniques of rationalization used by women who are in relationships where battering has occurred. We then turn to catalysts which may serve as forces to reevaluate rationalizations and to initiate serious attempts at escape. Various physical and emotional responses to battering are described, and finally, we outline the consequences of leaving or attempting to leave a violent relationship.

THE DATA

The data for this study were drawn from diverse sources. From July, 1978 to September, 1979 we were participant observers at a shelter for battered women located in the southwestern United States. The shelter was located in a suburban city of a major urban center. The shelter served five cities as well as the downtown population, resulting in a service population of 170,000.

It was funded primarily by the state through an umbrella agency concerned with drug, mental health, and alcoholism problems. It was initially staffed by paraprofessionals and volunteers, but since this research it has become professionalized and is run by several professional social workers.

During the time of the research, 120 women passed through the shelters; they brought with them 165 children. The women ranged in age from 17 to 68, generally had family incomes below $15,000, and did not work outside the home. The characteristics of shelter residents are summarized in Table 1.

We established personal relationships with each of these women, and kept records of their experiences and verbal accounts. We also tape-recorded informal conversations, staff meetings, and crisis phone conversations with battered women. This daily interaction with shelter residents and staff permitted first-hand observation of feelings and thoughts about the battering experience. Finally, we taped interviews with 10 residents and five battered women who had left their abusers without entering the shelter. All quotes in this paper are taken from our notes and tapes.

Table 1 / Demographic Characteristics of Shelter Residents during First Year of Operation ($N = 120$)

Age		Education	
−17	2%	Elementary school	2%
18–24	33%	Junior high	8%
25–34	43%	Some high school	28%
35–44	14%	High school graduate	43%
45–54	6%	Some college	14%
55+	1%	College graduate	2%
		Graduate school	1%
Ethnicity		**Number of Children**	
White	78%	0	19%
Black	3%	1	42%
Mexican-American	10%	2	21%
American Indian	8%	3	15%
Other	1%	4	2%
		5+	1%
		Pregnant	7%
Family Income		**Employment Status**	
−$5,000	27%	Full time	23%
$ 6,000–10,000	36%	Part time	8%
$11,000–15,000	10%	Housewife	54%
$16,000+	10%	Student	5%
No response*	17%	Not employed	8%
		Receiving welfare	2%

*Many women had no knowledge of their husbands' income.

In addition to this participant study, both authors have been involved with the problem of domestic violence for more than 10 years. In 1976–77, Ferraro worked as a volunteer at Rainbow Retreat, the oldest shelter still functioning in the United States. In 1977–78, we both helped to found a shelter for battered women in our community. This involvement has led to direct contact with hundreds of women who have experienced battering, and many informal talks with people involved in the shelter movement in the United States and Europe.

The term battered woman is used in this paper to describe women who are battered repeatedly by men with whom they live as lovers. Marriage is not a prerequisite for being a battered woman. Many of the women who entered the shelter we studied were living with, but were not legally married to, the men who abused them.

Rationalizing Violence

Marriages and their unofficial counterparts develop through the efforts of each partner to maintain feelings of love and intimacy. In modern, Western cultures, the value placed on marriage is high; individuals invest a great amount of emotion in their spouses, and expect a return on that investment. The majority of women who marry still adopt the roles of wives and mothers as primary identities, even when they work outside the home, and thus have a strong motivation to succeed in their domestic roles. Married women remain economically dependent on their husbands. In 1978, married men in the United States earned an average of $293 a week, while married women earned $167 a week (U.S. Department of Labor, 1980). Given these high expectations and dependencies, the costs of recognizing failures and dissolving marriages are significant. Divorce is an increasingly common phenomenon in the United States, but it is still labeled a social problem and is seldom undertaken without serious deliberations and emotional upheavals (Bohannan, 1971). Levels of commitment vary widely, but some degree of commitment is implicit in the marriage contract.

When marital conflicts emerge there is usually some effort to negotiate an agreement or bargain, to ensure the continuity of the relationship (Scanzoni, 1972). Couples employ a variety of strategies, depending on the nature and extent of resources available to them, to resolve conflicts without dissolving relationships. It is thus possible for marriages to continue for years, surviving the inevitable conflicts that occur (Sprey, 1971).

In describing conflict-management, Spiegel (1968) distinguishes between "role induction" and "role modification." Role induction refers to conflict in which "one or the other parties to the conflict agrees, submits, goes along with, becomes convinced, or is persuaded in some way" (1968:402). Role modification, on the other hand, involves adaptations by both partners. Role induction seems particularly applicable to battered women who accommodate their husbands' abuse. Rather than seeking help or escaping, as people typically do when attacked by strangers, battered women often rationalize violence from their husbands, at least initially. Although remaining with a violent man does not indicate that a woman views violence as an acceptable aspect of the relationship, the length of time that a woman stays in the marriage after abuse begins is a rough index of her efforts to accommodate the situation. In a U.S. study of 350 battered women, Pagelow (1981) found the median length of stay after violence began was four years; some left in less than one year, others stayed as long as 42 years.

Battered women have good reasons to rationalize violence. There are few institutional, legal, or cultural supports for women fleeing violent marriages. In Roy's (1977:32) survey of 150 battered women, 90 percent said they "thought of leaving and would have done so had the resources been available to them." Eighty percent of Pagelow's (1981) sample indicated previous, failed attempts to leave their husbands. Despite the development of the international shelter movement, changes in police practices, and legislation to protect battered women since 1975, it remains extraordinarily difficult for a battered woman to escape a violent husband determined to maintain his control. At least one woman, Mary Parziale, has been murdered by an abusive husband while residing in a shelter (Beverly, 1978); others have been murdered after leaving shelters to establish new, independent homes (Garcia, 1978). When these practical and social constraints are combined with love for and commitment to an abuser, it is obvious that there is a strong incentive—often a practical necessity—to rationalize violence.

Previous research on the rationalizations of deviant offenders has revealed a typology of "techniques of neutralization," which allow offenders to view their actions as normal, acceptable, or at least justifiable (Sykes and Matza, 1957). A similar typology can be constructed for victims. Extending the concepts developed by Sykes and Matza, we assigned the responses of battered women we interviewed to one of six categories of rationalization: (1) the appeal to the salvation ethic; (2) the denial of the victimizer; (3) the denial of injury; (4) the denial of victimization; (5) the denial of options; and (6) the appeal to higher loyalties. The women usually employed at least one of these techniques to make sense of their situations; often they employed two or more, simultaneously or over time.

1) *The appeal to the salvation ethic:* This rationalization is grounded in a woman's desire to be of service to others. Abusing husbands are viewed as deeply troubled, perhaps "sick," individuals, dependent on their wives' nurturance for survival. Battered women place their own safety and happiness below their commitment to "saving my man" from whatever malady they perceive as the source of their husbands' problems (Ferraro, 1979a). The appeal to the salvation ethic is a common response to an alcoholic or drug-dependent abuser. The battered partners of substance-abusers frequently describe the charming, charismatic personality of their sober mates, viewing this appealing personality as the "real man" being destroyed by disease. They then assume responsibility for helping their partners to overcome

their problems, viewing the batterings they receive as an index of their partners' pathology. Abuse must be endured while helping the man return to his "normal" self. One woman said:

> I thought I was going to be Florence Nightingale. He had so much potential; I could see how good he really was, and I was going to "save" him. I thought I was the only thing keeping him going, and that if I left he'd lose his job and wind up in jail. I'd make excuses to everybody for him. I'd call work and lie when he was drunk, saying he was sick. I never criticized him, because he needed my approval.

2) *The denial of the victimizer:* This technique is similar to the salvation ethic, except that victims do not assume responsibility for solving their abusers' problems. Women perceive battering as an event beyond the control of both spouses, and blame it on some external force. The violence is judged situational and temporary, because it is linked to unusual circumstances or a sickness which can be cured. Pressures at work, the loss of a job, or legal problems are all situations which battered women assume as the causes of their partners' violence. Mental illness, alcoholism, and drug addiction are also viewed as external, uncontrollable afflictions by many battered women who accept the medical perspective on such problems. By focusing on factors beyond the control of their abuser, women deny their husbands' intent to do them harm, and thus rationalize violent episodes.

> He's sick. He didn't used to be this way, but he can't handle alcohol. It's really like a disease, being an alcoholic....I think too that this is what he saw at home, his father is a very violent man, and alcoholic too, so it's really not his fault, because this is all he has ever known.

3) *The denial of injury:* For some women, the experience of being battered by a spouse is so discordant with their expectations that they simply refuse to acknowledge it. When hospitalization is not required—and it seldom is for most cases of battering[1]—routines quickly return to normal. Meals are served, jobs and schools are attended, and daily chores completed. Even with lingering pain, bruises, and cuts, the normality of everyday life overrides the strange, confusing memory of the attack. When husbands refuse to discuss or acknowledge the event, in some cases even accusing their wives of insanity, women sometimes come to believe the violence never occurred. The denial of injury does not mean that women feel no pain. They know they are hurt, but define the hurt as tolerable or normal. Just as individuals tolerate a wide range of physical discomfort before seeking medical help, battered women tolerate a wide range of physical abuse before defining it as an injurious assault. One woman explained her disbelief at her first battering:

> I laid in bed and cried all night. I could not believe it had happened, and I didn't want to believe it. We had only been married a year, and I was pregnant and excited about starting a family. Then all of a sudden, this! The next morning he

told me he was sorry and it wouldn't happen again, and I gladly kissed and made up. I wanted to forget the whole thing, and wouldn't let myself worry about what it meant for us.

4) *The denial of victimization*: Victims often blame themselves for the violence, thereby neutralizing the responsibility of the spouse. Pagelow (1981) found that 99.4 percent of battered women felt they did not deserve to be beaten, and 51 percent said they had done nothing to provoke an attack. The battered women in our sample did not believe violence against them was justified, but some felt it could have been avoided if they had been more passive and conciliatory. Both Pagelow's and our samples are biased in this area, because they were made up almost entirely of women who had already left their abusers, and thus would have been unlikely to feel major responsibility for the abuse they received. Retrospective accounts of victimization in our sample, however, did reveal evidence that some women believed their right to leave violent men was restricted by their participation in the conflicts. One subject said:

> Well, I couldn't really do anything about it, because I did ask for it. I knew how to get at him, and I'd keep after it and keep after it until he got fed up and knocked me right out. I can't say I like it, but I shouldn't have nagged him like I did.

As Pagelow (1981) noted, there is a difference between provocation and justification. A battered woman's belief that her actions angered her spouse to the point of violence is not synonymous with the belief that violence was therefore *justified*. But belief in provocation may diminish a woman's capacity for retaliation or self-defense, because it blurs her concept of responsibility. A woman's acceptance of responsibility for the violent incident is encouraged by an abuser who continually denigrates her and makes unrealistic demands. Depending on the social supports available, and the personality of the battered woman, the man's accusations of inadequacy may assume the status of truth. Such beliefs of inferiority inhibit the development of a notion of victimization.

5) *The denial of options*: This technique is composed of two elements: practical options and emotional options. Practical options, including alternative housing, source of income, and protection from an abuser, are clearly limited by the patriarchal structure of Western society. However, there are differences in the ways battered women respond to these obstacles, ranging from determined struggle to acquiescence. For a variety of reasons, some battered women do not take full advantage of the practical opportunities which are available to escape, and some return to abusers voluntarily even after establishing an independent lifestyle. Others ignore the most severe constraints in their efforts to escape their relationships. For example, one resident of the shelter we observed walked 30 miles in her bedroom slippers to get to the shelter, and required medical attention for blisters and cuts to her feet. On the other hand, a woman who had a full-time job, had rented an apartment, and had been given by the shelter all the clothes, furniture,

and basics necessary to set up housekeeping, returned to her husband two weeks after leaving the shelter. Other women refused to go to job interviews, keep appointments with social workers, or move out of the state for their own protection (Ferraro, 1981b). Such actions are frightening for women who have led relatively isolated or protected lives, but failure to take action leaves few alternatives to a violent marriage. The belief of battered women that they will not be able to make it on their own—a belief often fueled by years of abuse and oppression—is a major impediment to [acknowledgment] that one is a victim and taking action.

The denial of *emotional* options imposes still further restrictions. Battered women may feel that no one else can provide intimacy and companionship. While physical beating is painful and dangerous, the prospect of a lonely, celibate existence is often too frightening to risk. It is not uncommon for battered women to express the belief that their abuser is the only man they could love, thus severely limiting their opportunities to discover new, more supportive relationships. One woman said:

> He's all I've got. My dad's gone, and my mother disowned me when I married him. And he's really special. He understands me, and I understand him. Nobody could take his place.

6) *The appeal to higher loyalties:* This appeal involves enduring battering for the sake of some higher commitment, either religious or traditional. The Christian belief that women should serve their husbands as men serve God is invoked as a rationalization to endure a husband's violence for later rewards in the afterlife. Clergy may support this view by advising women to pray and try harder to please their husbands (Davidson, 1978; McGlinchey, 1981). Other women have a strong commitment to the nuclear family, and find divorce repugnant. They may believe that for their children's sake, any marriage is better than no marriage. One woman we interviewed divorced her husband of 35 years after her last child left home. More commonly women who have survived violent relationships for that long do not have the desire or strength to divorce and begin a new life. When the appeal to higher loyalties is employed as a strategy to cope with battering, commitment to and involvement with an ideal overshadows the mundane reality of violence.

CATALYSTS FOR CHANGE

Rationalization is a way of coping with a situation in which, for either practical or emotional reasons, or both, a battered woman is stuck. For some women, the situation and the beliefs that rationalize it, may continue for a lifetime. For others, changes may occur within the relationship, within individuals, or in available resources which serve as catalysts for redefining the violence. When battered women reject prior rationalizations and begin to view themselves as true victims of abuse, the victimization process begins.[2]

There are a variety of catalysts for redefining abuse; we discuss six: (1) a change in the level of violence; (2) a change in resources; (3) a change in the relationship; (4) despair; (5) a change in the visibility of violence; and (6) external definitions of the relationship.

1) *A change in the level of violence:* Although Gelles (1976) reports that the severity of abuse is an important factor in women's decisions to leave violent situations, Pagelow (1981) found no significant correlation between the number of years spent cohabiting with an abuser and the severity of abuse. On the contrary: the longer women lived with an abuser, the more severe the violence they endured, since violence increased in severity over time. What does seem to serve as a catalyst is a sudden change in the relative level of violence. Women who suddenly realize that battering may be fatal may reject rationalizations in order to save their lives. One woman who had been severely beaten by an alcoholic husband for many years explained her decision to leave on the basis of a direct threat to her life:

> It was like a pendulum. He'd swing to the extremes both ways. He'd get drunk and beat me up, then he'd get sober and treat me like a queen. One day he put a gun to my head and pulled the trigger. It wasn't loaded. But that's when I decided I'd had it. I sued for separation of property. I knew what was coming again, so I got out. I didn't want to. I still loved the guy, but I knew I had to for my own sanity.

There are, of course, many cases of homicide in which women did not escape soon enough. In 1979, 7.6 percent of all murders in the United States where the relationship between the victim and the offender was known were murders of wives by husbands (Flanagan *et al.*, 1982). Increases in severity do not guarantee a reinterpretation of the situation, but may play a part in the process.

2) *A change in resources:* Although some women rationalize cohabiting with an abuser by claiming they have no options, others begin reinterpreting violence when the resources necessary for escape become available. The emergence of safe homes or shelters since 1970 has produced a new resource for battered women. While not completely adequate or satisfactory, the mere existence of a place to go alters the situation in which battering is experienced (Johnson, 1981). Public support of shelters is a statement to battered women that abuse need not be tolerated. Conversely, political trends which limit resources available to women, such as cutbacks in government funding to social programs, increase fears that life outside a violent marriage is economically impossible. One 55-year-old woman discussed this catalyst:

> I stayed with him because I didn't want my kids to have the same life I did. My parents were divorced, and I was always so ashamed of that.... Yes, they're all on their own now, so there's no reason left to stay.

3) *A change in the relationship:* Walker (1979), in discussing the stages of a battering relationship, notes that violent incidents are usually followed by periods of remorse and solicitude. Such phases deepen the emotional bonds, and make rejection of an abuser more difficult. But as battering

progresses, periods of remorse may shorten, or disappear, eliminating the basis for maintaining a positive outlook on the marriage. After a number of episodes of violence, a man may realize that his victim will not retaliate or escape, and thus feel no need to express remorse. Extended periods devoid of kindness or love may alter a woman's feelings toward her partner so much so that she eventually begins to define herself as a victim of abuse. One woman recalled:

> At first, you know, we used to have so much fun together. He has kind've, you know, a magnetic personality; he can be really charming. But it isn't fun anymore. Since the baby came, it's changed completely. He just wants me to stay at home, while he goes out with his friends. He doesn't even talk to me, most of the time.... No, I don't really love him anymore, not like I did.

4) *Despair:* Changes in the relationship may result in a loss of hope that "things will get better." When hope is destroyed and replaced by despair, rationalizations of violence may give way to the recognition of victimization. Feelings of hopelessness or despair are the basis for some efforts to assist battered women, such as Al-Anon.[3] The director of an Al-Anon organized shelter explained the concept of "hitting bottom":

> Before the Al-Anon program can really be of benefit, a woman has to hit bottom. When you hit bottom, you realize that all of your own efforts to control the situation have failed; you feel helpless and lost and worthless and completely disenchanted with the world. Women can't really be helped unless they're ready for it and want it. Some women come here when things get bad, but they aren't really ready to be committed to Al-Anon. Things haven't gotten bad enough for them, and they go right back. We see this all the time.

5) *A change in the visibility of violence:* Creating a web of rationalizations to overlook violence is accomplished more easily if no intruders are present to question their validity. Since most violence between couples occurs in private, there are seldom conflicting interpretations of the event from outsiders. Only 7 percent of the respondents in Gelles' (1974) study who discussed spatial location of violence indicated events which took place outside the home, but all reported incidents within the home. Others report similar findings (Pittman and Handy, 1964; Pokorny, 1965; Wolfgang, 1958). If violence does occur in the presence of others, it may trigger a reinterpretation process. Battering in private is degrading, but battering in public is humiliating, for it is a statement of subordination and powerlessness. Having others witness abuse may create intolerable feelings of shame which undermine prior rationalizations.

> He never hit me in public before—it was always at home. But the Saturday I got back (returned to husband from shelter), we went Christmas shopping and he slapped me in the store because of some stupid joke I made. People saw it, I know, I felt so stupid, like, they must all think what a jerk I am, what a sick couple, and I thought, "God, I must be crazy to let him do this."

6) *External definitions of the relationship:* A change in visibility is usually accomplished by the interjection of external definitions of abuse. External definitions vary depending on their source and the situation; they either reinforce or undermine rationalizations. Battered women who request help frequently find others—and especially officials—don't believe their story or are unsympathetic (Pagelow, 1981; Pizzey, 1974). Experimental research by Shotland and Straw (1976) supports these reports. Observers usually fail to respond when a woman is attacked by a man, and justify nonintervention on the grounds that they assumed the victim and offender were married. One young woman discussed how lack of support from her family left her without hope:

> It wouldn't be so bad if my own family gave a damn about me.... Yeah, they know I'm here, and they don't care. They didn't care about me when I was a kid, so why should they care now? I got raped and beat as a kid, and now I get beat as an adult. Life is a big joke.

Clearly, such responses from family members contribute to the belief among battered women that there are no alternatives and that they must tolerate the abuse. However, when outsiders respond with unqualified support of the victim and condemnation of violent men, their definitions can be a potent catalyst toward victimization. Friends and relatives who show genuine concern for a woman's well-being may initiate an awareness of danger which contradicts previous rationalizations.

> My mother-in-law knew what was going on, but she wouldn't admit it.... I said, "Mom, what do you think these bruises are?" and she said "Well, some people just bruise easy. I do it all the time, bumping into things." ... And he just denied it, pretended like nothing happened, and if I'd said I wanted to talk about it, he'd say, "life goes on, you can't just dwell on things." ... But this time, my neighbor *knew* what happened, she saw it, and when he denied it, she said, "I can't believe it! You know that's not true!" ... and I was so happy that finally, somebody else saw what was goin' on, and I just told him then that this time I wasn't gonna' come home!

Shelters for battered women serve not only as material resources, but as sources of external definitions which contribute to the victimization process. They offer refuge from a violent situation in which a woman may contemplate her circumstances and what she wants to do about them. Within a shelter, women meet counselors and other battered women who are familiar with rationalizations of violence and the reluctance to give up commitment to a spouse. In counseling sessions, and informal conversations with other residents, women hear horror stories from others who have already defined themselves as victims. They are supported for expressing anger and rejecting responsibility for their abuse (Ferraro, 1981a). The goal of many shelters is to overcome feelings of guilt and inadequacy so that women can make choices in their best interests. In this atmosphere, violent incidents are reexamined and redefined as assaults in which the woman was victimized.

How others respond to a battered woman's situation is critical. The closer the relationship of others, the more significant their response is to a woman's perception of the situation. Thus, children can either help or hinder the victim. Pizzey (1974) found adolescent boys at a shelter in Chiswick, England, often assumed the role of the abusing father and themselves abused their mothers, both verbally and physically. On the other hand, children at the shelter we observed often became extremely protective and nurturing toward their mothers. This phenomenon has been thoroughly described elsewhere (Ferraro, 1981a). Children who have been abused by fathers who also beat their mothers experience high levels of anxiety, and rarely want to be reunited with their fathers. A 13-year-old, abused daughter of a shelter resident wrote the following message to her stepfather:

> I am going to be honest and not lie. No, I don't want you to come back. It's not that I am jealous because mom loves you. It is [I] am afraid I won't live to see 18. I did care about you a long time ago, but now I can't care, for the simple reason you['re] always calling us names, even my friends. And another reason is, I am tired of seeing mom hurt. She has been hurt enough in her life, and I don't want her to be hurt any more.

No systematic research has been conducted on the influence children exert on their battered mothers, but it seems obvious that the willingness of children to leave a violent father would be an important factor in a woman's desire to leave.

The relevance of these catalysts to a woman's interpretation of violence vary with her own situation and personality. The process of rejecting rationalizations and becoming a victim is ambiguous, confusing, and emotional. We now turn to the feelings involved in a victimization.

THE EMOTIONAL CAREER
OF VICTIMIZATION

As rationalizations give way to perceptions of victimization, a woman's feelings about herself, her spouse, and her situation change. These feelings are imbedded in a cultural, political, and interactional structure. Initially, abuse is contrary to a woman's cultural expectations of behavior between intimates, and therefore engenders feelings of betrayal. The husband has violated his wife's expectations of love and protection, and thus betrayed her confidence in him. The feeling of betrayal, however, is balanced by the husband's efforts to explain his behavior, and by the woman's reluctance to abandon faith. Additionally, the political dominance of men within and outside the family mediate women's ability to question the validity of their husband's actions.

At the interpersonal level, psychological abuse accompanying violence often invokes feelings of guilt and shame in the battered victim. Men define violence as a response to their wives' inadequacies or provocations, which leads battered women to feel that they have failed. Such character assaults are devastating, and create long-lasting feelings of inferiority (Ferraro, 1979b):

> I've been verbally abused as well. It takes you a long time to... you may say you feel good and you may... but inside, you know what's been said to you and it hurts for a long time. You need to build up your self-image and make yourself feel like you're a useful person, that you're valuable, and that you're a good parent. You might think these things, and you may say them.... I'm gonna prove it to myself.

Psychologists working with battered women consistently report that self-confidence wanes over years of ridicule and criticism (Hilberman and Munson, 1978; Walker, 1979).

Feelings of guilt and shame are also mixed with a hope that things will get better, at least in the early stages of battering. Even the most violent man is nonviolent much of the time, so there is always a basis for believing that violence is exceptional and the "real man" is not a threat. The vacillation between violence and fear on the one hand, and nonviolence and affection on the other was described by a shelter resident:

> First of all, the first beatings—you can't believe it yourself. I'd go to bed, and I'd cry, and I just couldn't believe this was happening. And I'd wake up the next morning thinking that couldn't of happened, or maybe it was my fault. It's so unbelievable that this person that you're married to and you love would do that to you but yet you can't leave either because, ya' know, for the other 29 days of the month that person loves you and is with you.

Hope wanes as periods of love and remorse dwindle. Feelings of love and intimacy are gradually replaced with loneliness and pessimism. Battered women who no longer feel love for their husbands but remain in their marriages enter a period of emotional dormancy. They survive each day, performing necessary tasks, with a dull depression and lack of enthusiasm. While some battered women live out their lives in this emotional desert, others are spurred by catalysts to feel either the total despair or mortal fear which leads them to seek help.

Battered women who perceive their husbands' actions as life-threatening experience a penetrating fear that consumes all their thoughts and energies. The awareness of murderous intent by a presumed ally who is a central figure in all aspects of her life destroys all bases for safety. There is a feeling that death is imminent, and that there is nowhere to hide. Prior rationalizations and beliefs about a "good marriage" are exploded, leaving the woman in a crisis of ambiguity (Ridington, 1978).

Feelings of fear are experienced physiologically as well as emotionally. Battered women experience aches and fatigue, stomach pains, diarrhea or constipation, tension headaches, shakes, chills, loss of appetite, and insomnia. Sometimes, fear is expressed as a numbed shock, similar to rape trauma syndrome (Burgess and Holmstrom, 1974), in which little is felt or communicated.

If attempts to seek help succeed, overwhelming feelings of fear subside, and a rush of new emotions are felt: the original sense of betrayal re-emerges, creating strong feelings of anger. For women socialized to reject angry feelings as unfeminine, coping with anger is difficult. Unless the expression of anger is encouraged in a supportive environment, such women may suppress anger and feel only depression (Ball and Wyman, 1978). When anger is expressed, it often leads to feelings of strength and exhilaration. Freedom from threats of violence, the possibility of a new life, and the unburdening of anger create feelings of joy. The simple pleasures of going shopping, taking children to the park, or talking with other women without fear of criticism or punishment from a husband, constitute amazing freedoms. One middle-aged woman expressed her joy over her newly acquired freedom this way:

> Boy, tomorrow I'm goin' downtown, and I've got my whole day planned out, and I'm gonna' do what *I* wanna' do, and if somebody doesn't like it, to *hell* with them! You know, I'm having so much fun, I should've done this years ago!

Probably the most typical feeling expressed by women in shelters is confusion. They feel both sad and happy, excited and apprehensive, independent, yet in need of love. Most continue to feel attachment to their husbands, and feel ambivalent about divorce. There is grief over the loss of an intimate, which must be acknowledged and mourned. Although shelters usually discourage women from contacting their abusers while staying at the shelter, most women do communicate with their husbands—and most receive desperate pleas for forgiveness and reconciliation. If there is not strong emotional support and potential material support, such encouragement by husbands often rekindles hope for the relationship. Some marriages can be revitalized through counseling, but most experts agree that long-term batterers are unlikely to change (Pagelow, 1981; Walker, 1979). Whether they seek refuge in shelters or with friends, battered women must decide relatively quickly what actions to take. Usually, a tentative commitment is made, either to independence or working on the relationship, but such commitments are usually ambivalent. As one woman wrote to her counselor:

> My feelings are so mixed up sometimes. Right now I feel my husband is really trying to change. But I know that takes time. I still feel for him some. I don't know how much. My mind still doesn't know what it wants. I would really like when I leave here to see him once in a while, get my apartment, and sort of like start over with our relationship for me and my baby and him, to try and make it work. It might. It kind of scares me. I guess I am afraid it won't. . . . I can only hope this works out. There's no telling what could happen. No one knows.

The emotional career of battered women consists of movement from guilt, shame, and depression to fear and despair, to anger, exhilaration, and confusion. Women who escape violent relationships must deal with strong, sometimes conflicting, feelings in attempting to build new lives for themselves free of violence. The kind of response women receive when they seek help largely determines the effects these feelings have on subsequent decisions.

*   *   *

Notes

1. National crime survey data for 1973–76 show that 17 percent of persons who sought medical attention for injuries inflicted by an intimate were hospitalized. Eighty-seven percent of injuries inflicted by a spouse or ex-spouse were bruises, black eyes, cuts, scratches, or swelling (National Crime Survey Report, 1980).

2. Explanation of why and how some women arrive at these feelings is beyond the scope of this paper. Our goal is to describe feelings at various stages of the victimization process.

3. Al-Anon is the spouse's counterpart to Alcoholics Anonymous. It is based on the same self-help, 12-step program that A.A. is founded on.

References

Ball, Patricia G., and Elizabeth Wyman
    1978 "Battered wives and powerlessness: What can counselors do?" Victimology 2(3–4):545–552.
Beverly
    1978 "Shelter resident murdered by husband." Aegis, September/October:13.
Bohannan, Paul (ed.)
    1971 Divorce and After. Garden City, New York: Anchor.
Burgess, Ann W., and Linda Lytle Holmstrom
    1974 Rape: Victims of Crisis. Bowie, Maryland: Brady.
Colorado Association for Aid to Battered Women
    1978 Services to Battered Women. Washington, D.C.: Office of Domestic Violence, Department of Health, Education and Welfare.
Davidson, Terry
    1978 Conjugal Crime. New York: Hawthorn.
Dobash, R. Emerson, and Russell P. Dobash
    1979 Violence Against Wives. New York: Free Press.
Ferraro, Kathleen J.
    1979a "Hard love: Letting go of an abusive husband." Frontiers 4(2):16–18.
    1979b "Physical and emotional battering: Aspects of managing hurt." California Sociologist 2(2):134–149.
    1981a "Battered women and the shelter movement." Unpublished Ph.D. dissertation, Arizona State University.
    1981b "Processing battered women." Journal of Family Issues 2(4):415–438.
Flanagan, Timothy J., David J. van Alstyne, and Michael R. Gottfredson (eds.)
    1982 Sourcebook of Criminal Justice Statistics: 1981. U.S. Department of Justice, Bureau of Justice Statistics, Washington, D.C.: U.S. Government Printing Office.

Gacquin, Deidre A.
  1978 "Spouse abuse: Data from the National Crime Survey." Victimology 2: 632–643.
Garcia, Dick
  1978 "Slain women 'lived in fear.'" The Times (Erie, Pa.) June 14:B1.
Gelles, Richard J.
  1974 The Violent Home. Beverly Hills: Sage.
  1976 "Abused wives: Why do they stay?" Journal of Marriage and the Family 38(4):659–668.
Hilberman, Elaine
  1980 "Overview: The 'wife-beater's wife' reconsidered." American Journal of Psychiatry 137(11):1336–1347.
Hilberman, Elaine, and Kit Munson
  1978 "Sixty battered women." Victimology 2(3–4):460–470.
Johnson, John M.
  1981 "Program enterprise and official cooptation of the battered women's shelter movement." American Behavioral Scientist 24(6):827–842.
McGlinchey, Anne
  1981 "Woman battering and the church's response." Pp. 133–140 in Albert R. Roberts (ed.), Sheltering Battered Women. New York: Springer.
Martin, Del
  1976 Battered Wives. San Francisco: Glide.
National Crime Survey Report
  1980 Intimate Victims. Washington, D.C.: U.S. Department of Justice.
O'Brien, John E.
  1971 "Violence in divorce-prone families." Journal of Marriage and the Family 33(4):692–698.
Pagelow, Mildred Daley
  1981 Woman-Battering. Beverly Hills: Sage.
Pittman, D. J. and W. Handy
  1964 "Patterns in criminal aggravated assault." Journal of Criminal Law, Criminology, and Police Science 55(4):462–470.
Pizzey, Erin
  1974 Scream Quietly or the Neighbors Will Hear. Baltimore: Penguin.
Pokorny, Alex D.
  1965 "Human violence: A comparison of homicide, aggravated assault, suicide, and attempted suicide." Journal of Criminal Law, Criminology, and Police Science 56(December):488–497.
Ridington, Jillian
  1978 "The transition process: A feminist environment as reconstitutive milieu." Victimology 2(3–4):563–576.
Roberts, Albert R.
  1981 Sheltering Battered Women. New York: Springer.
Roy, Maria (ed.)
  1977 Battered Women. New York: Van Nostrand.
Saul, Leon J.
  1972 "Personal and social psychopathology and the primary prevention of violence." American Journal of Psychiatry 128(12):1578–1581.

Scanzoni, John
  1972 Sexual Bargaining. Englewood Cliffs, N.J.: Prentice-Hall.
Shotland, R. Lance, and Margret K. Straw
  1976 "Bystander response to an assault: When a man attacks a woman." Journal of Personality and Social Psychology 34(5):990–999.
Snell, John E., Richard Rosenwald, and Ames Robey
  1964 "The wifebeater's wife: A study of family interaction." Archives of General Psychiatry 11(August):107–112.
Spiegel, John P.
  1968 "The resolution of role conflict within the family." Pp. 391–411 in N. W. Bell and E. F. Vogel (eds.), A Modern Introduction to the Family. New York: Free Press.
Sprey, Jetse
  1971 "On the management of conflict in families." Journal of Marriage and the Family 33(4):699–706.
Steinmetz, Suzanne K.
  1978 "The battered husband syndrome." Victimology 2(3–4):499–509.
Steinmetz, Suzanne K., and Murray A. Straus (eds.)
  1974 Violence in the Family. New York: Harper & Row.
Straus, Murray A.
  1978 "Wife beating: How common and why?" Victimology 2(3–4):443–458.
  1979 "Measuring intrafamily conflict and violence: The conflict tactics (CT) scales." Journal of Marriage and the Family 41(1):75–88.
Straus, Murray A., Richard J. Gelles, and Suzanne K. Steinmetz
  1980 Behind Closed Doors: Violence in the American Family. Garden City: Doubleday.
Sykes, Gresham M., and David Matza
  1957 "Techniques of neutralization: A theory of delinquency." American Sociological Review 22(6):667–670.
Tierney, Kathleen J.
  1982 "The battered women movement and the creation of the wife beating problem." Social Problems 29(3):207–220.
U.S. Department of Labor
  1980 Handbook of Labor Statistics. Washington, D.C.: U.S. Government Printing Office.
Walker, Lenore E.
  1979 The Battered Woman. New York: Harper & Row.
Wolfgang, Marvin E.
  1958 Patterns in Criminal Homicide. New York: John Wiley.
Women's Advocates
  1980 Women's Advocates: The Story of a Shelter. St. Paul, Minnesota: Women's Advocates.

Part 4 / The Production of Institutional Careers and Identities

In Part 3, I described how deviant behavior may initially be managed in a private setting. The material that was presented demonstrated how such behavior may become subject to regulation by a social-control agent or agency. When such regulation occurs, the actor's behavior is screened by the institution and its staff, and a label may be placed on him or her. The individual then becomes an institutional deviant, expected thereafter to conform to the institution's definition of the label. Some people will accept this labeling. In this event, the person's public identity (how others view him or her) meshes with personal identity (how the person views himself or herself), so that we can speak of the secondary, or career, deviant. Other deviants, however, will reject the label and attempt to structure and present to others a nondeviant image of self. The selections in this part explore such possibilities as these; they also illustrate clearly how institutional careers are initiated, perpetuated, and transformed. Throughout the following discussion of the various articles, the "organizational paradigm," which was presented in the general introduction, is applied.

ORGANIZATIONAL STRUCTURES, IDEOLOGIES, SOCIAL-CONTROL AGENTS, AND RECRUITMENT: THE INSTITUTIONAL BACKDROP

I have argued previously that it is difficult to understand the processes behind the production of deviance and deviants unless we first analyze the institution out of which a specific social-control agent operates. It is particularly important to know how the prevailing theory of the office, existing deviant categories, and diagnostic stereotypes are applied to clients. The first selection, "Bureaucratic Slots and Client Processing," from my book *Creating School Failure, Youth Crime, and Deviance,* not only elaborates on these ideas but presents an in-depth analysis of how the "organizational paradigm" can be applied to the study of social deviance. I initially stress the importance of analyzing how social institutions are structured. Here, by drawing particularly upon the works of Cicourel and Kitsuse, and Hargreaves, I describe the origin of a range of school career lines (e.g., ability groups and track systems). I note, for example, in terms of actor selection and placement, that students who give teachers a hard time or are perceived as troublemakers often land in the low, basic, or non-college-prep tracks. After describing selected organizational structures and components, I move to a general discussion of how clients are identified, selected, sorted, and processed by bureaucrats. Critical to an understanding of this process is the *content* of an agency's existing theory of the office and associated working ideology. Not only is the theory of the office embedded within an agency's organizational fabric (see Part 1), but it becomes, through socializing experiences in formal and informal settings, inculcated within relevant actors, audiences, and third parties.

I use certain aspects of the structure and process of schooling to underscore the importance of locating, describing, and characterizing the content of an agency's theory of the office. If, as I argue, society and its educational institutions are predicated firmly on an ideology that *presumes differential ability,* then we can expect to obtain outcomes commensurate with that view. Hence, some students will be destined to fail while others will be programmed for success. Ability groups, track systems, and other means for stratifying students offer graphic representations of how a society's educational philosophy becomes translated into bureaucratic entities. Actually predicting who will succeed or fail requires an analysis of how existing student stratification systems articulate with student attributes. For example, is the person of color more likely, independent of demonstrated academic success and competence, to be relegated to a low or basic track? If this happens (and there is increasing evidence that it does), then what can we say about the educational decision maker? Is he or she, either advertently or inadvertently, acting in a discriminatory or bigoted fashion? After addressing questions such as these, I provide additional observations on what I term the *bureaucratic matching game,* the decision-making process whereby a bureaucrat or decision maker assesses a client's attributes or traits and then renders an assignment decision. One of the better illustrations of this matching game is offered by Wiseman's data on the sentencing of skid-row alcoholics. I conclude by offering an overview of how client processing can destroy an actor's personal and public identity, as well as produce an erosion of self-image. I also comment on how institutions create, use, and misuse records.

Social-control agents, both formal (e.g., the police) and semi-formal (e.g., the school administrator), must become familiar with and act according to the agency's theory of the office. This socialization takes place within formal and informal domains. We have police academies and we have on-the-job training. We have teacher education programs and we have teacher lounges. Regardless of the specific institution or interactional context considered, however, a novice must "learn the ropes." And what he or she is taught in a formal setting (e.g., the police academy) may not mesh with what is expected in an informal context (e.g., the streets). The official mandate or theory of the office might be "to protect and serve all" or "to provide equal access for all to educational opportunities." An important question arises: How is an agency's theory of the office or official perspective translated into action? Are all citizens actually accorded equal protection under the law? Are all students provided equal access to educational opportunities? We need to examine how the theory of the office actually becomes translated into action; is there a direct correspondence between an agency's official perspective and its actual working ideology? Answering these questions requires an ongoing examination of how social-control agents go about processing clients. In a very real sense, we need to get inside the minds of the bureaucrats and examine their decision-making processes. For example, what can we say about the content and range of diagnostic stereotypes that are used to identify, select, sort, process, sanction, and treat clients? Is one hiding under the cloak of bureaucratic competence?

The selection by Jennifer Hunt and Peter K. Manning, "The Social Context of Police Lying," provides an account of how social-control agents become familiar with an agency's theory of the office and working ideology, in both formal and informal settings. Hunt and Manning use as their source of data an eighteen-month field study of a large urban police force, and they operate on the assumption that police, like many people in official positions, lie. Hunt and Manning analyze the types of lies police tell and the ways in which they lie. They note initially that instructors in the police academy not only often encourage recruits to lie but tell the recruits that lying is an element of "good police work." During classes on the law and courts, however, recruits receive a different message; they are taught that the best way to win in court is by presenting a factual account of an event. Once the rookie is on the job the situation changes, and he or she is taught when it is appropriate to lie. In fact, learning to lie is a prerequisite to gaining membership on the force. This is particularly important in view of the observation that the police in Metro City routinely engage in a range of illicit activities such as drinking and sleeping on the job. And those rookies who show little skill in constructing or using lies are often subject to criticism. Associated with lies is a range of acceptable justifications and excuses which the officers can use. Accounts, however, are often audience-specific. For example, a story directed at an "external" audience such as an attorney or the media is often viewed as more problematic than one directed at a supervisor. Hunt and Manning offer various illustrations of how case lies are used in court to obtain a conviction. For example, "probable cause" can be constructed in numerous ways (e.g., by adding to the facts). The researchers also report how the court can be manipulated to gain a conviction. The case of the boy who "hung out" with a corner group offers an excellent example. Throughout this specific analysis, the involved officer, who believes the boy is guilty, constructs and presents an account consisting of a combination of excuses and justifications. The researchers then describe cover stories, or those lies that officers tell in an attempt to shield themselves against disciplinary action. For example, one who does not respond to a radio call may claim that his or her radio was dead. Similarly, an officer who uses brutal force is often expected to lie to protect himself or herself. Hunt and Manning conclude by noting that the extent to which an organization uses lies varies across selected dimensions.

SOCIAL-CONTROL AGENTS AND THE APPLICATION OF DIAGNOSTIC STEREOTYPES: THE BEGINNING DESTRUCTION OF PUBLIC IDENTITY

Quite clearly, social-control agents must become familiar with an agency's theory of the office, its working ideology, associated diagnostic stereotypes, and the like. Once we have located and described an institution's underlying formal and informal organizational structures, components, and decision-making processes, much more attention and research must be focused on the decision makers themselves; this is one of the messages of Hunt and Manning's research. We can ask: Are the decision makers rendering decisions on the basis of organizational and/or individual stereotypes? Stated differently, are selected bureaucrats applying a range of gender, racial, and class stereotypes in the identifying, processing, and sanctioning of clients? Evidence suggests that some agents may very well be doing this. We need to reconsider Becker's discussion (in Part 1) of how "public branding" or labeling can initiate the deviant-defining process and how it becomes virtually impossible to reverse the labeling process once it has begun, especially because of how labels become disseminated to others in a range of interactional domains.

The research by Elijah Anderson, "The Police and the Black Male," offers a contemporary account of how racial stereotypes may be applied by bureaucrats. He focuses on the police and particularly on how the officers perceive and respond to young black males. According to Anderson's observations, the black male is especially vulnerable to being selected to play the role of the "suspect" or social deviant. In his words, "to be black and male, particularly when young, is to be suspect." The researcher notes that even when he reported his car stolen, he was perceived and responded to on the basis of his gender and color. He describes how whites are treated more deferentially than blacks. A cause of this difference in treatment, Anderson reasons, may be that many white officers have grown up in various ethnic neighborhoods and, hence, they may be bent on protecting their own community and class interests. The translation of the police officers' views into action often means that attempts are made to keep blacks out of the white communities. The police perceptions also seem to be associated with an informal policy whereby the police, in an effort to curb crime, monitor the activities and routines of young black men. Anderson describes how the objects of this racism attempt to cope. The black male may change his style of dress so that it meshes with the uniforms and emblems of "legitimate" society. Especially important to some is the identification card. Possession of such a middle-class emblem seems to reduce the number of police stops encountered, and it serves as a reminder to the police that the black male is "somebody." Anderson's comparison of "downtown" and "local" police is insightful, particularly in terms of how they relate to black males. For example, the local police spend time in the area and know more of the residents, whereas downtown police are from the outside, are distant and impersonal, and seem to be looking for trouble. Anderson offers material describing how downtown police perceive, interact with, and treat black males. Singling out or labeling the black male as the "bad" element is not without its repercussions. Not only does such treatment breed a sense of hostility, contempt, and distrust for the police, but it also helps to drive a wedge between the black ghetto and middle- and upper-class white communities. Anderson concludes by describing how drugs have affected various communities.

The tendency to respond, bureaucratically, on the basis of embedded typifications or diagnostic stereotypes receives further treatment in research by Leslie Margolin. In "Deviance on Record: Techniques for Labeling Child Abusers in Official Documents," Margolin examines how social workers go about "proving" that someone committed child abuse. His research underscores the need for understanding how decision makers arrive at their decisions—decisions that may begin the ritualistic and ultimate destruction of an actor's personal and public identity. Margolin begins by analyzing the bureaucratic context in which decisions are made. For example, are the bureaucrats under a range of pressures to produce selected organizational products (e.g., the requirement that a certain number of clients be processed)? Margolin comments on such pressures and then moves to a general discussion of how bureaucracies operate on the basis of social types, typifications, and "normal crimes." He contends that the more hurried the bureaucrat is, the greater the tendency to rely on stereotypes in processing clients. Another pressure is the need to produce records in an effort to convince others that the job is getting done. Margolin proceeds to analyze how social workers actually label child abusers. His data are drawn from the analysis of 120 official case records of child abuse. He notes that, in the production of the organizational record or document reality, social workers are guided and constrained by an official perspective that requires that two criteria be satisfied or met: (1) the child care provider's acts were damaging and exploitive and (2) the provider intended to damage or exploit the child. How these criteria were translated into action is interesting. Over half (50) of the suspects denied the accusations and many (14) were not interviewed; this seemed to be related to the view that suspects were "noncredible" witnesses. Victims, by contrast, were not only viewed as "credible," but even when they claimed suspects were innocent, such testimony was rejected. Part of the discrediting or status-degradation process can be found in the nature of the labels applied by the social workers. Even though in theory the accused is to be viewed legally as a "suspect," in practice he or she is often perceived and responded to as a "perpetrator." Margolin contends that, although it is obviously desirable to keep dangerous people away from children, the negative aspects of such simplified and perfunctory labeling of actors as child abusers must be addressed and examined, especially in view of the personal, social, and legal stigma associated with the application of this label. He comments on the growing number of people labeled as child abusers and suggests that this increase can probably be traced to several factors, such as demands by a range of professional and lay people that something be done about child abuse, and repeated, sensational media coverage of child abuse. The vested interests of bureaucracies and bureaucrats must also be considered seriously.

SOCIAL-CONTROL AGENTS, SANCTIONING, AND THE PRODUCTION OF INSTITUTIONAL CAREERS AND IDENTITIES

In the previous section I focused on organizational structures, ideologies, and the beginning destruction of public identities. Here I shift my focus to examine how social-control agents and the identifying and sanctioning processes operate to produce institutional careers and identities. The next two selections provide a feel for how bureaucrats go about the organizational production of a perceived "institutional misfit."

In her illuminating study "Getting Rid of Troublemakers: High School Disciplinary Procedures and the Production of Dropouts," Christine Bowditch examines how, by using such disciplinary procedures as suspensions, transfers, and involuntary drops, school officials get rid of "troublemakers." She focuses on how the disciplinarian identifies and processes the students who will be "dropped" involuntarily. Bowditch draws on observations of Du Bois High School, an all-black, inner-city school situated in a highly segregated northern city. She describes the nature of the discipline office and its associated responsibilities, rules, and regulations. The disciplinarian, for example, is expected, at least formally, to assess the nature of a student's infraction, determine its seriousness, and then take action; this often entails dealing with students who are late, cut classes, and disrupt teaching. Bowditch observes that the official view is rarely translated into action. Rather, disciplinarians operate on the basis of an informal system that can be characterized by a different set of definitions, routines, and expectations. Even though workers engage in ongoing disagreements over issues of work, lines of authority, and responsibilities, both within and outside the school, they operate on the basis of a shared understanding about the office's goals, the forms of student conduct that should be treated, the types of students who create the problems, and the specific sanctions for handling the misconduct cases.

After outlining the actual working ideology of the discipline office, Bowditch analyzes how the troublemaker is constructed socially. The bureaucrat is allowed a great deal of discretion, partly because what actually constitutes misconduct is often problematic. For example, a student's demeanor or attitude (e.g., acting either silly or mature) can change the meaning of an act. Bowditch offers some case material to illustrate how the construction process works. Bowditch observes that disciplinarians rarely inquire about the nature of the infraction; they are concerned primarily about the student's overall academic profile. In Bowditch's words, "they sought to punish 'types of students' more than 'types of behavior.'" Predictably, students with high grades, if caught up in the sanctioning system, are viewed and treated differently. Bowditch notes that parental involvement could have a direct bearing on the identification of a student as "troublemaker." In effect, disciplinarian personnel expect the parents to accept the authority of the school and to force their children to go along with the rules. Parents who fail to do so, or who challenge the authorities, could expect to feel the brunt of a range of discrediting tactics. Disciplinarians might belittle or denigrate their parenting skills, or threaten their children with failure, arrest, and expulsion.

Once the label of "troublemaker" has been bestowed upon a student, the discipline office uses two strategies for getting rid of the organizationally-defined misfit or deviant; it can either transfer the individual or else drop him or her from the roll. The researcher offers evidence of how this process works. Particularly illuminating is the documentation of how students with various academic biographies or profiles and varying degrees of parental involvement are removed from the school grounds. Bowditch concludes by commenting on how the school perceives and responds to the troubled student. These students expect the school to provide some semblance of service; however, they are often reconceptualized, defined as troublemakers, and then dropped. The students most "at risk" are African American and Hispanic. Processes such as these, she contends, perpetuate the racial and class distinctions that exist in larger society. I would add that anyone who occupies a marginal position in our society or is perceived as lacking power, resources, and an effective network of support systems, is eminently more vulnerable or susceptible to being selected to play the role of institutional deviant.

Gray Cavender and Paul Knepper, in "Strange Interlude: An Analysis of Juvenile Parole Revocation Decision Making," offer another piece of research documenting how decision makers or bureaucrats routinely apply an agency's existing social types, typifications, or diagnostic stereotypes to clients. They examine the juvenile parole revocation hearing and use as their source the data obtained from 114 revocation hearings. Like several of the preceding pieces in Part 4 (e.g., Margolin's research), the researchers initially stress the importance of zeroing in on an agency's theory of the office and its range of diagnostic stereotypes. They then analyze how prehearing conferences by board members are conducted "backstage." By making appeals to existing typologies, the participants reconstruct a view of "what happened" to bring the client back to the court. Reconstructing what happened, the authors observe, not only involves examining a juvenile's biography, but also entails matching selected actor attributes with a set of typologies—typologies that might, for example, be based on an assessment of character or personality traits (e.g., "he has a negative attitude"), or behavior (e.g., "he's been a bad boy"). Cavender and Knepper note that once created, reconstructions of what happened are rarely refuted. In those cases in which a negative typology was applied, 94 percent resulted in revoked parole. The researchers describe how, once the outcome has been decided backstage, a script is written for the formal revocation hearing; this often involves a degree of collusion and fabrication on the part of the involved parties. At the formal hearing, the participants act in accord with the script. Because they operate on the *presumption of guilt,* decision makers are more concerned with disposition than with a juvenile's guilt or innocence. Admissions of guilt were obtained, particularly if evidence was questionable or shaky. Even when juveniles protested or refused to accept the script and the associated disposition, they lost. Rarely were they able to convince the board to change its decision. Cavender and Knepper conclude by commenting on how board members were aware of the organizational context in which they were operating. They were required, for example, to consider how a particular disposition might affect other cases, institutional overcrowding, and the evidence reviewed in companion cases.

MANAGING INSTITUTIONAL CAREERS AND IDENTITIES

I have argued previously that the labeling ceremony or institutional processing can be viewed from two major perspectives—the institution's or the actor's. Thus far, the selections have dealt with processing primarily from the institution's perspective and little direct attention has been given to the actor's perceptions and responses. If we are to approach a more complete understanding of the range of effects that various types of bureaucratic processing can produce at selected stages, then we must try to assume the perspective of individuals who become caught up in the deviant-defining process. How, for example, does being identified, selected, and processed, and ultimately accorded the status of social deviant affect one's public and personal identity and one's self-image? Does the organizationally-created deviant accept his or her new status and associated labels, or does the newly-created deviant reject such organizational products and tags? Perhaps the patient will, in a therapeutic setting, accept the "sick role," but out on the ward the patient may reject the role and protest that he or she is not sick. Predicting which type of outcome is likely to occur is problematic.

Erving Goffman's work, "The Moral Career of the Mental Patient," examines contingencies such as these. Goffman is concerned with analyzing the *moral career* of the mental patient, particularly in terms of how patients perceive and respond to their treatment. Of major concern is the impact of the ward experience upon *self*. He points out initially that very few patients come willingly to the hospital. Rather, many arrive as a result of family or police action. (In this sense, the article further substantiates the discussion of the ways in which behavior in private domains may become regulated by some institution.) Goffman argues that the prepatient career can be analyzed in terms of an "extrusory model." In essence, this means that the patient initially has certain relationships and rights; however, he or she is left with very few after admission. Through Goffman's insightful analysis, one understands how the actor's public identity becomes transformed into a "deviant" identity—in this case, that of a mental patient. Important to this process are such phenomena as the "alienative coalition" and the "betrayal funnel." Goffman argues further that "the last step in the prepatient career can involve his realization—justified or not—that he has been deserted by society and turned out of relationships by those closest to him." At this stage the patient may begin to orient himself or herself to the "ward system." Some patients may, for example, accept the "sick role" and develop a set of rationalizations to "explain" their hospitalization. Such strategies enable the patient to regain and sustain a certain semblance of self—a self that has been subjected to a frontal assault from the institution, its personnel, family members and relatives, and, frequently, other patients. With his or her acceptance of this label, the individual begins to take on the identity of the secondary, or career, deviant.

Thomas J. Schmid and Richard S. Jones, in "Suspended Identity: Identity Transformation in a Maximum Security Prison," present an interesting variant of the identity change process. They examine inmates incarcerated in a maximum security prison. Of interest are not only the ways in which inmates may suspend their preprison identities but how inauthentic prison identities may be constructed. They note initially that most inmates have little in common prior to their imprisonment; they also have little knowledge about what prison is like. However, inmates are required to come to grips with the fact of their incarceration. An inmate often finds himself trying to manage a dualistic self, trying to balance his "true" identity (i.e., his preprison identity) with his "false" identity (i.e., his prison identity). The researchers note that this separation of identities "represents two conscious and interdependent identity-preservation tactics, formulated through self-dialogue and refined through tentative interaction with others." Schmid and Jones present an excellent diagram illustrating the major features involved in the identity change process. They conclude by discussing how an inmate's postprison identity may be influenced in various domains.

24 / Bureaucratic Slots and Client Processing

DELOS H. KELLY

I have illustrated how actors may become progressively defined by a range of others as societal misfits. Understanding this process, I have argued, requires a preliminary consideration of how, over time, individual traits, features, and biographies articulate with organizational components and processes to produce selected organizational products (e.g., the academic failure, troublemaker, or school dropout). Even more basic than this, I have argued that one must initially describe, as well as dissect, an institution's underlying organizational structure; this need was documented most graphically by Cicourel and Kitsuse's (1963) research on the origin of school career lines. They, it may be recalled, were able to locate three distinct career lines (i.e., the academic, clinical, and delinquent). These career lines not only composed an integral element of the school's organizational structure but they also provided the molds for student placement. Another significant finding of the Cicourel-Kitsuse (1963) study that should be made note of, once again, is the fact that the career lines could be characterized by a set of deviant and non-deviant labels. Teachers, for example, referred to those who gave them trouble or who were late as delinquents or predelinquents. The significance of this observation becomes especially meaningful when we find these same labels being invoked in the student selection and assignment processes. Thus, students who were late, did not work, or gave the teachers difficulty were more apt to be relegated to the delinquent career line. Thereafter, they became subject to the values associated with their low or deviant school status. The research by Hargreaves (1967) was used to buttress this observation, as well as claim.

Like the Cicourel-Kitsuse (1963) evidence, Hargreaves' (1967) observations point to the need for dissecting and understanding organizational structures. At Lumley, not only were student and teacher attitudes, reactions, and behaviors stream-specific, but the streaming system itself operated in such a fashion as to cut off effectively interaction between the lowest and highest streams; this organizational impediment to communication was also linked to subcultural differentiation. Hence, Lumley came to be characterized by two basic subcultures (i.e., the academic and the delinquescent), each possessing a set of dominant values. Low-stream students, it may be remembered, received positive sanctions by teachers and peers when they acted in accordance with the reigning values. The content of some of these values was such that misbehavior, even petty delinquency, was encouraged and supported by group members.

In effect, then, approaching a feeling for the structural roots or origins of school crime requires a basic and initial examination and documentation of the school's underlying organizational structure. Not only must the career lines and their labels be noted, but the corresponding value systems must also be mapped out; these comprise the basic structures to which individuals become molded.

Once the basic structural features of the educational system have been fixed, one can begin to examine student identifying, selecting, sorting, and processing. In this respect, I have argued that teachers-educators play a critical role in the initiation of a range of deviant careers; they are what I have termed "initiators of status degradation ceremonies." Several works were offered to support the fact that many teachers do invoke non-academic criteria (e.g., class, color, stigma symbols) in deciding which students will occupy the deviant, delinquent, or non-academic career lines. The importance of these observations, however, is found in the fact that once a pupil is assigned to a low school status or deviant career line, then that student must become subject to and be influenced by the prevailing value system, the general content of which is frequently non-academic in nature. It is in this way that a deviant, delinquent, and, perhaps ultimately, a criminal career is launched. The impact of the school experience and associated deviant labels is frequently more critical and wide-ranging than this. The efforts by Cicourel and Kitsuse (1963), and Polk (1975) were used to underscore this point.

As Cicourel and Kitsuse (1963) acknowledge, the school actually serves as a clearing house, and in this capacity it both sends and receives information about its students. Selected bits of biographical or stigmatizing material, however, seem especially vulnerable to dissemination and particularly that which evolves out of what I have termed "the success-fail philosophy" that permeates our society and its basic institutions. Thus, to fail academically, most assuredly, foretells of failure in other domains. In this regard, Polk (1975) noted that students who had been formally tagged as an academic failure by the school (i.e., a socializing institution) *and* who also had been adjudicated as a delinquent by the court (i.e., a social control institution) were more likely to possess an adult criminal record. Specific labels, or combinations of labels, thus assume a certain priority in our society, most notably those associated with the educational and social control apparatus. In fact, such labels have common meanings and are used interchangeably by institutions.

THE ORGANIZATIONAL PARADIGM AND INSTITUTIONAL PROCESSING

...Most interactions or status degradation ceremonies become eminently more meaningful when examined within an institutional context. Once we understand, for example, how the school is structured (i.e., the type and range of career lines), then the exchanges between teachers and pupils, or between students, make more sense. Similarly, after one becomes familiar with and understands how a law enforcement agency is structured in terms of its available career lines, then citizen-agent encounters take on added meaning and significance. Thus, the institutional fabric provides the backdrop against which interactions must be evaluated.

Elsewhere, in my studies of deviance (Kelly, 1979) and crime (Kelly, 1980), I have developed an analytical tool that can be used to gain an understanding of how organizations, in general, are structured and function. I have termed this the *organizational paradigm*; this basic paradigm or tool can be applied to the study of school crime.

What must be recognized initially is that the educational system has been given the major task of socializing or educating our youth. In this capacity, the educational decision makers must, as the major differentiators of academic talent, decide which students possess ability and which do not; this task, however, is not especially difficult, nor is it, necessarily, left to chance, primarily because the educators operate on the basis of a theory of the office which is, as I have stressed, predicated fundamentally upon the presumption of differential ability—a working ideology that guarantees the continued production of winners and losers. Not only have educators, parents, students, and others been effectively socialized into this dominant, all-pervading educational philosophy but, and upon closer examination, it becomes obvious that the success-fail philosophy can be characterized by a range of school labels (i.e., diagnostic stereotypes) and associated career lines. The career lines, however, become the most objective, bureaucratic representation of this ideology; they can, as Cicourel and Kitsuse (1963) demonstrated, be located and described. Moreover, the career lines or organizational entities constitute the molds into which students, once identified and tagged by the authorized school personnel, are placed. The paradigm illuminates this process very nicely.

THE ORGANIZATIONAL PARADIGM AND CLIENT PROCESSING: A BRIEF OVERVIEW

Conceptually, the major audience in the case of the school is usually the counselor; this institutional representative or agent has, during the course of formal and informal socializing experiences and influences, been indoctrinated with the school's theory of the office and associated elements (i.e., the diagnostic stereotypes and career lines).... The diagnostic stereotypes, once mastered, serve as the criteria by which actors (i.e., students) are selected out and placed into the existing career lines.... If, for example, and to sketch a brief scenario, an actor (i.e., student) violates a school rule, regulation, or expectation (i.e., this is the act in terms of the paradigm), and is observed doing so by the primary audience (i.e., the counselor), this violation may, and depending upon the content of the audience's diagnostic stereotypes (e.g., the counselor may, and probably does, feel that problem or difficult students belong in the non-academic career lines), be enough to result in placement in a deviant or delinquent career line. In this event, not only has the status degradation ceremony been initiated, but the student may, by virtue of his or her implication in a deviant status, be on the road to the development of a delinquent career and identity. Quite obviously, a single act of defiance, deviance, or misconduct may not constitute sufficient grounds for such treatment.

The probability, however, increases with repeated violations, and particularly so if the acts are observed by others (i.e., third parties or witnesses in terms of my paradigm); this, it may be recalled, is one of the major messages offered by the works of Tannenbaum (1938), Becker (1963), and Lemert (1951). Stated somewhat more directly, if others report acts of misbehavior to the counselor, then a conception of an individual may evolve to the effect that he or she is truly an academic misfit and should be processed and treated accordingly. Thus, third parties or witnesses are often important in structuring a degree of *consensus* about an actor (e.g., that he or she is evil, a troublemaker, a gang member, an academic failure, and the like).

As I indicated previously, the organizational paradigm can be used to refine Polk's (1975) "status flow chart." ... Specifically, the paradigm can be applied in such a way as to *flesh out* the underlying organizational structure. For example, and in looking at the school—the domain Polk (1975) considers critical in the generation of delinquent careers and identities, his conceptualization of the role and significance of academic performance could be easily recast into a discussion of career lines. Thus, and similar to Cicourel and Kitsuse (1963), we can speak of deviant and non-deviant career lines, as well as the dominant value systems that, according to Hargreaves' (1967) research, characterize a school's career lines. Also evident in Polk's (1975) analysis of status flows is the idea that certain students, by virtue of their status origins (e.g., low social class or minority status), are more apt to land in a low school status or deviant career line; this notion, too, can be handled very easily by the paradigm, particularly if we incorporate a concern for the role that the educational decision maker (i.e., the school's primary audience) plays. In effect, and as the evidence by Schafer and Olexa (1971), Pink and Sweeney (1978), Kelly (1976), Kelly and Grove (1981), and others indicates clearly, decision makers often apply non-academic criteria (i.e., class and race) in the selection and assignment processes, and, accordingly, students who fit the diagnostic stereotypes are selected out to play the role of the deviant, delinquent, or academic misfit. Polk's (1975) treatment of the interconnections between the educational system (i.e., a major socializing institution) and other social control institutions (i.e., police units, courts, and training schools) can also benefit from this type of refinement.

Not only do social control institutions become attuned to and act on the basis of a selected range of institutional labels (i.e., diagnostic stereotypes) but they, like the educational system, can also be described in terms of their underlying organizational structure. Thus, each agency can be analyzed relative to its prevailing theory of the office, diagnostic stereotypes, career lines, staff socializing procedures (both the formal and informal aspects), client selection and assignment routines (i.e., the application of diagnostic stereotypes to actors), and the like.

The police, by way of illustration, are expected to maintain peace and enforce the law. In this capacity, they are generally guided and constrained by what I would term a "good guy-bad guy" philosophy or, perhaps more generally, a "we-they" working ideology. Rookies, as do any other novices (Scheff, 1966), become socialized into this ideology, and they soon learn how to recognize the good guys from the bad guys; this is accomplished through familiarity with and application of a department's diagnostic stereotypes to clients or suspected clients. Officers, for example, develop conceptions of the "typical" features of the burglar, how the act of burglary is apt to be committed, where the event is likely to occur, and the range of possible victims. Similarly, the officer is taught how to spot, classify, and handle suspected cases of rape, homicide, spouse abuse, child molestation, and the like; these typical cases, or "normal crimes" in Sudnow's (1965) usage, are extremely important in the initiation of a *public* deviant identity and career, primarily because the initial classification of an actor (e.g., police labeling as a drunk driver or suspected rapist) has a direct bearing upon how that individual will be processed. Stated somewhat differently, the law enforcement apparatus contains a set of career lines commensurate with the diagnostic stereotypes or normal crimes; therefore, if a person is tagged as a child molester, murderer, or rapist, then he or she will be treated as such throughout the system. Not only this but what is often lost sight of is the fact that the suspected or adjudicated criminal, delinquent, or deviant is expected to act in accordance with the new public identity, status and associated roles. In effect, then, clients are examined with an eye toward seeing if they match the organization's selection criteria or standards.

DIAGNOSTIC STEREOTYPES AND CLIENT PROCESSING: THE MATCHING GAME

One of the best illustrations of this matching process is found in Wiseman's (1970) research on skid row alcoholics, particularly her description of the judicial screening process. By using various combinations of physical appearance, past performance, and social position, she was able to produce a paradigm of expected social types and matching sentences....

Of significance is the observation that there was an excellent fit between the derived social types and actual sentencing. Derelicts, for example, who looked rough, as well as men who were repeaters, were more apt to serve time and receive the longest sentences. Similarly, derelicts who appeared rough were "the least likely of any social type to escape jail" (Wiseman, 1970:93).

Even though the judge must, according to my paradigm, be conceptualized as occupying the position as major audience in the court, it must recognized that, in the determination of a sentence, he or she often relies heavily on the inputs from others. In Pacific City, two court helpers—"the Rapper" and "the Knocker"—assumed a major role in the sentencing process. Specifically, the Rapper, an ex-alcoholic himself, not only claimed intimate knowledge of the skid row alcoholics and their life style, but he acted as the major advisor to the judge. Thus, and as each case passed before the judge, the Rapper would offer a recommended case disposition and the judge then passed sentence (Wiseman, 1970:94). The Knocker, operating in his capacity as record keeper, also supplied information to the judge. In fact, and according to Wiseman (1970:95–96), it was often difficult to distinguish the Knocker's role (i.e., supplier of information to the judge) from the Rapper's (i.e., recommender of sentence to the judge). A major conclusion Wiseman (1970:97) offers is that:

> Far from freeing the judge to make idiosyncratic personalized decisions, the result of the drunk court system is to *standardize drunks on the basis of social types* and then with the *assistance of court aides objectify them in such a way as to fit the predetermined types.* Thus the decision of the patrolman in typification of the Skid Row Drinker is not only accepted in the court without question—it is reinforced and embellished. [Italics mine]

Thus, and as I have argued, the initial typification or labeling of an actor contains certain consequences for subsequent processing and treatment. In the case of the public drunk, the police type this person in a specified way (e.g., as a derelict, young repeater, or out-of-towner) and this designation then determines how the individual will be handled. Emerson's (1969) research on the court processing of juveniles also illustrates very nicely how clients are identified and processed in accordance with existing organizational categories or career lines and associated diagnostic stereotypes.

Emerson (1969:83) makes a beginning statement to the effect that juveniles appearing before the court have created problems for some institution:

> ...youths brought before the juvenile court generally represent "trouble" for some caretaking or control institution. In this sense every delinquent is "trouble" for someone. It may be added here that every delinquency complaint represents a plea that the court "do something" to remedy or alleviate that "trouble." Hence, one fundamental set of problems and demands confronting the juvenile court arises from the pressures and expectations of those initiating court action that "something be done." In this sense the court must work out practical solutions to cases that satisfy, or at least take some cognizance of, the concerns of complainants.

DIAGNOSTIC STEREOTYPES AND CLIENT PROCESSING: THE DESTRUCTION OF IDENTITY

Not all cases, however, represent "trouble" in the eyes of the court. Rather, cases are subjected to two rather distinct phases of organizational screening or sorting. During phase one, troubled cases are separated from the untroubled or, more specifically, attempts are made to distinguish between cases requiring special handling as opposed to those that can be released. Assessing a juvenile's moral character triggers the subsequent, second phase of screening. At this juncture, the court specifies how the case is to be processed. If a decision is reached that no trouble exists, then the assumption is the delinquent's moral character is *normal*. If, by contrast, trouble is found to exist, then one's moral character is viewed as being *problematic* in nature; this latter decision brings about additional scrutiny by court personnel. Emerson (1969:90–91) maintains that, during the decision-making process, court staff endeavor to fit the juvenile into one of three kinds of moral character:

> ...First, a youth may be *normal,* i.e., basically like most children, acting for basically normal and conventional reasons, despite some delinquent behavior. Second, a youth may be regarded as a *hard-core* or *criminal-like* delinquent, maliciously or hostilely motivated, consciously pursuing illegal ends. Third, a youth may be *disturbed,* driven to acting in senseless and irrational ways by obscure motives or inner compulsions. [Italics his]

Emerson (1969:91) goes on to say that the existing categories of moral character not only "provide institutionally relevant means for 'explaining' or 'accounting for' the patterns of behavior that led to the identification of 'trouble'" but placement in a category "both suggests and justifies particular court actions to deal with it." To determine that a person is "disturbed" explains or accounts for one's "bizarre" behavior. Such a finding would indicate a need for psychiatric treatment. It would also justify such care or institutionalization. Categories of moral character are thus associated with rather specific courses of action. In Emerson's (1969:91) words:

> ...The three classes of moral character recognized by the court—normal, criminal, and disturbed—correspond to the following general reactions which the court may try to implement: (a) routine handling of the case: generally probation and the relatively minor obligations and checks accompanying it; (b) incarceration in reform school or some other institution of that nature; and (c) special care and treatment, especially in a psychiatric setting.

Even though the court looks for trouble and then assesses moral character, this does not mean that a decision relative to character will be linked to a specific outcome or disposition. Rather, and as Emerson (1969:96–97) points out, an initial decision often represents nothing more than a recommendation, primarily because the court must deal with several practical considerations (e.g., those of placement and treatment). As an illustration, he cites the case of the "disturbed" delinquent. Specifically, the decision makers may decide that such an individual needs hospitalization, yet the youth may never be institutionalized. To obtain the desired recommendation (i.e., institutionalization), psychiatrists must validate the "disturbed" or "sick" diagnosis, and the court must convince the mental hospital to accept the case. If these contingencies are not met, the youth's case will be disposed of differently.

> ... Contingencies surrounding the actual "solution" of a case may lead to different case outcomes despite common assessments of moral character. For example, the juvenile court may come to classify a boy as a dangerous, criminally motivated person, in which case some penal sanction such as commitment to reform school would seem indicated. But the decision actually to invoke this sanction is influenced by factors such as the boy's home situation and the availability of alternatives to reform school. Thus a boy who is a state ward is more likely to be committed to reform school than a boy judged just as criminally inclined but from a stable home. Commitment follows for the first case because there is no other place to put the public ward. [Emerson, 1969:97]

THE DESTRUCTION OF IDENTITY: THE ROLE OF WITNESSES

Once a youth has been initially typed (e.g., by a police officer) relative to moral character, efforts must be made, thereafter, to convince others (e.g., the probation officer), and even the actor, of the correctness of the decision. As Emerson (1969:101) stresses:

> Moral character is not passively established. It is the product of interaction and communicative work involving the delinquent, his family, enforcers, complainants generally, and the court itself. *Specific versions of moral character must be successfully presented if they are to be adopted by others* (Garfinkel, 1956). Officials, who play the dominant role in this process, both directly communicate their opinions of the moral character of the youth involved and more indirectly make selective reports of incidents and information pertinent to the court's evaluation of this character. In general, *the version of moral character finally established is negotiated from among these presented "facts," opinions, and reports.* [Italics mine]

In effect, then, competing versions of moral character are presented to the court, and the judge, acting in his or her capacity as the major audience or decision maker, must decide ultimately which version of moral character will prevail; this, according to Emerson (1969:102), often leads to contests over moral character:

> Character-related presentations are inextricably linked to issues of disposition. For moral character is established in the process of negotiating a disposition of a case among the various expectations and demands of the parties involved. In

this process, the court determines an outcome not by balancing the relative merits and demerits of possible disposition alternatives, but by attempting to establish a correspondence between a youth's moral character and a particular alternative. As a result, issues of disposition lead to contests over moral character, and parties to these contests, who seek to influence the outcome of a particular case, have to marshal and present evidence to establish a version of moral character appropriate to their desired outcome.

Not only is the court concerned with establishing a linkage between a juvenile's moral character and a particular disposition but the success of this process depends heavily upon inputs from other third parties or witnesses. In this respect, the probation officer frequently plays a central role in the construction of one's moral character. Similar to the Knocker and the Rapper in Wiseman's research, he or she attempts to convey a specific image of character to the judge; this is especially evident in the following case reported in Emerson's (1969:102–103) research:

> Rodney Knight, a 16-year-old Negro boy, was accused of stealing a handbag from a woman in a subway station. The police told of the arrest, and complained that the boy had given them "difficulties," particularly by using false names, address, and age. The probation officer recommended that Knight be held in county jail under $1,000 bail until the hearing. The judge reacted: "My only problem is the county jail. I can understand the $1,000 bail for this crime—it's serious enough to warrant it. But I'm curious about the recommendation of county jail." Probation officer replied that the boy had a previous record for use without authority at the municipal court. In addition he had been "uncooperative-information limited" with the police. Judge: "Let me put it this way: Is this something that in your opinion could not be handled at the YCA [Detention Center]?" Probation Officer (hesitating): "It's a problem of either the one or the other. (pause) I think that possibly the YCA is more of a picnic grounds." Judge: "Are you making this recommendation because of uncooperativeness, or because of some knowledge you have of his previous conduct?" Probation officer replied that he knew nothing about the boy's prior life and conduct. But another probation officer reported that the municipal court had told him that Knight had not done well while on probation there. The arresting policeman again told of how much trouble the boy had given them. The judge finally agreed to county jail, but with considerable reluctance.

In the preceding case, the probation officer obviously tries to convince the judge that the youth's moral character is criminal in nature. The judge initially balks at this suggestion; however, additional witnesses (i.e., the second probation officer and policeman) are brought into the picture, and they testify in such a manner as to corroborate or validate the probation officer's image of Knight. Thus consensus is reached (i.e., that the youth is criminal) and the judge uses this information as a basis for sentencing to jail. At this point, a beginning delinquent career becomes solidified, at least in terms of the individual's public identity.

What the research by Emerson (1969) and others (e.g., Wiseman, 1970) indicates very clearly is that organizational personnel are interested in matching clients with the existing organizational categories or career lines. And if the efforts in this direction are successful, then the actor does, at least in the eyes of the institution, become effectively molded to the category or line he or she has been cast into. Emerson's (1969) observations also provide additional substance to my claim that there is often a high degree of correspondence between one social control agency's diagnostic stereotypes and another's; this is probably most apparent in Emerson's discussion of how the first probation officer used statements by the policeman—the actual initiator of the status degradation ceremony—and another probation officer to convince the judge that the court was dealing with a young criminal. What should be noted, however, is the fact that processes and associated outcomes such as these are not only routine and recurring features of the court but they become eminently more meaningful once we realize that the underlying organizational structure of the judicial system guarantees this kind of handling. Stated very simply, the court does not deal in individuals per se. It deals in social types, categories, and labels. Thus, and similar to the statements and research by Wiseman, court personnel, and especially the probation officer, are concerned primarily with the "typicalness" of their cases. Can, for example, a delinquent act be classified and processed in accordance with any of the court's existing categories of "typical delinquencies?" This is the basic question.

ORGANIZATIONAL SLOTS AND PROCESSING: FURTHER OBSERVATIONS ON BECOMING A CLIENT

Organizational constructs (e.g., categories of typical academic types or delinquencies), once mastered, provide for the smooth and efficient processing of clients; this was pointed out by Scheff (1966). In effect, once a staff member has been effectively inculcated with the current diagnostic stereotypes, he or she becomes more proficient in the screening and processing of prospective clients (i.e., in the application of diagnostic stereotypes). Unfortunately, and as also suggested by Scheff's (1966) comments, the perceptions of many staff members seem to be locked in at the stereotypic level. Hence, the individual merits or demerits of a case are often lost sight of or else ignored. Of major concern to the staff member or social control agent is whether or not there are enough typical features of an event or case to allow for classification in terms of reigning categories. Emerson (1969), in drawing upon the work by Sudnow, stresses the important role that "typical delinquencies" play in the structuring of a successful degradation ceremony.

> Court personnel regularly deal with a recurring sequence of delinquent acts. In this activity, they come to make certain characterizations about routinely encountered delinquencies and delinquents. *A given delinquent act is understood in terms of these characterizations; that is, its organizationally relevant meaning derives from*

its membership in a known class of "typical delinquencies." Typical delinquencies are constructs of the typical features of regularly encountered delinquent acts, embodying the court staff's previous experience with and common-sense knowledge of the situations and setting of delinquent acts.... [Emerson, 1969:106–107] [Italics mine]

To illustrate the substantive nature of typical delinquencies, Emerson (1969:107) offers some comments made by probation officers:

Boy shoplifters: "Usually it's very mild type of boy. There are not many seriously delinquent boys." Generally no previous record. Often from "well-to-do families" and taking goods "for kicks." "Usually they're pretty nice children. They give you no trouble." Seldom in court again. "Usually they're not thieves at heart. They're in the store and they succumb to a beautiful display or something that looks good to them."

Typical delinquencies, according to Emerson (1969:107), actually "indicate *the kind of actor* typically involved." Similar to Sudnow's usage, typical delinquencies (1) "identify typical actors in terms of such *social characteristics* as age, sex, class, and residence," (2) "provide explanations or 'reasons' for the particular delinquent act, including but not limited to the actor's *immediate motives*;" and (3) "identify the kind of typical actor in terms of *moral character*" (Emerson, 1969:107–108) [italics his].

Throughout court processing or, for that matter, any status degradation ceremony, an actor's public identity is under attack. And if the assault is successful, an individual becomes viewed, at least in the eyes of others, as a new or different person; this, it may be recalled, is one of the basic messages contained in the works by Werthman (1967), Tannenbaum (1938), Garfinkel (1956), Becker (1963), Hughes (1945), and Lemert (1951). I argued subsequently, however, that prior to making any statements or conducting any analysis relative to status denunciation ceremonies or institutional handling, one must see the underlying organizational structure. The research by especially Wiseman and Emerson illustrates the need for doing so. Evidence of this type also indicates that potential clients are processed in accordance with the existing organizational categories or career lines. Not only this, but fitting a candidate to a particular career line often involves various stages of screening. For example, Emerson's juveniles were subjected to two distinct stages of screening. Another excellent illustration of this process is contained in McCleary's (1978) research with parolees, particularly his discussion of those stages involved in becoming a client....

McCleary (1978:124–127) points out that parole officers work with a set of social types. Thus when a prisoner's dossier is received, the officer must decide how to classify the individual; this is an important decision, primarily because, and as illustrated by the efforts of Wiseman and Emerson, each decision and corresponding type or organizational category is associated with a specific line of action. In terms of actual typing, the officer must decide initially whether the prisoner should be typed as a criminal or non-criminal. If the decision is to the effect that the person is a non-criminal, the decision-making process moves to stage four where the individual will be labeled subsequently as a client or paper man. If, by contrast, the parole officer decides that the parolee is a criminal, then another decision must be made: Is the parolee controllable? This is determined during the site visit. For example, if selected environmental factors exist (e.g., a good job or stable family) as potential controls, then, and similar to the non-criminal's processing, the prisoner will be designated as a client or paper man. Some parolees, however, are not only viewed as criminals and uncontrollable but they are perceived as dangerous; these men are kept under surveillance and returned to prison at the first sign of trouble. A parolee who is judged as sincere becomes transformed into a client; this person interacts frequently with the officer and if problems develop, attempts will be made to "save" the client. The paper man category or type comprises those who have been judged as insincere, yet controllable, and those who have not been judged; these men remain on the books, however, they experience very little interaction with the parole officer. Most see the officer a couple of times a year. Clients and dangerous men usually see the officer once a week. In fact, McCleary (1978) characterizes the interaction between the officer and the paper man as being one of "mutual disinterested toleration."

INSTITUTIONAL RECORDS: THEIR CREATION, USE, AND MISUSE

Even though it may be assumed that parole records accurately describe a parolee's behavior relative to the classification criteria, this is often not the case. Rather, McCleary (1978:129) maintains that "parole records are more likely to reflect the needs and problems of the POs [parole officers];" this produces a bureaucratic dysfunction, one that can be related directly to the discretionary license allowed the officer, particularly in the creation or production of parole records. In McCleary's (1978:129) words:

> ... [the] bureaucratic dysfunction can be attributed to the great discretion allowed POs in the gathering and reporting of information. In most cases, the PO himself decides what portion of the information he has gathered will actually go into the official record. By exercising editorial discretion in this area, the PO can suppress information that might make his job more difficult or complex and can include information that might facilitate work goals or objectives. This is how POs "use" their records.

Although rarely acknowledged, the parole officer, like any other bureaucrat, must come to grips with several bureaucratic demands—considerations that have a significant impact upon the production of records. In fact, and according to McCleary (1978:129), the parole officer's work environment consists of two distinct halves: PO-parolee interaction and PO-bureaucracy interaction. McCleary (1978:129–130) points out that successful parole officers must not only control their clients but they must satisfy the bureaucracy's explicit and implicit demands. A feature common to both halves, however, is record-keeping and successful POs know how to "use" their records. Record-keeping is not necessarily a simple or straightforward task, primarily because the officers must weigh the costs or benefits that may ensue from "using" their records. McCleary's (1978:130) major argument is that, other things being equal,

> ...a PO will not report any of the minor crimes, incidents, or violations he observes in his caseload. When a PO does report an incident, he is creating records that will accomplish some end, the benefits of which are expected to outweigh the practical costs of reporting the incident. The implication of this argument is that parole records do not accurately reflect the behavior of parolees, but rather, reflect the many problems that arise in the PO's work environment. Three general problems... lead to the three most common "uses" of records: (1) records created to threaten parolees, (2) records created to get rid of troublesome parolees, and (3) records created to protect the PO and his superiors.

Not only is the creation of a record associated with potential costs but organizational incentives exist for underreporting. McCleary (1978:131–136) lists and describes several practical considerations a parole officer must deal with. For example, the complete or full reporting of each event may cut into the parole officer's "free" time (e.g., many of them moonlight) or place the officer in jeopardy (e.g., a lengthy hearing may result). Full reporting may also create a great deal of "busy work" for the officer, as well as restrict his or her options (e.g., most feel that their job is to counsel and not catch clients).

The significance of the preceding observations can be found in the fact that not only do bureaucratic factors affect the production of records but they must also impact significantly on client processing. Teachers, I might add, are not immune from these influences; they, too, must come to grips with demands of their profession, as well as the bureaucracy they are immersed in.

References

Becker, H. S. (1963) *Outsiders: Studies in the Sociology of Deviance*. New York: Free Press.

Cicourel, A. V. and J. I. Kitsuse (1963) *The Educational Decision Makers*. New York: Free Press.

Emerson, R. M. (1969) *Judging Delinquents*. Chicago: Aldine.

Garfinkel, H. (1956) "Conditions of successful degradation ceremonies." *The American Journal of Sociology* 61:420–424.

Hargreaves, D. (1967) *Social Relations in a Secondary School*. New York: Humanities Press.

Hughes, E. C. (1945) "Dilemmas and contradictions of status." *The American Journal of Sociology* 50:353–359.

Kelly, D. H., Ed. (1980) *Criminal Behavior*. New York: St. Martin's.

Kelly, D. H., Ed. (1979) *Deviant Behavior*. New York: St. Martin's.

Kelly, D. H. (1976) "The role of teachers' nominations in the perpetuation of deviant adolescent careers." *Education* 96:209–217.

Kelly, D. H. and W. D. Grove (1981) "Teachers' nominations and the production of academic 'misfits'." *Education* 101:246–263.

Lemert, E. M. (1951) *Social Pathology*. New York: McGraw-Hill.

McCleary, R. (1978) *Dangerous Men*. Beverly Hills: Sage.

Pink, W. T. and M. E. Sweeney (1978) "Teacher nomination, deviant career lines and the management of stigma in the junior high school." *Urban Education* 13:361–380.

Polk, K. (1975) "Schools and the delinquency experience." *Criminal Justice and Behavior* 2:315–338.

Schafer, W. E. and C. Olexa (1971) *Tracking and Opportunity*. Scranton: Chandler.

Scheff, T. J. (1966) "Typification in the diagnostic practices of rehabilitation agencies." In M. B. Sussman, Ed., *Sociology and Rehabilitation*. Washington, D.C.: American Sociological Association.

Sudnow, D. (1965) "Normal crimes: sociological features of the penal code in a public defender office." *Social Problems* 12:255–276.

Tannenbaum, F. (1938) *Crime and Community*. New York: Ginn and Company.

Werthman, C. (1967) "The function of social definitions in the development of delinquent careers." In the President's Commission on Law Enforcement and Administration of Justice, *Task Force Report: Juvenile Delinquency and Youth Crime*. Washington, D.C.: U.S. Government Printing Office.

Wiseman, J. P. (1970) *Stations of the Lost*. Chicago: University of Chicago Press.

25 / The Social Context of Police Lying

JENNIFER HUNT
PETER K. MANNING

INTRODUCTION

Police, like many people in official capacities, lie. We intend here to examine the culturally grounded bases for police lying using ethnographic materials.[1] Following the earlier work of Manning (1974), we define lies as speech acts which the speaker knows are misleading or false, and are intended to deceive. Evidence that proves the contrary must be known to the observer.[2] Lying is not an obvious matter: it is always socially and contextually defined with reference to what an audience will credit; thus, its meaning changes and its effects are often ambiguous (Goffman 1959, pp. 58–66). The moral context of lying is very important insofar as its definition may be relative to membership status. The outsider may not appreciate distinctions held scrupulously within a group; indeed, differences between what is and is not said may constitute a lie to an outsider, but these distinctions may not be so easily made by an insider. In a sense, lies do not exist in the abstract; rather they are objects within a negotiated occupational order (Maines 1982). In analytic terms, acceptable or normal lies become one criteria for membership within a group, and inappropriate lying, contextually defined, sets a person on the margins of that order.

The structural sources of police lying are several. Lying is a useful way to manipulate the public when the applying of the law and other threats are of little use (see Bittner 1970; Westley 1970; Skolnick 1966; Klockars 1983, 1984; Wilson 1968; Stinchcombe 1964). The police serve as gatherers and screeners of facts, shaping them within the legal realities and routines of court settings (Buckner 1978). The risks involved in establishing often problematic facts and the adversarial context of court narratives increases the value of secrecy and of concealing and controlling information generally (Reiss 1974). Police are protected for their lies by law under stipulated circumstances (see McBarnett 1981; Ericson and Shearing 1986).[3] The internal organization of policing as well as the occupational culture emphasize control, punishment, and secrecy (Westley 1970; Manning 1977).

Some police tasks, especially those in specialized police units such as vice, narcotics and internal affairs, clearly require and reward lying skills more than others, and such units may be subject to periodic scandals and public outcry (Manning 1980). The unfilled and perhaps impossible expectations in drug enforcement may escalate the use of lies in the "war on drugs," further reducing public trust when officers' lies are exposed. Most police officers in large forces at one time or another participate in some form of illicit or illegal activity, from the violation of departmental morals codes to the use of extra-legal force. Perhaps more importantly, there is an accepted view that it is impossible to "police by the book;" that any good officer, in the course of a given day, will violate at least one of the myriad rules and regulations governing police conduct. This is certain; what is seen as contingent is when, how and where detection by whom will take place.

Lying is a sanctioned practice, differentially rewarded and performed, judged by local occupationally-grounded standards of competence.[4] However, it is likely that these standards are changing; as police claims to professional competence and capacity to control crime and incivilities in cities are validated, and absent any changes in internal or external sources of control and accountability (cf. Reiss 1974), police may encounter less external pressure and public support in routine tasks and are less likely to be called into account. Policing has emerged as a more "professional" occupation and may be less at risk generally to public outcry. One inference of this line of conjecture is that lying is perceived as less risky by police. The occupational culture in departments studied by researchers contains a rich set of stories told to both colleagues and criminals. However, like the routinely required application of violence, some lies are "normal," and acceptable to audiences, especially colleagues, whereas others are not.

Given the pervasiveness of police lies, it is surprising that no research has identified and provided examples of types of lies viewed from the officers' perspective. We focus here on patrol officers' lies and note the skill with which they cope with situations in which lies are produced. Some officers are more frequently in trouble than others, and some more inclined to lie. We suggest a distinction between lies that excuse from those that justify an action, between troublesome and non-troublesome lies, and between case and cover lies. Lies are troublesome when they arise in a context such as a courtroom or a report in which the individual is sworn to uphold the truth. In such a context, lying may risk legal and/or moral sanctions, resulting in punishment and a loss in status. *Case lies* and *cover stories* are routinely told types of troublesome lies. Case lies are stories an officer utilizes systematically in a courtroom or on paper to facilitate the conviction of a suspect. Cover stories are lies an officer tells in court, to supervisors, and to colleagues in order to provide a verbal shield or mitigation in the event of anticipated discipline.

METHODOLOGY

The senior author was funded to study police training in a large Metropolitan police department ("Metro City"). Continuous fieldwork, undertaken as a known observer-participant for eighteen months, focused on the differences and similarities in the socialization experiences of young female and male officers.[5] The fieldwork included observation, participation in training with an incoming class in the policy academy, tape-recording interviews in relaxing informal settings with key informants selected for their verbal skills and willingness to give lengthy interviews. The social milieu encouraged them to provide detailed and detached stories. The observer had access to the personnel files of the two hundred officers who entered the force during the research period. She attended a variety of off-duty events and activities ranging from meetings of the Fraternal Order of the Police, sporting events, parties, and funerals (for further details see Hunt 1984). The data presented here are drawn primarily from tape recorded interviews.

LEARNING TO LIE

In the police academy, instructors encouraged recruits to lie in some situations, while strongly discouraging it in others. Officers are told it is "good police work," and encouraged to lie, to substitute guile for force, in situations of crisis intervention, investigation and interrogation, and especially with the mentally ill (Harris 1973).[6] During classes on law and court testimony, on the other hand, students were taught that the use of deception in court was illegal, morally wrong, and unacceptable and would subject the officer to legal and departmental sanctions. Through films and discussions, recruits learned that the only appropriate means to win court cases was to undertake and complete a "solid," "by the books" investigation including displaying a professional demeanor while delivering a succinct but "factual" narrative in court testimony.

Job experience changes the rookies' beliefs about the circumstances under which it is appropriate to lie. Learning to lie is a key to membership. Rookies in Metro City learn on the job, for example, that police routinely participate in a variety of illicit activities which reduce the discomfort of the job such as drinking, sleeping on duty, and staying inside during inclement weather. As these patterns of work avoidance may result in discovery, they demand the learning of explanatory stories which rationalize informal behavior in ways that jeopardize neither colleagues nor supervisors (Cain 1973; Chatterton 1975). Rookies and veteran police who demonstrate little skill in constructing these routine lies were informally criticized. For example, veteran officers in Metro City commented sympathetically about rookies who froze on footbeats because they were too green to know that "a good cop never gets cold or wet ... " and too new to have attained expertise in explaining their whereabouts if they were to leave their beats. After a few months in the district, several veteran officers approvingly noted that most of the rookies had learned not only where to hide but what to say if questioned by supervisors.

Rookies also learn the situational utility of lying when they observe detectives changing reports to avoid unnecessary paperwork and maintain the clearance rate. In the Metro City police department, some cases defined initially as robberies, assaults, and burglaries were later reduced to less serious offenses (cf. Sudnow 1965). Police argued that this practice reduced the time and effort spent on "bullshit jobs" little likely to be cleared. Rookies who opposed this practice and insisted on filing cases as they saw fit were ridiculed and labeled troublemakers. As a result, most division detectives provided minimal cooperation to these "troublemakers." This added the task of reworking already time-consuming and tedious reports to the workload of young officers who were already given little prospective guidance and routine assistance in completing their paperwork.

Young police also observe veterans lying in court testimony regarding, for example, the presence of probable cause in situations of search, seizure and arrest (see, for example, McClure 1986, pp. 230–232).

There are also counter-pressures. While learning to lie, rookies also recognize that the public and court officials disapprove of lying, and that if caught in a serious lie, they may be subject to either legal sanctioning and/or departmental punishment. But recognizing external standards and their relevance does not exhaust the learning required. There are also relevant tacit rules within the occupational culture about what constitutes a normal lie. Complexity and guile, and agile verbal constructions are appreciated, while lying that enmeshes or makes colleagues vulnerable or is "sloppy" is condemned. Lying is judged largely in pragmatic terms otherwise. Soon, some rookies are as skillful as veterans at lying.[7]

POLICE ACCOUNTS OF LYING

Lies are made normal or acceptable by means of socially approved vocabularies for relieving responsibility or neutralizing the consequences of an event. These accounts are provided *after* an act if and when conduct is called into question (see the classic, Mills 1940; Sykes and Matza 1957; Scott and Lyman 1968). Police routinely normalize lying by two types of accounts, excuses and justifications (Van Maanen 1980; Hunt 1985; Waegel 1984). These accounts are not mutually exclusive, and a combination is typically employed in practice. The greater the number of excuses and justifications condensed in a given account, the more the police officer is able to reduce personal and peer related conflicts. These accounts are typically tailored to an audience. A cover story directed to an "external" audience such as the district attorneys, courts, or the media is considered more problematic than a lie directed to supervisors or peers (Manning 1974). Lies are more troublesome also when the audience is perceived as less trustworthy (Goffman 1959, p. 58).

Excuses deny full responsibility for an act of lying but acknowledge its inappropriateness. Police distinguish passive lies which involve omission, or covering oneself, from active lies such as a "frame," of a person for a crime by, for example, planting a gun, or the construction of a sophisticated story. The latter are more often viewed as morally problematic.

Justifications accept responsibility for the illegal lie in question but deny that the act is wrongful or blameworthy. They socially construct a set of justifications, used with both public and other police, according to a number of principles (These are analogous to the neutralizations found by Sykes and Matza 1957 in another context). When lying, police may appeal to "higher" loyalties that justify the means used, deny that anyone is truly hurt or a victim of the lies. Police may also deny injury by claiming that court testimony has little consequence as it is merely an extension of the "cops and robbers" game. It is simply a tool in one's repertoire that requires a modicum of verbal skill (see Sudnow 1965; Blumberg 1967). Finally, as seen in "cover stories," officers justify lies instrumentally and pragmatically (see Van Maanen 1980; Waegel 1984).

LYING IN ACTION

Case Stories and the Construction of Probable Cause

The most common form of case lying, used to gain a conviction in court, involves the construction of probable cause for arrest, or search and seizure in situations where the legally required basis in the street encounter is weak or absent.[8] Probable cause can be constructed by reorganizing the sequence of events, "shading" or adding to the facts, omitting embarrassing facts, or entering facts into a testimony that were not considered at the time of arrest or while writing the report.

The following is a typical case story-account chosen from a taped interview in which probable cause was socially constructed. The officer was called to a "burglary in progress" with no further details included and found a door forced open at the back of the factory.

> So I arrive at the scene, and I say, I know: I do have an open property and I'm going in to search it. And I'm looking around, and I hear noise. Then, I hear glass break. And I run to the window, and obviously something just jumped out the window and is running and I hear skirmishing. So I run, and I still don't see anyone yet. I just hear something. I still haven't seen anyone. You hear a window, you see a window and you hear footsteps running. Then you don't hear

it anymore. I don't find anybody. So I say to myself "whoever it is is around here somewhere." So, fifteen minutes go by, twenty go by. The job resumes.

One cop stays in the front and about a half an hour or forty-five minutes later, low and behold, I see someone half a block away coming out of a field. Now, the field is on the other side of the factory. It's the same field that I chased this noise into. So a half hour later I see this guy at quarter to four in the morning just happened to be walking out of this field. So I grab him. "Who are you? What are you doing?" Bla bla bla.... And I see that he has flour on him, like flour which is what's inside of this factory. So I say to myself, "you're the suspect under arrest for burglary." Well, I really, at this point it was iffy if I had probable cause or not.... A very conservative judge would say that that was enough.... But probably not, because the courts are so jammed that that weak probable cause would be enough to have it thrown out. So in order to make it stick, what I said was "As I went to the factory and I noticed the door open and I entered the factory to search to see if there was anybody inside. Inside, by the other side of the wall, I see a young black male, approximately twenty two years old, wearing a blue shirt and khaki pants, jump out of the window, and I chase him and I lost him in the bushes. An hour later I saw this very same black male walking out of the field and I arrested him. He was the same one I saw inside." O.K.?...

What I did was to construct probable cause that would definitely stick in court and I knew he was guilty. So in order to make it stick.... That's the kind of lies that happen all the time. I would defend that.[9]

The officer's account of his activity during the arrest of a suspect and subsequent testimony in court reveals a combination of excuses and justifications which rationalize perjury. He clearly distinguishes the story he tells the interviewer from the lie he told in court. Near the end of the vignette, by saying "O.K.?," he seeks to emphasize phatic contact as well to establish whether the interviewer understood how and why he lied and how he justified it. Within the account, he excuses his lies with reference to organizational factors ("conservative judges"—those who adhere to procedural guarantees—and "overcrowded courts"), and implies that these are responsible for releasing guilty suspects who should be jailed. These factors force the officer to lie in court in order to sustain an ambiguous and weak probable cause. The officer further justifies his lies by claiming that he believes the suspect to be guilty and responsible for perpetrating crime more serious than the lie used to convict him. He ends by claiming that such lies are acceptable to his peers—they "happen all the time"—and implicitly appeals to the higher goal of justice. As in this case, officers can shape and combine observed and invented facts to form a complex, elaborate yet coherent, picture which may help solve a crime, clear a case, or convict a criminal.

Case Stories and the Manipulation of the Court as an Informal Entity

As a result of community pressure in Metro City, a specialized unit was created to arrest juveniles who "hung out" on street corners and disturbed neighborhoods. The unit was considered a desirable assignment because officers worked steady shifts and were paid overtime for court appearances. They were to be judged by convictions obtained, not solely upon their arrests. An officer in this unit explains some of the enforcement constraints produced by the law and how they can be circumvented:

> Legally...when there's any amount of kids over five there is noise, but it's not really defined legally being unruly even though the community complains that they are drunk and noisy. Anyway, you get there, you see five kids and there's noise. It's not really criminal, but you gotta lock them up, particularly if someone had called and complained. So you lock them up for disorderly conduct and you tell your story. If they plead not guilty then you have to actually tell a story.
> ...It's almost like a game. The kids know that they can plead guilty and get a $12.50 fine or a harder judge will give them a $30.50 fine or they can plead not guilty and have the officer tell their story of what occurred which lead to the arrest.
> ...The game is who manipulates better, the kid or the cop? The one who lies better wins.
> Well, the kids are really cocky. I had arrested this group of kids, and when we went to court the defense attorney for the kids was arguing that all of the kids, who I claimed were there the first time that I warned them to get offa the corner, weren't there at all. Now, you don't really have to warn them to get offa the corner before you arrest them, but the judge likes it if you warn them once.
> Meanwhile, one of the kids is laughing in the courtroom, and the judge asks why he's laughing in her courtroom and showing disrespect.
> At this point, the kid's attorney asks me what the kid was wearing when I arrested him. I couldn't remember exactly what he had on so I just gave the standard uniform; dungarees, shirt, sneakers....Then, the defense attorney turns around and asks the kid what he was wearing and he gives this description of white pants with a white sports jacket. Now, you just know the kid is lying because there ain't a kid in that neighborhood who dresses like that. But, anyway, I figure they got me on this one.
> But then I signal the District Attorney to ask me how I remembered this kid outta the whole bunch who was on the corner. So the District Attorney asks me, "Officer, what was it that made you remember this male the first time?" And I said, "Well, your honor, I referred this one here because the first time that I warned the group to get off the corner, this male was the one that laughed the hardest." I know this would get the Judge because the kid has pissed her off in the first place by laughing in the courtroom. Well, the judge's eyes lit up like she knew what I was talking about.
> "Found guilty....60 dollars." (The Judge ruled).

In this case, the officer believed the boy was guilty because he "hung out" regularly with the juvenile corner group. Although the officer forgot the boy's dress on the day he was arrested, he testifies in court that it was the "standard [juvenile] uniform." The boy, however, claims he wore pants and a sports jacket. The officer was in a potentially embarrassing and awkward spot. In order to affirm the identification of the suspect and win the case, the officer constructs another lie using the District Attorney's question. He manipulates the emotions of the judge whose authority was previously threatened by the boy's disrespectful courtroom demeanor. He claims that he knows this was the boy because he displayed arrogance by laughing when arrested just as he had in court.

The officer's account of the unit's organization, the arrest, and his courtroom testimony reveals a combination of excuses and justifications. He justifies his lie to make the arrest without probable cause and to gain a conviction citing the organizational and community pressures. He also justifies perjury by denying the reality and potential injury to the suspect caused by his actions. He sees courtroom communications as a game, and argues that the penalty is minor in view of the offense and the age of the suspect. The officer argues instrumentally that the lie was a means to gain or regain control as well as a means to punish an offender who has not accepted the police definition of the situation. The latter is evident in the officer's assertion that the boys are "really cocky." Their attempts to question the police version of the story by presenting themselves as clean cut children with good families is apparently viewed as a demonstration of deliberate arrogance deserving of retaliation in the form of a lie which facilitates their conviction.

Another officer from the same unit describes a similar example of case construction to gain a conviction. The clumsy character of the lie suggests that the officer believes he is at little risk of perjury. According to a colleague's account:

> We arrested a group of kids in a park right across from the hospital. They all know us and we know them, so they are getting as good as we are at knowing which stories go over better on the judge. So the kids in this instance plead not guilty which is a real slap in the face because you know that they are going to come up with a story that you are going to have to top [That is, the case will go to court and require testimony].
>
> So, the kids' story was that they were just sitting in the park and waiting for someone and that they were only having a conversation. [The police officer's testimony was]: "The kids were making so much noise, the kids were so loud.... They had this enormous radio blasting and the people in the hospital were so disturbed that they were just hanging outta the windows. And some nuns, some of the nuns that work in the hospital, they were coming outside because it was so loud." And the thing that appalled the officer the most was that this was going on right in front of the entrance to the hospital. The kids were acting in such a manner that the officer immediately arrested them without even a warning.
>
> Well, the kid, when he hears this, likely drops dead. He kept saying "what radio, what radio?" The funny part of it was that the other police officers who were in the back of the courtroom watching the cop testify kept rolling their eyes at him. First of all, because when he said that the people were hanging outta the hospital windows, the windows in the hospital don't open. They're sealed. Another thing was that the cop said this occurred at the entrance of the hospital.

Two years ago this was the entrance to the hospital. But it's not the entrance now. Another thing was that there never was a radio. But when the officer testified regarding the radio, he got confused. He actually did think there was one but in fact, the radio blasting was from another job. The cop realized after he testified that the kid didn't have a radio blasting.

The lies are described as instrumental: they are designed to regain control in court and to punish the offender for violating the officer's authority by verbally "slapping him in the face." In addition, the court-as-a-game-metaphor is evident in the notion that each participant must top the other's story in court. The amused reaction evidenced by peers listening to what they viewed as absurd testimony, rolling their eyes, also suggests their bemused approval. The informant's ironic identification of his colleague's factual errors points out the recognized and displayed limits and constraints upon lying. The officers recognized the difference between a rather sloppy or merely effective lie and an admired lie that artfully combines facts, observations, and subtle inferences. Perhaps it is not unimportant to note that the police engaged in the first instance in a kind of social construction of the required social order. The police lied in virtually every key facet of this situation because they believed that the juveniles should be controlled. What might be called the police ordering of a situation was the precondition for both of these court lies. Such decisions are potentially a factor in community policing when police define and then defend in court with lies their notions of public order (see Wilson and Kelling 1982).

Cover Stories

A cover story is the second kind of legal lie that police routinely tell on paper, in court, and to colleagues. Like most case stories, cover stories are constructed using sub-cultural nuances to make retelling the dynamics of encounters legally rational. Maintaining the capacity to produce a cover story is viewed as an essential skill required to protect against disciplinary action.

A cover story may involve the manipulation of legal and departmental rules, or taken-for-granted-knowledge regarding a neighborhood, actions of people and things. A common cover story involves failure to respond to a radio call. Every officer knows, for example, that some districts have radio "dead spots" where radio transmissions do not reach. If "radio" (central communications) calls an officer who doesn't respond or accept, "pick up the job," radio will usually recall. If he still doesn't respond, another officer typically takes the job to cover for him, or a friendly dispatcher may assign the job to another unit. However, if radio assigns the same job to the same car a third time and the unit still doesn't accept the job, the officer may be subject to formal disciplinary action. One acceptable account for temporary unavailability (for whatever reason) is to claim that one's radio malfunctioned or that one was in a "dead spot" (see Rubinstein 1973; Manning 1988).

The most common cover stories involving criminal matters are constructed to protect the officer against charges of brutality or homicide. Such cover stories serve to bridge the gap between the normal use of force which characterizes the informal world of the street and its legal use as defined by the court.

Self-protection is the presumed justification for cover stories. Since officers often equate verbal challenges with actual physical violence, both of which are grounds for retaliatory violence, either may underlie a story.[10] Threats of harm to self, partner, or citizens, are especially powerful bases for rationalizations. Even an officer who is believed by colleagues to use brutal force and seen as a poor partner as a result, is expected to lie to protect himself (see Hunt 1985; Waegel 1984). He or she would be considered odd, or even untrustworthy, if he or she did not. There is an interaction between violence and lying understood by police standards.

In the following account, the officer who fired his weapon exceeded "normal" force and committed a "bad shooting" (see Van Maanen 1980). Few officers would condone the shooting of an unarmed boy who they did not see commit a crime. Nevertheless, the officers participate in the construction of a cover story to protect their colleague against disciplinary action and justify it on the basis of self-defense and loyalty. Officers arrived at a scene that had been described mistakenly in a radio call as a "burglary in progress" (in fact, boys were stripping a previously stolen car). Since this is a call with arrest potential, it drew several police vehicles and officers soon began to chase the suspect(s):

Then they get into a back yard chasing one kid. The kid starts running up a rain spout like he's a spider man, and one of the cops took a shot at him. So now they're all panicky because the kid made it to the roof and he let out a scream and the cops thought that they hit him. And that was a bad shooting! What would you think if you was that kid's mother? Not only did they not have an open property, but they don't know if it's a stolen car at all. Well, when they shot the kid I gave them an excuse by mistake, inadvertently. I was on the other side of the place with my partner when I heard the one shot. [The officer telling the story is on one side of an iron gate, and another officer J.J. was on the other side. He kicks open the gate, thinking it is locked. It is not locked and swings wildly open, striking J.J. in the head] . . .

J.J. keeps stepping backward like he wanted to cry . . . like he was in a daze. "It's all right, it's not bleeding." I says to him . . . like he was stunned.

So then the Sergeant gets to the scene and asks what happened, cause this shot has been fired, and the kid screamed, and you figure some kid's been hit and he's up on the roof.

They gotta explain this dead kid and the shot to the sergeant when he gets there. So J.J. and Eddy discuss this. Eddy was the cop who'd fired the shot at the kid climbing up the rain spout, and all of a sudden they decide to claim he got hit with something in the head, and J.J. yells, "I'm hit, I'm hit." Then Eddy, thinking his partner's been shot, fires a shot at the kid. So they reported this all to the Captain and J.J. gets reprimanded for yelling "I'm shot" when he said, "I'm hit."

J.J. was never involved at all, but he just says this to cover for Eddy.

Meanwhile, the fire department is out there looking on the roof for the kid and they never found him so you figure he never got hit.

Here, the officer telling the story demonstrates his solidarity with colleagues by passively validating (refusing to discredit) the construction of an episode created by collusion between two other officers. The moral ambiguity of participation in such a troublesome lie is recognized and indicated by the interviewed officer. He disclaims responsibility for his involvement in the lie by insisting that he was not at the scene of the shooting and only "by mistake . . . inadvertently . . . gave them [the other officers] an excuse" used to create the cover story. In such morally ambiguous situations, individual officers remain in some moral tension. Note the officers' role-taking capacity, empathy, and concern for the generalized other when he asks in the vignette what the interviewer's thoughts would be if " . . . you was that kid's mother?" Such views may conflict with those of peers and supervisors. Moral tensions also arise in situations producing case stories.

The Morally Ambiguous Lie in a Case Story

Occasionally, officers cannot fully neutralize their sense of self-responsibility in the context of the police role. Their lies remain troubling in a moral sense. Such lies suggest the moral limits of pragmatism within the police, but in this case, the lie may be also a sign of the youth and gender of the officer involved. In the following example, a five-year veteran police officer experiences a profound moral dilemma as a result of pressures to frame a boy for a burglary she did not see him commit and did not believe he had committed. She refuses, even under peer and supervisory officers' pressure to do so, to produce a case story lie. Refusing to lie in this instance does not constitute a violation of police officers' sense of mutual obligation since she does not jeopardize peers. She sets the scene by noting that she and her partner are talking to John near his butcher shop when Frankie, a powerful and well-connected community member, approaches her and wants her to watch his shop. He claims a guy is trying to pass a bad check. She continues:

Well, Frankie's a close friend of the Police Commissioner and his sister's married to the owner of a drug manufacturing company. He donated a lot of money to the mayor's political campaign. . . . The police commissioner vacations at Frankie's sister's summer home in [an elite resort location]. . . . Frankie has "a lot of pull" and we [the police] sometimes call ourselves "Frankie's private little army."

Anyway, I tell Frankie, "O.K. I'll watch the store." But I don't think anything's really gonna happen. Frankie's just jealous because I'm spending more time with John than with him. Anyway, I go in the butcher shop and talk to John and when I come out, I hear Frankie screaming, "Stop him, stop him!" I respond, "Stop who?" Frankie says, "Stop the guy walking with the bag." I see a black kid walking away from the store with a bag in his hand and I call him over. I ask Frankie "What's going on?" He responds, "Something's fishy, something fishy's going on." At this point, the kid opens the bag in front of me and there's nothing in it and I search the kid.... The so called bad check that the kid was trying to cash at Frankie's store turned out to be a valid money order. I ask the kid to come over to the car and make out a ped stop. Thank God, I made up a good ped stop.... I got all the information on the kid.

At this point a "man with a gun" [call] comes over the radio. As no one else picks up the job, we take it. It was unfounded and I tell my partner that we'd better go back and check on Frankie because there might be trouble. When we return I ask Frankie, "Is everything all right?" He responds, "No it isn't." I say, "What's wrong?" Frankie says, "I told you he took something." I say, "That's not good enough, you have to tell me what he took ... not that 'something's fishy and he must have taken something.'... Did you see him take anything?" Frankie responds, "Three radios."

I go inside the appliance store to see the missing radios and there are a number of radios on a shelf way above the counter where it would be difficult for anyone to reach them, particularly a kid. I ask Frankie if he wants me to take the report or if he would prefer a regular district car to do it. He tells me, "You take it!" I take a report and right away call a 43rd district car to take it into the detectives.

An hour later, I got a call to go to the district. The captain asks me again, "What did you do to Frankie?" I tell him, "nothing." The captain asks me again, "What did you do to Frankie?" I say "nothing," and tell him exactly what had occurred at the incident. The captain says, "Did you run him [the suspect] through the computer?" I say, "No, I didn't ... because he had legitimate identification." The captain then tells me, "Well, you better get your story together because Frankie's going before the Board of Inquiry. You fucked up. Now, tomorrow you're gonna apologize!" I say, "But if I apologize, it makes it seem like I did something wrong. I did nothing wrong." The captain adds, "Don't argue with me, I told you what you're gonna do."

An hour later, I receive a call from the Division detective and he wants to know my side of the story. I tell him what happened. The detective says, "Well, we have to put out a warrant for the kid's arrest." I say, "For what?" The detective explains, "Believe me, the only reason this kid is getting locked up is because it's Frankie.... Have you ever been burnt by Frankie? Do you know who Frankie is?"

The detective then asks, "Will you go to court?" I say, "Why should I go to court, I didn't make the arrest." The detective says, "Well, you're the key to the identification of the kid." I respond, "O.K. you send me to court and I'll make the asshole out of him that he is." The detective then says, "O.K. if I'm not man enough to stand this up in court, then I won't ask you to do it.... Let the old bastard do it himself."

Later, I'm called back into the Captain's office ... and he tells me that "You're in for it now ... the detectives have put out a warrant for the kid's arrest and that makes you look foolish...." He then orders me to tell my story again. I tell it again. Finally, I say, "I didn't lock the kid up because I had no probable cause and to this day, I have no probable cause." The Captain warns me, "Well, you're going to the Board of Inquiry and there's nothing you can say that will get you out of this one.... I hope your partner's a good front man." I told him, "My partner don't need to lie."

In this incident, the officer is unwilling, in spite of quite direct threats and pressures, to neutralize her felt responsibility by constructing a case story lie. She believed that the boy was innocent and did not believe that "higher truth" was served by participating in a lie that would have framed the boy and saved Frankie's face. She also thought her lie would facilitate the conviction of the boy for burglary, an offense that was so serious that injury to him could not be denied. The officer not only refused to lie but agreed to testify for the boy if subpoenaed to appear in court.

This ambiguous lie highlights several important subpoints. The officer clung to a version of the situation that denied the relevance of lying, and featured her view of the facts, her duty and her distrust of Frankie. The pressure to lie illustrated here makes evident some divergence of opinions about what is acceptable practice by rank and function. She refuses to lie in part because neither she nor her partner were at fault in her eyes (in contrast to the other examples in this article in which officers understood that both the public and themselves viewed a story as a lie), and her refusal does not jeopardize other officers. The officer first is confronted by her Captain who tells her she "fucked up" and should apologize. He implies that she should agree with Frankie's view (which she, in turn, views as a lie), be prepared to apologize, and to go before a Board of Inquiry. The division detective is ambivalent and unsure of what to do, and passes responsibility on to her. He asks her if she will go to court. The Captain again calls her in and by telling her that a warrant has been issued by detectives, i.e., that there is probable cause in the case, and that she will look foolish for persisting in her story. He does not go into the details of the case with her, just listens to her story and then implies that she is lying and that her partner will have to lie for her before the Board of Inquiry.

While officers are oriented to peers and their sergeants and are sensitive to those loyalties (Cain 1973), administrative officers may justify their actions with regard to higher political obligations, organizational pressures or even loyalty to the Police Commissioner or the Mayor (even though such politicians may have no direct involvement in the case). If a case involves for an officer such higher loyalties and patronage as well as political corruption, there is more to be lost by *not* lying.[11] Detectives are more cynical and view their role as mediating between the street realities and those of the courtroom. Their standards for judging normal lies differ from those of uniformed officers. This patrol officer, however, defined her loyalties in terms of her immediate peers and the public rather than officials whom she viewed as corrupt. Rank, age, and other factors not explored here may mediate an officer's relationship with the community, his/her allegiance to the police department, and sense of right and wrong.

CONCLUSION

This ethnographic analysis relies principally upon the perspective of the officers observed and interviewed. It draws, however, on broad ethnographic accounts or general formulations of the police mandate and tasks. We attempt to integrate the pressures inherent in the inevitable negotiation within hierarchical systems between official expectations and roles, and one's individual sense of self. Officers learn how to define and control the public and other officers, and to negotiate meanings. The social constructions or lies which arise result from situational integration of organizational, political and moral pressures. These are not easily captured in rules, norms, or values. Repeatedly, officers must negotiate organizational realities *and* maintain self-worth. Police lies, serving in part to maintain a viable self, are surrounded by cultural assumptions and designations, a social context which defines normal or acceptable lies and distinguishes them from those deviant or marginal to good practice. The meanings imputed to the concepts "lie," "lying," and "truth" are negotiated and indicate or connote subtle intergroup relationships. In a crisis, ability to display solidarity by telling a proper and effective lie is highly valued and rewarded. The ironic epithet "police liar" is neutralized. Subtle redefinition of truth includes forms of group-based honesty that are unrecognized by legal standards or by the standards of outsiders. These findings have implications that might be further researched.

Lying is a feature of everyday life found in a variety of personal, occupational and political interactions. Although telling the full truth may be formally encouraged throughout life, it is not always admired or rewarded. Neither truth nor lies are simple and uniform; cultural variation exists in the idea of normal lying and its contrast conception. Those who continue to tell the truth and do not understand communications as complex negotiations of formal and informal behavioral norms, find themselves in social dilemmas, and are vulnerable to the variety of labels used in everyday life like "tactless," "undersocialized," "deviant," or "mentally ill." The application of the label is contingent upon taken-for-granted modes of deception that structure interpersonal relations. As the last few years have shown, given the impossible mandate of the police, certain police tasks are more highly visible, e.g., drug enforcement, and even greater pressure to lie may emerge. Thus, the mandate is shaped and patterned by tasks as well as general social expectations; the sources of lying may differ as well.

The cultural grounds explored here are features of any organization which lies as a part of its routine activities, such as government agencies carrying out domestic intelligence operations and covert foreign activities. Standards of truth and falsehood drawn from everyday life do not hold here, and this shifting ground of fact and reality is often difficult to grasp and hold for both insiders and outsiders. As a result, organization members, like the police, develop sophisticated and culturally sanctioned mechanisms for neutralizing the guilt and responsibility that troublesome and even morally ambiguous lying may often entail. In time, accounts which retrospectively justify and excuse a lie may become techniques of neutralization which prospectively facilitate the construction of new lies with ready-made justifications. When grounds for lying are well-known in advance, it takes a self-reflective act to tell the truth, rather than to passively accept and use lies when they are taken-for-granted and expected. Police, like politicians, look to "internal standards" and practices to pin down the meaning of events that resonate with questions of public morality and propriety (Katz 1977). When closely examined in a public inquiry, the foreground of everyday internal standards may become merely the background for a public scandal. Normal lies, when revealed and subjected to public standards, can become the basis for scandals. This may be the first occasion on which members of the organization recognize their potential to be seen in such a fashion.

Finally, the extent to which an organization utilizing lies or heavily dependent upon them perceives that it is "under siege" varies. In attempts to shore up their mandate, organizations may tacitly justify lying. As a result, the organization may increase its isolation, lose public trust and credibility, and begin to believe its own lies. This differentially occurs within policing, across departments, and in agencies of control generally. Such dynamics are suggested by this analysis.

Acknowledgment

20 June 89. Revision of a paper presented by the senior author to The Society for the Study of Social Problems, New York, 1986. We acknowledge the very useful comments from this journal's reviewers as well as from Betsy Cullum-Swan, and Peter and Patti Adler.

Notes

1. The many social functions of lying, a necessary correlate of trust and symbolic communication generally, are noted elsewhere (Ekman 1985; Simmel 1954; Manning 1977). Our focus is restricted. We do not discuss varieties of concealment, falsification and leakage (Ekman 1985, pp. 28–29), nor interpersonal dynamics, such as the consequence of a sequence of lies and cover lies that often occur. We omit the case in which the target, such as a theater audience or someone conned, is prepared in advance to accept lies (Ekman 1984, p. 28). Nor do we discuss in detail horizontal or vertical collusions within organizations that generate and sustain lying (e.g., Honeycombe 1974).

2. We do not distinguish "the lie" from the original event, since we are concerned with verbal rationalizations in the sense employed by Mills (1940), Lindesmith and Strauss (1956) and Scott and Lyman (1968). We cluster what might be called accounts for lies (lies about lies found in the interview material included here) with lies, and argue that the complexity of the formulations, and their embeddedness in any instance (the fact that a story may include several excuses, and justifications, and may include how these, in turn, were presented to a judge) makes it misleading to adhere to a strict typology of lies such as routine vs. non-routine, case lies (both justifications and excuses) vs. cover stories (both justifications and excuses), and troublesome vs. not troublesome lies. If each distinction were worked out in a table, as one reader noted, omitting ambiguous lies, at least 16 categories of lies would result. After considering internal distinctions among lies in policing, we concluded that a typology would

suggest a misleading degree of certainty and clarity. More ethnographic material is required to refine the categories outlined here.

3. Police organization, courts, and the law permit sanctioned freedom to redefine the facts of a case, the origins of the case, the bases of the arrest and the charge, the number of offenders and the number of violations. Like many public officials, they are allowed to lie when public well-being is at issue (for example, posing as drug dealers, buying and selling drugs, lying about their personal biographies and so on. See Manning 1980). Officers are protected if they lie in order to enter homes, to encourage people to confess, and to facilitate people who would otherwise be committing crimes to commit them. They have warrant to misrepresent, dissemble, conceal, and reveal as routine aspects of an investigation.

4. Evidence further suggests, in a point we do not examine here, that departments differ in the support given for lies. This may be related to legalistic aspects of the social organization of police departments (cf. Wilson 1968, Ch. 6). Ironically, for members of specialized units like "sting operations" or narcotics, the line between truth and lies becomes so blurred that according to Ekman's definition (the liar must know the truth and intend to lie), they are virtually always "telling the truth." Furthermore, as noted above, such units are more vulnerable to public criticism because they are held to unrealistic standards, and feel greater pressure to achieve illegally what cannot be accomplished legally. Marx (1988) argues that increased use of covert deceptive operations leads to further penetration of private life, confusion of public standards, and reduced expectations of police morality.

5. She spent some 12 weeks in recruit classes at the academy. For fifteen months, she rode as a non-uniformed research observer, usually in the front seat of a one officer car, from 4–midnight and occasionally on midnight to eight shifts. Although she rode with veteran officers for the first few weeks in order to learn official procedures, the remainder of the time was spent with rookie officers. Follow-up interviews were conducted several years after the completion of the initial 18 months of observation.

6. Typically, recruits were successful in calming the "psychotic" actor when they demonstrated convincingly that they shared the psychotic's delusion and would rescue him/her from his/her persecutors by, for instance, threatening to shoot them. Such techniques were justified scientifically by trained psychologists who also stressed their practical use to avoid violence in potentially volatile situations.

7. Previous research has shown how detailed the knowledge is of officers of how and why to lie, and it demonstrates that trainees are taught to lie by specific instructions and examples (see Harris 1973; McClure 1986; Fielding 1988).

8. Technically, adding facts one recalls later, even in court, are not the basis for lies. Lies, in our view, must be intended.

9. This is taken verbatim from an interview, and thus several rather interesting linguistic turns (especially changes in perspective) are evidenced. Analysis of this sociolinguistically might suggest how this quote replicates in microcosm the problem officers have in maintaining a moral self. They dance repeatedly along the edges of at least two versions of the truth.

10. Waegel (1984) explores the retrospective and prospective accounts police use to excuse and justify the use of force. However, he does not distinguish accounts told by colleagues which are viewed as true by the speaker and those told to representatives of the legal order which are viewed as lies and fit the description of a cover story. For example, the account of accidental discharge which Waegel perceives as a denial of responsibility may also be a cover story which itself is justified as "self defense" against formal reprimand. In contrast, other police excuses and justifications invoked to account for the use of force are often renditions of events that present the officer in the morally favorable light rather than actual lies (see Van Maanen 1980; Hunt 1985; Waegel 1984). Whether the police categorize their use of force as "normal" or "brutal" (Hunt 1985) also structures the moral assessment of a lie, a point which Waegel also overlooks. Thus, acts of normal force which can be excused or justified with reference to routine accounting practices may necessitate the construction of cover stories which became morally neutral by virtue of the act they disguise. Other acts of violence viewed as demonstrating incompetence or brutality may not be excused or justified according to routine accounting practices. Although cover stories in such cases are perceived as rational, they may not provide moral protection for the officer because the lie takes on aspects of moral stigma associated with the act of violence which it conceals.

11. Supervisors and higher administrators, of course, collude in maintaining the viability of lies because they *share* the beliefs of officers that it is not possible to police by the book, and that one should not rock the boat and should keep your head down (Van Maanen 1975). It is

viewed as impossible to manage routine tasks without lying both to colleagues and supervisors (Punch 1985). The working bases of corruption are thus laid, as well as the potential seen in so many corruption scandals of cover-ups, lies about lies, and vertical and horizontal collusion in lying as seen in both the Watergate and the Iran-Contra affairs.

References

Bittner, E. 1970. *Functions of the Police in an Urban Society.* Bethesda: NIMH.
———. 1974. "A Theory of Police: Florence Nightingale in Pursuit of Willie Sutton." In *The Potential for Reform of Criminal Justice,* edited by H. Jacob. Beverly Hills: Sage.
Blumberg, A. 1967. *Criminal Justice.* Chicago: Quadrangle Books.
Buckner, H. T. 1978. "Transformations of Reality in the Legal Process," *Social Research* 37:88–101.
Cain, M. 1973. *Society and the Policeman's Role.* London: Routledge & Kegan Paul.
Chatterton, M. 1975. "Organizational Relationships and Processes in Police Work: A Case Study of Urban Policing." Unpublished Ph.D. thesis, University of Manchester.
———. 1979. "The Supervision of Patrol Work Under the Fixed Points System." In *The British Police,* edited by S. Holdaway. London: Edward Arnold.
Ekman, P. 1985. *Telling Lies.* New York: W.W. Norton.
Ericson, R. and C. Shearing. 1986. "The Scientification of the Police." In *The Knowledge Society,* edited by G. Bohme and N. Stehr. Dordrecht and Boston: D. Reidel.
Fielding, N. 1988. *Joining Forces.* London: Tavistock.
Goffman, E. 1959. *The Presentation of Self in Everyday Life.* New York: Doubleday Anchor Books.
Harris, R. 1973. *The Police Academy.* New York: Wiley.
Honeycombe, G. 1974. *Adam's Tale.* London: Arrow Books.
Hunt, J. C. 1985. "Police Accounts of Normal Force." *Urban Life* 13:315–342.
———. 1984. "The Development of Rapport Through the Negotiation of Gender in Fieldwork among the Police." *Human Organization.*
Katz, J. 1977. "Cover-up and Collective Integrity: on the Natural Antagonisms of Authority Internal and External to Organizations." *Social Problems* 25:3–17.
Klockars, C. 1983. "The Dirty Harry Problem." *Annals of the American Academy of Political and Social Science* 452 (November):33–47.
———. 1984. "Blue Lies and Police Placebos." *American Behavioral Scientist* 27:529–544.
Lindesmith, A. and A. Strauss. 1956. *Social Psychology.* New York: Holt, Dryden.
McBarnett, D. 1981. *Conviction.* London: MacMillan.
McClure, J. 1986. *Cop World.* New York: Laurel/Dell.
Maines, D. 1982. "In Search of Mesostructure: Studies in the Negotiated Order." *Urban Life* 11:267–279.
Manning, P. K. 1974. "Police Lying." *Urban Life* 3:283–306.
———. 1977. *Police Work.* Cambridge: MA: M.I.T. Press.
———. 1980. *Narc's Game.* Cambridge: MA: M.I.T. Press.
———. 1988. *Symbolic Communication: Signifying Calls and the Police Response.* Cambridge, MA: M.I.T. Press.

Marx, G. 1988. *Undercover. Policework in America: Problems and Paradoxes of a Necessary Evil.* Berkeley: University of California Press.

Mills, C. W. 1940. "Situated Actions and Vocabularies of Motive." *ASR* 6 (December): 904–913.

Punch, M. 1985. *Conduct Unbecoming.* London: Tavistock.

Reiss, A. J., Jr. 1971. *The Police and the Public.* New Haven: Yale University Press.

———. 1974. "Discretionary Justice." Pp. 679–699 in *The Handbook of Criminal Justice,* edited by Daniel Glaser. Chicago: Rand McNally.

Rubinstein, J. 1973. *City Police.* New York: Farrar, Straus and Giroux.

Scott, M. B. and S. Lyman. 1968. "Accounts." *American Sociological Review* 33:46–62.

Simmel, G. 1954. *The Society of Georg Simmel,* edited by Kurt Wolff. Glencoe: Free Press.

Skolnick, J. 1966. *Justice Without Trial.* New York: Wiley.

Stinchcombe, A. 1964. "Institutions of Privacy in the Determination of Police Administrative Practice." *American Journal of Sociology* 69:150–160.

Sudnow, D. 1965. "Normal Crimes: Sociological Features of the Penal Code in a Public Defender Office." *Social Problems* 12:255–276.

Sykes, G. M. and D. Matza. 1957. "Techniques of Neutralization: A Theory of Delinquency." *American Sociological Review* 22:664–670.

Van Maanen, J. 1974. "Working the Street..." in *Prospects for Reform in Criminal Justice,* edited by H. Jacob. Newbury Park, CA: Sage.

———. 1975. "Police Socialization: A Longitudinal Examination of Job Attitudes in an Urban Police Department." *Administrative Science Quarterly* 20 (June): 207–228.

———. 1980. "Beyond Account: The Personal Impact of Police Shootings." *Annals of the American Academy of Political and Social Science* 342: 145–156.

Waegel, W. 1984. "How Police Justify the Use of Deadly Force." *Social Problems* 32: 144–155.

Westley, W. 1970. *Violence and the Police.* Cambridge: MA: M.I.T. Press.

Wilson, J. Q. 1968. *Varieties of Police Behavior.* Cambridge: Harvard University Press.

Wilson, J. Q. and G. Kelling. 1982. "The Police and Neighborhood Safety: Broken Windows." *Atlantic* 127 (March): 29–38.

26 / The Police and the Black Male

ELIJAH ANDERSON

The police, in the Village-Northton as elsewhere, represent society's formal, legitimate means of social control.[1] Their role includes protecting law-abiding citizens from those who are not law-abiding, by preventing crime and by apprehending likely criminals. Precisely how the police fulfill the public's expectations is strongly related to how they view the neighborhood and the people who live there. On the streets, color-coding often works to confuse race, age, class, gender, incivility, and criminality, and it expresses itself most concretely in the person of the anonymous black male. In doing their job, the police often become willing parties to this general color-coding of the public environment, and related distinctions, particularly those of skin color and gender, come to convey definite meanings. Although such coding may make the work of the police more manageable, it may also fit well with their own presuppositions regarding race and class relations, thus shaping officers' perceptions of crime "in the city." Moreover, the anonymous black male is usually an ambiguous figure who arouses the utmost caution and is generally considered dangerous until he proves he is not.

In July 1988, in the area just south of the Village, my own automobile was taken from its parking place on a main thoroughfare. Convinced that a thief had stolen the car, I quickly summoned the police. Within ten minutes of my calling 911 a police car arrived, driven by a middle-aged white officer. He motioned for me to get in. Because the front seat was cluttered with notebooks and papers, I opened the back door and got in on the right-hand side. I introduced myself to Officer John Riley, mentioning that I was a professor, mainly to help establish myself with him. He was courteous, commiserated with me, then asked for the basic information. What time did I park the car? Could a friend or relative have taken it? During our exchanges I said that my family and I were planning a trip to the Midwest the next day to attend a family reunion, and I could feel his empathy. He said he would call in the report right away, and since the case was "hot," meaning the theft had just occurred, there might be a good chance of getting the car back soon, if not that very night. He then reported the theft and put out a bulletin. Into his radio he said, "Be on the lookout for a maroon 1982 Oldsmobile four-door sedan, heading northwest on Warrington Avenue."

Every police car in the city, particularly those in the same district, was thus given a description of my car and would presumably be on the lookout for it. I was pleased with his attention to my misfortune.

As we sat in the patrol car, the officer interviewed me; and I took the opportunity to interview him as well. We spoke about policing the local area, about car thefts, and about the general crime rate. We discussed the characteristics of car thieves, robbers, muggers, and other antisocial persons in the area. I did not tell him I was a sociologist. I think he thought of himself as simply doing his job, treating me as just another victim of local crime—which I was indeed.

During this conversation the police officer seemed to be feeling me out, attempting to get a fix on me as a person, perhaps wondering where I stood politically. At one point we discussed jobs and crime and their relation to one another. Then the officer mentioned the way "he" had messed up this city and how the "big boys" had already gotten to "him." I took this as implicit criticism of the city's black mayor, so I deferred and listened intently, thinking I could learn something about his attitude concerning local city politics. But I also did not want to alienate this person who was trying to find my car. Hence I played along, pointing out that the mayor's stock had declined in the black community, that even many blacks were not satisfied with his performance.

After this conversational give and take, the officer seemed favorably impressed. He appeared genuinely sympathetic with my fear of missing my family reunion. More than once he suggested that I try to forget the theft for now, rent a Lincoln Town Car like his own, and drive to the reunion. I demurred, insisting that I wanted my own car back as soon as possible.

Through our conversation, he seemed to open up and trust me. Then he offered, "Listen, why don't we drive around and see if we can spot your car. Maybe some kids just took it for a joyride and ditched it." I was appreciative and encouraged him, but I stayed in the backseat, wondering where he would take me to look for my car. We headed north through the Village, across Bellwether, and into Northton. After driving up and down a number of the familiar streets of Northton, we headed for "the projects," about a mile northwest of the Village. When I asked why he had chosen to come here, he replied, "This is where they usually take them [cars]." It seemed he had a definite idea who he was talking about. *They* were the thieves, the robbers, the muggers, and generally the people who cause trouble. And they lived in Northton. As we proceeded, we passed numerous street corner groups of young black men, with some young women among them. Many were simply loitering. He knew some of them and greeted them in a familiar way as we slowly drove past. He would wave and say, "How y'all doin'" in what sounded like affected Black English. By showing this level of familiarity, he let me know he knew the community: it was to some degree his turf.

As we drove through the projects and the neighborhoods of Northton, ostensibly looking for my car, I felt strange—as though I was somehow identified with "the enemy"—though I was safe in the backseat. Also, when a young black man is sitting in a police car, most people perceive him to be in custody, in some kind of trouble, regardless of the real circumstances. This seems to go with the general definition of affairs in the neighborhood—that to be black and male, particularly when young, is to be suspect; that the young man must prove he is law-abiding. Even though I was sitting in the backseat, so that many onlookers might know the officer considered me "safe" or a victim to be aided, this reality goes strongly against the common sense of the community: a young black male is a suspect until he proves he is not. The burden of proof is not easily lifted.

After riding around Northton for about twenty minutes, we met another police car. The driver, who was white, middle-aged, and alone, had stopped at the corner, preparing to make a right-hand turn. My driver turned left onto the same street, and both stopped with the two cars facing in opposite directions. As they exchanged pleasantries, the second policeman kept looking at me with puzzlement. Black male alone in rear seat. Officer Riley felt the need to explain me and said, "Oh, somebody stole his car, and we're out looking for it. It's a maroon '82 Delta 88." The other policeman nodded. The two continued to make small talk, but the second officer could not keep his eyes off me. I felt that if I made a false move he would come after me. In essence the policeman played his role, and I played mine; notwithstanding that I was a victim of crime, my color and gender seemed to outweigh other claims.

Such roles are expected by the young black men of the neighborhood, who have a clear sense of who they are and what they mean to the police. It is from this knowledge that they infer how to act, and how the police will act, believing both must behave according to an elaborate script of the streets. Much of this may be viewed as symbolic display, but it works to maintain a certain ordering of affairs in the public arena.

In the presence of police officers, who clearly have the upper hand, black youths check themselves. They defer to the police or try to avoid them. And some black men, because of their profound distrust of the criminal justice system, say they would never allow a white policeman to arrest them. A young black male told me, "A white policeman would never go out of his way for a black man."

After about fifteen minutes the policemen finished their talk and said their good-byes. Meanwhile I was simply a nonperson, not their equal, and my time and business were clearly secondary in their minds. As we drove slowly up and down the streets, Officer Riley continued to nod, speak, and wave to people. Finally he gave up, saying he was "sorry, but maybe we'll have some luck tonight or tomorrow. I'll stay on it, and hopefully we'll get your car back." He then offered me a ride home, which I gladly accepted.

On the way Officer Riley talked about his own misfortunes with theft, attempting to commiserate with me. I saw one of my white colleagues on a street corner near my house, reading a newspaper while waiting for a bus. As the patrol car pulled up to the light, he casually looked over at me, looked away, then looked again with astonishment. "Eli! Is that you? Are you okay? What's the trouble?" I quickly assured him that everything was all right, that I was with the policeman because my car had been stolen. But my colleague looked unconvinced. The light changed, and Officer Riley drove toward my house. He again expressed his regret for my predicament but said he was hopeful. We parted company, and I never saw him again. But the next morning at 9:00 I got a call that my car had been found and I could come and retrieve it.

There are some who charge—and as this account indicates, perhaps with good reason—that the police are primarily agents of the middle class who are working to make the area more hospitable to middle-class people at the expense of the lower classes. It is obvious that the police assume whites in the community are at least middle class and are trustworthy on the streets. Hence the police may be seen primarily as protecting "law-abiding" middle-class whites against anonymous "criminal" black males.

To be white is to be seen by the police—at least superficially—as an ally, eligible for consideration and for much more deferential treatment than that accorded blacks in general. This attitude may be grounded in the backgrounds of the police themselves. Many have grown up in Eastern City's "ethnic" neighborhoods.[2] They may serve what they perceive as their own class and neighborhood interests, which often translates as keeping blacks "in their place"—away from neighborhoods that are socially defined as "white." In trying to do their job, the police appear to engage in an informal policy of monitoring young black men as a means of controlling crime, and often they seem to go beyond the bounds of duty. The following field note shows what pressures and racism young black men in the Village may endure at the hands of the police:

At 8:30 on a Thursday evening in June I saw a police car stopped on a side street near the Village. Beside the car stood a policeman with a young black man. I pulled up behind the police car and waited to see what would happen. When the policeman released the young man, I got out of my car and asked the youth for an interview.

"So what did he say to you when they stopped you? What was the problem?" I asked. "I was just coming around the corner, and he stopped me, asked me what was my name, and all that. And what I had in my bag. And where I was coming from. Where I lived, you know, all the basic stuff, I guess. Then he searched me down and, you know, asked me who were the supposedly tough guys around here? That's about it. I couldn't tell him who they are. How do I know? Other gang members could, but I'm not from a gang, you know. But he tried to put me in a gang bag, though." "How old are you?" I asked. "I'm seventeen, I'll be eighteen next month." "Did he give any reason for stopping you?" "No, he didn't. He just wanted my address, where I lived, where I was coming from, that kind of thing. I don't have no police record or nothin'. I guess he stopped me on principle, 'cause I'm black." "How does that make you feel?" I asked. "Well, it doesn't bother me too much, you know, as long as I know that I hadn't done nothin', but I guess it just happens around here. They just stop young black guys and ask 'em questions, you know. What can you do?"

On the streets late at night, the average young black man is suspicious of others he encounters, and he is particularly wary of the police. If he is dressed in the uniform of the "gangster," such as a black leather jacket, sneakers, and a "gangster cap," if he is carrying a radio or a suspicious bag (which may be confiscated), or if he is moving too fast or too slow, the police may stop him. As part of the routine, they search him and make him sit in the police car while they run a check to see whether there is a "detainer" on him. If there is nothing, he is allowed to go on his way. After this ordeal the youth is often left afraid, sometimes shaking, and uncertain about the area he had previously taken for granted. He is upset in part because he is painfully aware of how close he has come to being in "big trouble." He knows of other youths who have gotten into a "world of trouble" simply by being on the streets at the wrong time or when the police were pursuing a criminal. In these circumstances, particularly at night, it is relatively easy for one black man to be mistaken for another. Over the years, while walking through the neighborhood I have on occasion been stopped and questioned by police chasing a mugger, but after explaining myself I was released.

Many youths, however, have reason to fear such mistaken identity or harassment, since they might be jailed, if only for a short time, and would have to post bail money and pay legal fees to extricate themselves from the mess (Anderson 1986). When law-abiding blacks are ensnared by the criminal justice system, the scenario may proceed as follows. A young man is arbitrarily stopped by the police and questioned. If he cannot effectively negotiate with the officer(s), he may be accused of a crime and arrested. To resolve this situation he needs financial resources, which for him are in short supply. If he does not have money for an attorney, which often happens, he is left to a public defender who may be more interested in going along with the court system than in fighting for a poor black person. Without legal support, he may well wind up "doing time" even if he is innocent of the charges brought against him. The next time he is stopped for questioning he will have a record, which will make detention all the more likely.

Because the young black man is aware of many cases when an "innocent" black person was wrongly accused and detained, he develops an "attitude" toward the police. The street word for police is "the man," signifying a certain machismo, power, and authority. He becomes concerned when he notices "the man" in the community or when the police focus on him because he is outside his own neighborhood. The youth knows, or soon finds out, that he exists in a legally precarious state. Hence he is motivated to avoid the police, and his public life becomes severely circumscribed.

To obtain fair treatment when confronted by the police, the young man may wage a campaign for social regard so intense that at times it borders on obsequiousness. As one streetwise black youth said: "If you show a cop that you nice and not a smartass, they be nice to you. They talk to you like the man you are. You gonna get ignorant like a little kid, they gonna get ignorant with you." Young black males often are particularly deferential toward the police even when they are completely within their rights and have done nothing wrong. Most often this is not out of blind acceptance or respect for the "law," but because they know the police can cause them hardship. When confronted or arrested, they adopt a particular style of behavior to get on the policeman's good side. Some simply "go limp" or politely ask, "What seems to be the trouble, officer?" This pose requires a deference that is in sharp contrast with the youths' more usual image, but many seem to take it in stride or not even to realize it. Because they are concerned primarily with staying out of trouble, and because they perceive the police as arbitrary in their use of power, many defer in an equally arbitrary way. Because of these pressures, however, black youths tend to be especially mindful of the police and, when they are around, to watch their own behavior in public. Many have come to expect harassment and are inured to it; they simply tolerate it as part of living in the Village-Northton.

After a certain age, say twenty-three or twenty-four, a black man may no longer be stopped so often, but he continues to be the object of police scrutiny. As one twenty-seven-year-old black college graduate speculated:

> I think they see me with my little bag with papers in it. They see me with penny loafers on. I have a tie on, some days. They don't stop me so much now. See, it depends on the circumstances. If something goes down, and they hear that the guy had on a big black coat, I may be the one. But when I was younger, they could just stop me, carte blanche, any old time. Name taken, searched, and this went on endlessly. From the time I was about twelve until I was sixteen or seventeen, endlessly, endlessly. And I come from a lower-middle-class black neighborhood, OK, that borders a white neighborhood. One neighborhood is all black, and one is all white. OK, just because we were so close to that neighborhood, we were stopped endlessly. And it happened even more when we went up into a suburban community. When we would ride up and out to the suburbs, we were stopped every time we did it.
>
> If it happened today, now that I'm older, I would really be upset. In the old days when I was younger, I didn't know any better. You just expected it, you knew it was gonna happen. Cops would come up, "What you doing, where you coming from?" Say things to you. They might even call you nigger.

Such scrutiny and harassment by local police makes black youths see them as a problem to get beyond, to deal with, and their attempts affect their overall behavior. To avoid encounters with the man, some streetwise young men camouflage themselves, giving up the urban uniform and emblems that identify them as "legitimate" objects of police attention. They may adopt a more conventional presentation of self, wearing chinos, sweat suits, and generally more conservative dress. Some youths have been known to "ditch" a favorite jacket if they see others wearing one like it, because wearing it increases their chances of being mistaken for someone else who may have committed a crime.

But such strategies do not always work over the long run and must be constantly modified. For instance, because so many young ghetto blacks have begun to wear Fila and Adidas sweat suits as status symbols, such dress has become incorporated into the public image generally associated with young black males. These athletic suits, particularly the more expensive and colorful ones, along with high-priced sneakers, have become the leisure dress of successful drug dealers, and other youths will often mimic their wardrobe to "go for bad" in the quest for local esteem. Hence what was once a "square" mark of distinction approximating the conventions of the wider culture has been adopted by a neighborhood group devalued by that same culture. As we saw earlier, the young black male enjoys a certain power over fashion: whatever the collective peer group embraces can become "hip" in a manner the wider society may not desire (see Goffman 1963). These same styles then attract the attention of the agents of social control.

THE IDENTIFICATION CARD

Law-abiding black people, particularly those of the middle class, set out to approximate middle-class whites in styles of self-presentation in public, including dress and bearing. Such middle-class emblems, often viewed as "square," are not usually embraced by young working-class blacks. Instead, their connections with and claims on the institutions of the wider society seem to be symbolized by the identification card. The common identification card associates its holder with a firm, a corporation, a school, a union, or some other institution of substance and influence. Such a card, particularly from a prominent establishment, puts the police and others on notice that the youth is "somebody," thus creating an important distinction between a black man who can claim a connection with the wider society and one who is summarily judged as "deviant." Although blacks who are established in the middle class might take such cards for granted, many lower-class blacks, who continue to find it necessary to campaign for civil rights denied them because of skin color, believe that carrying an identification card brings them better treatment than is meted out to their less fortunate brothers and sisters. For them this link to the wider society, though often tenuous, is psychically and socially important. The young college graduate continues:

I know [how] I used to feel when I was enrolled in college last year, when I had an ID card. I used to hear stories about the blacks getting stopped over by the dental school, people having trouble sometimes. I would see that all the time. Young black male being stopped by the police. Young black male in handcuffs. But I knew that because I had that ID card I would not be mistaken for just somebody snatching a pocketbook, or just somebody being where maybe I wasn't expected be. See, even though I was intimidated by the campus police—I mean, the first time I walked into the security office to get my ID they all gave me the double take to see if I was somebody they were looking for. See, after I got the card, I was like, well, they can think that now, but I have this [ID card]. Like, see, late at night when I be walking around, and the cops be checking me out, giving me the looks, you know. I mean, I know guys, students, who were getting stopped all the time, sometimes by the same officer, even though they had the ID. And even they would say, "Hey, I got the ID, so why was I stopped?"

The cardholder may believe he can no longer be treated summarily by the police, that he is no longer likely to be taken as a "no count," to be prejudicially confused with that class of blacks "who are always causing trouble on the trolley." Furthermore, there is a firm belief that if the police stop a person who has a card, they cannot "do away with him without somebody coming to his defense." This concern should not be underestimated. Young black men trade stories about mistreatment at the hands of the police; a common one involves policemen who transport youths into rival gang territories and release them, telling them to get home the best way they can. From the youth's perspective, the card signifies a certain status in circumstances where little recognition was formerly available.

"DOWNTOWN" POLICE AND LOCAL POLICE

In attempting to manage the police—and by implication to manage themselves—some black youths have developed a working conception of the police in certain public areas of the Village-Northton. Those who spend a good amount of their time on these corners, and thus observing the police, have come to distinguish between the "downtown" police and the "regular" local police.

The local police are the ones who spend time in the area; normally they drive around in patrol cars, often one officer to a car. These officers usually make a kind of working peace with the young men on the streets; for example, they know the names of some of them and may even befriend a young boy. Thus they offer an image of the police department different from that displayed by the "downtown" police. The downtown police are distant, impersonal, and often actively looking for "trouble." They are known to swoop down arbitrarily on gatherings of black youths standing on a street corner; they might punch them around, call them names, and administer other kinds of abuse, apparently for sport. A young Northton man gave the following narrative about his experiences with the police.

And I happen to live in a violent part. There's a real difference between the violence level in the Village and the violence level in Northton. In the nighttime it's more dangerous over there.

It's so bad now, they got downtown cops over there now. They doin' a good job bringin' the highway patrol over there. Regular cops don't like that. You can tell that. They even try to emphasize to us the certain category. Highway patrol come up, he leave, they say somethin' about it. "We can do our job over here." We call [downtown police] Nazis. They about six feet eight, seven feet. We walkin', they jump out. "You run, and we'll blow your nigger brains out." I hate bein' called a nigger. I want to say somethin' but get myself in trouble.

When a cop do somethin', nothing happen to 'em. They come from downtown. From what I heard some of 'em don't even wear their real badge numbers. So you have to put up with that. Just keep your mouth shut when they stop you, that's all. Forget about questions, get against the wall, just obey 'em. "Put all that out right there"—might get rough with you now. They snatch you by the shirt, throw you against the wall, pat you hard, and grab you by the arms, and say, "Get outta here." They call you nigger this and little black this, and things like that. I take that. Some of the fellas get mad. It's a whole different world.

Yeah, they lookin' for trouble. They gotta look for trouble when you got five, eight police cars together and they laughin' and talkin', start teasin' people. One night we were at a bar, we read in the paper that the downtown cops comin' to straighten things out. Same night, three police cars, downtown cops with their boots on, they pull the sticks out, beatin' around the corner, chase into bars. My friend Todd, one of 'em grabbed him and knocked the shit out of him. He punched 'im, a little short white guy. They start a riot. Cops started that shit. Everybody start seein' how wrong the cops was—they start throwin' bricks and bottles, cussin' 'em out. They lock my boy up; they had to let him go. He was just standin' on the corner, they snatch him like that.

One time one of 'em took a gun and began hittin' people. My boy had a little hickie from that. He didn't know who the cop was, because there was no such thing as a badge number. They have phony badge numbers. You can tell they're tougher, the way they dress, plus they're bigger. They have boots, trooper pants, blond hair, blue eyes, even black [eyes]. And they seven feet tall, and six foot six inches and six foot eight inches. Big! They the rough cops. You don't get smart with them or they beat the shit out of you in front of everybody, they don't care.

We call 'em Nazis. Even the blacks among them. They ride along with 'em. They stand there and watch a white cop beat your brains out. What takes me out is the next day you don't see 'em. Never see 'em again, go down there, come back, and they ride right back downtown, come back, do their little dirty work, go back downtown, and put their real badges on. You see 'em with a forty-five or fifty-five number: "Ain't no such number here, I'm sorry, son." Plus, they got unmarked cars. No sense takin' 'em to court. But when that happened at that bar, another black cop from the sixteenth [local] district, ridin' a real car, came back and said, "Why don't y'all go on over to the sixteenth district and file a complaint? Them musclin' cops was wrong. Beatin' people." So about ten people went over there; sixteenth district knew nothin' about it. They come in unmarked cars, they must have been downtown cops. Some of 'em do it. Some of 'em are off duty, on their way home. District commander told us they do that. They have a patrol over there, but them cops from downtown have control of them cops. Have bigger ranks and bigger guns. They carry .357s and regular cops carry little .38s. Downtown cops are all around. They carry magnums.

Two cars the other night. We sittin' on the steps playing cards. Somebody called the cops. We turn around and see four regular police cars and two highway police cars. We drinkin' beer and playin' cards. Police get out and say you're gamblin'. We say we got nothin' but cards here, we got no money. They said all right, got back in their cars, and drove away. Downtown cops dressed up like troopers. That's intimidation. Damn!

You call a cop, they don't come. My boy got shot, we had to take him to the hospital ourselves. A cop said, "You know who did it?" We said no. He said, "Well, I hope he dies if y'all don't say nothin'." What he say that for? My boy said, "I hope your mother die," he told the cop right to his face. And I was grabbin' another cop, and he made a complaint about that. There were a lot of witnesses. Even the nurse behind the counter said the cop had no business saying nothin' like that. He said it loud, "I hope he dies." Nothin' like that should be comin' from a cop.

Such behavior by formal agents of social control may reduce the crime rate, but it raises questions about social justice and civil rights. Many of the old-time liberal white residents of the Village view the police with some ambivalence. They want their streets and homes defended, but many are convinced that the police manhandle "kids" and mete out an arbitrary form of "justice." These feelings make many of them reluctant to call the police when they are needed, and they may even be less than completely cooperative after a crime has been committed. They know that far too often the police simply "go out and pick up some poor black kid." Yet they do cooperate, if ambivalently, with these agents of social control.

In an effort to gain some balance in the emerging picture of the police in the Village-Northton, I interviewed local officers. The following edited conversation with Officer George Dickens (white) helps place in context the fears and concerns of local residents, including black males:

I'm sympathetic with the people who live in this neighborhood [the Village-Northton], who I feel are victims of drugs. There are a tremendous number of decent, hardworking people who are just trying to live their life in peace and quiet, not cause any problems for their neighbors, not cause any problems for themselves. They just go about their own business and don't bother anyone. The drug situation as it exists in Northton today causes them untold problems. And some of the young kids are involved in one way or another with this drug culture. As a result, they're gonna come into conflict even with the police they respect and have some rapport with.

We just went out last week on Thursday and locked up ten young men on Cherry Street, because over a period of about a week, we had undercover police officers making drug buys from those young men. This was very well documented and detailed. They were videotaped selling the drugs. And as a result, right now, if you walk down Cherry Street, it's pretty much a ghost town; there's nobody out. [Before, Cherry Street was notorious for drug traffic.] Not only were people buying drugs there, but it was a very active street. There's been some shock value as a result of all those arrests at one time.

Now, there's two reactions to that. The [television] reporters went out and interviewed some people who said, "Aw, the police overreacted, they locked up innocent people. It was terrible, it was harassment." One of the neighbors from Cherry Street called me on Thursday, and she was outraged. Because she said, "Officer, it's not fair. We've been working with the district for well over a year trying to solve some of the problems on Cherry Street." But most of the neighbors were thrilled that the police came and locked all those kids up. So you're getting two conflicting reactions here. One from the people that live there that just wanta be left alone, alright? Who are really being harassed by the drug trade and everything that's involved in it. And then you have a reaction from the people that are in one way or another either indirectly connected or directly connected, where they say, "You know, if a young man is selling drugs, to him that's a job." And if he gets arrested, he's out of a job. The family's lost their income. So they're not gonna pretty much want anybody to come in there to make arrests. So you've got contradicting elements of the community there. My philosophy is that we're going to try to make Northton livable. If that means we have to arrest some of the residents of Northton, that's what we have to do.

You talk to Tyrone Pitts, you know the group that they formed was formed because of a reaction to complaints against one of the officers of how the teenagers were being harassed. And it turned out that basically what he [the officer] was doing was harassing drug dealers. When Northton against Drugs actually formed and seemed to jell, they developed a close working relationship with the police here. For that reason, they felt the officer was doing his job.

I've been here eighteen months. I've seen this neighborhood go from... Let me say, this is the only place I've ever worked where I've seen a rapport between the police department and the general community like the one we have right now. I've never seen it anyplace else before coming here. And I'm not gonna claim credit because this happened while I happened to be here. I think a lot of different factors were involved. I think the community was ready to work with the police because of the terrible situation in reference to crack. My favorite expression when talking about crack is "crack changed everything." Crack changed the rules of how the police and the community have to interact with each other. Crack changed the rules about how the criminal justice system is gonna work, whether it works well or poorly. Crack is causing the prisons to be overcrowded. Crack is gonna cause the people that do drug rehabilitation to be overworked. It's gonna cause a wide variety of things. And I think the reason the rapport between the police and the community in Northton developed at the time it did is very simply that drugs to a certain extent made many areas in this city unlivable.

In effect the officer is saying that the residents, regardless of former attitudes, are now inclined to be more sympathetic with the police and to work with them. And at the same time, the police are more inclined to work with the residents. Thus, not only are the police and the black residents of Northton working together, but different groups in the Village and Northton are working with each other against drugs. In effect, law-abiding citizens are coming together, regardless of race, ethnicity, and class. He continues:

> Both of us [police and the community] are willing to say, "Look, let's try to help each other." The nice thing about what was started here is that it's spreading to the rest of the city. If we don't work together, this problem is gonna devour us. It's gonna eat us alive. It's a state of emergency, more or less.

In the past there was significant negative feeling among young black men about the "downtown" cops coming into the community and harassing them. In large part these feelings continue to run strong, though many young men appear to "know the score" and to be resigned to their situation, accommodating and attempting to live with it. But as the general community feels under attack, some residents are willing to forgo certain legal and civil rights and undergo personal inconvenience in hopes of obtaining a sense of law and order. The officer continues:

> Today we don't have too many complaints about police harassment in the community. Historically there were these complaints, and in almost any minority neighborhood in Eastern City where I ever worked there was more or less a feeling of that [harassment]. It wasn't just Northton; it was a feeling that the police were the enemy. I can honestly say that for the first time in my career I don't feel that people look at me like I'm the enemy. And it feels nice; it feels real good not to be the enemy, ha-ha. I think we [the police] realize that a lot of the problems here [in the Village-Northton] are related to drugs. I think the neighborhood realizes that too. And it's a matter of "Who are we gonna be angry with? Are we gonna be angry with the police because we feel like they're this army of occupation, or are we gonna argue with these people who are selling drugs to our kids and shooting up our neighborhoods and generally causing havoc in the area? Who deserves the anger more?" And I think, to a large extent, people of the Village-Northton decided it was the drug dealers and not the police.
>
> I would say there are probably isolated incidents where the police would stop a male in an area where there is a lot of drugs, and this guy may be perfectly innocent, not guilty of doing anything at all. And yet he's stopped by the police because he's specifically in that area, on that street corner where we know drugs are going hog wild. So there may be isolated incidents of that. At the same time, I'd say I know for a fact that our complaints against police in this division, the whole division, were down about 45 percent. If there are complaints, if there are instances of abuse by the police, I would expect that our complaints would be going up. But they're not; they're dropping.

Such is the dilemma many Villagers face when they must report a crime or deal in some direct way with the police. Stories about police prejudice against blacks are often traded at Village get-togethers. Cynicism about the effectiveness of the police mixed with community suspicion of their behavior toward blacks keeps middle-class Villagers from embracing the notion that they must rely heavily on the formal means of social control to maintain even the minimum freedom of movement they enjoy on the streets.

Many residents of the Village, especially those who see themselves as the "old guard" or "old-timers," who were around during the good old days when antiwar and antiracist protest was a major concern, sigh and turn their heads when they see the criminal justice system operating in the ways described here. They express hope that "things will work out," that tensions will ease, that crime will decrease and police behavior will improve. Yet as incivility and crime become increasing problems in the neighborhood, whites become less tolerant of anonymous blacks and more inclined to embrace the police as their heroes.

Such criminal and social justice issues, crystallized on the streets, strain relations between the newcomers and many of the old guard, but in the present context of drug-related crime and violence in the Village-Northton, many of the old-timers are adopting a "law and order" approach to crime and public safety, laying blame more directly on those they see as responsible for such crimes, though they retain some ambivalence. Newcomers can share such feelings with an increasing number of old-time "liberal" residents. As one middle-aged white woman who has lived in the Village for fifteen years said:

> When I call the police, they respond. I've got no complaints. They are fine for me. I know they sometimes mistreat black males. But let's face it, most of the crime is committed by them, and so they can simply tolerate more scrutiny. But that's them.

Gentrifiers and the local old-timers who join them, and some traditional residents continue to fear, care more for their own safety and well-being than for the rights of young blacks accused of wrongdoing. Yet reliance on the police, even by an increasing number of former liberals, may be traced to a general feeling of oppression at the hands of street criminals, whom many believe are most often black. As these feelings intensify and as more yuppies and students inhabit the area and press the local government for services, especially police protection, the police may be required to "ride herd" more stringently on the youthful black population. Thus young black males are often singled out as the "bad" element in an otherwise healthy diversity, and the tensions between the lower-class black ghetto and the middle- and upper-class white community increase rather than diminish.

Notes

1. See Rubinstein (1973); Wilson (1968); Fogelson (1977); Reiss (1971); Bittner (1967); Banton (1964).

2. For an illuminating typology of police work that draws a distinction between "fraternal" and "professional" codes of behavior, see Wilson (1968).

References

Anderson, Elijah. 1986. Of old heads and young boys: Notes on the urban black experience. Unpublished paper commissioned by the National Research Council, Committee on the Status of Black Americans.

Banton, Michael. 1964. *The policeman and the community*. New York: Basic Books.

Bittner, Egon. 1967. The police on Skid Row. *American Sociological Review* 32(October): 699-715.

Fogelson, Robert. 1977. *Big city police*. Cambridge: Harvard University Press.

Goffman, Erving. 1963. *Behavior in public places*. New York: Free Press.

Reiss, Albert J. 1971. *The police and the public*. New Haven: Yale University Press.

Rubinstein, Jonathan. 1973. *City police*. New York: Farrar, Straus & Giroux.

Wilson, James Q. 1968. The police and the delinquent in two cities. In *Controlling delinquents*, ed. Stanton Wheeler. New York: John Wiley.

27 / Deviance on Record: Techniques for Labeling Child Abusers in Official Documents

LESLIE MARGOLIN

Some sociologists believe that wrong-doers have considerable capacity to defend and mollify attributions of deviance by offering excuses, apologies, and expressions of sorrow. For example, conceptual formulations such as Mills' (1940) "vocabularies of motive," Scott and Lyman's (1968) "accounts," Sykes and Matza's (1957) "techniques of neutralization," and Hewitt and Stokes' (1975) "disclaimers" reflect a belief in the almost limitless reparative potential of talk. In the parlance of these sociologists, deviant identities are negotiable because attributions of wrong-doing are seen to depend not only on an assessment of what the wrong-doer did but on an understanding of his or her mental state during and after the violation. As Douglas (1970:12) observes, "an individual is considered responsible for his actions if and only if ... he has intended to commit those actions and knows the rules relevant to them. ... "

Given these conditions, accused persons may argue that the violation in question was unanticipated, unplanned, and contrary to what they wished. Still, limited evidence exists that people win such arguments. Although account theorists (e.g., Scott and Lyman 1968:46–47) claim that "the timbers of fractured sociations" can be repaired through talk, investigators addressing the ways social control agents process putative deviants have found few instances of people talking their way out of deviant labels (cf. Margolin 1990). On the whole, social control agents tend to pigeon-hole clients fairly quickly. As Waegel (1981) has shown, the organizational demand to meet deadlines, process an expected number of cases, and turn out paperwork reduces the amount of time agents can give their clients. The more bureaucrats are hurried, the greater their need to rely on shorthand methods for dealing with clients, and thus, the greater the necessity to interpret people and situations by means of stereotypes. In this regard, stereotypical or "normal" case conceptions guide responses to homicide defendants (Swigert and Farrell 1977), juvenile delinquents (Piliavin and Briar 1964), clients in a public defender's office (Sudnow 1965), skid-row residents (Bittner 1967), and shoplifters (Steffensmeier and Terry 1973).

The paperwork demand has a second effect on the putative deviant's capacity to negotiate effectively. Because oral and written communication have different potentialities for conveying information and structuring argument, agencies emphasizing the creation of records place a proportional pressure on bureaucrats to note the "recordable" features of their clients' situations. By implication, the contingencies of a case which best lend themselves to being described in written language are given the most prominence in records, and those contingencies most difficult to capture on paper (those aspects of a case best understood through face-to-face interaction) are minimized or neglected.

Studies examining the types of information bureaucrats leave out of written accounts have shown that clients' feelings are often omitted because the inner life of the individual is not only difficult to defend as objective evidence, but it is difficult to defend as evidence in writing (Kahn 1953, Lemert 1969). In face-to-face encounters, however, feelings and intentions are available through a series of gestures, tonal changes, and bodily movements which accompany the other's words (Schutz and Luckmann 1973). There is continual exchange between words and gestures. Such reciprocity cannot be duplicated in written communication, particularly when the writing is part of an official document. This means that putative deviants' capacity to argue their cases is seriously reduced when cases must be made in writing.

While documents may be a poor medium for describing internal states, bureaucrats are also reluctant to designate deviance on something as indefinite as "feelings"—theirs or the client's. The primary risk of citing the client's mental state at the time of the violation as a criterion for labeling or not labeling is that it makes agents vulnerable to accusations of subjectivity and personal bias. Since records are permanently available to supervisory scrutiny, agents feel pressure to make written assessments defendable displays of bureaucratic competence (Meehan 1986). For this reason, agents must use records to display not only "what happened" but that they performed their jobs rationally and objectively (Garfinkel 1967, Zimmerman 1969). These practical considerations oblige agents whose decision processes are recorded to place singular emphasis on the tangible aspects of the case—what the putative deviant's behavior was and what harm resulted—at the same time giving relatively little weight to clients' excuses, apologies, and expressions of sorrow.

Conceptualizing the deviant identity, then, as a mosaic assembled out of imputations of behavior and intention, this study examines how such a mosaic is pieced together in written documents. I explore how the "deviant's" point of view is documented and displayed, and how evidence is organized on paper to create the appearance that "deviance" has occurred. These dynamics are addressed through the examination of 120 case records designating child abuse.

Since the documentary reality of child abuse provides the vehicle and substantive focus of the analysis, what follows shows how child care providers are constituted as intentionally harmful to children. Like other "dividing practices" which categorize people as either healthy/sick, law abiding/criminal, or sane/insane, the separation of child abusers from normals is seen as an accomplishment of asymmetric power relations (cf. Foucault 1965, 1973, 1977). This article focuses on the power imbalance between child abuse investigators and suspects and the means by which the former impose their version of reality on the latter. Since this imposition is an accomplishment of contemporary modes of discourse (cf. Foucault 1978), I focus on investigators' vocabularies, the structure of their arguments, and the types of common sense reasoning they utilize.

METHODS

The idea for this research emerged while I was involved in a study of child abuse by babysitters. As part of that study, I had to read "official" case records documenting that child abuse had occurred. The more records I read, the more it appeared that the social workers devoted a rather large portion of their writing to describing children's injuries, as well as the violent and sexual interactions which often preceded and followed them. By contrast, the alleged perpetrator's intentions, feelings, and interpretations of what happened appeared to occupy a relatively small portion of the documents. This imbalance roused interest in view of the agency's formal regulations that social workers satisfy two criteria to establish that a caregiver committed child abuse: (1) They must establish that a caregiver performed acts which were damaging or exploitive to a child; (2) They must prove that the caregiver *intended* to damage or exploit the child—that the trauma was non-accidental. In the article I examine how social workers managed to label child abusers in a manner consistent with these regulations without appearing to give much weight to subjective factors such as suspects' excuses and justifications.

The sample consisted of 60 case records documenting physical abuse and 60 records documenting sexual abuse. They were randomly selected from all case records of child abuse by babysitters substantiated by a state agency during a two year period (N = 537). A babysitter was defined as someone who took care of a child who was not a member of the child's family, was not a boyfriend or girlfriend of the child's parent, and was not employed in a registered or licensed group care facility.

I do not treat these records as ontologically valid accounts of "what happened;" rather, I treat them as a "documentary reality" (Smith 1974), indicating the ways the social workers who constructed them want to be seen by their superiors. As such, the records provide evidence that the social workers utilized the unstated yet commonly known procedures which represent "good work." The following analysis attempts to make these procedures explicit and to show how the social workers who used them "prove" that child abuse took place by constructing good (bureaucratically sound) arguments supporting the view that a specific person intentionally damaged a child. I also explore the degree to which deviants' excuses, denials, and other accounts were incorporated into these decision processes. Finally, I look at how each type of information—descriptions of the injuries and accounts of what happened—was used as evidence that child abuse occurred and could have only been performed by the person who was labeled.

DISPLAYING VIOLENCE AND SEXUALITY

At the beginning of each record, the social worker described the physical injuries which were believed to have been inflicted on the child by the babysitter. These descriptions did not specify how the child's health or functioning were impaired but were presented as evidence that an act of transformative social import had occurred (cf. Denzin 1989). To illustrate this reporting style, one three-year-old who was spanked by his babysitter was described by the physician as having "a contusion to the buttocks and small superficial lacerations." However, the social worker who used these injuries as evidence of child abuse described them as follows:

> The injuries gave the appearance of an ink blot, in that they were almost mirror images of each other, positioned in the center of each buttock. The bruising was approximately four inches long by about two and a half inches wide, and was dark red on the perimeter and had a white cast to the inside of the bruise. There was a long linear line running across the bottom of both buttocks extending almost the entire width of the child's buttock. There was lighter reddish bruising surrounding the two largest bruises on each buttock and faint bluish-red bruising extending up to the lower back. The bruising would be characterized as being red turning to a deeper reddish-purple than true bright red.

This unusually graphic style of presentation gave the bruises a special status. They were no longer simply bruises but were now defined as out of the ordinary, strange, and grotesque. By removing the bruises from everyday experience, the stage was set for redefining the babysitter who supposedly did this to the child. In this manner, a person whose social status had been taken for granted could now be seen as potentially suspicious, foreign, and malevolent (Garfinkel 1956).

A parallel line of reportage was apparent in the sexual abuse cases. To the degree that the available information permitted, reports contained no obscurity in the descriptions of sexual interactions. No detail of what happened appeared too small to be pursued, named, and included in the records as evidence (cf. Foucault 1978). This excerpt from a social worker's recorded interview with an eight-year-old girl illustrates:

S.W.: How did the bad touch happen? Can you think?
Child: I can't remember.
S.W.: Did you ever have to kiss?
Child: No.
S.W.: Anybody?
Child: Uh uh.
S.W.: Did you have to touch anybody?
Child: Yeah.
S.W.: Ah, you had to touch 'em. Where did you have to touch 'em?
Child: Down below.
S.W.: Oh, down below. Do you have a word for that body part?
Child: A thing-a-ma-jig.
S.W.: A thing-a-ma-jig. OK, let's look.... Is P [the suspect] a man?
Child: Yeah.
S.W.: OK, let's take a look at the man doll. Can you show me on the man doll what part you're talking about?
Child: This part.
S.W.: Oh, the part that sticks out in front. We have another word for that. Do you know the other word for that part?
Child: Dick.
S.W.: Yeah. Dick is another word for it. Another word is penis.
Child: Penis?
S.W.: Yeah.
Child: Oh.
S.W.: Can you tell me what—Did you see his body? Did you see his penis with your eyes?
Child: No.
S.W.: OK. Did he have his pants on or off?
Child: Unzipped.
S.W.: Unzipped. I see. How did his penis happen to come out of his pants?
Child: By the zipper.
S.W.: I see. Who took his penis out of his pants?
Child: He did.
S.W.: What did you have to touch his penis with?
Child: My fingers.
S.W.: I see. How did you know you had to do that?
Child: He told me to.
S.W.: What did he say?
Child: Itch it.
S.W.: Itch it. I see. Did he show you how to itch it? How did he have to itch it? One question at a time. Did he show you how to itch it?
Child: He said just go back.
S.W.: So you showed me that you're kind of scratching on it.
Child: Um hum.
S.W.: Did anything happen to his penis or his thing-a-ma-jig when you did that?
Child: No.

S.W.:   OK. When he took his penis out of his pants, how did it look?
Child: Yucky.
S.W.:   Yeah, I know you think it's yucky, but um, what does yucky mean? Can you tell me with some other words besides yucky?
Child: Slimy.
S.W.:   Looked slimy. OK. Was it big?
Child: Yeah.
S.W.:   Was it hard or soft.
Child: Soft and hard.
S.W.:   OK. Explain how you mean that....

I offer this dialogue not as evidence that sexual abuse did or did not occur, but rather, to display the means by which equivocal behavior is translated into the "fact" of sexual abuse. Whatever it is that "really happened" to this child, we see that her experience of it is not a concern when "documentation" is being gathered. She is an object of inquiry, not a participant (Cicourel 1968, Smith 1974). Whatever reasons compel social workers to bring her to their offices and ask these questions are their reasons not hers. And as the child learns, even features of the "event"—such as the size, hardness, and overall appearance of a penis—can assume critical importance within interviewers' frames of reference.

While social workers used these details of sexual interactions and injuries to set the stage for the attribution of deviance, I noted four cases in which the analysis of the injuries themselves played a conspicuously larger role in determining who was responsible. In these cases the injured children were too young to explain how their injuries were caused, the babysitters denied causing the injuries, and there were no witnesses. This meant that the only way the investigators were able to label the babysitters as abusive was to argue that the injuries occurred during the time the suspects were taking care of the children. The parents of the injured children testified that the children were sent to the babysitters in good health, without any marks, but returned from the babysitters with a noticeable injury. This allowed the social workers to determine responsibility through the following method: if a babysitter cannot produce any plausible alternative explanation for the child's injuries, the babysitter must be responsible for the injuries.

Since children who had allegedly been sexually abused did not have conspicuous or easily described injuries, attributing sexual abuse in the absence of any plausible alternative explanation for the injury was, of course, impossible. This would appear to severely limit social workers' capacity to document that a babysitter committed sexual abuse when the babysitter denied the charges, when the child was too young to provide coherent testimony, and when there were no other witnesses. However, this was not always the case. Like the investigators described by Garfinkel (1967:18) who were able to determine the cause of death among possible suicides with only "*this* much; *this* sight; *this* note; *this* collection of whatever is at hand," child abuse investigators showed the capacity to "make do" with whatever information was available. In one case of sexual abuse, for example, there were no witnesses, no admission from the suspect, no physical evidence, and no charge from the alleged victim; still, "evidence" was summoned to establish a babysitter's guilt. Here, the social worker cited a four-year-old girl's fears, nightmares, and other "behavior consistent with that of a child who was sexually traumatized by a close family friend." Additionally, the babysitter in question was portrayed as a "type" capable of doing such things:

> Having no physical evidence, and no consistent statement from the alleged victim, I am forced to make a conclusion based on the credibility of the child as opposed to that of the perpetrator. This conclusion is supported by similar allegations against him from an independent source. It is also supported by behavioral indications and what we know of his history.

In a second case, a social worker showed that information pointing to the suspect's homosexuality and history of sexual victimization could be used to support charges of sexual abuse when other kinds of evidence were lacking:

> Although the babysitter denied having sexual contact with this child when interviewed, he did leave a note to the effect that he was attracted to males and thought that he was homosexual, and records indicate that he, himself, was sexually abused at the age of eight. Based on the interview done, the past history, and his own previous victimization, this worker feels that he did, in fact, penetrate and perpetrate himself upon the victim.

In most cases, however, portraying the suspect as a "type" was not critical to the finding of child abuse. The rationale for labeling was primarily constructed out of witnesses' testimony showing "who did what to whom."

USING WITNESSES TO DETERMINE WHO DID WHAT TO WHOM

Since the children and alleged child abusers often had different versions of what happened (40 cases), social workers needed a decision-rule to settle the question of who had the correct story. The rule used for resolving disagreements was fairly simple: The child's version was considered the true one. The children were called "credible" witnesses when describing assaults which were done to them because it was assumed they had nothing to gain by falsely accusing the babysitter. The babysitters, on the other hand, were seen as "non-credible" (when they attempted to establish their innocence) because they had everything to gain by lying. Even children as young as two- and three-years-old were believed in preference to their adult babysitters. In fact, the main reason given for interpreting children as superior witnesses was precisely their youth, ignorance, and lack of sophistication. As one social worker observed, "It's my experience that a four-year-old would not be able to maintain such a consistent account of an incident if she was not telling the truth." Particularly in cases of sexual abuse, it was believed that the younger the witness, the more credible his or her testimony was. Social workers made the point that children who were providing details of sexual behavior would not know of such things unless they had been abused (cf. Eberle and Eberle 1986).

The children's accounts were rejected in only three instances. In one of these cases, two teenage boys claimed they witnessed a babysitter abuse a child as they peered through a window. Both the babysitter and the child said this was not true. The social worker did not feel it was necessary to explain why the babysitter would deny the allegations, but the child's denial was seen as problematic. Therefore, the social worker offered the following rationale for rejecting the child's account: "The child's refusal to say anything is not unusual because her mother was so verbally upset when she was informed of the allegations." A child's version of what happened (his denial of abuse) was rejected in a second case on the grounds that he was protecting a babysitter described as his "best friend." Finally, a 12-year-old female who repeatedly denied that anyone had touched her sexually was seen as non-credible because of her "modesty." As the social worker put it, "She did seem to have a very difficult time talking about it, and I feel she greatly minimized the incident due to her embarrassment about it."

In general, however, testimony from children was treated as the most credible source of evidence of what happened, since most social workers believe that children do not lie about the abuse done to them. By contrast, babysitters were presented as credible witnesses only when they agreed with the allegations made against them (56 cases). When they testified to the contrary, they were portrayed as biased. What does *not* happen, therefore, is the child implicating someone, the accused saying nothing happened, and the investigator siding with the accused. This suggests an underlying idealization that precedes and supports the ones operating on the surface of most cases: *the accused is guilty.* It goes without saying that this organizational stance runs roughly opposite to the Constitutional one of "innocent until proven guilty."

Here, it might be useful to draw an analogy between the child protection workers' "investigative stance" and that of welfare investigators responsible for determining applicants' eligibility (Zimmerman 1974). In both cases, investigators adopt a thorough-going skepticism designed "to locate and display the potential discrepancy between the applicant's [or suspect's] subjective and 'interested' claims and the factual and objective (i.e., rational) account that close observance of agency procedure is deemed to produce" (Zimmerman 1974:131). However, an important difference should be noted: during the conduct of welfare investigations, the investigated party is referred to as the "applicant," indicating that the investigation could end in a determination of either eligibility or ineligibility; by contrast, during the conduct of child abuse investigations, the investigated party is routinely identified as the "perpetrator," suggesting a previously concluded status. To illustrate, these notations documented one worker's activities during the first days of a child abuse investigation:

> 3/24: Home visit with police, interviewed parents, child not at home—perpetrator not in home.
>
> 3/26: Interview with detective J at Police station with CPI and child. Perpetrator arrested.

While babysitters accused of child abuse may in theory be only "suspects," at the level of practice, they are "perpetrators." This discrepancy between "theory" and "practice" is more than an example of how the formal structures of organizations are accompanied by unintended and unprogrammed structures (Bittner 1965). In this instance, child protection workers are formally enjoined to gather evidence about "perpetrators," not "suspects." Consider these guidelines from the agency's official handbook:

> Information collected from the person [witness] should include precise description of size, shape, color, type, and location of injury. It may be possible to establish the credibility of the child, the responsible caretaker or the *perpetrator* as a source of this information.... The *perpetrator* and victim may be credible persons and need to be judged on the basis of the same factors as any other persons. [Italics added.]

The implicit message is that the goal of the child abuse investigation is not to determine an individual's guilt or innocence but to find evidence to be used in recording or "documenting" what is already taken for granted, that parties initially identified as the "perpetrator" and "victim" are in fact the "perpetrator" and "victim." Strictly speaking, then, the goal is not to determine "who did what to whom," since that information is assumed at the outset, but rather, to document that agency rules have been followed, and that the investigation was conducted in a rational, impersonal manner.

DETERMINING INTENTIONALITY

A decision-rule was also needed to determine the babysitter's intentions. While babysitters were portrayed in the allegations as malicious or exploitive, many babysitters offered a different version of their motivations. Among the babysitters accused of physical abuse, 25 acknowledged hitting the children but also claimed they intended no harm. Three said they were having a bad day, were under unusual stress, and simply "lost it." They attributed their violence to a spontaneous, non-instrumental, expression of frustration. For example, one male caregiver took a two-year-old to the potty several times but the child did not go. Later he noticed that the child's diaper was wet; so he hurried him to the potty. However, just before being placed on the potty the child had a bowel movement. At that point the caregiver lost his temper and hit the child.

One woman who was labeled abusive claimed she was ill and never wanted to babysit in the first place. She only agreed to take care of a two-year-old girl because the girl's mother insisted. The mother had an unexpected schedule change at work and needed child care on an emergency basis. The abusive event occurred soon after the babysitter served lunch to the child. While the sitter rested on a couch in the living room, she observed the girl messing with her lunch. The sitter got up and tried to settle the child. When this did not work, she took away the girl's paper plate and threw it in the garbage. At that point the girl began to cry for her mother. The babysitter returned to the living room to lie down on the couch. But the girl followed her, wailing for her mother. When the girl reached the couch, the babysitter sat up and slapped her.

Other babysitters described their violence in instrumental terms: their goal was to discipline the children and not to hurt or injure them. They said that whatever injuries occurred were the accidental result of hitting (in one case, biting) the children harder than they meant to do. Some sitters indicated that the only reason children were injured during a disciplinary action was that the children moved just as they were being hit, exposing a sensitive part of the body to the blow. Others protested that the child's movements made it impossible to aim the blows accurately or to assess how hard they were hitting. In one case, the sitter said she was trying to hit the child across the buttocks with a stick, but the child put her hand across her buttocks to protect herself, receiving "non-intentional" bruising and swelling to the hand. A different sitter asked that the social worker consider that at the time of the violation he did not know it was against the law to beat a child with a belt. Another said he had been given permission to spank the child by the child's mother and was only following her orders. This was confirmed by the mother. After a two-and-a-half-year-old bit another child, his sitter bit him to show him "what it felt like." The sitter argued that she had done this in the past and had even told the child's mother. Thus, she believed that this was tacitly approved. Still another babysitter claimed that he struck the 11-year-old girl who was in his care in self-defense. He said that when he told her it was time for bed she began to bite and kick him. He said her injuries resulted from his efforts to calm and restrain her.

To sift out the babysitters' "official" intentions from the versions offered by the sitters themselves, several social workers explicitly invoked the following reasoning: Physical damage to the child would be considered "intentional" if the acts which produced them were intentional. Thus, a social worker wrote:

> I am concluding that this injury to the child was non-accidental in that the babysitter did have a purpose in striking the child, that purpose being to discipline her in hopes of modifying her behavior.

While close examination of this logic reveals an absurdity (the injury was seen as "intentional" despite the fact that it was produced by an act aimed at an entirely different outcome, "modifying her behavior"), the practical consequence of such a formula was a simple method for determining a suspect's intentions: If a babysitter was known to intentionally hit a child, causing an injury, the social worker could conclude the babysitter intended to cause the injury. Through such a formula, the most common excuse utilized by babysitters to account for their actions, that the injury was the accidental result of a disciplinary action, was interpreted as a confession of responsibility for physical abuse.

To give another example of how this formula provided a short-cut to determining intentionality, one social worker concluded her recording as follows:

> Physical abuse is founded in that the caretaker did hit the child on the face because she was throwing a temper tantrum and left a bruise approximately one inch long under the right eye. This constitutes a non-accidental injury. The bruise is still visible after five days.

In cases involving allegations of physical abuse, the problem of figuring out what the babysitter was really contemplating at the time of the violation never came up as a separate issue because the alleged perpetrator's motivation to injure the child was seen as the operational equivalent of two prior questions, "Does the child have an injury resulting from a blow?" and "Did the babysitter intentionally strike the child?" When each of these questions was answered affirmatively, intent to harm the child was inferred. Thus, it was possible for a social worker to observe, "It was this writer's opinion that the babysitter was surprised at the injury she left on the child by spanking the child," and later conclude, "the injury occurred as a result of a non-accidental incident."

One record included comments from witnesses which stated that a babysitter pushed a five-year-old boy after the child socked a cat. All agreed that the injury was not a direct consequence of the push but resulted when the child lost balance and fell over. Despite the social worker's explicit recognition that the child's injury was neither planned nor anticipated (she wrote that "the injury will probably not be repeated due to the sitter's awareness of the seriousness of disciplining a child by reacting rather than thinking"), the report of physical abuse was, nonetheless, founded "due to the fact that the injury occurred in the course of a disciplinary action."

In another record, a male babysitter admitted to spanking a child, causing red marks on his buttocks. Although the child's father said he "did not believe the sitter meant to spank as hard as he did," and the police officer who was present concluded that "based on the information obtained in this investigation, I could find no intent on the sitter's part to assault this child," the social worker found the determination of physical abuse nonproblematic. Since the child received the injury in the course of a spanking, child abuse occurred.

There were only two cases of sexual abuse in which the alleged abuser acknowledged touching the child in a manner consistent with the allegations, but at the same time denied sexual intent. In one of these cases, the alleged abuser said he only touched a 10-year-old boy's genitals in the process of giving him a bath. In the other case, the alleged abuser claimed he only touched the girl's body as part of an anatomy lesson, to show her where her rib and pelvic bones were located. Both of these accounts were dismissed as preposterous. The social workers expressed the opinion that sexual intent was the only possible reason anyone would enact the types of behavior attributed to the accused in the allegations. In short, an equation was drawn between specific behaviors attributed to the accused and their states of mind. If it was established that the babysitter behaved toward the child in ways commonly understood as sexual (e.g., fondling), establishing intent, as a separate dimension of the investigation, was seen as redundant. Thus, social workers were able to conclude their investigations of sexual abuse, as one investigator did, by utilizing the following formula: "The child, a credible witness, indicated that her babysitter did fondle her genitals. Therefore, this is a founded case of intent to commit sexual abuse."

To summarize, in cases of both physical and sexual abuse, the intent to commit these acts was seen as a necessary component of the specific behaviors used to accomplish them. Hitting which resulted in an injury was always treated as if it was a direct indicator of the motivation to injure. Similarly, behavior commonly known as "sexual" was always treated as if it was identical with the suspect's intent to sexually exploit. The fact that social workers sometimes described the suspects' surprise and horror at the physical damage their violence caused the child did not make the attribution of "intent to harm" more problematic because suspects' accounts were not organizationally defined as indicators of intent. Consistent with Mills (1940), motives for child abuse are not features of the perpetrator's psyche, but rather, of the bureaucracy and profession. That 50 of the babysitters labeled as abusive denied performing the actions imputed to them, and another 14 were not interviewed at all (either because they could not be located or refused to speak to the social worker) demonstrated that it was possible to "officially" determine babysitters' intentions without confirmatory statements from the babysitters themselves.

DISCUSSION

Sociologists have often questioned official records on the grounds of their accuracy, reliability, and representativeness. However, the methods through which and by which deviance is routinely displayed in records have rarely been investigated (cf. Cicourel and Kitsuse 1963, Kitsuse and Cicourel 1963). This study has treated as problematic the standardized arguments and evidence which social workers use in official documents to prove that child abuse has taken place. In this regard, child abuse is seen as an accomplishment of a bureaucratic system in which members agree to treat specific phenomena as if they were "child abuse."

The proof of abuse was problematic since more than half of the suspects either denied the accusations or were not interviewed. Social workers "made do" without supportive testimony from suspects by routinely defining them as "non-credible" witnesses. Also, social workers managed to conform to agency regulations requiring proof that suspects intended to harm or exploit children by agreeing to treat specific observables as if they represented the intent to harm or exploit.

Thus, the designation of child abuse was simplified. Testimony from the person most likely to disagree with this label, the accused, did not have to be considered. This is not to say that testimony from the accused might overcome the processes of institutional sense-making. It is to suggest, rather, that defining the accused as non-credible makes the designation of child abuse more "cut and dried," defendable, and recordable, since abuse that might otherwise be denied, excused, or justified, either in whole or in part, can then be fully attributed to suspects.

While it can be argued that simplifying the means by which suspects are labeled is desirable for a society concerned about keeping dangerous people away from children, the negative consequences should be acknowledged. As already shown, individuals who assign child abuse labels have more power than suspects, making it impossible for parties at risk of being labeled to "negotiate" on an equal footing with labelers. Indeed, any disjunctures between suspects' and investigators' versions of "what really happened" do not have to be resolved prior to the attribution of child abuse (cf. Pollner 1987:77–81). Since investigators have the capacity to impose their versions of reality on suspects, the only "resolution" needed from the investigators' perspective entails finding ways to make their decisions defendable in writing.

As might also be expected, the personal, social, and legal stigma resulting from designating this label is enormous. Once the impression has been formed that a person is a child abuser, the expectation exists that he or she will continue to be abusive. Moreover, there is little a person can do to remove this label. It exists as part of a permanent record that can be recalled whenever a person's child care capacities or moral standing are questioned (cf. Rosenhan 1973). If, as Smith (1974:259) argues, the creation of written records "mediates relations among persons in ways analogous to how Marx conceived commodities mediating relations among individuals," then for the relations (and identities) constituted by records, there is no intersubjective world in which members share the passage of time, and, in the words of Schutz, "grow old together" (cited in Smith 1974:259). There is no interpersonal negotiation or becoming, but only "fact" as sedimented in the records themselves.

While most who write about child abuse are enmeshed in that system, either as practitioners or idealogues and so are strained to defend its existence, in recent years critics have shown concern about the growing numbers of people labeled as child abusers (Besharov 1986, Eberle and Eberle 1986, Elshtain 1985, Johnson 1985, Pride 1986, Wexler 1985). Most trace this "overattribution" of child abuse to professional and lay people's "emotionally charged desire to 'do something' about child abuse, fanned by repeated and often sensational media coverage" (Besharov 1986:19). However, Conrad and Schneider (1980:270) provide a more general explanation: "bureaucratic 'industries' with large budgets and many employees . . . depend for their existence on the acceptance of a particular deviance designation. They become 'vested interests' in every sense of the term." To take their analysis one step farther, "bureaucratic industries" have a vested interest not only in a label, but in a labeling process—specifically, in finding ways of reducing complexity and making labeling accomplishable.

Piven and Cloward's (1971) analysis of the regulating functions of welfare programs suggests why these bureaucracies have expanded in recent years. If income support programs expand and contract to control turmoil resulting from instability in labor markets, it is possible that social agencies geared to controlling child care grow in response to instability in the child care system. This hypothesis warrants attention if for no other reason than that mothers' dramatic increases in labor force participation over the last three decades, and the commensurate increase in young children's time in nonparental care, have closely paralleled the emergence of child abuse as a major social issue. However, this single causal mode of explanation would be more compelling if it were not that history reveals other periods in which institutional momentum developed around "saving children" under a variety of different conditions (Best 1990, Finestone 1976, Platt 1969). This suggests that any explanation of why such social movements wax and wane, taking their particular form at each point in history, needs to account for many interacting factors, including the prevailing moralities and family institutions as well as opportunities for effectively marketing these problems to a wide audience (cf. Best 1990).

To conclude, this study has shown some of the ways in which the construction of documents labels deviance. The main findings include bureaucrats' determination to translate sex and violence into endlessly accumulated verbal detail, to "make do" with whatever information is available, to fashion proofs of child abuse based on the new "common sense" that children's testimony is more credible than adults', and to develop simple, accomplishable ways of imputing intentionality that are unaffected by suspects' accounts.

References

Besharov, Douglas J.
1986 "Unfounded allegations—A new child abuse problem." The Public Interest 83:18–33

Best, Joel
1990 Threatened Children: Rhetoric and Concern about Child-Victims. Chicago: The University of Chicago Press.

Bittner, Egon
1965 "The concept of organization." Social Research 32:239–255.
1967 "The police on skid row: A study of peace keeping." American Sociological Review 32:699–715.

Cicourel, Aaron V.
1968 The Social Organization of Juvenile Justice. New York: John Wiley and Sons.

Cicourel, Aaron V., and John I. Kitsuse
1963 The Educational Decision-Makers. New York: Bobbs-Merrill.

Conrad, Peter, and Joseph W. Schneider
1980 Deviance and Medicalization. St. Louis: C.V. Mosby.

Denzin, Norman K.
1989 Interpretive Interactionism. Newbury Park, Calif.: Sage.

Douglas, Jack D.
1970 "Deviance and respectability: The social construction of moral meanings." In Deviance and Respectability, ed. Jack D. Douglas, 3–30. New York: Basic Books.

Eberle, Paul, and Shirley Eberle
1986 The Politics of Child Abuse. Secaucus, N.J.: Lyle Stuart.

Elshtain, Jean Bethke
1985 "Invasion of the child savers: How we succumb to hype and hysteria." The Progressive 49:23–26.

Finestone, Harold
1976 Victims of Change: Juvenile Delinquents in American Society. Westport, Conn.: Greenwood Press.

Foucault, Michel
1965 Madness and Civilization. New York: Random House.
1973 The Birth of the Clinic. New York: Pantheon.
1977 Discipline and Punishment. New York: Pantheon.
1978 The History of Sexuality. Vol. 1. New York: Pantheon.

Garfinkel, Harold
1956 "Conditions of successful degradation ceremonies." American Journal of Sociology 61:420–424.
1967 Studies in Ethnomethodology. Englewood Cliffs, N.J.: Prentice Hall.

Hewitt, John P., and Randall Stokes
1975 "Disclaimers." American Sociological Review 40:1–11.

Johnson, John M.
1985 "Symbolic salvation: The changing meanings of the child maltreatment movement." Studies in Symbolic Interaction 6:289–305.

Kahn, Alfred, J.
1953 A Court for Children. New York: Columbia University Press.

Kitsuse, John I., and Aaron V. Cicourel
  1963 "A note on the use of official statistics." Social Problems 11:131–139.
Lemert, Edwin M.
  1969 "Records in juvenile court." In On Record: Files and Dossiers in American
  Life, ed. Stanton Wheeler, 355–389. New York: Russell Sage Foundation.
Margolin, Leslie
  1990 "When vocabularies of motive fail: The example of fatal child abuse."
  Qualitative Sociology 13:373–385.
Meehan, Albert J.
  1986 "Record-keeping practices in the policing of juveniles." Urban Life 15:70–
  102.
Mills, C. Wright
  1940 "Situated actions and vocabularies of motive." American Sociological
  Review 5:904–913.
Piliavin, Irving, and Scott Briar
  1964 "Police encounters with juveniles." American Sociological Review 70:206–
  214.
Piven, Frances Fox, and Richard A. Cloward
  1971 Regulating the Poor: The Functions of Public Welfare. New York: Pantheon Books.
Platt, Anthony M.
  1969 The Child Savers: The Invention of Delinquency. Chicago: The University
  of Chicago Press.
Pollner, Melvin
  1987 Mundane Reason: Reality in Everyday and Sociological Discourse. Cambridge: Cambridge University Press.
Pride, Mary
  1986 The Child Abuse Industry. Westchester, Ill.: Crossway.
Rosenhan, D.L.
  1973 "On being sane in insane places." Science 179:250–258.
Schutz, Alfred, and Thomas Luckmann
  1973 The Structures of the Life-World. Translated by R.M. Zaner and H.T.
  Engelhardt, Jr. Evanston, Ill.: Northwestern University Press.
Scott, Marvin B., and Stanford M. Lyman
  1968 "Accounts." American Sociological Review 22:664–670.
Smith, Dorothy E.
  1974 "The social construction of documentary reality." Sociological Inquiry
  44:257–268.
Steffensmeier, Darrell J., and Robert M. Terry
  1973 "Deviance and respectability: An observational study of reactions to
  shoplifting." Social Forces 51:417–426.
Sudnow, David
  1965 "Normal crimes: Sociological features of the penal code in a public
  defender office." Social Problems 12:255–276.
Swigert, Victoria, and Ronald Farrell
  1977 "Normal homicides and the law." American Sociological Review 42:16–32.
Sykes, Gresham M., and David Matza
  1957 "Techniques of neutralization: A theory of delinquency." American Sociological Review 22:664–670.

Waegel, William B.
1981 "Case routinization in investigative police work." Social Problems 28:263–275.
Wexler, Richard
1985 "Invasions of the child savers: No one is safe in the war against abuse." The Progressive 49:19–22.
Zimmerman, Don H.
1969 "Record-keeping and the intake process in a public welfare agency." In On Record: Files and Dossiers in American Life, ed. Stanton Wheeler, 319–354. New York: Russell Sage Foundation.
1974 "Fact as a practical accomplishment." In Ethnomethodology, ed. Roy Turner, 128–143. Middlesex, Eng.: Penguin Books.

28 / Getting Rid of Troublemakers: High School Disciplinary Procedures and the Production of Dropouts

CHRISTINE BOWDITCH

Questions about schools and stratification have been addressed at both the macro- and the microlevel and from the full spectrum of theoretical perspectives (Karabel and Halsey 1977). Although the dominant research tradition has looked to the characteristics of students or their families to explain patterns of school performance and subsequent occupational placement, a significant and growing body of scholarship has underscored the role played by the organization of schools and the practices of school personnel (e.g., Anderson 1982; Cicourel and Kitsuse 1977; Connell et al. 1982; Corcoran 1985; Fine 1991; Rutter et al. 1979; Weis, Farrar, and Petrie 1989). Both lines of research, until quite recently, have focused on differences between college-bound students and those who move into the work force after graduation. However, since the mid-1980s, resurgent interest in urban poverty has directed attention to high school dropouts and to the factors that distinguish them from graduates (Ekstrom et al. 1987; Fine 1986; Hahn and Danzberger 1987; Morrow 1986; Peng 1983; Rumberger 1983).

Dropout research has found that a disproportionate number of inner-city Hispanic and black students leave school before graduation and has identified a series of factors that place such students "at risk"[1] of dropping out: students are least likely to complete high school if they come from a low-income background, are frequently absent or truant, have a record of school disciplinary problems, are failing classes, and are overage in grade (Borus and Carpenter 1983; Ekstrom et al. 1987; Peng 1983; Rumberger 1983). Dropouts are also more likely to feel alienated from school and less likely to get along with their teachers (Wagenaar 1987). According to one conventional interpretation of these data, students become discouraged with multiple experiences of failure and walk away from school (see Finn 1989); hence a proposed solution to the dropout problem has been to convince "at risk" students to remain in school and to support them in their struggle to graduate.

370

Although this goal has become the publicly stated objective of many urban school districts, experience as well as research teaches that other pressures can subvert such ideals (see Fine 1991; Kozol 1991). This paper examines some of those countervailing forces. Specifically, this paper analyzes the routine disciplinary activities in an inner-city high school and shows that these policies and practices encouraged school workers to "get rid of" students deemed to be "troublemakers." Significantly, the indicators used to identify "troublemakers" were the very "risk factors" that emerge in the research on dropouts. The exclusion of "troublemakers," sometimes explicitly against their wishes, calls into question precisely why such students are "at risk." Are students at risk because they truly cannot or will not finish school? Or, are they at risk because school personnel label their behaviors or attitudes as troublesome and, on that basis, encourage their departure from school? Answers to these questions can help us understand the role schools play in perpetuating social inequality.

DISCIPLINE AND DROPOUT

As previous scholarship has noted, the category "dropout," as employed by school districts and educational researchers, often includes "pushouts," "stopouts,"[2] and those who fail academically, as well as disaffected students who decide to leave (Fine 1991; Hahn and Danzberger 1987; Morrow 1986). The number of students who leave via these routes is unknown since these paths to early school withdrawal are masked in the official statistics. Yet, in at least one study, as many as a quarter of the "dropouts" reported that they were discharged coercively (Fine 1991).

Recent scholarship has raised questions about how student characteristics interact with institutional practices in producing dropouts (Farrell 1988; Fine 1991; Miller 1988; Pittman 1986; Toles, Schulz, and Rice 1986; Weis, Farrar, and Petrie 1989). Even though research has begun to examine how school environments produce truancy, academic failure, or disobedience, the relationship between these student behaviors and dropping out is either ignored or treated as essentially unproblematic (Fine 1991, is a notable exception). Little has been done to examine how schools selectively label and respond to student actions.

The fact that African-American students experience a significantly higher rate of school suspension than do whites (Hahn and Danzberger 1987; Yudof 1975), as well as a higher dropout rate, underscores the importance of looking at disciplinary procedures. Recent findings seem to refute charges of racism in the use of suspension, but research in other institutional settings gives us reason to remain skeptical. When a student's past disciplinary record, grades, and demeanor are taken into account, neither race nor socioeconomic status explains the type of disciplinary action taken by school officials (McCarthy and Hoge 1987). Parallel findings emerge from research on juvenile court dispositions (Cohen and Kleugel 1987; see also Empey 1982; Tittle 1980); however, the way certain youth come to police attention in the first place and the factors that influence police decisions to take official action—in other words, to construct a "prior" record— is connected to race and class (e.g., Morash 1984; Sampson 1986). We need to question, therefore, how school workers construct the records that "explain" suspensions. We need a much clearer understanding of how grades, demeanor, and prior record are linked in practice to suspensions, since a record of suspensions increases a student's "dropout" risk.

THEORETICAL PERSPECTIVE

Following the research tradition established by Cicourel and Kitsuse (1977), this paper investigates how routine administrative decisions and actions affect a student's passage through high school. Whereas Cicourel and Kitsuse looked at the counselor's role in selecting students who will go on to college, this paper examines the disciplinarian's role in selecting students who will be "dropped."

The theoretical framework for this investigation borrows from both the labeling perspective in criminology, which itself is informed by both conflict theory and symbolic interactionism (Paternoster and Iovanni 1989), and the "negotiated-order" approach to the study of organizations (Maines and Charlton 1985). According to the labeling perspective,[3] people in positions of formal authority—such as school board members or state legislators— define "deviance" through a process of conflict and negotiation with other interested players. Practices at the organizational level—in this case, within schools—determine whose behavior fits those formal definitions of deviance. Analysis of school practices draws on the negotiated-order approach to the study of organizations. That approach acknowledges that formal rules organize and define an agency's work, but calls attention to the fact that workers' informal, negotiated understandings determine the meaning and implementation of rules. Workers use and interpret the formal rules governing client interactions in ways that allow them to simplify their own work conditions; accommodate co-workers' expectations or routines; and pursue their own, unofficial understanding of the agency's proper goals (Lipsky 1980). Although research findings have been mixed, some labeling studies have concluded that the accused person's class or racial status makes him or her more vulnerable to being officially labeled (Paternoster and Iovanni 1989).

Labeling theory also addresses the source of "secondary deviance" (Becker 1963; Lemert 1967). In some instances, labeling produces additional deviance by strengthening identification with and commitment to deviance. However, since the accused individual's social, political, and economic resources shape the capacity to reject or mitigate the stigma of a deviant label, labeling may produce additional deviance merely by cutting off access to legitimate resources and opportunities. Alternatively, a social network which provides support and resources may allow an individual to renegotiate or disavow a deviant label (Paternoster and Iovanni 1989). Thus, the power and social resources attached to class and racial status may affect both the initial interpretation of a person's actions and the consequences following from that interpretation.

METHODOLOGICAL APPROACH

A labeling or interactionist perspective calls for an investigation of the tacit, unofficial rules employed by school workers as they engage in routine organizational activities, and thus favors an ethnographic approach to research (Cicourel and Kitsuse 1977; Mehan 1992). Accordingly, this paper draws on qualitative data collected as part of a case study of DuBois High School conducted between the spring of 1984 and the spring of 1987; the bulk of classroom observation was done during the 1985/86 school year. (All names, including the school's, have been changed.) Although I spoke regularly, throughout the study, to the school's disciplinary workers and security staff, most of the material considered in this paper comes from two ten-day periods of intensive observation in the boys' discipline office. The materials include written observations of daily disciplinary activities; notes on frequent *in situ* discussions with teachers, disciplinarians, nonteaching assistants (NTA), students, and a small number of parents; tape-recorded *post hoc* interviews with key players in a particular case of a "troublemaker"; and publicly available disciplinary documents generated by the district and the school. I did not have access to confidential materials in student records except in cases where the materials were presented in a conference I attended or when a disciplinarian chose to show me a student file he or she thought I might find interesting.

THE FIELD SETTING

DuBois High was a troubled, inner-city school. Its all-black student body[4] came from an area of a highly segregated northern city where half of the adults never completed high school (Bureau of the Census 1983), almost half of the school's students lived in poverty, and more than 60 percent had only one parent or guardian at home (school figures 1984).[5] Many of the teenage girls had children of their own and most of the boys belonged to one of the area's five or six corner groups or neighborhood gangs.

In the decade before my study, enrollment at DuBois had declined steadily as many students in its catchment area found their way to city magnet schools or private or parochial high schools. Of the more than 1,600 students still on the school's roll, many came late, cut classes, or just did not attend. While I was there, as many as 400 missed school daily. Another 100 or more

Table 1 / California Achievement Test
Schoolwide Distribution for Reading

Percentile	1980	1981	1982	1983
< 16th	49	48	47	53
16th–49th	42	43	44	40
50th–84th	8	8	8	8
85th–100	0	1	1	0

students arrived late. Two hundred or more students cut certain classes on a regular basis; perhaps as many or more skipped some of their classes on occasion.

Most of the students worked substantially below grade level. California Achievement Test scores for 1983 showed that while no student scored above the 85th percentile in reading, 53 percent scored below the 16th percentile and another 40 percent scored between the 16th and 49th percentiles. Records of school grades provided additional evidence of low achievement. Figures from the math department for the 1984/85 school year, for instance, showed that 74 percent of all tenth graders failed math. As a consequence of the widespread academic failure, each year the school retained in grade approximately a quarter of all its tenth graders.

Student disorder and disobedience figured prominently both in the public's perception of the school and in the school's self-assessment. DuBois frequently suspended a half dozen or more students each day; by the end of the year, more than a quarter of its students were suspended at least once, and many had multiple or serial suspensions.

Despite these facts, I did not encounter scenes of violence or chaos. Teachers did not complain of belligerence or open hostility; instead they talked about apathy, silliness, inattention, and poor attendance. During my months of fieldwork, I witnessed daily the essentially familiar scenes of high school life.

Students sent from class; picked up in the halls; or brought in by the police for truancy, misbehavior, or more serious misconduct all went to the discipline office, a crowded, first floor office divided into a small waiting area and four inner offices. Although they shared a physical space, girls' and boys' discipline was administered separately. Three disciplinarians handled cases involving boys and two disciplinarians dealt with girls.

The discipline office could go from complete quiet to the confusion of three or four cases without notice. In addition to the discipline staff, three or four nonteaching assistants, two district security officers assigned to the school, two city police officers assigned to the school, various teachers, one or two of the school's counselors, twenty or thirty students, and five to ten parents moved in and out of the office in the course of a day. The design of the office ensured little privacy or protection from the noise and confusion of other cases. Just inside the door to the office, a half dozen mismatched classroom chairs placed between a couple of battered file cabinets and a table scattered with outdated school notices formed a waiting area. But, since the partitions that separated the disciplinarians' offices from that area did not rise completely to the ceiling and were fitted with opaque glass, waiting parents and students could monitor much of the "private" conversation and activity; shouted comments or angry remarks made in one conference often intruded upon other conferences.[6]

DISCIPLINARY WORK

Within the school's bureaucratic organization, the discipline office staff's specialized tasks were to maintain files on the documented misbehavior of DuBois students, confer with students charged with rule violations, determine punitive actions to be taken against students, contact the parents of students who had violated school rules, and process the forms documenting disciplinary actions and protecting due process. Specific and extensive rules from the school district defined misconduct and outlined policies, procedures, and proper documentation for disciplinary actions.

The disciplinarian's responsibility, when a student entered the office, was to determine what the student had done, assess the seriousness of the offense, and take the appropriate disciplinary action. Most of the routine work involved either dealing with students who were late for class, caught cutting class, or accused of disrupting class, or meeting with students and their parents for the required conference following a suspension. Less routine, but still fairly common work involved determining punishments for students who were caught fighting; found in possession of marijuana; accused of theft, vandalism, or wall-writing; caught drinking alcohol; or charged with threatening a teacher. In rare instances, the disciplinary office handled cases involving a weapon, the sale of drugs, or violence directed against a teacher.[7]

Neither the formal description of disciplinary activities nor the rules and procedures governing the discipline office fully captured its operational practice. Disciplinary practice reflected the negotiated definitions, routines, and expectations developed among co-workers, and ongoing contests over work, authority, and responsibility within the school and between the school and parents. Disciplinarians relied on informally developed understandings about the discipline office's goals, the typical forms of student misconduct the office should handle, the types of students who normally caused trouble, and the standard strategies for dealing with misconduct (cf. Sudnow 1965, see also Waegel 1981). Within this context, official rules became a resource for workers to regulate the conditions of their work and to pursue informally identified goals (see Lipsky 1980).

To complete its work, the discipline staff interacted with teachers, NTAs, security personnel, administrators, parents, and students. Although school workers' jobs were formally coordinated, they frequently contested the boundaries of their authority and responsibility. Teachers, for example, negotiated their own strategies of classroom control—some taking a "hard line" allowing no deviation from formal rules, some using rules selectively to "contain problems" rather than to enforce obedience—and therefore made different demands on the discipline office (cf. Bittner 1967; Rubinstein 1973). Each student a teacher sent to the discipline office was, in essence, a test case of that teacher's authority. The discipline office's handling of the student determined whether the school's coercive power endorsed the teacher's definition of the situation or refuted it.

The nature of the disciplinarians' work meant the student's behavior was not interpreted in terms of its threat to one teacher's struggle for authority and classroom control. Instead, a student's behavior was judged in relation to the other students processed through the office. The staff was concerned with regulating and controlling its work, protecting its authority, and, most important, maintaining the institution's authority.

Because disciplinarians judged student misconduct with reference to the concerns of the school as a whole, they sometimes disagreed with teachers over what types of problems required the intervention of their office, complaining "this is something the teacher should have handled." In those instances, they typically took no action or very limited action against a student. In other cases, where the disciplinarian agreed with the teacher's assessment, punitive actions, especially severe punitive actions, were occasionally blocked by the principal. The principal shared their concern for the school's interests, but nonetheless had to evaluate both student behavior and staff authority within the context of complaints or pressures from parents and the district, or with regard to the school's public image.

Disciplinary Penalties

The sanctions available to the disciplinary staff were few. Beyond talking to students, and short of transferring or expelling them, disciplinarians could hold students out of class, contact their parents, or enforce one- to five-day suspensions. Disciplinarians rarely, if ever, contacted parents outside the context of a suspension. Official responses to misbehavior were, thus, limited in practice to either a simple reprimand, holding the student in the office until the next class period, or a suspension.

The district's "Code Prohibiting Serious Student Misconduct" identified and defined the nine categories of misconduct that warranted suspension: (1) disruption of the school, (2) damage, destruction or theft of school property, (3) damage, destruction or theft of private property, (4) assault on a school employee, (5) physical abuse of a student or other person not employed by the school, (6) possession of weapons and dangerous instruments, (7) possession or use of narcotics, alcoholic beverages, and stimulant drugs,

(8) repeated school violations, and (9) disruptive and/or offensive use of language (District manual on policies and procedures 1984).[8]

At DuBois High, an estimated 35.2 percent of the boys' suspensions were for "repeated school violations."[9] That figure jumped to 63 percent with the inclusion of suspensions for which no specific reason was listed. Presumably, most unspecified cases were repeated school violations rather than some more specific and serious violation. A full 81.4 percent of the suspensions could be accounted for by adding the category "disruptive and offensive use of language." These figures demonstrate how heavily the discipline staff at DuBois, in accord with national patterns (see note 7), relied on suspensions to punish behaviors that threatened the school's authority rather than its safety. The figures also emphasize the amount of discretion called for in disciplinary work. The issue of "labeling" enters when we examine how disciplinarians determine the definition of "repeated" violations and the instances when profane or obscene language warrants punishment.

The procedural instructions in the district manual for "repeated school violations" explained that the rule "basically...is aimed at those students whose conduct is consistently at odds with normal school discipline"; these were the students disciplinarians defined as "troublemakers." The instructions went on to caution that a pupil should be suspended only when unacceptable behavior continued after all available school resources and services were tried or when an exceptionally serious act that warranted such action was committed.

Since the instructions did not define "available school resources and services," the discipline staff, in practice, operated as if any "legitimate" case entering their office came there either because it was "an exceptionally serious act," or because previous efforts by teachers, or perhaps counselors, had

Table 2 / Reasons for the Suspension of Boys ($N = 244$)

	Oct. 1986	Feb. 1987	Mar. 1987	Total	Percentage
Disruption of school	6	1	3	10	4.1
Damage/theft of school property	1	1	1	3	1.2
Damage/theft of private property	1	1	0	2	0.8
Assault on school employee	0	0	1	1	0.4
Physical abuse of another student	5	5	11	21	8.6
Possession of weapon	0	0	2	2	0.8
Possession of drugs or alcohol	0	1	5	6	2.4
Repeated school violations	28	22	36	86	35.2
Disruptive/offensive language	14	19	12	45	18.4
No reason listed	27	6	35	68	27.8
Total	82	56	35	244	99.7

failed. Thus, beyond assessing whether "a teacher should have handled this," disciplinarians made little or no effort to consider other school services.[10]

THE SOCIAL CONSTRUCTION OF A TROUBLEMAKER

Conflicts over disciplinary practice arose because the definition of what constituted misconduct was itself problematic. Although the authors of the school's rules identified the categories of punishable student behavior, they realized judgments about the meaning and seriousness of any particular behavior depended upon its specific social setting, the student's intent, and the responses of others present. Understandably, some categories of misconduct, such as "disrupting class," were necessarily vague or ambiguous. The immediate context of a student's actions distinguished silliness or immaturity from insubordination or disruptiveness. Situational factors such as intent or provocation changed the meaning of an act. For that very reason, district regulations allowed disciplinarians considerable discretion.

In practice, disciplinarians rarely questioned students about the details of their misbehavior or the reasons behind them. Instead, after identifying the charge against the student, they moved on to a series of questions about grades, attendance, previous suspensions, and, in some instances, the student's year in school, age, or plans for employment. A student's answers, rather than the particular circumstances of his actions, identified the misconduct's meaning to the disciplinarians. Only when a student's academic profile seemed to violate the disciplinarian's expectations would he or she inquire further about the charges against the student. They sought to punish "types of students" more than "types of behavior."

Whereas most students occasionally violated school rules, the proper role of the discipline office, as its staff understood it, was to deal with troublemakers who persistently disregarded the institution's authority. Information on grades, attendance, and prior disciplinary problems created a profile of the student's relationship to the school used to interpret the meaning of misconduct and the appropriateness of disciplinary intervention.[11] Students who failed classes, played hookey, used drugs, or frequently troubled teachers with disruptive behavior were students who, in the minds of most school workers, did not belong in school.

The following example illustrates the use of questions to interpret the significance of a student's behavior:

Mr. Leary picked up the next file on his desk and called out, "Is Kenneth Watson out there?" Kenneth stood up and walked over to Mr. Leary's doorway.
Leary: "Kenneth?"
Kenneth: "Yeah."
Leary: "Sit down." Kenneth slumped into the chair in front of Mr. Leary's desk. In a combative voice: "I've got a pink slip here that says you were

	disrupting class. Talking. I thought we had this straightened out. Wasn't this straightened out?"
Kenneth:	Muttering, "Yeah, I guess so."
Leary:	"What do you mean, 'I guess so'? If it was straightened out, you wouldn't be here." He paused, looking down at the pink slip. "It says here you were talking in class. So what is this? *I've got three others here for the same thing.* Now what's the problem?"
Kenneth:	"I don't know."
Leary:	"Well, we already brought your mother in, didn't we?" Kenneth shook his head slightly, looking puzzled. "Yeah, you were present at the meeting." Mr. Leary looked again at the file. "What class is it?"
Kenneth:	"Math."
Leary:	"How are you doing in it?" Kenneth shrugged. "Well, *did you pass math in the last report?*" Kenneth nodded. "What grade did you get, then?" Mr. Leary shouted, clearly exasperated.
Kenneth:	After a slight hesitation, "Two As and a B. I think I had an 89 for the last report and As for the ones before."
Leary:	Visibly surprised, "You have As and Bs in math?" Slight pause, then, "You're in what, general math?"
Kenneth:	"Algebra."
Leary:	*"Are you passing all your classes?"*
Kenneth:	"Yeah."
Leary:	"Were you on the honor roll?"
Kenneth:	"I don't know," still mumbling, still sullen.
Leary:	"What do you mean you don't know! Were you in the lottery?"
Kenneth:	He gestured over his shoulder in the direction of the main hallway, "That attendance thing?"
Leary:	"No! We have one for grades, too. Didn't you go to the awards assembly?"
Kenneth:	"Oh, yeah. I went to that. I got a slip ... said to report ... I didn't know."
Leary:	Quite frustrated, "Yeah, well I was there. I gave out the certificate and prize." He paused and looked down at the file again. *"What does this mean, 'talking in class'?"*
Kenneth:	Still mumbling, "We have these preclass exercises on the board. When I got that done, I end up talking."
Leary:	"What, you have a problem to do when you get to class?"
Kenneth:	"Yeah."
Leary:	In a reasoning tone, "Well, if you finish up early can't you help out someone who isn't as bright as you, who has trouble in math?"
Kenneth:	"He wants us to do our own work."
Leary:	"Yeah, well, ok. That doesn't mean you have to talk. You make it sound like you can't control yourself. Why don't you do some studying for another class? *A bright boy like you shouldn't have to go through all this.* So what's the solution to this problem?"
Kenneth:	"I guess I shouldn't talk in class."
Leary:	"Alright. *This is Mickey Mouse stuff.*" He paused, "You wait outside until the next period." After Kenneth left the office, Mr. Leary turned to me and explained, *"Clearly a classroom problem. A kid like that can understand if you reason with him. It's not like some of the*

barely educable kids we see in here. The teacher—I don't know what the problem is—just wants to pass along the problem to us. We get a lot of that here. This teacher should just take him aside and talk to him, even if he has to do it every week" (April 1984, italics added).

During my observation, three pink slips for disrupting class, a prior interview with a parent, and a sullen and uncooperative demeanor normally led to a student's suspension, a significant act in the creation of an official record. Disciplinarians typically did not ask students, "What does this mean?" Instead, they took "talking in class" as a known and unproblematic form of disruption.

In the case above, Mr. Leary began with the assumption that Kenneth, a student repeatedly sent to the office for disrupting class, must be a troublemaker. In the course of their interaction, however, Kenneth became a kid you could reason with; the talking in class became "Mickey Mouse stuff"; the whole problem became something the teacher should have dealt with. Each of these reconstructions occurred because Kenneth's grades altered the meaning of his behavior.

In most school workers' minds, students who received high grades demonstrated that they accepted the school's requirements and, presumably, acknowledged the value of the school's work. According to this reasoning, Kenneth obviously posed no challenge to the school's aims or operation—and indeed was one of its few success stories. Therefore, his talking in class, even if it recurred weekly, represented not a "repeated violation of school rules" but a problem with the teacher's ability to control the class.

PARENTAL INVOLVEMENT

A student's vulnerability to suspension, and to identification as a "troublemaker," may also depend upon his or her parents' ability to influence the actions of school personnel. As one NTA observed, "The only time you ever see a parent is when the kid is suspended and they have to come in." Indeed, according to district policy, "The primary purpose for the use of suspension is for the involvement of parents in the remediation of a problem."[12] In interviews, disciplinarians confirmed this objective. Ms. Gordon, an NTA working as a disciplinarian, told me: "Suspension is strictly for communication. Not to hurt the student or punish the student." Both she and the others did, however, qualify that objective with conditions such as "unless we can't keep the kid in school because it was something serious or he completely defies authority."

Although all agreed that suspensions served to bring parents into the school, the understanding among most school workers about what constituted "involvement of the parent in the remediation of a problem" challenged the claim that suspensions had no punitive intent. School workers expected parents to accept the school's authority and to support its goals and practices. They expected parents to force their children to comply with the school's rules. If parents suggested, through their words and demeanor, that they accepted the school's authority and shared its judgment of their child, then disciplinarians interpreted "involvement" as "notification." They informed the parents of the student's misbehavior and, frequently, suggested strategies for controlling the student's actions. However, if a parent either challenged the disciplinarian's version of events or argued that the student was responsible for him or herself, "involvement" became more punitive in intent. One teacher explained how a student's suspension would punish the parent and thereby encourage her to support the school's efforts:

> If you got to take a day off from work because of something your child has done, that's going to make you put more pressure on him. If you can't come up here, then you keep him home until you can come up here. He becomes *your* problem for four or five days. You got to worry about what he's doing in your apartment or your house while you're at work. Now you're a little more concerned about this (Mr. Fisk May 1987).

The relatively disadvantaged status of most parents *vis-a-vis* school workers meant that many parents received disrespectful and dismissive treatment.[13] Parents had few, if any, social or political resources with which to challenge a disciplinarian's actions. Freed from the constraints more powerful, higher status parents might have imposed, disciplinarians reverted to three tactics when they faced opposition from students and parents: (1) they denigrated the parenting skills of the mother or father; (2) they threatened the student with failure, arrest, or expulsion—frequently without the power or intent to make good their threat; (3) they explicitly denied any personal responsibility or concern for resolving the problem.

In the course of a reinstatement conference, Carl told Mr. Weis, "She [the teacher] seen me, I was coming out of the bathroom, but she closed the door and wouldn't let me in." His mother characterized this as an "involuntary cut." Weis countered by repeating the rule, "If you're late to class, you're not allowed in class. It's a cut." The mother muttered something about knowing all about it since she'd gone to school, too.

Weis:	*"Perhaps if you talked to your son—"*
Mother:	"I talk to Carl every day . . . but I have to go to work, and sleep, I can't watch him every minute. And he is sixteen. . . ."
Weis (to Carl):	*"You want to go to disciplinary school? Or drop out?"* (To mother): "Cuz that's where he's headed. *We won't take him for a third year in tenth grade. Not at seventeen.* (Mother mutters something.) You have a complaint that you're not getting serviced properly, there's a principal . . . I really have a problem that you didn't insist on getting his second report [card]. *How important is education to you? I know if I had kids, I wouldn't let them get away with that* . . . unless you're going to support him for the rest of your life" (March 1987, italics added).

Mr. Weis told Carl's mother that he needed more responsibility and discipline at home. She claimed that her son acted responsibly at home, it was only when he came to school that he "acted like a fool." During the course of this discussion, someone delivered Carl's grades to Mr. Weis which showed he was failing all of his classes. After a few minutes of berating Carl for his grades, Mr. Weis said, *"I have no time for this. I am writing here, 'to be dropped from school at age seventeen if there is no improvement in grades and attendance.'* So you'll receive a letter this summer, when we make our review." As they left the office, Mr. Weis turned to me and said, "All bluff." I asked, "You can't drop him?" Weis said, "Naw." "Will he get a letter?" I asked. He answered, "No."

Mr. Weis admitted to me that he was bluffing; but in such an example his threat's impact came less from his actual power to expel the student—which, informally, he could and had done—than from his presentation of the school as unforgiving and unconcerned. It was not, in fact, unusual to hear him say to a parent: "This is your problem. You'll have to deal with it. I'll readmit him, but—I don't mind, I'll keep suspending him. It's not my problem" (April 1984).

This posture by a school official seems likely to affect "secondary deviance," that is, the student's continued violation of the school's expectations. Mr. Weis has emphasized to Carl that the school has little stake in his success and a primarily negative vision of his social value and personal worth—the very conditions which may strengthen his hostility toward the school and to foster his commitment to the troublemaker role.[14] Even if Carl does not want to adopt the troublemaker identity, Mr. Weis has made it clear that he will be treated as one, in any case.[15] Moreover, as I have suggested above, it seems likely that Mr. Weis's easy rejection of Carl and his mother, and his willingness to push Carl out of school, is connected to their social position. A higher status mother might have been successful in her efforts to define Carl's behavior as an "involuntary cut" and to forestall his classification as a troublemaker.

GETTING RID OF TROUBLEMAKERS

The discipline office had two strategies to get rid of students identified as troublemakers. One was to transfer the student; the other to drop the student from the roll. Transfers were of two types: "regular" transfers, arranged when students moved out of the school's catchment area; and "disciplinary transfers," known by their code as "21s." Dropping a student from the roll required that the student be 17 years old. At that age, schooling was no longer compulsory and the discipline office interpreted this to mean the school no longer had to keep the student.

Typically, if a disciplinarian sought a regular transfer for a troublesome student, arrangements were made for the student to shift his or her legal residence to the address of a relative in another part of the district. This procedure avoided the paperwork and legal proceedings of a disciplinary transfer. In the following incident, however, Mr. Weis discovered he could get rid of a troublemaker who already lived outside the normal bounds of the school. Mr. Weis began a conference with John, a boy I had seen in the office on two previous occasions, by asking, "What's your address?" After questioning, Weis discovered John's address put him in another school's catchment area. Weis called John's house:

> Hello, Mrs. Preston?... well you'll have to wake her up. This is DuBois High School calling... Mrs. Preston, this is Carl Weis. John has been acting up again. He refused to take off his hat and has been disruptive. I have five pink slips on him. Look, I don't know why he's here and not at Northern Heights to start with. ... Yeah, well, I'm going to write up a transfer for him and get all his records together. You'll have to come down tomorrow and take him over there and enroll him.

After John left the office, Weis turned to me and said:

> We didn't solve anything. We just sent the problem along to Northern Heights. But we have to look out for ourselves. That's the way it is—crazy system (April 1984, italics added).

Although this case was unusual in that the student already lived in another school's catchment area, it was absolutely standard in intent. The goal of the discipline office, as Mr. Weis explained, was not to solve any problems a student might have, but to protect the school's operation. Thus, in the case of another transfer, Mr. Leary confirmed Mr. Weis's assessment of their goals. Mr. Leary escorted a boy and his mother out of the office and then sat down next to me. He explained:

> Now that mother came in here, her son was suspended weeks ago for having a weapon, marijuana. Now she wants him transferred to Washington High. You know, for us, that's fine. We get rid of one.

I asked if 21 transfers helped. He said:

> They help this school. They don't help the kid. But then, you can't do anything with those kids, anyway (March 1986, italics added).

Transfers were, thus, seen as an important resource for the discipline office. If they could build a sufficiently strong case, they could get rid of a troublemaker, even if he wanted to remain in the school, through the use of a disciplinary transfer. Because district rules prohibited the use of 21s on students whose only offenses were cutting class or missing school, the disciplinarians took pains to document all other forms of misconduct on potential or identified troublemakers. Since they would be used for a 21, Mr. Leary stressed the importance of being detailed and complete when making out "pink slips."

> You don't just write, "picked up for cutting class." You write, "cutting class, ran away from officer, used abusive language," all of which is true, but if you don't write it down—or if there's a disturbance in class, you write down, "shoved desks, said 'fuck you' to teacher"—you know, we're not squeamish. We write down just what they say, "fuck you" or "fuck you white mother."

Since the projected future or "career" of the forms influenced their form and content,[16] the pink slips represent an important point at which discretion or "bias" can enter into the construction of an official disciplinary record.

Once disciplinarians filed the paperwork on a 21, a parent had to come in for a conference. The parent has the right to a hearing in the district superintendent's office. If a parent does not want a hearing, he or she can sign a form during the conference transferring the child. The discipline staff and the principal work toward that goal, since all the paperwork goes to the district superintendent's office for review when the parent wants a hearing. As Mr. Leary complained: "Then they mostly do nothing. Send the kid back. Decide he needs another chance."

Student transfers were not the only means available to get rid of trouble-makers. Another option used by the school was the informal expulsion of overage students. Although the state granted all students the right to attend public school until the age of twenty-one, it did not require attendance past the age of sixteen. At DuBois, school workers understood that to mean that they were not required to keep a student in school once he or she turned seventeen.[17] It was not unusual, therefore, for disciplinarians to reason: "Look, he's already eighteen and only in tenth grade. You know he can only stay in school 'til he's twenty-one. I don't want him here. I'm going to talk to [the principal]." That logic also permitted the following scene. A police officer escorted four boys into the discipline office. The officer stopped at Weis's door. Weis sent the boys into Leary's office.

The officer: Two with, two without IDs.
Weis: This one I don't know. He might be an adult. I don't know if he's a juvenile. This one's a student. Doesn't come in very often.

Weis asked the boy he didn't recognize how old he was. The boy said he was seventeen, went to DuBois, and was in tenth grade.

Weis: You don't go to DuBois. I just dropped you as of now. *I'm not suspending you. I'm dropping you from school.*

Weis said to the officer, in reference to the other boy who was younger:

You're going to leave the building right now.
Older boy: How many days suspension?
Weis: I just told him. Two months, three months, 'til his mother comes in (April 1986).

Although in this example the student demonstrated little interest in attending school,[18] other students who did want to attend but who ran into problems with the discipline office were also subject to the informal expulsion of an "overage drop." In the following instance, Nicholas had missed most of his first period math classes because of familial responsibilities.

Weis: What're you in for?
Nicholas: Mr. Fisk suspended me cuz I missed his class.
Weis: Let me get your folder.

He left the office and returned with the folder. To Nicholas's stepfather he said:

As you are aware, sir, Nicholas was out of school and then let back in school. When he was readmitted, he signed a contract that he would attend school and behave himself. *Right now, he's overage, still in tenth grade, not passing* [one class]. *I recommend dropping him.*
Nicholas: That's only one class!
Weis: But that's enough. You are overage in tenth grade. You have to pass....
Nicholas: Don't you want to know why I missed—
Weis: No reason is—you signed a contract.
Nicholas: I had to do something for my mother.
Weis: *You're eighteen years old, third year in tenth grade, you have to set priorities. If that's to do something for your mother—you signed a contract that you would obey all the rules and attend all your classes.* You know, we wanted to transfer you before. Do you have a relative in another neighborhood (March 1987, italics added)?

The conference established that Nicholas was a classic troublemaker. He had previously been dropped from school, and was overage, behind in grade, and failing a class. Mr. Weis wanted him out of the school. Since he could not initiate a disciplinary transfer on the grounds of cutting class, Mr. Weis explored his two other options: an "overage" drop pressed on Nicholas because he had violated the terms of his readmission contract, and a regular transfer based on the pretense that Nicholas had changed residence.

It is important to note that because he did not conform to all of the school's demands, the school workers focused on how to exclude Nicholas rather than on how to solve his problems or to work around them. As I learned from lengthy interviews with both Nicholas and his stepfather, Nicholas had tried to work within the system. As he told me:

I have this first period class and I'm supposed to be there at five minutes before eight. And I have to take my nieces to day care in the morning.... They live with me, and there's no one else there, you know, that could take them. It's inconvenient for my mother cuz she leaves so early. And their mom is in Florida. So I was the only one that could take them. So I was taking them, and I wasn't making the class. But I was bringing notes and stuff in to show them.... Mr. Fisk wouldn't contact my mother or nothing. He just kept on telling me the notes aren't going to do no good.... I talked to my mother at one time. And that's when she told me she was going to try to work something out [about taking the girls to day care]. But at the moment to keep taking them.... You know, so that's when I went to see the counselor. She told me to see [someone else]... he was absent two days I brought in the note.... Probably if I went to see [the counselor] earlier, I would have probably got help. But I didn't know who to go see. I thought he was the teacher, I was supposed to give the notes and all that to him.... [When I did see the counselor], she was saying there's not much you can do, and everything. I could have got a roster change if it was like the beginning.

The school workers blamed his mother for putting Nicholas in the position of having to care for his sister's daughters and blamed him for accepting that responsibility. Mr. Fisk explained:

> Why should that responsibility become his? The parent has to take more active— why would you thrust that responsibility on your offspring if it's creating problems in the school? ... If he's thrust into this situation and he knows it's threatening his possibilities for graduation, for promotion, for passing this class, if he's truly serious about passing, he has to lighten the load. And there's only one load he can lighten. And that's the supervision of this [niece]. So that means sitting down with whomever.

Mr. Fisk assumed that the solution to the problem involved "sitting down" with someone. Nicholas, therefore, was penalized for his mother's inability or unwillingness to make his education the family's priority.

Nicholas confronted a system which his parents had little skill in handling or power to influence, and which rejected his own efforts. Had he come from a middle-income family, it is likely he would have fared better. Not only would it have been less likely for such a family/school conflict to arise, but a middle-income parent would have had greater success in manipulating the bureaucratic requirements of the school system. As it was, Nicholas's family circumstances allowed—one might even argue, encouraged—both Mr. Fisk and Mr. Weis to dismiss him as another troublemaker who did not value education.

BEING "AT RISK"

When I spoke to Ms. Riley, the vice principal of DuBois High, she was not "amazed" that 335 of her students had "dropped out" in the previous year. Instead, citing how many kids faced problems at home or on the streets, she was amazed that so many of them "made it." DuBois High students who faced disruption, violence, substance abuse, or conflicting obligations to school and family were understandably distracted, uncooperative, or truant. Manifesting those symptoms of broader social ills, however, brought them into contact with the discipline office. There troubled students were rather easily reconceptualized as troublemakers. And troublemakers were readily seen as undeserving of the school's services. This process is all the more disturbing when we consider that inner-city African Americans and Hispanics are disproportionately likely to suffer from such social ills. The activities of the discipline office, which routinely identified "troublemakers" and "got rid of" them through suspensions and involuntary drops, may be one important but largely unacknowledged mechanism through which schools perpetuate the racial and class stratification of the larger society.

Ironically, educational research has served to legitimate the actions of the disciplinarians. In a conference to reinstate a student following his suspension for poor attendance, Mr. Leary remarked:

I'm talking to you like a man...*this is a turning point in your life. You can go either way: follow the rules and graduate, or drop out of the whole school system.* You signed this contract. I'm going to reinstate you. But I tell you quite frankly, you got to get up, whatever you got to do, and get to school. I know, there's no doubt in my mind, [the principal] *is going to want to drop you. Not because he wants to be mean, but statistics prove it out* (March 1986, italics added).

Indeed, the statistics prove that students are most likely to "drop out" of high school if they come from a low-income background, are frequently absent or truant, have a record of school suspensions, are failing classes, and are overage in grade (Hahn and Danzberger 1987; Natriello 1986). But what is proven? Those factors are the very indicators that disciplinarians used to define troublemakers and that led to suspensions, disciplinary transfers, and involuntary drops. Although it is unwise to generalize from the findings of one case study, we can nevertheless ask: are "risk factors" correlated with "dropping out" because they are used routinely by school workers to expel students? If that is the case, then disciplinarians' daily activities play an important role in regulating social mobility.

Notes

1. For a critical discussion of "at risk" see Margonis (1992).

2. "Pushouts" refers to students who are forced to leave school. "Stopouts" refers to students who withdraw from school and then return.

3. See Rist (1977) for an explanation of labeling theory's utility in the study of schools.

4. Although all of the students were African Americans, the faculty's racial composition reflected the metropolitan area's labor pool and thus included many whites.

5. These figures come from a report prepared by the school for the visiting committee of the association charged with evaluating the school for accreditation. For reasons of confidentiality, I cannot give the full name of this publication or of other reports issued by the school or the school district.

6. The irregular tempo of activity in the discipline office made it difficult to gather accurate, quantifiable data on the number, type, and disposition of cases. Although I solicited staff members' help at one point, asking each of them to mark on a chart the type and disposition of each case they handled, I found their recordkeeping unreliable. Moreover, such records masked the very assumptions and decisions I sought to investigate.

7. National studies report that most high school suspensions are for nonthreatening behavior—defying authority, chronic tardiness, chronic absence, and use of profanity and vulgarity. Black students are suspended three times as often as whites (Hahn and Danzberger 1987:19).

8. The physical education department also suspended students who were unprepared for gym class on three occasions. Those "one day" suspensions were not processed through the discipline office and are not a part of my report.

9. These figures come from the suspension reports compiled by one of the disciplinarians for the district. I selected three months, at random, from the 1986/87 school year and computed the percentages. These figures are compatible with my observations in the discipline office. The total number of boys suspended in those three months was 244.

10. Students had extremely limited access to any form of counseling. The few "guidance counselors" in the school each had responsibility for hundreds of students and seemed to limit their "guidance" to brief conferences on scheduling or attendance problems. The only other counselor I was aware of was a part-time drug counselor from a private agency.

11. McCarthy and Hoge (1987) found that school disciplinary sanctions were influenced by the student's past official record, grades, and "general demeanor in school." These findings suggest that the practices of the discipline staff at DuBois conform to those at other schools.

12. The other purposes of suspension noted in the district's guidelines were: removing the student from the scene of difficulty, diffusing a situation when the final outcome is not yet assured, and displaying the school's dissatisfaction with the student's behavior.

13. The relatively homogeneous background of DuBois students prohibited a comparative assessment of how a parent's race and class affected her or his treatment by disciplinarians.

14. Crespo (1974) found that a school's disciplinary responses to "skippers" (truants) did indeed lead to the amplification of deviance and, in many cases, encouraged students to drop out.

15. See Anderson's discussion of how "social selves" are constructed in social interaction; as he states, "a person is somebody because others allow him to be" (1976:38).

16. See Meehan (1986) for a discussion of how the projected use of police records shapes their form and content as well as for a discussion of how police officers infer the meaning or accuracy of a record.

17. In the official statistics for the 1985/86 school year, all but six of the 335 dropouts were categorized as "overage."

18. Crespo noted, "students who do not find school rewarding are more prepared to consider missing it. In this sense, the tracking system provides the invitational edge to the activity of skipping" (1974:133). Students in lower tracks are offered less stimulating and less valuable educational experiences (Oakes 1985). We must remember, therefore, that the school bears some responsibility for its students' attitudes and behaviors.

References

Anderson, Carolyn
1982 "The search for school climate: A review of the research." Review of Educational Research 52:368–420.

Anderson, Elijah
1976 A Place on the Corner. Chicago: University of Chicago Press.

Becker, Howard
1963 Outsiders. New York: Free Press.

Bittner, Egon
1967 "The police on skid-row: A 'study of peace keeping.'" American Sociological Review 32:699–715.

Borus, Michael E., and Susan A. Carpenter
1983 "A note on the return of dropouts to high school." Youth and Society 14:501–507.

Cicourel, Aaron V., and John I. Kitsuse
1977 "The school as a mechanism of social differentiation." In Power and Ideology in Education, ed. Jerome Karabel and A.H. Halsey, 282–292. New York: Oxford University Press.

Cohen, Lawrence, and James Kleugel
1987 "Determinants of juvenile court dispositions: Ascriptive and achieved factors in two metropolitan courts." American Sociological Review 43:162–176.

Connell, R. W., D. J. Ashenden, S. Kessler, and G.W. Dowsett
1982 Making the Difference: Schools, Families and Social Division. Boston: George Allen & Unwin.

Corcoran, Thomas
1985 "Effective secondary schools." In Reaching for Excellence: An Effective Schools Sourcebook, 71–97. Washington, D.C.: U.S. Department of Education.

Crespo, Manuel
1974 "The career of the school skipper." In Decency and Deviance: Studies in Deviant Behavior, ed. Jack Haas, 129–145. Toronto: McClelland and Stewart.

Ekstrom, Ruth B., Margaret E. Goertz, Judith M. Pollack, and Donald A. Rock
1987 "Who drops out of high school and why? Findings from a national study."

In School Dropouts: Patterns and Policies, ed. Gary Natriello, 52–69. New York: Teachers College Press.

Empey, Lamar
1982 American Delinquency: Its Meaning and Construction. Homewood, Ill.: Dorsey.

Farrell, Edwin
1988 "Giving voice to high school students: Pressure and boredom, ya know what I'm sayin'?" American Educational Research Journal 25:489–502.

Fine, Michelle
1986 "Why urban adolescents drop into and out of public high school." In School Dropouts: Patterns and Policies, ed. Gary Natriello, 89–105. New York: Teachers College Press.
1991 Framing Dropouts: Notes on the Politics of an Urban Public High School. Albany, N.Y.: State University of New York Press.

Finn, Jeremy D.
1989 "Withdrawing from school." Review of Educational Research 59:117–142.

Hahn, Andrew, and Jacqueline Danzberger
1987 Dropouts in America: Enough is Known for Action. Washington, D.C.: Institute for Educational Leadership.

Karabel, Jerome, and A.H. Halsey, eds.
1977 Power and Ideology in Education. New York: Oxford University Press.

Kozol, Jonathan
1991 Savage Inequalities: Children in American Schools. New York: Crown Publishers, Inc.

Lemert, Edwin M.
1967 Human Deviance. Englewood Cliffs. N.J.: Prentice Hall.

Lipsky, Michael
1980 Street-Level Bureaucracy: Dilemmas of the Individual in Public Services. New York: Russell Sage.

Maines, David R., and Joy C. Charlton
1985 "Negotiated order approach to the analysis of social organization." In Foundations of Interpretive Sociology: Original Essays in Symbolic Interaction, ed. Harvey A. Faberman and R.S. Perinbanayagam, 271–308. Greenwich, Conn.: JAI Press Inc.

Margonis, Frank
1992 "The cooptation of "at risk": Paradoxes of policy criticism." Teachers College Record 94:343–364.

McCarthy, John, and Dean Hoge
1987 "The social construction of school punishment: Racial disadvantage out of universalistic process." Social Forces 65:1101–1120.

Meehan, Albert J.
1986 "Record-keeping practices in the policing of juveniles." Urban Life 15:70–102.

Mehan, Hugh
1992 "Understanding inequality in schools: The contribution of interpretive studies." Sociology of Education 65:1–20.

Miller, Sandra E.
1988 "Influencing engagement through accommodation: An ethnographic study of at-risk students." American Education Research Journal 25:465–487.

Morash, Merry
1984 "Establishment of a juvenile police record." Criminology 22:97–111.
Morrow, George
1986 "Standardizing practice in the analysis of school dropouts." In School Dropouts: Patterns and Policies, ed. Gary Natriello, 38–51. New York: Teachers College Press.
Natriello, Gary, ed.
1986 School Dropouts: Patterns and Policies. New York: Teachers College Press.
Oakes, Jeannie
1985 Keeping Track: How Schools Structure Inequality. New Haven, Conn.: Yale University Press.
Paternoster, Raymond, and Leeann Iovanni
1989 "The labeling perspective and delinquency: An elaboration of the theory and an assessment of the evidence." Justice Quarterly 6:359–394.
Peng, Samuel S.
1983 "High school dropouts: Descriptive information from high school and beyond." National Center for Education Statistics Bulletin.
Pittman, R. B.
1986 "Importance of personal, social factors as potential means for reducing high school dropout rate." The High School Journal 70:7–13.
Rist, Ray C.
1977 "On understanding the processes of schooling: The contributions of labeling theory." In Power and Ideology in Education, ed. Jerome Karabel and A.H. Halsey, 292–305. New York: Oxford University Press.
Rubinstein, Jonathan
1973 City Police. Farrar, Straus & Giroux.
Rumberger, Russell W.
1983 "Dropping out of high school: The influence of race, sex, and family background." American Educational Research Journal 20:199–220.
Rutter, Michael, B. Maughan, R. Moritmore, J. Ouston, and A. Smith
1979 Fifteen Thousand Hours: Secondary Schools and Their Effects on Children. Cambridge, Mass.: Harvard University Press.
Sampson, Robert J.
1986 "Effects of socioeconomic context on official reaction to juvenile delinquency." American Sociological Review 51:876–885.
Skolnich, Jerome H.
1975 Justice Without Trial. New York: John Wiley.
Sudnow, David
1965 "Normal crimes: Sociological features of the penal code in a public defender's office." Social Problems 12:255–276.
Tittle, Charles
1980 "Labelling and crime: An empirical evaluation." In The Labelling of Deviance, ed. Walter Gove, 241–263. Beverly Hills, Calif.: Sage.
Toles, T., E. M. Schulz, and W. K. Rice Jr.
1986 "A study of variation in dropout rates attributable to effects of high schools." Metropolitan Education 2:30–38.
Waegel, William B.
1981 "Case routinization in investigative police work." Social Problems 28: 263–275.

Wagenaar, Theodore C.
1987 "What do we know about dropping out of high school?" In Research in Sociology of Education and Socialization, ed. Ronald G. Corwin, 161–190. Greenwich, Conn.: JAI Press.

Weis, Lois, Eleanor Farrar, and Hugh G. Petrie, ed.
1989 Dropouts from school: Issues, dilemmas, and solutions. New York: State University of New York Press.

Yudof, Mark G.
1975 "Suspension and expulsion of black students from the public schools: Academic capital punishment and the Constitution." Law and Contemporary Problems 39:374–411.

29 / Strange Interlude: An Analysis of Juvenile Parole Revocation Decision Making

GRAY CAVENDER
PAUL KNEPPER

Sociologists who study decision making in the justice system are confronted with an interesting task when they consider juvenile justice. The adult system's rational model of decision making, with its emphasis on formal legal criteria, is largely inapplicable in juvenile justice. Juvenile justice's underlying ideology of "individualized justice" is operationalized through the paternalistic *parens patriae* doctrine. Decisions reflect the "best interests of the child and society," not traditional due process guarantees (Bernard 1992; Champion 1992). Today, despite 25 years of efforts to "reform" its ideology and operational strategies, "flexibility, informality, and discretion" still characterize juvenile justice (Bortner 1988:43). The transfer of jurisdiction and the specter of the death penalty may produce an "adult" version of juvenile justice, yet *parens patriae* remains in place.

Because the rational model is inconsistent with the data, researchers turn to other models for analyzing juvenile justice decision making. Some address the effects on outcomes of extralegal factors such as gender, race, and social class (Black and Reiss 1970; Cohen and Kluegel 1978; Dannefer and Schutt 1982; Piliavin and Briar 1964). Others, using a "process" model, suggest that the extralegal factors that inform decisions may be masked as legal factors in subsequent stages (Bortner and Reed 1985; McCarthy and Smith 1986; Zatz 1987).

An alternative approach considers the gestalt of juvenile justice decision making (Emerson 1969, 1983). Rather than focusing on outcomes or the criteria on which they are based, the gestalt perspective emphasizes the social production of decisions (Drass and Spencer 1987). Important considerations include case sequence and flow, decision maker/client interactions, professional norms, organizational goals, and situational context (Emerson 1983; also see Maynard 1982). Sociologists focus on three aspects of decision making in the gestalt perspective: (1) theory of office, (2) organizational context, and (3) accounts.

Theory of office, which refers to the working ideology of decision makers, consists of typologies and outcomes (Drass and Spencer 1987; Kelly 1979; Rubington and Weinberg 1981). Some research focusing on theory of office emphasizes case types (e.g., Sudnow's [1965] normal crimes); some emphasizes client types (e.g., Emerson's [1969] moral character of delinquents). Decision makers' reliance on case or client typologies is based on their assumption of symmetry between behavior and character (Maynard 1982:356; also see Garfinkel 1967:106; Goffman 1959:1). Moreover, personal attributes may contribute to offense types (see Sudnow 1965:243–244), and prior offenses sometimes are treated as offender attributes (see Maynard 1982:250–251).

Relying on legal factors, attitudinal impressions, training and experience, decision makers construct a client/case typology, usually at the initial meeting with a client (Sudnow 1965). They then seek information that confirms the typology and the "appropriate" case outcome (Rosecrance 1988). They learn a theory of office through professional socialization; it is embedded in their organization (Drass and Spencer 1987:279; Sudnow 1965:248).

Organizational context is a second aspect of the gestalt of juvenile justice decision making. Decision makers perform certain tasks, for example, disposing of cases, to accomplish the goals of their agencies. Disposing of cases may be more important than a particular defendant's guilt or innocence (Maynard 1982:351). They also must consider how one disposition affects other cases, and what is "reasonable" in a situation (Emerson 1983:443; Sudnow 1965:248).

Decisions thus require sensitivity to organizational resources such as available bed space (Emerson 1983:444–46). Decision makers also must be sensitive to the various occupational roles within their organizations, and to the special relationships of such roles. Some roles may enjoy greater privilege than others in decision making. For example, in involuntary commitment hearings, the psychiatrist's opinion tends to prevail because organizational work arrangements give him or her special access to and knowledge of the client (Decker 1987:159). Knowledge, thus, is situationally organized (Decker 1987:163).

Criminal justice case dispositions are usually rendered in a formal ceremonial context by courts or administrative boards (see Hagan, Hewitt, Alwin 1979). Ceremonies are more than simple "pomp and circumstance," and they produce more than dispositions: they are staged to confront juveniles with their wrongdoing, perhaps to elicit commitment to improvement (Emerson 1969, 1983; see Goffman 1959). Ceremonies also subordinate defendants/clients and reinforce organizational authority and solidarity (Emerson 1969; Garfinkel 1956). They perpetuate the organization's working ideology. Decision makers appeal to that ideology to justify case disposition to the client, to themselves, and for the record. The official record and other justifications are an account.

Accounts are a third aspect of the gestalt of decision making. They are the language people use to make actions intelligible to evaluative inquiry (Scott and Lyman 1968:46). The intelligibility of an account depends on its context; like a disposition, it must be reasonable in the situation (Garfinkel 1967:3). However, they are neither an after-the-fact matter nor are they limited to problematic behavior. Rather, they are a dynamic, unavoidable feature of all social life (Garfinkel 1967:1). The anticipation of accountability shapes and is concurrent with the production of actions.

Decision makers in justice organizations offer accounts. By emphasizing some aspects of a situation and de-emphasizing others, accounts help justify particular outcomes (Garfinkel 1967). Indeed, they are constructed so that the outcome appears to be the only possibility. Accounts are designed to "cool out" defendants/clients. They also "cool out" reluctant decision makers, inviting them to see themselves as professionals who agree with an outcome (Emerson 1983:441–42; Garfinkel 1967:108–111). Accounts are an aspect of the professional socialization of decision makers; they refer to and validate the theory of office (Drass and Spencer 1987:279; Spencer 1983).

Goffman's (1959) dramaturgical framework adds insight to the gestalt perspective. He notes that individuals in social settings sometimes act together as a professional team (1959:79). They may reach consensual definitions about the situations in which they find themselves, or plan upcoming performances (1959:9–19). Goffman suggests that they accomplish these activities "backstage" without an audience. Familiarity and collusion are the norm (1959:182–186). In contrast, when the team performs before an audience, formality and decorum rule (1959:108–12). The team dramatizes certain activities to convey the correct meaning and sustain its underlying definition of the situation (1959:141). Performances become institutionalized, taking on abstract, stereotypic meanings that reflect idealized/official values (1959:30–35). Goffman's dramaturgical framework is especially applicable to decision making in the juvenile justice system.

A caveat must be interposed here. Unlike most theatrical performances, audience members are not always passive observers. Clients in criminal justice settings are an active part of the decision-making gestalt. They may resist, with varying degrees of success, the imposition of a typology or its typical outcome (see Emerson 1969; Piliavin and Briar 1964).

Sociologists have considered client involvement and other aspects of the decision-making gestalt in analyses of juvenile justice and juvenile courts (Emerson 1969), and juvenile probation (Cicourel 1968). However, there is little research on juvenile corrections from the gestalt or other perspectives (Krisberg et al. 1986). Accordingly, we consider the gestalt of decision making in juvenile parole revocation hearings.

DATA SOURCES AND RESEARCH METHODS

The Setting

The analysis is based on observations of 114 hearings held by a western state juvenile parole board. The board comprises a chairperson and two trainees. The chairperson or case management coordinator (CMC) is appointed by the director of the state department of corrections. The CMC, the only permanent board member, has final authority on all decisions. The trainees are parole officers who maintain their caseloads while serving a three-month term on the board. During our research, there were two CMCs and four trainees.

The juvenile parole board is an administrative tribunal, not a court of law. Attorneys are rarely present, and rules of evidence and other criminal trial procedures are inapplicable. Although there are formal guidelines, the board enjoys wide latitude in deciding cases. Several potential dispositions are available. The board may revoke parole and remand the juvenile to a correctional facility. The board may reinstate parole and allow the juvenile to live at home, at a foster home, or at a placement facility such as a halfway house or group home. If parole is reinstated, the board may impose additional conditions, for example, requiring the juvenile to participate in a drug treatment program. Decisions may be postponed while waiting for more information or for other reasons. The board's decisions are binding.

The juveniles who appear before the board are charged with parole violations. These may be technical violations, such as being AWOL from a placement facility, or new criminal offenses. Usually, hearings for technical violations are initiated by the juvenile's parole officer (PO) or by a representative of the placement facility where the juvenile resides, and hearings for new offenses are initiated by police arrest. Often, the board members know the juvenile on a first name basis. The juvenile may have appeared before the board in the past, or may be supervised by a trainee parole officer.

The juveniles were held in a disciplinary/detention unit at the juvenile correctional facility for an average of ten days pending their hearings. The department of corrections held revocation hearings for males and females on separate days. Due to limited resources, the research team attended only the revocation hearings for males, who constituted the vast majority of the board's workload. The board met weekly, and heard an average of 12 cases a day. To a degree, cases were scheduled for the convenience of the POs. All hearings for juveniles under parole officer A would be sequenced in order, then those of parole officer B, and so on.

On the day of the hearing, a security officer accompanied each juvenile to a staff lounge where the board conducted its business. After announcing the juvenile, the security officer stood in front of the door through which the juvenile had entered. A long, cafeteria-style table divided the room roughly in half. The board members (the CMC in the middle flanked by the trainees) were seated on one side of the table. The juvenile, wearing a bright-orange jumpsuit—the uniform for the detention unit—was seated across the table from them. The juvenile's PO and occasionally placement staff, if he resided in such a facility, sat beside the juvenile. Additional chairs behind the juvenile remained empty except when occupied by family members or legal counsel. The researchers were seated about ten feet from the table. The table was piled high with case files. The CMC used a small, hand-held tape recorder to record the board's decisions and rationales for them; hearings and other discussions were not recorded.

Data Collection

Our research team was made up of professors and students. Members of the team attended revocation hearings for two weeks, and developed a protocol that was discussed and revised by the full team. Two members "tested" the protocol at another revocation hearing, and then revised it. We developed a protocol because we could not tape-record hearings. It streamlined the collection of information common to all hearings. Because we could simply check off standard information, we were free to focus on the dynamics of the decision-making process. This permitted greater sensitivity to the gestalt of the process and to emergent categories of analysis and unanticipated findings (see Glaser and Strauss 1967). After the second week of attendance, the participants treated the researchers more as colleagues than as an audience.

Our data include protocol information and nearly verbatim transcripts of the hearings and attendant discussions (for a rationale for do-it-yourself transcripts, see Atkinson and Drew 1979; Holstein 1988:460). The transcripts include incomplete sentences, organizational jargon, slang, and profanity, all of which are important for understanding the decision-making gestalt. We conducted preliminary data collection sessions and research team review sessions to enhance the reliability of the observations.

THE PREHEARING CONFERENCE

We made an interesting discovery during our preliminary observations. Before the official parole revocation hearing, the board held a kind of informal conference during which it determined the facts, the outcome, a "script," and also offered accounts for these actions. These decisions and the process through which they were made reflected a shared theory of office and an awareness of the organizational context of decisions.

Goffman's (1959) "backstage" metaphor is especially apt for the prehearing conferences. Aside from the researchers, no audience was present. The participants knew one another as colleagues and sometimes as friends; the atmosphere was relaxed.

The prehearing conferences were embedded in a melange of interactions and activities that occurred between the formal revocation hearings: tape-recording the previous decision, thumbing through a stack of folders for the next case, ordinary social interactions, departmental gossip (see Maynard 1988:320–322). At any point during these activities, a PO might focus the discussion with, "Let me tell you a little story about this kid" (Case 96). The prehearing conference had begun.

An informal conference occurred in 106 of the 114 cases we observed. Only when an attorney was present or the PO was absent did a case proceed without one. The exceptions are instructive. The presence of an attorney constituted an audience which negated the backstage atmosphere and precluded the conference. The lack of a conference when the PO was absent points up the PO's centrality in decision making.

The prehearing conferences ranged from 1 to 17 minutes in duration; they lasted an average of 6 minutes, with a modal length of 2 minutes. The participants exchanged a wealth of information during these brief conferences, communicating through an organizational shorthand underpinned by a shared theory of office. They were a professional team with tasks to accomplish (see Goffman 1959:79).

What Happened

First, the participants decided "what happened," that is, they reconstructed the facts leading to the revocation hearing. With technical violations, the facts might include the details of being AWOL from a placement facility and any ensuing mischief. In 67 percent of the cases, the juvenile was charged with a new offense. Here, "what happened" included details about the offense or the arrest. For example, in one case, a PO explained "the police had [the juvenile] on trespass, and, while they were looking for another kid, he kicked out the police car windows and escaped" (Case 135).

Reconstructing "what happened" was not simply a matter of fact-finding with respect to the current allegation. Rather, it entailed a broader consideration of the juvenile's social history. For example, as they discussed "what happened," the participants in the discussion offered typologies. Some typologies referred to character or personality traits: "he's a manipulator" (Cases 81, 86), "he has a negative attitude" (Case 115). Others referred to behavior on the street or in detention: "he's been a bad boy" (Case 136), "he's been a real flame in here" (Case 80). Occasionally, the participants offered positive typologies: "he's not a criminal offender" (Case 83). Some participants stated a typology in professional vernacular: "he has a substance abuse problem" (Case 114), "he's a sociopathic personality" (Case 105). Others used common parlance: "he's a jerk" (Case 116), "he's an asshole" (Case 120). All participants enjoyed a license to offer a typology and everyone seemed to understand its contribution to reconstructing "what happened." Typologies contributed to a definition of the situation (Goffman 1959:4).

Accounts often accompanied and were compatible with typologies. The participants offered biographical social histories that explained how the juveniles were the sorts of people who get involved in such situations (Decker 1987; Garfinkel 1967:106), and they usually attributed responsibility for violations to the juveniles.

As they tried to discover what happened and to decide what to do, the board relied heavily on the PO's definition of the situation. This is not surprising since the PO probably had the most thorough knowledge of the juvenile's social history and of the alleged violation. Moreover, the trainees were POs and one CMC was a former PO. One board member asked the PO to "Tell me what happened so I won't have to read the file" (Case 135). The PO's importance even extended to quality of evidence issues, as this exchange suggests,

PO: I know he did it. He has a power booster, and didn't have one before.
CMC: Will he cop to it if you confront him...?
PO: No, he'll deny it. Can't we lock him up?
CMC: ...If there's a preponderance of evidence.
PO: There is, we've got him (Case 80).

These discussions were commonplace, and seemed to assume the juvenile's guilt (see Sudnow 1965:253).

Once determined, typologies and reconstructions of "what happened" were rarely refuted. The board revoked parole in 94 percent of the cases in which a negative typology was offered during the pretrial conference.

What Should Be Done

Theory of office consists of typologies and outcomes. At the prehearing conference, the participants chose outcomes that were appropriate to the typologies and their determination of "what happened." They also offered accounts for the outcomes. The board was sensitive to the organizational context, including resource limitations and work roles.

The following exchange occurred in a case where a juvenile had assaulted a staff member at a placement facility.

Placement: We won't tolerate hands on staff, but it would be countertherapeutic to charge him with assault.
CMC: Just revoke without the assault charge?
Placement: Yes.
CMC: We'll revoke him for inappropriate behavior (Case 117).

This example illustrates two important points. First, the "counterther-apeutic" reference demonstrates the links among the working ideology (individualized justice), a recommended outcome, and an account for it (see Drass and Spencer 1987:285). Second, it reveals the board's concern for a participant's work situation. Placement staff manage halfway houses populated by juveniles who often are reluctant guests; their behavior may present a control problem for the entire facility.

Recommendations by POs were very important. Some POs volunteered a recommendation: "He should go to [an institution] and do no less than four months." The board revoked parole and sentenced the juvenile to 4 months, although he denied the charge (Case 81). In other cases, the board solicited a PO's recommendation.

CMC: What do you want us to do?
PO: Oh, send him back to [placement].
CMC: Will they take him?
PO: Yes.

The board reinstated parole and assigned the juvenile to the placement facility (Case 112).

The participants also addressed organizational barriers, including other criminal justice agencies, that impinged on their decisions; they noted, for example, whether the county attorney would transfer a juvenile to adult criminal court (Case 88). They also were aware of internal constraints. Institutional overcrowding was frequently a problem, as when the CMC said his superior told him not to send any juveniles with only misdemeanor charges to a particular institution that day (Case 120; Case 130). The board's decisions had to be reasonable within the organizational context (Sudnow 1965:248).

In 93 percent of the cases we observed, the final outcome was consistent with the decision made at the prehearing conference.

A Script

Once they decided on an outcome, the participants, still backstage, developed a script for the formal revocation hearing. There was collusion in its fabrication, even in the assignment of the parts they would play (Goffman 1959:176–177). Scripts were an aspect of outcome, and the participants accounted for them. Often, the accounts and the parts played depended on organizational roles.

For example, at one conference, the PO said, "I'm willing to reinstate but he has to get the message about the responsibility to report. He needs a lecture." The board honored the PO's request and castigated the juvenile at the formal hearing (Case 96). In another, the participants agreed that the first placement had been inappropriate, and that a second facility would be better, if there was bed space.

Placement #2: We have a bed for him.
Placement #1: Don't let him know that you're taking him in; make him impress you.
Placement #2: I'll make him sweat.

Placement #2 was rough on the juvenile at the formal hearing before accepting him in the second facility (Case 106). Sometimes, more positive scripts were planned; the board had to deal with the juvenile's parole violation, but also wanted to reinforce otherwise positive behavior (Case 135).

The prehearing conference usually ended when the board had enough information to reach a decision. The PO's recommendation often signalled the end of the conference. At that point, the CMC would instruct the security officer to bring in the juvenile.

FORMAL HEARING

The board officially decided a case outcome at the parole revocation hearing. The formal hearings manifested the performance characteristics Goffman (1959) describes. They were devoted to confirmations—of "what happened," of typologies, of the juvenile's guilt—that sustained the definition of the agreement reached backstage. The participants, especially the board, exhibited demeanors in stark contrast to the casual atmosphere backstage; they managed ceremonial hearings that impressed upon the juveniles the gravity of their situation and that subjugated them to the board's authority. The board maintained the trappings of individualized justice as it performed. It appealed to the juveniles' "best interests" while holding them responsible for parole violations. At the same time, the board reinforced the various organizational roles of team members. Participants also offered accounts as they performed their scripted parts.

The formal hearing began when the juvenile entered the room. Formal hearings ranged from 3 to 42 minutes in duration; they averaged 12 minutes, with a modal length of 9 minutes.

Confirmation

At the formal hearing, the participants followed the agreed upon script. In one case, before the formal hearing began placement staff reported that the juvenile and others had been drinking and were arrested for burglary. The PO warned that he would be rough on the juvenile. The juvenile entered and the PO brusquely interrogated him (Case 81). In another case, the security officer said that the juvenile was injured in a fall from a stolen truck. The accident set the agenda for the formal hearing.

Placement: How come you're walking so slow?
Juvenile: Fell.
CMC: Off a roof?
Juvenile: Out of a truck.
Trainee: What'd you do?
Juvenile: Left [placement] in a stolen truck (Case 139).

The board tried to confirm its backstage construction of "what happened," and its presumption of the juvenile's guilt.

The literature suggests that because guilt is presumed, decision makers are more concerned with disposition than with guilt or innocence (Maynard 1982:351; Sudnow 1965:253). While we tend to agree, the decision makers we observed often solicited an admission of guilt from the juvenile. Admissions were especially important when the evidence was shaky. In one case, overcrowding had generated a "revoke only for felony" rule. The board repeatedly tried to make the juvenile "fess up" to a felony charge, but he consistently denied it. Finally, the CMC told the juvenile, "We don't believe you, but we don't have enough evidence." The board reluctantly reinstated parole amid stern warnings to the juvenile (Case 120). Sometimes, the board solicited admissions of guilt even when there were no criminal charges. The CMC asked a juvenile, who had worked at a fair while AWOL, "What kind of illegal activities have you been into with the carnival?" (Case 98). The juveniles never confessed to any unknown crimes.

Refusal to admit guilt in such cases was but one example of the juveniles' active participation in the decision-making gestalt. Some argued with board members; others were deferential, contrite, and admitted guilt. Some were articulate; others stammered and cried. In any case, some juveniles resisted the typologies and outcomes that were being imposed on them (see Decker 1987:158). Their resistance occasionally paid off, as in the case noted previously where the board failed to elicit a felony-level admission (Case 120), or where a juvenile brought up information that changed the board members' minds (Case 80). However, for the most part, they rarely overcame the board's determination of what happened and what should be done about it.

The participants employed a variety of methods to overcome the juveniles' resistance. Some grounded their actions in "best interests" and encouraged the juvenile to "stop fighting them" (Case 93). For the most part, they interpreted a juvenile's resistance (or any other aspect of behavior) as a confirmation of assessments made backstage (Case 86). Juveniles who resisted too vehemently were condemned for violating decorum.

Ceremony

The formal hearing was a ceremonial affair intended to "shake up" the juvenile. Decision makers staged their performances in order to intimidate, incriminate, and degrade the juvenile (Emerson 1969:172–215).

To do this, decision makers frequently voiced defining attributes of juvenile justice. Participants frequently invoked the language of "treatment," although with varying implications. One PO told a juvenile, "You keep on with a negative attitude and you'll end up at [the adult prison]." A trainee added, "The juvenile system is for treatment; [adult prison] is for punishment" (Case 81). In another case, the board assigned a juvenile to a placement facility after he first served some "treatment time" in detention (Case 135).

As the performances unfolded, the participants tried to convey an air of informality, of negotiable outcomes. One PO asked the juvenile, "What should I recommend?" (Case 109). The CMC exhorted another juvenile to "Tell the truth; this isn't a court" (Case 83).

There was an etiquette of parole revocation hearings. Juveniles waited outside until summoned, and were then led into the room by the security officer. Once inside, the seating arrangements—the juvenile across from the board—added to the formality of the proceedings. A question and answer format contributed to the sense of ceremony (see Holstein 1988:460). The following exchange occurred in a case where a juvenile was charged with possessing marijuana at a placement facility.

CMC: Can you maintain till you get off parole?
Juvenile: Yes.
Trainee: Can you stay off marijuana till you get your GED?
Juvenile: Yes.
Trainee: Till you complete the program at [placement]?
Juvenile: Yes.
Trainee: Till you finish vocational school?
Juvenile: Yes.
Trainee: Talk's cheap.
Placement: Why should I take another chance on you?
Juvenile: I thought about it a lot.
Placement: Let's not play word games (Case 132).

The board protected decorum by condemning breaches of ceremony. One juvenile who was angered when the board revoked parole, tore some official papers and cursed. The CMC ordered him to "Watch your language!" (Case 137). When another juvenile called the security officer a liar, the CMC said, "Hey! Don't call staff members liars" (Case 192). Some interactions escalated into status degradation ceremonies.

Placement: You're so goddamn stupid I can't stand it. How many times could I have sent you back but didn't? Everyone was doing for you, and you weren't doing for yourself.
Trainee: You're off parole.
Placement: You think you're smarter than everyone else—do you think you're smarter than everyone else now? (Case 116).

Status degradation ceremonies, like other aspects of performance, reflected idealized social values (kids should not curse), and also maintained the board's authority over the juveniles (see Garfinkel 1956:56; Goffman 1959:35). Such displays did not occur in the few cases where attorneys were present. Either their presence imposed certain due process requirements, or simply constituted an external audience.

The board's ultimate control rested in its authority to revoke or reinstate parole. In some cases, the board expressly reminded the juvenile of its power and of the juvenile's situation. In other cases, the board used its power to persuade rather than threaten. The use of persuasion had two advantages over the exercise of raw power. It encouraged a juvenile to acknowledge his wrongdoing, and then to negotiate a commitment to a disposition with the board (Darrough 1984). Such negotiations appeared to give the juvenile a more active role in the decision. Persuasion also enabled the board to portray a participant in a positive light and perhaps improve his or her working relationship with the juvenile (see Emerson 1969:180–181). In one case the CMC said, "You'd better thank your PO. He's the one who put you back on the street" (Case 109).

Accounts were a part of the ceremony. Some were in the form of denunciations; the board revoked parole because the juvenile had "blown chances" (Case 116). Others referred to the juvenile's best interest: "We're doing this for your own good" (Case 109). The formal parole revocation hearing ended when the juvenile left the room with the security officer.

POSTHEARING DISCUSSION

The participants usually continued discussion after a juvenile had left the room. During the posthearing discussion, the participants completed the circle of decision making: they confirmed the constructions and decisions made at the prehearing conference and the formal hearing. They addressed organizational matters and offered accounts for the dispositions and their performance. The discussions reflected and reinforced their theory of office and its organizational context.

Performance

Backstage again, everyone relaxed as they analyzed their performance and its effects (Goffman 1959). At one posthearing discussion, after the board had lectured a juvenile at the PO's request, a trainee said, "I think he got the message" (Case 96). Some participants joked about their performance, in one instance, the placement staff referred to his performance as "bad ass routine number 14" (Case 106). Some jokes produced subsequent scripts. The CMC laughed about using "Christmas in the institution" to pressure a juvenile and one trainee thought the threat might work in other cases that day (Case 125).

Organizational Context

The board members' discussions often referred to organizational issues. For example, they considered the impact of a disposition on upcoming cases

(Cases 101, 130). Such considerations frequently pertained to institutional overcrowding (see Emerson 1983:446). At other times, they discussed a case in terms of its evidentiary relationship to a companion case (Cases 81, 82).

Team members usually maintained a unified front during the formal hearing performance. Afterwards, backstage, they dealt with any differences of opinion that emerged during the formal hearing; there were a few heated arguments. The following exchange occurred in a case where the board allowed a juvenile to continue living with his mother. The placement representative had favored assignment to a halfway house because the mother allegedly used marijuana.

Placement: I have reservations about this.
CMC: The system is overloaded. If he's doing well, why keep him in a halfway house?
Placement: They need to go after his mother, slam her ass in jail, the bitch.
PO: Don't say that.
CMC: Lots of people smoke pot, even people in the department.

The CMC recorded the decision, noting that the juvenile had been doing well (Case 105). Such discussions were couched in the theory of office, and they referred to organizational context. They were designed to "cool out" dissenters and to preserve the working consensus (Garfinkel 1967:111; Goffman 1959:85–86).

The board members maintained a sense of propriety for the record. In one case, while the CMC recorded the disposition, the other participants discussed the juvenile's personality problems. The CMC switched off the tape recorder, said "He's a simple-minded young man," switched on the machine, and continued to record (Case 138). Although rarely mentioned in the official record, the posthearing discussions also featured accounts.

Confirmatory Accounts

The participants constructed and offered accounts throughout the entire revocation process. However, the posthearing discussion provided a natural setting for accounts: the performance was over, the results were in, and the participants were backstage.

The most obvious posthearing account was the official one tape-recorded by the CMC. Along with the disposition, the CMC stated a brief rationale that included "what happened," recommendations, an admission of guilt when possible, and, sometimes, treatment language.

Frequently, the posthearing discussion featured confirmatory accounts. Some reasserted earlier typologies offered to justify the board's decision (e.g., Case 86). Often, accounts confirmed both the board's construction of "what happened" and the juvenile's guilt. Of course, some juveniles denied guilt. The participants overcame such resistance in several ways. Sometimes, they gave more credibility to a team member's allegations than to the juvenile's denial (see Holstein 1988:466). In one case, after the board deferred a decision pending more information, the placement representative reported a conversation with the juvenile held in the hall.

Placement: He practically admitted the burglary to me. I told him. "You can admit it and be treated as a juvenile, or I'd personally like to see that the department transfers you [to adult court]."
PO: I'll go talk to him and tell him the same thing.
Placement: He did it, and if you play him, he'll cop to it.
PO: OK.
CMC: I know he did it (Case 80).

At other times, an account reinterpreted resistance so that it actually confirmed a disposition (see Decker 1987:158). In one case, the board revoked parole, and a trainee said the juvenile was guilty because he had not protested enough—"not claiming he's been railroaded" (Case 84).

The participants also accounted for reinstatements of parole, explaining such dispositions by a juvenile's positive behavior and demeanor. Sometimes they used "treatment" to account for reinstatement (Case 135).

Regardless of whether the board reinstated or revoked parole, their accounts always made reference to the juvenile's "best interests." One case richly illustrates the gestalt of the entire process. A juvenile was charged with possession of marijuana. In the prehearing conference, the security officer said the juvenile had been a "jerk" and had "an attitude." The participants asked rhetorical questions at the formal hearing, and lectured and degraded the juvenile before revoking parole. The following exchange occurred during the posthearing discussion.

Placement: I'd like to wring his neck.
Security: I'd like to help you. You should have heard his mouth. That trade school was an alibi for smoking marijuana.
CMC: We'll do this kid more good by locking him up than by putting him on the street. We could do him more good with thump therapy. I wish we could (Case 116).

The participants defined the situation and decided on an outcome as a team at the prehearing conference. The formal hearing was a ritualistic performance that maintained their authority over the juvenile. Posthearing accounts confirmed their definitions and decisions. Throughout, they justified their actions (and desires) by the tenets of individualized justice.

CONCLUSION

This paper is concerned with the gestalt of decision making when juveniles are charged with parole violations, and with how the gestalt reflects and reproduces individualized justice as a working ideology. Informal prehearing conferences represented an interlude in the day's agenda, not for the personnel involved—it was a normal part of their workday—but rather in terms of the parole revocation hearings in which dispositions were officially made. We found Goffman's (1959) drama metaphors helpful in understanding this interlude and the proceedings within it. Working together backstage without an audience, the participants decided "what happened" and what should be done. They also developed a script for the team to perform at the formal hearing.

In following the script during the parole revocation hearings, they confirmed the definitions and decisions made backstage. The revocation hearings, although ostensibly informal, were ceremonial performances in which the board strictly maintained its and the organization's authority over the juvenile. During performances, the team consistently invoked the language of individualized justice, mixing this with a focus on individual responsibility.

From the prehearing conference through the posthearing discussion, the participants constructed accounts as they made decisions. Accounts were especially prominent after the formal revocation hearing; participants had one last chance to explain their decisions and performances.

Through our analysis, we see a theory of office, its organizational context, and accompanying accounts as integrated features of the decision-making gestalt. The theory of office, which included typologies of juveniles, guided the participants in their decisions about what happened and about appropriate case outcomes. The PO emerged as a key participant in these decisions, which made organizational sense given his or her supervisory role over the juvenile. The team was aware of occupational roles and other organizational matters. Their accounts reflected their roles, and the theory of office or working ideology.

Some scholars have characterized individualized justice as a myth that decision makers carefully perpetuate (Rosecrance 1988). Our observation of backstage decisions and scripted performances to an extent confirms that characterization. Further, our analysis reveals how active juveniles are overcome by the weight of typologies, decision makers' authority, or the juveniles' very status as alleged parole violators. At the same time, individualized justice is not a myth to the personnel we observed—it is their working ideology, guiding their decisions and accounts.

Their working ideology reflects the traditions of juvenile justice. The participants invoked the language of "best interests," albeit in ritualized fashion. They exhibited the "expert knows best" paternalism that is the hallmark of the *parens patriae* doctrine. As always, paternalism can go either way; we observed personnel who were caring and compassionate in one case, but frustrated and mean-spirited in another. Sometimes "treatment" meant treatment; at other times it was a euphemism for punishment.

The working ideology of juvenile justice is not static. The due process "reforms" of the 1960s and the sterner, crime control "reforms" of the 1980s have changed juvenile justice. We observed the coexistence of two ideologies. Some actions and explanations were steeped in the *parens patriae* tradition. Others reflected the sterner 1980s approach; transfer of jurisdiction to adult criminal court was a typical part of the work environment and the lexicon of individual responsibility was common. We saw little of the due process legacy.

However, this paper is not a paean to due process. An attorney might have prevented some of the abusive degradations we observed, but probably could not have altered the overall gestalt of decision making. Individualized justice, as modified by a crime control ideology, *is* the working ideology of juvenile justice. Participants' typologies—the very way they see the juveniles under their supervision or before the board—are steeped in it; organizational roles and tasks are structured around it. If individualized justice is a myth, it is a myth to which the personnel we observed owe fealty. The gestalt of juvenile parole revocation decision making maintains it.

References

Atkinson, Maxwell, and Paul Drew
 1979 Order in Court. Atlantic Highlands, N.J.: Humanities Press.
Bernard, Thomas J.
 1992 The Cycle of Juvenile Justice. New York: Oxford University Press.
Black, Donald, and Albert Reiss
 1970 "Police control of juveniles." American Sociological Review 35:63–77.
Bortner, M.A.
 1988 Delinquency and Justice: An Age of Crisis. New York: McGraw-Hill Book Company.
Bortner, M.A., and Wornie Reed
 1985 "The preeminence of process: An example of refocused justice research." Social Science Quarterly 66:413–425.
Champion, Dean J.
 1992 The Juvenile Justice System. New York: Macmillan.
Cicourel, Aaron
 1968 The Social Organization of Juvenile Justice. New York: Wiley.
Cohen, Lawrence, and James Kluegel
 1978 "Determinants of juvenile court dispositions: Ascriptive and achieved factors in two metropolitan courts." American Sociological Review 43:162–176.
Dannefer, Dale, and Russel K. Schutt
 1982 "Race and juvenile processing in court and police agencies." American Journal of Sociology 87:1113–1132.
Darrough, William
 1984 "In the best interests of the child: Negotiating parental cooperation for probation placement." Urban Life 13:123–153.
Decker, Frederick
 1987 "Psychiatric management of legal defense in period commitment hearings." Social Problems 34:156–171.
Drass, Kriss, and William Spencer
 1987 "Accounting for pre-sentencing recommendations: Typologies and probation officers' theory of office." Social Problems 34:277–293.
Emerson, Robert
 1969 Judging Delinquents: Context and Process in Juvenile Court. Chicago: Aldine Publishing.

1983 "Holistic effects in social control decision-making." Law and Society Review 17:425–455.

Garfinkel, Harold
1956 "Conditions of successful degradation ceremonies." American Journal of Sociology 61:420–424.
1967 Studies in Ethnomethodology. Englewood Cliffs, N.J.: Prentice Hall.

Glaser, Barney, and Anselm Strauss
1967 The Discovery of Grounded Theory. Chicago: Aldine.

Goffman, Erving
1959 The Presentation of Self in Everyday Life. Garden City, N.Y.: Doubleday Anchor Books.

Hagan, John, John Hewitt, and Duane Alwin
1979 "Ceremonial justice: Crime and punishment in a loosely coupled system." Social Forces 58:506–527.

Holstein, James
1988 "Court ordered incompetence: Conversational organization in involuntary commitment hearings." Social Problems 35:458–473.

Kelly, Delos
1979 Deviant Behavior. New York: St. Martin's Press.

Krisberg, Barry, Ira Schwartz, Paul Litsky, James Austin
1986 "The Watershed of Juvenile Justice Reform." Crime and Delinquency 32:5–38.

Maynard, Douglas
1982 "Defendant attributes in plea bargaining: Notes on the modeling of sentencing decisions." Social Problems 29:347–360.
1988 "Language, interaction, and social problems." Social Problems 35:311–334.

McCarthy, Belinda, and Brent Smith
1986 "The conceptualization of discrimination in the juvenile justice process: The impact of administrative factors and screening decisions on juvenile court dispositions." Criminology 24:41–58.

Piliavin, Irving, and Scott Briar
1964 "Police encounters with juveniles." American Journal of Sociology 70:206–214.

Rosecrance, John
1988 "Maintaining the myth of individualized justice: Probation presentence reports." Justice Quarterly 5:235–256.

Rubington, Earl, and Martin Weinberg
1981 Deviance: The Interactionist Perspective. 4th ed. New York: Macmillan.

Scott, Marvin, and Stanford Lyman
1968 "Accounts." American Sociological Review 33:46–62.

Spencer, Jack
1983 "Accounts, attitudes, and solutions: Probation officer-defendant negotiations of subjective orientations." Social Problems 30:570–581.

Sudnow, David
1965 "Normal crimes: Sociological features of the penal code in a public defender office." Social Problems 12:255–270.

Zatz, Marjorie
1987 "The changing forms of racial/ethnic biases in sentencing." Journal of Research in Crime and Delinquency 24:69–92.

30 / The Moral Career of the Mental Patient

ERVING GOFFMAN

Traditionally the term *career* has been reserved for those who expect to enjoy the rises laid out within a respectable profession. The term is coming to be used, however, in a broadened sense to refer to any social strand of any person's course through life. The perspective of natural history is taken: unique outcomes are neglected in favor of such changes over time as are basic and common to the members of a social category, although occurring independently to each of them. Such a career is not a thing that can be brilliant or disappointing; it can no more be a success than a failure. In this light, I want to consider the mental patient, drawing mainly upon data collected during a year's participant observation of patient social life in a public mental hospital,[1] wherein an attempt was made to take the patient's point of view.

One value of the concept of career is its two-sidedness. One side is linked to internal matters held dearly and closely, such as image of self and felt identity; the other side concerns official position, jural relations, and style of life, and is part of a publicly accessible institutional complex. The concept of career, then, allows one to move back and forth between the personal and the public, between the self and its significant society, without having overly to rely for data upon what the person says he thinks he imagines himself to be.

This paper, then, is an exercise in the institutional approach to the study of self. The main concern will be with the *moral* aspects of career—that is, the regular sequence of changes that career entails in the person's self and in his framework of imagery for judging himself and others.[2]

The category "mental patient" itself will be understood in one strictly sociological sense. In this perspective, the psychiatric view of a person becomes significant only in so far as this view itself alters his social fate—an alteration which seems to become fundamental in our society when, and only when, the person is put through the process of hospitalization.[3] I therefore exclude certain neighboring categories: the undiscovered candidates who would be judged "sick" by psychiatric standards but who never come to be viewed as such by themselves or others, although they may cause everyone a great deal of trouble;[4] the office patient whom a psychiatrist feels he can handle with drugs or shock on the outside; the mental client who engages in psychotherapeutic relationships. And I include anyone, however robust in temperament, who somehow gets caught up in the heavy machinery of mental hospital servicing. In this way the effects of being treated as a mental patient can be kept quite distinct from the effects upon a person's life of traits a clinician would view as psychopathological.[5] Persons who become mental hospital patients vary widely in the kind and degree of illness that a psychiatrist would impute to them, and in the attributes by which laymen would describe them. But once started on the way, they are confronted by some importantly similar circumstances and respond to these in some importantly similar ways. Since these similarities do not come from mental illness, they would seem to occur in spite of it. It is thus a tribute to the power of social forces that the uniform status of mental patient cannot only assure an aggregate of persons a common fate and eventually, because of this, a common character, but that this social reworking can be done upon what is perhaps the most obstinate diversity of human materials that can be brought together by society. Here there lacks only the frequent forming of a protective group-life by ex-patients to illustrate in full the classic cycle of response by which deviant subgroupings are psychodynamically formed in society.

This general sociological perspective is heavily reinforced by one key finding of sociologically oriented students in mental hospital research. As has been repeatedly shown in the study of nonliterate societies, the awesomeness, distastefulness, and barbarity of a foreign culture can decrease in the degree that the student becomes familiar with the point of view to life that is taken by his subjects. Similarly, the student of mental hospitals can discover that the craziness or "sick behavior" claimed for the mental patient is by and large a product of the claimant's social distance from the situation that the patient is in, and is not primarily a product of mental illness. Whatever the refinements of the various patients' psychiatric diagnoses, and whatever the special ways in which social life on the "inside" is unique, the researcher can find that he is participating in a community not significantly different from any other he has studied.[6] Of course, while restricting himself to the off-ward grounds community of paroled patients, he may feel, as some patients do, that life in the locked wards is bizarre; and while on a locked admissions or convalescent ward, he may feel that chronic "back" wards are socially crazy places. But he need only move his sphere of sympathetic participation to the "worst" ward in the hospital, and this too can come into social focus as a place with a livable and continuously meaningful social world. This in no way denies that he will find a minority in any ward or patient group that continues to seem quite beyond the capacity to follow rules of social organization, or that the orderly fulfillment of normative expectations in patient society is partly made possible by strategic measures that have somehow come to be institutionalized in mental hospitals.

The career of the mental patient falls popularly and naturalistically into three main phases: the period prior to entering the hospital, which I shall call the *prepatient phase*; the period in the hospital, the *inpatient phase*; the period after discharge from the hospital, should this occur, namely, the *ex-patient phase*.[7] This paper will deal only with the first two phases.

THE PREPATIENT PHASE

A relatively small group of prepatients come into the mental hospital willingly, because of their own idea of what will be good for them, or because of wholehearted agreement with the relevant members of their family. Presumably these recruits have found themselves acting in a way which is evidence to them that they are losing their minds or losing control of themselves. This view of oneself would seem to be one of the most pervasively threatening things that can happen to the self in our society, especially since it is likely to occur at a time when the person is in any case sufficiently troubled to exhibit the kind of symptom which he himself can see. As Sullivan described it,

> What we discover in the self-system of a person undergoing schizophrenic changes or schizophrenic processes, is then, in its simplest form, an extremely fear-marked puzzlement, consisting of the use of rather generalized and anything but exquisitely refined referential processes in an attempt to cope with what is essentially a failure at being human—a failure at being anything that one could respect as worth being.[8]

Coupled with the person's disintegrative re-evaluation of himself will be the new, almost equally pervasive circumstance of attempting to conceal from others what he takes to be the new fundamental facts about himself, and attempting to discover whether others too have discovered them.[9] Here I want to stress that perception of losing one's mind is based on culturally derived and socially engrained stereotypes as to the significance of symptoms such as hearing voices, losing temporal and spatial orientation, and sensing that one is being followed, and that many of the most spectacular and convincing of these symptoms in some instances psychiatrically signify merely a temporary emotional upset in a stressful situation, however terrifying to the person at the time. Similarly, the anxiety consequent upon this perception of oneself, and the strategies devised to reduce this anxiety, are not a product of abnormal psychology, but would be exhibited by any person socialized into our culture who came to conceive of himself as someone losing his mind. Interestingly, subcultures in American society apparently differ in the amount of ready imagery and encouragement they supply for such self-views, leading to differential rates of *self*-referral; the capacity to take this disintegrative view of oneself without psychiatric prompting seems to be one of the questionable cultural privileges of the upper classes.[10]

For the person who has come to see himself—with whatever justification—as mentally unbalanced, entrance to the mental hospital can sometimes bring relief, perhaps in part because of the sudden transformation in the structure of his basic social situations; instead of being to himself a questionable person trying to maintain a role as a full one, he can become an officially questioned person known to himself to be not so questionable as that. In other cases, hospitalization can make matters worse for the willing patient, confirming by the objective situation what has theretofore been a matter of the private experience of self.

Once the willing prepatient enters the hospital, he may go through the same routine of experiences as do those who enter unwillingly. In any case, it is the latter that I mainly want to consider, since in America at present these are by far the more numerous kind.[11] Their approach to the institution takes one of three classic forms: they come because they have been implored by their family or threatened with the abrogation of family ties unless they go "willingly"; they come by force under police escort; they come under misapprehension purposely induced by others, this last restricted mainly to youthful prepatients.

The prepatient's career may be seen in terms of an extrusory model; he starts out with relationships and rights, and ends up, at the beginning of his hospital stay, with hardly any of either. The moral aspects of this career, then, typically begin with the experience of abandonment, disloyalty, and embitterment. This is the case even though to others it may be obvious that he was in need of treatment, and even though in the hospital he may soon come to agree.

The case histories of most mental patients document offense against some arrangement for face-to-face living—a domestic establishment, a work place, a semipublic organization such as a church or store, a public region such as a street or park. Often there is also a record of some *complainant*, some figure who takes that action against the offender which eventually leads to his hospitalization. This may not be the person who makes the first move, but it is the person who makes what turns out to be the first effective move. Here is the *social* beginning of the patient's career, regardless of where one might locate the psychological beginning of his mental illness.

The kinds of offenses which lead to hospitalization are felt to differ in nature from those which lead to other extrusory consequences—to imprisonment, divorce, loss of job, disownment, regional exile, noninstitutional psychiatric treatment, and so forth. But little seems known about these differentiating factors; and when one studies actual commitments, alternate outcomes frequently appear to have been possible. It seems true, moreover, that for every offense that leads to an effective complaint, there are many psychiatrically similar ones that never do. No action is taken; or action is taken which leads to other extrusory outcomes; or ineffective action is taken, leading to the mere pacifying or putting off of the person who complains. Thus, as Clausen and Yarrow have nicely shown, even offenders who are eventually hospitalized are likely to have had a long series of ineffective actions taken against them.[12]

Separating those offenses which could have been used as grounds for hospitalizing the offender from those that are so used, one finds a vast number of what students of occupation call career contingencies.[13] Some of these contingencies in the mental patient's career have been suggested, if not explored, such as socio-economic status, visibility of the offense, proximity to a mental hospital, amount of treatment facilities available, community regard for the type of treatment given in available hospitals, and so on.[14] For information about other contingencies one must rely on atrocity tales: a psychotic man is tolerated by his wife until she finds herself a boyfriend, or by his adult children until they move from a house to an apartment; an alcoholic is sent to a mental hospital because the jail is full, and a drug addict because he declines to avail himself of psychiatric treatment on the outside; a rebellious adolescent daughter can no longer be managed at home because she now threatens to have an open affair with an unsuitable companion; and so on. Correspondingly there is an equally important set of contingencies causing the person to bypass this fate. And should the person enter the hospital, still another set of contingencies will help determine when he is to obtain a discharge—such as the desire of his family for his return, the availability of a "manageable" job, and so on. The society's official view is that inmates of mental hospitals are there primarily because they are suffering from mental illness. However, in the degree that the "mentally ill" outside hospitals numerically approach or surpass those inside hospitals, one could say that mental patients *distinctively* suffer not from mental illness, but from contingencies.

Career contingencies occur in conjunction with a second feature of the prepatient's career—the *circuit of agents*—and agencies—that participate fatefully in his passage from civilian to patient status.[15] Here is an instance of that increasingly important class of social system whose elements are agents and agencies, which are brought into systemic connection through having to take up and send on the same persons. Some of these agent-roles will be cited now, with the understanding that in any concrete circuit a role may be filled more than once, and a single person may fill more than one of them.

First is the *next-of-relation*—the person whom the prepatient sees as the most available of those upon whom he should be able to most depend in times of trouble; in this instance the last to doubt his sanity and the first to have done everything to save him from the fate which, it transpires, he has been approaching. The patient's next-of-relation is usually his next of kin; the special term is introduced because he need not be. Second is the *complainant*, the person who retrospectively appears to have started the person on his way to the hospital. Third are the *mediators*—the sequence of agents and agencies to which the prepatient is referred and through which he is relayed and processed on his way to the hospital. Here are included police, clergy, general medical practitioners, office psychiatrists, personnel in public clinics, lawyers, social service workers, school teachers, and so on. One of these agents will have the legal mandate to sanction commitment and will exercise it, and so those agents who precede him in the process will be involved in something whose outcome is not yet settled. When the mediators retire from the scene, the prepatient has become an inpatient, and the significant agent has become the hospital administrator.

While the complainant usually takes action in a lay capacity as a citizen, an employer, a neighbor, or a kinsman, mediators tend to be specialists and differ from those they serve in significant ways. They have experience in handling trouble, and some professional distance from what they handle. Except in the case of policemen, and perhaps some clergy, they tend to be more psychiatrically oriented than the lay public, and will see the need for treatment at times when the public does not.[16]

An interesting feature of these roles is the functional effects of their interdigitation. For example, the feelings of the patient will be influenced by whether or not the person who fills the role of complainant also has the role of next-of-relation—an embarrassing combination more prevalent, apparently, in the higher classes than in the lower.[17] Some of these emergent effects will be considered now.[18]

In the prepatient's progress from home to the hospital he may participate as a third person in what he may come to experience as a kind of *alienative coalition*. His next-of-relation presses him into coming to "talk things over" with a medical practitioner, an office psychiatrist, or some other counselor. Disinclination on his part may be met by threatening him with desertion, disownment, or other legal action, or by stressing the joint and explorative nature of the interview. But typically the next-of-relation will have set the interview up, in the sense of selecting the professional, arranging for time, telling the professional something about the case, and so on. This move effectively tends to establish the next-of-relation as the responsible person to whom pertinent findings can be divulged, while effectively establishing the other as the patient. The prepatient often goes to the interview with the understanding that he is going as an equal of someone who is so bound together with him that a third person could not come between them in fundamental matters; this, after all, is one way in which close relationships are defined in our society. Upon arrival at the office the prepatient suddenly finds that he and his next-of-relation have not been accorded the same roles, and apparently that a prior understanding between the professional and the next-of-relation has been put in operation against him. In the extreme but common case the professional first sees the prepatient alone, in the role of examiner and diagnostician, and then sees the next-of-relation alone, in the role of advisor, while carefully avoiding talking things over seriously with them both together.[19] And even in those nonconsultative cases where public officials must forcibly extract a person from a family that wants to tolerate him, the next-of-relation is likely to be induced to "go along" with the official action, so that even here the prepatient may feel that an alienative coalition has been formed against him.

The moral experience of being third man in such a coalition is likely to embitter the prepatient, especially since his troubles have already probably led to some estrangement from his next-of-relation. After he enters the hospital, continued visits by his next-of-relation can give the patient the "insight" that his own best interests were being served. But the initial visits may temporarily strengthen his feeling of abandonment; he is likely to beg his visitor to get him out or at least to get him more privileges and to sympathize with the monstrousness of his plight—to which the visitor ordinarily can respond only by trying to maintain a hopeful note, by not "hearing" the requests, or by assuring the patient that the medical authorities know about these things and are doing what is medically best. The visitor then nonchalantly goes back into a world that the patient has learned is incredibly thick with freedom and privileges, causing the patient to feel that his next-of-relation is merely adding a pious gloss to a clear case of traitorous desertion.

The depth to which the patient may feel betrayed by his next-of-relation seems to be increased by the fact that another witnesses his betrayal—a factor which is apparently significant in many three-party situations. An offended person may well act forbearantly and accommodatively toward an offender when the two are alone, choosing peace ahead of justice. The presence of a witness, however, seems to add something to the implications of the offense. For then it is beyond the power of the offended and offender to forget about, erase, or suppress what has happened; the offense has become a public social fact.[20] When the witness is a mental health commission, as is sometimes the case, the witnessed betrayal can verge on a "degradation ceremony."[21] In such circumstances, the offended patient may feel that some kind of extensive reparative action is required before witnesses, if his honor and social weight are to be restored.

Two other aspects of sensed betrayal should be mentioned. First, those who suggest the possibility of another's entering a mental hospital are not likely to provide a realistic picture of how in fact it may strike him when he arrives. Often he is told that he will get required medical treatment and a rest, and may well be out in a few months or so. In some cases they may thus be concealing what they know, but I think, in general, they will be telling what they see as the truth. For here there is a quite relevant difference between patients and mediating professionals; mediators, more so than the public at large, may conceive of mental hospitals as short-term medical establishments where required rest and attention can be voluntarily obtained, and not as places of coerced exile. When the prepatient finally arrives he is likely to learn quite quickly, quite differently. He then finds that the information given him about life in the hospital has had the effect of his having put up less resistance to entering than he now sees he would have put up had he known the facts. Whatever the intentions of those who participated in his transition from person to patient, he may sense they have in effect "conned" him into his present predicament.

I am suggesting that the prepatient starts out with at least a portion of the rights, liberties, and satisfactions of the civilian and ends up on a psychiatric ward stripped of almost everything. The question here is *how* this stripping is managed. This is the second aspect of betrayal I want to consider.

As the prepatient may see it, the circuit of significant figures can function as a kind of *betrayal funnel*. Passage from person to patient may be effected through a series of linked stages, each managed by a different agent. While each stage tends to bring a sharp decrease in adult free status, each agent may try to maintain the fiction that no further decrease will occur. He may even manage to turn the prepatient over to the next agent while sustaining this note. Further, through words, cues, and gestures, the prepatient is implicitly asked by the current agent to join with him in sustaining a running line of polite small talk that tactfully avoids the administrative facts of the situation, becoming, with each stage, progressively more at odds with these facts. The spouse would rather not have to cry to get the prepatient to visit a psychiatrist; psychiatrists would rather not have a scene when the prepatient learns that he and his spouse are being seen separately and in different ways; the police infrequently bring a prepatient to the hospital in a strait jacket, finding it much easier all around to give him a cigarette, some kindly words, and freedom to relax in the back seat of the patrol car; and finally, the admitting psychiatrist finds he can do his work better in the relative quiet and luxury of the "admission suite" where, as an incidental consequence, the notion can survive that a mental hospital is indeed a comforting place. If the prepatient heeds all of these implied requests and is reasonably decent about the whole thing, he can travel the whole circuit from home to hospital without forcing anyone to look directly at what is happening or to deal with the raw emotion that his situation might well cause him to express. His showing consideration for those who are moving him toward the hospital allows them to show consideration for him, with the joint result that these interactions can be sustained with some of the protective harmony characteristic of ordinary face-to-face dealings. But should the new patient cast his mind back over the sequence of steps leading to hospitalization, he may feel that everyone's *current* comfort was being busily sustained while his long-range welfare was being undermined. This realization may constitute a moral experience that further separates him for the time from the people on the outside.[22]

I would now like to look at the circuit of career agents from the point of view of the agents themselves. Mediators in the person's transition from civil to patient status—as well as his keepers, once he is in the hospital—have an interest in establishing a responsible next-of-relation as the patient's deputy or *guardian*; should there be no obvious candidate for the role, someone may be sought out and pressed into it. Thus while a person is gradually being transformed into a patient, a next-of-relation is gradually being transformed into a guardian. With a guardian on the scene, the whole transition process can be kept tidy. He is likely to be familiar with the prepatient's civil involvements and business, and can tie up loose ends that might otherwise be left to entangle the hospital. Some of the prepatient's abrogated civil rights can be transferred to him, thus helping to sustain the legal fiction that while the prepatient does not actually have his rights he somehow actually has not lost them.

Inpatients commonly sense, at least for a time, that hospitalization is a massive unjust deprivation, and sometimes succeed in convincing a few persons on the outside that this is the case. It often turns out to be useful, then, for those identified with inflicting these deprivations, however justifiably, to be able to point to the cooperation and agreement of someone whose relationship to the patient places him above suspicion, firmly defining him as the person most likely to have the patient's personal interest at heart. If the guardian is satisfied with what is happening to the new inpatient, the world ought to be.[23]

Now it would seem that the greater the legitimate personal stake one party has in another, the better he can take the role of guardian to the other. But the structural arrangements in society which lead to the acknowledged merging of two persons' interests lead to additional consequences. For the person to whom the patient turns for help—for protection against such threats as involuntary commitment—is just the person to whom the mediators and hospital administrators logically turn for authorization. It is understandable, then, that some patients will come to sense, at least for a time, that the closeness of a relationship tells nothing of its trustworthiness.

There are still other functional effects emerging from this complement of roles. If and when the next-of-relation appeals to mediators for help in the trouble he is having with the prepatient, hospitalization may not, in fact, be in his mind. He may not even perceive the prepatient as mentally sick, or, if he does, he may not consistently hold to this view.[24] It is the circuit of mediators, with their greater psychiatric sophistication and their belief in the medical character of mental hospitals, that will often define the situation for the next-of-relation, assuring him that hospitalization is a possible solution and a good one, that it involves no betrayal, but is rather a medical action taken in the best interests of the prepatient. Here the next-of-relation may learn that doing his duty to the prepatient may cause the prepatient to distrust and even hate him for the time. But the fact that this course of action may have had to be pointed out and prescribed by professionals, and be defined by them as a moral duty, relieves the next-of-relation of some of the guilt he may feel.[25] It is a poignant fact that an adult son or daughter may be pressed into the role of mediator, so that the hostility that might otherwise be directed against the spouse is passed on to the child.[26]

Once the prepatient is in the hospital, the same guilt-carrying function may become a significant part of the staff's job in regard to the next-of-relation.[27] These reasons for feeling that he himself has not betrayed the patient, even though the patient may then think so, can later provide the next-of-relation with a defensible line to take when visiting the patient in the hospital and a basis for hoping that the relationship can be re-established after its hospital moratorium. And of course this position, when sensed by the patient, can provide him with excuses for the next-of-relation, when and if he comes to look for them.[28]

Thus while the next-of-relation can perform important functions for the mediators and hospital administrators, they in turn can perform important functions for him. One finds, then, an emergent unintended exchange or reciprocation of functions, these functions themselves being often unintended.

The final point I want to consider about the prepatient's moral career is its peculiarly *retroactive* character. Until a person actually arrives at the hospital there usually seems no way of knowing for sure that he is destined to do so, given the determinative role of career contingencies. And until the point of hospitalization is reached, he or others may not conceive of him as a person who is becoming a mental patient. However, since he will be held against his will in the hospital, his next-of-relation and the hospital staff will be in great need of a rationale for the hardships they are sponsoring. The medical elements of the staff will also need evidence that they are still in the trade they were trained for. These problems are eased, no doubt unintentionally, by the case-history construction that is placed on the patient's past life, this having the effect of demonstrating that all along he had been becoming sick, that he finally became very sick, and that if he had not been hospitalized much worse things would have happened to him—all of which, of course, may be true. Incidentally, if the patient wants to make sense out of his stay in the hospital, and, as already suggested, keep alive the possibility of once again conceiving of his next-of-relation as a decent, well-meaning person, then he too will have reason to believe some of this psychiatric work-up of his past.

Here is a very ticklish point for the sociology of careers. An important aspect of every career is the view the person constructs when he looks backward over his progress; in a sense, however, the whole of the prepatient career derives from this reconstruction. The fact of having had a prepatient career, starting with an effective complaint, becomes an important part of the mental patient's orientation, but this part can begin to be played only after hospitalization proves that what he had been having, but no longer has, is a career as a prepatient.

THE INPATIENT PHASE

The last step in the prepatient's career can involve his realization—justified or not—that he has been deserted by society and turned out of relationships by those closest to him. Interestingly enough, the patient, especially a first admission, may manage to keep himself from coming to the end of this trail, even though in fact he is now in a locked mental hospital ward. On entering the hospital, he may very strongly feel the desire not to be known to anyone as a person who could possibly be reduced to these present circumstances, or as a person who conducted himself in the way he did prior to commitment. Consequently, he may avoid talking to anyone, may stay by himself when possible, and may even be "out of contact" or "manic" so as to avoid ratifying any interaction that presses a politely reciprocal role upon him and opens him up to what he has become in the eyes of others. When the next-of-relation makes an effort to visit, he may be rejected by mutism, or by the patient's refusal to enter the visiting room, these strategies sometimes suggesting that the patient still clings to a remnant of relatedness to those who made up his past, and is protecting this remnant from the final destructiveness of dealing with the new people that they have become.[29]

Usually the patient comes to give up this taxing effort at anonymity, at not-hereness, and begins to present himself for conventional social interaction to the hospital community. Thereafter he withdraws only in special ways—by always using his nickname, by signing his contribution to the patient weekly with his initial only, or by using the innocuous "cover" address tactfully provided by some hospitals; or he withdraws only at special times, when, say, a flock of nursing students makes a passing tour of the ward, or when, paroled to the hospital grounds, he suddenly sees he is about to cross the path of a civilian he happens to know from home. Sometimes this making of oneself available is called "settling down" by the attendants. It marks a new stand openly taken and supported by the patient, and resembles the "coming out" process that occurs in other groupings.[30]

Once the prepatient begins to settle down, the main outlines of his fate tend to follow those of a whole class of segregated establishments—jails, concentration camps, monasteries, work camps, and so on—in which the inmate spends the whole round of life on the grounds, and marches through his regimented day in the immediate company of a group of persons of his own institutional status.[31]

Like the neophyte in many of these "total institutions," the new inpatient finds himself cleanly stripped of many of his accustomed affirmations, satisfactions, and defenses, and is subjected to a rather full set of mortifying experiences: restriction of free movement; communal living; diffuse authority of a whole echelon of people; and so on. Here one begins to learn about the limited extent to which a conception of oneself can be sustained when the usual setting of supports for it are suddenly removed.

While undergoing these humbling moral experiences, the inpatient learns to orient himself in terms of the "ward system."[32] In public mental hospitals this usually consists of a series of graded living arrangements built around wards, administrative units called services, and parole statuses. The "worst" level involves often nothing but wooden benches to sit on, some quite indifferent food, and a small piece of room to sleep in. The "best" level may involve a room of one's own, ground and town privileges, contacts with staff that are relatively undamaging, and what is seen as good food and ample recreational facilities. For disobeying the pervasive house rules, the inmate will receive stringent punishments expressed in terms of loss of privileges; for obedience he will eventually be allowed to reacquire some of the minor satisfactions he took for granted on the outside.

The institutionalization of these radically different levels of living throws light on the implications for self of social settings. And this in turn affirms that the self arises not merely out of its possessor's interactions with significant others, but also out of the arrangements that are evolved in an organization for its members.

There are some settings which the person easily discounts as an expression or extension of him. When a tourist goes slumming, he may take pleasure in the situation not because it is a reflection of him but because it so assuredly is not. There are other settings, such as living rooms, which the person manages on his own and employs to influence in a favorable direction other persons' views of him. And there are still other settings, such as a work place, which express the employee's occupational status, but over which he has no final control, this being exerted, however tactfully, by his employer. Mental hospitals provide an extreme instance of this latter possibility. And this is due not merely to their uniquely degraded living levels, but also to the unique way in which significance for self is made explicit to the patient, piercingly, persistently, and thoroughly. Once lodged on a given ward, the patient is firmly instructed that the restrictions and deprivations he encounters are not due to such things as tradition or economy—and hence dissociable from self—but are intentional parts of his treatment, part of his need at the time, and therefore an expression of the state that his self has fallen to. Having every reason to initiate requests for better conditions, he is told that when the staff feels he is "able to manage" or will be "comfortable with" a higher ward level, then appropriate action will be taken. In short, assignment to a given ward is presented not as a reward or punishment, but as an expression of his general level of social functioning, his status as a person. Given the fact that the worst ward levels provide a round of life that inpatients with organic brain damage can easily manage, and that these quite limited human beings are present to prove it, one can appreciate some of the mirroring effects of the hospital.[33]

The ward system, then, is an extreme instance of how the physical facts of an establishment can be explicitly employed to frame the conception a person takes of himself. In addition, the official psychiatric mandate of mental hospitals gives rise to even more direct, even more blatant, attacks upon the inmate's view of himself. The more "medical" and the more progressive a mental hospital is—the more it attempts to be therapeutic and not merely custodial—the more he may be confronted by high-ranking staff arguing that his past has been a failure, that the cause of this has been within himself, that his attitude to life is wrong, and that if he wants to be a person he will have to change his way of dealing with people and his conceptions of himself. Often the moral value of these verbal assaults will be brought home to him by requiring him to practice taking this psychiatric view of himself in arranged confessional periods, whether in private sessions or group psychotherapy.

Now a general point may be made about the moral career of inpatients which has bearing on many moral careers. Given the stage that any person has reached in a career, one typically finds that he constructs an image of his life course—past, present, and future—which selects, abstracts, and distorts in such a way as to provide him with a view of himself that he can usefully expound in current situations. Quite generally, the person's line concerning self defensively brings him into appropriate alignment with the basic values of his society, and so may be called an *apologia*. If the person can manage to present a view of his current situation which shows the operation of favorable personal qualities in the past and a favorable destiny awaiting him, it may be called a *success story*. If the facts of a person's past and present are extremely dismal, then about the best he can do is to show that he is not responsible for what has become of him, and the term *sad tale* is appropriate. Interestingly enough, the more the person's past forces him out of apparent alignment with central moral values, the more often he seems compelled to tell his sad tale in any company in which he finds himself. Perhaps he partly responds to the need he feels in others of not having their sense of proper life courses affronted. In any case, it is among convicts, "wino's," and prostitutes that one seems to obtain sad tales the most readily.[34] It is the vicissitudes of the mental patient's sad tale that I want to consider now.

In the mental hospital, the setting and the house rules press home to the patient that he is, after all, a mental case who has suffered some kind of social collapse on the outside, having failed in some overall way, and that here he is of little social weight, being hardly capable of acting like a full-fledged person at all. These humiliations are likely to be most keenly felt by middle-class patients, since their previous condition of life little immunizes them against such affronts; but all patients feel some downgrading. Just as any normal member of his outside subculture would do, the patient often responds to this situation by attempting to assert a sad tale proving that he is not "sick," that the "little trouble" he did get into was really somebody else's fault, that his past life course had some honor and rectitude, and that the hospital is therefore unjust in forcing the status of mental patient upon him. This self-respecting tendency is heavily institutionalized within the patient society where opening social contacts typically involve the participants' volunteering information about their current ward location and length of stay so far, but not the reasons for their stay—such interaction being conducted in the manner of small talk on the outside.[35] With greater familiarity, each patient usually volunteers relatively acceptable reasons for his hospitalization, at the same time accepting without open immediate question the lines offered by other patients. Such stories as the following are given and overtly accepted.

> I was going to night school to get a M.A. degree, and holding down a job in addition, and the load got too much for me.

> The others here are sick mentally but I'm suffering from a bad nervous system and that is what is giving me these phobias.

> I got here by mistake because of a diabetes diagnosis, and I'll leave in a couple of days. [The patient had been in seven weeks.]

> I failed as a child, and later with my wife I reached out for dependency.

> My trouble is that I can't work. That's what I'm in for. I had two jobs with a good home and all the money I wanted.[36]

The patient sometimes reinforces these stories by an optimistic definition of his occupational status: A man who managed to obtain an audition as a radio announcer styles himself a radio announcer; another who worked for some months as a copy boy and was then given a job as a reporter on a large trade journal, but fired after three weeks, defines himself as a reporter.

A whole social role in the patient community may be constructed on the basis of these reciprocally sustained fictions. For these face-to-face niceties tend to be qualified by behind-the-back gossip that comes only a degree closer to the "objective" facts. Here, of course, one can see a classic social function of informal networks of equals: they serve as one another's audience for self-supporting tales—tales that are somewhat more solid than pure fantasy and somewhat thinner than the facts.

But the patient's *apologia* is called forth in a unique setting, for few settings could be so destructive of self-stories except, of course, those stories already constructed along psychiatric lines. And this destructiveness rests on more than the official sheet of paper which attests that the patient is of unsound mind, a danger to himself and others—an attestation, incidentally, which seems to cut deeply into the patient's pride, and into the possibility of his having any.

Certainly the degrading conditions of the hospital setting belie many of the self-stories that are presented by patients; and the very fact of being in the mental hospital is evidence against these tales. And of course, there is not always sufficient patient solidarity to prevent patient discrediting patient, just as there is not always a sufficient number of "professional-ized" attendants to prevent attendant discrediting patient. As one patient informant repeatedly suggested to a fellow patient:

> If you're so smart, how come you got your ass in here?

The mental hospital setting, however, is more treacherous still. Staff has much to gain through discreditings of the patient's story—whatever the felt reason for such discreditings. If the custodial faction in the hospital is to succeed in managing his daily round without complaint or trouble from him, then it will prove useful to be able to point out to him that the claims about himself upon which he rationalizes his demands are false, that he is not what he is claiming to be, and that in fact he is a failure as a person. If the psychiatric faction is to impress upon him its views about his personal make-up, then they must be able to show in detail how their version of his past and their version of his character hold up much better than his own.[37] If both the custodial and psychiatric factions are to get him to cooperate in the various psychiatric treatments, then it will prove useful to disabuse him of *his* view of their purposes, and cause him to appreciate that they know what they are doing, and are doing what is best for him. In brief, the difficulties caused by a patient are closely tied to his version of what has been happening to him, and if cooperation is to be secured, it helps if this version is discredited. The patient must "insightfully" come to take, or affect to take, the hospital's view of himself.

Notes

1. The study was conducted during 1955–56 under the auspices of the Laboratory of Social-environmental Studies of the National Institute of Mental Health. I am grateful to the Laboratory Chief, John A. Clausen, and to Dr. Winfred Overholser, Superintendent, and the late Dr. Jay Hoffman, then First Assistant Physician of Saint Elizabeths Hospital, Washington, D.C., for the ideal cooperation they freely provided. A preliminary report is contained in Goffman, "Interpersonal Persuasion," pp. 117–193; in *Group Processes: Transactions of the Third Conference*, edited by Bertram Schaffner: New York, Josiah Macy, Jr. Foundation, 1957. A shorter version of this paper was presented at the Annual Meeting of the American Sociological Society, Washington, D.C., August 1957.

2. Material on moral career can be found in early social anthropological work on ceremonies of status transition, and in classic social psychological descriptions of those spectacular changes in one's view of self that can accompany participation in social movements and sects. Recently new kinds of relevant data have been suggested by psychiatric interest in the problem of "identity" and sociological studies of work careers and "adult socialization."

3. This point has recently been made by Elaine and John Cumming, *Closed Ranks;* Cambridge, Commonwealth Fund, Harvard Univ. Press, 1957; pp. 101–102. "Clinical experience supports the impression that many people define mental illness as 'That condition for which a person is treated in a mental hospital.' ... Mental illness, it seems, is a condition which afflicts people who must go to a mental institution, but until they do almost anything they do is normal." Leila Deasy has pointed out to me the correspondence here with the situation in white collar crime. Of those who are detected in this activity, only the ones who do not manage to avoid going to prison find themselves accorded the social role of the criminal.

4. Case records in mental hospitals are just now coming to be exploited to show the incredible amount of trouble a person may cause for himself and others before anyone begins to think about him psychiatrically, let alone take psychiatric action against him. See John A. Clausen and Marian Radke Yarrow, "Paths to the Mental Hospital," *J. Social Issues* (1955) 11:25–32; August B. Hollingshead and Fredrick C. Redlich, *Social Class and Mental Illness;* New York, Wiley, 1958: pp. 173–174.

5. An illustration of how this perspective may be taken to all forms of deviancy may be found in Edwin Lemert, *Social Pathology;* New York, McGraw-Hill, 1951; see especially pp. 74–76. A specific application to mental defectives may be found in Stewart E. Perry, "Some Theoretic Problems of Mental Deficiency and Their Action Implications," *Psychiatry* (1954) 17:45–73; see especially p. 68.

6. Conscientious objectors who voluntarily went to jail sometimes arrived at the same conclusion regarding criminal inmates. See, for example, Alfred Hassler, *Diary of a Self-made Convict;* Chicago, Regnery, 1954; p. 74.

7. This simple picture is complicated by the somewhat special experience of roughly a third of ex-patients—namely, readmission to the hospital, this being the recidivist or "repatient" phase.

8. Harry Stack Sullivan, *Clinical Studies in Psychiatry;* edited by Helen Swick Perry, Mary Ladd Gawel, and Martha Gibbon; New York, Norton, 1956; pp. 184–185.

9. This moral experience can be contrasted with that of a person learning to become a marihuana addict, whose discovery that he can be "high" and still "op" effectively without being detected apparently leads to a new level of use. See Howard S. Becker, "Marihuana Use and Social Control," *Social Problems* (1955) 3:35–44; see especially pp. 40–41.

10. See footnote 4: Hollingshead and Redlich, p. 187, Table 6, where relative frequency is given of self-referral by social class grouping.

11. The distinction employed here between willing and unwilling patients cuts across the legal one, of voluntary and committed, since some persons who are glad to come to the mental hospital may be legally committed, and of those who come only because of strong familial pressure, some may sign themselves in as voluntary patients.

12. Clausen and Yarrow; see footnote 4.

13. An explicit application of this notion to the field of mental health may be found in Edwin M. Lemert, "Legal Commitment and Social Control," *Sociology and Social Research* (1946) 30:370–378.

14. For example, Jerome K. Meyers and Leslie Schaffer, "Social Stratification and Psychiatric Practice: A Study of an Outpatient Clinic," *Amer. Sociological Rev.* (1954) 19:307–310, Lemert, see footnote 5; pp. 402–403. *Patients in Mental Institutions*, 1941; Washington, D.C., Department of Commerce, Bureau of Census, 1941; p. 2.

15. For one circuit of agents and its bearing on career contingencies, see Oswald Hall, "The Stages of a Medical Career," *Amer. J. Sociology* (1948) 53:227–336.

16. See Cumming, footnote 3; p. 92.

17. Hollingshead and Redlich, footnote 4; p. 187.

18. For an analysis of some of these circuit implications for the inpatient, see Leila C. Deasy and Olive W. Quinn, "The Wife of the Mental Patient and the Hospital Psychiatrist," *J. Social Issues* (1955) 11:49–60. An interesting illustration of this kind of analysis may also be found in Alan G. Gowman, "Blindness and the Role of Companion," *Social Problems* (1956) 4:68–75. A general statement may be found in Robert Merton, "The Role Set: Problems in Sociological Theory," *British J. Sociology* (1957) 8:106–120.

19. I have one case record of a man who claims he thought *he* was taking his wife to see the psychiatrist, not realizing until too late that his wife had made the arrangements.

20. A paraphrase from Kurt Riezler, "The Social Psychology of Shame," *Amer. J. Sociology* (1943) 48:458.

21. See Harold Garfinkel, "Conditions of Successful Degradation Ceremonies," *Amer. J. Sociology* (1956) 61:420–424.

22. Concentration camp practices provide a good example of the function of the betrayal funnel in inducing cooperation and reducing struggle and fuss, although here the mediators could not be said to be acting in the best interests of the inmates. Police picking up persons from their homes would sometimes joke good-naturedly and offer to wait while coffee was being served. Gas chambers were fitted out like delousing rooms, and victims taking off their clothes were told to note where they were leaving them. The sick, aged, weak, or insane who were selected for extermination were sometimes driven away in Red Cross ambulances to camps referred to by terms such as "observation hospital." See David Boder, *I Did Not Interview the Dead;* Urbana, Univ. of Illinois Press, 1949; p. 81; and Elie A. Cohen, *Human Behavior in the Concentration Camp;* London, Cape, 1954; pp. 32, 37, 107.

23. Interviews collected by the Clausen group at NIMH suggest that when a wife comes to be a guardian, the responsibility may disrupt previous distance from in-laws, leading either to a new supportive coalition with them or to a marked withdrawal from them.

24. For an analysis of these nonpsychiatric kinds of perception, see Marian Radke Yarrow, Charlotte Green Schwartz, Harriet S. Murphy, and Leila Calhoun Deasy, "The Psychological Meaning of Mental Illness in the Family," *J. Social Issues* (1955) 11:12–24; Charlotte Green Schwartz, "Perspectives on Deviance: Wives' Definitions of their Husbands' Mental Illness," *Psychiatry* (1957) 20:275–291.

25. This guilt-carrying function is found, of course, in other role-complexes. Thus, when a middle-class couple engages in the process of legal separation or divorce, each of their lawyers

usually takes the position that his job is to acquaint his client with all of the potential claims and rights, pressing his client into demanding these, in spite of any nicety of feelings about the rights and honorableness of the ex-partner. The client, in all good faith, can then say to self and to the ex-partner that the demands are being made only because the lawyer insists it is best to do so.

26. Recorded in the Clausen data.

27. This point is made by Cumming, see footnote 3; p. 129.

28. There is an interesting contrast here with the moral career of the tuberculosis patient. I am told by Julius Roth that tuberculosis patients are likely to come to the hospital willingly, agreeing with their next-of-relation about treatment. Later in their hospital career, when they learn how long they yet have to stay and how depriving and irrational some of the hospital rulings are, they may seek to leave, be advised against this by the staff and by relatives, and only then begin to feel betrayed.

29. The inmate's initial strategy of holding himself aloof from ratifying contact may partly account for the relative lack of group-formation among inmates in public mental hospitals, a connection that has been suggested to me by William R. Smith. The desire to avoid personal bonds that would give license to the asking of biographical questions could also be a factor. In mental hospitals, of course, as in prisoner camps, the staff may consciously break up incipient group-formation in order to avoid collective rebellious action and other ward disturbances.

30. A comparable coming out occurs in the homosexual world, when a person finally comes frankly to present himself to a "gay" gathering not as a tourist but as someone who is "available." See Evelyn Hooker, "A Preliminary Examination of Group Behavior of Homosexuals," *J. Psychology* (1956) 42:217–225; especially p. 221. A good fictionalized treatment may be found in James Baldwin's *Giovanni's Room;* New York, Dial, 1956; pp. 41–63. A familiar instance of the coming out process is no doubt to be found among prepubertal children at the moment one of these actors sidles *back* into a room that had been left in an angered huff and injured *amour-propre*. The phrase itself presumably derives from a *rite-de-passage* ceremony once arranged by upper-class mothers for their daughters. Interestingly enough, in large mental hospitals the patient sometimes symbolizes a complete coming out by his first active participation in the hospital wide patient dance.

31. See Goffman, "Characteristics of Total Institutions," pp. 43–84; in *Proceedings of the Symposium of Preventive and Social Psychiatry;* Washington, D.C., Walter Reed Army Institute of Research, 1958.

32. A good description of the ward system may be found in Ivan Belknap, *Human Problems of a State Mental Hospital;* New York, McGraw-Hill, 1956; see especially p. 164.

33. Here is one way in which mental hospitals can be worse than concentration camps and prisons as places in which to "do" time; in the latter, self-insulation from the symbolic implications of the settings may be easier. In fact, self-insulation from hospital settings may be so difficult that patients have to employ devices for this which staff interpret as psychotic symptoms.

34. In regard to convicts, see Anthony Heckstall-Smith, *Eighteen Months;* London, Wingate, 1954; pp. 52–53. For "wino's" see the discussion in Howard G. Bain, "A Sociological Analysis of the Chicago Skid-Row Lifeway;" unpublished M.A. thesis, Dept. of Sociology, pp. 141–146. Bain's neglected thesis is a useful source of material on moral careers.

Apparently one of the occupational hazards of prostitution is that clients and other professional contacts sometimes persist in expressing sympathy by asking for a defensible dramatic explanation for the fall from grace. In having to bother to have a sad tale ready, perhaps the prostitute is more to be pitied than damned. Good examples of prostitute sad tales may be found in Sir Henry Mayhew, "Those that Will Not Work," pp. 210–272; in his *London Labour and the London Poor,* Vol. 4; London, Griffin, Bohn, and Cox, 1862. For a contemporary source, see *Women of the Streets,* edited by C. H. Rolph; London, Zecker, and Warburg, 1955; especially p. 6. "Almost always, however, after a few comments on the police, the girl would begin to explain how it was that she was in the life, usually in terms of self-justification." Lately, of course, the psychological expert has helped out the profession in the construction of wholly remarkable sad tales. See, for example, Harold Greenwald, *Call Girl;* New York, Ballantine, 1958.

35. A similar self-protecting rule has been observed in prisons. Thus, Hassler, see footnote 6, in describing a conversation with a fellow-prisoner: "He didn't say much about why he

was sentenced, and I didn't ask him, that being the accepted behavior in prison" (p. 76). A novelistic version for the mental hospital may be found in J. Kerkhoff, *How Thin the Veil: A Newspaperman's Story of His Own Mental Crack-up and Recovery;* New York, Greenberg, 1952; p. 27.

36. From the writer's field notes of informal interaction with patients, transcribed as near verbatim as he was able.

37. The process of examining a person psychiatrically and then altering or reducing his status in consequence is known in hospital and prison parlance as *bugging*, the assumption being that once you come to the attention of the testers you either will automatically be labeled crazy or the process of testing itself will make you crazy. Thus psychiatric staff are sometimes seen not as *discovering* whether you are sick, but as *making* you sick; and "Don't bug me, man," can mean, "Don't pester me to the point where I'll get upset." Sheldon Messinger has suggested to me that this meaning of bugging is related to the other colloquial meaning, of wiring a room with a secret microphone to collect information usable for discrediting the speaker.

31 / Suspended Identity: Identity Transformation in a Maximum Security Prison

THOMAS J. SCHMID
RICHARD S. JONES

The extent to which people hide behind the masks of impression management in everyday life is a point of theoretical controversy (Goffman 1959; Gross and Stone 1964; Irwin 1977; Douglas et al. 1980; Douglas and Johnson 1977; Messinger et al. 1962; Blumer 1969, 1972). A variety of problematic circumstances can be identified, however, in which individuals find it necessary to accommodate a sudden but encompassing shift in social situations by establishing temporary identities. These circumstances, which can range from meteoric fame (Adler and Adler 1989) to confinement in total institutions, place new identity demands on the individual, while seriously challenging his or her prior identity bases.

A prison sentence constitutes a "massive assault" on the identity of those imprisoned (Berger 1963: 100–101). This assault is especially severe on first-time inmates, and we might expect radical identity changes to ensue from their imprisonment. At the same time, a prisoner's awareness of the challenge to his identity affords some measure of protection against it. As part of an ethnographic analysis of the prison experiences of first-time, short-term inmates, this article presents an identity transformation model that differs both from the gradual transformation processes that characterize most adult identity changes and from such radical transformation processes as brainwashing or conversion.

Data for the study are derived principally from ten months of participant observation at a maximum security prison for men in the upper midwest of the United States. One of the authors was an inmate serving a felony sentence for one year and one day, while the other participated in the study as an outside observer. Relying on traditional ethnographic data collection and analysis techniques, this approach offered us general observations of hundreds of prisoners, and extensive fieldnotes that were based on repeated, often daily, contacts with about fifty inmates, as well as on personal relationships established with a smaller number of inmates. We subsequently

Figure 1 / Prison Images and Strategies of New Inmates

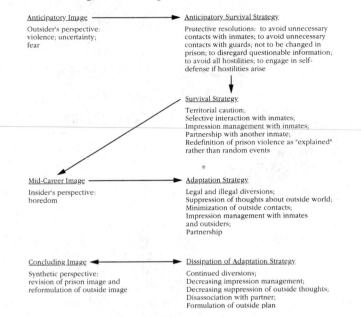

returned to the prison to conduct focused interviews with other prisoners; using information provided by prison officials, we were able to identify and interview twenty additional first-time inmates who were serving sentences of two years or less. See Schmid and Jones (1987) for further description of this study.

Three interrelated research questions guided our analysis: How do first-time, short-term inmates define the prison world, and how do their definitions change during their prison careers? How do these inmates adapt to the prison world, and how do their adaptation strategies change during their prison careers? How do their self-definitions change during their prison careers? Our analyses of the first two questions are presented in detail elsewhere (Schmid and Jones 1987, 1990); an abbreviated outline of these analyses, to which we will allude throughout this article, is presented in Figure 1. The identity transformation model presented here, based on our analysis of the third question, is outlined in Figure 2.

PREPRISON IDENTITY

Our data suggest that the inmates we studied have little in common before their arrival at prison, except their conventionality. Although convicted of felonies, most do not possess "criminal" identities (cf. Irwin 1970: 29–34). They begin their sentences with only a vague, incomplete image

Figure 2 / Suspended Identity Dialectic

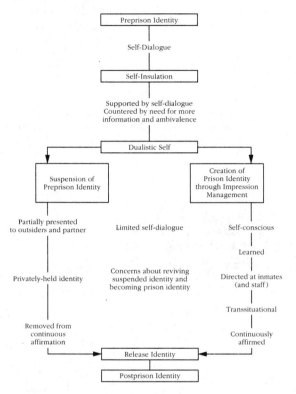

(Boulding 1961) of what prison is like, but an image that nonetheless stands in contrast to how they view their own social worlds. Their prison image is dominated by the theme of violence: they see prison inmates as violent, hostile, alien human beings, with whom they have nothing in common. They have several specific fears about what will happen to them in prison, including fears of assault, rape, and death. They are also concerned about their identities, fearing that—if they survive prison at all—they are in danger of changing in prison, either through the intentional efforts of rehabilitation personnel or through the unavoidable hardening effects of the prison environment. Acting on this imagery (Blumer 1969)—or, more precisely, on the inconsonance of their self-images with this prison image—they develop an anticipatory survival strategy (see Figure 1) that consists primarily of protective resolutions: a resolve to avoid all hostilities; a resolve to avoid all nonessential contacts with inmates and guards; a resolve to defend themselves in any way possible; and a resolve not to change, or to be changed, in prison.

A felon's image and strategy are formulated through a running self-dialogue, a heightened state of reflexive awareness (Lewis 1979) through which he ruminates about his past behavior and motives, and imaginatively projects himself into the prison world. This self-dialogue begins shortly after his arrest, continues intermittently during his trial or court hearings, and becomes especially intense at the time of his transfer to prison.

> You start taking a review—it's almost like your life is passing before your eyes. You wonder how in the heck you got to this point and, you know, what are— what's your family gonna think about it—your friends, all the talk, and how are you going to deal with that—and the kids, you know, how are they gonna react to it? . . . All those things run through your head. . . . The total loss of control—the first time in all my life that some other people were controlling my life.

*   *   *

> My first night in the joint was spent mainly on kicking myself in the butt for putting myself in the joint. It was a very emotional evening. I thought a lot about all my friends and family, the good-byes, the things we did the last couple of months, how good they had been to me, sticking by me. I also thought about my fears: Am I going to go crazy? Will I end up fighting for my life? How am I going to survive in here for a year? Will I change? Will things be the same when I get out?

His self-dialogue is also typically the most extensive self-assessment he has ever conducted; thus, at the same time that he is resolving not to change, he is also initiating the kind of introspective analysis that is essential to any identity transformation process.

SELF-INSULATION

A felon's self-dialogue continues during the initial weeks and months of his sentence, and it remains a solitary activity, each inmate struggling to come to grips with the inconsonance of his established (preprison) identity and his present predicament. Despite the differences in their preprison identities, however, inmates now share a common situation that affects their identities. With few exceptions, their self-dialogues involve feelings of vulnerability, discontinuity, and differentiation from other inmates, emotions that reflect both the degradations and deprivations of institutional life (cf. Goffman 1961; Sykes 1958; and Garfinkel 1956) and their continuing outsiders' perspective on the prison world. These feelings are obviously the result of everything that has happened to the inmates, but they are something else as well: they are the conditions in which every first-time, short-term inmate finds himself. They might even be called the common attributes of the inmates' selves-in-prison, for the irrelevance of their preprison identities within the prison world reduces their self-definitions, temporarily, to the level of pure emotion.[1] These feelings, and a consequent emphasis on the "physical self" (Zurcher 1977: 176), also constitute the essential motivation for the inmates' self-insulation strategies.[2]

An inmate cannot remain wholly insulated within the prison world, for a number of reasons. He simply spends too much of his time in the presence of others to avoid all interaction with them. He also recognizes that his prison image is based on incomplete and inadequate information, and that he must interact with others in order to acquire first-hand information about the prison world. His behavior in prison, moreover, is guided not only by his prison image but by a fundamental ambivalence he feels about his situation, resulting from his marginality between the prison and outside social worlds (Schmid and Jones 1987). His ambivalence has several manifestations throughout his prison career, but the most important is his conflicting desires for self-insulation and for human communication.

MANAGING A DUALISTIC SELF

An inmate is able to express both directions of his ambivalence (and to address his need for more information about the prison) by drawing a distinction between his "true" identity (i.e., his outside, preprison identity) and a "false" identity he creates for the prison world. For most of a new inmate's prison career, his preprison identity remains a "subjective" or "personal" identity while his prison identity serves as his "objective" or "social" basis for interaction in prison (see Weigert 1986; Goffman 1963). This bifurcation of his self (Figure 2) is not a conscious decision made at a single point in time, but it does represent two conscious and interdependent identity-preservation tactics, formulated through self-dialogue and refined through tentative interaction with others.

First, after coming to believe that he cannot "be himself" in prison because he would be too vulnerable, he decides to "suspend" his preprison identity for the duration of his sentence. He retains his resolve not to let prison change him, protecting himself by choosing not to reveal himself (his "true" self) to others. Expressions of a suspension of identity emerged repeatedly and consistently in both the fieldwork and interview phases of our research through such statements as

> I was reserved....I wouldn't be very communicative, you know. I'd try to keep conversation to a minimum....I wasn't interested in getting close to anybody... or asking a lot of questions. You know, try to cut the conversation short...go my own way back to my cell or go to the library or do something.

* * *

> I didn't want nobody to know too much about me. That was part of the act.

An inmate's decision to suspend his preprison identity emanates directly from his feelings of vulnerability, discontinuity and differentiation from other inmates. These emotions foster something like a "proto-sociological attitude" (Weigert 1986: 173; see also Zurcher 1977), in which new inmates find it necessary to step outside their taken-for-granted preprison identities. Rather than viewing these identities and the everyday life experience in which they are grounded as social constructions, however, inmates see the *prison* world as an artificial construction, and judge their "naturally occurring" preprison identities to be out of place within this construction. By attempting to suspend his preprison identity for the time that he spends in prison an inmate believes that he will again "be his old self" after his release.

While he is in confinement, an inmate's decision to suspend his identity leaves him with little or no basis for interaction. His second identity tactic, then, is the creation of an identity that allows him to interact, however cautiously, with others. This tactic consists of his increasingly sophisticated impression management skills (Goffman 1959; Schlenker 1980), which are initially designed simply to hide his vulnerability, but which gradually evolve into an alternative identity felt to be more suitable to the prison world. The character of the presented identity is remarkably similar from inmate to inmate:

> Well, I learned that you can't act like—you can't get the attitude where you are better than they are. Even where you might be better than them, you can't strut around like you are. Basically, you can't stick out. You don't stare at people and things like that. I knew a lot of these things from talking to people and I figured them out by myself. I sat down and figured out just what kind of attitude I'm going to have to take.

* * *

> Most people out here learn to be tough, whether they can back it up or not. If you don't learn to be tough, you will definitely pay for it. This toughness can be demonstrated through a mean look, tough language, or an extremely big build.... One important thing is never to let your guard down.

An inmate's prison identity, as an inauthentic presentation of self, is not in itself a form of identity transformation but is rather a form of identity construction. His prison identity is simply who he must pretend to be while he is in prison. It is a false identity created for survival in an artificial world. But this identity nonetheless emerges in the same manner as any other identity: it is learned from others, and it must be presented to, negotiated with, and validated by others. A new inmate arrives at prison with a general image of what prisoners are like, and he begins to flesh out this image from the day of his arrival, warily observing others just as they are observing him. Through watching others, through eavesdropping, through cautious conversation and selective interaction, a new inmate refines his understanding of what maximum security prisoners look like, how they talk, how they move, how they act. Despite his belief that he is different from these other prisoners, he knows that he cannot appear to be too different from them, if he is to hide his vulnerability. His initial image of other prisoners, his early observations, and his concern over how he appears to others thus provide a foundation for the identity he gradually creates through impression management.

Impression management skills, of course, are not exclusive to the prison world; a new inmate, like anyone else, has had experience in the creation of his prison identity. He has undoubtedly even had experience in presenting a "front" to others, and he draws upon his experience in projecting the very attributes—strength, stoicism, aplomb—required by his prison identity. Impression management in prison differs, however, in the totality with which it governs interactions and in the perceived costs of failure: humiliation, assault, or death. For these reasons the entire impression management process becomes a more highly conscious endeavor. When presenting himself before others, a new inmate pays close attention to such minute details of his front as eye contact, posture, and manner of walking:

> I finally got out of orientation. I was going out with the main population, going down to get my meals and things. The main thing is not to stare at a bunch of people, you know. I tried to just look ahead, you know, not stare at people. 'Cause I didn't really know; I just had to learn a little at a time.

*   *   *

> The way you look seems to be very important. The feeling is you shouldn't smile, that a frown is much more appropriate. The eyes are very important. You should never look away; it is considered a sign of weakness. Either stare straight ahead, look around, or look the person dead in the eyes. The way you walk is important. You shouldn't walk too fast; they might think you were scared and in a hurry to get away.

To create an appropriate embodiment (Weigert 1986; Stone 1962) of their prison identities, some new inmates devote long hours to weightlifting or other body-building exercises, and virtually all of them relinquish their civilian clothes—which might express their preprison identities—in favor of the standard issue clothing that most inmates wear. Whenever a new inmate is open to the view of other inmates, in fact, he is likely to relinquish most overt symbols of his individuality, in favor of a standard issue "prison inmate" appearance.

By acting self-consciously, of course, a new inmate runs the risk of exposing the fact that he *is* acting. But he sees no alternative to playing his part better; he cannot "not act" because that too would expose the vulnerability of his "true" identity. He thus sees every new prison experience, every new territory that he is allowed to explore, as a test of his impression management skills. Every nonconfrontive encounter with another inmate symbolizes his success at these skills, but it is also a social validation of his prison identity. Eventually he comes to see that many, perhaps most, inmates are engaging in the same kind of inauthentic presentations of self (cf. Glaser and Strauss 1964). Their identities are as "false" as his, and their validations of his identity may be equally false. But he realizes that he is powerless to change this state of affairs, and that he must continue to present his prison identity for as long as he remains in prison.

A first-time inmate enters prison as an outsider, and it is from an outsider's perspective that he initially creates his prison identity. In contrast to his suspended preprison identity, his prison identity is a *shared* identity, because it is modeled on his observations of other inmates. Like those of more experienced prisoners, his prison identity is tied directly to the social role of "prison inmate" (cf. Scheff 1970; Solomon 1970); because he is an outsider, however, his prison identity is also severely limited by his narrow understanding of that role. It is based on an outsider's stereotype of who a maximum security inmate is and what he acts like. It is, nonetheless, a *structural* identity (Weigert 1968), created to address his outsider's institutional problems of social isolation and inadequate information about the prison world.

By the middle of his sentence, a new inmate comes to adopt what is essentially an insider's perspective on the prison world. His prison image has evolved to the point where it is dominated by the theme of boredom rather than violence. (The possibility of violence is still acknowledged and feared, but those violent incidents that do occur have been redefined as the consequences of prison norm violations rather than as random predatory acts; see Schmid and Jones 1990.) His survival strategy, although still extant, has been supplemented by such general adaptation techniques as legal and illegal diversionary activities and conscious efforts to suppress his thoughts about the outside world (Figure 1). His impression management tactics have become second nature rather than self-conscious, as he routinely interacts with others in terms of his prison identity.

An inmate's suspension of his preprison identity, of course, is never absolute, and the separation between his suspended identity and his prison identity is never complete. He continues, to interact with his visitors at least partially in terms of his preprison identity, and he is likely to have acquired at least one inmate "partner" with whom he interacts in terms of his preprison as well as his prison identity. During times of introspection, however—which take place less frequently but do not disappear—he generally continues to think of himself as being the same person he was before he came to prison. But it is also during these periods of self-dialogue that he begins to have doubts about his ability to revive his suspended identity.

That's what I worry about a lot. Because I didn't want to change....I'm still fighting it, 'cause from what I understood, before, I wasn't that bad—I wasn't even violent. But I have people say stuff to me now, before I used to say "O.k., o.k."—but now it seems like I got to eye them back, you know.

* * *

I don't know, but I may be losing touch with the outside. I am feeling real strange during visits, very uncomfortable. I just can't seem to be myself, although I am not really sure what myself is all about. My mind really seems to be glued to the inside of these walls. I can't even really comprehend the outside. I haven't even been here three months, and I feel like I'm starting to lose it. Maybe I'm just paranoid. But during these visits I really feel like I'm acting. I'm groping for the right words, always trying to keep the conversation going. Maybe I'm just trying to present a picture that will relieve the minds of my visitors, I just don't know.

* * *

I realized that strength is going to be an important factor whether I'm going to turn into a cold person or whether I'm going to keep my humanitarian point of view. I knew it is going to be an internal war. It's going to take a lot of energy to do that....I just keep telling myself that you gotta do it and sometimes you get to the point where you don't care anymore. You just kinda lose it and you get so full of hate, so full of frustration, it gets wound up in your head a lot.

At this point, both the inmate's suspended preprison identity and his created prison identity are part of his "performance consciousness" (Schechner 1985), although they are not given equal value. His preprison identity is grounded primarily in the memory of his biography (Weigert 1986) rather than in self-performance. His concern, during the middle of his sentence, is that he has become so accustomed to dealing with others in terms of his prison identity—that he has been presenting and receiving affirmation of this identity for so long—that it is becoming his "true" identity.[3]

An inmate's fear that he is becoming the character he has been presenting is not unfounded. All of his interactions within the prison world indicate the strong likelihood of a "role-person merger" (Turner 1978). An inmate views his presentation of his prison identity as a necessary expression of his inmate status. Unlike situational identities presented through impression management in the outside world, performance of the inmate role is transsituational and continuous. For a new inmate, prison consists almost exclusively of front regions, in which he must remain in character. As long as he is in the maximum security institution, he remains in at least partial view of the audience for which his prison identity is intended: other prison inmates.[4] Moreover, because the stakes of his performance are so high, there is little room for self-mockery or other forms of role distance (Ungar

1984; Coser 1966) from his prison identity, and there is little possibility that an inmate's performance will be "punctured" (Adler and Adler 1989) by his partner or other prison acquaintances. And because his presentation of his prison identity is continuous, he also receives continuous affirmation of this identity from others—affirmation that becomes more significant in light of the fact that he also remains removed from day-to-day reaffirmation of his preprison identity by his associates in the outside world. The inauthenticity of the process is beside the point: Stone's (1962: 93) observation that "one's identity is established when others *place* him as a social object by assigning him the same words of identity that he appropriates for himself or *announces*" remains sound even when both the announcements and the placements are recognized as false.

Standing against these various forms of support for an inmate's prison identity are the inmate's resolve not to be changed in prison, the fact that his sentence is relatively brief (though many new inmates lose sight of this brevity during the middle of their careers) and the limited reaffirmation of his preprison identity that he receives from outsiders and from his partner. These are not insubstantial resources, but nor do they guarantee an inmate's future ability to discard his prison identity and revive the one he has suspended.

IDENTITY DIALECTIC

When an inmate's concerns about his identity first emerge, there is little that he can do about them. He recognizes that he has no choice but to present his prison identity so, following the insider's perspective he has now adopted, he consciously attempts to suppress his concerns. Eventually, however, he must begin to consider seriously his capacity to revive his suspended identity; his identity concerns, and his belief that he must deal with them, become particularly acute if he is transferred to the minimum security unit of the prison for the final months of his sentence.[5] At the conclusion of his prison career, an inmate shifts back toward an outsider's perspective on the prison world (see Figure 1); this shift involves the dissipation of his maximum security adaptation strategy, further revision of his prison image, reconstruction of an image of the outside world, and the initial development of an outside plan.[6] The inmate's efforts to revive his suspended identity are part of this shift in perspectives.

It is primarily through a renewed self-dialogue that the inmate struggles to revive his suspended identity—a struggle that amounts to a dialectic between his suspended identity and his prison identity. Through self-dialogue he recognizes, and tries to confront, the extent to which these two identities really do differ. He again tries to differentiate himself from maximum security inmates.

There seems to be a concern with the inmates here to be able to distinguish...
themselves from the other inmates. That is—they feel they are above the others....
Although they may associate with each other, it still seems important to degrade
the majority here.

And he does have some success in freeing himself from his prison identity.

Well, I think I am starting to soften up a little bit. I believe the identity I picked
up in the prison is starting to leave me now that I have left the world of the
[maximum security] joint. I find myself becoming more and more involved with
the happenings of the outside world. I am even getting anxious to go out and see
the sights, just to get away from this place.

But he recognizes that he *has* changed in prison, and that these changes run
deeper than the mask he has been presenting to others. He has not returned
to his "old self" simply because his impression management skills are used
less frequently in minimum security. He raises the question—though he
cannot answer it—of how permanent these changes are. He wonders how
much his family and friends will see him as having changed. As stated by
one of our interview respondents:

I know I've changed a little bit. I just want to realize how the people I know
are going to see it, because they [will] be able to see it more than I can see
it.... Sometimes I just want to go somewhere and hide.

He speculates about how much the outside world—especially his own
network of outside relationships—has changed in his absence. (It is his life,
not those of his family and friends, that has been suspended during his
prison sentence; he knows that changes have occurred in the outside world,
and he suspects that some of these changes may have been withheld from
him, intentionally or otherwise.) He has questions, if not serious doubts,
about his ability to "make it" on the outside, especially concerning his
relationships with others; he knows, in any case, that he cannot simply
return to the outside world as if nothing has happened. Above all, he
repeatedly confronts the question of who he is, and who he will be in the
outside world.

An inmate's struggle with these questions, like his self-dialogue at the
beginning of his prison career, is necessarily a solitary activity. The identity
he claims at the time of his release, in contrast to his prison identity,
cannot be learned from other inmates. Also like his earlier periods of
self-dialogue, the questions he considers are not approached in a rational,
systematic manner. The process is more one of rumination—of pondering
one question until another replaces it, and then contemplating the new
question until it is replaced by still another, or suppressed from his thoughts.
There is, then, no final resolution to any of the inmate's identity questions.
Each inmate confronts these questions in his own way, and each arrives at his

own understanding of who he is, based on this unfinished, unresolved self-dialogue. In every case, however, an inmate's release identity is a synthesis of his suspended preprison identity and his prison identity.[7]

POSTPRISON IDENTITY

Because each inmate's release identity is the outcome of his own identity dialectic, we cannot provide a profile of the "typical" release identity. But our data do allow us to specify some of the conditions that affect this outcome. Reaffirmations of his preprison identity by outsiders—visits and furloughs during which others interact with him as if he has not changed—provide powerful support for his efforts to revive his suspended identity. These efforts are also promoted by an inmate's recollection of his preprison identity (i.e., his attempts, through self-dialogue, to assess who he was before he came to prison), by his desire to abandon his prison identity, and by his general shift back toward an outsider's perspective. But there are also several factors that favor his prison identity, including his continued use of diversionary activities; his continued periodic efforts to suppress thoughts about the outside world; his continued ability to use prison impression management skills; and his continuing sense of injustice about the treatment he has received. Strained or cautious interactions with outsiders, or unfulfilled furlough expectations, inhibit the revival of his preprison identity. And he faces direct, experiential evidence that he has changed: when a minimum security resident recognizes that he is now completely unaffected by reports of violent incidents in maximum security, he acknowledges that he is no longer the same person that he was when he entered prison. Turner (1978: 1) has suggested three criteria for role-person merger: "failure of role compartmentalization, resistance to abandoning a role in the face of advantageous alternative roles, and the acquisition of role-appropriate attitudes"; at the time of their release from prison, the inmates we studied had already accrued some experience with each of these criteria.

Just as we cannot define a typical release identity, we cannot predict these inmates' future, postprison identities, not only because we have restricted our analysis to their prison experiences but because each inmate's future identity is inherently unpredictable. What effect an ex-inmate's prison experience has on his identity depends on how he, in interaction with others, defines this experience. Some of the men we have studied will be returned to prison in the future; others will not. But all will have been changed by their prison experiences. They entered the prison world fearing for their lives; they depart with the knowledge that they have survived. On the one hand, these men are undoubtedly stronger persons by virtue of this accomplishment. On the other hand, the same tactics that enabled them to survive the prison world can be called upon, appropriately or not, in difficult situations in the outside world. To the extent that these men draw upon their prison survival tactics to cope with the hardships of the outside world—to the extent that their prison behavior becomes a meaningful part of their "role repertoire" (Turner 1978) in their everyday lives—their prison identities will have become inseparable from their "true" identities.

THE SUSPENDED IDENTITY MODEL

As identity preservation tactics, an inmate's suspension of his preprison identity and development of a false prison identity are not, and cannot be, entirely successful. At the conclusion of his sentence, no inmate can ever fully revive his suspended identity; he cannot remain the same person he was before he came to prison. But his tactics do not fail entirely either. An inmate's resolve not to change, his decision to suspend his preprison identity, his belief that he will be able to revive this identity, and his subsequent struggle to revive this identity undoubtedly minimize the identity change that would otherwise have taken place. The inmate's tactics, leading up to his suspended identity dialectic, constitute an identity transformation process, summarized in Figure 2, that differs from both the gradual, sequential model of identity transformation and models of radical identity transformation (Strauss 1959). It also shares some characteristics with each of these models.

As in cases of brainwashing and conversion, there is an external change agency involved, the inmate does learn a new perspective (an insider's perspective) for evaluating himself and the world around him, and he does develop new group loyalties while his old loyalties are reduced. But unlike a radical identity transformation, the inmate does not interpret the changes that take place as changes in a *central* identity; the insider's perspective he learns and the new person he becomes in prison are viewed as a false front that he must present to others, but a front that does not affect who he really is. And while suspending his preprison identity necessarily entails a weakening of his outside loyalties, it does not, in most cases, destroy them. Because he never achieves more than a marginal status in the prison world, the inmate's ambivalence prevents him from accepting an insider's perspective too fully, and thus prevents him from fully severing his loyalties to the outside world (Schmid and Jones 1987). He retains a fundamental, if ambivalent, commitment to his outside world throughout his sentence, and he expects to reestablish his outside relationships (just as he expects to revive his suspended identity) when his sentence is over.

Like a religious convert who later loses his faith, an inmate cannot simply return to his old self. The liminal conditions (Turner 1977) of the prison world have removed him, for too long, from his accustomed identity bearings in everyday life. He does change in prison, but his attempts to suspend and subsequently revive his preprison identity maintain a general sense of identity continuity for most of his prison career. As in the gradual identity transformation process delineated by Strauss (1959), he recognizes changes in his identity only at periodic "turning points," especially his mid-career doubts about his ability to revive his suspended identity and his self-dialogue at the end of his sentence. Also like a gradual identity transformation, the extent of his identity change depends on a balance between the situational adjustments he has made in prison and his continuing commitments to the outside world (Becker 1960, 1964). His identity depends, in other words, on the outcome of the dialectic between his prison identity and his suspended preprison identity.

The suspended identity model is one component and a holistic analysis of the experiences of first-time, short-term inmates at a specific maximum security prison. Like any holistic analysis, its usefulness lies primarily in its capacity to explain the particular case under study (Deising 1971). We nonetheless expect similar identity transformation processes to occur under similar circumstances: among individuals who desire to preserve their identities despite finding themselves involved in temporary but encompassing social situations that subject them to new and disparate identity demands and render their prior identities inappropriate. The suspended identity model presented here provides a basis for further exploration of these circumstances.

Acknowledgments

We wish to thank Jim Thomas, Patricia A. Adler and the reviewers of *Symbolic Interaction* for their useful comments and suggestions.

Notes

1. This is a matter of some theoretical interest. Proponents of existential sociology (cf. Douglas and Johnson 1977) view feelings as the very foundation of social action, social structures, and the self. From this theoretical framework, a new inmate would be viewed as someone who has been stripped to that core of primal feelings that constitutes his existential self; the symbolic constructions of his former world, including his cognitive definition of himself (learned from the definitions that others hold of him) are exposed as artificial, leaving the individual at least partially free to choose for himself what he wants to be and how he wants to present himself to others. Whether or not we view the feelings of vulnerability, discontinuity, and differentiation as the core of an inmate's self, or even as attributes of his self, we must note that the inmate does not reject his earlier self-image (or other symbolic constructions) as artificial. He continues to hold on to his preprison identity as his "true" self and he continues to view the outside world as the "real" world. It is the prison world that is viewed as artificial. His definitions of the outside world and the prison world do change during his prison career, but he never fully rejects his outsider's perspective.

2. There are four principal components to the survival strategies of the inmates we studied, in the early months of their prison sentences. "Selective interaction" and "territorial caution" are essentially precautionary guidelines that allow inmates to increase their understanding of the prison world while minimizing danger to themselves. "Partnership" is a special friendship bond between two inmates, typically based on common backgrounds and interests (including

a shared uncertainty about prison life) and strengthened by the inmates' mutual exploration of a hostile prison world. The fourth component of their strategies, impression management, is discussed in subsequent sections of this article.

3. Clemmer (1958: 299) has defined "prisonization" as the "taking on in greater or less degree of the folkways, mores, customs, and general culture of the penitentiary." Yet new inmates begin to "take on" these things almost immediately, as part of the impression they are attempting to present to other inmates. Thus, we would argue instead that prisonization (meaning assimilation to the prison world) begins to occur for these inmates when their prison identities become second nature—when their expressions of prison norms and customs are no longer based on self-conscious acting. A new inmate's identity concerns, during the middle of his sentence, are essentially a recognition of this assimilation. For other examples of problems associated with double identity, see Warren and Ponse (1977) and Lemert (1967); Adler and Adler (1989) describe self-diminishment problems, as well as self-aggrandizement effects, that accompany even highly valued identity constructions.

4. This finding stands in contrast to other works on total institutions, which suggest that inmates direct their impression management tactics toward the staff. See, for example, Goffman (1961: 318) and Heffernan (1972; chapter VI). First-time, short-term inmates certainly interact with guards and other staff in terms of their prison identities, but these personnel are neither the primary source of their fear nor the primary objects of their impression management. Interactions with staff are limited by a concern with how other inmates will define such interactions; in this sense, presentation of a new inmate's prison identity to staff can be viewed as part of the impression he is creating for other inmates.

5. Not all prisoners participate in this unit; inmates must apply for transfer to the unit, and their acceptance depends both on the crimes for which they were sentenced and staff evaluation of their potential for success in the unit. Our analysis focuses on those inmates who are transferred.

6. There are three features of the minimum security unit that facilitate this shift in perspectives: a more open physical and social environment; the fact that the unit lies just outside the prison wall (so that an inmate who is transferred is also physically removed from the maximum security prison); and greater opportunity for direct contact with the outside world, through greater access to telephones, an unrestricted visitor list, unrestricted visiting hours and, eventually, weekend furloughs.

7. This is an important parallel with our analysis of the inmate's changing prison definitions: his concluding prison image is a synthesis of the image he formulates before coming to prison and the image he holds at the middle of his prison career; see Schmid and Jones 1990.

References

Adler, Patricia A. and Peter Adler. 1989. "The Gloried Self: The Aggrandizement and the Constriction of Self." *Social Psychology Quarterly* 52:299–310.

Becker, Howard S. 1960. "Notes on the Concept of Commitment." *American Journal of Sociology* 66:32–40.

———. "Personal Change in Adult Life." 1964. *Sociometry* 27:40–53.

Berger, Peter L. 1963. *Invitation to Sociology: A Humanistic Perspective.* Garden City, NY: Doubleday Anchor Books.

Blumer, Herbert. 1972. "Action vs. Interaction: Review of *Relations in Public* by Erving Goffman." *Transaction* 9:50–53.

———. 1969. *Symbolic Interactionism: Perspective and Method,* Englewood Cliffs, NJ: Prentice Hall.

Boulding, Kenneth. 1961. *The Image.* Ann Arbor: University of Michigan Press.

Clemmer, Donald. 1958. *The Prison Community.* New York: Holt, Rinehart & Winston.

Coser, R. 1966. "Role Distance, Sociological Ambivalence and Traditional Status Systems." *American Journal of Sociology* 72:173–187.

Deising, Paul. 1971. *Patterns of Discovery in the Social Sciences*. Chicago: Aldine-Atherton.

Douglas, Jack D., Patricia A. Adler, Peter Adler, Andrea Fontana, Robert C. Freeman, and Joseph A. Kotarba. 1980. *Introduction to the Sociologies of Everyday Life*. Boston: Allyn and Bacon.

Douglas, Jack D. and John M. Johnson. 1977. *Existential Sociology*. Cambridge: Cambridge University Press.

Garfinkel, Harold. 1956. "Conditions of Successful Degradation Ceremonies." *American Journal of Sociology* 61:420–424.

Glaser, Barney G. and Anselm L. Strauss. 1964. "Awareness Contexts and Social Interaction." *American Sociological Review* 29:269–279.

Goffman, Erving. 1961. *Asylums*. Garden City, NY: Doubleday Anchor Books.

———. 1959. *The Presentation of Self in Everyday Life*. Garden City, NY: Doubleday Anchor Books.

———. 1963. *Stigma: Notes on the Management of Spoiled Identity*. Englewood Cliffs, NJ: Prentice Hall.

Gross, Edward and Gregory P. Stone. 1964. "Embarrassment and the Analysis of Role Requirements." *American Journal of Sociology* 70:1–15.

Heffernan, Esther. 1972. *Making It in Prison: The Square, the Cool and the Life*. New York: Wiley-Interscience.

Irwin, John. 1970. *The Felon*. Englewood Cliffs, NJ: Prentice Hall.

———. 1977. *Scenes*. Beverly Hills: Sage.

Lemert, Edwin. 1967. "Role Enactment, Self, and Identity in the Systematic Check Forger." Pp. 119–134 in *Human Deviance, Social Problems and Social Control*. Englewood Cliffs, NJ: Prentice Hall.

Lewis, David J. 1979. "A Social Behaviorist Interpretation of the Median I." *American Journal of Sociology* 84:261–287.

Messinger, Sheldon E., Harold Sampson, and Robert D. Towne. 1962. "Life as Theater: Some Notes on the Dramaturgic Approach to Social Reality." *Sociometry* 25:98–111.

Schechner, Richard. 1985. *Between Theater and Anthropology*. Philadelphia: University of Pennsylvania Press.

Scheff, Thomas. 1970. "On the Concepts of Identity and Social Relationships" Pp. 193–207 in *Human Nature and Collective Behavior*, edited by T. Shibutani. Englewood Cliffs, NJ: Prentice Hall.

Schlenker, B. 1980. *Impression Management: The Self Concept, Social Identity and Interpersonal Relations*. Belmont, CA: Wadsworth.

Schmid, Thomas and Richard Jones. 1987. "Ambivalent Actions: Prison Adaptation Strategies of New Inmates." American Society of Criminology, annual meetings, Montreal, Quebec.

Schmid, Thomas and Richard Jones. 1990. "Experiential Orientations to the Prison Experience: The Case of First-Time, Short-Term Inmates." Pp. 189–210 in *Perspectives on Social Problems*, edited by Gale Miller and James A. Holstein. Greenwich, CT: JAI Press.

Solomon, David N. 1970. "Role and Self-Conception: Adaptation and Change in Occupations." Pp. 286–300 in *Human Nature and Collective Behavior*, edited by T. Shibutani. Englewood Cliffs, NJ: Prentice Hall.

Stone, Gregory P. 1962. "Appearance and the Self." Pp. 86–118 in *Human Behavior and Social Processes*, edited by Arnold Rose. Boston: Houghton Mifflin.

Strauss, Anselm L. 1959. *Mirrors and Masks: The Search for Identity.* Glencoe: The Free Press.

Sykes, Gresham. 1958. *The Society of Captives: A Study of a Maximum Security Prison.* Princeton: Princeton University Press.

Turner, Ralph H. 1978. "The Role and the Person." *American Journal of Sociology* 84:1–23.

Turner, Victor. 1977. *The Ritual Process: Structure and Anti-Structure.* Ithaca, NY: Cornell University Press.

Ungar, Sheldon. 1984. "Self-Mockery: An Alternative Form of Self-Presentation." *Symbolic Interaction* 7:121–133.

Warren, Carol A. and Barbara Ponse. 1977. "The Existential Self in the Gay World." Pp. 273–289 in *Existential Sociology,* edited by Jack D. Douglas and John M. Johnson. Cambridge: Cambridge University Press.

Weigert, Andrew J. 1986. "The Social Production of Identity: Metatheoretical Foundations." *Sociological Quarterly* 27:165–183.

Zurcher, Louis A. 1977. *The Mutable Self.* Beverly Hills: Sage.

Part 5 / Building Deviant Careers and Identities

In Part 4, I described how institutional careers and identities may be produced. The material in that section examined how various types of institutional typing and processing may affect an actor's personal and public identity, as well as self-image. An equally important concern is the way in which noninstitutional careers evolve. As I noted earlier, such careers or activities generally arise as a result of an actor's own desires and needs; this means that frequently the actor plays an assertive role in moving into a particular type of activity, consciously structuring and presenting a specific image of self to others. Often, as the general introduction indicates, there may be a degree of overlap between institutional and noninstitutional careers. For instance, prostitutes, skid-row alcoholics, homosexuals, and thieves may be arrested and thus pulled into, rather than intentionally entering, an institutional career. Although the distinction between institutional and noninstitutional careers is useful analytically, we must recognize that if an actor is to assume the status of a secondary or career deviant, he or she must become familiar with and act in accord with existing ideology, culture, practices, and traditions. Obtaining a more complete understanding of how a deviant career or identity is actually built, however, requires that we initially examine an occupation's or profession's underlying organizational structures and associated ideologies. Once such elements have been located, characterized, described, and set, we are in a much better position to understand such processes as recruitment and socialization.

ORGANIZATIONAL STRUCTURES, IDEOLOGIES, AND RECRUITMENT: THE NONINSTITUTIONAL BACKDROP

"The Social Organization of Deviants," by Joel Best and David F. Luckenbill, provides an excellent framework for understanding the social organizations in which deviants become involved. The authors make an initial distinction between the social organization of *deviants* and the social organization of *deviance*. The former refers to the "patterns of relationships between deviant actors," whereas the latter refers to the "patterns of

445

relationships between the various roles performed in deviant transactions." Best and Luckenbill elect to focus on the social organization of deviants. Deviant organizations, they reason, can vary along certain dimensions, most notably in terms of their sophistication (i.e., complexity, degree of coordination, and purposiveness). For example, with regard to complexity, organizations can have varying divisions of labor, degrees of stratification, and degrees of role specialization. Best and Luckenbill note that, in terms of sophistication, deviants organize in identifiable ways. They discuss five organizational forms: loners, colleagues, peers, mobs, and formal organizations. Each of these forms can be analyzed relative to four variables: whether the deviants associate with each other, whether they engage in deviance together, whether there is an elaborate division of labor, and whether activities extend over time and space. The authors describe various types of each organizational form. They then examine the consequences of organizing as loners, colleagues, peers, mobs, or formal organizations. Best and Luckenbill argue that the degree of sophistication of a deviant organization has consequences for deviants and social-control agents. Five propositions are advanced in support of this argument. The authors' second hypothesis is especially relevant for the next section on entering and learning about deviant cultures. Specifically, they hypothesize that "the more sophisticated the form of deviant organization, the more elaborate the socialization of its members." The underlying assumption here is that "neophyte deviants" not only must learn how to perform deviant acts and attain the appropriate skills and techniques, but they must also develop a *cognitive perspective* (e.g., learn the relevant rationalizations and language). For example, loners do not depend on others for instruction, but pool hustlers do.

In "The Voluntary Recruitment of 'Deviants': The Examples of Homosexuality, Prostitution, and Alcoholism" from my book *Creating School Failure, Youth Crime, and Deviance,* I move beyond Best and Luckenbill's description of organizational forms of deviants to an examination of the actual underlying organizational structures of various types of deviant enterprises and activities. In keeping with Part 4, I first focus on the ideologies and recruitment offices that characterize deviant and semideviant activities, occupations, and professions. Because of the availability of relevant material, I examine homosexuality, prostitution, and alcoholism. Of significance is not only the way in which an actor or novice gains exposure to or entry into a deviant enterprise but also how, as a result of socializing experiences, he or she may ultimately acquire a deviant career and identity. I use Bryan's research on call girls to describe these processes. He insightfully analyzes how the *content* of the call-girl profession becomes inculcated in the novice, and he discusses the "philosophical" versus the "interpersonal" ideology. The former refers to the official perspective, whereas the latter (i.e., the working ideology) refers to the dos and don'ts of dealing with johns. Interesting, too, is the nature and content of the rationalizations taught (e.g., "all men are corrupt and deserve exploitation"). The research by Wallace on skid-row alcoholics also describes the various entry routes actors may take on their "routes to homelessness." I observe that exposure may not lead to participation, nor does participation necessarily lead to a stable career as a skid rower. In effect, one can have exposure to, enter in, and participate for a spell, yet not become a skid rower. Regardless of whether an actor stays or goes, he or she must become familiar with and act according to the underlying normative structure of the skid-row world. Becoming a regular member of the skid-row culture, Wallace notes, is associated with some noticeable changes in identity, dress, manners, and appearance. Skid rowers may, for example, neglect their appearance or sell their clothes or razors for money. I conclude by discussing the important role that rationalization plays in the assumption of the status of a career deviant.

ENTERING AND LEARNING DEVIANT CULTURES AND PRACTICES: THE BUILDING OF DEVIANT CAREERS AND IDENTITIES

The statements by Best and Luckenbill indicate that deviant organizations can be characterized in terms of their relative degree of sophistication. Best and Luckenbill also emphasize that a person can gain initial entry to organizations through various channels. Once individuals gain entry, however, they must, if they elect to stay, learn the existing culture and traditions. A similar requirement exists with respect to the institutional deviant. Failure to meet expectations may result in such penalties as ostracism or exclusion from the group. (The general social-psychological processes involved in learning deviant cultures were highlighted in my discussion of the cultural transmission model in Part 2.) The selections in this section deal primarily with entry routes and offer specific illustrations of how actors become socialized into deviant or semideviant careers.

In "Drifting into Dealing: Becoming a Cocaine Seller," Sheigla Murphy, Dan Waldorf, and Craig Reinarman outline the various modes and levels of entry into the world of cocaine sales. Their observations are based on interviews with eighty ex-cocaine sellers. All had sold cocaine for at least a year; however, none had done so for a period of six months prior to the interviews. Actual entry into the world of cocaine sales is, according to the researchers, a fluid process, with most sellers drifting into their dealing career. The authors go on to describe five basic ways that people begin to sell cocaine. The first mode of entry is the *go-between,* in which a person who initially buys for his or her friends begins to envision the profits that may result from selling. The second avenue is the *stash dealer,* in which a user sells small amounts to support his or her own cocaine needs. The *connoisseur,* the third mode of entry, includes those who seek to buy high-quality drugs through wholesale purchases, and the fourth entry route entails the *apprenticeship,* a trainee-style of connection. In this situation, the novice takes over all aspects of an established dealer's business after learning the ropes. The fifth and final entry route described involves what is termed the *product line expansion.* Here dealers start selling other drugs (e.g., marijuana) and then move into cocaine sales when a supply becomes available. Of importance, too, is the authors' analysis of how a seller may exhibit a subtle transformation of his or her identity. Once situated in the role of the dealer, selling often becomes viewed as a job or career. Significant, too, is the observation that the "dealer identity" did not seem to replace former "legitimate" identities but was, instead, added to a subject's other conventional identities. Thus, sellers would, and depending upon the situation, emphasize different aspects of their identities. The researchers end by describing some of the values and expectations that characterize the business relationships existing between sellers and customers.

In "Confronting Deadly Disease: The Drama of Identity Construction among Gay Men with AIDS," Kent L. Sandstrom uses interview data to describe how gay men attempt to construct an AIDS-related identity and integrate it with other positive aspects of self; this is a particularly important requirement for those who are inflicted with AIDS. Persons with AIDS (PWAs), the author notes, are acutely aware of the stigma associated with their illness, and they often encounter some very difficult emotional and social reactions. How do the PWAs deal with such responses? The researcher sheds some light on this question by describing a range of identity management strategies (e.g., passing, covering, isolation, and insulation) that can be used to avoid potentially threatening social occasions and interactions. Whether a specific technique is useful or not depends on several factors. If, for example, facial lesions are apparent or one has a pale complexion, then passing or covering is not especially effective. Pursuing isolation also produces differential effects on the PWAs. Exclusive reliance on such attempts to shield one's self from the stigma of AIDS not only is defensive in nature but is not associated with any significant efforts to reformulate or reconstruct one's personal and public identity, or view of self. Sandstrom then outlines the various types of *identity work* that the PWAs engage in, with the most prominent one being *identity embracement.* Through use of new memberships and support groups, the PWAs build and come to embrace a positive AIDS-related identity. They reject public impu-tations that they are "AIDS victims" and promote a different image. The view promoted might be that the PWAs are individuals who are "living and thriving with the illness." Sandstrom concludes by describing how subcul-tures and such processes as ideological embracement are used by the PWAs to revitalize their identities and views of self. His concluding comments are especially relevant to those sections of this book in which I describe how deviant categories are created (Part 1) and how they may be transformed

(Part 6). In this case, the category of "AIDS victim" and its associated range of negative labels appear to have undergone some significant redefinition. Hence, anyone occupying this status may, both in terms of self and other perceptions, be cast in a more positive light.

DEVIANT CAREERS AND IDENTITIES: SOME ADDITIONAL FORMS AND SHAPES—PEERS, GANGS, AND ORGANIZATIONS

As the preceding descriptions reveal, deviant or semideviant occupations vary in terms of their sophistication and corresponding organizational structure; the house prostitute, given the particular nature of the profession, is subjected to a more elaborate and intense degree of socialization than is the call girl. This means that deviance and the deviant career can exhibit a variety of patterns, each with its own recruiting offices, entry routes, career lines, socialization mechanisms, and career shifts. Deviant pursuits can also exhibit (in accord with Best and Luckenbill's concern over the social organization of deviance), a range of mutually beneficial relationships; this is especially evident in the next two selections.

Patricia Yancey Martin and Robert A. Hummer, in "Fraternities and Rape on Campus," note that fraternities are rarely examined in terms of their underlying structure, values, and group processes. The authors focus specifically on those organizational contexts and associated practices that create an abusive social context for women. The researchers, in their examination of rapes in college fraternities, draw on data obtained from a range of newspaper accounts, judges, attorneys, and fraternity members. They initially find that fraternities are vitally concerned with promoting the image of *masculinity*. The researchers observe that fraternities work hard to create a macho image and context, and, accordingly, they avoid any suggestions or indicators of "wimpishness," homosexuality, and femininity. Not only are such values as winning, athleticism, willingness to drink, and sexual prowess stressed, but prospective members who do not measure up to such standards are rejected. Alcohol and activities associated with its use form the cornerstones of the fraternity's social life. Martin and Hummer then move to an analysis of the status and norms associated with pledgeship. Of significance is their description of how the new recruit, who is given a trial membership, is actually socialized by other brothers, most notably by his "Big Brother." It is during this process that the prevailing norms and values are inculcated in the pledge. The pledging experience itself can involve physical abuse, harsh discipline, demands to obey and follow orders, and demeaning activities and rituals. Such emphasis on toughness and obedience to superiors creates a brother who is non-caring and insensitive. Once the status of brother is actually occupied, it is expected that the occupant abide by the practices of brotherhood. At this point, the researchers describe the practices that are especially conducive to the sexual exploitation and coercion of women. For example, the use of alcohol to obtain sex is pervasive. It is often used as a weapon to counter sexual resistance or reluctance. The researchers present materials illustrating how this works, both individually and collectively. Martin and Hummer conclude by describing how women are treated as commodities (i.e., how "fraternities knowingly, and intentionally, *use* women for their benefit"). In this respect, they are used as bait to attract new members, as servers of the members' needs, and as sexual prey. Here, Martin and Hummer describe how the group known as "Little Sisters," because of its virtual lack of affiliation with any other groups (e.g., sororities) and its lack of peer group support, is particularly susceptible to forced sexual encounters with the brothers. Access to such women for sexual gratification is not only a presumed benefit of membership but, and at the individual and collective levels, the brothers develop and execute strategies aimed at achieving sexual gratification. Getting a woman drunk, or inviting women to fraternity parties, getting them drunk, and then forcing sex on them, are but two of the strategies frequently employed. If such organizational contexts and associated practices remain intact, we can expect to obtain outcomes similar to those noted in this research. Clearly, such observations emphasize the need for the complete elimination or radical restructuring of those institutions which, by way of a particularly demeaning ideology, place selected categories of actors in especially vulnerable or susceptible positions. Part 6 of this book examines how those perceived as powerless by organizations can be empowered to effect change in an agency's underlying organizational structure, theory of the office, diagnostic stereotypes, working ideology, and staff-socializing practices. Part 6 also calls for increased monitoring of the activities and routines of bureaucrats and others.

Andrew Szasz, in "Corporations, Organized Crime, and The Disposal of Hazardous Waste: An Examination of the Making of a Criminogenic Regulatory Structure," offers another interesting account of the types of relationships that can exist among legitimate and illegitimate enterprises or entrepreneurs. He focuses on the disposal of toxic waste, particularly the way in which organized crime became involved in its disposal. Szasz argues that corporate generators of hazardous waste products helped to create a regulatory structure that was accessible and attractive to organized crime. Szasz begins by describing how attempts were made to regulate the disposal of hazardous waste—efforts that resulted in the creation of the federal Resource Conservation and Recovery Act (RCRA). RCRA established procedures for the safe disposal of hazardous substances and authorized states to register the corporate generators of the waste. RCRA also mandated the licensing of hauling and disposal firms. Given organized crime's traditionally heavy involvement in garbage hauling and landfilling, extension of their influence to the illegal disposal of hazardous wastes was relatively straightforward. For example, when RCRA mandated the licensing of firms, mob-connected haulers acquired state permits and called themselves hazardous waste haulers. Organized crime also controlled some final disposal sites; hence, it was easy to have the manifest signed and then state that the waste had been disposed of properly. Other organized crime figures seized control of phony disposal sites and treatment facilities. Szasz continues by describing those political and social-structural factors that enabled organized crime to "'colonize' the hazardous waste disposal industry." Specifically, lax implementation and incompetent enforcement of the provisions of RCRA allowed organized crime to gain a strong foothold in the hazardous waste business. Interim licenses were granted and the manifest system was monitored loosely. Szasz also points to the role of generators of waste. For example, corporate generators lobbied for narrow definitions of hazardous waste as well as less stringent rules for disposal.

MANAGING DEVIANT CAREERS AND IDENTITIES

Involvement in activities, careers, and professions that are commonly viewed as deviant by others is not without its personal and social costs. If, for example, deviance becomes known, the actor may become stigmatized and subsequently discredited. Thus, those who engage in potentially discrediting behavior must manage their "front" in such a way as to avoid detection by socially significant "straights." The articles in this section focus directly on the social actor, particularly on the management strategies that may be invoked to protect a person's identity and self-image from erosion, damage, or outright destruction.

In "Management of Deviant Identity among Competitive Women Bodybuilders," Robert W. Duff and Lawrence K. Hong explore how women who participate in what many would view as a semideviant or deviant occupation attempt to minimize, as well as to prevent, damage to their personal identity and self-image. The researchers' guiding assumption is that with relatively few exceptions (e.g., the acceptance of attractive women bodybuilders who appear in television commercials), women bodybuilders, as a group, are perceived unfavorably by society at large. They also contend that the "deviant character" of the sport seems to be fueled by persistent rumors of drug use among its participants. Duff and Hong examine contingencies such as these through use of survey data obtained from the responses of 205 women bodybuilders. These data exhibit some interesting patterns. Over one half of the women, for example, indicated that, even though they are "proud to be known as a bodybuilder," they are very much aware of the controversial nature of their sport. Many (i.e., over fifty percent) felt that the media, by portraying the bodybuilder in an inaccurate and negative manner, helped to perpetuate and feed the various stereotypes surrounding the profession. The researchers present additional evidence indicating how the participants attempt to deal with the negative image of female masculinity. Selected "neutralization techniques" seem most effective in this regard. For example, by claiming some benefit (e.g., the sport enables them to develop strong and healthy bodies) or "blasting" the detractors, the women can deflect any negative reactions that are cast their way and they can, in doing so, maintain a positive image of self. Duff and Hong conclude with a discussion of what they term "the unprecedented women"—women who not only reject the prevailing stereotypes but who also try to introduce a new set of conceptions (e.g., the notion that bodybuilders should "maximize muscular development").

In "Topless Dancers: Managing Stigma in a Deviant Occupation," William E. Thompson and Jackie L. Harred present another account of how actors attempt to protect their identity and self-image from various threats, attacks, and assaults. They note initially that not only does a person's occupation form a basic ingredient of his or her personal and public identity, but knowledge of one's occupation often gives one a sense of social acceptance and prestige. Disclosing to others, however, that one is engaged in a deviant occupation, profession, enterprise, or pursuit can prove embarrassing and potentially stigmatizing. Hence, the researchers focus on this basic question: How do social actors engaged in deviant occupations manage their involvement so as to reduce or neutralize any negative attitudes, behaviors, and reactions that may be levied at them and their chosen profession? The researchers draw on data obtained from over 40 topless dancers to provide some insight. Thompson and Harred begin by pointing out that all dancers feel stigmatized, at least by certain groups, because of the nature of their occupation; they then describe the various recruitment offices and entry routes (e.g., being intoxicated and issued a challenge to dance, being in need of a job, and responding to encouragement from a network of social friends) that are associated with the process of becoming a topless dancer. Assuming the status of topless dancer, the researchers note, is linked with conscious attempts to manage and overcome the perceived stigma of the occupation. They describe two basic techniques: (1) dividing the social world and (2) rationalization and neutralization. In terms of the former, dancers band together in small groups and share potentially discrediting information; this not only reduces the probability that the dancer will come to be revealed as a discredited person but it also helps to create a strong sense of group cohesion. Most, in terms of information control, do tell their close friends and boyfriends what they do for a living. They do not disclose this information to acquaintances, casual friends, or parents. Many attempt to pass as waitresses, entertainers, and the like. Although most of the dancers indicate that they divide their social world, they are aware of the potentially stigmatizing nature of their work, at least in the eyes of some. Still, most see nothing wrong with being a topless dancer. What the researchers observe, however, is that most dancers employ a range of techniques to legitimate their involvement in this world. For example, most feel that topless dancing is harmless and, hence, they do not understand why so many people are opposed to it. In fact, and as part of their working ideology or rationale, many dancers promote the image of themselves as entertainers, therapists (e.g., they are protecting society against sexual assaults and rapes), and educators (e.g., by exposing the body they are making men and women more comfortable with nudity). The authors conclude by raising several questions that deserve future research. For example, do male strippers experience the same level and type of stigma as female dancers? Or, given the double standards relating to sex and nudity, do male strippers experience less need to manage any potentially stigmatizing information about the nature of their occupation?

32 / The Social Organization of Deviants

JOEL BEST
DAVID F. LUCKENBILL

Ethnographic research on particular social scenes provides data for general, grounded theories (Glaser and Strauss, 1967). For the study of deviance, field studies have supplied the basis for the development of general theories of the social psychology of deviance (Goffman, 1963; Lofland, 1969; Matza, 1969). However, while several reports about specific forms of deviance focus on social organization (Einstader, 1969; McIntosh, 1971; Mileski and Black, 1972; Shover, 1977; Zimmerman and Wieder, 1977), there is no satisfactory general theory of the social organization of deviance.

Sociologists of varying perspectives have debated the nature of social organization among juvenile delinquents, professional criminals, organized criminals and white-collar criminals. Others have developed typologies of deviants that include social organizational features (Clinard and Quinney, 1973; Gibbons, 1965, 1977; Miller, 1978). However, these treatments of social organization suffer from several flaws. First, they are often too narrow, focusing on a single type of deviance, such as burglary or more broadly, crime. Second, they usually are content with describing the organizational forms of different types of deviance. They fail to locate such forms along a dimension of organization or examine the consequences of organizational differences for deviants and social control agents. Third, they typically confuse two different bases for analyzing social organization: a general theory must distinguish between the social organization of *deviants* (the patterns of relationships between deviant actors) and the social organization of *deviance* (the patterns of relationships between the various roles performed in deviant transactions).

In this paper, we present a framework for understanding the social organization of deviants.[1] By examining reports of field research, several forms of social organization are identified and located along a dimension of organizational sophistication. Then some propositions are developed regarding the consequences of organizational variation for deviants and social control agents. Finally, some implications for the study of social organization are considered.

FORMS OF DEVIANT ORGANIZATION

The social organization of deviants refers to the structure or patterns of relationships among deviant actors in the context of deviant pursuits. The social organization of deviants varies along a dimension of sophistication. Organizational sophistication involves the elements of complexity, coordination and purposiveness (cf. Cressey, 1972). Organizations vary in the complexity of their division of labor including the size of membership, degree of stratification, and degree of specialization of organizational roles. Organizations also vary in their coordination among roles including the degree to which rules, agreements, and codes regulating relationships are formalized and enforced. Finally, organizations vary in the purposiveness with which they specify, strive toward, and achieve their objectives. Forms of organization which display high levels of complexity, coordination, and purposiveness are more sophisticated than those forms with lower levels.

Research reports suggest that deviants organize in several identifiable ways along the dimension of sophistication. Beginning with the least sophisticated, we will discuss five forms: loners, colleagues, peers, mobs and formal organizations. These organizational forms can be defined in terms of four variables: (1) whether the deviants associate with one another; (2) whether they participate in deviance together; (3) whether their deviance requires an elaborate division of labor; and (4) whether their organization's activities extend over time and space (see Table 1). *Loners* do not associate with other deviants, participate in shared deviance, have a division of labor, or maintain their deviance over extended time and space. *Colleagues* differ from loners because they associate with fellow deviants. *Peers* not only associate with one another, but also participate in deviance together. In *mobs*, the shared participation requires an elaborate division of labor. Finally, *formal organizations* involve mutual association and participation, an elaborate division of labor, and deviant undertakings extended over time and space.

Table 1 / Characteristics of Different Forms of the Social Organization of Deviants

| | Type of Organization | | | | |
Variable	LONERS	COLLEAGUES	PEERS	MOBS	FORMAL ORGANIZATIONS
Mutual association	−	+	+	+	+
Mutual participation	−	−	+	+	+
Division of labor	−	−	−	+	+
Extended organization	−	−	−	−	+

The descriptions of these forms of organization must be qualified in two ways. First, the forms are presented as ideal types. There is variation among the types of deviants within each form, as well as between one form and another. The intent is to sketch out the typical features of each form, recognizing that particular types of deviants may not share all of the features of their form to the same degree. Organizational sophistication can be viewed as a continuum, with deviants located between, as well as on, the five points. Describing a number of forms along this continuum inevitably understates the complexities of social life. Second, the descriptions of these forms draw largely from field studies of deviance in the contemporary United States, and attempt to locate the deviants studied along the dimension of organizational sophistication. A particular type of deviant can be organized in various ways in different societies and at different times. The references to specific field studies are intended to place familiar pieces of research within this framework; they are not claims that particular types of deviants invariably organize in a given way.

Loners

Some deviants operate as individuals. These loners do not associate with other deviants for purposes of sociability, the performance of deviant activities, or the exchange of supplies and information. Rather, they must supply themselves with whatever knowledge, skill, equipment and ideology their deviance requires. Loners lack deviant associations, so they cannot receive such crucial forms of feedback as moral support or information about their performance, new opportunities, or changes in social control strategies. They often enter deviance as a defensive response to private troubles (Lofland, 1969). Because their entry does not require contact with other deviants, as long as they can socialize themselves, loners frequently come from segments of the population which are less likely to be involved in the more sophisticated forms of deviance; it is not uncommon for loners to be middle-aged, middle-class or female. Because their deviance often is defensive, and because they lack the support of other deviants, loners' careers typically are short-lived. Examples of loners include murderers (Luckenbill, 1977), rapists (Amir, 1971), embezzlers (Cressey, 1953), check forgers (Lemert, 1967:99–134; Klein and Montague, 1977), physician narcotic addicts (Winick, 1961), compulsive criminals (Cressey, 1962), heterosexual transvestites (Buckner, 1970), amateur shoplifters (Cameron, 1964), some gamblers (Lesieur,1977), and many computer criminals (Parker, 1976).[2]

Colleagues

Like loners, colleagues perform as individuals. Unlike loners, however, colleagues associate with others involved in the same kind of deviance. Colleagues thus form a simple group which provides important services for members. First, colleagues often socialize newcomers, providing training in deviant skills as well as an ideology which accounts for and justifies their deviance. Association also offers sociability among members with whom one's deviant identity need not be concealed: an actor can take down his or her guard without fear of discovery by agents of social control (Goffman, 1959, 1963). Also, association provides a source of information about ways to obtain deviant equipment, new techniques, new opportunities for engaging in deviance, and strategies for avoiding sanctioning. Colleagues learn and are held to a loose set of norms which direct conduct in both deviant and respectable activities. "Don't inform on a colleague" and "Never cut in on a colleague's score" exemplify such norms. The moral climate established by these expectations increases the stability of colleagues' social scene. At the same time, only some deviant activities and some people are suited for such a loose form of organization. A successful career as a colleague depends ultimately on the individual's performance when operating alone. As a result, newcomers often sample the scene and, when they encounter difficulties, drift away. Only the more successful colleagues maintain extended deviant careers. Some examples of colleagues include most prostitutes (Hirschi, 1962; Bryan, 1965, 1966), pimps (Milner and Milner, 1972), and pool hustlers (Polsky, 1967).

Peers

Like colleagues, peers associate with one another and benefit from services provided by their fellows. Peers are involved in the socialization of novices, considerable sociable interaction, and the maintenance of a loose, unwritten code of condut to be followed by individuals who wish to remain in the peer group. Unlike colleagues, peers participate in deviant acts together; they are involved in deviant transactions at the same time and in the same place. In some cases, such mutual participation is required by the nature of the deviant activity. This is exemplified in the performance of homosexual acts, or in the "task force raids" where a collection of young men engages in simple acts of violence such as gang fighting or rolling drunks (Cressey, 1972). In other cases, mutual participation is required because peers form a network for supplying one another with essential goods and services, as found in the distribution of illicit drugs. In either event, peers interact basically as equals; there is a minimal division of labor and specialized roles are uncommon. Although individuals pass through these social scenes, peer groups often are quite stable, perhaps because peer groups solve structural problems within society for their members. Two common varieties of deviant peers are young people who have not yet entered integrated adult work roles, and those who frequent a deviant marketplace and depend on their contacts with one another for the satisfaction of illicit needs. Examples of peers include hobos (Anderson,

1923), homosexuals (Humphreys, 1970; Mileski and Black, 1972; Warren, 1974), group-oriented gamblers (Lesieur, 1977), swingers (Bartell, 1971), gang delinquents (Shaw, 1930; Matza, 1964; Rosenberg and Silverstein, 1969), motorcycle outlaws (Thompson, 1966), skid row tramps (Wiseman, 1970; Rubington, 1978), and illicit drug users (Blumer, 1967; Carey, 1968; Feldman, 1968; Stoddart, 1974).

Mobs

Mobs are small groups of professional or career deviants organized to pursue specific, profitable goals.[3] Their deviance requires the coordinated actions of members performing specialized roles—a more sophisticated division of labor than that found among peers. Thus, work is divided among confidence artists (the inside man and the outside man), pickpockets (the tool and the stall), or card and dice hustlers (the mechanic and the shootup man; Maurer, 1962, 1964; Prus and Sharper, 1977). Ordinarily, at least one of the roles in the mob is highly skilled, requiring considerable practice and training to perfect. This training (normally via apprenticeship), the need for on-the-job coordination, and the common practice of traveling from city to city as a mob lead to intensive interaction between mobsters. Elaborate technical argots develop, as well as elaborate codes specifying mobsters' obligations to each other.

Mobs have complex links to outsiders. They are organized to accomplish profitable yet safe crimes. McIntosh (1971) describes the historical shift from craft thieving, where mobs develop routine procedures for stealing relatively small sums from individuals, to project thieving, where larger amounts are taken from corporate targets using procedures specifically tailored to the particular crime. In either case, mob operations are planned and staged with an eye toward avoiding arrest. Also, mobs may attempt to neutralize the criminal justice system by bribing social control agents not to make arrests, "fixing" those cases where arrests take place, or making restitution to victims in return for dropped charges. Mobs also have ties to others who purchase stolen goods, provide legal services, and supply information and deviant equipment. Finally, a network of sociable and business contacts ties mobs to one another, enabling strategic information to spread quickly. These arrangements ensure that mobs can operate at a consistently profitable level with minimal interference. Consequently, the careers of individual mobsters, as well as those of specific mobs, seem to be more stable than those of deviants organized in less sophisticated ways.[4] Examples of mobs are the groups of professional criminals specializing in confidence games (Sutherland, 1937; Maurer, 1962), picking pockets (Maurer, 1964), shoplifting (Cameron, 1964), armed robbery (Einstader, 1969; Letkemann, 1973), burglary (Shover, 1977), and card and dice hustling (Prus and Sharper, 1977).

Formal Organizations

Formal organizations of deviants differ from mobs in the scope of their actions.[5] Normally they involve more people, but, more importantly, their actions are coordinated to efficiently handle deviant tasks on a routine basis over considerable time and space. While mobsters work as a group in a series of episodic attacks, formal organizations are characterized by delegated responsibility and by routine and steady levels of productivity. In many ways, formal organizations of deviants share the features which characterize such respectable bureaucracies as military organizations, churches, and business firms. They have a hierarchal division of labor, including both vertical and horizontal differentiation of positions and roles and established channels for vertical and horizontal communication. A deviant formal organization may contain departments for planning, processing goods, public relations and rule enforcement, with positions for strategists, coordinators, accountants, lawyers, enforcers, and dealers in illicit goods. There may be recruitment policies for filling these diversified positions, and entry into the organization may be marked by a ritual ceremony of passage. Formal organizations usually have binding, but normally unwritten, rules and codes for guiding members in organizational action, and these rules are actively enforced.

Formal organizations of deviants can make large profits by operating efficiently. At the same time, they must protect themselves from harm or destruction. As in less sophisticated forms of organization, loyal members are expected to maintain the group's secrets. In addition, deviant formal organizations attempt to locate power in the office, rather than in an individual charismatic leader. Although charismatic leadership obviously plays a part in some deviant formal organizations, the successful organization is able to continue operations when a leader dies or is arrested. Finally, deviant formal organizations typically invest considerable energy in neutralizing the criminal justice system by corrupting both high- and low-level officials. The scope and efficiency of their operations, their organizational flexibility, and their ties to agencies of social control make formal organizations of deviants extremely stable. Examples of such deviant formal organizations include very large urban street gangs (Keiser, 1969; Dawley, 1973), smuggling rings (Green, 1969), and organized crime "families" (Cressey, 1969; Ianni, 1972).

THE SIGNIFICANCE OF THE SOCIAL ORGANIZATION OF DEVIANTS

The identification and description of these different organizational forms permit a comparative analysis. What are the consequences of organizing as loners, colleagues, peers, mobs, or formal organizations? A comparison suggests that the sophistication of a form of deviant social organization has several consequences for both deviants and social control agents. Five propositions can be advanced.

I. *The more sophisticated the form of deviant organization, the greater its members' capability for complex deviant operations.* Deviant activities, like conventional activities, vary in their complexity. The complexity of a deviant operation refers to the number of elements required to carry it through; the more component parts to an activity, the more complex it is.[6] Compared to simple activities, complex lines of action demand more careful preparation and execution and take longer to complete. The complexity of a deviant activity depends upon two identifiable types of elements. First, there are the *resources* which the actors must be able to draw upon. Some activities require that the deviant utilize special knowledge, skill, equipment, or social status in order to complete the operation successfully, while simple acts can be carried out without such resources. Second, the *organization of the deviant transaction* affects an activity's complexity.[7] Some deviant acts can be accomplished with a single actor, while others require two or more people. The actors in a transaction can share a common role, as in a skid row bottle gang, or the transaction may demand different roles, such as offender and victim or buyer and seller. Furthermore, the degree to which these roles must be coordinated, ranging from the minimal coordination of juvenile vandals to the precision routines performed by mobs of pickpockets, varies among situations. The more people involved, the more roles they perform; and the more coordination between those roles, the more complex the deviant transaction's organization. The more resources and organization involved in a deviant operation, the more complex the operation is.

In general, deviants in more sophisticated forms of organization commit more complex acts.[8] The deviant acts of loners tend to be simple, requiring little in the way of resources or organization. Although colleagues work apart from one another, they generally share certain resources, such as shared areas. The hustlers' pool hall and the prostitutes' red light district contain the elements needed to carry out deviant operations, including victims and clients. Peers may interact in situations where they are the only ones present, performing complementary or comparable roles, as when two people engage in homosexual intercourse or a group of motorcycle outlaws makes a "run." Peers also may undertake activities which involve nonmembers, as when members of a delinquent gang rob a passerby. The activities carried out by mobs involve substantially more coordination among the members' roles. In an armed robbery, for instance, one member may be assigned to take the money, while a second provides "cover" and a third waits for the others in the car, ready to drive away on their return. Finally, the activities of formal organizations tend to be particularly complex, requiring substantial resources and elaborate organization. Major off-track betting operations, with staff members at local, district and regional offices who carry out a variety of clerical and supervisory tasks on a daily basis, represent an exceedingly complex form of deviance.

The relationship between the sophistication of organization and the complexity of deviant activities is not perfect. Loners can engage in acts of considerable complexity, for example. The computer criminal who single-handedly devises a complicated method of breaking into and stealing from computerized records, the embezzler who carries through an elaborate series of illicit financial manipulations, and the physician who juggles drug records in order to maintain his or her addiction to narcotics are engaged in complex offenses requiring substantial resources. However, these offenses cannot be committed by everyone. These loners draw upon resources which they command through their conventional positions, turning them to deviant uses. The computer criminal typically is an experienced programmer, the embezzler must occupy a position of financial trust, and the physician has been trained in the use of drugs. Possessing these resources makes the loner's deviance possible. Thus, the more concentrated the resources necessary for a deviant operation, the less sophisticated the form of organization required. However, when resources are not concentrated, then more sophisticated forms of organization are necessary to undertake more complex deviant operations.

Sophisticated forms of deviant organization have advantages beyond being able to undertake complex operations by pooling resources distributed among their members. Some deviant activities require a minimal level of organization; for example, homosexual intercourse demands the participation of two parties. In many other cases, it may be possible to carry out a deviant line of action using a relatively unsophisticated form of organization, but the task is considerably easier if a sophisticated form of organization can be employed. This is so because more sophisticated forms of deviant organization enjoy several advantages: they are capable of conducting a larger number of deviant operations; the operations can occur with greater frequency and over a broader range of territory; and, as discussed below, the members are better protected from the actions of social control agents. Of course, sophisticated organizations may engage in relatively simple forms of deviance, but the deviant act is often only one component in a larger organizational context. Taking a particular bet in the policy racket is a simple act, but the racket itself, handling thousands of bets, is complex indeed. Similarly, a murder which terminates a barroom dispute between two casual acquaintances is very different from an execution which is ordered and carried out by members of a formal organization, even though the two acts may appear equally simple. In the latter case, the killing may be intended as a means of maintaining discipline by demonstrating the organization's ability to levy sanctions against wayward members.

II. *The more sophisticated the form of deviant organization, the more elaborate the socialization of its members.* Neophyte deviants need to acquire two types of knowledge: (1) they must learn how to perform deviant acts, and how to gain appropriate *skills and techniques*; (2) they must develop a *cognitive perspective*, a distinctive way of making sense of their new, deviant world (cf. Shibutani, 1961:118–127). Such a perspective includes an ideology which accounts for the deviance, the individual's participation in deviance, and the organizational form, as well as a distinctive language for speaking about these and other matters.

As forms of deviant organization increase in sophistication, socialization becomes more elaborate. Loners do not depend upon other deviants for instruction in deviant skills or for a special cognitive perspective; they learn through their participation in conventional social scenes. Murderers, for instance, learn from their involvement in conventional life how to respond in situations of interpersonal conflict, and they employ culturally widespread justifications for killing people (Bohannon, 1960; Wolfgang and Ferracuti, 1967). Embezzlers learn the technique for converting a financial trust in the course of respectable vocational training, adapting justifications such as "borrowing" from conventional business ideology (Cressey, 1953). In contrast, colleagues teach one another a great deal. Although pool hustlers usually know how to shoot pool before they enter hustling, their colleagues provide a rich cognitive perspective, including a sense of "we-ness," some norms of behavior, a system for stratifying the hustling world, and an extensive argot (Polsky, 1967).[9] Peers receive similar training or, in some cases, teach one another through a process of emerging norms (Turner, 1964). Juvenile vandals, for example, can devise new offenses through their mutually constructed interpretation of what is appropriate to a particular situation (Wade, 1967). Sometimes, the knowledge peers acquire has largely symbolic functions that affirm the group's solidarity, as when a club of motorcycle outlaws devises a written constitution governing its members (Reynolds, 1967:134–136). In mobs and formal organizations, the cognitive perspective focuses on more practical matters; their codes of conduct specify the responsibilities members have in their dealings with one another, social control agents and others. Greater emphasis is also placed on the acquisition of specialized skills, with an experienced deviant coaching an apprentice, frequently over an extended period of time.

Two circumstances affect the socialization process in different forms of deviant organization. First, the sophistication of the organization affects the scope and style of the training process. The amount of training tends to increase with the sophistication of the organization. The skills required to perform deviant roles vary, but there is a tendency for more sophisticated forms of organization to incorporate highly skilled roles. Further, the more sophisticated forms of organization often embody cognitive perspectives of such breadth that the deviant must acquire a large body of specialized knowledge. In addition, the socialization process tends to be organized differently in different forms of deviant organization. While loners serve as their own agents of socialization, and colleagues and peers may socialize one another, mobs and formal organizations almost always teach newcomers through apprenticeship to an experienced deviant. Second, the socialization process is affected by the newcomer's motivation for entering deviance. Loners, of course, choose deviance on their own. In the more sophisticated forms, newcomers may ask for admission, but they often are recruited by experienced deviants. While peers may recruit widely, as when a delinquent gang tries to enlist all of the neighborhood boys of a given age, mobs and formal organizations recruit selectively, judging the character and commitment of prospective members and sometimes demanding evidence of skill or prior experience. For loners, entry into deviance frequently is a defensive act, intended to ward off some immediate threat. Peers, on the other hand, often are using deviance to experience stimulation; their deviance has an adventurous quality (Lofland, 1969). In contrast, mobs and formal organizations adopt a more professional approach: deviance is instrumental, a calculated means of acquiring economic profits.[10] These differences in the scope of socialization, the way the process is organized, and the neophyte's motivation account for the relationship between sophistication of organization and the elaborateness of the socialization.

III. *The more sophisticated the form of deviant organization, the more elaborate the services provided its members.* Every social role poses practical problems for its performers. In some cases these problems can be solved by providing the actors with supplies of various sorts. Actors may require certain *equipment* to perform a role. They may also need *information* about their situation in order to coordinate their behavior with the ongoing action and successfully accomplish their part in an operation. One function of deviant social organization is to solve such practical problems by supplying members with needed equipment and information. More sophisticated forms of social organization are capable of providing more of these services.

Deviants differ in their requirements for equipment. Some need little in the way of equipment; a mugger may be able to get by with a piece of pipe. In other cases, deviants make use of specialized items which have few, if any, respectable uses (e.g., heroin or the booster boxes used in shoplifting).[11] Most loners require little equipment. When specialized needs exist, they are met through conventional channels accessible to the deviants, as when a physician narcotic addict obtains illicit drugs from hospital or clinic supplies. Colleagues also supply their own equipment, for the most part, although they may receive some assistance; pool hustlers, for example, provide their own cues, but they may rely on financial backers for funding. Peers adopt various patterns toward equipment. In some cases, peer groups develop to facilitate the distribution and consumption of deviant goods, such as illicit drugs. In other instances, peers use equipment as a symbol of their deviant status, as when gang members wear special costumes. The equipment used by mobsters is more utilitarian; many of their trades demand specialized tools, for safecracking, shoplifting and so forth. In addition to a craftsman's personal equipment, the mob may require special materials for a specific project. Norms often exist that specify the manner in which these equipment purchases will be financed. In still other instances, some mobsters with expensive pieces of equipment may cooperate with several different mobs who wish to make use of them (such as the "big store" which is centrally located for the use of several confidence mobs). Formal organizations also have extensive equipment requirements. Because their operations extend over considerable time, formal organizations may find it expedient to invest in an elaborate array of fixed equipment. Off-track bookmaking, for example, may involve the purchase or rental of offices, desks, calculators, computer lines, special telephone lines, office supplies and automobiles. Special staff members may have the responsibility for maintaining this equipment (Bell, 1962:134). In addition, some formal organizations are involved in producing or distributing deviant equipment for the consumption of other deviants; drug smuggling offers the best example.

Deviants need information in order to determine their courses of action. To operate efficiently, they need to know about new opportunities for deviant action; to operate safely, they need to know about the movements of social control agents. The more sophisticated forms of organization have definite advantages in acquiring and processing information. Loners, of course, depend upon themselves for information; opportunities or threats outside their notice cannot be taken into account. Colleagues and peers can learn more by virtue of their contacts with the deviant "grapevine," and they may have norms regarding a member's responsibility to share relevant information. In mobs, information is sought in more systematic ways. In the course of their careers, mobsters develop perceptual skills, enabling them to "case" possible targets (Letkemann, 1973). In addition, some mobs rely on outsiders for information; spotters may be paid a commission for pointing out opportunities for theft. A formal organization can rely upon its widely distributed membership for information and its contacts with corrupted social control agents.

The degree to which deviants need special supplies varies with the requirements of their operations, the frequency with which they interact with victims or other nondeviants, and their visibility to social control agents. Supplies other than equipment and information may be required in some instances. However, for most supply problems, sophisticated forms of social organization enjoy a comparative advantage.

IV. *The more sophisticated the form of deviant organization, the greater its members' involvement in deviance.* Complex deviant operations require planning and coordinated action during the deviant act. Socialization and supply also involve interaction among an organization's members. More sophisticated forms of deviant organization, featuring complex operations and elaborate socialization and supply, are therefore more likely to involve intensive social contact with one's fellow deviants. Furthermore, because deviants face sanctions from social control agents and respectable people, their contacts with other deviants are an important source of social support. The differences in the ability of forms and social organization to provide support for their members have important social psychological consequences for deviants' careers and identities.

The dimensions of deviant careers vary from the form of deviant organization. Longer deviant careers tend to occur in more sophisticated forms of organization. For naive loners, deviance can comprise a single episode, a defensive act to ward off an immediate threat. For systematic loners, and many colleagues and peers, involvement in deviance is limited to one period in their life. Prostitutes grow too old to compete in the sexual marketplace, delinquents move into respectable adult work roles, and so forth. Members of mobs and formal organizations are more likely to have extended careers. Where the roles are not too physically demanding, deviance can continue until the individual is ready to retire from the work force (Inciardi, 1977). Deviant careers also vary in the amount of time they demand while the individual is active; some kinds of deviance take up only a small portion of the person's hours, but other deviant roles are equivalent to full-time, conventional jobs. Although the relationship is not perfect, part-time deviance is associated with less sophisticated forms of deviant organization.[12]

Social organization is also related to the relative prominence of the deviant identity in the individual's self-concept. Individuals may view their deviance as tangential to the major themes in their lives, or as a central focus, an identity around which much of one's life is arranged. The latter pattern is more likely to develop in sophisticated forms of deviant organization, for, as Lofland (1969) points out, several factors associated with deviant social organization facilitate the assumption of deviant identity, including frequenting places populated by deviants, obtaining deviant equipment, and receiving instruction in deviant skills and ideology. These factors also would appear to be associated with the maintenance of deviance as a central identity. Loners seem especially adept at isolating their deviance, viewing it as an exception to the generally conventional pattern their lives take. This is particularly true when the deviance was initially undertaken to defend that conventional life style from some threat. Even when an individual is relatively committed to deviance, normal identities can serve as an important resource. In his discussion of the World War II underground, Aubert (1965) notes that normal identities served to protect its members. In the same way, an established normal status shields the deviant from the suspicion of social control agents and, if the members refrain from revealing their conventional identities to one another, against discovery brought about by deviant associates who invade their respectable lives. Such considerations seem to be most important in middle-class peer groups organized around occasional leisure-time participation in a deviant marketplace, such as homosexuality and swinging.[13] Other deviants, particularly members of mobs and formal organizations, may associate with their fellows away from deviant operations, so that both their work and their sociable interaction take place among deviants. This is also true for peer groups that expand into "communities" and offer a wide range of services to members. Active members of urban gay communities can largely restrict their contacts to other homosexuals (Harry and Devall, 1978; Wolf, 1979). In these cases there is little need to perform conventional roles, aside from their obvious uses as concealment, and the deviant identity is likely to be central for the individual.

The degree to which an individual finds a deviant career and a deviant identity satisfying depends, in part, on the form of deviant organization of which he or she is a part. As in any activity, persons continue to engage in deviance only as long as the rewards it offers are greater than the rewards which could be obtained through alternative activities. The relevant rewards vary from one person to the next and from one type of deviance to another; a partial list includes money, physical and emotional satisfaction, valued social contacts, and prestige. Because the relative importance of these rewards varies with the individual, it is impossible to measure the differences in rewards between forms of deviant organization. There is some evidence that monetary profits are generally higher in more sophisticated forms of deviant organization. While an occasional loner can steal a very large sum through an embezzlement or a computer crime, most mobs can earn a reasonably steady income, and rackets run by formal organizations consistently bring in high profits. A more revealing measure of satisfaction is career stability; members of more sophisticated forms of deviant organization are more likely to remain in deviance. Loners' careers are short-lived, even when they are involved in systematic deviance. Lemert's (1967) account of the failure of professional forgers to remain at large suggests that the lack of social support is critical. As noted above, persons frequently drift out of their roles as colleagues and peers when other options become more attractive. The long-term careers of members of mobs and formal organizations suggest that these forms are more likely to satisfy the deviant.[14]

V. *The more sophisticated the form of deviant organization, the more secure its members' deviant operations.* The social organization of deviants affects the interaction between deviants and social control agents. This relationship is complicated because increased sophistication has consequences which would seem to make social control effects both easier and more difficult. On the one hand, the more sophisticated the deviant organization, the greater its public visibility and its chances of being subject to social control actions. Because more sophisticated forms of organization have more complex deviant operations, there are more people involved with the organization as members, victims, customers and bystanders. Therefore, there are more people capable of supplying the authorities with information about the identities, operations, and locations of organizational members. On the other hand, more sophisticated forms of organization are more likely to have codes of conduct requiring their members to be loyal to the organization and to maintain its secrets. Further, more sophisticated forms of organization command resources which can be used to protect the organization and its members from social control agents. While highly sophisticated organizations find it more difficult to conceal the fact that deviance is taking place, they often are more successful at shielding their members from severe sanctions.

Notes

1. A second paper, in preparation, will discuss the social organization of deviance.

2. Following Lemert (1967), loners can be subdivided into naive loners, for whom deviance is an exceptional, one-time experience, and systematic loners, whose deviance forms a repeated pattern. Lemert's analysis of the problems confronting systematic check forgers, who have trouble maintaining a deviant identity with little social support, suggests that systematic loners may have particularly instable careers.

3. The term "mob," as it is used here, is drawn from the glossary in Sutherland: "A group of thieves who work together; same as 'troupe' and 'outfit'" (1937:239; cf. Maurer, 1962, 1964). A more recent study uses the term "crew" (Prus and Sharper, 1977).

4. Although the mob is able to accomplish its ends more efficiently, the same tasks are sometimes handled by loners. For example, see Maurer (1964:166–168) and Prus and Sharper (1977:22).

5. Our use of the term "formal organization" is not meant to imply that these organizations have all of the characteristics of an established bureaucracy. Rather, "formal" points to the deliberately designed structure of the organization—a usage consistent with Blau and Scott (1962:5).

6. The complexity of a deviant activity must be distinguished from two other types of complexity. First, the definition of organizational sophistication, given above, included the complexity of the division of labor among the deviants in a given organizational form as one criterion of sophistication. Second, the complexity of an activity should not be confused with the complexity of its explanation. A suicide, for example, can be easily accomplished, even though a complex social-psychological analysis may be required to explain the act.

7. This point illustrates the distinction, made earlier, between the social organization of deviance (the pattern of relationships between the roles performed in a deviant transaction) and the social organization of deviants (the pattern of relationships between deviant actors). The former, not the latter, affects an activity's complexity.

8. In most cases, loners do not possess the resources required for more than one type of complex deviance; physicians, for instance, are unable to commit computer thefts. In contrast, members of more sophisticated forms of organization may be able to manage several types of operations, as when a mob's members shift from picking pockets to shoplifting in order to avoid the police, or when an organized crime family is involved in several different rackets simultaneously (Maurer, 1964; Ianni, 1972:87–106).

9. Within a given form of organization, some cognitive perspectives may be more elaborate than others. While pool hustlers have a strong oral tradition, founded on the many hours they share together in pool halls, prostitutes have a relatively limited argot. Maurer (1939) argues that this is due to the restricted contact they have with one another during their work.

10. Here and elsewhere, colleagues represent a partial exception to the pattern. Colleagues resemble members of mobs and formal organizations in that they adopt an instrumental perspective, view deviance as a career, are socialized through apprenticeship to an experienced deviant, and accept deviance as a central identity. While peers have a more sophisticated form of organization, their mutual participation in deviance is based on their shared involvement in an illicit marketplace or leisure-time activity. In contrast, colleagues usually are committed to deviance as means of earning a living.

Yet, because colleagues share a relatively unsophisticated form of organization, they labor under restrictions greater than those faced by mobs and formal organizations. Socialization is of limited scope; call girls learn about handling money and difficult clients, but little about sexual skills (Bryan, 1965). The code of conduct governing colleagues is less encompassing and less binding than those for more sophisticated forms, and the deviance of colleagues is usually less profitable. The absence of the advantages associated with organizational sophistication leads colleagues, despite their similarities to mobs and formal organizations, into an unstable situation where many individuals drift away from deviance.

11. Sometimes such equipment is defined as illicit, and its possession constitutes a crime.

12. Two reasons can be offered to explain this relationship. If a type of deviance is not profitable enough to support the individual, it may be necessary to take other work, as when a

pool hustler moonlights (Polsky, 1967). Also, many loners have only a marginal commitment to deviance and choose to allocate most of their time to their respectable roles. This is particularly easy if the form of deviance requires little time for preparation and commission.

13. Swingers meeting new couples avoid giving names or information which could be used to identify them (Bartell, 1971:92–95); and Humphreys (1970) emphasizes that many tearoom participants are attracted by the setting's assurance of anonymity.

14. During their careers, deviants may shift from one organizational form or one type of offense to another. The habitual felons interviewed by Petersilia et al. (1978) reported that, while many of their offenses as juveniles involved more than one partner (presumably members of a peer group), they preferred to work alone or with a single partner on the crimes they committed as adults. The most common pattern was for juveniles who specialized in burglaries to turn to robbery when they became adults.

References

Amir, Menachem
    1971 Patterns in Forcible Rape. Chicago: University of Chicago Press.
Anderson, Nels
    1923 The Hobo. Chicago: University of Chicago Press.
Aubert, Vilhelm
    1965 The Hidden Society. Totowa, N.J.: Bedminster.
Bartell, Gilbert
    1971 Group Sex. New York: New American.
Bell, Daniel
    1962 The End of Ideology. Revised edition. New York: Collier.
Blau, Peter M. and W. Richard Scott
    1962 Formal Organizations. San Francisco: Chandler.
Blumer, Herbert
    1967 The World of Youthful Drug Use. Berkeley: University of California Press.
Bohannon, Paul
    1960 African Homicide and Suicide. Princeton: Princeton University Press.
Bryan, James H.
    1965 "Apprenticeships in prostitution." Social Problems 12:287–297.
    1966 "Occupational ideologies and individual attitudes of call girls." Social Problems 13:441–450.
Buckner, H. Taylor
    1970 "The transvestic career path." Psychiatry 33:381–389.
Cameron, Mary Owen
    1964 The Booster and the Snitch. New York: Free Press.
Carey, James T.
    1968 The College Drug Scene. Englewood Cliffs, N.J.: Prentice Hall.
Clinard, Marshall B. and Richard Quinney
    1973 Criminal Behavior Systems: A Typology. Second edition. New York: Holt, Rinehart and Winston.
Cressey, Donald R.
    1953 Other People's Money. New York: Free Press.
    1962 "Role theory, differential association, and compulsive crimes." Pp. 443–467 in Arnold M. Rose (ed.), Human Behavior and Social Processes. Boston: Houghton Mifflin.
    1969 Theft of the Nation. New York: Harper & Row.
    1972 Criminal Organization. New York: Harper & Row.

Dawley, David
1973 A Nation of Lords. Garden City, N.Y.: Anchor.
Einstader, Werner J.
1969 "The social organization of armed robbery." Social Problems 17:64–83.
Feldman, Harvey W.
1968 "Ideological supports to becoming and remaining a heroin addict." Journal of Health and Social Behavior 9:131–139.
Gibbons, Don C.
1965 Changing the Lawbreaker. Englewood Cliffs, N.J.: Prentice-Hall.
1977 Society, Crime, and Criminal Careers. Third edition. Englewood Cliffs, N.J.: Prentice-Hall.
Glaser, Barney G. and Anselm L. Strauss
1967 The Discovery of Grounded Theory. Chicago: Aldine.
Goffman, Erving
1959 The Presentation of Self in Everyday Life. Garden City, N.Y.: Anchor.
1963 Stigma. Englewood Cliffs, N.J.: Prentice-Hall.
Green, Timothy
1969 The Smugglers. New York: Walker.
Harry, Joseph and William B. Devall
1978 The Social Organization of Gay Males. New York: Praeger.
Hirschi, Travis
1962 "The professional prostitute." Berkeley Journal of Sociology 7:33–49.
Humphreys, Laud
1970 Tearoom Trade. Chicago: Aldine.
Ianni, Francis A. J.
1972 A Family Business. New York: Sage.
Inciardi, James A.
1977 "In search of the class cannon." Pp. 55–77 in Robert S. Weppner (ed.), Street Ethnography. Beverly Hills, Calif.: Sage.
Keiser, R. Lincoln
1969 The Vice Lords. New York: Holt, Rinehart and Winston
Klein, John F. and Arthur Montague
1977 Check Forgers. Lexington, Mass.: Lexington.
Lemert, Edwin M.
1967 Human Deviance, Social Problems, and Social Control. Englewood Cliffs, N.J.: Prentice-Hall.
Lesieur, Henry R.
1977 The Chase. Garden City, N.Y.: Anchor.
Letkemann, Peter
1973 Crime as Work. Englewood Cliffs, N.J.: Prentice-Hall.
Lofland, John
1969 Deviance and Identity. Englewood Cliffs, N.J.: Prentice-Hall.
Luckenbill, David F.
1977 "Criminal homicide as a situated transaction." Social Problems 25:176–186.
Matza, David
1964 Delinquency and Drift. New York: Wiley.
1969 Becoming Deviant. Englewood Cliffs, N.J.: Prentice-Hall.
Maurer, David W.
1939 "Prostitutes and criminal argots." American Journal of Sociology 44:346–350.

1962 The Big Con. New York: New American.

1964 Whiz Mob. New Haven, Conn.: College and University Press.

McIntosh, Mary

1971 "Changes in the organization of thieving." Pp. 98–133 in Stanley Cohen (ed.), Images of Deviance. Baltimore, Maryland: Penguin.

Mileski, Maureen and Donald J. Black

1972 "The social organization of homosexuality." Urban Life and Culture 1:131–166.

Miller, Gale

1978 Odd Jobs: The World of Deviant Work. Englewood Cliffs, N.J.: Prentice-Hall.

Milner, Christina and Richard Milner

1972 Black Players. Boston: Little, Brown.

Parker, Donn B.

1976 Crime by Computer. New York: Scribner's.

Petersilia, Joan, Peter W. Greenwood and Marvin Lavin

1978 Criminal Careers of Habitual Felons. Santa Monica, Calif.: Rand.

Polsky, Ned

1967 Hustlers, Beats, and Others. Chicago: Aldine.

Prus, Robert C. and C. R. D. Sharper

1977 Road Hustler. Lexington, Mass.: Lexington.

Reynolds, Frank

1967 Freewheelin' Frank. New York: Grove.

Rosenberg, Bernard and Harry Silverstein

1969 Varieties of Delinquent Experience. Waltham, Mass.: Blaisdell.

Rubington, Earl

1978 "Variations in bottle-gang controls." Pp. 383–391 in Earl Rubington and Martin S. Weinberg (eds.), Deviance: The Interactionist Perspective. Third edition. New York: Macmillan.

Shaw, Clifford R.

1930 The Jack-Roller. Chicago: University of Chicago Press.

Shibutani, Tamotsu

1961 Society and Personality. Englewood Cliffs, N.J.: Prentice-Hall.

Shover, Neal

1977 "The social organization of burglary." Social Problems 20:499–514.

Stoddart, Kenneth

1974 "The facts of life about dope." Urban Life and Culture 3:179–204.

Sutherland, Edwin H.

1937 The Professional Thief. Chicago: University of Chicago Press.

Thompson, Hunter S.

1966 Hell's Angels. New York: Ballantine.

Turner, Ralph H.

1964 "Collective behavior." Pp. 382–425 in Robert E. L. Faris (ed.), Handbook of Modern Sociology. Chicago: Rand McNally.

Wade, Andrew L.

1967 "Social processes in the act of juvenile vandalism." Pp. 94–109 in Marshall B. Clinard and Richard Quinney (eds.), Criminal Behavior Systems: A Typology. New York: Holt, Rinehart and Winston.

Warren, Carol A. B.

1974 Identity and Community in the Gay World. New York: Wiley.

Winick, Charles
    1961 "Physician narcotic addicts." Social Problems 9:174–186.
Wiseman, Jacqueline P.
    1970 Stations of the Lost. Englewood Cliffs, N.J.: Prentice-Hall.
Wolf, Deborah G.
    1979 The Lesbian Community. Berkeley: University of California Press.
Wolfgang, Marvin E. and Franco Ferracuti
    1967 The Subculture of Violence. London: Tavistock.
Zimmerman, Don H. and D. Lawrence Wieder
    1977 "You can't help but get stoned." Social Problems 25:198–207.

33 / The Voluntary Recruitment of "Deviants": The Examples of Homosexuality, Prostitution, and Alcoholism

DELOS H. KELLY

... There are various ways in which one can gain exposure and subsequent entry into some type of grouping, collectivity, career line, or the like. Thus far, focus has been given to what I have termed the "involuntary route"—a career entry or initiation point that is characterized by relatively little individual choice. Quite clearly, students and involuntary mental patients, as well as the blacks and the "hoods" in the Piliavin-Briar research, are not, in any sense of the word, in control of their own destiny. Rather, once designated as "deviants," they became the bureaucratic pawns necessary for playing out "the matching game." There are, obviously, other situations and opportunities that afford the individual an eminently greater degree of choice. One may, for example, decide to investigate the possibility of becoming a "street walker" or house prostitute. Others may begin to push drugs, experiment with homosexuality, or become involved with some religious sect or cult. Still others may elect to move into a bookmaking operation, try their hand at shoplifting, or receive and sell stolen goods. The point that must be emphasized, however, is that people often have a say in whether or not they will become exposed to what may be defined as deviant or semi-deviant activities, occupations, and professions. In these situations, initial exposure and perhaps subsequent entry can be conceptualized as being of a voluntary nature. The choice, however, may not always be this simple or clear-cut. For example, in certain areas, a juvenile may experience pressures to join a gang, and he or she may resist. The possibility also exists that the youth may succumb to the recruitment efforts and become a gang member. Similarly, a young male or female may, as a matter of economic or personal survival, find it necessary to move into prostitution, homosexuality, drug pushing, and the like. In situations such as these, it becomes rather questionable as to whether or not the

473

actor has actually exercised any significant degree of choice. Thus, and even though it is useful to think primarily in terms of voluntary and involuntary exposure and entry routes, it must be recognized that the factors promoting eventual contact and involvement in deviant or semi-deviant activities and routines are often complex and interrelated. What this may mean for some individuals is that involvement is neither strictly voluntary or involuntary. Rather, it may be of a quasi-voluntary nature; this would appear to hold for our gang member. In terms of the choice dimension, then, we can think in terms of a continuum, one that ranges from real individual choice to a lack of choice. Thus far, the clearest examples of the latter (i.e., individuals lacking any significant choice or say) would be students and the involuntary mental patients.

In any event, and for a host of reasons, people will experience exposure to, as well as enter, various types of activities, routines, and groupings. And what must be recognized, once again, is that exposure carries with it the very real possibility that the actor will become inculcated with the existing ideology, values, norms, and traditions. Some of the better pieces of research relating to the issues of exposure and entry have been provided by Reiss (1961), Weinberg (1966), Bryan (1965), and Wallace (1965).

In terms of the Reiss research..., it can be added that boys who voluntarily established contacts with fellators were also delinquent in other respects. Learning how to make contact is, according to Reiss (1961:109), an institutionalized aspect of the delinquent group. What this means rather simply is that the novice, by virtue of membership, becomes inculcated with the existing traditions and culture—a portion of which includes instruction in how to actually establish contact with potential fellators. Critical to the success of this process is the role that the experienced gang members play. Not only do the regulars indoctrinate the novice, but they often accompany the uninitiated during his initial contacts. Doy L., one of Reiss' (1961:109) case studies, explains how he was initiated into the homosexual transaction:

> I went along with these older boys down to the bus station, and they took me along and showed me how it was done...they'd go in, get a queer, get blowed and get paid...if it didn't work right, they'd knock him in the head and get their money...they showed me how to do it, so I went in too.

Novices are also taught how to obtain money from fellators who refuse to pay, how much to charge, and what kind of behavior is acceptable. Reiss (1961:109) points out that males know most of the specifics *before* any contact is established. In effect, then, they become prepared both psychologically and socially for their first experience and the peers will become involved if the opportunity presents itself. Reiss (1961:110) provides a piece of case material illustrative of these dynamics:

> I was down in the Empress Theatre and this gay came over and felt me up and asked me if I'd go out...I said I would if he'd give me money as I'd heard they did, and I was gettin' low on it...so he took me down by the river and blowed me.

In terms of other exposure and entry routes, Reiss maintains that many boys become inducted into the peer-queer transaction by a brother. The comments of Jimmie M., another of Reiss' (1961:110) subjects, are typical of this pattern:

> Well, my younger brother came home and told me this gay'd blowed him and he told me where he lived.... And, I was scared to do it, but I figured I'd want to see what it was like since the other guys talked about it and my brother'd done it. So I went down there and he blowed me.

Not all lower-class males who are solicited will accept the initial solicitation. In fact, most will probably refuse. If, however, certain conditions are met, the probability of acceptance will increase rather markedly. Specifically, and according to Reiss (1961:110), the male must be a member of a group allowing this type of sexual encounter, the male must be inculcated with the appropriate codes or normative structure, and the group must sanction positively the male's participation in the peer-queer sexual transaction.

In his research on the pathways to becoming a nudist, Weinberg (1966:15) makes an initial observation to the effect that most people give relatively little thought to nudism; however, if they do, their conceptions of nudism and nudists are often laced with vague stereotypes. Weinberg (1966:15) offers the words of a practicing nudist:

> I never gave it too much thought. I thought it was a cult—a nut-eating, berry-chewing bunch of vegetarians, doing calisthenics all day, a gymno-physical society. I thought they were carrying health to an extreme, being egomaniacs about their body.

Others exhibited conceptions of the following nature:

> I'm afraid I had the prevailing notion that they were undignified, untidy places populated (a) by the very poor, and (b) by languishing bleached blonds, and (c) by greasy, leering bachelors. [Weinberg, 1966:15]

In terms of more systematic data, Weinberg (1966:15) reports that over one half of the nudist population studied exhibited positive attitudes prior to affiliation. A small percentage (i.e., 20 percent) exhibited negative prenudist attitudes.

These particular patterns lead Weinberg (1966:15) to ask the following question: "how does one become interested enough to make a first visit to a nudist camp?" Stated somewhat differently, what prompts the initial exposure to nudism? The data presented exhibit some rather striking differences by sex. Specifically, for males, the initial source of interest came from magazines, while for females it was the spouse. For both sexes, relationships with other people also played an important part. As an example of spousal pressure, Weinberg (1966:16) offers the comments of a man who did, in fact, persuade his spouse to become interested in nudism:

> I expected difficulty with my wife. I presented it to her in a wholesome manner. [Q] I had to convince her it was a wholesome thing, and that the people there were sincere.

...[Q] That they were sincere in efforts to sunbathe together and had only good purposes in mind when they did that. [Q] All the things that nudism stands for: A healthy body and a cleansed mind by killing sex curiosities.

Weinberg (1966:16) reports that, even though the respondents expressed a willingness to actually visit a nudist camp, most did not necessarily expect to become nudists. For many the trip was viewed as being nothing more than a joke or new experience, with the underlying motivation being one of curiosity. They were, for example, interested in seeing what kinds of people belonged, as well as "nude members of the opposite sex." Again, the motivations for the first visit varied by sex. In particular, 49 percent of the males did so because of curiosity (i.e., general curiosity, 33 percent; and sexual curiosity, 16 percent). The major motivating factor for females involved the attempt to satisfy a spouse or relative (i.e., 38 percent). A very small percentage (i.e., 2 percent) did so because of sexual curiosity. Another 13 percent reported that a combination of curiosity and spousal factors prompted their first visit to a nudist camp.

Predictably, and given a set of unknowns, many exhibited a degree of nervousness or anxiety upon their first visit; these feelings, however, soon dissipated and rapid adjustments were made to the camp. In terms of data, forty-six percent of Weinberg's (1966:17) subjects said their nervousness disappeared upon arrival, and another 31 percent reported feeling comfortable at the end of three hours. Fifteen percent of the respondents, however, did experience difficulty adjusting to the nudist way of life. Informal coaching by others (e.g., a husband) played a significant role in easing the adjustment problems. The following comments are typical of this process:

My husband said the men are gentlemen. He told me I'd have fun, like play in the sun, play games and swim.

*   *   *

She didn't want to undress.... [Q] I tried to talk to her and her husband did; she finally got convinced. [Q] I told her you feel better with them off, and that no one will pay any attention. [Weinberg, 1966:18]

Individuals who actually became nudists (i.e., in terms of their personal identity, conceived of self as such and adopted the nudist way of life) did so for a variety of reasons, and in most cases the motives for doing so differed from the motives that prompted the initial visit. The following responses illustrate the changing nature of one's motives:

[Q: *What was your main reason for wanting to attend camp the first time?*] Curiosity.
[Q] To see how people behave under such circumstances, and maybe also looking at the girls.
[Q] Just that it's interesting to see girls in the nude.
[Q: *What is the main reason you continue to attend?*] I found it very relaxing.
[Q] It's more comfortable to swim without a wet suit, and not wearing clothes when it's real warm is more comfortable and relaxing.

[I went up the first time] to satisfy my husband. He wanted me to go and I fought it. But he does a lot for me, so why not do him a favor. [She had told him that people went to nudist camps only for thrills and that she would divorce him before she would go. Although he talked her into it, she cried all the way to camp. Asked why she continued to attend, she looked surprised and replied:] Why, because I thoroughly enjoy it! [Weinberg, 1966:19]

Once exposed, the nudist, like the peer, may become indoctrinated with the existing normative system.

Another interesting account of exposure and entry routes is provided by Bryan. His research is focused on the type of call girl that obtains clients primarily by individual referrals. Thus, the prostitutes studied did not solicit clients through the use of the bars, streets, known houses of prostitution, or the like; they also initiated the contract in their residence or the client's. In terms of actual exposure and entrance into prostitution, Bryan (1965:289) notes that all girls but one experienced personal contact with someone already immersed in the call girl profession, usually another girl. The importance of this connection is most evident in the following interview:

I had been thinking about it [becoming a call girl] before a lot.... Thinking about wanting to do it, but I had no connections. Had I not had a connection, I probably wouldn't have started working.... I thought about starting out.... Once I tried it [without a contact].... I met this guy at a bar and I tried to make him pay me, but the thing is, you can't do it that way because they are romantically interested in you, and they don't think that it is on that kind of basis. You can't all of a sudden come up and want money for it, you have to be known beforehand.... I think that is what holds a lot of girls back who might work. I think I might have started a year sooner had I had a connection. You seem to make one contact or another...If it's another girl or a pimp or just someone who will set you up and get you a client.... You can't just say, get an apartment and get a phone in and everything and say, "Well, I'm gonna start business," because you gotta get clients from somewhere. There has to be a contact. [Bryan, 1965:289]

Almost one half of Bryan's (1965:289) sample of thirty-three prostitutes reported that their initial contact was with another "working girl." The nature of these contacts was, however, variable. Some had been friends prior to contact. Other novices had been sexually involved with a call girl. Most had not known each other very long and so the relationship was weak. In some cases, the aspirant actually sought out the contact. Regardless of the nature and source of contact, Bryan (1965:289) reports that whenever a professional call girl agrees to aid the novice, she also appears to assume the major responsibility for training her.

If the initial contact is with a pimp, the relationship, as well as the typical career sequence, often takes a different course. Usually, the connection between the pimp and the novice is, according to Bryan's (1965:289) data, typically that of lovers. In a few cases, however, the link is strictly business in nature.

Right now I am buying properties and as soon as I can afford it, I am buying stocks.... It is strictly a business deal. This man and I are friends, our relationship ends there. He handles all the money, he is making all the investments and I trust him. We have a legal document drawn up which states that half the investments are mine, half of them his, so I am protected. [Bryan, 1965:290]

Regardless of whether the relationship is one of love or business, the pimp not only solicits the girl, but he also plays a very important role in structuring her career. Bryan (1965:290) reports that once the girl agrees to become a call girl, the pimp, like his female counterpart, either elects to train the girl or else refers her to another call girl. Throughout the training period, the pimp continues to maintain his dominance.

After contact has been established and the girl decides to become a call girl, she moves into the next stage of her career: the apprenticeship period. Bryan (1965:290) notes that the apprenticeship is usually served under the supervision of another girl, although occasionally a pimp may conduct the training. In most cases the trainer's apartment becomes the classroom. The training itself often lasts an average of two or three months, and during this time, the trainer exerts virtually complete control over the novice's referrals and appointments.

Bryan (1965:291) maintains that the *content* of the training period consists of two rather broad but interrelated dimensions: the philosophical and the interpersonal. The former refers to the value system that the trainer attempts to inculcate within the novice, while the latter pertains to the "do's" and the "don'ts" of dealing with customers and other "working girls." As an example of the actual content of the value system taught, the ideology often promoted is to the effect that all men are corrupt and thus deserve exploitation, that all relationships are but part of a larger "con" game, and that the act of prostitution is probably more honest than the acts of the "johns" or "squares." The fact that a man will betray his wife is taken as evidence that man is basically corrupt. Values such as fairness to other girls or a pimp may also be taught. Bryan (1965:292) quotes a pimp:

So when you ask me if I teach a kind of basic philosophy, I would say that you could say that. Because you try to teach them in an amoral way that there is a right and wrong way as pertains to this game...and then you teach them that when working with other girls to try to treat the other girl fairly because a woman's worst enemy in the street [used in both a literal and figurative sense] is the other woman and only by treating the other women decently can she expect to get along.... Therefore the basic philosophy I guess would consist of a form of honesty, a form of sincerity and complete fidelity to her man [pimp].

As far as the interpersonal dimension is concerned, customers are to be seen as "marks" and "pitches" are to be made. Bryan (1965:292) offers the account of one call girl:

[Did you have a standard pitch?] It's sort of amusing. I used to listen to my girl friend [trainer]. She was the greatest at this telephone type of situation. She would call up and cry and say that people had come to her door.... She'd cry and she'd complain and she'd say "I have a bad check at the liquor store, and they sent the police over," and really... a girl has story she tells the man.... Anything, you know, so he'll help her out. Either it's the rent or she needs a car, or doctor's bills, or any number of things.

Girls are informed about certain customers, taught how to handle alcohol and drugs, as well as how to obtain fees and deal with customers. Occasionally, instruction in physical and sexual hygiene may be given. What is omitted should also be noted. In this respect Bryan (1965:293) reports that the novice receives very little training relative to sexual techniques, and what is taught revolves primarily around the act of fellation. Experiencing an orgasm does not appear to be encouraged.

Bryan (1965:294) goes on to note that, even though the occupational ideology is imparted to the novice, the main thrust of the apprenticeship appears to be centered around establishing and building a lucrative clientele. And the most frequent, as well as effective, method of accomplishing this seems to be through use of the contacts established while serving as an apprentice. During this time, the trainer not only refers customers to the girl, but he or she often monitors the apprentice's actual dealings with customers; this produces certain advantages for both parties. For the novice, a clientele is, in fact, built, while for the trainer, a fee, usually forty to fifty percent, is received for every referral that meets with success (i.e., a sexual contract is negotiated successfully). In a sense, then, both profit from the trainer-trainee relationship. Actually, according to Bryan (1965:295), early success with customers and the associated financial rewards can play an important part in a girl's decision to become a professional call girl. Implicit in this statement is the idea that some females, even though they may begin to participate in the call girl culture, may, ultimately, elect to leave. Put somewhat differently, exposure and participation do not guarantee that one will become a career or professional call girl. Nor should one assume, necessarily, that exposure to the peer-queer, nudist, or any other culture will produce regular membership. The road to career deviance or, for that matter, non-deviance is often a most difficult one to travel. Thus some will drop by the wayside, while others will continue the trek. The research by Wallace on the skid row culture is especially good in terms of sensitizing one to contingencies such as these.

Wallace (1965:163–164) offers some initial comments on the "routes to homelessness" and then proceeds to describe the actual entry routes that are used by the skid rowers:

The process of becoming a skid rower is not easy, rapid, or uniform. There are many pitfalls along the way, and the novice must be on the alert ere the Forces of Respectable Society swoop down and snatch up another hapless victim. It is a complex process whose description depends upon one's point of view. To the non-skid rower, the process appears to involve ever-increasing isolation from the larger society accompanied by ever-increasing deviance from its norms. From the point of view of the skid rower, on the other hand, the process is one of increasing participation in the life of the skid row community, and is accompanied by increasing conformity to its norms. In its totality, the process of becoming a skid rower combines both the push out of respectable society with the pull toward the society of skid row. To understand the final product of this process—the completely acculturated skid rower—the investigator must recognize these dual forces of rejection and attraction within the life history of the individual.

There are, according to Wallace (1965:164–165), three rather distinct phases involved in becoming a skid rower. Phase one involves a person's initial exposure to the culture. Wallace points out that since no one is actually born into this way of life, it is important to understand what he terms the skid row's "recruiting offices" (e.g., the characteristics of the skid rowers, their origins, and the pathways to exposure). Phase two occurs when the novice begins to exhibit regular participation in the skid row culture. Of concern here is why, given the negative community perceptions and sanctions he most certainly encounters, does the beginner continue to participate in the culture? The third and final stage occurs at the point of conformity to the skid row values. It is at this stage, too, that we can speak of the career skid rower. Not only has the recruit been socialized into the existing normative structure and associated values, but his personal view of self has undergone a corresponding change. In a sense, he comes to view self as a skid rower.

Wallace (1965:164–165) stresses the fact that exposure does not necessarily lead to participation, nor does participation necessarily lead to conformity to the skid row values. Some who are exposed will leave and some who participate will also leave. Thus, if one is to understand the process of becoming a career skid rower, one must be able to account for those who drop out, as well as for those who elect to continue.

According to Wallace (1965:165), three distinct categories of individuals have served as the primary recruits for the skid row life style. The majority, however, have been drawn from those occupations which are noted for separating "men from their fixed places in established society" (e.g., the migrant workers, lumberjacks, soldiers, seamen). The second source comes from the ranks of the welfare client (e.g., the displaced, homeless, jobless, hungry). Skid row *aficionados* provide the third source of recruits; these are the men (e.g., the wanderers, alcoholics, petty criminals, fringe members of society) whose life styles demand a degree of anonymity, as well as community tolerance and acceptance.

In terms of actual exposure and entry routes, the mobile or transient worker often becomes initially exposed through his job. It is in this setting that he meets fellow workers who are already immersed in the skid row culture. From various types of contacts with these individuals, the recruit becomes exposed to the skid row way of life, and he may begin to enter this world. Wallace (1965:166) comments on contingencies such as these:

> . . . In working, eating, talking, drinking, sleeping, and living with confirmed skid rowers on the job, the newcomer to the occupation is exposed to his first taste of skid row subculture. He learns of skid row attitudes toward the community, the

employer, the police, the welfare worker—and he learns of their attitudes toward him. To defend himself against the condemnation he experiences in dealing with the outside community, and to adjust to his companions on the job, he gradually begins to enter the world of the skid rower. He may take up the camaraderie of sharing, of heavy drinking, of casual womanizing, and other behavior patterns characteristic of the subculture. When the season's work is finished, or when his voyage is over, or when he simply quits his job, the newcomer may return home, or move directly onto skid row.

Upon his return home, the mobile or itinerant laborer often learns that his absence has created some problems. He knows, however, that if he does not like his living arrangements or conditions, he can leave. Wallace (1965:166–167) notes that the worker "is no longer necessarily or totally committed to the values of home and family any more than his family is totally committed to accepting him back in their midst." Of major significance at this stage is the fact that he is aware of an alternative way of life and, in effect, he becomes caught between two competing worlds (i.e., the conventional versus the skid row). It is at this stage, too, that family factors can be used to help explain a man's decision to move to skid row. In Wallace's (1965:167) words:

> It is at this point, and only at this point, that an unsatisfactory home situation becomes relevant in explaining a man's move to skid row. If before he left home he was at constant odds with his family, he may be less inclined than ever to "put up with it"—now that he knows another way of life complete with a few friends is open to him. Problems at home plus the weakening of family ties brought about by his absence reinforce his sense of isolation, push him further adrift, and help sever the few remaining roots he has in the world of respectable society. The skid row way of life—a life without care, worry, and responsibility, a life with friends, drink, and plenty of time in which to enjoy them—begins to look better and better.

Wallace (1965:167) maintains that the welfare client's route to skid row is often more direct. The client may be sent directly to skid row and, thereafter, fed, housed, and clothed by the same agencies which deal with the skid rower. Predictably, the client is apt to experience contact with skid rowers and their way of life; this pattern, Wallace (1965:168) points out, was probably more relevant in the past, and particularly when relief agencies were located in the skid row section of a community. Modern day attitudes, policies, and procedures have altered this picture considerably. For example, welfare agencies are not centered in slum or skid row areas, and other agencies or institutions have developed to care for the aged and the ill. In any event, the "down and out" may, for various reasons, be attracted to the skid row culture.

Skid row *aficionados*—the third main source of recruits—exhibit patterns of behavior that are, according to Wallace (1965:169), inherently deviant. In fact, not only does the deviance exist prior to contact, but the *aficionado* is the only type that is interested in disengaging himself from society. To him, skid row offers the refuge he is actively seeking. As an example of this type of motivation, Wallace (1965:169–170) cites the case of the salesman who moves to skid row in a deliberate effort to conceal his excessive drinking from his family, friends, and employer. Other examples include the aging prostitute who uses skid row as a source of clients, and the petty thief or racketeer who is trying to escape detection.

Wallace (1965:170–172) goes on to note that, over the years and due primarily to economic factors, changes have occurred with respect to the volume of men that enter skid row through these three main points and, correspondingly, the skid row population has experienced increases or decreases. What needs to be reemphasized at this stage is that, and virtually independent of composition and size, males *and* females will be exposed to the skid row way of life. And for some the exposure will be deliberately induced, while for others it will be more subtle and indirect. Once contact has been established, however, the process of socialization begins.

In terms of socialization per se, the newcomer must become familiar with, as well as act in accordance with, the dominant normative structure that guides interaction among the skid rowers. And learning the "argot" or language of the skid world does, according to Wallace (1965:173), help to facilitate this process. Increasing socialization into this world is coupled with increasing isolation from the conventional world. For example, the skid rower loses contact with his family, and his friends and neighbors are replaced by the men on skid row. In effect, and to use Wallace's (1965:174) term, the newcomer becomes *de-socialized* from the outside world and becomes socialized into a new world (i.e., the world of the skid row). Being publicly labeled or branded as a deviant (i.e., a skid rower) also helps in the socialization process, and most particularly labeling that occurs at the hands of official social control agents. In Wallace's (1965:175) words:

> ... If he is publicly and officially labeled a deviant through arrest, sentence, and incarceration, the newcomer's socialization is vastly intensified since those he lives with in jail and in the workhouse are also members of the skid row community. He spends all day long eating, working, and talking with his fellow community members and returns to skid row with a more intimate knowledge of its way of life. The public label of deviance also adds to the credentials he needs for admittance into the in-group on skid row.

Public labeling also produces another telling effect. At this point, the individual must recognize the fact that he is now a part of the skid row world—a realization that is often associated with other rather predictable outcomes. Wallace (1965:175–176) comments on the possibilities:

> Once he has been labeled a deviant, self-awareness is forced upon the individual. He must face the fact that he is now indeed on skid row. The same label increases his separation from the wider society and at the same time urges him to enter into ever closer participation with those similarly isolated. Thus is he pushed into still further deviance, additional arrests, workhouse socialization, and more

complete isolation until he is finally and completely a full-fledged member of the deviant community. Sooner or later private self-acceptance of the deviant label must inevitably follow public recognition, and thus this greatest of all barriers to reform is erected: he now thinks of himself as a skid rower.

Acceptance of the deviant label is, Wallace (1965:176) points out, associated with some rather significant changes. The skid rower may, for example, begin to neglect his appearance, and when in need of money he may actually sell his clothes or even his razor; these changes (i.e., acceptance of the label as a skid rower, as well as the corresponding normative structure) produces the skid rower. The availability of prevailing attitudes and beliefs is critical to the success of this process (i.e., the evolving career of the skid rower). Specifically, according to Wallace (1965:176), if the male is to protect his self-image from destruction by outside forces, as well as become a full-fledged member of the subculture, he must make effective use of the attitudes (i.e., the occupational ideology) that have, presumably, been inculcated within him.

Wallace (1965:179–180) contends that becoming a model skid rower is not easy. Some may be unable or unwilling to become totally committed to the skid row society. The degree of commitment is, however, a rather direct function of the career route one becomes caught up in. For some, exposure and perhaps participation may be casual and sporadic, while for others, contact may be deliberate and ongoing. Predictably, then, some novices will become career skid rowers and others will not. In terms of the skid row's status hierarchy, the drunk is accorded the highest degree of status; this social type also represents the epitome of what it means to be a career or model skid rower.

> To be completely acculturated in skid row subculture is to be a drunk—since skid rowers place strong emphasis on group drinking and the acculturated person is by definition a conformist. The drunk has rejected every single one of society's established values and wholly conformed to the basic values of skid row subculture. Food, shelter, employment, appearance, health, and all other considerations are subordinated by the drunk to the group's need for alcohol. This group constitutes the drunk's total social world and it in turn bestows upon him any status, acceptance, or security he may possess. [Wallace, 1965:181–182]

RECRUITMENT AND LEARNING TO RATIONALIZE: SOME FINAL COMMENTS

Regardless of whether exposure, entry, or participation is voluntary or not, the possibility exists that the novice may become a career deviant, delinquent, or criminal. Quite obviously, too, not all who experience some type of contact with a grouping, gathering, or subculture will become regular members. Some will continue, while others will drop out; this is one of the basic themes contained in Wallace's research. In fact, and as

Wallace also emphasizes, becoming a model skid rower is not especially easy. One must, for example, deal with a complex of identity and self-image problems—concerns, I might add, that are not, in any sense of the word, unique to the skid rower and his way of life. Stated somewhat differently, whenever people in general contemplate involvement in criminal, deviant, or delinquent activities, they must come to grips with some difficult issues. Probably of utmost concern, however, is the protection of their identity and self-image from possible destruction. How, for example, will generalized (e.g., a teacher, police officer, or judge) and significant (e.g., a family member or spouse) others perceive and react to knowledge about an individual's involvement in homosexuality, nudism, delinquency, crime, or some other form of deviance? Will they criticize the person and perhaps impute a deviant label to him or her? How about the person involved? Will he or she label self as a deviant or pervert and then begin to act accordingly? These are some of the basic questions that must be addressed.

What the preceding research and comments should indicate is that not only have people been socialized in certain ways but when deviation from these patterns is considered, they must weigh the consequences of their deviation. As an illustration, some parents may teach their sons and daughters that premarital sex, smoking marijuana, snorting coke, living with a person, and so on are wrong. And, obviously, some children will comply with their parent's wishes, while others will not. Their deviation, it should be noted, may not be necessarily easy, nor without its personal and social costs. Many deviators report initial feelings of guilt, anxiety, shame, humiliation, or remorse; these costs, however, can, in many cases, be lessened or assuaged a bit, particularly if the deviator is aware of, or perhaps even implicated in, alternative value and associated normative systems. Tannenbaum's (1938), Miller's (1958), and Cohen's (1965) males, for example, turned to the gang for relief, while Bryan's (1955) rookie prostitutes looked to their pimps and other call girls for training and advice. Whether processes such as these are effective for all is certainly problematic. The probability of success, it should be emphasized, is often notably higher when the individual is given some type of group support or encouragement. Perhaps an even better predictor of success, at least as far as reducing any real or potential threats to ego, identity, or self-image, would be the degree to which the deviator has actually internalized any justifications or rationalizations for his or her actions. And, predictably, those who possess an effective network of rationalizations, justifications, or defenses would probably be the most likely candidates for some type of deviation. In fact, some have gone so far as to argue that rationalizations precede deviation and therefore make it possible. One of the better statements on the use and function of rationalization techniques is provided by the work of Sykes and Matza (1957).

A basic part of their thesis is to the effect that children probably internalize certain demands for conformity. Hence, most retain some type of commitment to the existing social order. Not only this but few can escape criticism for their deviant acts. In Sykes and Matza's (1957:666) words:

...No matter how deeply enmeshed in patterns of delinquency he may be and no matter how much this involvement may outweigh his associations with the law-abiding, he cannot escape the condemnation of his deviance. Somehow the demands for conformity must be met and answered...

To support their claim that juvenile delinquents often have some type of commitment to larger society, Sykes and Matza (1957:666) cite evidence indicating that delinquents frequently exhibit shame and guilt when they deviate, accord approval to certain individuals, and distinguish between acceptable and unacceptable targets. How, then, do they handle any criticism, guilt, or shame? Sykes and Matza (1957) reason that they do so through the use and extension of many of the common "defenses to crimes" (e.g., insanity, drunkenness, self-defense, and so on). If, for example, the individual can remove blame from self, then he or she is in better position to deal with any pressing identity or self-image problems. It is at this point that Sykes and Matza (1957) argue that the rationalizations or justifications not only *follow* deviation and hence protect the person "from self-blame and the blame of others," but they also *precede* the deviation and thus make the behavior possible. As Sykes and Matza (1957:666–667) state it:

...Disapproval flowing from internalized norms and conforming others in the social environment is neutralized, turned back, or deflected in advance. Social controls that serve to check or inhibit deviant motivational patterns are rendered inoperative, and the individual is freed to engage in delinquency without serious damage to his self-image. In this sense, the delinquent both has his cake and eats it too, for he remains committed to the dominant normative system and yet so qualifies its imperatives that violations are "acceptable" if not "right."

Sykes and Matza (1957:667) refer to these justifications for deviance as *techniques of neutralization*. It is by learning these techniques that a juvenile becomes delinquent. Sykes and Matza (1957:667–669) divide the techniques into five major types: (1) the denial of responsibility, (2) the denial of injury, (3) the denial of the victim, (4) the condemnation of the condemners, and (5) the appeal to higher authorities. As an illustration, and in terms of the first technique, if the individual can define himself or herself as lacking responsibility for delinquent actions, then the criticism of self or others is reduced markedly. It may be argued that delinquent acts are due to forces beyond the control of the individual (e.g., unloving parents, bad companions, or a bad neighborhood). Sykes and Matza (1957:667) note that those who neutralize in this fashion seem to possess a "billiard ball" conception of self—a conception in which the individual does not see self as being in control of his or her destiny. Similarly, if harm or injury can be denied (i.e., invoking the denial of injury technique), the individual can, once again, reduce the effects of any disapproval or criticism. Vandalism, for example, may be defined as mischief, while auto theft may be viewed as joy riding. Claiming that homosexuals or suspected homosexuals deserve to be assaulted (i.e., the denial of the victim), that the police are brutal (i.e., the condemnation of the condemners), or that one must not squeal on a friend or buddy (i.e., the appeal to higher loyalties) provide additional examples of the justifications that may be used by delinquents.

Sykes and Matza (1957:669) note that the techniques of neutralization may not be powerful enough to protect selected individuals from the force of their own values, as well as the reactions of conformists. And for others, especially those who are not a part of the conforming world, there exists no obvious need to learn and use the justifications or defenses to crimes. Overall, however, it is Sykes and Matza's (1957:669) conclusion that the techniques are "...critical in lessening the effectiveness of social controls and that they lie behind a large share of delinquent behavior...." They also point out that very little research has been conducted in this area—an observation, I might add, that continues to hold for this point in time.

Even though the research on neutralization techniques is, at best, sketchy, it is my position that any discussion or analysis of the evolution of delinquent, criminal or deviant careers must give central theoretical and empirical focus to the use and function of rationalization or neutralization techniques. Quite clearly, and as the evidence in this book indicates, those who can rationalize are more apt to become involved in deviant pursuits; they are also more likely to become secondary or career deviants.

References

Bryan, J. H. (1965) "Apprenticeships in prostitution." *Social Problems* 12:287–297.

Cohen, A. K. (1955) *Delinquent Boys*. New York: Free Press.

Miller, W. B. (1958) "Lower class culture as a generating milieu of gang delinquency." *The Journal of Social Issues* 14:5–19.

Piliavin, I. and S. Briar (1964) "Police encounters with juveniles." *The American Journal of Sociology* 70:206–214.

Reiss, A. J., Jr. (1961) "The social integration of queers and peers." *Social Problems* 9:102–120.

Sykes, G. M. and D. Matza (1957) "Techniques of neutralization: a theory of delinquency." *American Sociological Review* 22:664–670.

Tannenbaum, F. (1938) *Crime and the Community*. New York: Ginn and Company.

Wallace, S. E. (1965) *Skid Row as a Way of Life*. Totowa, N.J.: Bedminster.

Weinberg, M. S. (1966) "Becoming a nudist." *Psychiatry* 29:15–24.

34 / Drifting into Dealing: Becoming a Cocaine Seller

SHEIGLA MURPHY
DAN WALDORF
CRAIG REINARMAN

INTRODUCTION

No American who watched television news in the 1980s could have avoided images of violent drug dealers who brandished bullets while driving BMW's before being hauled off in handcuffs. This new stereotype of a drug dealer has become a staple of popular culture, the very embodiment of evil. He works for the still more vile villains of the "Columbian cartel," who make billions on the suffering of millions. Such men are portrayed as driven by greed and utterly indifferent to the pain from which they profit.

We have no doubt that some such characters exist. Nor do we doubt that there may be a new viciousness among some of the crack cocaine dealers who have emerged in ghettos and barrios already savaged by rising social problems and falling social programs. We have grave doubts, however, that such characterizations tell us anything about cocaine sellers more generally. If our interviews are any guide, beneath every big-time dealer who may approximate the stereotype there are hundreds of smaller sellers who do not.

This paper describes such sellers, not so much as a way of debunking a new devil but rather as a way of illuminating how deviant careers develop and how the identities of the individuals who move into this work are transformed. Along with the many routine normative strictures against drug use in our culture, there has been a mobilization in recent years for a "war on drugs" which targets cocaine dealers in particular. Many armaments in the arsenal of social control from propaganda to prisons have been employed in efforts to dissuade people from using/selling such substances. In such a context it is curious that ostensibly ordinary people not only continue to use illicit drugs but also take the significant additional step of becoming drug sellers. To explore how this happens, we offer an analysis of eighty depth interviews with former cocaine sellers. We sought to learn something about how it is that otherwise conventional people—some legally employed, many well educated—end up engaging in a sustained pattern of behavior that their neighbors might think of as very deviant indeed.

DEVIANT CAREERS AND DRIFT

Our reading of this data was informed by two classic theoretical works in the deviance literature. First, in *Outsiders,* Howard Becker observed that, "The career lines characteristic of an occupation take their shape from the problems peculiar to that occupation. These, in turn, are a function of the occupation's position vis-a-vis other groups in society" (1963:102). He illustrated the point with the dance musician, caught between the jazz artist's desire to maintain creative control and a structure of opportunities for earning a living that demanded the subordination of this desire to mainstream musical tastes. Musicians' careers were largely a function of how they managed this problem. When the need to make a living predominated, the basis of their self conceptions shifted from art to craft.

Of course, Becker applied the same proposition to more deviant occupations. In the next section, we describe five discrete modes of becoming a cocaine seller which center on "the problems peculiar to" the world of illicit drug use and which entail a similar shift in self conception. For example, when a drug such as cocaine is criminalized, its cost is often greatly increased while its availability and quality are somewhat limited. Users are thus faced with the problems of avoiding detection, reducing costs, and improving availability and quality. By becoming involved in sales, users solve many of these problems and may also find that they can make some money in the bargain. As we will show, the type of entree and the level at which it occurs are functions of the individual's relationship to networks of other users and suppliers. At the point where one has moved from being a person who *has* a good connection for cocaine to a person who *is* a good connection for cocaine, a subtle shift in self conception and identity occurs.

Becker's model of deviant careers entails four basic steps, three of which our cocaine sellers took. First, the deviant must somehow avoid the impact of conventional commitments that keep most people away from intentional non-conformity. Our cocaine sellers passed this stage by ingesting illegal substances with enough regularity that the practice became normalized in their social world. Second, deviant motives and interests must develop. These are usually learned in the process of the deviant activity and from interaction with other deviants. Here too our cocaine sellers had learned the pleasures of cocaine by using it, and typically were moved toward involvement in distribution to solve one or more problems entailed in such use. Once involved, they discovered additional motivations which we will describe in detail below.

Becker's third step in the development of deviant careers entails public labeling. The person is caught, the rule is enforced, and his or her public identity is transformed. The new master status of "deviant," Becker argues, can be self fulfilling when it shapes others' perceptions of the person and limits his or her possibilities for resuming conventional roles and activities. Few of our respondents had been publicly labeled deviant, but they did describe a gradual change in identity that may be likened to self-labeling. This typically occurred when they deepened their deviance by dealing on top of using cocaine. This shift in self conception for our subjects was more closely linked to Becker's fourth step—movement into an organized deviant group in which people with a common fate and similar problems form subcultures. There they learn more about solving problems and ideologies which provide rationales for continuing the behavior, thus further weakening the hold of conventional norms and institutions and solidifying deviant identities. In the case of our subjects, becoming sellers further immersed them into deviant groups and practices to the point where many came to face the problems of, and to see themselves as, "dealers."

The fact that these processes of deeper immersion into deviant worlds and shifts in self conception were typically gradual and subtle brought us to a second set of theoretical reference points in the work of David Matza (1964; 1969).[1] In his research on delinquency, Matza discovered that most so-called delinquents were not self-consciously committed to deviant values or lifestyles, but on the contrary continued to hold conventional beliefs. Most of the time they were law abiding, but because the situation of "youth" left them free from various restraints, they often *drifted* in and out of deviance. Matza found that even when caught being delinquent, young people tended to justify or rationalize their acts through "techniques of neutralization" (Sykes and Matza, 1957) rooted in conventional codes of morality. Although we focus on *entering* selling careers, we found that Matza's concept of drift (1964) provided us with a useful sensibility for making sense of our respondents' accounts. The modes of entree they described were as fluid and non-committal as the drift into and out of delinquency that he described.

None of the career paths recounted by our subjects bear much resemblance to stereotypes of "drug dealers."[2] For decades the predominant image of the illicit drug dealer was an older male reprobate sporting a long, shabby overcoat within which he had secreted a cornucopia of dangerous consciousness-altering substances. This proverbial "pusher" worked school yards, targeting innocent children who would soon be chemically enslaved repeat customers. The newer villains have been depicted as equally vile but more violent. Old or new, the ideal-typical "drug dealer" is motivated by perverse greed and/or his own addiction, and has crossed a clearly marked moral boundary, severing most ties to the conventional world.

The cocaine sellers we interviewed, on the other hand, had more var-ied and complex motives for selling cocaine. Moreover at least within their subcultures, the moral boundaries were both rather blurry and as often wandered along as actually crossed. Their life histories reminded us of

Matza's later but related discussion of the *overlap* between deviance and conventionality:

> Overlap refers to . . . the marginal rather than gross differentiation between deviant and conventional folk and the considerable though variable interpenetration of deviant and conventional culture. Both themes sensitize us to the regular exchange, traffic, and flow—of persons as well as styles and precepts—that occur among deviant and conventional worlds. (1969:68)

Our subjects were already seasoned users of illicit drugs. For years their drug use coexisted comfortably with their conventional roles and activities; having a deviant dimension to their identities appeared to cause them little strain. In fact, because their use of illicit drugs had gone on for so long, was so common in their social worlds, and had not significantly affected their otherwise normal lives, they hardly considered it deviant at all.

Thus, when they began to sell cocaine as well as use it, they did not consider it a major leap down an unknown road but rather a series of short steps down a familiar path. It was not as if ministers had become mobsters; no sharp break in values, motives, world views, or identities was required. Indeed, few woke up one morning and made a conscious decision to become sellers. They did not break sharply with the conventional world and actively choose a deviant career path; most simply drifted into dealing by virtue of their strategies for solving the problems entailed in using a criminalized substance, and only then developed additional deviant motives centering on money.

To judge from our respondents, then, dealers are not from a different gene pool. Since the substances they enjoy are illegal, most regular users of such drugs become involved in some aspect of distribution. There is also a growing body of research on cocaine selling and distribution that has replaced the simplistic stereotype of the pusher with complex empirical evidence about underground economies and deviant careers (e.g., Langer, 1977; Waldorf et al., 1977, 1991; Adler, 1985; Plasket and Quillen, 1985; Morales, 1986a, 1986b; Sanchez and Johnson, 1987; Sanabria, 1988; and Williams, 1989). Several features of underground economies or black markets in drugs contribute to widespread user participation in distribution. For example, some users who could obtain cocaine had other user-friends who wanted it. Moreover, the idea of keeping such traffic among friends offered both sociability and safety. For others, cocaine's high cost inspired many users to become involved in purchasing larger amounts to take advantage of volume discounts. They then sold part of their supply to friends in order to reduce the cost of personal use. The limited supply of cocaine in the late seventies and early eighties made for a sellers' market, providing possibilities for profits along with steady supplies. For most of our subjects, it was not so much that they learned they could make money and thus decided to become dealers but rather, being involved in distribution anyway, they learned they could make money from it. As Becker's model suggests, deviant motives are learned in the course of deviant activities; motivation follows behavior, not the other way around.

After summarizing our sampling and interviewing procedures, we describe in more detail (1) the various modes and levels of entree into cocaine sales; (2) some of the practices, rights and responsibilities entailed in dealing; and (3) the subtle transformation of identity that occurred when people who consider themselves rather conventional moved into careers considered rather deviant.

SAMPLE AND METHODS

The sample consists of 80 ex-sellers who sold cocaine in the San Francisco Bay Area. We interviewed them in 1987 and 1988. Most had stopped selling before crack sales peaked in this area. Only five of the eighty had sold crack or rock. Of these five, two had sold on the street and two had sold in "rock party houses"[3] as early as 1978. It is important to note, therefore, that the sellers we describe are very likely to be different from street crack dealers in terms of the product type, selling styles, visibility, and thus the risks of arrest and attendant violence.

The modes and levels of entree we describe should not be considered exhaustive. They are likely to vary by region, subculture, and level of dealing. For example, our sample and focus differed from those of Adler (1985), who studied one community of *professional* cocaine dealers at the *highest levels* of the distribution system. Her ethnographic account is rich in insights about the lifestyles and career contingencies of such high-level dealers and smugglers. These subjects decided to enter into importing and/or dealing and to move up the ranks in this deviant occupation in order to obtain wealth and to live the sorts of lives that such wealth made possible. Adler's dealers were torn, however, between the lures of fast money and the good life and the stress and paranoia inherent in the scene. Thus, she reported "oscillations" wherein her dealers moved in and out of the business, usually to be lured back in by the possibility of high profits. Our dealers tended to have different motivations, career trajectories, and occupational exigencies. Most were lower in the hierarchy and non-professional (some maintained "straight" jobs); few set out to achieve success in an explicitly deviant career, to amass wealth, or to live as "high rollers." Moreover, our study was cross-sectional rather than longitudinal, so our focus was on how a wide variety of cocaine sellers entered careers rather than on the full career trajectories of a network of smugglers and sellers.

To be eligible for the study our respondents had to have sold cocaine steadily for at least a year and to have stopped selling for at least 6 months. We designed the study to include only *former* sellers so that respondents would feel free to describe all their activities in detail without fear that their accounts could somehow be utilized by law enforcement authorities.

They spoke of six different levels or types of sellers: smugglers, big dealers, dealers, sellers (unspecified), bar dealers, and street dealers. The social organization of cocaine sales probably varies in other areas. We located and interviewed ex-sellers from the full range of these dealer-identified sales levels, but we have added two categories in order to provide a more detailed typology. Our eight levels of sales were defined according to the units sold rather than the units bought. So, for example, if a seller bought quarters or eighths of ounces and regularly sold grams, we categorized him or her as a gram dealer rather than a part-ounce dealer.

Levels of Sales	Number of Interviews
Smugglers	2
Kilograms/pounds	13
Parts of kilos and pounds	6
Ounce dealers	18
Part-ounce dealers	13
Gram dealers	12
Part-gram dealers	11
Crack dealers	5
Total	80

Unlike most other studies of dealing and the now infamous street crack dealers, the majority of our respondents sold cocaine hydrochloride (powder) in private places. There are a number of styles of selling drugs—selling out of homes, selling out of rock houses and shooting galleries, selling out of party houses, selling out of rented "safe houses" and apartments, delivery services (using telephone answering, answering machines, voice mail and telephone beepers), car meets,[4] selling in bars, selling in parks, and selling in the street. Within each type there are various styles. For example, in some African-American communities in San Francisco a number of sellers set up business on a street and respond to customers who come by on foot and in automobiles. Very often a number of sellers will approach a car that slows down or stops to solicit customers; drugs and money are exchanged then and there. Such sales activities are obvious to the most casual observers; even television camera crews often capture such transactions for the nightly news. On certain streets in the Mission District, a Latino community in San Francisco, street drug sales are less blatant. Buyers usually walk up to sellers who stand on the street among numerous other people who are neither buyers nor sellers. There, specific transactions rarely take place on the street itself; the participants generally retreat to a variety of shops and restaurants. Buyers seldom use cars for transactions and sellers tend not to approach a car to solicit customers.

Despite the ubiquity of street sales in media accounts and the preponderance of street sellers in arrest records, we set out to sample the more
hidden and more numerous sellers who operate in private. Most users of
cocaine hydrochloride are working- or middle-class. They generally avoid
street sellers both because they want to avoid being observed and because
they believe that most street sellers sell inferior quality drugs (Waldorf et
al., 1991). Further, we found that people engaged in such illegal and furtive
transactions tend to prefer dealing with people like themselves, people
they know.

We located our respondents by means of chain referral sampling techniques (Biernacki and Waldorf, 1981; Watters and Biernacki, 1989). This is a
method commonly used by sociologists and ethnographers to locate hard-to-
find groups and has been used extensively in qualitative research on drug use
(Lindesmith, 1947; Becker, 1953; Feldman, 1968; Preble and Casey, 1969;
Rosenbaum, 1981; Biernacki, 1986). We initiated the first of our location
chains in 1974–75 in the course of a short-term ethnography of cocaine use
and sales among a small friendship network (Waldorf et al., 1977). Other
chains were developed during a second study of cocaine cessation conducted
during 1986–1987 (Reinarman et al., 1988; Macdonald et al., 1988; Murphy et al., 1989; Waldorf et al., 1991). Another three chains were developed
during the present study. We located the majority of our respondents via
referral chains developed by former sellers among their previous customers
and suppliers. Initial interviewees referred us to other potential respondents
whom we had not previously known. In this way we were able to direct our
chains into groups of ex-sellers from a variety of backgrounds.

We employed two interview instruments: an open-ended, exploratory
interview guide designed to maximize discovery of new and unique types
of data, and a more structured survey designed to gather basic quantifiable
data on all respondents. The open-ended interviews were tape-recorded,
transcribed, and content-analyzed. These interviews usually took from 2
to 4 hours to complete, but when necessary we conducted longer and/or
follow-up interviews (e.g., one woman was interviewed for 10 hours over
three sessions). The data analyzed for this paper was drawn primarily from
the tape-recorded depth interviews.

There is no way to ascertain if this (or any similar) sample is representative of all cocaine sellers. Because the parameters of the population are
unknowable, random samples on which systematic generalizations might
be based cannot be drawn. We do know that, unlike other studies of drug
sellers, we placed less emphasis on street sellers and included dealers at all
levels. We also attempted to get a better gender and ethnic mix than studies
based on captive samples from jails or treatment programs. Roughly one in
three (32.5%) of our dealers are female and two of five (41.2%) are persons
of color.

Our respondents ranged in age from 18 to 60, with a mean age of 37.1
years. Their education level was generally high, presumably an indication
of the relatively large numbers of middle-class people in the sample.

Table 1 / Demographics (N = 80)

Age: Range = 18–60 years
Mean 37.1
Median = 35.4

	Number	Percent
Sex:		
Male	54	67.5
Female	26	32.5
Ethnicity:		
African-American	28	35.0
White	44	58.8
Latino(a)	4	5.0
Asian	1	1.2
Education:		
Less than high school grad	11	13.8
High school graduate	18	22.5
Some college	31	38.8
B.A. or B.S. degree	12	15.0
Some graduate	3	3.8
Graduate degree	5	6.3

[Percentages may not equal 100% due to rounding]

DEALERS

Dealers are people who are "fronted" (given drugs on consignment to be paid for upon sale) and/or who buy quantities of drugs for sale. Further, in order to be considered a dealer by users or other sellers a person must: (1) have one or more reliable connections (suppliers); (2) make regular cocaine purchases in amounts greater than a single gram (usually an eighth of an ounce or greater) to be sold in smaller units; (3) maintain some consistent supplies for sale; and (4) have a network of customers who make purchases on a regular basis. Although the stereotype of a dealer holds that illicit drug sales are a full-time occupation, many dealers, including members of our sample, operate part-time and supplement income from a legal job.

As we noted in the introduction, the rather average, ordinary character of the respondents who fit this definition was striking. In general, without prior knowledge or direct observation of drug sales, one would be unable to distinguish our respondents from other, non-dealer citizens. When telling their career histories, many of our respondents invoked very conventional, middle-class American values to explain their involvement in dealing (e.g., having children to support, mortgages or rent to pay in a high-cost urban area, difficulty finding jobs which paid enough to support a family). Similarly, their profits from drug sales were used in "normal" ways—to buy children's clothes, to make house or car payments, to remodel a room. Moreover, like Matza's delinquents, most of our respondents were quite law-abiding, with the obvious exception of their use and sales of an illicit substance.

When they were not dealing, our respondents engaged in activities that can only be described as mainstream American. For example, one of our dealers, a single mother of two, found herself with a number of friends who used cocaine and a good connection. She needed extra income to pay her mortgage and to support her children, so she sold small amounts of cocaine within her friendship network. Yet while she sold cocaine, she worked at a full-time job, led a Girl Scout troop, volunteered as a teacher of cardio-pulmonary resuscitation (CPR) classes for young people, and went to Jazzercize classes. Although she may have been a bit more civic-minded than many others, her case served to remind us that cocaine sellers do not come from another planet.

MODES OF ENTRÉE INTO DEALING

Once they began selling cocaine, many of our respondents moved back and forth between levels in the distribution hierarchy. Some people dealt for short periods of time and then quit, only to return several months later at another level of sales.[5] The same person may act as a broker on one deal, sell a quarter gram at a profit to a friend on another, and then pick up an ounce from an associate and pass it on to another dealer in return for some marijuana in a third transaction. In a few instances each of these roles were played by the same person within the same twenty-four hour period.

But whether or not a dealer/respondent moved back and forth in this way, s/he usually began selling in one of five distinct ways. All five of these modes of entree pre-suppose an existing demand for cocaine from people known to the potential dealers. A person selling any line of products needs two things, a group of customers and a product these customers are interested in purchasing. Cocaine sellers are no different. In addition to being able and willing to pay, however, cocaine customers must also be trustworthy because these transactions are illegal.

The first mode of entree, *the go-between,* is fairly straightforward. The potential seller has a good cocaine connection and a group of friends who place orders for cocaine with him/her. If the go-between's friends use cocaine regularly enough and do not develop their own connections, then a period of months or even years might go by when the go-between begins to spend more and more time and energy purchasing for them. Such sellers generally do not make formal decisions to begin dealing; rather, opportunities regularly present themselves and go-betweens gradually take advantage of them. For example, one 30-year-old African-American who became a gram dealer offered this simple account of his passage from go-between to seller:

> Basically, I first started because friends pressured me to get the good coke I could get. I wasn't even making any money off of it. They'd come to me and I'd call up my friend who had gotten pretty big selling a lot of coke. (Case # E-5)

This went on for six months before he began to charge his friends money for it. Then his connection started fronting him eighths of ounces at a time, and he gradually became an official dealer, regularly selling drugs for a profit. Others who began in this way often took only commissions-in-kind (a free snort) for some months before beginning to charge customers a cash mark-up.

Another African-American male began selling powdered cocaine to snorters in 1978 and by the mid-eighties had begun selling rock cocaine (crack) to smokers. He described his move from go-between to dealer as follows:

> Around the time I started indulging [in cocaine] myself, people would come up and say, "God, do you know where I can get some myself?" I would just say, "Sure, just give me your money," I would come back and either indulge with them or just give it to them depending on my mood. I think that's how I originally set up my clientele. I just had a certain group of people who would come to me because they felt that I knew the type of people who could get them a real quality product.
>
> And pretty soon I just got tired of, you know, being taken out of situations or being imposed upon....I said that it would be a lot easier to just do it myself. And one time in particular, and I didn't consider myself a dealer or anything, but I had a situation one night where 5 different people called me to try to get cocaine...not from me but it was like, "Do you know where I can get some good cocaine from?" (Case # E-11)

Not all go-betweens-cum-dealers start out so altruistically. Some astute businessmen and women spot the profit potential early on and immediately realize a profit, either in-kind (a share of the drugs purchased) or by tacking on a surcharge to the purchase price. The following respondent, a 39-year-old African-American male, described this more profit-motivated move from go-between to formal seller:

> Well, the first time that I started it was like I knew where to get good stuff...and I had friends that didn't know where to get good stuff. And I knew where to get them really good stuff and so I would always put a couple of dollars on it, you know, if I got it for $20 I would sell it to them for $25 or $30 or whatever.
>
> It got to be where more and more people were coming to me and I was going to my man more and I would be there 5 or 6 times a day, you know. So he would tell me, "Here, why don't you take this, you know, and bring me x-amount of dollars for it." So that's how it really started. I got fronted and I was doing all the business instead of going to his house all the time, because he had other people that were coming to his house and he didn't want the traffic. (Case # E-13)

The second mode of entree is the *stash dealer,* or a person who becomes involved in distribution and/or sales simply to support or subsidize personal use. The name is taken from the term "stash," meaning a personal supply of marijuana (see Fields, 1985, on stash dealers in the marijuana trade). This 41-year-old white woman who sold along with her husband described her start as a stash dealer this way:

Q: So what was your motivation for the sales?
A: To help pay for my use, because the stuff wasn't cheap and I had the means and the money at the time in order to purchase it, where our friends didn't have that amount of money without having to sell something. . . . Yeah, friendship, it wasn't anything to make money off of, I mean we made a few dollars. . . . (Case # E-7)

The respondents who entered the dealing world as stash dealers typically started out small (selling quarter and half grams) and taking their profits in product. However, this motivation contributed to the undoing of some stash dealers in that it led to greater use, which led to the need for greater selling, and so on. Unless they then developed a high-volume business that allowed them to escalate their cocaine use and still make profits, the reinforcing nature of cocaine tempted many of them to use more product than was good for business.

Many stash dealers were forced out of business fairly early on in their careers because they spent so much money on their own use they were financially unable to "re-cop" (buy new supplies). Stash dealers often want to keep only a small number of customers in order to minimize both the "hassle" of late-night phone calls and the risk of police detection, and they do not need many customers since they only want to sell enough to earn free cocaine. Problems arise, however, when their small group of customers do not buy the product promptly. The longer stash dealers had cocaine in their possession, the more opportunities they had for their own use (i.e., for profits to "go up your nose"). One stash dealer had an axiom about avoiding this: "It ain't good to get high on your own supply" (Case # E-57). The predicament of using rather than selling their product often afflicts high-level "weight dealers" as well, but they are better able to manage for longer periods of time due to larger volumes and profit margins.

The third mode of entry into cocaine selling had to do with users' desire for high-quality, unadulterated cocaine. We call this type the *connoisseur.* Ironically, the motivation for moving toward dealing in this way is often health-related. People who described this mode of entree described their concerns, as users, about the possible dangers of ingesting the various adulterants or "cuts" commonly used by dealers to increase profits. User folklore holds that the larger the quantity purchased, the purer the product. This has been substantiated by laboratory analysis of the quality of small amounts of street drugs (typically lower) as opposed to larger police seizures (typically higher).

The connoisseur type of entry, then, begins with the purchase of larger quantities of cocaine than they intend to use in order to maximize purity. Then they give portions of the cocaine to close friends at a good price. If the members of the network start to use more cocaine, the connoisseurs begin to make bigger purchases with greater regularity. At some point they begin to feel that all this takes effort and that it makes sense to buy large quantities not only to get purer cocaine but to make some money for their efforts. The following 51-year-old, white business executive illustrated the connoisseur route as follows:

> I think the first reason I started to sell was not to make money or even to pay for my coke, because I could afford it. It was to get good coke and not to be snorting a lot of impurities and junk that people were putting into it by cutting it so much. So I really think that I started to sell it or to get it wholesale so that I would get the good stuff. And I guess my first, ... what I did with it in the beginning, because I couldn't use all that I had to buy to get good stuff, I sold it to some of my friends for them to sell it, retail it. (Case # E-16)

Connoisseurs, who begin by selling unneeded quantities, often found they unlearned certain attitudes when they moved from being volume buyers looking for quality toward becoming dealers looking for profit. It was often a subtle shift, but once their primary motivation gradually changed from buying-for-purity to buying-to-sell they found themselves beginning to think and act like dealers. The shift usually occurred when connoisseurs realized that the friends with whom they had shared were in fact customers who were eager for their high quality cocaine and who often made demands on their time (e.g., friends seeking supplies not merely for themselves, but for other friends a step or two removed from the original connoisseur). Some connoisseurs also became aware of the amount of money that could be made by becoming business-like about what had been formerly friendly favors. At such points in the process they began to buy-to-sell, for a profit, as well as for the purpose of obtaining high-quality cocaine for personal use. This often meant that, rather than buying sporadically, they had to make more regular buys; for a successful businessperson must have supplies when customers want to buy or they will seek another supplier.

The fourth mode of entree into cocaine selling is an *apprenticeship.* Like the other types, apprentices typically were users who already had loosened conventional normative strictures and learned deviant motives by interacting with other users and with dealers; and they, too, drifted into dealing. However, in contrast to the first three types, apprentices moved toward dealing less to solve problems inherent in using a criminalized substance than to solve the problems of the master dealer. Apprenticeships begin in a personal relationship where, for example, the potential seller is the lover or intimate of a dealer. This mode was most often the route of entry for women, although one young man we interviewed learned to deal from his father. Couples often start out with the man doing the dealing— picking up the product, handling the money, weighing and packaging, etc. The woman gradually finds herself acting as an unofficial assistant—taking telephone messages, sometimes giving people prepackaged cocaine and collecting money. Apprentices frequently benefit from being involved with the experienced dealer in that they enjoy both supplies of high-quality cocaine and indirect financial rewards of dealing.

Some of our apprentices moved into official roles or deepened their involvement when the experienced dealer began to use too much cocaine to function effectively as a seller. In some such cases the abuse of the product led to an end of the relationship. Some apprentices then left dealing altogether while others began dealing on their own. One 32-year-old African-American woman lived with a pound dealer in Los Angeles in 1982. Both were freebasers (cocaine smokers) who sold to other basers. She described her evolution from apprentice to dealer this way:

> I was helping him with like weighing stuff and packaging it and I sort of got to know some of the people that were buying because his own use kept going up. He was getting more out of it, so I just fell into taking care of it partly because I like having the money and it also gave me more control over the situation, too, for awhile, you know, until we both got too out of it. (Case # E-54)

The fifth mode of entree into cocaine selling entailed the *expansion of an existing product line.* A number of the sellers we interviewed started out as marijuana salespersons and learned many aspects of the dealers' craft before they ever moved to cocaine. Unlike in the other modes, in this one an existing marijuana seller already had developed selling skills and established a network of active customers for illicit drugs. Expansion of product line (in business jargon, horizontal integration) was the route of entry for many of the multiple-ounce and kilo cocaine dealers we interviewed. The combination of the availability of cocaine through their marijuana connection and their marijuana customers' interest in purchasing cocaine, led many marijuana sellers to add cocaine to their product line.

Others who entered dealing this way also found that expanding from marijuana to cocaine solved some problems inherent in marijuana dealing. For example, cocaine is far less bulky and odoriferous than marijuana and thus did not present the risky and costly shipping and storage problems of multiple pounds of marijuana. Those who entered cocaine selling via this product line expansion route also recognized, of course, that there was the potential for higher profits with cocaine. They seemed to suggest that as long as they were already taking the risk, why shouldn't they maximize the reward? Some such dealers discontinued marijuana sales altogether and others merely added cocaine to their line. One white, 47-year-old mother of three grown children described how she came to expand her product line:

Q: How did you folks [she and her husband] get started dealing?
A: The opportunity just fell into our lap. We were already dealing weed and one of our customers got this great coke connection and started us onto dealing his product. We were selling him marijuana and he was selling us cocaine.
Q: So you had a network of weed buyers, right? So you could sell to those...?

A: There was a shift in the market. Yeah, because weed was becoming harder [to find] and more expensive and a bulkier product. The economics of doing a smaller, less bulkier product and more financially rewarding product like cocaine had a certain financial appeal to the merchant mentality. (Case # E-1)

CONSCIOUS DECISION TO SELL

As noted earlier, the majority of our sample were middle class wholesalers who, in the various ways just described, drifted into dealing careers. The few street sellers we interviewed did not drift into sales in the same way. We are obliged to note again that the five modes of entry into cocaine selling we have identified should not be taken as exhaustive. We have every reason to believe that for groups and settings other than those we have studied there are other types of entree and career trajectories. The five cases of street sellers we did examine suggest that entree into street-level sales was more of a conscious decision of a poor person who decided to enter an underground economy, not an effort to solve a user's problems. Our interviews with street sellers suggest that they choose to participate in an illicit profit-generating activity largely because licit economic opportunities were scarce or nonexistent. Unlike our other types, such sellers sold to strangers as well as friends, and their place of business was more likely to be the street corner rather than homes, bars, or nightclubs. For example, one 30-year-old Native American ex-prostitute described how she became a street crack dealer this way:

I had seen in the past friends that were selling and stuff and I needed extra money so I just one day told one of my friends, you know, if he could help me, you know, show me more or less how it goes. So I just went by what I seen. So I just started selling it. (Case # E-AC 1)

A few higher-level dealers also made conscious decisions to sell (see Adler, 1985), particularly when faced with limited opportunity structures. Cocaine selling, as an occupation, offers the promise of lavish lifestyles otherwise unattainable to most ghetto youth and other impoverished groups. Dealing also provides an alternative to the low-paying, dead-end jobs typically available to those with little education and few skills. A 55-year-old African-American man who made his way up from grams to ounce sales described his motivation succinctly: "The chance presented itself to avoid the 9 to 5" (Case # E-22).

Street sellers and even some higher-level dealers are often already participating in quasi-criminal lifestyles; drug sales are simply added to their repertoire of illicit activities. The perceived opportunity to earn enormous profits, live "the good life," and set your own work schedule are powerful enticements to sell. From the perspective of people with few life chances, dealing cocaine may be seen as their only real chance to achieve the "American Dream" (i.e., financial security and disposable income). Most of our sample were not ghetto dwellers and/or economically disadvantaged.

But for those who were, there were different motivations and conscious decisions regarding beginning sales. Popular press descriptions of cocaine sellers predominantly portray just such street sellers. Although street sellers are the most visible, our data suggest that they represent what might be called the tip of the cocaine dealing iceberg.

LEVELS OF ENTRY

The levels at which a potential dealer's friends/connections were selling helped determine the level at which the new dealer entered the business. If the novitiate was moving in social scenes where "big dealers" are found, then s/he is likely to begin by selling grams and parts of grams. When supplies were not fronted, new dealers' personal finances, i.e., available capital, also influenced how much they could buy at one time.

Sellers move up and down the cocaine sales ladder as well as in and out of the occupation (see Adler, 1985). Some of our sellers were content to remain part-ounce dealers selling between a quarter and a half an ounce a week. Other sellers were more ambitious and eventually sought to become bigger dealers in order to increase profits. One interviewee reported that her unusually well organized suppliers had sales quotas, price fixing, and minimum purchase expectations which pushed her toward expansion. The levels of sales and selling styles of the new dealer's suppliers, then, interacted with personal ambitions to influence eventual sales careers.

Another important aspect of beginning to sell cocaine is whether the connection is willing to "front" the cocaine (risk a consignment arrangement) rather than requiring the beginner to pay in full. Having to pay "up front" for one's inventory sometimes slowed sales by tying up capital, or even deterred some potential dealers from entering the business. Fronted cocaine allowed people with limited resources to enter the occupation. Decisions to front or not to front were based primarily on the connection's evaluation of the new seller's ability to "move" the product. This was seen as a function of the potential volume of business the beginning seller could generate among his/her networks of friends and/or customers. The connection/fronter also evaluates the trustworthiness of the potential dealer, as well as their own capability of absorbing the loss should the deal "go bad" and the frontee be unable to pay. The judgment of the fronter is crucial, for a mistake can be very costly and there is no legal recourse.

LEARNING TO DEAL

In the go-between, stash and connoisseur modes of entree, novices gradually learn the tricks of the trade by observing the selling styles of active dealers, and ultimately by doing. Weighing, packaging, and pricing the product are basic techniques. A scale, preferably a triple-beam type . . . accurate to the tenth of a gram, is a necessary tool. In the last ten years answering machines, beepers, and even cellular phones have become important tools as well. Learning how to manage customers and to establish selling routines and rules of procedure are all essential skills that successful dealers must master.

The dealers who enter sales through the apprenticeship and product line expansion modes have the advantage of their own or their partner/seller's experience. Active marijuana sellers already have a network of customers, scales, familiarity with metric measures, and, most important, a connection to help them move into a new product line. Apprentices have lived with and/or observed the selling styles of their dealer/mentors and have access to their equipment, connections and customers. Both apprentices and marijuana dealers who have expanded into cocaine also know how to "maintain a low profile" and avoid any kind of attention that might culminate in arrest. In this way they were able to reduce or manage the paranoia that often inheres in drug dealing circles.

Many sellers learn by making mistakes, often expensive mistakes. These include: using too much cocaine themselves, fronting drugs to people who do not pay for them, and adding too much "cut" (usually an inactive adulterant such as vitamin B) to their product so they develop a reputation for selling inferior cocaine and sometimes have difficulty selling the diluted product. One 32-year-old African-American male made one such error in judgment by fronting to too many people who did not "come through." It ended up costing him $15,000:

> It was because of my own recklessness that I allowed myself to get into that position. There was a period where I had a lot of weight that I just took it and just shipped it out to people I shouldn't have shipped it out to....I did this with 10 people and a lot of them were women to be exact. I had a lot of women coming over to my house and I just gave them an ounce apiece one time....So when maybe 6 of those people didn't come through...there was a severe cramp in my cash flow. This made me go to one of the family members to get the money to re-cop. (Case # E-11)

Business Sense/People Sense

Many people have a connection, the money to make the initial buy, a reputation for being reliable, and a group of friends interested in buying drugs, but still lack the business sense to be a successful dealer. Just because a person drifts into dealing does not mean that he or she will prosper and stay in dealing. We found a variety of ways in which people initially became dealers, few of which hinged on profits. But what determined whether they continued dealing was their business sense. Thus even though a profit orientation had little to do with becoming a dealer, the ability to consistently realize profits had a major influence over who remained a dealer. In this sense, cocaine selling was like any other capitalist endeavor.

According to our respondents, one's ability to be a competent dealer depended on being able to separate business from pleasure. Success or failure at making this separation over time determined whether a profit was realized. Certain business practices were adopted by prosperous dealers to assist them in making this important distinction. For example, prepackaging both improves quality control and helps keep inventory straight; establishing rules for customers concerning when they can purchase and at what prices reduces the level of hassle; limiting the amount of fronting can reduce gross sales volume, but it also reduces financial risk and minimizes the amount of debt collection work; and limiting their own personal use keeps profits from disappearing up one's nose or in one's pipe.

Being a keen judge of character was seen as another important component of being a skilled dealer. Having the "people skills" to judge whether a person could be trusted to return with the money for fronted supplies, to convince people to pay debts that the dealer had no legal mechanisms for collecting, and to engender the trust of a connection when considerable amounts of money were at stake, are just a few of the sophisticated interpersonal skills required of a competent dealer.

Adler also discusses the importance of a "good personal reputation" among upper level dealers and smugglers:

> One of the first requirements for success, whether in drug trafficking, business enterprise broadly, or any life undertaking, is the establishment of a good personal reputation. To make it in the drug world, dealers and smugglers had to generate trust and likability. (1985:100)

Adler's general point applies to our respondents as well, although the experiences of some of our middle and lower level dealers suggested a slight amendment: A likable person with a good reputation could sell a less than high quality product, but an unlikable person, even one with a bad reputation, could still do a considerable amount of business if s/he had an excellent product. One 47-year-old white woman described her "difficult" husband/partner, "powder keg Paul":

> He would be so difficult, you couldn't believe it. Somebody [this difficult] better have a super primo product to make all this worthwhile. . . . He's the kind of guy you don't mind buying from because you know you'll get a good product, but he's the kind of guy you never want to sell to . . . he was that difficult. (Case # E-1)

High quality cocaine, in other words, is always at a premium in this subculture, so even without good people skills a dealer or connection with "good product" was tolerated.

FROM USER TO DEALER: THE TRANSFORMATION OF IDENTITY

In each of our respondents' deviant careers there occurred what Becker referred to as a change in self conception. Among our respondents, this took the form of a subtle shift in identity from a person who *has* a good connection for cocaine to a person who *is* a good connection for cocaine. There is a corresponding change in the meaning of, and the motives for, selling. The relationship between the seller and the customer undergoes a related transformation, from "picking up something for a friend" to conducting a commercial transaction. In essence, dealing becomes a business quite like most others, and the dealer gradually takes on the professional identity of a business person. Everett Hughes, writing on the sociology of work, urged social scientists to remember that when we look at work,

> We need to rid ourselves of any concepts which keep us from seeing that the essential problems of men at work are the same whether they do their work in the laboratories of some famous institution or in the messiest vat of a pickle factory. (1951:313)

When they had fully entered the dealer role, our respondents came to see selling cocaine as a job—work, just like other kinds of work save for its illegality. For most, selling cocaine did not mean throwing out conventional values and norms. In fact, many of our respondents actively maintained their conventional identities (see Broadhead, 1983). Such identities included those of parents, legally employed workers, neighbors, church-goers and softball players, to list just a few. Dealer identities tended not to replace former, "legitimate" identities but were added to a person's repertoire of more conventional identities.

Like everyone else in modern life, sellers emphasized one or another dimension of their identities as appropriate to the situation. In his study of heroin addicts Biernacki notes that, "The arrangement of identities must continuously be managed in such a way as to stress some identities at certain points in particular social worlds and situations, and at the same time to de-emphasize others" (1986:23). Our sellers, too, had to become adept at articulating the proper identity at the proper time. By day, one woman dealer was a concerned mother at her daughter's kindergarten field trip, and that same evening she was an astute judge of cocaine quality when picking up an ounce from her connection. At least for our interviewees, selling cocaine rarely entailed entirely terminating other social roles and obligations.

Yet, at some point in all of our sellers' careers, they found themselves transformed from someone who has a good connection to someone who is a good connection, and they gradually came to accept the identity of dealer as a part of their selves. Customers began to treat them like a salesperson, expecting them to be available to take calls and do business and even for services such as special off-hour pick-ups and deliveries or reduced rates for volume purchases. When dealers found themselves faced with such demands, they typically began to feel *entitled* to receive profits from selling. They came to be seen as dealers by others, and in part for this reason, came to see themselves as dealers. As Becker's (1963) model suggests, selling *behavior* usually preceded not only motivation but also changes in attitude and identity. As one 38-year-old white woman put it,

I took over the business and paid all my husband's debts and started to make some money. One day I realized I was a coke dealer. . . . It was scary, but the money was good. (Case # E-75)

Acceptance of the dealer identity brings with it some expectations and values shared by dealers and customers alike. Customers have the expectation that the dealer will have a consistent supply of cocaine for sale. Customers also expect that the dealer will report in a fairly accurate manner the quality of his/her present batch of drugs within the confines of the *caveat emptor* philosophy that informs virtually all commercial activities in market societies. Buyers do not expect sellers to denigrate their product, but they do not expect the dealer to claim that their product is "excellent" if it is merely "good." Customers assume the dealer will make a profit, but dealers should not be "too greedy." A greedy dealer is one who makes what is estimated by the buyer to be excessive profits. Such estimations of excessiveness vary widely among customers and between sellers and buyers. But the fact that virtually all respondents spoke of some unwritten code of fairness suggests that there is, in E. P. Thompson's (1971) phrase, a "moral economy" of drug dealing that constrains the drive for profit maximization even within an illicit market.[6]

For their part, dealers expect that customers will act in a fashion that will minimize their chances of being arrested by being circumspect about revealing their dealer status. One simply did not, for example, bring to a dealer's house friends whom the dealer had not met. Dealers want customers to appreciate the risks undertaken to provide them with cocaine. And dealers come to feel that such risks deserve profits. After all, the seller is the one who takes the greatest risks; s/he could conceivably receive a stiff jail sentence for a sales conviction. While drifting into dealing and selling mostly to friends and acquaintances mitigated the risks of arrest and reduced their paranoia, such risks remained omnipresent.

In fact, the growing realization of such risks—and the rationalization it provided for dealing on a for-profit basis—was an integral part of becoming a cocaine seller. As our 38-year-old white woman dealer put it, "When it's all said and done, I'm the one behind bars, and I had better have made some money while I was selling or why in the hell take the risk?" (Case # E-75)

Acknowledgment

The research reported herein was funded by a grant from the National Institute of Justice (#7-0363-9-CA-IJ), Bernard A. Gropper, Ph.D., Program Manager, Drugs, Alcohol and Crime Programs, Center for Crime Control Research. The views expressed herein are those of the authors alone. The authors are grateful to the anonymous reviewers of *Qualitative Sociology* for helpful comments.

Address correspondence to Sheigla Murphy, Institute for Scientific Analysis, 2235 Lombard Street, San Francisco, CA, 94123.

Notes

1. Adler also refers briefly to Matza's formulations within her discussion of becoming a dealer (pp. 127–128, 1985).

2. It must be noted at the outset that the predominately white, working and middle-class cocaine sellers we interviewed are very likely to differ from inner-city crack dealers depicted in the media. While there is now good reason to believe that both the profits and the violence reported to be endemic in the crack trade have been exaggerated (e.g., Reuter, 1990, and Goldstein et al., 1989, respectively), our data are drawn from a different population, selling a different form of the drug, who were typically drawn to selling for different reasons. Thus the exigencies they faced and their responses to them are also likely to differ from those of inner-city crack sellers.

3. Rock party houses are distinct from "rock houses" or "crack houses." In the former, sellers invite only selected customers to their homes to smoke rock and "party." Unlike crack houses, where crack is sold to all comers, outsiders are never invited to rock party houses, and the arrangement is social and informal. Proprietors of both types, however, charge participants for the cocaine.

4. Car meets are transactions that take place in cars. Arrangements are made over the telephone in advance and both buyer and seller arrange to meet at parking lots, usually at busy shopping centers, and exchange drugs and money. Each arrives in his or her own car and leaves separately.

5. These movements back and forth among different levels of involvement in dealing were different from the "shifts and oscillations" found among the cocaine dealers studied by Adler (1985:133–141). She studied a circle of high-level dealers over an extended period of field work and found that the stresses and strains of dealing at the top of the pyramid often led her participants to attempt to get out of the business. While many of our interviewees felt similar pressures later in their careers and subsequently quit, our focus here is on becoming a cocaine seller.

6. In addition to lore about "righteous" and "rip off" dealers, there were present other norms that suggested the existence of such an unwritten code or moral economy, e.g., refusing to sell to children or to adults who "couldn't handle it" (i.e., had physical, financial, familial, or work-related problems because of cocaine use).

References

Adler, P. (1985). *Wheeling and Dealing: An Ethnography of an Upper-Level Drug Dealing Community*. New York: Columbia University Press.

Becker, H. S. (1953). "Becoming a marijuana user." *American Journal of Sociology* 59:235–242.

Becker, H. S. (1963). *Outsiders*. New York: Free Press.

Becker, H. S. (1986). *Pathways from Heroin Addiction*. Philadelphia: Temple University Press.

Biernacki, P., and Waldorf, D. (1981). "Snowball sampling: problems and techniques of chain referral sampling." *Sociological Methods and Research* 10:141–163.

Broadhead, R. (1983). *The Private Lives and Professional Identity of Medical Students*. New Brunswick, NJ: Transaction Books.

Feldman, H. W. (1968). "Ideological supports to becoming and remaining a heroin addict." *Journal of Health and Social Behavior* 9:131–139.

Fields, A. (1985). "Weedslingers: a study of young black marijuana dealers." *Urban Life* 13:247–270.

Goldstein, P., Brownstein, H., Ryan, P., and Belucci, P. (1989). "Crack and homicide in New York City, 1988." *Contemporary Drug Problems* 16:651–687.

Grinspoon, L., and Bakalar, J. (1976). *Cocaine: A Drug and Its Social Evolution.* New York: Basic Books.

Hughes, E. (1951). "Work and the self." In John Rohrer and Muzafer Sherif (eds.), *Social Work at the Crossroads.* New York: Harper and Brothers, 313–323.

Langer, J. (1977)."Drug entrepreneurs and dealing culture." *Social Problems* 24:377–386.

Lindesmith, A. (1947). *Addiction and Opiates.* Chicago: Aldine Press.

Macdonald, P., Waldorf, D., Reinarman, C., and Murphy, S. (1988). "Heavy cocaine use and sexual behavior." *Journal of Drug Issues* 18:437–455.

Matza, D. (1964). *Delinquency and Drift.* New York: Wiley.

Matza, D. (1969). *Becoming Deviant.* Englewood Cliffs, NJ: Prentice Hall.

Morales, E. (1986a). "Coca culture: the white gold of Peru." *Graduate School Magazine of City University of New York* 1:4–11.

Morales, E. (1986b). "Coca and cocaine economy and social change in the Andes in Peru." *Economic Development and Social Change* 35:143–161.

Morales, E. (1988). *Cocaine: The White Gold Rush in Peru.* Tucson, AZ: University of Arizona Press.

Murphy, S., Reinarman, C., and Waldorf, D. (1989). "An eleven year follow-up of a network of cocaine users." *British Journal of the Addictions* 84:427–436.

Plasket, B., and Quillen, E. (1985). *The White Stuff.* New York: Dell Publishing Company.

Preble, E., and Casey, J. H., Jr. (1969). "Taking care of business: the heroin user's life on the streets." *The International Journal of the Addictions* 4:1–24.

Reinarman, C., Waldorf, D., and Murphy, S. (1988). "Scapegoating and social control in the construction of a public problem: empirical and critical findings on cocaine and work." *Research in Law, Deviance and Social Control* 9:37–62.

Reuter, P. (1990). *Money from Crime: The Economics of Drug Dealing.* Santa Monica, CA: Rand Corporation.

Rosenbaum, M. (1981). *Women on Heroin.* New Brunswick, NJ: Rutgers University Press.

Sanabria, H. (1988). *Coca, Migration and Socio-Economic Change in a Bolivian Highland Peasant Community.* Ph.D. thesis, University of Wisconsin.

Sanchez, J., and Johnson, B. (1987). "Women and the drug crime connection: crime rates among drug abusing women at Riker's Island." *Journal of Psychoactive Drugs* 19:205–215.

Sykes, G., and Matza, D. (1957). "Techniques of neutralization." *American Sociological Review* 22:664–670.

Thompson, E. P. (1971). "The moral economy of the English crowd in the eighteenth century." *Past and Present* 50:76–136.

Waldorf, D., Reinarman, C., Murphy, S., and Joyce, B. (1977). *Doing Coke: An Ethnography of Cocaine Snorters and Sellers.* Washington, DC: Drug Abuse Council.

Waldorf, D., Reinarman, C., and Murphy, S. (1991). *Cocaine Changes.* Philadelphia: Temple University Press.

Watters, J. K., and Biernacki, P. (1989). "Targeted sampling: options for the study of hidden populations." *Social Problems* 36:416–430.

Williams, T. (1989). *The Cocaine Kids.* New York: Addison-Wesley.

35 / Confronting Deadly Disease: The Drama of Identity Construction among Gay Men with AIDS

KENT L. SANDSTROM

The phenomenon of AIDS (acquired immunodeficiency syndrome) has been attracting increased attention from sociologists. A number of observers have examined the social meanings of the illness (Conrad 1986; Sontag 1989; Palmer 1989), the social influences and behavior involved in its onset and progression (Kaplan et al. 1987) and the larger social consequences of the AIDS epidemic (Ergas 1987). Others have studied the "psychosocial" issues faced by individuals who are either diagnosed with the illness (Nichols 1985; Baumgartner 1986: Weitz 1989) or closely involved with someone who has been diagnosed (Salisbury 1986; Geiss, Fuller and Rush 1986; Macklin 1988).

Despite this growing interest in the social and psychosocial dimensions of AIDS, little attention has been directed toward the processes of social and self-interaction (Denzin 1983) by which individuals acquire and personalize an AIDS-related identity. Further, given the stigmatizing implications of AIDS, there has been a surprising lack of research regarding the strategies of stigma management and identity construction utilized by persons with this illness.

This article presents an effort to address these issues. It examines the dynamics of identity construction and management which characterize the everyday lives of persons with AIDS (PWAs). In doing so, it highlights the socially ambiguous status of PWAs and considers (a) the processes through which they personalize the illness, (b) the dilemmas they encounter in their interpersonal relations, (c) the strategies they employ to avoid or minimize potentially discrediting social attributions, and (d) the subcultural networks and ideologies which they draw upon as they construct, avow and embrace AIDS-related identities. Finally, these themes are situated within the unfolding career and lived experience of people with AIDS.

METHOD AND DATA

The following analysis is based on data gathered in 56 in-depth interviews with 19 men who had been diagnosed with HIV (human immunodeficiency virus) infections. On the average, each individual was interviewed on three separate occasions and each of these sessions lasted from 1 to 3 hours. The interviews, conducted between July 1987 and February 1988, were guided by 60 open-ended questions and were audiotaped. Most interviews took place in the participants' homes. However, a few participants were interviewed in a private university office because their living quarters were not conducive to a confidential conversation.

Participants were initially recruited through two local physicians who treat AIDS patients and through a local self-help organization that provides support groups and services for people with HIV infections. Those individuals who agreed to be interviewed early in the study spoke with friends or acquaintances and encouraged them to become involved. The majority of interviews were thus obtained through "snowball" or chain-referral sampling.

By employing a snowball sampling procedure, we were able to gain fairly rapid access to persons with AIDS-related diagnoses and to discuss sensitive issues with them. However, due to its reliance on self-selection processes and relatively small social networks, this method is not likely to reflect the range of variation which exists in the population of persons with advanced AIDS-related infections. This study is thus best regarded as exploratory.

All respondents were gay males who lived in a metropolitan area in the Midwest. They varied in age, income, and the stage of their illness. In age, they ranged from 19 to 46 years, with the majority in the 28 to 40 age bracket. Six persons were currently employed in professional or white-collar occupations. The remaining 13 were living marginally on Social Security or disability benefits. Several members of this latter group had previously been employed in either blue-collar or service occupations. Seven individuals were diagnosed with AIDS, 10 were diagnosed with ARC (AIDS-related complex), and 2 were diagnosed as HIV positive but both had more serious HIV-related health complications (e.g., tuberculosis).

ON BECOMING A PWA: THE REALIZATION OF AN AIDS IDENTITY

For many of these men, the transformation of physical symptoms into the personal and social reality of AIDS took place most dramatically when they received a validating diagnosis from a physician. The following account reveals the impact of being officially diagnosed:

> She [the doctor] said, "Your biopsy did come out for Kaposi's sarcoma. I want you to go to the hospital tomorrow and to plan to spend most of the day there."

While she is telling me this, the whole world is buzzing in my head because this is the first confirmation coming from outside as opposed to my own internal suspicions. I started to cry—it (AIDS) became very real... *very real*....

Anyway, everything started to roller coaster inside me and I was crying in the office there. The doctor said "You knew this was the way it was going to come out, didn't you?" She seemed kind of shocked about why I was crying so much, not realizing that no matter how much you are internally aware of something, to hear it from someone else is what makes it real. For instance, the first time I really accepted being gay was when other people said "You are gay!"...It's a social thing—you're not real until you're real to someone else.

This quote illustrates the salience of social processes for the validation and realization of an identity—in this case, an AIDS-related identity. Becoming a PWA is not simply a matter of viral infection, it is contingent on interpersonal interaction and definitions. As depicted in the quote, a rather momentous medical announcement facilitates a process of identity construction which, in turn, entails both interpersonal and subjective transformation. Within the interpersonal realm, the newly diagnosed "AIDS patient" is resituated as a social object and placed in a marginal or liminal status. He is thereby separated from many of his prior social moorings. On the subjective level, this separation produces a crisis, or a disruption of the PWA's routine activities and self-understanding. The diagnosed individual is prompted to "make sense" of the meaning of his newly acquired status and to feel its implications for future conceptions and enactments of self....

INTERPERSONAL DILEMMAS ENCOUNTERED BY PWAS

Stigmatization

Stigmatization is one of the most significant difficulties faced by people with AIDS as they attempt to fashion a personal and social meaning for their illness. The vast majority of our informants had already experienced some kind of stigma because of their gay identities. When they were diagnosed with AIDS, they usually encountered even stronger homophobic reactions and discreditation efforts. An especially painful form of stigmatization occurred when PWAs were rejected by friends and family members after revealing their diagnosis. Many respondents shared very emotional accounts of how they were ostracized by parents, siblings, or colleagues. Several noted that their parents and family members had even asked them to no longer return home for visits. However, rejections were not always so explicit. In many cases, intimate relationships were gradually and ambiguously phased out rather than abruptly or clearly ended.

A few PWAs shared stories of being stigmatized by gay friends or acquaintances. They described how some acquaintances subtly reprimanded them when seeing them at gay bars or repeatedly reminded them to "be careful" regarding any sexual involvements. Further, they mentioned that certain gay friends avoided associating with them after learning of their AIDS-related diagnoses. These PWAs thus experienced the problem of being "doubly stigmatized" (Kowalewski 1988), that is, they were devalued within an already stigmatized group, the gay community.

PWAs also felt the effects of stigmatization in other, more subtle ways. For example, curious and even sympathetic responses on the parts of others, especially strangers, could lead PWAs to feel discredited. One PWA, reflecting on his interactions with hospital staff, observed:

> When they become aware [of my diagnosis], it seemed like people kept looking at me...like they were looking for something. What it felt like was being analyzed, both physically and emotionally. It also felt like being a subject or guinea pig... like "here's another one." They gave me that certain kind of look. Kind of that look like pity or that said "what a poor wretch," not a judgmental look but rather a pitying one.

An experience of this nature can precipitate a crisis of identity for a person with AIDS. He finds himself being publicly stigmatized and identified as a victim. Such an identifying moment can seriously challenge prior conceptions of self and serve as a turning point from which new self-images or identities are constructed (Charmaz 1980). That is, it can lead a PWA to internalize stigmatizing social attributions or it can incite him to search for involvements and ideologies which might enable him to construct a more desirable AIDS identity.

Counterfeit Nurturance

Given the physical and social implications of their illness, PWAs typically desire some kind of special nurturing from friends, partners, family members, or health practitioners. Yet displays of unusual concern or sympathy on the part of others can be threatening to self. People with AIDS may view such expressions of nurturance as counterfeit or harmful because they highlight their condition and hence confirm their sense of difference and vulnerability.

The following observation illustrates the sensitivity of PWAs to this problem:

> One thing that makes you feel kind of odd is when people come across supportive and want to be supportive but it doesn't really feel like they are supportive. There is another side to them that's like, well, they are being nice to you because they feel sorry for you, or because it makes them feel good about themselves to help someone with AIDS, not because they really care about you.

PWAs often find themselves caught in a paradox regarding gestures of exceptional help or support. They want special consideration at times, but if they accept support or concern which is primarily focused on their condition, they are likely to feel that a "victim identity" is being imposed on them. This exacerbates some of the negative self-feelings that have already been triggered by the illness. It also leads PWAs to be more wary of the motivations underlying others' expressions of nurturance.

Given these dynamics, PWAs may reach out to each other in an effort to find relationships that are more mutually or genuinely nurturing. This strategy is problematic, though, because even PWAs offer one another support which emphasizes their condition. They are also likely to remind each other of the anomalous status they share and the "spoiled" features (Goffman 1963) of their identities qua PWAs.

Ultimately, suspicions of counterfeit nurturance can lead those diagnosed with AIDS to feel mistreated by almost everyone, particularly by caregivers who are most directly involved in helping them. Correctly or incorrectly, PWAs tend to share some feelings of ambivalence and resentment towards friends, lovers, family members, and medical personnel.

Fears of Contagion and Death Anxiety

Fears of contagion present another serious dilemma for PWAs in their efforts to negotiate a functional social identity. These fears are generated not only by the fact that people with AIDS are the carriers of an epidemic illness but also because, like others with a death taint, they are symbolically associated with mass death and the contagion of the dead (Lifton 1967). The situation may even be further complicated by the contagion anxiety which homosexuality triggers for some people.

In general, others are tempted to withdraw from an individual with AIDS because of their fears of contracting the virus. Even close friends of a PWA are apt to feel more fearful or distant toward him, especially when first becoming aware of the diagnosis. They may feel anxious about the possibility of becoming infected with the virus through interactions routinely shared with him in the past (e.g., hugging and kissing). They may also wish to avoid the perils of being stigmatized themselves by friends or associates who fear that those close to a PWA are a potential source of contagion.

Another dimension of contagion anxiety is reflected in the tendency of significant others to avoid discussing issues with a PWA that might lead them to a deeper apprehension of the death-related implications of his diagnosis. As Lifton (1967) suggested, the essence of contagion anxiety is embodied in the fear that "if I come too close to a death tainted person, I will experience his death and his annihilation" (p. 518).

This death-related contagion anxiety often results in increased strain and distance in a PWA's interactions with friends or family members. It can also inhibit the level of openness and intimacy shared among fellow PWAs when they gather together to address issues provoked by their diagnoses. Responses of grief, denial, and anxiety in the face of death make in-depth discussions of the illness experience keenly problematic. According to one respondent:

> Usually no one's ever able to talk about it [their illness and dying] without going to pieces. They might start but it only takes about two minutes to break into tears. They might say something like "I don't know what to do! I might not even be here next week!" Then you can just see the ripple effect it has on the others sitting back and listening. You have every possible expression from anger to denial to sadness and all these different emotions on people's faces. And mostly this feeling of "what can we do? Well...Nothing!"

Problems of Normalization

Like others who possess a stigmatizing attribute, people with AIDS come to regard many social situations with alarm (Goffman 1971) and uncertainty (Davis 1974). They soon discover that their medical condition is a salient aspect of all but their most fleeting social encounters. They also quickly learn that their diagnosis, once known to others, can acquire the character of a *master status* (Hughes 1945; Becker 1963) and thus become the focal point of interaction. It carries with it, "the potential for inundating the expressive boundaries of a situation" (Davis 1974, 166) and hence for creating significant strains or rupture in the ongoing flow of social intercourse.

In light of this, one might expect PWAs to prefer interaction contexts characterized by "closed" awareness (Glaser and Strauss 1968). Their health status would be unknown to others and they would presumably encounter fewer problems when interacting. However, when in these situations, they must remain keenly attuned to controlling information and concealing attributes relevant to their diagnosis. Ironically, this requirement to be dramaturgically "on" may give rise to even more feelings of anxiety and resentment.

The efforts of persons with AIDS to establish and maintain relationships within more "open" contexts are also fraught with complications. One of the major dilemmas they encounter is how to move interactions beyond an atmosphere of fictional acceptance (Davis 1974). A context of fictional acceptance is typified by responses on the part of others which deny, avoid, or minimize the reality of an individual's diagnosis. In attempting to grapple with the management of a spoiled identity, PWAs may seek to "break through" (Davis 1974) relations of this nature. In doing so, they often try to broaden the scope of interactional involvement and to normalize problematic elements of their social identity. That is, they attempt to project "images, attitudes and concepts of self which encourage the normal to identify with [them] (i.e., 'take [their] role') in terms other than those associated with imputations of deviance" (Davis 1974, 168).

Yet even if a PWA attains success in "breaking through," it does not necessarily diminish his interactional difficulties. Instead, he can become caught in an ambiguous dilemma with respect to the requisites of awareness and normalization. Simply put, if others begin to disregard his diagnosis and treat him in a normal way, then he faces the problem of having to remind them of the limitations to normalcy imposed by this condition. The person with AIDS is thus required to perform an intricate balancing act between encouraging the normalization of his relationships and ensuring that others remain sensitized to the constraining effects of such a serious illness. These dynamics promote the construction of relationships which, at best, have a qualified sense of normalcy. They also heighten the PWA's sense that he is located in an ambiguous or liminal position.

AVOIDING OR MINIMIZING DILEMMAS

In an attempt to avoid or defuse the problematic feelings, attributions, and ambiguities which arise in their ongoing interactions, PWAs engage in various forms of identity management. In doing so, they often use strategies which allow them to minimize the social visibility of their diagnoses and to carefully control interactions with others. These strategies include *passing, covering, isolation, and insulation.*

The particular strategies employed vary according to the progression of their illness, the personal meanings they attach to it, the audiences serving as primary referents for self-presentations, and the dynamics of their immediate social situation.

Passing and Covering

As Goffman (1963) noted in his classic work on stigma, those with a spoiled identity may seek to pass as normal by carefully suppressing information and thereby precluding others' awareness of devalued personal attributes. The PWAs we interviewed mentioned that "passing" was a maneuver they had used regularly. It was easily employed in the early stages of the illness when more telltale physical signs had not yet become apparent and awareness of an individual's diagnosis was [confined] to a small social circle.

However, as the illness progresses, concealing the visibility of an AIDS-related diagnosis becomes more difficult. When a person with AIDS begins to miss work frequently, to lose weight noticeably, and to reduce his general level of activity, others become more curious or suspicious about what ailment is provoking such major changes. In the face of related questions, some PWAs elected to devise a "cover" for their diagnosis which disguised troubling symptoms as products of a less discrediting illness.

One informant decided to cover his AIDS diagnosis by telling co-workers that he was suffering from leukemia:

> There was coming a point, I wasn't feeling so hot. I was tired and the quality of my life was decreasing tremendously because all of my free time was spent

resting or sleeping. I was still keeping up with work but I thought I'd better tell them something before I had to take more days off here and there to even out the quality of my life. I had already had this little plan to tell them I had leukemia... but I thought how am I going to tell them, what am I going to tell them, how am I going to convince them? What am I going to do if someone says, "You don't have leukemia, you have AIDS!"? This was all stuff clicking around in my mind. I thought, how could they possibly know? They only know as much as I tell them.

This quote reveals the heightened concern with information control that accompanies decisions to conceal one's condition. Regardless of the psychic costs, though, a number of our informants opted for this remedial strategy. A commonly used technique consisted of informing friends, parents, or co-workers that one had cancer or tuberculosis without mentioning that these were the presenting symptoms of one's AIDS diagnosis. Covering attempts of this kind were most often employed by PWAs when relating to others who were not aware of their gay identity. These relationships were less apt to be characterized by the suspicions or challenges offered by those who knew that an individual was both gay and seriously ill.

Isolation and Insulation

For those whose diagnosis was not readily visible, dramaturgical skills, such as passing and covering, could be quite useful. These techniques were not so feasible when physical cues, such as a pale complexion, emaciated appearance, or facial lesion made the nature of a PWA's condition more apparent. Under these circumstances, negotiations with others were more alarming and they were more likely to include conflicts engendered by fear, ambiguity, and expressions of social devaluation.

In turn, some PWAs came to view physical and social isolation as the best means available to them for escaping from both these interpersonal difficulties and their own feelings of ambivalence. By withdrawing from virtually all interaction, they sought to be spared the social struggles and psychic strains that could be triggered by others' recognition of their condition. Nonetheless, this strategy was typically an unsuccessful one. Isolation and withdrawal often exacerbated the feelings of alienation that PWAs were striving to minimize in their social relationships. Moreover, their desire to be removed from the interactional matrix was frequently overcome by their need for extensive medical care and interpersonal support as they coped with the progressive effects of the illness.

Given the drawbacks of extreme isolation, a number of PWAs used a more selective withdrawal strategy. It consisted of efforts to disengage from many but not all social involvements and to interact regularly with only a handful of trusted associates (e.g., partners, friends, or family members). Emphasis was placed on minimizing contacts with those outside of this circle because they were likely to be less tolerant or predictable. PWAs engaging in this type of selective interaction tried to develop a small network of intimate others who could insulate them from potentially threatening interactions. Ideally, they were able to form a reliable social circle within which they felt little need to conceal their diagnosis. They could thereby experience some relief from the burden of stigma management and information control.

BUILDING AND EMBRACING AN AIDS IDENTITY

Strategies such as passing, covering, isolation, and insulation are used by PWAs, especially in the earlier stages of their illness, to shield themselves from the stigma and uncertainty associated with AIDS. However, these strategies typically require a high level of personal vigilance, they evoke concerns about information control, and they are essentially defensive in nature. They do not provide PWAs with a way to reformulate the personal meaning of their diagnosis and to integrate it with valued definitions of self.

In light of this, most PWAs engage in more active types of *identity work* which allow them to "create, present and sustain personal identities which are congruent with and supportive of the(ir) self-concept[s]" (Snow and Anderson 1987, 1348). Certain types of identity work are especially appealing because they help PWAs to gain a greater sense of mastery over their condition and to make better use of the behavioral possibilities arising from their liminal condition.

The most prominent type of identity work engaged in by the PWAs we interviewed was embracement. As Snow and Anderson (1987) argued, embracement refers to "verbal and expressive confirmation of one's acceptance of and attachment to the social identity associated with a general or specific role, a set of social relationships, or a particular ideology" (p. 1354). Among the PWAs involved in this study, embracement was promoted and reinforced through participation in local AIDS-related support groups.

Support Groups and Associational Embracement

People facing an existential crisis often make use of new memberships and social forms in their efforts to construct a more viable sense of self (Kotarba 1984). The vast majority of respondents in this study became involved in PWA support groups in order to better address the crisis elicited by their illness and to find new forms of self-expression. They typically joined these groups within a few months of receiving their diagnosis and continued to attend meetings on a fairly regular basis.

By and large, support groups became the central focus of identity work and repair for PWAs. These groups were regarded as a valuable source of education and emotional support that helped individuals to cope better with the daily exigencies of their illness. At support group meetings, PWAs could exchange useful information, share feelings and troubles, and relate to others who could see beyond the negative connotations of AIDS.

Support groups also facilitated the formation of social ties and feelings of collective identification among PWAs. Within these circles, individuals learned to better nurture and support one another and to emphasize the shared nature of their problems. Feelings of guilt and isolation were transformed into a sense of group identification. This kind of *associational embracement* (Snow and Anderson 1987) was conveyed in the comments of one person who proclaimed:

> I spend almost all of my time with other PWAs. They're my best friends now and they're the people I feel most comfortable with. We support one another and we know that we can talk to each other any time, day or night.

For some PWAs, especially those with a troubled or marginal past, support group relationships provided an instant "buddy system" that was used to bolster feelings of security and self-worth. Recently formed support group friendships even took on primary importance in their daily lives. Perhaps because of the instability and isolation which characterized their life outside of support groups, a few of these PWAs tended to exaggerate the level of intimacy which existed in their newly found friendships. By stressing a romanticized version of these relationships, they were able to preserve a sense of being cared for even in the absence of more enduring social connections.

Identity Embracement and Affirmation

Most of the PWAs we interviewed had come to gradually affirm and embrace an AIDS-related identity. Participation in a support group exposed them to alternative definitions of the reality of AIDS and an ongoing system of identity construction. Hence, rather than accepting public imputations which cast them as "AIDS victims," PWAs learned to distance themselves from such designations and to avow more favorable AIDS-associated identities. In turn, the process of *identity embracement* was realized when individuals proudly announced that they were PWAs who were "living and thriving with the illness."

Continued associations with other PWAs could also promote deepening involvement in activities organized around the identity of being a person with AIDS. A case in point is provided by a man who recounted his progression as a PWA:

> After awhile, I aligned myself with other people with AIDS who shared my beliefs about taking the active role. I began writing and speaking about AIDS and I became involved in various projects. I helped to create and promote a workshop for people with AIDS.... I also got involved in organizing a support group for family members of PWAs.

As involvement in AIDS-related activities increases, embracement of an AIDS-centered identity is likely to become more encompassing. In some cases, diagnosed individuals found themselves organizing workshops on AIDS, coordinating a newsletter for PWAs, and delivering speeches regularly at schools and churches. Virtually all aspects of their lives became associated with their diagnosis. Being a PWA thus became both a master status and a valued career. This process was described by a person who had been diagnosed with ARC for two years:

> One interesting thing is that when you have AIDS or ARC and you're not working anymore, you tend to become a veteran professional on AIDS issues. You get calls regularly from people who want information or who want you to get involved in a project, etc. You find yourself getting drawn to that kind of involvement. It becomes almost a second career!

This kind of identity embracement was particularly appealing for a few individuals involved in this study. Prior to contracting an AIDS-related infection, they had felt rejected or unrecognized in many of their social relationships (e.g., family, work, and friendships). Ironically, their stigmatized AIDS diagnosis provided them with an opportunity for social affirmation. It offered them a sense of uniqueness and expertise that was positively evaluated in certain social and community circles (e.g., public education and church forums). It could even serve as a springboard for a new and more meaningful biography.

Ideological Embracement: AIDS as a Transforming Experience

Support groups and related self-help networks are frequently bases for the production and transmission of subcultural perspectives which controvert mainstream social definitions of a stigma. As Becker (1963) argued, when people who share a deviant attribute have the opportunity to interact with one another, they are likely to develop a system of shared meanings emphasizing the differences between their definitions of who they are and the definitions held by other members of the society. "They develop perspectives on themselves and their deviant [attributes] and on their relations with other members of the society" (p. 81). These perspectives guide the stigmatized as they engage in processes of identity construction and embracement.

Subcultural perspectives contain ideologies which assure individuals that what they do on a continuing basis has moral validity (Lofland 1969). Among PWAs, these ideologies were grounded in metaphors of transformation which included an emphasis on *special mission* and *empowerment*.

One of the most prominent subcultural interpretations of AIDS highlighted the spiritual meaning of the illness. For PWAs embracing this viewpoint, AIDS was symbolically and experientially inverted from a "curse" to a "blessing" which promoted a liberating rather than a constricting form of identity transformation. The following remarks illustrate this perspective:

I now view AIDS as both a gift and a blessing. That sounds strange, I suppose, in a limited context. It sounds strange because we [most people] think it's so awful, but yet there are such radical changes that take place in your life from having this illness that's defined as terminal. You go through this amazing kind of *transformation.* You look at things for the first time, in a powerful new way that you've never looked at them before in your whole life.

A number of PWAs similarly stressed the beneficial personal and spiritual transitions experienced as a result of their diagnosis. They even regarded their illness as a motivating force that led them to grapple with important existential questions and to experience personal growth and change that otherwise would not have occurred.

For many PWAs, *ideological embracement* (Snow and Anderson 1987) entailed identity constructions based on a quasi-religious sense of "special mission." These individuals placed a premium on disseminating information about AIDS and promoting a level of public awareness which might inhibit the further transmission of this illness. Some felt that their diagnosis had provided them with a unique opportunity to help and educate others. They subsequently displayed a high level of personal sacrifice and commitment while seeking to spread the news about AIDS and to nurture those directly affected by this illness. Most crucially, their diagnosis provided them with a heightened sense of power and purpose:

Basically I feel that as a person with ARC I can do more for humanity in general than I could ever do before. I never before in my life felt like I belonged here. For the most part, I felt like I was stranded on a hostile planet—I didn't know why. But now with the disease and what I've learned in my life, I feel like I really have something by which I can help other people. It gives me a special sense of purpose.

I feel like I've got a mission now and that's what this whole thing is about. AIDS is challenging me with a question and the question it asks is: If I'm not doing something to help others regarding this illness, then why continue to use up energy here on this earth?

The idea of a "special mission" is often a revitalizing formulation for those who carry a death taint (Lifton 1967). It helps to provide PWAs with a sense of mastery and self-worth by giving their condition a more positive or redemptive meaning. This notion also gives form and resolution to painful feelings of loss, grief, guilt, and death anxiety. It enables individuals to make use of these emotions, while at the same time transcending them. Moreover, the idea of special mission provides PWAs with a framework through which they can moralize their activities and continuing lives.

Beliefs stressing the empowering aspects of AIDS also served as an important focus of identity affirmation. These beliefs were frequently rooted in the sense of transformation provoked by the illness. Many of those interviewed viewed their diagnosis as empowering because it led them to have a concentrated experience of life, a stronger sense of purpose, a better understanding of their personal resources and a clearer notion of how to prioritize their daily concerns. They correspondingly felt less constrained by mundane aspects of the AIDS experience and related symptoms.

A sense of empowerment could additionally be derived from others' objectification of PWAs as sources of danger, pollution, or death. This was illustrated in the remarks of an informant who had Kaposi's sarcoma:

> People hand power to me on a silver platter because they are afraid. It's not fear of catching the virus or anything, I think it is just fear of identification with someone who is dying.

The interactional implications of such attributions of power were also recognized by this same informant:

> Because I have AIDS, people leave me alone in my life in some respects if I want them to. I never used to be able to get people to back off and now I can. I'm not the one who is doing this, so to speak. They are giving me the power to do so.

Most PWAs realized their condition offered them an opportunity to experience both psychological and social power. They subsequently accentuated the empowering dimensions of their lived experience of AIDS and linked these to an encompassing metaphor of transformation.

SUMMARY AND CONCLUSIONS

People with AIDS face many obstacles in their efforts to construct and sustain a desirable social identity. In the early stages of their career, after receiving a validating diagnosis, they are confronted by painful self-feelings such as grief, guilt, and death anxiety. These feelings often diminish their desire and ability to participate in interactions which would allow them to sustain favorable images of self.

PWAs encounter additional difficulties as a result of being situated (at least initially) as liminal persons. That is, their liminal situation can heighten negative self-feelings and evoke a sense of confusion and uncertainty about the social implications of their illness. At the same time, however, it releases them from conventional roles, meanings, or expectations and provides them with a measure of power and maneuverability in the processes of identity construction.

In turn, as they construct and negotiate the meaning of an AIDS-related identity, PWAs must grapple with the effects of social reactions such as stigmatization, counterfeit nurturance, fears of contagion, and death anxiety. These reactions both elicit and reinforce a number of interactional ambiguities, dilemmas, and threats to self.

In responding to these challenges, PWAs engage in various types of identity management and construction. On one hand, they may seek to disguise their diagnoses or to restrict their social and interactional involvements. PWAs are most likely to use such strategies in the earlier phases of the illness. The disadvantage of these strategies is that they are primarily defensive. They provide PWAs with a way to avoid or adjust to the effects of problematic social reactions, but they do not offer a means for affirming more desirable AIDS-related identities.

On the other hand, as their illness progresses and they become more enmeshed in subcultural networks, most PWAs are prompted to engage in forms of identity embracement which enable them to actively reconstruct the meaning of their illness and to integrate it with valued conceptions of self. In essence, through their interactions with other PWAs, they learn to embrace affiliations and ideologies which accentuate the transformative and empowering possibilities arising from their condition. They also acquire the social and symbolic resources necessary to fashion revitalizing identities and to sustain a sense of dignity and self-worth.

Ultimately, through their ongoing participation in support networks, PWAs are able to build identities which are linked to their lived experience of AIDS. They are also encouraged to actively confront and transform the stigmatizing conceptions associated with this medical condition. Hence, rather than resigning themselves to the darker implications of AIDS, they learn to affirm themselves as "people with AIDS" who are "living and thriving with the illness."

References

Baumgartner, G. 1986. *AIDS: Psychosocial factors in the acquired immune deficiency syndrome.* Springfield, IL: Charles C. Thomas.

Becker, H. S. 1963. *Outsiders.* New York: Free Press.

Charmaz, K. 1980. The social construction of pity in the chronically ill. *Studies in Symbolic Interaction* 3:123–45.

Conrad, P. 1986. The social meaning of AIDS. *Social Policy* 17:51–56.

Davis, F. 1974. Deviance disavowal and the visibly handicapped. In *Deviance and liberty,* edited by L. Rainwater, 163–72. Chicago: Aldine.

Denzin, N. 1983. A note on emotionality, self and interaction. *American Journal of Sociology* 89:402–9.

Ergas, Y. 1987. The social consequences of the AIDS epidemic. *Social Science Research Council/Items* 41:33–39.

Geiss, S., R. Fuller, and J. Rush. 1986. Lovers of AIDS victims: Psychosocial stresses and counseling needs. *Death Studies* 10:43–53.

Goffman, E. 1963. *Stigma.* Englewood Cliffs, NJ: Prentice Hall.

———. 1971. *Relations in public.* New York: Harper & Row.

Glaser, B. S., and A. L Strauss. 1968. *Awareness of dying.* Chicago: Aldine.

Hughes, E. C. 1945. Dilemmas and contradictions of status. *American Journal of Sociology* 50:353–59.

Kaplan, H., R. Johnson, C. Bailey, and W. Simon. 1987. The sociological study of AIDS: A critical review of the literature and suggested research agenda. *Journal of Health and Social Behavior* 28:140–57.

Kotarba, J. 1984. A synthesis: The existential self in society. In *The existential self in society,* edited by J. Kotarba and A. Fontana, 222–33. Chicago: Aldine.

Kowalewski, M. 1988. Double stigma and boundary maintenance: How gay men deal with AIDS. *Journal of Contemporary Ethnography* 7:211–28.

Lifton, R. J. 1967. *Death in life.* New York: Random House.

Lofland, J. 1969. *Deviance and identity.* Englewood Cliffs, NJ: Prentice Hall.

Macklin, E. 1988. AIDS: Implications for families. *Family Relations* 37:141–49.

Nichols, S. 1985. Psychosocial reactions of persons with AIDS. *Annals of Internal Medicine* 103:13–16.

Palmer, S. 1989. AIDS as metaphor. *Society* 26:45–51.

Salisbury, D. 1986. AIDS: Psychosocial implications. *Journal of Psychosocial Nursing* 24 (12): 13–16.

Snow, D., and L. Anderson. 1987. Identity work among the homeless: The verbal construction and avowal of personal identities. *American Journal of Sociology* 1336–71.

Sontag, S. 1989. *AIDS and its metaphors.* New York: Farrar, Straus & Giroux.

Weitz, R. 1989. Uncertainty and the lives of persons with AIDS. *Journal of Health and Social Behavior* 30:270–81.

36 / Fraternities and Rape on Campus

PATRICIA YANCEY MARTIN
ROBERT A. HUMMER

Rapes are perpetrated on dates, at parties, in chance encounters, and in specially planned circumstances. That group structure and processes, rather than individual values or characteristics, are the impetus for many rape episodes was documented by Blanchard (1959) 30 years ago (also see Geis 1971), yet sociologists have failed to pursue this theme (for an exception, see Chancer 1987). A recent review of research (Muehlenhard and Linton 1987) on sexual violence, or rape, devotes only a few pages to the situational contexts of rape events, and these are conceptualized as potential risk factors for individuals rather than qualities of rape-prone social contexts.

Many rapes, far more than come to the public's attention, occur in fraternity houses on college and university campuses, yet little research has analyzed fraternities at American colleges and universities as rape-prone contexts (cf. Ehrhart and Sandler 1985). Most of the research on fraternities reports on samples of individual fraternity men. One group of studies compares the values, attitudes, perceptions, family socioeconomic status, psychological traits (aggressiveness, dependence), and so on, of fraternity and nonfraternity men (Bohrnstedt 1969; Fox, Hodge, and Ward 1987; Kanin 1967; Lemire 1979; Miller 1973). A second group attempts to identify the effects of fraternity membership over time on the values, attitudes, beliefs, or moral precepts of members (Hughes and Winston 1987; Marlowe and Auvenshine 1982; Miller 1973; Wilder, Hoyt, Doren, Hauck, and Zettle 1978; Wilder, Hoyt, Surbeck, Wilder, and Carney 1986). With minor exceptions, little research addresses the group and organizational context of fraternities or the social construction of fraternity life (for exceptions, see Letchworth 1969; Longino and Kart 1973; Smith 1964).

Gary Tash, writing as an alumnus and trial attorney in his fraternity's magazine, claims that over 90 percent of all gang rapes on college campuses involve fraternity men (1988, p. 2). Tash provides no evidence to substantiate this claim, but students of violence against women have been concerned with fraternity men's frequently reported involvement in rape episodes (Adams and Abarbanel 1988). Ehrhart and Sandler (1985) identify over 50 cases of gang rapes on campus perpetrated by fraternity men, and their analysis points to many of the conditions that we discuss here. Their analysis is unique in focusing on conditions in fraternities that make gang

523

rapes of women by fraternity men both feasible and probable. They identify excessive alcohol use, isolation from external monitoring, treatment of women as prey, use of pornography, approval of violence, and excessive concern with competition as precipitating conditions to gang rape (also see Merton 1985; Roark 1987).

The study reported here confirmed and complemented these findings by focusing on both conditions and processes. We examined dynamics associated with the social construction of fraternity life, with a focus on processes that foster the use of coercion, including rape, in fraternity men's relations with women. Our examination of men's social fraternities on college and university campuses as groups and organizations led us to conclude that fraternities are a physical and sociocultural context that encourages the sexual coercion of women. We make no claims that all fraternities are "bad" or that all fraternity men are rapists. Our observations indicated, however, that rape is especially probable in fraternities because of the kinds of organizations they are, the kinds of members they have, the practices their members engage in, and a virtual absence of university or community oversight. Analyses that lay blame for rapes by fraternity men on "peer pressure" are, we feel, overly simplistic (cf. Burkhart 1989; Walsh 1989). We suggest, rather, that fraternities create a sociocultural context in which the use of coercion in sexual relations with women is normative and in which the mechanisms to keep this pattern of behavior in check are minimal at best and absent at worst. We conclude that unless fraternities change in fundamental ways, little improvement can be expected.

METHODOLOGY

Our goal was to analyze the group and organizational practices and conditions that create in fraternities an abusive social context for women. We developed a conceptual framework from an initial case study of an alleged gang rape at Florida State University that involved four fraternity men and an 18-year-old coed. The group rape took place on the third floor of a fraternity house and ended with the "dumping" of the woman in the hallway of a neighboring fraternity house. According to newspaper accounts, the victim's blood-alcohol concentration, when she was discovered, was .349 percent, more than three times the legal limit for automobile driving and an almost lethal amount. One law enforcement officer reported that sexual intercourse occurred during the time the victim was unconscious: "She was in a life-threatening situation" (*Tallahassee Democrat,* 1988b). When the victim was found, she was comatose and had suffered multiple scratches and abrasions. Crude words and a fraternity symbol had been written on her thighs (*Tampa Tribune,* 1988). When law enforcement officials tried to investigate the case, fraternity members refused to cooperate. This led, eventually, to a five-year ban of the fraternity from campus by the university and by the fraternity's national organization.

In trying to understand how such an event could have occurred, and how a group of over 150 members (exact figures are unknown because the fraternity refused to provide a membership roster) could hold rank, deny knowledge of the event, and allegedly lie to a grand jury, we analyzed newspaper articles about the case and conducted open-ended interviews with a variety of respondents about the case and about fraternities, rapes, alcohol use, gender relations, and sexual activities on campus. Our data included over 100 newspaper articles on the initial gang rape case; open-ended interviews with Greek (social fraternity and sorority) and non-Greek (independent) students (N = 20); university administrators (N = 8, five men, three women); and alumni advisers to Greek organizations (N = 6). Open-ended interviews were held also with judges, public and private defense attorneys, victim advocates, and state prosecutors regarding the processing of sexual assault cases. Data were analyzed using the grounded theory method (Glaser 1978; Martin and Turner 1986). In the following analysis, concepts generated from the data analysis are integrated with the literature on men's social fraternities, sexual coercion, and related issues.

FRATERNITIES AND THE SOCIAL CONSTRUCTION OF MEN AND MASCULINITY

Our research indicated that fraternities are vitally concerned—more than with anything else—with masculinity (cf. Kanin 1967). They work hard to create a macho image and context and try to avoid any suggestion of "wimpishness," effeminacy, and homosexuality. Valued members display, or are willing to go along with, a narrow conception of masculinity that stresses competition, athleticism, dominance, winning, conflict, wealth, material possessions, willingness to drink alcohol, and sexual prowess vis-à-vis women.

Valued Qualities of Members

When fraternity members talked about the kind of pledges they prefer, a litany of stereotypical and narrowly masculine attributes and behaviors was recited and feminine or woman-associated qualities and behaviors were expressly denounced (cf. Merton 1985). Fraternities seek men who are "athletic," "big guys," good in intramural competition, "who can talk college sports." Males "who are willing to drink alcohol," "who drink socially," or "who can hold their liquor" are sought. Alcohol and activities associated with the recreational use of alcohol are cornerstones of fraternity social life. Nondrinkers are viewed with skepticism and rarely selected for membership.[1]

Fraternities try to avoid "geeks," nerds, and men said to give the fraternity a "wimpy" or "gay" reputation. Art, music, and humanities majors, majors in traditional women's fields (nursing, home economics, social work, education), men with long hair, and those whose appearance or dress violate current norms are rejected. Clean-cut, handsome men who dress well (are clean, neat, conforming, fashionable) are preferred. One sorority woman commented that "the top ranking fraternities have the best looking guys."

One fraternity man, a senior, said his fraternity recruited "some big guys, very athletic" over a two-year period to help overcome its image of wimpiness. His fraternity had won the interfraternity competition for highest grade-point average several years running but was looked down on as "wimpy, dancy, even gay." With their bigger, more athletic recruits, "our reputation improved; we're a much more recognized fraternity now." Thus a fraternity's reputation and status depends on members' possession of stereotypically masculine qualities. Good grades, campus leadership, and community service are "nice" but masculinity dominance—for example, in athletic events, physical size of members, athleticism of members—counts most.

Certain social skills are valued. Men are sought who "have good personalities," are friendly, and "have the ability to relate to girls" (cf. Longino and Kart 1973). One fraternity man, a junior, said: "We watch a guy [a potential pledge] talk to women...we want guys who can relate to girls." Assessing a pledge's ability to talk to women is, in part, a preoccupation with homosexuality and a conscious avoidance of men who seem to have effeminate manners or qualities. If a member is suspected of being gay, he is ostracized and informally drummed out of the fraternity. A fraternity with a reputation as wimpy or tolerant of gays is ridiculed and shunned by other fraternities. Militant heterosexuality is frequently used by men as a strategy to keep each other in line (Kimmel 1987).

Financial affluence or wealth, a male-associated value in American culture, is highly valued by fraternities. In accounting for why the fraternity involved in the gang rape that precipitated our research project had been recognized recently as "the best fraternity chapter in the United States," a university official said: "They were good-looking, a big fraternity, had lots of BMWs [expensive, German-made automobiles]." After the rape, newspaper stories described the fraternity members' affluence, noting the high number of members who owned expensive cars (*St. Petersburg Times*, 1988).

The Status and Norms of Pledgeship

A pledge (sometimes called an associate member) is a new recruit who occupies a trial membership status for a specific period of time. The pledge period (typically ranging from 10 to 15 weeks) gives fraternity brothers an opportunity to assess and socialize new recruits. Pledges evaluate the fraternity also and decide if they want to become brothers. The socialization experience is structured partly through assignment of a Big Brother to each pledge. Big Brothers are expected to teach pledges how to become a brother and to support them as they progress through the trial membership period.

Some pledges are repelled by the pledging experience, which can entail physical abuse; harsh discipline; and demands to be subordinate, follow orders, and engage in demeaning routines and activities, similar to those used by the military to "make men out of boys" during boot camp.

Characteristics of the pledge experience are rationalized by fraternity members as necessary to help pledges unite into a group, rely on each other, and join together against outsiders. The process is highly masculinist in execution as well as conception. A willingness to submit to authority, follow orders, and do as one is told is viewed as a sign of loyalty, togetherness, and unity. Fraternity pledges who find the pledge process offensive often drop out. Some do this by openly quitting, which can subject them to ridicule by brothers and other pledges, or they may deliberately fail to make the grades necessary for initiation or transfer schools and decline to reaffiliate with the fraternity on the new campus. One fraternity pledge who quit the fraternity he had pledged described an experience during pledgeship as follows:

> This one guy was always picking on me. No matter what I did, I was wrong. One night after dinner, he and two other guys called me and two other pledges into the chapter room. He said, "Here, X, hold this 25 pound bag of ice at arms' length 'til I tell you to stop." I did it even though my arms and hands were killing me. When I asked if I could stop, he grabbed me around the throat and lifted me off the floor. I thought he would choke me to death. He cussed me and called me all kinds of names. He took one of my fingers and twisted it until it nearly broke.... I stayed in the fraternity for a few more days, but then I decided to quit. I hated it. Those guys are sick. They like seeing you suffer.

Fraternities' emphasis on toughness, withstanding pain and humiliation, obedience to superiors, and using physical force to obtain compliance contributes to an interpersonal style that de-emphasizes caring and sensitivity but fosters intragroup trust and loyalty. If the least macho or most critical pledges drop out, those who remain may be more receptive to, and influenced by, masculinist values and practices that encourage the use of force in sexual relations with women and the covering up of such behavior (cf. Kanin 1967).

Norms and Dynamics of Brotherhood

Brother is the status occupied by fraternity men to indicate their relations to each other and their membership in a particular fraternity organization or group. Brother is a male-specific status; only males can become brothers, although women can become "Little Sisters," a form of pseudomembership. "Becoming a brother" is a rite of passage that follows the consistent and often lengthy display by pledges of appropriately masculine qualities and behaviors. Brothers have a quasi-familial relationship with each other, are normatively said to share bonds of closeness and support, and are sharply set off from nonmembers. Brotherhood is a loosely defined term used to represent the bonds that develop among fraternity members and the obligations and expectations incumbent upon them (cf. Marlowe and

Auvenshine [1982] on fraternities' failure to encourage "moral development" in freshman pledges).

Some of our respondents talked about brotherhood in almost reverential terms, viewing it as the most valuable benefit of fraternity membership. One senior, a business-school major who had been affiliated with a fairly high-status fraternity throughout four years on campus, said:

> Brotherhood spurs friendship for life, which I consider its best aspect, although I didn't see it that way when I joined. Brotherhood bonds and unites. It instills values of caring about one another, caring about community, caring about ourselves. The values and bonds [of brotherhood] continually develop over the four years [in college] while normal friendships come and go.

Despite this idealization, most aspects of fraternity practice and conception are more mundane. Brotherhood often plays itself out as an overriding concern with masculinity and, by extension, femininity. As a consequence, fraternities comprise collectivities of highly masculinized men with attitudinal qualities and behavioral norms that predispose them to sexual coercion of women (cf. Kanin 1967; Merton 1985; Rapaport and Burkhart 1984). The norms of masculinity are complemented by conceptions of women and femininity that are equally distorted and stereotyped and that may enhance the probability of women's exploitation (cf. Ehrhart and Sandler 1985; Sanday 1981, 1986).

Practices of Brotherhood

Practices associated with fraternity brotherhood that contribute to the sexual coercion of women include a preoccupation with loyalty, group protection and secrecy, use of alcohol as a weapon, involvement in violence and physical force, and an emphasis on competition and superiority.

Loyalty, group protection, and secrecy. Loyalty is a fraternity preoccupation. Members are reminded constantly to be loyal to the fraternity and to their brothers. Among other ways, loyalty is played out in the practices of group protection and secrecy. The fraternity must be shielded from criticism. Members are admonished to avoid getting the fraternity in trouble and to bring all problems "to the chapter" (local branch of a national social fraternity) rather than to outsiders. Fraternities try to protect themselves from close scrutiny and criticism by the Interfraternity Council (a quasi-governing body composed of representatives from all social fraternities on campus), their fraternity's national office, university officials, law enforcement, the media, and the public. Protection of the fraternity often takes precedence over what is procedurally, ethically, or legally correct. Numerous examples were related to us of fraternity brothers' lying to outsiders to "protect the fraternity."

Group protection was observed in the alleged gang rape case with which we began our study. Except for one brother, a rapist who turned state's evidence, the entire remaining fraternity membership was accused by university and criminal justice officials of lying to protect the fraternity. Members consistently failed to cooperate even though the alleged crimes were felonies, involved only four men (two of whom were not even members of the local chapter), and the victim of the crime nearly died. According to a grand jury's findings, fraternity officers repeatedly broke appointments with law enforcement officials, refused to provide police with a list of members, and refused to cooperate with police and prosecutors investigating the case (*Florida Flambeau*, 1988).

Secrecy is a priority value and practice in fraternities, partly because full-fledged membership is premised on it (for confirmation, see Ehrhart and Sandler 1985; Longino and Kart 1973; Roark 1987). Secrecy is also a boundary-maintaining mechanism, demarcating in-group from out-group, us from them. Secret rituals, handshakes, and mottoes are revealed to pledge brothers as they are initiated into full brotherhood. Since only brothers are supposed to know a fraternity's secrets, such knowledge affirms membership in the fraternity and separates a brother from others. Extending secrecy tactics from protection of private knowledge to protection of the fraternity from criticism is a predictable development. Our interviews indicated that individual members knew the difference between right and wrong, but fraternity norms that emphasize loyalty, group protection, and secrecy often overrode standards of ethical correctness.

Alcohol as weapon. Alcohol use by fraternity men is normative. They use it on weekdays to relax after class and on weekends to "get drunk," "get crazy," and "get laid." The use of alcohol to obtain sex from women is pervasive—in other words, it is used as a weapon against sexual reluctance. According to several fraternity men whom we interviewed, alcohol is the major tool used to gain sexual mastery over women (cf. Adams and Abarbanel 1988; Ehrhart and Sandler 1985). One fraternity man, a 21-year-old senior, described alcohol use to gain sex as follows: "There are girls that you know will fuck, then some you have to put some effort into it.... You have to buy them drinks or find out if she's drunk enough...."

A similar strategy is used collectively. A fraternity man said that at parties with Little Sisters: "We provide them with 'hunch punch' and things get wild. We get them drunk and most of the guys end up with one." " 'Hunch punch,' " he said, "is a girls' drink made up of overproof alcohol and powdered Kool-Aid, no water or anything, just ice. It's very strong. Two cups will do a number on a female." He had plans in the next academic term to surreptitiously give hunch punch to women in a "prim and proper" sorority because "having sex with prim and proper sorority girls is definitely a goal." These women are a challenge because they "won't openly consume alcohol and won't get openly drunk as hell." Their sororities have "standards committees" that forbid heavy drinking and easy sex.

In the gang rape case, our sources said that many fraternity men on campus believed the victim had a drinking problem and was thus an "easy make." According to newspaper accounts, she had been drinking alcohol on the evening she was raped; the lead assailant is alleged to have given her a bottle of wine after she arrived at his fraternity house. Portions of the rape occurred in a shower, and the victim was reportedly so drunk that her assailants had difficulty holding her in a standing position (*Tallahassee Democrat*, 1988a). While raping her, her assailants repeatedly told her they were members of another fraternity under the apparent belief that she was too drunk to know the difference. Of course, if she was too drunk to know who they were, she was too drunk to consent to sex (cf. Allgeier 1986; Tash 1988).

One respondent told us that gang rapes are wrong and can get one expelled, but he seemed to see nothing wrong in sexual coercion one-on-one. He seemed unaware that the use of alcohol to obtain sex from a woman is grounds for a claim that a rape occurred (cf. Tash 1988). Few women on campus (who also may not know these grounds) report date rapes, however; so the odds of detection and punishment are slim for fraternity men who use alcohol for "seduction" purposes (cf. Byington and Keeter 1988; Merton 1985).

Violence and physical force.   Fraternity men have a history of violence (Ehrhart and Sandler 1985; Roark 1987). Their record of hazing, fighting, property destruction, and rape has caused them problems with insurance companies (Bradford 1986; Pressley 1987). Two university officials told us that fraternities "are the third riskiest property to insure behind toxic waste dumps and amusement parks." Fraternities are increasingly defendants in legal actions brought by pledges subjected to hazing (Meyer 1986; Pressley 1987) and by women who were raped by one or more members. In a recent alleged gang rape incident at another Florida university, prosecutors failed to file charges but the victim filed a civil suit against the fraternity nevertheless (*Tallahassee Democrat*, 1989).

Competition and superiority.   Interfraternity rivalry fosters in-group identification and out-group hostility. Fraternities stress pride of membership and superiority over other fraternities as major goals. Interfraternity rivalries take many forms, including competition for desirable pledges, size of pledge class, size of membership, size and appearance of fraternity house, superiority in intramural sports, highest grade-point averages, giving the best parties, gaining the best or most campus leadership roles, and, of great importance, attracting and displaying "good looking women." Rivalry is particularly intense over members, intramural sports, and women (cf. Messner 1989).

Fraternities' Commodification of Women

In claiming that women are treated by fraternities as commodities, we mean that fraternities knowingly, and intentionally, *use* women for their benefit.

Fraternities use women as bait for new members, as servers of brothers' needs, and as sexual prey.

Women as bait. Fashionably attractive women help a fraternity attract new members. As one fraternity man, a junior, said, "They are good bait." Beautiful, sociable women are believed to impress the right kind of pledges and give the impression that the fraternity can deliver this type of woman to its members. Photographs of shapely, attractive coeds are printed in fraternity brochures and videotapes that are distributed and shown to potential pledges. The women pictured are often dressed in bikinis, at the beach, and are pictured hugging the brothers of the fraternity. One university official says such recruitment materials give the message: "Hey, they're here for you, you can have whatever you want," and, "we have the best looking women. Join us and you can have them too." Another commented: "Something's wrong when males join an all-male organization as the best place to meet women. It's so illogical."

Fraternities compete in promising access to beautiful women. One fraternity man, a senior, commented that "the attraction of girls [i.e., a fraternity's success in attracting women] is a big status symbol for fraternities." One university official commented that the use of women as a recruiting tool is so well entrenched that fraternities that might be willing to forgo it say they cannot afford to unless other fraternities do so as well. One fraternity man said, "Look, if we don't have Little Sisters, the fraternities that do will get all the good pledges." Another said, "We won't have as good a rush [the period during which new members are assessed and selected] if we don't have these women around."

In displaying good-looking, attractive, skimpily dressed, nubile women to potential members, fraternities implicitly, and sometimes explicitly, promise sexual access to women. One fraternity man commented that "part of what being in a fraternity is all about is the sex" and explained how his fraternity uses Little Sisters to recruit new members:

> We'll tell the sweetheart [the fraternity's term for Little Sister], "You're gorgeous; you can get him." We'll tell her to fake a scam and she'll go hang all over him during a rush party, kiss him, and he thinks he's done wonderful and wants to join. The girls think it's great too. It's flattering for them.

Women as servers. The use of women as servers is exemplified in the Little Sister program. Little Sisters are undergraduate women who are rushed and selected in a manner parallel to the recruitment of fraternity men. They are affiliated with the fraternity in a formal but unofficial way and are able, indeed required, to wear the fraternity's Greek letters. Little Sisters are not full-fledged fraternity members, however; and fraternity national offices and most universities do not register or regulate them. Each fraternity has an officer called Little Sister Chairman who oversees their organization and activities. The Little Sisters elect officers among themselves, pay monthly dues to the fraternity, and have well-defined roles. Their dues are used to pay for the fraternity's social events, and Little Sisters are expected to attend and hostess fraternity parties and hang around the house to make it a "nice place to be." One fraternity man, a senior, described Little Sisters this way: "They are very social girls, willing to join in, be affiliated with the group, devoted to the fraternity." Another member, a sophomore, said: "Their sole purpose is social—attend parties, attract new members, and 'take care' of the guys."

Our observations and interviews suggested that women selected by fraternities as Little Sisters are physically attractive, possess good social skills, and are willing to devote time and energy to the fraternity and its members. One undergraduate woman gave the following job description for Little Sisters to a campus newspaper:

> It's not just making appearances at all the parties but entails many more responsibilities. You're going to be expected to go to all the intramural games to cheer the brothers on, support and encourage the pledges, and just be around to bring some extra life to the house. [As a Little Sister] you have to agree to take on a new responsibility other than studying to maintain your grades and managing to keep your checkbook from bouncing. You have to make time to be a part of the fraternity and support the brothers in all they do. (*The Tomahawk*, 1988)

The title of Little Sister reflects women's subordinate status; fraternity men in a parallel role are called Big Brothers. Big Brothers assist a sorority primarily with the physical work of sorority rushes, which, compared to fraternity rushes, are more formal, structured, and intensive. Sorority rushes take place in the daytime and fraternity rushes at night so fraternity men are free to help. According to one fraternity member, Little Sister status is a benefit to women because it gives them a social outlet and "the protection of the brothers." The gender-stereotypic conceptions and obligations of these Little Sister and Big Brother statuses indicate that fraternities and sororities promote a gender hierarchy on campus that fosters subordination and dependence in women, thus encouraging sexual exploitation and the belief that it is acceptable.

Women as sexual prey. Little Sisters are a sexual utility. Many Little Sisters do not belong to sororities and lack peer support for refraining from unwanted sexual relations. One fraternity man (whose fraternity has 65 members and 85 Little Sisters) told us they had recruited "wholesale" in the prior year to "get lots of new women." The structural access to women that the Little Sister program provides and the absence of normative supports for refusing fraternity members' sexual advances may make women in this program particularly susceptible to coerced sexual encounters with fraternity men.

Access to women for sexual gratification is a presumed benefit of fraternity membership, promised in recruitment materials and strategies and through brothers' conversations with new recruits. One fraternity man said: "We

always tell the guys that you get sex all the time, there's always new girls....
After I became a Greek, I found out I could be with females at will." A
university official told us that, based on his observations, "no one [i.e.,
fraternity men] on this campus wants to have 'relationships.' They just want
to have fun [i.e., sex]." Fraternity men plan and execute strategies aimed
at obtaining sexual gratification, and this occurs at both individual and
collective levels.

Individual strategies include getting a woman drunk and spending a great
deal of money on her. As for collective strategies, most of our undergraduate
interviewees agreed that fraternity parties often culminate in sex and that
this outcome is planned. One fraternity man said fraternity parties often
involve sex and nudity and can "turn into orgies." Orgies may be planned
in advance, such as the Bowery Ball party held by one fraternity. A former
fraternity member said of this party:

> The entire idea behind this is sex. Both men and women come to the party wearing
> little or nothing. There are pornographic pinups on the walls and usually porno
> movies playing on the TV. The music carries sexual overtones.... They just get
> schnockered [drunk] and, in most cases, they also get laid.

When asked about the women who come to such a party, he said: "Some
Little Sisters just won't go.... The girls who do are looking for a good time,
girls who don't know what it is, things like that."

Other respondents denied that fraternity parties are orgies but said that
sex is always talked about among the brothers and they all know "who
each other is doing it with." One member said that most of the time, guys
have sex with their girlfriends "but with socials, girlfriends aren't allowed to
come and it's their [members'] big chance [to have sex with other women]."
The use of alcohol to help them get women into bed is a routine strategy at
fraternity parties.

CONCLUSIONS

In general, our research indicated that the organization and membership of
fraternities contribute heavily to coercive and often violent sex. Fraternity
houses are occupied by same-sex (all men) and same-age (late teens, early
twenties) peers whose maturity and judgment is often less than ideal. Yet
fraternity houses are private dwellings that are mostly off-limits to, and
away from scrutiny of, university and community representatives, with the
result that fraternity house events seldom come to the attention of outsiders.
Practices associated with the social construction of fraternity brotherhood
emphasize a macho conception of men and masculinity, a narrow, stereotyped conception of women and femininity, and the treatment of women
as commodities. Other practices contributing to coercive sexual relations
and the cover-up of rapes include excessive alcohol use, competitiveness,

and normative support for deviance and secrecy (cf. Bogal-Allbritten and Allbritten 1985; Kanin 1967).

Some fraternity practices exacerbate others. Brotherhood norms require "sticking together" regardless of right or wrong; thus rape episodes are unlikely to be stopped or reported to outsiders, even when witnesses disapprove. The ability to use alcohol without scrutiny by authorities and alcohol's frequent association with violence, including sexual coercion, facilitates rape in fraternity houses. Fraternity norms that emphasize the value of maleness and masculinity over femaleness and femininity and that elevate the status of men and lower the status of women in members' eyes undermine perceptions and treatment of women as persons who deserve consideration and care (cf. Ehrhart and Sandler 1985; Merton 1985).

Androgynous men and men with a broad range of interests and attributes are lost to fraternities through their recruitment practices. Masculinity of a narrow and stereotypical type helps create attitudes, norms, and practices that predispose fraternity men to coerce women sexually, both individually and collectively (Allgeier 1986; Hood 1989; Sanday 1981, 1986). Male athletes on campus may be similarly disposed for the same reasons (Kirshenbaum 1989; Telander and Sullivan 1989).

Research into the social contexts in which rape crimes occur and the social constructions associated with these contexts illumine rape dynamics on campus. Blanchard (1959) found that group rapes almost always have a leader who pushes others into the crime. He also found that the leader's latent homosexuality, desire to show off to his peers, or fear of failing to prove himself a man are frequently an impetus. Fraternity norms and practices contribute to the approval and use of sexual coercion as an accepted tactic in relations with women. Alcohol-induced compliance is normative, whereas, presumably, use of a knife, gun, or threat of bodily harm would not be because the woman who "drinks too much" is viewed as "causing her own rape" (cf. Ehrhart and Sandler 1985).

Our research led us to conclude that fraternity norms and practices influence members to view the sexual coercion of women, which is a felony crime, as sport, a contest, or a game (cf. Sato 1988). This sport is played not between men and women but between men and men. Women are the pawns or prey in the interfraternity rivalry game; they prove that a fraternity is successful or prestigious. The use of women in this way encourages fraternity men to see women as objects and sexual coercion as sport. Today's societal norms support young women's right to engage in sex at their discretion, and coercion is unnecessary in a mutually desired encounter. However, nubile young women say they prefer to be "in a relationship" to have sex while young men say they prefer to "get laid" without a commitment (Muehlenhard and Linton 1987). These differences may reflect, in part, American puritanism and men's fears of sexual intimacy or perhaps intimacy of any kind. In a fraternity context, getting sex without giving emotionally demonstrates "cool" masculinity. More important, it poses no threat to the bonding and loyalty of the fraternity brotherhood (cf. Farr 1988). Drinking large quantities of alcohol before having sex suggests that "scoring" rather than intrinsic sexual pleasure is a primary concern of fraternity men.

Unless fraternities' composition, goals, structures, and practices change in fundamental ways, women on campus will continue to be sexual prey for fraternity men. As all-male enclaves dedicated to opposing faculty and administration and to cementing in-group ties, fraternity members eschew any hint of homosexuality. Their version of masculinity transforms women, and men with womanly characteristics, into the out-group. "Womanly men" are ostracized; feminine women are used to demonstrate members' masculinity. Encouraging renewed emphasis on their founding values (Longino and Kart 1973), service orientation and activities (Lemire 1979), or members' moral development (Marlowe and Auvenshine 1982) will have little effect on fraternities' treatment of women. A case for or against fraternities cannot be made by studying individual members. The fraternity qua group and organization is at issue. Located on campus along with many vulnerable women, embedded in a sexist society, and caught up in masculinist goals, practices, and values, fraternities' violation of women—including forcible rape—should come as no surprise.

Note

1. Recent bans by some universities on open-keg parties at fraternity houses have resulted in heavy drinking before coming to a party and an increase in drunkenness among those who attend. This may aggravate, rather than improve, the treatment of women by fraternity men at parties.

References

Allgeier, Elizabeth. 1986. "Coercive Versus Consensual Sexual Interactions." G. Stanley Hall Lecture to American Psychological Association Annual Meeting, Washington, DC, August.

Adams, Aileen and Gail Abarbanel. 1988. *Sexual Assault on Campus: What Colleges Can Do.* Santa Monica, CA: Rape Treatment Center.

Blanchard, W. H. 1959. "The Group Process in Gang Rape." *Journal of Social Psychology* 49:259–66.

Bogal-Allbritten, Rosemarie B. and William L Allbritten. 1985. "The Hidden Victims: Courtship Violence Among College Students." *Journal of College Student Personnel* 43:201–4.

Bohrnstedt, George W. 1969. "Conservatism, Authoritarianism and Religiosity of Fraternity Pledges." *Journal of College Student Personnel* 27:36–43.

Bradford, Michael. 1986. "Tight Market Dries Up Nightlife at University." *Business Insurance* (March 2): 2, 6.

Burkhart, Barry. 1989. Comments in Seminar on Acquaintance/Date Rape Prevention: A National Video Teleconference, February 2.

Burkhart, Barry R. and Annette L Stanton. 1985. "Sexual Aggression in Acquaintance Relationships." Pp. 43–65 in *Violence in Intimate Relationships,* edited by G. Russell. Englewood Cliffs, NJ: Spectrum.

Byington, Diane B. and Karen W. Keeter. 1988. "Assessing Needs of Sexual Assault Victims on a University Campus." Pp. 23–31 in *Student Services: Responding to Issues and Challenges.* Chapel Hill: University of North Carolina Press.

Chancer, Lynn S. 1987. New Bedford, Massachusetts, March 6, 1983–March 22, 1984: The 'Before and After' of a Group Rape. *Gender & Society* 1:239–60.

Ehrhart, Julie K. and Bernice R. Sandler. 1985. *Campus Gang Rape: Party Games?* Washington, DC: Association of American Colleges.

Farr, K. A. 1988. "Dominance Bonding Through the Good Old Boys Sociability Network." *Sex Roles* 18:259–77.

Florida Flambeau. 1988. "Pike Members Indicted in Rape." (May 19):1, 5.

Fox, Elaine, Charles Hodge, and Walter Ward. 1987. "A Comparison of Attitudes Held by Black and White Fraternity Members." *Journal of Negro Education* 56:521–34.

Geis, Gilbert. 1971. "Group Sexual Assaults." *Medical Aspects of Human Sexuality* 5:101–13.

Glaser, Barney G. 1978. *Theorical Sensitivity: Advances in the Methodology of Grounded Theory.* Mill Valley, CA: Sociology Press.

Hood, Jane. 1989. "Why Our Society Is Rape-Prone." *New York Times,* May 16.

Hughes, Michael J. and Roger B. Winston, Jr. 1987. "Effects of Fraternity Membership on Interpersonal Values." *Journal of College Student Personnel* 45:405–11.

Kanin, Eugene J. 1967. "Reference Groups and Sex Conduct Norm Violations." *The Sociological Quarterly* 8:495–504.

Kimmel, Michael, ed. 1987. *Changing Men: New Directions in Research on Men and Masculinity.* Newbury Park, CA: Sage.

Kirshenbaum, Jerry. 1989. "Special Report, An American Disgrace: A Violent and Unprecedented Lawlessness Has Arisen Among College Athletes in all Parts of the Country." *Sports Illustrated* (February 27): 16–19.

Lemire, David. 1979. "One Investigation of the Stereotypes Associated with Fraternities and Sororities." *Journal of College Student Personnel* 37:54–57.

Letchworth, G. E. 1969. "Fraternities Now and in the Future." *Journal of College Student Personnel* 10:118–22.

Longino, Charles F., Jr., and Cary S. Kart. 1973. "The College Fraternity: An Assessment of Theory and Research." *Journal of College Student Personnel* 31:118–25.

Marlowe, Anne F. and Dwight C. Auvenshine. 1982. "Greek Membership: Its Impact on the Moral Development of College Freshmen." *Journal of College Student Personnel* 40:53–57.

Martin, Patricia Yancey and Barry A. Turner. 1986. "Grounded Theory and Organizational Research." *Journal of Applied Behavioral Science* 22:141–57.

Merton, Andrew. 1985. "On Competition and Class: Return to Brotherhood." *Ms.* (September): 60–65, 121–22.

Messner, Michael. 1989. "Masculinities and Athletic Careers" *Gender & Society* 3:71–88.

Meyer, T. J. 1986. "Fight Against Hazing Rituals Rages on Campuses." *Chronicle of Higher Education* (March 12):34–36.

Miller, Leonard D. 1973. "Distinctive Characteristics of Fraternity Members." *Journal of College Student Personnel* 31:126–28.

Muehlenhard, Charlene L. and Melaney A. Linton. 1987. "Date Rape and Sexual Aggression in Dating Situations: Incidence and Risk Factors." *Journal of Counseling Psychology* 34:186–96.

Pressley, Sue Anne. 1987. "Fraternity Hell Night Still Endures." *Washington Post* (August 11):B1.

Rapaport, Karen and Barry R. Burkhart. 1984. "Personality and Attitudinal Characteristics of Sexually Coercive College Males." *Journal of Abnormal Psychology* 93:216–21.

Roark, Mary L. 1987. "Preventing Violence on College Campuses." *Journal of Counseling and Development* 65:367–70.

Sanday, Peggy Reeves. 1981. "The Socio-Cultural Context of Rape: A Cross-Cultural Study." *Journal of Social Issues* 37:5–27.

———. 1986. "Rape and the Silencing of the Feminine." Pp. 84–101 in *Rape,* edited by S. Tomaselli and R. Porter. Oxford: Basil Blackwell.

St. Petersburg Times. 1988. "A Greek Tragedy." (May 29):1F, 6F.

Sato, Ikuya. 1988. "Play Theory of Delinquency: Toward a General Theory of 'Action.' " *Symbolic Interaction* 11:191–212.

Smith, T. 1964. "Emergence and Maintenance of Fraternal Solidarity." *Pacific Sociological Review* 7:29–37.

Tallahassee Democrat. 1988a. "FSU Fraternity Brothers Charged" (April 27):1A, 12A.

———. 1988b. "FSU Interviewing Students About Alleged Rape" (April 24):1D.

———. 1989. "Woman Sues Stetson in Alleged Rape" (March 19):3B. *Tampa Tribune.* 1988. "Fraternity Brothers Charged in Sexual Assault of FSU Coed." (April 27):6B.

Tash, Gary B. 1988. "Date Rape." *The Emerald of Sigma Pi Fraternity* 75(4):1–2.

Telander, Rick and Robert Sullivan. 1989. "Special Report, You Reap What You Sow." *Sports Illustrated* (February 27):20–34.

The Tomahawk. 1988. "A Look Back at Rush, A Mixture of Hard Work and Fun" (April/May):3D.

Walsh, Claire. 1989. Comments in Seminar on Acquaintance/Date Rape Prevention: A National Video Teleconference, February 2.

Wilder, David H., Arlyne E. Hoyt, Dennis M. Doren, William E. Hauck, and Robert D. Zettle. 1978. "The Impact of Fraternity and Sorority Membership on Values and Attitudes." *Journal of College Student Personnel* 36:445–49.

Wilder, David H., Arlyne E. Hoyt, Beth Shuster Surbeck, Janet C. Wilder, and Patricia Imperatrice Carney. 1986. "Greek Affiliation and Attitude Change in College Students." *Journal of College Student Personnel* 44:510–19.

37 / Corporations, Organized Crime, and the Disposal of Hazardous Waste: An Examination of the Making of a Criminogenic Regulatory Structure

ANDREW SZASZ

The generation of hazardous waste is a necessary side effect of modern industrial production. Factories must cope daily with large accumulations of unrecyclable chemical byproducts generated by normal production techniques. The processing or disposal of these byproducts is a significant cost of production, a cost that, like all other costs of production, the prudent owner or manager minimizes.

Until recently, industrial hazardous waste was not legally distinguished from municipal garbage and other solid wastes. It was disposed of with ordinary garbage, at very low cost to the generator, mostly in coastal waters or in landfills unfit to adequately contain it. However, concern grew during the 1970s that improper disposal of hazardous waste was creating an environmental and public health burden of unknown but potentially massive scale. This concern finally moved some states and eventually the federal government to begin to legislate new regulations. The centerpiece of this regulatory effort was the federal Resource Conservation and Recovery Act (RCRA) of 1976. On paper, RCRA mandated comprehensive mechanisms to guarantee the safe disposal of hazardous waste. It established standards and procedures for classifying substances as hazardous. It authorized the states to register corporate generators of hazardous waste and license hauling and disposal firms. It mandated the creation of a manifest system that would document the movement of hazardous waste "from cradle to grave," from the generator, through the hands of the transporter, to the shipment's final destination at a licensed disposal site.

By legally distinguishing hazardous waste from other wastes and by directing that such wastes be treated differently than municipal solid waste, the new regulations dramatically increased, almost overnight, the

538

demand for hazardous waste hauling and disposal services. Unhappily, recent state and federal investigations have documented both that illegal waste disposal is widespread (U.S. General Accounting Office, 1985; U.S. House of Representatives, 1980) and that organized crime elements traditionally active in garbage hauling and landfilling have entered this burgeoning and potentially profitable new market (Block and Scarpitti, 1985; U.S. House of Representatives, 1980, 1981a). Although the exact extent of organized crime involvement in hazardous waste hauling and disposal is uncertain,[1] the fact of that involvement is beyond question. A situation exists, then, in which corporations, some at the heart of the American economy, discharge their regulatory obligations under RCRA by entering into direct contractual relationships with firms dominated by organized crime. The goal in this paper is to analyze in detail the complex nature of this relationship between corporate generators of hazardous waste and elements of organized crime that are active in industrial waste disposal. This goal will be approached by analyzing the formation and implementation of RCRA legislation.

The subject of this paper speaks to two distinct criminological literatures: works that examine the relationship between legitimate and illicit enterprise and works that examine crimogenic market structures. Recent scholarship has challenged the commonsense distinction between legitimate business and organized crime. Schelling (1967), Smith and Alba (1979), Smith (1980), and Albanese (1982) all argue that the most fundamental aspect of organized crime is that it is a form of entrepreneurial activity and that its ethnic or conspiratorial nature is of secondary importance. Recent scholarship also challenges the equally widely held belief that the relationship between the underworld and legitimate business consists solely of the former exploiting the latter through extortion, racketeering, and so on (Drucker, 1981). At minimum, it is argued that the relationship is one of mutually beneficial interdependence (Martens and Miller-Longfellow, 1982). This is clearly supported by excellent case studies of labor racketeering (Block and Chambliss, 1981), organized crime on the waterfront (Block, 1982), and arson (Brady, 1983). Chambliss (1978: 181–182) argues the even stronger view that organized crime can exist only because the structure of the legitimate economy and its accompanying political organization make its emergence possible and even inevitable. In a similar vein, Smith (1980) and Smith and Alba (1979) challenge the very distinction between business and organized crime and begin to dissolve that distinction in the common dynamic of a market economy. The study of organized crime participation in hazardous waste disposal presents an opportunity to once again examine this relationship between legitimate and illegitimate entrepreneurship.

The story of RCRA may also have links to the concept of crimogenic market processes. Farberman's (1975) and Leonard and Weber's (1977) studies of auto retailing and Denzin's (1977) study of the liquor industry showed that the normal operating logic of an industry may force some sectors of that industry into illegal activity in order to survive, much less thrive, in doing their part of the business. Needleman and Needleman (1979) subsequently expanded the concept by describing a second type of criminogenesis in which the criminal activity is not forced. It is, instead, an unwelcome drain on business, but it is unavoidable because the conditions that make it possible are necessary to the overall functioning of that industry and could not be altered without fundamentally affecting how business is conducted in that industry. Needleman and Needleman discussed securities fraud as an example of what they call a "crime-facilitative," as opposed to a "crime-coercive" market sector. The fact that RCRA not only cannot prevent illegal hazardous waste dumping but has also attracted organized crime participation in illegal hazardous waste activity suggests that the concept of criminogenesis may be fruitfully extended to regulatory processes as well.

In the first sections of this paper, some background is presented on hazardous waste as a social issue and the nature and extent of organized crime involvement in hazardous waste hauling and disposal is summarized. At the core of the paper, the conditions that made this involvement possible are analyzed. It is shown that the most common explanations—lax implementation and enforcement by state and local officials—are incomplete. Analysis of the formation of RCRA legislation shows that corporate generators of hazardous waste were instrumental in securing a regulatory structure that would prove highly attractive to and well suited for organized crime participation. In other words, generators are deeply implicated in the creation of conditions that have their relationship to organized crime possible. This finding is used to critique two explanations of this relationship suggested during Congressional hearings, generator "ignorance" and generator "powerlessness." It is then argued that the relationship has two other important aspects: generators did not consciously desire or intend this outcome, but they nonetheless benefited from it once it occurred. The paper concludes with a discussion of the relevance of the findings to the two areas of criminological research mentioned above.

THE ISSUE BACKGROUND: HAZARDOUS WASTE FACTS

The Environmental Protection Agency (EPA) defines waste products as "hazardous" if they are flammable, explosive, corrosive, or toxic. Major industries central to the modern national economy, such as the petroleum, chemical, electronic, and pharmaceutical industries, generate copious amounts of hazardous waste. Although there is still great uncertainty about the exact effect of industrial hazardous waste on public health (Greenberg and Anderson, 1984: 84–105), improper management may result in explosions, fires, pollution of water resources, and other uncontrolled releases that put surrounding communities at risk and may result in physical harm ranging from skin irritation to increased incidence of cancer, lung disease, birth defects, and other serious illnesses.

How much hazardous waste has accumulated? How much is currently generated? Neither question can be answered confidently at this time. The generation and disposal of hazardous waste was completely unregulated until the late 1970s. In the absence of regulation, there was no systematic data-gathering effort. Consequently, there is great uncertainty about the magnitude and composition of hazardous waste accumulated up to the passage of the RCRA. Estimates have risen regularly as more sites are located and assessed. The EPA's most recent estimate is that there are 25,000 sites nationally that contain some hazardous waste. Of these, about 2,500 are priority sites judged by the EPA to be imminently hazardous to public health. More recent research by the General Accounting Office (GAO) and the Office of Technology Assessment (OTA) suggests that there may be 378,000 total sites nationally, perhaps 10,000 of them requiring priority attention (Shabecoff, 1985).

In theory, at least, the availability of data should have improved greatly following passage of the RCRA. Generators of hazardous waste were now required to create written documentation—the manifest—of the amount and content of every shipment of hazardous waste signed over to outside haulers and disposers. This documentation would be forwarded to state agencies following final disposition of each waste shipment. However, the actual quality of the data produced was compromised by several factors. First, there was little agreement over what substances should be defined as hazardous. Congressional and EPA testimony (U.S. Environmental Protection Agency, 1976, 1979; U.S. House of Representatives, 1975, 1976; U.S. Senate, 1974, 1979) shows that industrial spokesmen argued that too many substances had been unjustifiably included, while environmentalists argued that some materials had been improperly excluded. Second, firms generating less than one metric ton (2,200 lbs.) of hazardous waste per month are exempt from RCRA regulation (U.S. House of Representatives, 1983: 56, 60). There are over four million privately owned industrial sites in the nation. The "small generator" exemption leaves all but a few tens of thousands of these sites out of RCRA's registration and manifest system. Third, some firms that generate significant amounts of hazardous waste have either failed to cooperate with EPA requests for data (Williams and Matheny, 1984: 436–437) or have failed to identify themselves to the EPA as regulable generators (U.S. General Accounting Office, 1985: 14–20). Fourth, even those firms that appear to comply with reporting requirements may not be reporting accurately the types and quantities of hazardous waste they generate (U.S. GAO, 1985: 20–23). Consequently, knowledge of the amount and content of current hazardous waste generation is still imprecise. Estimates, like estimates of historical accumulation, have been rising. In 1974, the EPA was estimating hazardous waste generation at 10 million metric tons per year (U.S. Senate, 1974: 70). In 1980, the EPA estimate had risen to 40 million metric tons. In 1983, new research led the EPA to nearly quadruple its estimate to 150 million metric tons (Block and Scarpitti, 1985: 46), while the OTA was estimating 250 million metric tons per year (U.S. House of Representatives, 1983: 1).[2]

Where does hazardous waste end up? In response to EPA inquiries in 1981, 16% of generating firms reported treating their wastes completely on site and another 22% reported treating part of their wastes on site. The remaining 62% contracted with other parties to handle all of their wastes (Block and Scarpitti, 1985: 48–49). Where do transported wastes actually end up? The exemptions and noncooperation cited above leave an unknown fraction of total hazardous waste movement out of the paperwork of the manifest system (U.S. GAO, 1985: 3–4, 14–24). The manifests that are filed are poorly monitored and vulnerable to undetected falsification (Greenberg and Anderson, 1984: 242; U.S. GAO, 1985: 25–31; U.S. House of Representatives, 1980: 140, 1981b: 124). Consequently, this question also cannot be answered with great certainty. On the basis of admittedly poor and incomplete data, the OTA estimates that no more than 10% to 20% of all hazardous waste is rendered harmless by incineration or by chemical or biological treatment. There are few facilities that can treat wastes in these ways and the price of treatment is much higher than the price of other means of disposal (U.S. House of Representatives, 1983: 2, 5–6). The remaining 80% to 90% is either landfilled or disposed of illegally. Only a small proportion of hazardous waste goes into landfills that have the siting studies, proper containment practices, and continuous monitoring to be fully licensed by the EPA, since there are only about 200 such landfills in the nation (Block and Scarpitti, 1985: 49; U.S. House of Representatives, 1981b: 187). Even these top landfills are only required by the EPA to keep wastes contained for 30 years (U.S. House of Representatives, 1983: 2).[3] Most hazardous waste goes to landfills that have only interim license to operate, landfills that are of much poorer quality and are likely to pollute the surrounding land and water within a few years.

Illegal hazardous waste dumping is even more likely to have adverse short-term environmental and public health consequences. The full extent of illegal hazardous waste disposal is not known. State officials interviewed by the GAO agreed that illegal disposal was occurring, but had no firm information on the scope of this activity (U.S. GAO, 1985: 10). One study done for the EPA surveyed hazardous waste generators in 41 cities and estimated that one in seven generators had illegally disposed some of their wastes during the two years preceding the study (U.S. GAO, 1985: 10). A wide array of illegal disposal practices have been documented. Waste shipments may end up commingled with ordinary garbage. A 20 cubic yard "dumpster" full of dry garbage can be made to absorb up to sixty 55 gallon drums of liquid hazardous waste (U.S. House of Representatives, 1980: 63) and then be deposited in unlicensed municipal landfills never designed to contain hazardous waste. Liquid hazardous waste may be released along a roadway. An 8,000 gallon truck can be emptied in 8 minutes (U.S. House of Representatives, 1980: 101). Shipments may simply be stockpiled at sites awaiting alleged transfer that never happens or at disposal facilities that have no real disposal capability (U.S. House of Representatives, 1980: 10). Wastes may be drained into local city sewer systems, rivers, and oceans, or dumped in out-of-the-way rural spots (U.S. House of Representatives, 1980: 93). Flammable hazardous waste may be commingled with fuel oil and sold as pure heating oil (U.S. House of Representatives, 1980: 63–64) or sprayed on unsuspecting communities' roads for dust control (U.S. House of Representatives, 1980: 151).

ORGANIZED CRIME PARTICIPATION IN THE HAZARDOUS WASTE DISPOSAL INDUSTRY

Congressman Albert Gore: "At what point did companies picking up garbage begin to get into the toxic waste disposal business?"

Harold Kaufman: "To my knowledge, it's when the manifest system came out is when they found out the profit motive" (U.S. House of Representatives, 1980: 8).

New Jersey Attorney General John J. Degnan pointed out to a Congressional audience that organized crime activity accounts for only a fraction of the illegal dumping taking place in the United States (U.S. House of Representatives, 1980: 87). Nonetheless, organized crime was ideally suited to develop the methodology of illegal hazardous waste practices to the fullest. In those parts of the nation where garbage hauling and landfilling was historically controlled by organized crime, their movement into the newly created hazardous waste market was an obvious extension of current activity. In New Jersey, for example, organized crime had controlled the garbage industry through ownership of garbage hauling firms, through ownership of or control of landfills, and through labor racketeering (U.S. House of Representatives, 1981: 1–45). The new regulations governing hazardous waste would have had to have been carefully written and tenaciously enforced were organized crime to be kept from applying this highly developed infrastructure to the new market. In fact, as will be shown below, the opposite happened and organized crime easily entered both the hauling and the disposal phases of the hazardous waste handling industry.

Hauling. Organized crime had dominated traditional garbage hauling in states like New York and New Jersey for decades. Once associates of organized crime owned a number of hauling firms in any geographical area, they established an organizational infrastructure that governed their relationships and ensured high profits. Threats and violence persuaded other firms to join that infrastructure and abide by its rules or to sell and get out. The keystone of this infrastructure was the concept of "property rights" or "respect." Municipal solid waste hauling contracts were illegally apportioned among haulers. Having a property right meant that a hauler held rights to continue picking up the contract at sites he currently serviced without competition from others. Other firms would submit artificially high bids or would not bid at all when a contract came up for renewal, thereby assuring that the contractor kept his traditional site. This system of *de facto* territorial monopolies permitted noncompetitive pricing and made the lowly business of garbage hauling a very lucrative activity. Property rights were recognized and enforced by organized crime authorities. Conflicts were adjudicated in meetings of the Municipal Contractors Association. Decisions of the MCA were enforced by threats and, if necessary, violence (U.S. House of Representatives, 1981a: 1–42).[4] As is shown below, when the RCRA mandated the licensing of firms deemed fit to transport hazardous waste, mob-connected garbage haulers found it easy to acquire state permits and declare themselves to be hazardous waste haulers. Quite naturally, they brought their traditional forms of social organization with them. Individual haulers holding established property rights assumed that they would transfer those property rights to a new type of waste (U.S. House of Representatives, 1980: 22). They also met as a group to set up a Trade Waste Association modeled after the Municipal Contractors Association to apportion and enforce property rights in the new market (U.S. House of Representatives, 1980: 9–10, 1981a: 1–12, 212).

Disposal. The manifest system requires that someone will be willing to sign off on the manifest and declare that a waste shipment has been properly disposed of. This means, as Congressman Florio (Democrat, New Jersey) pointed out (U.S. House of Representatives, 1980: 30), that mob control over hauling is not enough: organized crime figures had to have ownership of, or at least influence over, final disposal sites. This requirement did not prove to be a serious stumbling block, however. Many landfills were already owned wholly or in part by organized crime figures, a legacy of past mob involvement in the garbage business. These sites readily accepted dubious shipments of hazardous waste thinly disguised as ordinary municipal waste (U.S. House of Representatives 1981a: 228, 1981b). Landfill owners not directly associated with organized crime could be bribed to sign manifests for shipments never received or to accept hazardous waste that was manifested elsewhere (U.S. House of Representatives, 1980: 70, 90). In addition, known organized crime figures started or seized control of a network of phony disposal and "treatment" facilities such as Chemical Control Corporation, Elizabeth, New Jersey; Modern Transportation, Kearny, New Jersey; and Duane Marine, Perth Amboy, New Jersey.[5] Licensed by the state, these outfits could legally receive hazardous waste and sign off on the manifest. They would then either stockpile it on site (where it would stay until it exploded, burned, or otherwise came to the attention of authorities) or dump it along roadways, down municipal sewers, into the ocean, or elsewhere (Block and Scarpitti, 1985: 145, 158, 298; U.S. House of Representatives, 1980: 25). In the extreme, actual ownership of or access to disposal sites was unnecessary for those willing to file totally fanciful manifests. Congressman

Gore cited one case in which several major corporations signed over their wastes to an out-of-state facility that subsequently was shown to simply not exist (U.S. House of Representatives, 1980: 70, 135).[6]

ENABLING CAUSES: THE MAKING OF A VULNERABLE REGULATORY STRUCTURE

In retrospect, it is hardly surprising that, given the opportunity, organized crime would enter the newly created market for hazardous waste handling. It was an extension of their current business activity. They had the equipment and organization. They had both the know-how and the will to corrupt the manifest system. It was an attractive prospect. Both the potential size of the market and the potential profits were enormous. Even if they charged only a fraction of the true price of legitimate disposal, that price would be much higher than the price they charged to move the same stuff when it was legally just garbage, but their operating expenses would stay the same (if they commingled hazardous waste with ordinary garbage) or decrease (if they simply dumped). Why organized crime would want to enter into relationship with corporate generators when the opportunity presented itself needs no subtle unraveling. The more complex task is to determine what political and social-structural conditions made it possible for them to "colonize" the hazardous waste disposal industry.

Lax Implementation, Incompetent and/or Corrupt Enforcement

Explanations of organized crime presence in hazardous waste handling focused on lax implementation and improper enforcement. Congressional hearings produced dramatic evidence that, at least in New Jersey, the state where organized crime intrusion into hazardous waste is most thoroughly documented, the major provisions of the RCRA were poorly implemented and enforced. Interim hauling and disposal licenses were freely granted. The manifest system was not sufficiently monitored.

Interim Licensing. Congress had mandated an extended transition period during which both transporters and disposal firms would operate under temporary permits until an adequate national hazardous waste industry developed. Generators lobbied quite heavily on this point (U.S. EPA, 1976: 238, 1979: 153, 307; Gansberg, 1979) and Congress had to agree to this provision because the shortage of adequate hazardous waste facilities was so severe. American industry would have choked in its own accumulating wastes had it not been permitted to continue to use less-than-adequate means of disposal. A reasonable concession to economic realities, implementation of interim licensing was poorly managed. House of Representatives testimony shows that New Jersey issued hauling permits to any applicant who paid a nominal $50 fee (U.S. House of Representatives, 1980: 14–15). Existing landfills and even totally bogus firms with no real disposal facilities found it equally easy to get interim disposal permits (U.S. House of Representatives, 1980: 10).

Harold Kaufman (key FBI informant on mob involvement in hazardous waste disposal, testifying about his old firm, Duane Marine): The State licensed us. We were the first ones licensed....

Gore: And this was a chemical waste disposal facility, is that right?

Kaufman: Well, that is what it was called. It never disposed of anything, but you can call it that.

Manifest Oversight. Once a license was obtained, lax supervision of the manifest system made illegal and unsafe disposal of hazardous waste a relatively straightforward, low-risk activity (U.S. House of Representatives, 1980: 140).

Gore: What enforcement efforts are you making to prevent the abuse of the manifest system?

Edwin Stier (New Jersey Division of Criminal Justice): The only way the manifest system is going to be properly, effectively enforced is through the proper analysis of the information that comes from the manifest.... Anyone who assumes that a manifest system which looks good on paper can control the flow and disposition of toxic waste without the kind of support both technical and manpower support that is necessary to make it effective, I think, is deluding himself. [However]... we aren't looking specifically for manifest case violations. We aren't pulling every manifest in that is filed with the department of environmental protection and looking for falsification of manifests specifically because we don't have the time, the resources, or the specific lead information to do that.

Congressional testimony revealed that until 1980 New Jersey did not have a single person assigned to monitor the manifests being filed in Trenton (U.S. House of Representatives, 1981b: 124). A recent study by the General Accounting Office (U.S. GAO, 1985: 25–31) found that the manifest system does not detect illegal disposal, in part because of inadequate monitoring.

Congressional hearings also produced evidence suggesting that the relevant New Jersey agencies—the Interagency Hazardous Waste Strike Force, the Division of Criminal Justice, and the Division of Environmental Protection—were incapable of producing effective enforcement even when tipped off to specific instances of hazardous waste dumping (U.S. House of Representatives, 1980: 144–146, 1981b: 110–124). Block and Scarpitti (1985) present many other examples that appear to show corruption or, at best, ineptitude on the part of state officials responsible for investigation and prosecution of illegal hazardous waste practices.

Lax implementation and enforcement undoubtedly played a big role in facilitating organized crime entry into the hazardous waste disposal industry. There are, however, more fundamental conditioning factors that logically and temporally preceded these causes. RCRA is a regulatory structure ripe with potential for subversion. Why did Congress create a regulatory structure so vulnerable to lax enforcement? A review of RCRA's legislative history shows quite clearly that corporate generators moved decisively to shape the emerging federal intervention to their liking. They determinedly fought for and achieved a regulatory form that would demand of them the least real change and a form that would minimize their liability for potential violations of the new regulations.

GENERATORS' STRATEGIC INTERVENTION IN THE LEGISLATIVE DEBATE OVER THE FORM OF POLICY

Compared to the regulatory mechanism written into the final language of the RCRA, some potential alternative forms that were proposed and then rejected would have proved much less hospitable to noncompliance in general and to the entry of organized crime in particular. The federal government could have mandated specific treatment and disposal practices, or directed generators to treat all of their wastes themselves, or legislated that generators retain full responsibility for their wastes even if they assign them to other parties for shipping and disposal. Generators, led by representatives of major oil and chemical corporations, explicitly and vigorously opposed any such language. They hammered away with striking unanimity at two fundamental points: that the government should in no way interfere in firms' production decisions, and that generators should not be held responsible for the ultimate fate of their hazardous wastes.

Generators repeatedly warned Congress neither to appropriate to itself the power to intervene in production processes nor to require generators to follow specific waste treatment practices. They stressed, instead, that regulatory controls are more properly imposed at the stage of final disposition. Here are some representative statements:

> We believe that the disposal of wastes ought to be regulated instead of regulating the nature and use of the product or the type of manufacturing process used (E.I. DuPont de Nemours and Co., U.S. Senate, 1974: 454).

> Authority to control production, composition, and distribution of products... would be devastating to free enterprise commerce (Dow Chemical, U.S. Senate, 1974: 1,478).

> [Stauffer Chemical opposes generator permits which] would place controls on raw materials, manufacturing processes, products and distribution (Stauffer, U.S. Senate, 1974: 1,745).

> ...legislation should not impede the natural interaction of raw materials, market and other forces that ultimately control the nature, quality, price, and success of products developed in our free enterprise system (Union Carbide, U.S. Senate, 1974: 1,748).

No specific requirements or prohibitions should be set governing the recovery, reuse or disposal of industrial wastes.... Generators should be free to increase or decrease waste production rates, terminate waste production, treat their own wastes, and negotiate treatment or disposal service contracts in a free and competitive market (American Petroleum Institute, U.S. EPA, 1976: 1,406, 1,410).

... the generator should be free to decide whether to treat or dispose of wastes (Manufacturing Chemists Association, U.S. EPA, 1976: 565).

... economic incentive alone should determine the degree of waste recycle and recovery.... We are opposed to regulations specifying the kind and amount of processing and recycle of wastes [by the generator]. [The] greatest emphasis should be placed on establishing standards which assure that the ultimate disposal method is satisfactory (DuPont, U.S. EPA, 1976: 72–73).[7]

Generator unanimity was equally impressive on the second issue of responsibility. They were willing to have limited responsibility, to label their wastes, and make sure they contracted only with firms approved by state authorities, but they vehemently opposed the idea that generators should bear legal responsibility for their wastes from cradle to grave. They argued that responsibility should pass to the party in physical possession of the hazardous waste. Under such a system, they further pointed out, only the hauler and disposer need to be licensed and the government should not license generators. Here are some representative statements:

We agree that the generator has some responsibility in the area,... [i.e.] make some determination that the disposer is competent and has the proper permits for disposal.... However, the waste hauler and disposer have responsibility to assure, respectively, that the wastes are delivered for disposal at the proper location and are properly disposed. Irresponsible action is invited if the person holding the waste has no responsibility for it (DuPont, U.S. EPA, 1976: 73–74).

[The generator should] confirm the competence and reliability of transporters, treaters and processors to whom the waste may be transferred.... Each transporter, treater and disposer should be responsible for his individual activities while the waste is in his possession (Monsanto, U.S. EPA, 1976: 410–411).

MCA recommends that the responsibility for the waste should be associated with physical possession of the waste, so that the generator should not be held liable for negligence of the transporter and the disposer of the waste. (Manufacturing Chemists Association, U.S. EPA, 1976: 565).

We feel that permits should only be required of the disposal site operator (B.F. Goodrich, U.S. Senate, 1974: 1,441).

... permits for both generation and disposal of hazardous waste is doubly redundant.... A permit system for generators of wastes is unneeded and would tend to stagnate technology at the level prevailing at the time the permit was issued (Dow Chemical, U.S. Senate, 1974: 1,478–1,479).

... we consider permits for the generation of hazardous wastes to be unneeded, and could result in unnecessary restriction of manufacturing operations (Union Carbide, U.S. Senate, 1974: 464).[8]

The generators also lobbied for the other provisions to their liking—a narrow definition of what substances should be regulated as hazardous, flexible time frames for implementation, and less stringent rules for on-site disposal[9]—but the two points above were the heart of their legislative intervention. In the end, they didn't get everything they wanted. The government would make generators register with the EPA. On-site, generator self-disposal would be subject to the same rules that governed off-site disposal firms. However, the overall forms of RCRA passed by Congress embodied both of their major demands.

THE LEGACY OF GENERATOR INATTENTION AND INACTION

The generators also contributed indirectly to the shaping of RCRA legislation through their historical lack of attention to proper hazardous waste disposal. The EPA estimated in 1974 that ocean dumping and improper landfilling cost about 5% of the price of environmentally adequate disposal and it reported that

> Given this permissive legislative climate, generators of waste are under little or no pressure to expend resources for adequate management of their hazardous wastes. (U.S. Senate, 1974: 71)

Lack of generator demand for adequate disposal facilities discouraged the inflow of investment capital, and an adequate waste disposal industry had failed to develop by the time RCRA legislation was being debated. Had legislators ignored this situation and required an immediate shift to proper disposal, a production crisis could have been triggered as wastes accumulated and firms found few legal outlets for them. Industrial spokesmen predicted dire consequences. In a representative statement, a Union Carbide spokesman warned legislators:

> Those wastes which are non-incinerable and have no commercial value must be disposed of. To deny opportunity for disposal would effectively eliminate much of the chemical process industry. Disposal in or on the land or disposal in the oceans are the only viable alternatives available. (U.S. Senate, 1974: 461)

Neither individual officeholders nor whole governments stay in office long if they pass legislation which, even for the best and most popular of reasons, brings to a halt industrial sectors central to the national economy. Congressmen had to be realistic and mandate years of transition during which hazardous waste would be hauled and disposed by operators having only interim licenses. This reasonable concession to the reality of the situation, a legacy of generator inattention, created a loophole through which many less-than-qualified parties could legally participate as providers in the hazardous waste market.[10]

Notes

I wish to gratefully acknowledge that this paper has benefited from comments by Frank Henry, Judith Gerson, Wendy Strimling, Vern Baxter, John Campbell, Carroll Estes, members of the Pew Writing Seminar, and several anonymous reviewers.

1. The extent of involvement is unclear for two reasons:

First, investigation has focused on the New York, Connecticut, and New Jersey region. This is a strategic site for investigation because so much hazardous waste is produced in the Tri-State area (for example, New Jersey ranks number one in the nation in annual hazardous waste generation) and because mob involvement in garbage in this region has been thoroughly documented. But, for the same reasons, this region may not be typical of the rest of the nation. Recent investigatory reporting concerning environmental pollution and political corruption in Louisiana (Getschow and Petzinger, 1984; Petzinger and Getschow, 1984a, 1984b; Snyder, 1985a, 1985b, 1985c, 1985d, 1985e, 1985f) shows that waste disposal is a corrupt business there as well, but that corruption grows out of the specific history of oil industry domination of that state's economy and its politics and appears to be quite different from patterns of corruption in the Northeast. This suggests that the post-RCRA relationship between corporate generators and waste disposers may be heavily influenced by variations in regional history predating RCRA.

Second, on a more theoretical level, the boundary between organized crime and legitimate business is, at points, somewhat ambiguous. Take, for example, SCA, the nation's third largest hazardous waste company. SCA undertook a vigorous acquisition program in New Jersey and quickly bought up about 20 garbage hauling and landfill companies. Some of these were formerly owned by organized crime figures. SCA is a corporation whose stock is traded on the New York Stock Exchange and its corporate board boasts outside directors associated with IBM, Houghton-Mifflin Co., MIT, and the Boston Co. (U.S. House of Representatives, 1980, 1981a), but Congressional testimony indicates that when SCA bought mob-owned firms, it hired the former owners as managers and appears to have allowed them free hand to run their business as they had before acquisition.

2. Methods of estimation are discussed in depth by Greenberg and Anderson (1984).

3. It is generally admitted that even the best landfill is only temporary and inadequate: "No landfill can be made safe from all substances"—Albert Gore (U.S. House of Representatives, 1983: 2). George J. Tyler, Assistant Commissioner of the New Jersey Department of Environmental Protection, speaking about the Lone Pine landfill in Freehold, New Jersey (U.S. House of Representatives, 1981b: 188): "The landfill is leaking into the water, but so does every landfill in the country." The landfill at Wilsonville, Illinois, owned and operated by SCA (see Note 1), is, according to Dr. Raymond D. Harbison, a toxicologist, EPA consultant, and professor of pharmacology at Vanderbilt University, "the most scientific landfill in this country" (U.S. House of Representatives, 1981a: 267). Geological and soil permeability feasibility tests were conducted before construction was begun. Trenches were carefully dug. Arriving waste is sampled and tested, then buried in either nonleaking 55 gallon drums or double-walled paper bags. Monitoring wells surround the site. Yet subsequent studies show that the soil is more porous than originally thought and water is seeping in at rates greater than predicted. Furthermore, the landfill is built over an abandoned coal mine and feasibility tests underestimated the likelihood of "subsidence," land sinkage that may compromise the site's ability to keep substances safely contained. If this is the best site in the nation, the Office of Technology Assessment is right to worry that current efforts to clean up the worst abandoned sites under the Superfund program only transfer the problem to other places and future times (Shabecoff, 1985: 31).

4. Of parenthetical interest here is the methodological similarity between organized crime's property rights system in garbage and price-fixing by Westinghouse, General Electric, and other firms in the famous heavy electrical equipment price fixing scandal of 1961 (Geis, 1977).

5. Modern Transportation, a firm that would ultimately receive half the manifested hazardous waste originating in northern New Jersey, was incorporated in 1972 by Richard Miele, co-owner with known organized crime figures of numerous garbage-related firms and landfills (Block and Scarpitti, 1985: 297). Chemical Control Corporation was taken over by Johnny Albert, one of the organizers of the New Jersey Trade Waste Association (Block and Scarpitti, 1985: 256–260; U.S. House of Representatives, 1980: 10). Duane Marine was so enmeshed in organized crime networks and activities that its former employee, Harold Kaufman, became the central federal informant on these activities.

6. Albert Gore in the case of Capital Recovery: "The subcommittee's investigation has uncovered evidence that since August, 1976, major industrial companies, such as Koppers, Inc., in one case Exxon, Union Chemical Company in the state of New Jersey certified that over 270,000 gallons of chemical waste were delivered to an out-of-state facility in Wilmington, Delaware, named Capital Recovery. From all the available evidence, Capital Recovery is nothing more than a paper corporation. It has no offices or any site in Wilmington. There is no phone listing, no city or State real estate tax or business tax information; no annual report has been filed . . . " (U.S. House of Representatives, 1980: 135–136).

7. Other companies and associations making the same argument during these hearings included Monsanto, Exxon, B.F. Goodrich, Alcoa, the Texas Chemical Council, and the Western Oil and Gas Association.

8. The same point was also raised by Stauffer Chemicals, Marathon Oil, American Cyanamid, Berylco, Shell, Alcoa, the Texas Chemical Council, the Western Oil and Gas Association, the American Petroleum Institute, and the New Jersey Manufacturers Association.

9. The issue of flexible time frames was raised by the National Association of Manufacturers (U.S. House of Representatives, 1976: 190) and Exxon (U.S. EPA, 1976: 940). Arguing for a restricted definition of what is regulable hazardous waste were DuPont (U.S. EPA, 1976: 69), the American Iron and Steel Institute (U.S. EPA, 1976: 100), American Cyanamid (U.S. EPA, 1976: 1,550), B.F. Goodrich (U.S. Senate, 1974: 1,440), Stauffer (U.S. Senate, 1974: 1,746). Monsanto (U.S. EPA, 1976: 406–407), and Dow (U.S. EPA, 1976: 956), argued for fewer restrictions for on-site disposal.

10. It should be noted that generators intervened not only in policy formation but also engaged in ongoing efforts to weaken regulatory impact during implementation. They appeared at EPA implementation hearings to emphasize that the criteria for declaring substances hazardous were still too broad, that proposed disposal requirements were too stringent, that interim standards were burdensome and inflexible, and that recordkeeping and reporting requirements were onerous. Especially active in this period were trade associations such as the Manufacturing Chemists Association, the Synthetic Organic Chemists Manufacturing Association, the American Petroleum Institute, and the National Paint and Coatings Association, as well as large individual corporations such as Dow and DuPont (U.S. EPA, 1979; U.S. Senate, 1979). EPA officials complained privately that "the millions of pages of testimony filed by representatives of industry on virtually each clause of every implementation proposal" created "a major obstacle" to timely implementation of RCRA (Shabecoff, 1979: 1).

References

Albanese, Jay S.
1982 What Lockheed and La Cosa Nostra have in common: The effect of ideology on criminal justice policy. Crime and Delinquency 28: 211–232.

Barnett, Harold C.
1981 Corporate capitalism, corporate crime. Crime and Delinquency 27: 4–23.

Block, Alan A.
1982 "On the Waterfront" revisited: The criminology of waterfront organized crime. Contemporary Crisis 6: 373–396.

Block, Alan A. and William J. Chambliss
1981 Organizing Crime. New York: Elsevier.

Block, Alan A. and Frank R. Scarpitti
1985 Poisoning for Profit: The Mafia and Toxic Waste in America. New York: William Morrow.

Brady, James
1983 Arson, urban economy and organized crime: The case of Boston. Social Problems 31: 1–27.

Chambliss, William J.
1978 On the Take: From Petty Crooks to Presidents. Bloomington: Indiana University Press.

Clinard, Marshall B., Peter C. Yeager, Jeanne M. Brissette, David Petrashek, and Elizabeth Harries
1979 Illegal Corporate Behavior. Washington, D.C.: U.S. Government Printing Office.

Clinard, Marshall B. and Peter C. Yeager
1980 Corporate Crime. New York: The Free Press.

Crenson, Matthew A.
1971 The Un-Politics of Air Pollution: A Study of Non-Decisionmaking in the Cities. Baltimore: Johns Hopkins University Press.

Denzin, Norman K.
1977 Notes on the crimogenic hypothesis: A case study of the American liquor industry. American Sociological Review 42: 905–920.

Drucker, Peter P.
1981 What is business ethics? The Public Interest 63: 18–36.

Etzioni, Amitai
1985 Shady corporate practices. New York Times. November 15.

Farberman, Harvey A.
1975 A crimogenic market structure: The automobile industry. Sociological Quarterly 16: 438–457.

Gansberg, Martin
1979 New Jersey Journal. New York Times. January 21.

Geis, Gilbert
1977 The heavy electrical equipment antitrust cases of 1961. In Gilbert Geis and Robert F. Meier (eds.), White-Collar Crime: Offenses in Business, Politics, and the Professions (rev. ed.). New York: Free Press.

Getschow, George and Thomas Petzinger, Jr.
1984 Oil's legacy: Louisiana marshlands, laced with oil canals, are rapidly vanishing. The Wall Street Journal. October 24.

Governor's Commission on Science and Technology for the State of New Jersey
1983 Report of the Governor's Commission on Science and Technology.

Greenberg, Michael R. and Richard F. Anderson
1984 Hazardous Waste Sites: The Credibility Gap. Piscataway, NJ: Center for Urban Policy Research.

Leonard, William N. and Marvin G. Weber
1977 Automakers and dealers: A study of crimogenic market forces. In Gilbert Geis and Robert F. Meier (eds.), White-Collar Crime: Offenses in Business, Politics, and the Professions (rev. ed.). New York: Free Press.

Martens, Frederick T. and Colleen Miller-Longfellow
1982 Shadows of substance: Organized crime reconsidered. Federal Probation 46: 3–9.

Marx, Karl
1967 Capital: A Critique of Political Economy, Vol. 1. New York: International Publishers.

Needleman, Martin L. and Carolyn Needleman
1979 Organizational crime: Two models of crimogenesis. Sociological Quarterly 20: 517–528.

Petzinger, Thomas, Jr. and George Getschow
1984a Oil's legacy: In Louisiana, big oil is cozy with officials and benefit is mutual. The Wall Street Journal. October 22.

1984b Oil's legacy: In Louisiana, pollution and cancer are rife in the petroleum area. The Wall Street Journal. October 23.

Shabecoff, Philip
1979 House unit attacks lags on toxic waste. New York Times. October 14.
1985 Toxic waste threat termed far greater than U.S. estimates. New York Times. March 10.

Schelling, Thomas C.
1967 Economics and criminal enterprise. The Public Interest 7: 61–78.

Smith, Dwight C., Jr.
1980 Paragons, pariahs, and pirates: A spectrum-based theory of enterprise. Crime and Delinquency 26: 358–386.

Smith, Dwight C., Jr., and Richard D. Alba
1979 Organized crime and American life. Society 3: 32–38.

Snyder, David
1985a Toxic scars crisscross Louisiana. The New Orleans Times-Picayune. September 8.
1985b Early action was met with disbelief. The New Orleans Times-Picayune. September 8.
1985c Wastes choke scenic bayous of St. Charles. The New Orleans Times-Picayune. September 10.
1985d Chemical specter fills Cajun paradise with sense of fear. The New Orleans Times-Picayune. September 11.
1985e He won't be stopped, landfill operator warns. The New Orleans Times-Picayune. September 11.
1985f 10-year struggle to shut down waste site stymied by state. The New Orleans Times-Picayune. September 12.

Szasz, Andrew
1982 The dynamics of social regulation: A study of the formation and evolution of the Occupational Safety and Health Administration. Unpublished doctoral dissertation. Madison: University of Wisconsin.
1984 Industrial resistance to occupational safety and health legislation: 1971–1981. Social Problems 32: 103–116.

U.S. Environmental Protection Agency
1976 Hazardous Waste Management: Public Meetings. December 2–11.
1979 Public Hearings on the Proposed Regulations Implementing Sections 3001 to 3004 of the Resource Conservation and Recovery Act. February 22–23.

U.S. General Accounting Office
1985 Illegal Disposal of Hazardous Waste: Difficult to Detect or Deter. Comptroller General's Report to the Subcommittee on Investigations and Oversight, Committee on Public Works and Transportation, House of Representatives.

U.S. House of Representatives
1975 Waste Control Act of 1975. Hearings held by the Subcommittee on Transportation and Commerce, Committee on Interstate and Foreign Commerce. April 8–11, 14–17.
1976 Resource Conservation and Recovery Act of 1976. Hearings held by the Subcommittee on Transportation and Commerce, Committee on Interstate and Foreign Commerce. June 29–30.
1980 Organized Crime and Hazardous Waste Disposal. Hearings held by Sub-

committee on Oversight and Investigations, Committee on Interstate and Foreign Commerce. December 16.

1981a Organized Crime Links to the Waste Disposal Industry. Hearings held by Subcommittee on Oversight and Investigations, Committee on Energy and Commerce. May 28.

1981b Hazardous Waste Matters: A Case Study of Landfill Sites. Hearings held by Subcommittee on Oversight and Investigations, Committee on Energy and Commerce. June 9.

1982 Hazardous Waste Enforcement. Hearings held by Subcommittee on Oversight and Investigations, Committee on Energy and Commerce. December.

1983 Hazardous Waste Disposal. Hearings held by Subcommittee on Oversight and Investigations. Committee on Science and Technology. March 30 and May 4.

U.S. Senate

1974 The Need for a National Materials Policy. Hearings held by the Subcommittee on Environmental Pollution, Committee on Public Works. June 11–13, July 9–11, 15–18.

1979 Oversight of RCRA Implementation. Hearings held by the Subcommittee on Environmental Pollution and Resource Protection, Committee on Environmental and Public Works. March 28–29.

Williams, Bruce A. and Albert R. Matheny

1984 Testing theories of social regulation: Hazardous waste regulation in the American states. Journal of Politics 46: 428–458.

38 / Management of Deviant Identity among Competitive Women Bodybuilders

ROBERT W. DUFF
LAWRENCE K. HONG

Thirty years ago, Sykes and Matza (1957) published a theoretical article on the management of deviant identity among juvenile delinquents, which has stimulated a spate of works (e.g., Ball, 1966; Priest and McGrath III, 1970; Dunford and Kunz, 1973; Friedman, 1974; Rogers and Buffalo, 1974; Hong and Duff, 1977; also see Kelly, 1984). Sykes and Matza (1957) postulated a number of mechanisms—namely, denial of injury, denial of victim, denial of responsibility, condemnation of the condemners, and the appeal of higher loyalties—employed by individuals to neutralize social disapprovals and moral constraints so that they may be freed to engage in deviant activities without serious damage to their self-images.

Since the appearance of Sykes and Matza's original work, two additional neutralization techniques have been proposed by others. Friedman (1974) added a "claim of benefits" technique and Richardson and Caildini (1981) a "BIRGing" (basking in reflected glory of related others) technique. A "blasting" technique has also been put forth by Richardson and Caildini (1981), but it is essentially the same as the "condemnation of the condemners" technique mentioned earlier.

We have found "neutralization theory" most helpful in the understanding of the management of deviant identity among the participants of one of the most publicized new sports in the 1980s. The sport of women bodybuilding has gained wide media attention since its inception a little more than 15 years ago. Today, magazines dedicated to bodybuilding, and specifically to woman participants, proliferate. Television routinely covers the major women's contests and a number of recent motion pictures have focused on the sport. Several thousand women are now competing in contests in virtually every state in the country and in many other countries (see Duff and Hong, 1984).

Socially, perhaps the greatest significance of this new phenomenon is that it may represent the profound breakthrough in gender definition that has been elegantly stated by Gaines and Butler (1984): a new image for women, an archetype—"the unprecedented woman." Scholars have become interested in the meaning of the sport and debate its merits (e.g., Freedman, 1986). However, beneath the glamour of media attention and sociological hyperbole, a very controversial world exists.

First, with the exception of a few exceptionally attractive women body-builders who frequently appear on television commercials and glaze the covers of national magazines, women bodybuilders as a group are not being perceived favorably by society at large. This is not surprising because male bodybuilding, in spite of its longer tradition in Western societies, is still being perceived as a form of "positive deviance" (Ewald and Joibu, 1985) because the activity, pronormative as it may seem, has been extended and intensified beyond the bounds deemed appropriate by the majority in society. Female bodybuilding clearly would seem to qualify as a form of deviant behavior with its very short history and its obvious departure from traditional normative expectation. Like male bodybuilding, the female activity may be argued as a form of positive deviance, in view of the recent societal interest in exercise, fitness, losing fat and toning up muscles for both men and women.

Second, the deviant character of the sport is further fueled by rumors of drug use. It is widely believed that women cannot develop large muscle mass without the aid of anabolic steroids which, incidentally, are also believed to be commonly used by male bodybuilders (Klein, 1986). Because of the negative image society has of drug use, women bodybuilders are being associated with a negative stereotype.

In sum the phenomenon of women bodybuilding represents an interesting paradox: glamorized by the media, intellectualized by academe, and stigmatized by many in society. In this article, it is our intention to examine the controversies of the sport of women bodybuilding as perceived by its participants and to attempt to understand how these women shield themselves from possible damage to their self-images. In the process of answering these questions, it is also our hope that some contribution can be made to the body of literature on neutralization techniques.

SOURCE OF DATA

The data (N = 205) presented in this paper are from a survey of women bodybuilders designed and conducted by the Women's Committee of the *International Federation of Body-Builders* (IFBB), and made available to the authors for analyses. Almost all responses were from a mail questionnaire sent to competitive women bodybuilders in late 1982 and early 1983; seven were from copies of the questionnaire published in a bodybuilding magazine.

The response rate was only 7% but the respondents did appear to represent a wide spectrum of women in the sport. Responses were received from 41 states. While ages ranged from 12 to 55 years, two-thirds were between 20 and 30. Seventy-four percent of respondents were active competitors at the time of the survey. Almost all of the rest were retired, sidelined because of injury, or contemplating entering their first contest in the near future.

The questionnaire consisted of a short background information section and 51 questions requiring fixed-choice answers, but many of the questions asked for elaboration on the answers. Most of the respondents supplemented their answers with pages of clarifications and comments. We found these free responses most illuminating and much more valuable than the fixed responses. Hence, the bulk of the data used in this article is derived from the elaborated answers.

EXTENT OF AWARENESS

While the women in this survey almost all contend that they are "proud to be known as a bodybuilder" (95.5%), and that they are developing their physiques "in a way that [they] personally prefer" (95.1%), responses to other questions indicate that they are very aware of the controversial character of their sport and that they are in fact deviating from the traditional norm of feminine appearance and body type. For example, while most (63%) respond that they personally receive positive or generally positive responses from the general public, less than half (46.8%) assert that the response has been completely positive. Forty-two percent indicate that they have personally experienced at least some negative feedback about their bodybuilding activity or their own personal appearance. Many female bodybuilders, even if they haven't personally experienced criticism, feel that the general public has a negative point of view of what they are doing.

> I would like to see the sport progress to the point where it is not misunderstood by the public as a bunch of frustrated women trying to look like men.

> Most men think it's weird... most women I know feel competitive bodybuilding is a freak show.

> Some females (and males for that matter) say that they don't want to get like a man and men don't want their women to feel like a man—you know, the usual.

> [They] say I'll look like a boy.

Additionally, more than half of those [who] responded to the question on the fairness of the media feel that the media portrays women bodybuilders in an inaccurate and negative fashion:

> They [media] tend to show the extremely developed women which makes the public see us as freaks.

> The female [bodybuilders] are not muscle bound brutes. Next time they televise a contest they should show the competitors off stage, more interviews, show them off season when they're not all ripped up, oiled up, and under the posing lights.

> Too much talk on lack of femininity and steroids. The news media is too negative and cynical.

This is an unexpected finding because, as mentioned earlier, television and magazines tend to idealize the sport. While the media may be inaccurate in portraying the sport, the inaccuracies tend to be in favor of the women bodybuilders. The fact that the respondents in this study perceive it very differently only buttresses the observation that there is a general concern among women bodybuilders about their public image.

NEUTRALIZATION TECHNIQUES

Claim of Benefit

In response to a generally acknowledged negative image of female muscularity, most women defend their participation in the sport by claiming they have healthy, strong, and attractive bodies and improved mental health.

> I'm encouraged because no matter what people think about bodybuilding, I know that my body looks and is 100% better than when I was in their shoes.

> The knowledge (hope?) that I can continue to look and feel better by training regularly spurs me on. The fact that a few others my age (50) have been able to attain the symmetry I have is heady.... I hope to serve as an image for other women over 35.

> I receive a lot of comments about what great shape I'm in for my age (41).

> I am encouraged by other women saying how good and firm my figure is. Most of these women have never been in a gym and are amazed at the results.

> I feel better and look better.

> It takes dedication and a lot of sweat. To be able to endure the pain and pleasure makes you feel like one of the "elite"... and I love it. It has made me a healthier happier person and I enjoy life so much more ... I feel so good so often that I wish I could encourage more people to do what it takes to feel the same.

One of the major positive characteristics emphasized by many of the respondents is the control over their own bodies which bodybuilding allows them. This may well be associated with a certain personality type being attracted to the sport.

> The ability to control your body, thus your life... the surpassing of limits within yourself. I have always been a competitor within my own self. Bodybuilding attracted me because of its nature to challenge the self.

> In bodybuilding you actually see with your own eyes your body conforming to the standards you set forth. You can actually mold your own physique. And anything that allows me that much control has got me hooked.

> [Bodybuilding] has made women aware that it is possible to create their body exactly the way they want to look, no matter what age, or what the body looked like before.

There are too many beautiful bodies that are being disguised by obesity. I want a 20-year-old figure always. Being physically fit feels good and looks good.

As is clear from these comments, overwhelming personal benefits are claimed as reason to continue in a sport which is acknowledged by many of the participants to be misunderstood and negatively perceived by the public at large. The popularity of this "claim of benefit" response is not unexpected because the sport, like most physical activities, does appear to be beneficial to health. Additionally, "claim of benefit" is a common technique that has been found to be employed by individuals to neutralize the negative aspects of roles and activities deemed to be deviant by society (Friedman, 1974; Hong and Duff, 1977).

Blasting and Aggressive Denial

Another tactic used by women in this sample to protect the image of bodybuilding is attacking persons who would criticize the sport. Richardson and Caildini (1981) referred to this tactic of attacking opponents for the purpose of enhancing one's own status as "blasting," while Sykes and Matza (1957) referred to it as "condemnation of the condemners." The respondents portray their critics as ignorant, jealous, unhealthy, fat, and lazy.

Most women envy my physique and the ones that feel it is disgusting (What? Muscles like men?) they have a terrible body themselves, but cannot pull themselves together to start to train.

Negative reactions usually come from people who are overweight, lazy and misinformed.

Women that are in shape compliment and encourage me. Women that are not in shape are disgusted and jealous.

I get very few negative reactions, but when I do, I'm still encouraged because it's always from a person who is out of shape and not very health conscious.

It's really kinda funny—it seems the overweight out of shape women are the first to say "yuck."

The claims of personal benefits and the blasting of non-bodybuilding critics are tactics employed by these women to defend their participation in the sport. However, a series of issues have evolved in the sport affecting the image of participants and about which the women in the survey feel vulnerable. These issues include the following: the use of anabolic steroids which are drugs that allow bodybuilders to add muscle mass and which are routinely used by competitive male bodybuilders; whether the development of very large muscle mass should be the goal of female bodybuilders or should women instead limit their muscle building to a more lithe, traditional level of development; the problems associated with extreme dieting or the use of diuretic drugs in preparing for competition; the use of breast implants and other forms of cosmetic surgery; and the issue of female exploitation in women's bodybuilding which encompasses a variety of topics such as the use of sensual expressions while posing in competition, posing for men's magazines, and bodybuilding as a new form of pornography.

All these issues threaten the image of the sport and its participants. An examination of two of these problems, the drug issue and the femininity issue, will be used to demonstrate how the female bodybuilders further utilize techniques of image management.

The drug issue is certainly one of the most damaging to the image of bodybuilders in general and female bodybuilders in particular. Research indicates that through the use of anabolic steroids, muscle mass and strength can be increased. Research also indicates that the use of these drugs by women produces a number of side effects including acne, lowering of the voice, hirsutism, baldness, enlargement of the clitoris, increased aggressiveness and mood changes, as well as heart and liver damage (Haupt and Rovere, 1984; Nayes, 1986; and Strauss, et al., 1985). The allegation that women bodybuilders use these drugs to develop their exceptional muscularity clearly hurts their self-image.

One of the common tactics employed by the women bodybuilders in this survey to defend their self-images is to deny personal use of these drugs, admit a serious problem does exist in the sport, and aggressively condemn those women who do use steroids. The condemnation of drug use is widespread, with almost 77% of the women expressing negative feelings toward the users, 14% saying it is "their decision" or holding "mixed feelings," and none expressing "positive feelings" toward steroid users. Over 94% deny that they would ever consider using these drugs, and only one woman in the survey actually admitted to ever having even experimented with steroids.

However, judging from their other responses, it is possible that many of these women have used the steroids, in spite of aggressive denials. The amount of advantage which the drug gives is medically debatable, but among the bodybuilders, steroids are believed to give a tremendous edge, and these women seem to believe in it.

I was told that if I didn't use steroids I would never get anywhere in bodybuilding.

People say I could get huge so fast if I take steroids.

When you reach sticking points or when you look at certain competitors and see what steroids have done for them it looks appealing....

I am often told what drugs could do to make my physique in their words unbeatable.

It is also interesting to note that even with this perception of heavy advantage going to the drug user, almost 69% of the women said that they would compete against drug users.

You have no choice but to compete against them—unless you don't want to compete.

I have no choice!

Most said that they have no choice because the use of steroids is so widespread.

I think I'd have to [compete against drug users]. If not I would not be able to compete. I think drug use is widespread.

Too many of the competitors use endless amounts of drugs and it is widely known!

The conversations about drug programs is constant. I know of *only* 2 drug free contestants who rank in the *top* 20 competitors here in this state.

One promoter questioned why I ever bothered with competing if I wasn't going to use drugs.

Another reason for having to compete against steroid users is that since there is no testing for drug use at the contest (at the time of the survey), it is impossible to detect who uses them and who doesn't. The large majority (85%) believe there should be testing for drug use, but only two-thirds (67%) say they would help pay for it.

The perception of widespread use of steroids is in total contradiction with the unanimous self-reported lack of use. While it is possible that the perception is simply incorrect, or that only non–drug users responded to the survey, the greater likelihood is that many of these women use steroids but deny it. The reality of their situation has to be read through the lines. These women don't want to use the drugs. They fear the side effects. But steroids are routinely used by the men in the gym (Klein, 1986), and the women often report being offered the drugs.

It was just a matter of days before my best friends' "dad" offered me steroids he said so I did not have to work so hard.

...the male bodybuilders often suggest the use of steroids.

When you work just as hard as the next person beside you but you know without a doubt that they use drugs or they brag about it, you say to yourself there is no hope unless I use drugs. Then someone comes to you sincerely and says try steroids.

...the guys in the gym think you can't win without their "wonder" steroids.

The women are embarrassed by the use of drugs. They wish that testing would be used to stop it. However, they are highly competitive and believe that the competitive advantage of using steroids is so strong that they must secretly take them to win.

Some of the respondents probably do not use drugs, and employ aggressive denial and blasting of users to dissociate themselves from this highly image-threatening element of the sport. However, we also have reason to believe that aggressive denial and blasting are very likely utilized as tactics by some women bodybuilders to protect their images while they secretly take steroids to maintain competitive advantage. Some support for this position can be gained by considering today's competitors. Only one top bodybuilder publicly admits to currently taking steroids. Yet comments are also common that probably all but a handful of top woman bodybuilders use steroids. Perhaps, the most telltale evidence is that the 1985 Ms. Olympia winner was, for the first time, required to take a drug test; it had been widely noted that relatively few of the women looked as muscular as they had in previous contests, which did not require any tests. Also in the past year a well-known woman bodybuilder, who had long been an outspoken critic of drug use, admitted that under pressure of competition she had employed steroids for a period of time even while denouncing their use in public (Pillow, 1985).

It must be pointed out that the use of aggressive denial and blasting to shield themselves from self-image damage of drug use is not limited to women bodybuilders. It is commonly found among male bodybuilders. In one of the most comprehensive and penetrating studies of male bodybuilding, Klein (1986) reported:

> In magazines bodybuilders espouse a competitive life free of steroids. Advice columns reject drugs as dangerous and not all that effective. Yet, among themselves they continue to consume dangerous quantities.

Basking in Reflected Glory (BIRGing)

A second major issue threatening to damage the image of women participating in bodybuilding is that the sport masculinizes women. Is a woman with very large, clearly defined musculature, and veins which are exposed under the skin, unattractive, unnatural, and unfeminine? Should a woman bodybuilder develop as large and defined muscularity and vascularity as possible? If a woman wishes to limit her development for the sake of maintaining her "feminine" shape, can she be considered a bodybuilder? Should she still be able to win bodybuilding contests against women with greater muscle development? If a woman strives for maximum muscular development is she destined to lose her feminine character? The women in this survey were very troubled over this issue of the relationship of heavy muscular development and femininity.

This issue is probably the most discussed about the sport in the popular media. It has also been the major focus of a number of articles in the academic press (Franck, 1984a and 1984b; Gaines and Butler, 1984; Duff and Hong, 1984).

While the large majority of the respondents (69%) admire muscle size on a woman ("large biceps and abdominals"), and an even larger proportion (73%) appreciate high definition ("striations and vascularity"), many, including some of the same individuals above, are concerned about women bodybuilders becoming too muscular. About half of the respondents (47%)

feel that a woman can be "too muscular"; 77% argue that a woman who refuses to develop beyond a certain point could still be considered a bodybuilder; 65% feel that some female competitors are going "too far"; and 38% select as their female idols women who are known for physiques with less muscular development and more emphasis on maintaining a "feminine" attractiveness. The last statistic is probably the best indicator of the size of a segment of respondents who are very sensitive to the criticism that women bodybuilders lack femininity. This group sees itself in a fight for control of the future of bodybuilding. These women aggressively employ the tactic of blasting the very muscular women in order to disassociate themselves from identification with the "bodybuilders are masculine" criticism.

In addition to blasting the bigger women by derogating their masculine look, this group of respondents employs BIRGing to seek enhancement of their self-images. They basked in reflected glory of the few glamorized women bodybuilders, such as Rachel McLish, Candy Csencsits, Shelly Gruwell, and Lisa Lyon, who are less muscular, more lithe and slender. A favorite BIRGing idol is the much publicized Rachel McLish.

Rachel McLish! She has proven that women can be both beautiful, graceful, and powerful! Without losing their femininity! She makes Playboy bunnies look bad! Rachel is very symmetrical, developed, charismatic, feminine and also my female idol. She is the ideal person or bodybuilder because she has proven to me you do not have to look like a man to win Ms. Olympia. Everyone I talk to about Rachel seems to be jealous of her. I am myself. What fool would not be? Keep the good and hard work up Rachel...I want to be present to see you win 1983 Olympia.

The ideal female bodybuilder [is] one who trains as hard as possible, stays in good shape all year round, eats good food, doesn't take any drugs, and enjoys taking care of herself as a bodybuilder—like Rachel McLish.

My body is developing much better than I had anticipated. My last competition I was compared to Rachel McLish which was an honor.

A number of these women commented in the survey, with seeming pride, that they are not easily recognized as bodybuilders in their street clothes.

Most of the time (because of my clothing) people don't know I'm a bodybuilder. They just comment on how trim and firm I am. You can't see a 13 in. bicep under a suit jacket.

Since I am very little, males and females look at me with clothes on and cannot believe I bodybuild. But when I show them pictures, they both are overwhelmed.

They can't believe I'm a bodybuilder. I go for the Rachel McLish look.

This may reflect the ambiguous identification with bodybuilding of some of these women who are especially sensitive to the allegation that muscularity and the sport of bodybuilding is unfeminine. These women seem to be responding to the allegation by saying, "It obviously doesn't apply to me, I am so clearly feminine that most people can't even tell I am a bodybuilder when I am not working out or competing." This approach may also point to the high admiration for control over body image discussed earlier in this paper which many in the group may have. Some of their idols, such as Rachel McLish, Candy Csencsits, Shelly Gruwell, and Lisa Lyon for instance, can pass as non-bodybuilding professional models when they are not in heavy training. In fact, they are often photographed as such. Then, with a few months of training they add enough muscles to successfully compete in the bodybuilding contests.

THE UNPRECEDENTED WOMEN

Not all respondents, however, find it necessary to be defensive about their sport, or to employ any of the neutralization tactics mentioned above. These women feel that bodybuilders should maximize muscular development, and should be less concerned with the "muscularity is not feminine" controversy. About 23% of our respondents belong to this group. Their responses to the issue seem to fall into three categories. First, some respondents reject outright the premise that large muscle development and femininity are incompatible:

...you can be muscular and feminine at the same time.

I don't think there is anything more attractive than a muscular, firm body.

I think the ideal female bodybuilder is someone who is developing and sculpting her body to the best it can be, while maintaining a certain feminine mystique along with fabulous glaring muscularity.

Or they consider the issue irrelevant:

I think massive women look great. The bigger the better.

I have not seen a "too" muscular woman yet.

I just wish everyone were not so afraid of muscles. Granted there are limits. I feel the public accepts muscle more than it realizes.

Women with these two perspectives seem either to be less concerned with their self-images or possibly identify more strongly with the bodybuilding subculture and its appreciation of muscular development than with the public definition of feminine appearance.

Other women in the survey who support maximum muscular development follow a third line of reasoning by pointing out the logical inconsistency between participation in the sport of competitive bodybuilding and the desire to limit muscularity:

And then we have all those who are trying to tell us we shouldn't go "too far" in development. Only in a beauty contest mentality is there a "too far." In a sport you go as far as possible.

More muscle! It's bodybuilding, isn't it?

I would like to see the sport progress as that, a *sport* and not a beauty contest.

Competitive athletes always go to the extreme. Nobody asks athletes in other sports if they are going "too far." Why should bodybuilders be accused of it?

The sport is bodybuilding, not semi-bodybuilding.

Women with these three perspectives who seem to see no inconsistencies between muscularity and femininity would also seem to be in the strongest position to continue on with the sport. They are emotionally less insecure and logically in a more comfortable position to continue participation in this sport where muscular development increases with length of participation in bodybuilding. They are also in an increasingly favorable position because more muscular women are now competing in contests, making it more difficult for those women who limit their development to be successful. In short, these may be the truly unprecedented women who are redefining femininity in a way that is unprecedented in the history of femininity as Gaines and Butler have asserted (1984)—no compromise, no holding back, and no apologies to what they are attempting to accomplish. They make very little use of the neutralization techniques because they have no need for them.

SUMMARY AND DISCUSSION

We have argued in this paper that identification with the sport of competitive female bodybuilding severely threatens the self-images of many women who participate in it. Traditionally the concept of femininity and feminine attractiveness are inconsistent with muscularity and physical strength. Even in this fitness conscious and more enlightened era, massive muscular development in women may still be considered by the public as pushing a healthy activity too far. Rumors of drug use further damage the image of women bodybuilders.

The women in this survey generally recognize the existence of negative images of women bodybuilders held by the general public, and appear to employ a number of techniques to neutralize, deflect, or turn back disapproval perceived in the social environment. These tactics include (1) claims of benefits from participation in the sport (i.e., better physical and mental health, youthful physical attractiveness, and extraordinary body control), (2) aggressive denial and blasting of their detractors as ignorant, jealous, unhealthy, overweight and/or lazy, and (3) basking in reflected glory of the few glamorized, exceptionally attractive women bodybuilders.

In contrast, there exists a somewhat smaller segment of the respondents who seem not to be concerned about the loss of femininity issue. These respondents feel strongly about the logical inconsistency between a sport of competitive bodybuilding and efforts to limit physical development. They employ no defenses against their actions because they either do not perceive any inconsistencies between their behavior and cultural expectations or they ignore it.

In examining the neutralization techniques used by the women in the study, it is of interest to note that almost all of them fall into three categories: claim of benefits, blasting, and BIRGing. We found little evidence of the other techniques described by Sykes and Matza, namely the denial of responsibility, the denial of injury, the denial of victim, and the appeal to the higher loyalties. In the main, the tactics employed by the respondents tend to be the ones that are *direct* and *aggressive*. They defend their self-images by extolling the benefits of their actions, by attacking the attackers, and by basking in reflected glory of the few superstars of their sport.

The conspicuous paucity of the other neutralization tactics leads us to speculate that perhaps the use of neutralization techniques is deviance specific, depending on whether the action is positively or negatively deviating from the norm. It has been argued that women's bodybuilding, like men's bodybuilding, may be a form of "positive deviance" under current cultural emphasis on health and fitness. Women who engage in bodybuilding may simply be carrying out a pronormative behavior to the extreme. If this is in fact the case, our data may suggest that the neutralization of positive deviances requires fewer devices and that the ones used are more likely to be the direct and aggressive techniques.

On the other hand, the neutralization of negative deviance, such as crimes and other clearly antinormative behavior, may require a better equipped repertoire of techniques, including both the direct and aggressive strategies and the indirect and defensive strategies. In addition to the direct and aggressive tactics, the neutralization of negative deviance may need to mobilize the other mechanisms originally proposed by Sykes and Matza, such as negating personal accountability; dismissing deviant behavior as harmless; redefining the victims as the transgressors (rather than as the transgressed); and attributing antinormative actions to the importance of social obligations to the primary group (as opposed to the larger society).

Our digression into theoretical discussion above, it must be pointed out, is based on very limited data. The present study does not allow us to offer a stronger conclusion than what has been stated. We are presenting the ideas here simply as hypotheses to stimulate interest for further research.

References

Ball, R.
  1966 "An empirical exploration of neutralization theory." Criminologica 4: 22–32.
Duff, Robert and Lawrence Hong
  1984 "Self-images of women bodybuilders." Sociology of Sport Journal 1: 374–380.
Dunford, F. and P. Kunz
  1973 "The neutralization of religious dissonance." Rev. of Religious Research 15:2–9.

Ewald, Keith and Robert Joibu
1985 "Explaining positive deviance: Becker's model and the case of runners and bodybuilders." Sociology of Sport Journal 2:144–155.

Franck, Loren
1984a "Exposure and gender effects in the social perception of women body-builders." Journal of Sport Psychology 6:239–245.
1984b "Some variables related to selected social desirability ratings of women bodybuilders." Unpublished manuscript, Brigham Young University.

Freedman, Rita
1986 Beauty Bound. Lexington, Massachusetts: D. C. Heath and Company.

Friedman, Norman
1974 "Cookies and contests: Notes on ordinary occupational deviance and its neutralization." Sociological Symposium 11:1–9.

Gaines, Charles and George Butler
1984 "Iron sisters." Psychology Today 17:65–69.

Haupt, Herbert and George Rovere
1984 "Anabolic steroids: A review of the literature." American Journal of Sports Medicine 12:460–484.

Hong, Lawrence K. and Robert W. Duff
1977 "Becoming a taxi-dancer: The significance of neutralization in a semi-deviant occupation." Sociology of Work and Occupations 4:327–342.

Kelly, Delos H.
1984 Deviant Behavior, 2nd ed. New York: St. Martin's Press.

Klein, Alan M.
1986 "Pumping irony: Crisis and contradiction in bodybuilding." Sociology of Sport Journal 3:112–133.

Nayes, Alan
1986 "Steroids: A clinical update." Muscle and Fitness 47:49–51, 171–173.

Pillow
1985 "I'm a natural... but it's time I came clean." Flex 3:38–39, 139–140.

Priest, M. and J. McGrath III
1970 "Techniques of neutralization: Young adult marijuana smokers." Criminology 8:185–194.

Richardson, Kenneth and Robert Caildini
1981 "Basking and blasting: Tactics of indirect self-preservation." In James Tedeschi (ed.), Impression Management Theory and Social Research. New York: Academic Press.

Rogers, J. and M. Buffalo
1974 "Neutralization techniques." Pacific Sociological Review 17:313–331.

Strauss, Richard, Marian Liggett, and Richard Lanese
1985 "Anabolic steroid use and perceived effects in ten weight-trained women athletes." Journal of the American Medical Association 253:2871–2873.

Sykes, G. and D. Matza
1957 "Techniques of neutralization: a theory of delinquency." American Sociological Review 26:664–670.

39 / Topless Dancers: Managing Stigma in a Deviant Occupation

WILLIAM E. THOMPSON
JACKIE L. HARRED

A person's occupation is one of the most important elements of his or her personal and social identity, and it is common for two strangers to "'break the ice' by indicating the kind of work they do" (Pavalko 1988, p. 4). Consequently, individuals often make a number of judgments about others based on preconceived notions about particular occupations. For many (e.g., doctors, judges, college professors), revealing their occupations almost immediately confers social acceptance and a certain amount of prestige. For others, especially those engaged in occupations regarded as deviant, disclosing how they make their living can be embarrassing and potentially stigmatizing. For "work provides identities as much as it provides bread for the table; ... [it] is as much an expression of who you are as what you want" (Friedland and Robertson 1990, p. 25).

This paper describes and analyzes how topless dancers manage the stigma related to their deviant occupation. Couched within a symbolic interactionist framework, it relies heavily on dramaturgical analysis, especially Erving Goffman's (1963) work on stigma and the management of "spoiled identities," to show how topless dancers socially and symbolically redefine their work in an effort to reduce or neutralize negative attitudes toward it and them. We also draw from social control theory, utilizing Sykes and Matza's (1957) theory of techniques of neutralization to show how dancers rationalize their actions in an effort to neutralize some of the stigma associated with their work.

METHOD

Data Collection

This study reflects approximately nine months of qualitative fieldwork including limited participant observation and ethnographic interviewing as outlined by Schatzman and Strauss (1973), Spradley (1979), and Berg (1989). Research was conducted at seven topless bars in a major metropolitan city in the Southwest with a population of approximately 1 million people. A structured interview schedule was used to collect data from over 40 topless dancers. In addition, a free-flowing interview technique was used so that dancers could provide any information they wished in addition to that obtained from the list of standardized questions. As with most ethnographic field work, some of the most insightful information was gained through casual conversation (Spradley 1979; Berg 1989).

All of our observations and interviews were conducted during the daytime, usually from 11:00 A.M. to approximately 6:00 P.M. because these clubs specialized in "daytime entertainment" targeted toward a business crowd. Although these bars also were open late at night, they had gained their reputations in the city as "gentlemen's clubs" that served lunch and did a substantial amount of their business during the daytime. Thus, our findings may not be generalizable to other types of topless clubs that cater primarily to a nighttime crowd. Most of the dancers we interviewed, however, also worked night shifts at these clubs and other nightclubs, so their comments regarding their work and how they managed the stigma may be generalizable beyond the scope of this particular study.

When possible, interviews were recorded on audiotape. One of the club managers permitted the researchers to interview dancers in the morning as they arrived at work before the club opened; all of these interviews (except two at the dancers' requests) were taped. Other interviews were conducted during business hours when the dancers were working. In those cases, it proved impossible to tape interviews because of the obtrusiveness of the tape recorder and interference from background noises, especially the loud music. On one occasion a female graduate student accompanied the researchers, conducted several interviews, and was allowed to go backstage to interview dancers in the dressing room as they prepared for their performances.

In addition to the structured interviews with dancers, information was obtained from unstructured interviews with at least 20 other dancers, numerous waitresses and bartenders in the clubs, two club managers, two assistant managers, and four former dancers still associated with topless clubs (as bartenders, waitresses, or door attendants).

Respondents

All of the dancers in this study were female. They ranged in age from 19 to 41 with a median age of 22. The vast majority of the dancers were white; one was black, five were Hispanic, and one was Oriental—describing herself as "half-Korean, half-American, and all woman." Approximately two-thirds (26) of the dancers had been married, but only one-third of them (13) currently lived with their spouses; the other one-third were either divorced or separated. Approximately one-third (14) of the dancers had never been married, but several of them indicated that they were either living with a boyfriend or had done so at some time in the past. Only one of the dancers interviewed was unmarried and living with a parent (her parents were divorced and she was living with her mother). Approximately one-half of the dancers (19) had at least one child, a few indicated that they had two children, and one was a mother of four.

The club managers and assistant managers were all male. One was Hispanic and in his early thirties; the other three were white and in their early to middle twenties. The waitresses and former dancers interviewed ranged in age from 21 to 43 years, with most being in their late twenties to early thirties; all were white.

Setting

All of the clubs in this study were located in the same metropolitan area (population approximately 1 million) in the Southwest. In a stratification hierarchy, these clubs represented the more elite so-called gentlemen's clubs, which were located in fairly nice areas of the city and, at least during the day, catered to middle class and upper middle class businessmen—"suits" as the dancers referred to them. The clubs had gained reputations of being "clean" and "safe," and all opened at 10:30 in the morning and served modestly priced luncheon and drink "specials" in an effort to attract businessmen from the surrounding area into the clubs over their lunch hours. In fact, two of the clubs featured well-known adult film stars and professional dancers who performed over the noon hour in addition to evening and nighttime shows.

The clubs were relatively attractive in appearance from the outside, offered plenty of free parking, and had names that, while provocative in nature, suggested that they were "high-class" clubs as opposed to "sleazy" bars. Most required customers to pay a modest cover charge for admission—in the words of two of the managers, to keep out the "riffraff" and the "gawkers." At the entrance of each of the clubs was a small entryway where the fee was paid or, if there was no cover charge, where customers were greeted by an attendant who checked coats and hats if desired, checked identification to verify age if necessary, and otherwise scrutinized customers before allowing entrance through the next set of doors into the actual club.

Although the specific layouts and decorating themes of the clubs varied, all had some common elements. There was at least one central bar (usually off to one side), and the larger clubs usually had one or two satellite bars in other areas that were used during peak business hours (the lunch hour and Friday and Saturday nights). Each also featured a main stage usually located at the front or center of the bar and from five to eight peripheral stages in various locations throughout the club. As each dancer was announced, she would dance one set[1] on the main stage and then move to one of the peripheral stages as the next dancer was introduced. Eventually, each dancer would work her way around all of the stages before she could take a "break" or be available for "table dances."[2]

All of the clubs attempted to establish a "fantasy" atmosphere. They were dark with special lights surrounding each of the stages and large spotlights focused on the main stage. Some showed videos of other dancers on the surrounding walls of the club; others used velvet draperies and other trappings to resemble early-day saloons or bordellos. All both explicitly and implicitly conveyed the message that this was a place where beautiful women were available to serve a gentleman's every whim. Conversely, all of the clubs studied had rather strict formal norms regarding customer-dancer interaction that prohibited males from mounting any of the stages (a rule that was strictly enforced), prohibited physical contact between dancers and customers (a rule that was routinely ignored if not flouted), and forbade dancers to expose the pubic area. In fact, due to some unusual zoning laws, several of the clubs required the dancers to wear clear latex over their nipples and "full-back" bottoms (equivalent to bikini underwear or bathing suit bottoms) so that at least technically the nipples and buttocks were "fully covered" at all times. These rules were attributed to city zoning laws that prohibited nudity in any club within 1000 feet of another club, a church, or a residential area. In clubs that were farther than 1000 feet from the prescribed areas, dancers were not required to cover their nipples and were allowed to wear "T-backs," which consisted of a thong-type bottom that exposes the buttocks but fully covers the pubic region.

Finally, whereas all of the clubs allowed both male and female patrons, they clearly were designed as male environments catering to male sexual fantasies. Each had a small "ladies room," but they all had large men's restrooms typically decorated with pictures of nude women and other forms of erotica. Disk jockeys always addressed the crowd as "gentlemen" regardless of whether female patrons were present, and the dancers said they were there to entertain and arouse men. Many had developed elaborate costumes and routines which they said were geared toward men's sexual fantasies (e.g., the little girl look with pigtails and baby doll pajamas or the librarian look with long hair initially drawn up in a tight bun, large-framed glasses, etc.).

Although no rules were posted, the researchers were informed that absolutely no illegal drugs were allowed on the premises and that club managers would not hesitate to call the police if either patrons or employees violated that rule. Also, although it was acknowledged that the "no-touching" rule was rarely strictly enforced, too much touching or kissing could result in a customer being asked to leave and the dancer being reprimanded. Solicitation and prostitution were strictly prohibited in all of the clubs, and all of the dancers interviewed denied that they participated in it. Interestingly, however, at each club dancers indicated that while they never engaged in prostitution, they were certain many of their fellow workers did. They had even coined the term "parking lot duty" to describe sexual encounters that supposedly occurred in the parking lots surrounding the clubs.

Within the confines of the club, topless dancing was "normalized" for both dancers and customers so that no hint of stigma or deviance was associated with the activity. Dancers used stage names[3] and customers enjoyed total anonymity if desired. As in most deviant settings, once inside the club, what typically would be viewed as deviant on the outside became the norm within.

STIGMA AND TOPLESS DANCING

Goffman (1963) defined *stigma* as any attribute that sets people apart and discredits them or disqualifies them from full social acceptance. This paper explores what happens when people are discredited (stigmatized) because of their work—in this case dancing topless—and how they attempt to reduce or eliminate the stigma.

People are most likely to be stigmatized because of their occupation if it is viewed as deviant by other members of society. Ritzer (1977) cited three criteria, any one of which can cause an occupation to be regarded as deviant: (1) if it is illegal, (2) if it is considered immoral, and (3) if it is considered improper. In the case of the topless dancers in this study, both the second and third criteria apply. Although topless dancing was legal in the city under study, it was governed by several legal statutes that set numerous restrictions on its practice, and because the city was located in the heart of what many local people refer to as the "Bible Belt," it is safe to assume that many people in the area certainly saw the behavior as "improper" and more than a few would contend that it was "immoral." In fact, a national poll conducted by *Time* magazine indicated that 52% of Americans considered topless nightclubs or bars pornographic and 38% thought they should be illegal (*Time* 1988, p. 22). In sociological terms, topless dancing is viewed as deviant because stripping constitutes what Bryant (1977, p. 5) referred to as "sexual deviancy in symbolic context." Moreover, popular conceptions of bars portray them as settings for deviant activities (e.g., drugs, prostitution, and other illicit activities) and certainly no place for any "self-respecting lady" to work (Cavan 1966; Detman 1990).

Skipper and McCaghy (1970, p. 392) found that stripping or dancing nude was viewed as an unusually low-status occupation, with many believing it was "outright promiscuous." When college students were asked what kind of women they thought took their clothes off for a living, they responded, "hard women," "dumb," "stupid," "uneducated," "lower class," "can't do anything else for a living," "oversexed," "immoral," and "prostitutes" (Skipper and McCaghy 1970, p. 392). Moreover, Skipper and McCaghy (1970, p. 392) found that strippers in their study were fully cognizant of the stigma directed at them and believed that most people viewed stripping as "dirty and immoral." As a result, most of the strippers attempted to keep their occupation secret and, if asked about their jobs, said they were dancers, entertainers, or something else.

Other studies also have documented the stigma directed at strippers and topless dancers (Boles and Garbin 1974, 1977; Enck and Preston 1988). For example, Boles and Garbin (1977, pp. 118–119) discovered that a major job complaint of strippers was their "objectification" by customers and their being viewed as "just a broad in a club." A senior student who served as a participation observer for $2\frac{1}{2}$ months, providing the primary source of data in another study, refused to allow her name to be attached to the published article "because of the stigma associated with being a topless waitress-dancer" (Enck and Preston 1988, p. 371).

All of the dancers indicated that they felt stigmatized, at least by certain groups of people, because of their occupation. Consequently, they adopted several strategies for managing the stigma associated with their work. In some ways, how dancers handled the stigma seemed related to their initial motivation for becoming a topless dancer. Therefore, a brief discussion of the process of becoming a topless dancer is in order.

BECOMING A TOPLESS DANCER

Skipper and McCaghy (1970) described a career sequence typical for most strippers: (1) a tendency toward exhibitionistic behavior for gain, (2) an opportunity structure making stripping an accessible occupational alternative, and (3) a sudden awareness of the easy economic rewards derived from stripping. Our data indicate an almost identical process for topless dancers, with four added dimensions often being present. A large proportion of the dancers (well over one-half) indicated that the first time they danced topless was the result of a combination of being slightly or highly intoxicated and being dared or challenged to do it. Also, a large number of the dancers indicated that they desperately needed a job and could not find one that paid better than topless dancing. Finally, many acquired the job through a recruitment process involving personal networks—friends, classmates, and other acquaintances. This was accompanied by anticipatory socialization and both formal and informal on-the-job socialization into the role similar to the socialization process experienced by novice prostitutes (e.g., Heyl 1977, 1979).

A common theme was summarized by one dancer who described her first time dancing topless on stage:

> My boyfriend took me to a topless bar with a couple of other friends. We were drinking and watching the girls dance, and one of my girlfriends and I started critiquing the dancers to our boyfriends. You know, we were just kind of jokin' around. I'd say, "she can't even dance," or "my tits are a lot better lookin' than hers." The next thing you know, everybody at the table was darin' me to get up on stage. Finally, I said I would, if the manager would let me. Well, one thing led to another. My boyfriend talked to the manager, and a few minutes later I was on stage. I was wearin' a pair of cut-offs and a tank top, so getting topless was simple—I just peeled off the top and started dancing. Well, guys started stuffing

dollar bills into my jeans' pockets and the more I was encouraged the more I shook and danced. I was only on stage for one song, and when I counted the money in my pockets, I had made $27! Can you imagine? Twenty-seven bucks for about three minutes? I thought, hey, this ain't bad. I really needed a job, so I talked to the manager the next day and he hired me—simple as that.

Another dancer who went by the stage name of "Sheena" confided:

I broke up with my boyfriend. I had a daughter to support and no job. So, I knew a friend who danced in one of the clubs. I went to watch her one night just to see what it was like. I got "wasted," and before the night was over she had dared me to get up on stage. I borrowed one of her outfits and did—and by closing time I had danced three sets and made over $200! I thought "Wow!, this is too easy!" I've been doin' it ever since.

Another dancer, "LaFonte," described her first experience:

I had won a couple of bikini contests. One night I was in a club competing in a "best legs" contest and one of the girls took her top off! The crowd all went wild and the MC made a big deal out of it, and it was obvious she was gonna win. Well, almost every girl after her took off their tops. By the time it was my turn to go out on stage, I'd had several drinks, and I thought "What the hell?" So, I pulled off my top, strutted my stuff, and it was no big deal. I didn't win the contest, but it made applying for this job easy. I thought, "Why show your tits for free?" So, now I do it for about $400–$500 a night—you can't beat it.

Finally, one dancer expressed the pragmatism shared by many of the dancers, which combined all of the elements found by Skipper and McCaghy with the dimensions we have added. A 31-year-old mother of two explained how and why she got into the business:

I've always had a good body, and I've never been ashamed of it. My parents were pretty casual about nudity, and I adopted their philosophy. In high school I found out that short skirts, skimpy tops, and other revealing clothing really turned guys on, so I used it to my advantage. You know, give a teacher a peek, let your date have a glimpse, it was fun—and harmless.

I got my B.S. degree in business and started selling real estate. I made pretty good money, but it was long hours. And, I noticed that male clients, even with their wives in the car, were always checking me out—trying to look down my blouse, or up my skirt. My boss was always hitting on me too.

One night a friend of mine who worked in one of the clubs invited me to come watch her dance. I went and had a few drinks and watched. She kept trying to get me up on stage, but I wouldn't do it. That night she made over $500! I thought, "Wait a minute, I have to work my butt off to make $500, then with taxes and everything... and I've got a better body than her... this is crazy." I danced the next night and made $400 and didn't even know what I was doing. At first I kept my job and started dancing three nights a week. Before long, I was making a lot more dancing than selling houses. I quit the real estate job and have been dancing ever since. I figure my time is limited—after all, I'm 31, but I'm in real good shape—in fact, the dancing helps, so as long as I can make this kind of money, why not? Once the body begins to go, I can always go back to selling houses.

The common elements of "chance," "economic need," "challenge," and "intoxication" permeated the stories of how and why many of the dancers first entered the trade. It should be noted that, because of the stigma associated with the job, these stories may represent a form of rationalization and neutralization similar to those discussed later. For, as previous studies have noted, many patrons ask strippers or topless dancers about their personal lives, the most frequently asked questions being "How did you get started at *this?*" or the proverbial "What's a nice girl like you...," and many of the dancers fabricate stories reminiscent of the "Perils of Pauline" to rationalize their entrance into a deviant occupation (Boles and Garbin 1977, p. 119).

MANAGING THE STIGMA OF BEING A TOPLESS DANCER

The topless dancers in our study used a variety of techniques to overcome the stigma associated with their occupation. For analytical purposes, we have created two "umbrella categories" under which the various techniques can be classified: (1) dividing the social world and (2) rationalization and neutralization. Most dancers employed some aspect of both of these techniques.

Dividing the Social World

Goffman (1963) indicated that information control was one of the most effective methods for managing stigma and suggested that one of the most practical ways to control information was to divide the social world. This involves establishing a relatively small group with which the discrediting information is shared, while keeping it hidden from the rest of the world. By implementing this technique, those "in the know" can help the potentially discreditable individual from being revealed to others. Dividing the social world also creates a strong sense of in-group alignments and cohesion that contributes to dancers identifying with one another and working to help conceal their stigmatizing occupational identities in other social arenas. This technique was widely employed by the dancers in this study.

When asked "What do you tell people you do for a living?" almost all of the dancers indicated that their close friends, spouses or boyfriends, and people they associated with on a regular basis knew they were "tittie dancers"[4] and had no problems with it. On the other hand, most did not tell new acquaintances, casual friends, or their parents the truth. Instead, most said they were waitresses, entertainers, or students. This technique of information control combines dividing the social world with *passing,* or trying to keep a potentially stigmatizing attribute hidden by posing as an individual who does not possess that attribute (Goffman 1963). Many of the dancers passed as waitresses because it was the most convenient way for their friends and co-workers to help cover for them. For example, one dancer who had a child in day care indicated:

> I had to tell the woman at day care where I worked because she needed the phone number. So, I just told her I was a waitress in a club. That way when she calls and they answer the phone with the club's name, she won't think anything. If she asks anybody here what I do, they'll just tell her I wait tables. It's cool.

Four of the clubs shared a common owner and many of the dancers in them indicated that they simply told people that they worked for the corporation (which was the man's name followed by the word Enterprises) and gave out the phone number of the central office rather than the number of the club.

A large number of the dancers passed as "entertainers" because, as one put it, "I'm not really lying—I *am* an entertainer, I'm just not telling the whole truth." Another dancer indicated:

> I'm an entertainer—plain and simple. If I were up on stage juggling oranges, nobody would think there was anything wrong with it. Instead I stand on stage and shake my tits and ass—big deal!

Many of the dancers expressed that their parents did not know they danced topless. Various reasons were given. For example, several simply indicated that they no longer lived with their parents and believed it was none of their parents' business. Others, however, admitted that they intentionally kept their job hidden from one or both of their parents for fear of how they would react. When asked if her parents knew what she did for a living, one dancer exclaimed, "Heavens no—they'd die!" Another said, "No, I just wouldn't know how to tell them—they'd never understand." And a third dancer responded, "Are you kidding?—they'd kill me."

Some of the dancers divided their social world by telling one parent, who then helped her conceal it from the other. In every case, it was the mother who was the confidant while the father was kept in the dark. One dancer said, "I told my mom, and she was real cool about it, even kind of excited, but she warned me, 'Don't tell your dad—he just couldn't take it.'" Another responded, "I told my mom right away because we don't keep any secrets, but we both agreed it would be a lot better if my dad didn't find out."

In some cases, dancers indicated they had attempted to keep their topless dancing secret but they were pretty sure their parents knew. In these cases, both they and their parents practiced *mutual denial.* For example, one dancer said:

> They have to know. My sisters know, my brother knows, even one of our neighbors came in the club one night and recognized me. So, I just don't see how they couldn't know. Still, I've never told them and they have never acted like they know. I tell them that I'm a waitress, and that's what they tell their friends.

Similarly, two dancers indicated that their husbands did not know they danced topless. Both told their husbands they were waitresses, but one indicated that she was pretty sure her husband was suspicious because she made more money than most waitresses. She had even started hiding some of her tip money in order to reduce his suspicions but indicated that "deep down I think he knows, but this way he doesn't have to admit it."

While most of the dancers indicated that they divided their social worlds in order to help hide their deviant occupation, most also were quick to point out that they did not see anything wrong with what they were doing. Many of them used some of the techniques of neutralization outlined by Sykes and Matza (1957).

Rationalization and Neutralization

In an article on juvenile delinquency, Sykes and Matza (1957) outlined five major techniques used by youths to rationalize their law-violating behavior and neutralize the stigma associated with it: (1) denial of responsibility, (2) denial of injury, (3) denial of the victim, (4) condemnation of the condemners, and (5) appeal to higher loyalties. These techniques employed an "unrecognized extension of defenses to crimes in the form of justifications for deviance that are seen as valid by the delinquent but not by the legal system or society at large" (Sykes and Matza 1957, p. 668). Our research shows that topless dancers employ many of these techniques to rationalize their deviant behavior—especially denial of injury, condemnation of the condemners, and, to some extent, appeal to higher loyalties.

Denial of Injury. Time and again the dancers in this study expressed bewilderment over why so many people were opposed to topless dancing and stigmatized them for doing it. One dancer complained:

Why does everybody make such a fuss over tittie dancing? It's not like we're hurting anybody or anything.... It's perfectly harmless, for God's sake!

Another pointed out:

People put us down like we're bad people or something. What are we doing wrong? Does it hurt anybody? These guys just want to have a few drinks and see some girls shake their tits—so what? It's not like we're dealin' drugs, or robbin' liquor stores or something.

Topless dancers not only rationalize their deviance by denying any harm but also often contend that they actually perform positive functions for society (Miller 1978). Research on stripping and topless dancing indicates that three rationales consistently are expressed. First is the assertion that strippers and topless dancers are legitimate entertainers and, as such, provide an important and harmless release from the stresses of everyday living. Second is the notion that strip shows and topless dancing clubs provide a form of "therapy"—protecting society from rapes, sexual assaults, and other offenses that might occur if the patrons of these clubs were forced to "act out" their sexual fantasies. Third, some strippers and topless dancers contend that they provide "educational services" by displaying the female anatomy in an unabashed fashion, thus reducing the stigma associated with nudity and making both men and women more comfortable with female nudity (Salutin 1971; Skipper and McCaghy 1970; Boles and Garbin 1974; Miller 1978).

Examples of all these rationales emerged in our study. Many dancers emphasized their role as "entertainers" and accentuated the harmless "fun" and "release from the stress of everyday living" they provided for customers. Others pointed to the "public service" they performed by, as one dancer put it, "keeping these perverts off the streets." Still another summarized the so-called educational aspect when she said:

> If I were a father, this is the first place I would want to bring my son when he became a teenager. Here, he could see some beautiful women, could see some tits and ass, have some fun, and not have to worry about getting in trouble, catching any diseases, or getting hurt. I think if kids 13 or 14 could come in here they'd probably develop a whole lot healthier attitude about sex.

Condemnation of the Condemners. One of the most consistent rationalization and neutralization techniques employed by topless dancers was condemnation of those who condemned them. Initially, in almost every interview, the dancers exhibited some defensiveness until they became convinced that the researchers were not making moral judgments about them or their work. When this hurdle was overcome, the entire nature of the interview usually changed, with the dancers becoming more comfortable and candid. Many confided that they enjoyed the chance to just sit and talk with somebody in the club without having to be "on" and without being "hit upon."

Virtually all of the dancers indicated that they resented the way they were treated and negatively viewed by many customers and the general public. One dancer commented:

> They're a bunch of hypocrites! Even the guys who come in here and drool and hit on us wouldn't give us the time of day if they ran into us on the streets. They will come in here on Saturday nights, get drunk, and play "grab-ass," and then go to church on Sunday and condemn what we do. In general, I think we're a whole lot more honest than they are.

Other research has also found a tendency for strippers and topless dancers to condemn those who condemn them. For example, Bryant (1982, p. 153) noted:

> They rationalize that what they do is no different from what all women do. All women as they see it, even wives, are really exhibitionists and prostitutes, but just charge a different kind of price, such as a dinner or marriage.

Like those in any other occupation that involves interaction with the public (e.g., sales clerks, waiters, and waitresses), topless dancers must hide their disapproval (or condemnation) from their customers. Enck and

Preston (1988, p. 372) noted that a topless dancer most effectively accomplishes this goal through the use of "counterfeit intimacy" that conveys the impression she is available "for informal recreational sex while, simultaneously, she goes about the real work of the club, namely, selling alcohol. . . . " Many of the customers dramaturgically engage in their own act of "counterfeit intimacy" by telling the dancers they "love" them, proposing marriage, etc., when in reality they are happily married men who have no interest in the dancer except for voyeuristic enjoyment.

A stigma management technique employed by those in many deviant occupations is the adoption of a sophisticated name that masks or reduces the stigma associated with the work. For example, dog catchers may be called animal control officers, garbage collectors become sanitation engineers, and undertakers are now funeral directors. Presumably a similar effort could be made to reduce the stigma of topless dancing symbolically by referring to it as ecdysiastic entertainment (Bryant 1982). The topless dancers in our study, however, not only did not attempt to use a less stigmatizing name for their work but instead used an even more stigma-laden term—"tittie dancers." In some ways this served to flaunt their deviance, especially to those who might condemn them. It basically conveyed the message "This is what I do—if you don't like it, that's too bad." In fact, some used those very words. Although, as we have indicated, many of the dancers were less than honest when people asked them what they did for a living, others were very frank about it. One dancer responded: "I tell people exactly what I do—I'm a tittie dancer—and if they don't like it, they can go to hell!"

Appeal to Higher Loyalties. A final rationalization-neutralization technique employed by topless dancers in this study was appeal to higher loyalties. This technique, as discussed by Sykes and Matza (1957), couches deviant behavior within an altruistic framework in which deviants neutralize stigma by contending they violate norms in order to benefit others. Most of the dancers in this study openly admitted they danced for the money. In the case of single mothers, wives who were attempting to support a husband and child(ren), or students who were paying their way through school, all cited the fact that they were helping others. For example, one dancer stated:

> I'm not proud of what I do—but I do it for my daughter. I figure if I can make enough money doin' this and raise her right, she won't ever have to stoop to doin' the same thing.

Another said:

> My parents would probably die if they knew I do this. But in a way, I do it for them. They couldn't possibly pay my way through school—so, whether they know it or not, this is making their lives a whole lot easier.

By rationalizing that others benefit from their deviance, topless dancers neutralize some of the stigma felt from external sources but, more importantly, deflect any internally generated or self-imposed stigma. By sharing these sentiments with other dancers, dancers reinforce in-group alignments, and their shared values and definition of the situation help manage stigma related to their deviant occupation while also helping to boost feelings of self-esteem associated with their work. A final quote from one of the dancers summarizes this idea:

> I'm not necessarily all that proud of what I do, but I'm not a criminal, and I ain't on welfare. I've managed to take care of myself, pay all my own bills, and take care of my little boy at the same time. I don't see why anybody should be ashamed of that. In fact, I'm damn proud of it!

SUMMARY AND CONCLUSION

Topless dancing constitutes a deviant occupation that carries a great deal of social stigma for those who are engaged in it. Because so much of a person's social and personal identity is related to his or her occupation, those engaged in topless dancing practice a variety of techniques in an effort to reduce and/or manage the stigma associated with their work.

Two overriding techniques of stigma-management were generally employed by the dancers in this study: dividing the social world and neutralization. Both of these stigma management strategies require a host of dramaturgical techniques on the part of the topless dancers to be effective. For the most part, by selectively allowing some people to know of their participation in topless dancing while keeping it hidden from others and by denying injury, condemning those who condemn them, and appealing to higher loyalties, the topless dancers in this study successfully manage the stigma associated with their deviant occupation.

This study raises some interesting questions for future research on topless dancing or stripping and other deviant occupations. For example, future research should compare and contrast female strippers or topless dancers with male nude and seminude dancers. Of special interest would be the issue of stigma related to the occupation. Do male dancers experience the same social stigma as female dancers? Do they feel the need to divide the social world and hide from others what they do? And are they viewed as being immoral, unintelligent, and otherwise less socially acceptable than other males?

Some studies have indicated that male strippers experience some of the same degradations from female customers as their female counterparts do from males (e.g., Peterson and Dressel 1982), but none has addressed the issue of social stigma and whether it is as great for male dancers. Our guess is that it probably is not. The "Chippendale" dancers and now their overweight counterparts the "Chunkendales" have appeared on television talk shows and at celebrity functions, have posed for calendars and posters, and otherwise have gained national public attention that seems devoid of the stigma directed at female dancers. Their acts appear to be viewed as either humorous or entertaining and, for the most part, quite harmless. Women apparently view the men as "studs" or "hunks," and the male dancers express that type of self-concept. Consequently, although nude and seminude dancing also constitutes deviant (norm-violating) behavior for males, it appears (at least on the surface) to carry much less stigma. Research should be conducted to see if this is indeed the case. Also, research should compare male dancers who perform in gay clubs for male audiences to those who dance in clubs with predominantly or exclusively female audiences.

Moreover, since the double standards related to sex and nudity for males and females may dictate the level of stigma associated with nude dancing, it probably can be assumed that they also dramatically shape the level to which those engaged in the deviant occupation must manage the personal and social stigma experienced. Researchers might pursue this issue by using Cooley's *looking-glass self* as a theoretical framework for analyzing the extent to which both male and female dancers develop their concept of *self* as a reflection of how they interpret their audience's feelings toward them. For example, does a female dancer look out from the stage at a crowd of leering males and interpret them as viewing her as "cheap," "easy," "immoral," "stupid," and nothing more than a "bimbo" and thus internalize the stigma associated with her work and feel compelled to rationalize and neutralize it? Do male dancers, on the other hand, peer out at a group of screaming female patrons and perceive that they are being viewed as "sexy," "irresistible," and the kind of men their women customers would like to marry? Future research should explore these questions and others in an effort to better understand stigma and deviant occupations.

Notes

1. At all of the clubs in this study each "set" involved dancing to two songs, usually one with the top on and one with the top off

2. "Table dances" consisted of going to a customer's table for a special "personalized" performance. Most of the dancers indicated that table dances brought the highest tips, usually a minimum of $20 per table dance and often as much as $100 to $200 in a single table dance. On the other hand, some dancers refused to do table dances, claiming that they sometimes involved more intense customer interaction (e.g., touching and kissing) and made them uncomfortable.

3. All of the dancers in our study used stage names instead of their real names while dancing. Many of the names were exotic sounding, such as "Sheena," "Sabrena," "LaFonte," "Sasha," "Cheyenne," and "Angelique." This might imply that the stage names were simply used to enhance the sensual image of the dancers on stage. However, many used very common names such as Lisa, Cindy, Tammy, or Linda, implying that at least part of the reason for using a stage name was to disguise their true identity. When we asked a dancer whose real name was Cathy why she danced by the stage name "Lisa," she responded, "If you got up on stage and shook your titties for a living would you want people to know your real name?"

4. All of the dancers referred to themselves as "tittie dancers" and punctuated their conversations with frequent reference to "titties" and "tits." When one of the authors asked a dancer why she called herself a "tittie dancer" instead of a "topless dancer," she responded, "Are you kidding, with a set of titties like these, would you call me topless?"

References

Berg, B. L.
   1989. *Qualitative Research Methods for the Social Sciences.* Boston: Allyn & Bacon.

Boles, J., and A. P. Garbin.
1974. "Stripping for a Living: An Occupational Study of the Night Club Stripper" (pp. 319–328). In *Deviant Behavior,* edited by Clifton D. Bryant. Chicago: Rand McNally.
———. 1977. "The Strip Club and Stripper-Customer Patterns of Interaction" (pp. 111–123). In *Sexual Deviancy in Social Context,* edited by Clifton D. Bryant. New York: New Viewpoints.

Bryant, C. D.
1977. "Sexual Deviancy in Social Context." Pp. 1–25 in *Sexual Deviancy in Social Context,* edited by Clifton D. Bryant. New York: New Viewpoints.
———. 1982. *Sexual Deviancy and Social Proscription: The Social Context of Carnal Behavior.* New York: Human Sciences Press.

Cavan, S.
1966. *Liquor License.* Chicago: Aldine.

Detman, L. A.
1990. "Women Behind Bars: The Feminization of Bartending." Pp. 241–55 in *Job Queues, Gender Queues,* edited by Barbara R. Reskin and Patricia A. Roos. Philadelphia: Temple University Press.

Enck, G. E., and J. D. Preston.
1988. "Counterfeit Intimacy: A Dramaturgical Analysis of an Erotic Performance." *Deviant Behavior* 9:369–81.

Friedland, R., and A. F. Robertson.
1990. "Beyond the Marketplace." Pp. 3–49 in *Beyond the Marketplace: Rethinking Economy and Society,* edited by Roger Friedland and A. F. Robertson. New York: Aldine de Gruyter.

Goffman, E.
1963. *Stigma: Notes on the Management of Spoiled Identity.* Englewood Cliffs, NJ: Prentice Hall.

Heyl, B. S.
1977. "The Madam as Teacher: The Training of House Prostitutes." *Social Problems* 24:545–55.
———. 1979. *The Madam as Entrepreneur: Career Management in House Prostitution.* New Brunswick, NJ: Transaction.

Miller, G.
1978. *Odd Jobs: The World of Deviant Work.* Englewood Cliffs, NJ: Prentice Hall.

Pavalko, R. M.
1988. *Sociology of Occupations and Professions* (2nd ed.). Itasca, IL: F. E. Peacock.

Peterson, D. M., and P. Dressel.
1982. "Notes on the Male Strip Show." *Urban Life and Culture* 11(July): 185–208.

Ritzer, G.
1977. *Working: Conflict and Change* (2nd ed.). Englewood Cliffs, NJ: Prentice Hall.

Salutin, M.
1971. "Stripper Morality." *Transaction* 8(June):12–22.

Schatzman, L. and A. L. Strauss.
1973. *Field Research: Strategies for a Natural Society.* Englewood Cliffs, NJ: Prentice Hall.

Skipper, J. K., Jr., and C. H. McCaghy.
    1970. "Stripteasers: The Anatomy and Career Contingencies of a Deviant Occupation." *Social Problems* 17(3):391–404.
Spradley, J. P.
    1979. *The Ethnographic Interview.* New York: Holt, Rinehart & Winston.
Sykes, G., and D. Matza.
    1957. "Techniques of Neutralization: A Theory of Delinquency." *American Sociological Review* 22(December):664–70.
Time.
    1988. "Pornography: A Poll." *Time* (July 21):22.

Part 6 / Changing Deviance

Parts 4 and 5 offered materials that demonstrate how, both voluntarily and involuntarily, a person's public identity becomes transformed into a "deviant" identity. Central to this process, at least in terms of bureaucratic processing, is the "status denunciation ceremony," in which a collective effort is made to place an institutional tag upon a person. This status-conferring process was especially evident in those articles dealing with the involuntary processing of students as troublemakers. The articles also helped to underscore the fact that the institutional deviant has relatively little to say about his or her processing. It has been emphasized, too, that the identity-transformation process is generally rather routine.

How the organizationally-labeled deviant actually perceives and responds to institutional processing is often difficult to judge. As we have seen, some will accept the label, while others will either reject or ignore it. The individual's response is critical in the alteration of a deviant career and identity—that is, in moving from a deviant to a nondeviant status, with the deviant label being removed during the process of change. For example, if an individual rejects an institutional label, he or she can expect to encounter various types of difficulties. The plight of McMurphy (discussed in the general introduction) offers an illustration of this. Not only did he reject the "sick role," but his resistance, when viewed from the institution's perspective, was taken as a sign that he needed help. In this instance, the prognosis for change—again from the institution's viewpoint (i.e., its theory of the office and associated diagnostic stereotypes)—was extremely poor. A patient may, however, accept the label and act according to institutional expectations. Such patients thus become willing parties in the transformation process.

Even if individuals decide to conform to social norms, they will most certainly encounter numerous structural and individual barriers—barriers that often reduce the probability that they will elect to change their behavior. The ex-deviant, as I have noted in the general introduction, frequently experiences difficulty finding housing and employment, primarily because others, in general, continue to react to the person as a deviant. Institutional processing is very systematic and efficient in tagging individuals as deviants. The reverse process, however, is anything but systematic and efficient. Specifically, there are few, if any, institutional mechanisms that can be used to systematically remove deviant labels (and the associated stigma) from individuals. Thus, deviants are often left to fend for themselves.

Obviously, giving ex-cons a bit of money and a suit of clothes, without helping them to deal with potential structural barriers (e.g., having to indicate they are ex-cons on job applications) and individual problems (e.g., feelings of low self-esteem) is not going to do much by way of "rehabilitating" them. A viable model of change, or "rehabilitation," must incorporate a concern for both individual and structural factors. Even this, however, is not enough.

Clearly, if the underlying images, conceptions, and categories of deviance are altered (as discussed in Part 1), then the picture of deviance and the deviant must undergo some corresponding changes. Analytically, it is useful to think in terms of the transformation of deviant categories, as well as the transformation of actors and structures. As an example, certain crimes may become decriminalized, and acts that were formerly perceived as deviant may become acceptable. The selections in this part explore possibilities such as these. The initial two pieces analyze how the *content* of prevailing conceptions and categories may be transformed. The next two selections examine how actors may attempt to transform their deviant identity by exiting a deviant career. The final selection illustrates some of the ways in which deviant organizations, decision makers, and structures can be altered.

DEVIANT CONCEPTIONS AND CATEGORIES AND THEIR TRANSFORMATION

A central theme in Part 1 was the idea that the reactions of social observers provide acts with meanings—that is, indicate whether the acts are deviant or nondeviant. In "Reform the Law: Decriminalization," Samuel Walker provides a provocative analysis of how removing selected types of behavior from the statutes may affect the picture of crime and deviance. He begins by drawing most heavily upon the classic work by Morris and Hawkins, *The Honest Politician's Guide to Crime Control,* and notes that these authors propose to decriminalize acts in seven areas: (1) drunkenness, (2) narcotics and drug abuse, (3) gambling, (4) disorderly conduct and vagrancy, (5) abortion, (6) sexual behavior, and (7) juvenile delinquency. The rationale for decriminalizing these domains is predicated primarily upon three arguments: many of the existing laws, in their applications, are "criminogenic" (i.e., produce more crime); they overburden the justice system; and they violate individual rights. Walker's working proposition, which centers on a major concern of his, is that "with the possible exception of heroin policy, decriminalization is simply irrelevant to the control of robbery and burglary." Hence, he is concerned mainly with what he views as being serious crime. In an effort to establish, as well as substantiate, the irrelevance of a link between most victimless crimes and the serious crimes of robbery and burglary, the author offers a balanced and insightful examination of the arguments and evidence associated with each of the areas listed by Morris and Hawkins. For example, in terms of the proposal to decriminalize most sexual activities (e.g., adultery, fornication, cohabitation, prostitution, and the like), he contends that many good arguments—some of which he reviews briefly—have been advanced for doing so. Walker does caution us, however, that decriminalization in a selected area may not reduce the ancillary crime connected with it. Customers may still be mugged or robbed before, during, or after their sexual encounter with a prostitute.

Renee R. Anspach, in "From Stigma to Identity Politics: Political Activism among the Physically Disabled and Former Mental Patients," focuses on how categories and conceptions of the physically disabled and mentally ill have undergone some significant transformation, due primarily to the efforts of political activism. She notes initially that increasing politicization by such groups differs qualitatively from the traditional self-help groups and voluntary associations of the past. The emerging activist groups, by contrast, comprise the disabled themselves, and it is they who seek social and policy changes on their own, instead of relying on surrogates or other advocates. In this sense, Anspach notes, they are political and not therapeutic in nature. These new activist groups, while seeking changes in public policy, are also concerned with one's *identity*, or being; this often means that conscious and deliberate attempts are made to change the self-concepts of the participants as well as societal conceptions of them. Disabled activists reject the "politics of pity" or "poster child" images and demand that they be viewed as self-determining and productive adults, capable of militant social protest. Anspach refers to this type of political activism as *identity politics*, with its focus on changing the images and conceptions of self and then disseminating the new self to other publics. Drawing on the work of Goffman and others, Anspach elaborates on the nature of political activism, noting that not only do most thinkers in the area of deviance give little attention to the political dimension underlying the production of deviance and deviants, but their notation of *power* is "limited and one-sided." Hence, deviants are often perceived and responded to as if they are powerless, passive, and weak. A product of such conceptions is that the stigmatized person accepts the prevailing definitions of what is "normal" and then structures his or her identity around those labels and imputations received from "wider society." The politically active patients, Anspach contends, repudiate these definitions. At this point, Anspach offers a fourfold typology based on two dimensions (i.e., self-concept and societal values) to illustrate how the stigmatized may manage stigma. For example, a person with a positive self-concept can either accept or reject societal values. If the values are accepted, however, he or she can be seen as engaged in the process of *normalization* where, if successful, the individual becomes committed to existing conceptions of normalcy and accepts the community's assumptions about how the "ideal" person should look and act. The author concludes by describing other stratagems of identity politics, focusing on how the disabled can repudiate societal values and elevate self.

DEVIANT ACTORS: ATTEMPTS AT EXITING AND RECOVERY

As I have suggested, noninstitutional deviants (e.g., drug addicts and prostitutes) and institutional deviants (e.g., mental patients and delinquents) who elect to change their deviant behavior can expect to encounter a range of structural and individual roadblocks—roadblocks that may ultimately produce a relapse or further deviance.

In "Return to Sender: Reintegrative Stigma-Management Strategies of Ex-Psychiatric Patients," Nancy J. Herman examines the postdeviant careers of 146 nonchronic ex-psychiatric patients. The author focuses on the exiting and the societal reintegration of these ex-patients, noting that very little attention has been given to these processes. What factors, both individual and structural, produce a successful exit and subsequent reintegration into society? Herman sheds some light on these twin concerns. She begins by noting the various ways in which patients learn they possess a stigmatizable trait (e.g., through institutional processing; rejection by society, family, and friends; and self-labeling) and then describing the individual strategies that ex-patients use to control social information about their past (e.g., selective concealment, therapeutic disclosures, and preventive disclosures). Collectively, political activism is also employed and, according to Herman, this strategy serves a threefold function: (1) it allows ex-patients to repudiate the standards of normalcy, as well as the labels that have been bestowed on them; (2) it offers them a new positive identity, enhances their self-image, and provides them with a renewed sense of purpose; and (3) it serves as a vehicle by which they can convey a new, positive image of the ex-patient to a range of publics. Herman ends by describing how the "ex-crazy" attempts to cast off old roles and identities and create new ones. Those most apt to exit and reintegrate successfully not only view themselves as occupying nondeviant roles but others also relate to them on the basis of these new roles.

J. David Brown, in "The Professional Ex-: An Alternative for Exiting the Deviant Career," offers another interesting twist on the processes involved in exiting from deviant careers. He notes that most material on exiting focuses on an actor's abandonment of deviant behavior, identity, and ideologies. Brown, however, contends that the exiting process does not have to entail the total abandonment of a deviant career and identity. Rather, the professionalization of a deviant identity might be more in order for selected types of occupations. In a sense, the contours of a deviant status can be expanded, redefined, and professionalized. And in a sense, a niche can be carved out for the institutionally perceived ex-deviant. Brown illustrates how this process works by using data obtained from interviews with some 35 professional "ex-s" who work in a variety of institutions that provide care for people with drug, drinking, and eating problems. He observes four main stages in the exiting and resocialization process: (1) the emulation of one's therapist, (2) the call to a counseling career, (3) status-set realignment, and (4) credentialization. For example, not only do many of the ex-s come to embrace the counseling profession but, through a process of resocialization and identity transformation, they create a counseling-related identity for themselves. Brown concludes by noting that many organizations are using ex-s in their social control efforts. He cites as examples the prison counselors who counsel delinquents, and the gang counselors who counsel present gang members.

DEVIANT ORGANIZATIONS, DECISION MAKERS, AND STRUCTURES

As is evident throughout this book, it is the social actor—usually a person who is relatively powerless—who becomes selected out and processed as a deviant by some type of people-processing or people-changing institution. As I have already argued, it is the actor who must alter behavior. Placing the burden for change exclusively upon the individual, however, means that the decision makers and their organizations escape scrutiny. Yet there is solid evidence of the need for such examinations. In Part 4, Margolin's data on the perfunctory treatment of suspected child abusers and Bowditch's research on the handling of troublemakers offer excellent examples. An important message about policy is also contained in research such as this: if an institution's underlying organizational structure (i.e., its theory of the office, diagnostic stereotypes, career lines, and staff socializing procedures) remains unaltered, then selected categories of clients can expect to be typed and treated in a routinized, stereotypical, and uncaring fashion. Predictably, if Cavender and Knepper's juveniles continue to be processed on the basis of a working ideology that presumes guilt, we can expect that these actors will have their parole revoked. Similarly, if low-income and minority students continue to be processed in accord with a theory of the office that presumes differential ability, we can expect failure, dropouts, and youth deviance. This need for focusing on underlying structures and ideologies applies not only to such formal, bureaucratic entities as the revocation hearing and the school, but to other types of groupings and organizations as well. Watson's description of the content of the outlaw motorcyclist subculture (Part 2), Hunt and Manning's analysis of police lying (Part 4), Best and Luckenbill's discussion of the social organization of deviants (Part 5), and Szasz's depiction of organized crime (Part 5) offer but a few examples that underscore the need for focusing on underlying organizational structures. More specifically, if the values and associated normative configurations of, for example, the outlaw motorist subculture remain intact, recruits, once socialized, will exhibit the expected behavior and attitudes. If, however, significant change is to occur on the part of the motorcyclists, it must come initially from a redefinition of those values and norms that are inculcated within the individual. The same applies to those who process juveniles, disadvantaged students, and other perceived "societal misfits." Clearly, a different theory of the office, once effectively ingrained in the decision makers, would produce changes in client processing. As an example, if educators and counselors presume that *all* students have strong abilities, the need for sorting, categorizing, or stratifying students would be reduced substantially. Thus, in analyzing change, we must attend not only to the social actor but to the decision makers, the institutions, and the underlying theories of the office.

The last selection, "Rehabilitating Social Systems and Institutions," is from my book *Creating School Failure, Youth Crime, and Deviance*. I initially describe how legislators, practitioners, professionals, and others, with their rather strict and exclusive focus on the individual, help to perpetuate what I have termed a "medical-clinical-individualistic" model of change and treatment. I then offer evidence demonstrating how such a model frequently affects the social actor, who may elect to alter his or her behavior. Most significantly, people become caught between two worlds—the conforming and the nonconforming. Not only does this dilemma give rise to a great deal of anxiety and self-debate, but the actor soon learns that neither world is likely to change much. Thus, "the individual must weigh the costs and benefits that may ensue by virtue of involvement with one culture as opposed to another." Frequently—and due to such factors as peer pressure or unsatisfactory experiences with former friends and family members—the actor will exhibit a relapse. Defining failure in *individual* terms and not in *structural-organizational* terms is associated with other serious limitations; most notably, this viewpoint protects the real culprits from scrutiny and analysis. I conclude by analyzing how the educational system, because of the way it is structured organizationally (i.e., its use of ability groups, track systems, and career lines), actually builds and perpetuates deviant careers for particularly vulnerable categories of students, such as black and low-income pupils. I also outline how changes could be produced by inculcating a different theory of the office in educators, parents, and others. These ideological and organizational alterations have implications for the rehabilitation of any social system or institution.

40 / Reform the Law: Decriminalization

SAMUEL WALKER

The "first principle" advanced by Norval Morris and Gordon Hawkins in the 1970 book, *The Honest Politician's Guide to Crime Control*, involved removing a broad range of crimes from the statutes. Decriminalization of certain types of behavior has long been a major item on the liberal crime control agenda. In his book *Crime and Punishment: A Radical Solution*, Aryeh Neier, then Executive Director of the ACLU, offered decriminalization as his most substantive crime reduction proposal.[1]

For liberals the problem is what Morris and Hawkins call the "overreach" of the criminal law. It covers too wide a range of human behavior. Too much of it expresses the moralistic concerns of particular groups who are offended by the behavior of others. Morris and Hawkins urge us to "strip off the moralistic excrescences on our criminal justice system so that it may concentrate on the essential." They propose decriminalization in seven general areas:

1. **Drunkenness.** Public drunkenness shall cease to be a criminal offense.

2. **Narcotics and drug abuse.** Neither the acquisition, purchase, possession, nor the use of any drug will be a criminal offense. The sale of some drugs other than by a licensed chemist (druggist) and on prescription will be criminally proscribed; proof of possession of excessive quantities may be evidence of a sale or of intent to sell.

3. **Gambling.** No form of gambling will be prohibited in the criminal law; certain fraudulent and cheating gambling practices will remain criminal.

4. **Disorderly conduct and vagrancy.** Disorderly conduct and vagrancy laws will be replaced by laws precisely stipulating the conduct proscribed and defining the circumstances in which the police should intervene.

5. **Abortion.** Abortion performed by a qualified medical practitioner in a registered hospital shall cease to be a criminal offense.

6. **Sexual behavior.** Sexual activities between consenting adults in private will not be subject to the criminal law. [In the following areas,] adultery, fornication, illicit cohabitation, statutory rape and carnal

knowledge, bigamy, incest, sodomy, bestiality, homosexuality, prostitution, pornography, and obscenity...the role of the criminal law is excessive.

7. **Juvenile delinquency.** The juvenile court should retain jurisdiction only over conduct by children which would be criminal were they adult.

THE RATIONALE

The rationale for decriminalization consists of three arguments. First, and of primary concern to us here, many of these laws are criminogenic. They produce crime through at least three different means: labeling, secondary deviance, and the creation of a crime tariff. According to labeling theory, the criminal process itself encourages criminal careers. Any contact with the system—arrest, prosecution, conviction, or incarceration—imposes a "criminal label" on the individual. The person internalizes the label and proceeds to act out the role, committing additional and more serious crimes. Decriminalization advocates argue that the laws covering essentially harmless behavior launch people onto criminal careers. Abolish those laws and these people will never become entangled in the criminal justice system to begin with. As a result, crime will be reduced.[2] The laws also create what is known as "secondary deviance." A person becomes addicted to heroin and then, because the drug is illegal and expensive, must turn to crime to support the habit. If addiction were handled as a medical problem, with appropriate treatment or maintenance programs, addicts would not have to rob and steal. Thus we would reduce much of the drug-related crime. Criminologists also refer to the "crime tariff" problem in this regard. Making a product illegal only drives up the price. Not only does this effect raise the amount of money the person needs to obtain illegally, but it encourages the development of criminal syndicates seeking to control the market. Thus, many decriminalization advocates charge that our gambling statutes are responsible for sustaining organized crime.

Overly broad criminal statutes undermine respect for the law. Prohibition is the classic example. The law made criminals out of millions of people who simply wanted a recreational drink. Today, it is argued that many young people lost respect for the law and the legal system by the illegal status of marijuana, a relatively harmless recreational drug.

In addition to actively generating more crime, the laws in question overburden the criminal justice system. Morris and Hawkins, along with many others, maintain that the police waste far too much time dealing with vagrancy, disorderly conduct, and public intoxication when they should be concentrating on serious crimes against people and property. Moreover, insofar as the gambling statutes sustain organized crime, they are also responsible for the most serious patterns of corruption in the criminal justice system.

The final decriminalization argument is that the laws violate individual rights. Much of the behavior covered by criminal statutes is a private matter: one's sexual preference or the decision to have an abortion, for example. As long as the behavior harms no one, it should not be criminalized. Most of the items on the Morris and Hawkins list are referred to as "victimless crimes."

There is room for debate on many of these issues. To what extent gambling should be legalized is an important social policy question, involving many considerations. Abortion is perhaps the most politically controversial moral issue in the United States today. Whether or not the drug addict is a "victim" is arguable. The debate between the libertarians, who wish to restrict the scope of the criminal law in order to enhance individual liberty, and the legal moralists, who argue that the law can and should reflect fundamental moral principles, has been going on for over a hundred years and will likely continue.

Here we are concerned with the control of serious crime. On the question of decriminalization, our position is:

PROPOSITION 26: With the possible exception of heroin policy, decriminalization is simply irrelevant to the control of robbery and burglary.

Placing decriminalization at the center of a crime control policy, as Morris and Hawkins and Neier do, evades the issue. There are no easy answers to the problem of serious crime. Conservatives and liberals respond to this dilemma in different ways. Conservatives focus on serious crime but tend to propose unworkable solutions. Liberals tend to shift the subject and talk about social reforms that are not directly related to serious crime at all.

The one possible exception to the general irrelevance of decriminalization involves heroin policy. The connection between heroin addiction and crime is clear, although experts disagree about the nature and extent of that connection. Nonetheless, as we shall see, there is no consensus on the effective solution to the heroin problem. Decriminalization is only one possible alternative, and its efficacy is not clearly established.

VICTIMLESS CRIMES AND SERIOUS CRIME

To establish the irrelevance of the connection between most of the victimless crimes and the serious crimes of robbery and burglary we should examine each of the items on Morris and Hawkin's list.

Public drunkenness, disorderly conduct, and vagrancy are public nuisances rather than predatory crimes. They harm no one, even though they may offend the sensibilities of many people. Traditionally, these three crimes have consumed the bulk of police time and energy.[3] In the nineteenth century as many as 80 percent of all arrests were in these three categories, and they still make up the largest single group of arrests. In 1981, they accounted for 18.5 percent of all arrests, or as many as all eight of the Index crimes and three times as many as robbery and burglary.

The public nuisance arrests are indeed a burden on the police, the lower courts, and city jails. There are many good reasons for decriminalizing all three offense categories. From our standpoint, the question is whether or not this step would help reduce serious crime, as it potentially could in two different ways.

The most direct effect would take the form of more efficient police work. In theory, police would be freed from about 20 percent of their arrest work load and would be able to concentrate on the more serious crimes against people and property. There are two reasons why this shift in police priorities would not significantly reduce serious crime. In our discussion of the conservative proposal to add more cops and/or improve detective work, we found that there are some basic limits to the crime control capacity of the police. Decriminalization is simply the liberal means to the same end of making more cops available for serious crime. For all the same reasons, it will not achieve the intended results. In poorly managed departments the savings in officer time will not be effectively used. In well-managed departments, as we have already learned, more patrol and more detectives will not lower the crime rate.

To a great extent, the decriminalization of public nuisances has been occurring gradually over the past fifteen years as a result of two factors. First, courts and legislatures have decriminalized some of the offenses in question. In *Easter v. District of Columbia*, a U.S. District Court ruled that chronic alcoholism was a condition and not a crime. Meanwhile, a number of states have repealed their public intoxication statutes and some cities have replaced arrest with referral to detoxification programs. These steps reflect a growing consensus that criminalization is not the appropriate response to social and medical problems. The arguments of the decriminalization advocates, in other words, have found some acceptance.[4]

On a de facto basis, the police have shifted their priorities away from public nuisance offenses. The percentage of all arrests in the categories of public intoxication, disorderly conduct, and vagrancy fell from 39.7 percent in 1969 to 18.5 percent in 1981. It is unlikely that the number of drunks and unemployed vagrants has declined in those years. If anything, their numbers have probably increased. Instead, the police have simply shifted their priorities to devote more time to serious crime. The redirection effort was probably not the result of a formal policy directive from the chief. Rather, individual patrol officers, perhaps in consultation with their sergeants, made a common-sense judgment about what was important.[5]

Not everyone, however, supports this reordering of police priorities. George L. Kelling and James Q. Wilson argue that the police should devote more attention to the little nuisance problems that define the quality of life on the neighborhood level. Police should be more aggressive in keeping drunks off the street (or at least out of the neighborhood), for example, as a way of maintaining a sense of public safety among law-abiding residents.

The police neglect of the small, "quality of life" issues, according to Kelling and Wilson, contributes to neighborhood deterioration.[6]

The second way in which decriminalization of nuisance offenses might reduce serious crime is by negating the labeling effect. The theory is generally applied to juvenile delinquents—and even then its validity remains a matter of debate. The people who are arrested for public intoxication and vagrancy are not the kind who graduate to predatory crime. For the most part they are the chronic alcoholics and the chronically unemployed. Often in helpless condition, they are commonly the victims of crime. Police frequently arrest them, in fact, in order to provide them some protection from either the elements or potential muggers. Being arrested does not encourage them to become predatory criminals. They are not the young, healthy, and aggressive males who become career criminals. Decriminalization of public intoxication, disorderly conduct, and vagrancy may well be sound social policy; but it is not a solution to the problem of serious crime.[7]

Much has happened since Morris and Hawkins recommended the decriminalization of abortion in 1970. Three years later the Supreme Court did just that in *Roe v. Wade.* One can debate the morality of abortion and the wisdom of the *Roe* decision as social policy. But it is hard to establish the connection between the old policy of criminal abortion and serious crime. There is nothing to suggest that a person is transformed into a robber or burglar because abortions are illegal. By the same token, the argument of many Right to Life advocates that abortion undermines the moral fabric of the nation, and thereby contributes to crime, is without foundation. Abortion is a supremely important social policy question, but it has no bearing on serious crime.

Much the same can be said for the proposal to decriminalize various sexual activities between consenting adults. The statutes are still filled with laws criminalizing adultery, fornication, cohabitation, statutory rape, homosexuality, and prostitution. Whether or not these activities are acceptable is a significant moral question. Good arguments can be advanced for removing them from their criminal status and, for the most part, police have accommodated themselves to changing moral standards by simply not enforcing them. Decriminalization, however, will not in any way reduce the level of predatory crime. The one possible exception is prostitution. A certain amount of ancillary crime accompanies this activity. Customers are occasionally mugged and robbed before or after their transactions with prostitutes. But those instances represent only a minor part of the total robbery picture.

A good case can be made that gambling sustains organized crime in America. Most experts on the subject agree that criminal syndicates generate not only a majority of revenues but their steadiest and most secure revenues from gambling. Our social policy of making many forms of gambling illegal creates a potentially lucrative area of enterprise for anyone willing to assume the risks of providing the necessary goods and services. The pernicious effects of criminal syndicates on our society are well known.

Organized crime money is the major corruptive force in the criminal justice system and a significant corrupter in politics. Criminal syndicates also invest their money in legitimate businesses and, using their accustomed methods, pervert the free enterprise system. Organized crime does generate some violent crime, but these murders and assaults are directed against other members of the criminal syndicates. To be sure, some threats and actual violence are directed against nonmembers—for example, owners of legitimate businesses that the syndicates are attempting to take over. But this category represents at most a tiny fraction of the violent crimes in this country. Decriminalization of gambling may or may not be a wise social policy. It may or may not strike at the roots of organized crime, as many people believe. But it will not reduce the incidence of robbery and burglary.

THE HEROIN PROBLEM

The one area in which decriminalization might help reduce crime involves heroin. There is no question that heroin is a terrible problem in our society and that a lot of predatory crime is committed by heroin addicts. Decriminalization is one possible remedy for these related problems, but it is not a self-evident solution. There is considerable disagreement over three central points: the number of heroin addicts, the amount of crime committed by addicts, and whether methadone maintenance or some other form of treatment effectively reduces addiction and crime.

The drug problem, unfortunately, has attracted more than its share of crusaders and quacks. Much of the information put out by drug crusaders is grossly wrong. Sorting our way through the misinformation is a difficult task by itself.

The first question concerns the number of heroin addicts in the United States. Official estimates range from 200,000 to 900,000, with about half of them in New York City alone. Use of the term "addict" is part of the problem. Not everyone who uses heroin is physically addicted. Antidrug propagandists created the myth that even the smallest use results in addiction. But there are large numbers of "weekend chippers" who use heroin occasionally as just another recreational drug. There are also many regular users who are not truly addicted. Even among addicts, there are great differences in the intensity of the addiction and the amount of heroin needed. As we shall see, these differences are important in estimating the amount of crime committed by heroin addicts. For the sake of the argument, let us accept the lower estimates and assume that there are between 200,000 and 300,000 regular users of heroin, including addicts, in the country and that 40 percent to 50 percent of them are in New York City.[8]

The second question is the amount of crime that is the direct result of heroin addiction. Or, to put it another way, how much crime could be eliminated by an effective heroin control policy (leaving the exact policy open for the moment)? On this issue we must sort our way through some truly fantastic estimates. The Rand Corporation estimated in 1969 that heroin addicts were responsible for $2 billion to $5 billion worth of crime in New York City. Frightening estimates of this sort are routine in the drug control business. They bear little relationship to reality, however.

In the pages of *The Public Interest*, Max Singer performed a devastating critique of the Rand heroin/crime estimates. If there were 100,000 addicts in New York City who needed $30 a day to maintain their habit, they would have to raise $1.1 billion over the course of a year (100,000 × $30 × 365). But criminals must sell their stolen goods to fences, who give them at most 25 percent of actual value (Singer may have been overly generous; some goods yield only 10 percent of their value from fences). Thus, the total value of stolen property would be in the neighborhood of $4 to $5 billion in New York City alone. By looking at the figures for particular crimes, Singer found that amount to be utterly absurd. Retail sales in New York City totaled $15 billion annually, and if addicts were responsible for half of the estimated 2 percent inventory loss they would realize only $150 million during the year. Likewise, 500,000 burglaries at an average loss of $200 would yield the addicts another $100 million. In 1969, however, there were only 196,397 reported burglaries in New York City (or about 400,000 total burglaries, if we assume that only half were reported). The same absurdity applies to robbery. At an average take of $100 (high by most recent estimates), 800,000 robberies would yield the addicts $80 million. Unfortunately there were only 61,209 reported robberies, or an estimated 120,000 actual robberies in New York City in 1969. Singer concludes that addicts are responsible for, at most, only one-tenth the amount of crime attributed to them by the Rand report.[9]

How could the Rand report and most of the other drug experts be so wrong? Easy. You begin with a high estimate of heroin users and assume that all users are addicts. Then you multiply the result by a relatively high estimate of the price of satisfying an intense level of addiction each day. This calculation ignores some well-known facts about heroin usage. Not all users are addicts. Neither regular users nor addicts have the same daily need. Some addicts can meet their needs through lawfully gained income. The cases of the addicted physicians and musicians are well known. Some blue-collar and now even white-collar workers can continue to work while addicted. Many addicts meet their financial needs through prostitution, pimping, and drug dealing. Only some heroin addicts, then, must turn to predatory crime to feed their habits. They are indeed responsible for a lot of crime, but it is much less than most of the sensational estimates would have us believe.

A realistic estimate of the amount of crime committed by heroin addicts must take into account the fluctuating intensity of addiction. During a "run" or a period of heavy addiction, an addict/criminal may rob or steal six times as much as during a period of less intense addiction.[10] Estimates based on interviews with addicts who report their needs during peak periods will inevitably result in gross exaggerations of the total heroin/crime picture. In short, there is no such thing as the "average" heroin addict (even forgetting, for the moment, about the nonaddicted users) and, as we discussed in relation to the problem of estimating average offense rates for career criminals, no meaningful "average" amount of crime committed by addicts.

The question of whether heroin causes predatory street crime has been hotly debated. The drug crusaders traditionally paint a picture of the addict driven to crime by the need to supply his or her habit. In this scenario, heroin causes crime. Criminologists tend to take a different view. Research has indicated that among addicts/criminals, the first arrest preceded the first use of heroin by about a year and a half. Crime and heroin use are seen as two parts of a deviant lifestyle, without a strong causal relationship working in either direction. Many factors lead people into this deviant lifestyle, but criminologists have yet to isolate any one of them as taking priority over the others. From our perspective this lack of established causality signifies that the effective control of heroin (by whatever means) would not in and of itself keep substantially more people from entering lives of crime.[11]

We now turn to the question of decriminalization as a method of controlling heroin-related crime. It is only one of several alternatives available. Law enforcement strategies may be divided into two classes: "supply reduction" and "demand reduction."[12] The former attempts to reduce the amount of heroin available on the streets, either by interdicting importation or by cracking down on major dealers. Decades of law enforcement effort have proven this approach to be a will-of-the-wisp. The potential sources of supply are simply too numerous and there are too many people willing to take the risks of becoming importers and major dealers. A number of supply reduction campaigns may actually have backfired. Supply reduction, of course, raises the price of the commodity in question and thus may only force current addicts to increase their criminal activity to meet the higher price. Or it may cause drug users to turn to other drugs to meet their recreational or physical needs.

Nor does demand reduction appear to be any more promising. The most notable effort in this regard is the 1973 New York drug law.... Despite its Draconian penalties, the law did not reduce the level of drug usage in New York City. Deterring people from wanting heroin is not a realistic goal.[13]

These lines of reasoning bring us to decriminalization. Many thoughtful observers have argued, quite persuasively, that the criminalization of heroin use has done incalculable damage to our society and our criminal justice system. Criminal penalties have brought suffering to addicts, sustained criminal syndicates, corrupted the criminal justice system, and brought the law and law enforcement into disrepute by exposing their helplessness. As a policy, decriminalization does not mean a total legalization of and disregard for heroin. Advocates of decriminalization acknowledge that the drug is a terribly destructive commodity that requires control. Decriminalization usually means removing criminal penalties for its *use* but not for its sale and distribution. Thus, the individual addict would not face criminal penalties. Heroin trafficking, however, would remain a crime. At the same time, most decriminalization proposals call for some form of treatment or maintenance for the addict. Methadone is the most popular form of maintenance, although some experts propose maintaining addicts through medically prescribed heroin.

The story of methadone maintenance is another example of a familiar syndrome in the treatment literature: a new treatment is announced, its proponents claim amazing success rates amid great publicity, independent evaluations reveal that the successes are greatly exaggerated, and a powerful backlash sets in. In the case of methadone maintenance, Vincent Dole, Marie Nyswander, and Alan Warner claimed, in the pages of the December 1968 issue of the *Journal of the American Medical Association*, a 90 percent success rate in treating heroin addicts. After four years of treatment through methadone maintenance, 88 percent of their 750 addicts with criminal records remained arrest-free. By comparison, 91 percent of the group had had some jail experience before entering treatment. Only 5.6 percent of the group were arrested and convicted while in methadone treatment. Dole, Nyswander, and Warner professed to have saved New York City over $1 million per day in prevented crime. A year later, Dr. Francis Gearing, of Columbia University School of Public Health, asserted that after three years of methadone maintenance his group of heroin addicts had an arrest rate lower than that of the general population.[14]

The backlash was not long in coming. A reevaluation of the Dole, Nyswander, and Warner data showed that while 94 percent of the addicts had not been arrested in the year following treatment, only 80 percent had not been arrested the year before treatment—a drop of but 14 percent. Further studies indicated that many methadone programs were not careful to ensure enrollment of true addicts rather than occasional heroin users. Some provided methadone but no other treatment services. Levels of dosage varied widely. Not all programs monitored the behavior of their clients carefully to ensure that they were not selling their methadone. As is the case with so many evaluations in other forms of correctional treatment, evaluators failed to use adequate controls, and the resulting findings are not reliable. Arnold Trebach concludes that there are "no definitive answers in the 'scientific' studies." The backlash reached its apogee with Edward Jay Epstein's 1974 article, "Methadone: the Forlorn Hope." Appearing in *The Public Interest* in the same year that the magazine published Martinson's "What Works?" article, Epstein's article denounced methadone as a complete failure. Not only was there no evidence of its success but, in many respects, it was as damaging as heroin itself.[15]

The truth is that methadone maintenance is partially but not completely successful. John Kaplan estimates that it achieves permanent success with about 40 percent of the addicts who receive treatment. That may not seem like a terribly high success rate, but, Kaplan argues, it is "about as well as we can do." Methadone maintenance is "the most cost-effective treatment we have today" for this destructive drug that has resisted every form of control and treatment. With respect to crime, it appears that methadone maintenance reduces but does not eliminate criminal activity. In one California experiment, income from criminal activity dropped from $3,900 to $400 a year for one group of former addicts, and from $7,200 to $1,700 for another group. Another study by Dr. Paul Cushman found that arrest rates for addicts fluctuated from 3.1 per 100 person/years before addiction to 35.1 per 100 during addiction (confirming other data indicating that addicts do indeed commit large numbers of crimes). During methadone maintenance, arrest rates dropped from 5.9 per 100 and then rose to 9.0 per 100 after the clients were discharged from the program. We can view this "success" from different perspectives. Discharged clients were committing about three times as much crime after treatment as before addiction, but less than during their addiction period.[16]

As John Kaplan suggests, heroin is indeed "the hardest drug." It is the hardest not just in terms of its addictive powers but also because it has resisted all our attempts to control it. He suggests that decriminalization is the wisest approach to this terrible problem. But he has no illusions about its being a total cure. Decriminalization, with methadone maintenance and accompanying treatment, might make some difference. But it will neither completely reduce addiction nor eliminate heroin-related crime.

Notes

1. Norval Morris and Gordon Hawkins, *The Honest Politician's Guide to Crime Control* (Chicago: University of Chicago Press, 1970), chap. 1; Aryeh Neier, *Crime and Punishment: A Radical Solution* (New York: Stein and Day, 1976).

2. Edwin M. Schur, *Crimes without Victims* (Englewood Cliffs, N.J.: Prentice Hall, 1965).

3. Raymond T. Nimmer, *Two Million Unnecessary Arrests* (Chicago: American Bar Foundation, 1971).

4. Nimmer, *Two Million Unnecessary Arrests.*

5. David E. Aaronson, C. Thomas Dienes, and Michael C. Mushneno, *Public Policy and Police Discretion* (New York: Clark Boardman, 1984).

6. George L. Kelling and James Q. Wilson, "Broken Windows: The Police and Neighborhood Safety," *Atlantic Monthly* 249 (March 1982), reprinted in James Q. Wilson, *Thinking about Crime*, rev. ed. (New York: Basic Books, 1983), chap. 5.

7. Nimmer, *Two Million Unnecessary Arrests*, chap. 2.

8. John Kaplan, *The Hardest Drug: Heroin and Public Policy* (Chicago: University of Chicago Press, 1983).

9. Max Singer, "The Vitality of Mythical Numbers," *The Public Interest* 23 (Spring 1971):3–9.

10. Kaplan, *The Hardest Drug*, pp. 55–57.

11. Kaplan, *The Hardest Drug*, p. 55.

12. Mark H. Moore, "Controlling Criminogenic Commodities: Drugs, Guns, and Alcohol," in James Q. Wilson, ed., *Crime and Public Policy* (San Francisco: ICS Press, 1983), pp. 125–144.

13. U.S. Department of Justice, *The Nation's Toughest Drug Law: Evaluating the New York Experience* (Washington, D.C.: U.S. Government Printing Office, 1978).

14. Arnold Trebach, *The Heroin Solution* (New Haven, Conn.: Yale University Press, 1982), pp. 259–260.

15. Edward Jay Epstein, "Methadone: The Forlorn Hope," *The Public Interest* 36 (Summer 1974).

16. Kaplan, *The Hardest Drug*, p. 222; Trebach, *The Heroin Solution*, p. 261.

41 / From Stigma to Identity Politics: Political Activism among the Physically Disabled and Former Mental Patients

RENEE R. ANSPACH

Among other legacies of the 1960s was what might be termed the "politicization of life." As political organizers extended their efforts to the most disenfranchised groups—welfare recipients, poor tenants, and prisoners—power, once seen as elusive, was now considered attainable. And as "deviant" groups such as hippies, Hell's Angels, and Gay Liberationists began to articulate their demands in quasi-political terms, the once hard-and-fast distinction between social deviance and political marginality became blurred [1]. Most significantly, the sixties witnessed a widening definition of politics to embrace all aspects of the person. An ever-increasing array of personal habits, from long hair to the discarding of brassieres to vegetarianism, came to be equated with conscious rebellion against the confines of the normative order. The language of political protest and persuasion, no longer a specialized vocabulary, became the available idiom for the expression of discontent. Sociologically, these developments pointed to the existence of a political as well as a social construction of reality.

This politically-charged climate set the stage for the subject of this paper: a nascent political activism among former mental patients and the physically disabled. On April 6, 1977, the politicization of the handicapped was dramatically and vividly displayed to the American public. About 300 blind, deaf, and physically disabled activists assembled in front of Washington's Department of Health, Education, and Welfare, carrying placards, shouting slogans, and chanting songs from the civil rights movement. The issue was H.E.W. Secretary Califano's failure to sign Section 504 of the Rehabilitation Act, which forbids architectural and economic discrimination on the basis of disability. The 30-hr sit-in coincided with demonstrations in other major cities. In San Francisco, the sit-in lasted almost a month, until final victory was achieved with the signing of the bill [2, 3]. Former mental patients, too, have recently joined the ranks of the politically active. In 1975, for example, 250 persons from several states and Canada and representing about twenty organizations attended a conference on "Human Rights and

Psychiatric Oppression." The names of the most militant organizations—
Mental Patients' Liberation Front, Network Against Psychiatric Assault,
and Committee Against Psychiatric Oppression—give testimony to their
concern with such issues as the quality of mental hospitals, aftercare, civil
rights, and forced medication and shock treatments. How many of the
nation's disabled and former mental patients have been swept up by this
tide of politicization, and how many others are "fellow travellers," passive
onlookers, apathetic, or opposed? No one knows. While the scope of the
new activism is elusive, it is clear from these events and from the spate of
publications such as *Mainstream* and *Madness Network News* that a social
movement has been born.

While it is difficult to delineate the contours of a social movement which
is only now taking shape, it is clear that this growing politicization differs
qualitatively from two traditional organizational modalities of the disabled,
the voluntary organization and the self-help group. Since various forms
of disability have historically captured the sympathetic imagination of the
American public, charitable voluntary associations, such as the Muscular
Dystrophy Association and the National Foundation for Infantile Paralysis,
have proliferated. The Mental Hygiene Movement, founded at the turn
of the century by Clifford Beers, established the tradition of advocacy and
social brokerage characteristic of contemporary Mental Health Associations
[4]. However, unlike these voluntary associations and lobbies, the new activist groups are composed of the disabled themselves, seeking social change
through their own efforts, rather than through others acting as surrogates.
The new activist groups also differ from self-help groups, such as colostomy
clubs and Recovery, Incorporated. While the emerging activist groups borrow from the self-help movements the emphasis on indigenous organization
and self-reliance, they are political, rather than therapeutic, in orientation.
They seek not to modify their own behavior in conformance to a pre-existing
normative mold, but rather to influence the behavior of groups, organizations, and institutions. For, unlike its predecessors, the new activism, with its
spate of organizations and its outpouring of publications, is self-consciously
polemical in tone, characterized by its open agitation for legislative change
and architectural reform, its militant opposition to job discrimination, and
its frequent reliance on demonstrations and the tactics of social protest.

This newly emergent political activism among the disabled and former mental patients is the subject of this paper. And, since this essay is
exploratory and speculative in scope, its conclusions await the test of empirical research. Such speculative work carries an obvious disadvantage:
it runs the risk of distorting, to a certain extent, the phenomenon under
study. The meaning of events may be misinterpreted and motives incorrectly
attributed to participants. However, speculation and theorizing may serve
as a basis for future empirical study, can provide novel and imaginative
ways of viewing subject matter, and are, therefore, an integral part of the
sociological enterprise.

The following pages will explore one facet of the politicization of the handicapped: the implications of such activism for the identity of its participants. Political activity will be viewed as a symbolic arena wherein selves are continually created, dramatized, and enacted.

The interface between politics and the self can, in my view, add a new dimension to the study of social movements. Political social movements have characteristically been classified according to the goals of the actors and/or the theorist's conception of their social function. In *Symbolic Crusade,* for example, Gusfield creates a taxonomy of political action. The categories he delineates are not mutually exclusive, for actual political social movements contain an admixture of elements. Nevertheless, political movements can be differentiated according to their salient foci. *Instrumental* politics involve actual conflicts of interest among social groups. By contrast, in *expressive* politics, political participation is "not a vehicle of conflict but of catharsis." Midway between the instrumental and expressive realms stand *symbolic* politics, typified by the Temperance Movement. In symbolic politics, participants are not concerned with actual changing of behavior, but rather seek institutional affirmation for their values, life styles, and normative standards of conduct. Symbolic politics, according to Gusfield, often fall within the realm of collective morality [5].

But the political activism of the handicapped and former mental patients seems to represent a style of politics not entirely captured by the labels "instrumental," "expressive," or "symbolic." This fourth political modality, while equally symbolic, primarily concerns not status, life style, or morality, but rather *identity* or being. This type of politics is characteristic not only of the disabled but of many recent social movements, such as the radical feminist movement, the black power movement, or gay liberation. While such social movements may have strong instrumental components, insofar as they seek to effect changes in public policy, they consciously endeavor to alter both the self-concepts and societal conceptions of their participants. Political goals and strategies often become a vehicle for the symbolic manipulation of persona and the public presentation of self. Hence many disabled activists are preoccupied with style and tactics, and imagery often takes precedence over substance. They eschew the telethon's "politics of pity" and abhor the "poster child" image [6], demanding instead to be regarded (by themselves and others) as self-determining adults, capable of militant political action. In the words of one articulate muscular dystrophy victim:

> Thriving on a climate of increasing public tolerance and kindness, we are becoming presumptuous. Now we reject any view of ourselves as being lucky to be allowed to live. We reject too all the myths and superstitions that have surrounded us in the past. We are challenging society to take account of us, to listen to what we have to say, to acknowledge us as an integral part of society itself. We do not want ourselves, or anyone else treated as second class citizens and put away out of sight and out of mind [7].

Political activism among the handicapped and former mental patients, then, exemplifies a type of politics which we will term *identity politics*. Among its goals are forging an image or conception of self and propagating this self to attentive publics.

Not only is the fashioning of collective identity an explicitly articulated *goal* of the politicized disabled, but the very act of political participation in itself induces others to impute certain characteristics to the activist. For once (s)he has entered the realm of polity, the political actor assumes a certain persona. We attribute certain qualities to political action which sharply contrast to personal deviation, which is assumed to be individualistic and non-rational, seemingly without purpose. Political action, on the other hand, is viewed as prima facie evidence of rational, goal-directed, voluntaristic, and change-oriented behavior. The agitation of the disabled and former mental patients demonstrates, in word and deed, that they are capable of purposive political action.

POLITICAL ACTIVISM OF THE DISABLED: AN ANOMALY

... Most of the prevailing thinking on deviance conceives of its phenomenon in a way that does not provide *sufficiently* for the possibility of politicized deviants, collectively engaged in attempts to reweave the fabric of identity. According to Horowitz and Liebowitz, theories which conceptualize deviance as a social, rather than as a political, problem tend to obscure its political dimensions. They fault prevailing theories for their reliance on a "social welfare model," which tends to evaluate deviance in largely therapeutic terms. Presumably, Horowitz and Liebowitz are referring to those structural-functional and sub-cultural perspectives which utilize notions of "improper socialization" or socially-induced individual pathology. Such theories, argue the authors, fail to recognize that deviance is a "conflict between superordinates who make the rules and subordinates whose behavior violates them" [1].

Instead, Horowitz and Liebowitz exhort sociologists to adopt a "conflict model" of deviance which turns out to be none other than labelling theory. In calling attention to the role of the responses of others and agents of social control in forging deviant identity, labelling theorists were among the first to take cognizance of issues of power and control. According to Becker:

> The question of the purpose or function of a group...is very often a political question. Factions within the group disagree and maneuver to have their definitions of the group's function accepted....If this is true, then it is likewise true that the question of what rules are to be enforced, what behavior regarded as deviant, and which people labeled as outsiders must also be regarded as political....
>
> Differences in the ability to make rules and apply them to other people are essentially power differentials [8].

But although labelling theorists may be credited with introducing a political dimension into the study of deviance, their notion of power ultimately proves to be limited and one-sided. Most studies of deviance generated by the labelling perspective portray the deviant as powerless, passive, and relatively uninvolved in the labelling process [9–11]. Part of this bias stems from the decision of many labelling theorists to focus on "total institutions" [12], where those labelled are perforce compelled to accept identities enforced by institutional dictates and where there is little latitude for negotiation with officials. But this portrait of the determined deviant goes much deeper, and is rooted in a *one-way* model of the role-taking process,[1] in which identities are simply *imposed* upon the deviant rather than negotiated. This problem is most apparent in the work of Scheff, who portrays the mental patient as a *tabula rasa,* who in one fell swoop casts off the trappings of an old self and steps into the strait jacket of an imposed, deviant role [13]. But the assumption of deviant passivity creeps into the work of almost all labelling theorists, reliant as they are on the notion of "victimization" and an ideological commitment to the "underdog." Labelling theory, then, is conceptually ill-equipped to deal with the identity politics of the "mentally ill" and the physically disabled. Demonstrations and social protest provide these politicized deviants with a forum where identity is negotiated on a grand scale with the American public.

Goffman's book-length essay, *Stigma* [14], is one of the most systematic attempts to deal with the problems of "spoiled" identity. It is an attempt which, in some senses, seems to avoid many of the pitfalls of labelling theory. Stigmatized persons emerge not as powerless victims, but as strategists and con artists, engaged in the work of "information control" and "tension management." Yet even in this more sophisticated framework we find the ever-present theme of passivity and imposed identity. The strategies of the stigmatized person are essentially *defensive maneuvers.* For the stigmatized person ultimately subscribes to the definitions of "normals" and derives his/her identity reactively, in response to the imputations of the "wider society." (S)he is fated to remain at the mercy of the Invisible Hand of the Generalized Other. Yet the political activism of the disabled and former mental patients is not an endorsement of but rather an *assault* upon the generalized other. Seeking the power to define their situation for themselves, disabled activists repudiate societal imputations. In the words of one politically active woman:

> As a kid I was labelled handicapped and I pretty much fit that role.... And then one day I thought, "Hey, *I don't want to be defined by others.* I want to be defined for and by myself." Because when you start accepting society's definition of the handicapped, then you are really different.
>
> When I was once asked by a reporter how old I was, I answered, "Does it really matter?" ... I think it's time that we stop judging people by their age, height, and weight. We've got to start looking at them as human beings, first and foremost ... (quoted in [6]).

The politicization of the disabled represents an attempt to wrest definitional control of identity from "normals." Goffman makes only passing reference to political activism of the stigmatized (for it had not yet come into being as a full-blown social movement), and he takes a somewhat fatalistic view of this phenomenon, emphasizing that, paradoxically, militant activity is ineluctably bound up with the world of "normals":

> The problems associated with militancy are well known. When the ultimate political objective is to remove the stigma from the differentness, the individual may find that his very efforts can politicize his own life, rendering it even more different from the normal life initially denied him. Further in *drawing attention to the situation of his own kind* [italics added] he is in some respects consolidating a public image of his own differentness as a real thing, as constituting a real group. On the other hand, if he seeks some kind of separateness, not assimilation, he may find that he is presenting his militant efforts in the language and style of his enemies. Moreover, the plea he presents, the plight he reveals, the strategies he advocates are all part of *an idiom* of expression and feeling that belongs to the whole society [14].

In Goffman's view, then, political activism is doomed to failure because assimilationist tactics only serve to reify their differentness and because separatists are compelled to rely on the pre-cast political idiom and imagery of "normals." Yet such a depiction does not, in my view, quite do justice to contemporary identity politics. The new activists do not seek to assimilate themselves; nor does their reliance on the political strategies of "normals" necessarily spell defeat. While the disabled activists do not operate in a political vacuum, their actions do testify to their ontological status as independent, politically active beings. Whether "normals" eventually accept or internalize the image they sell is, of course, a different matter....

I have been leading up to the following: sociological theories have, perhaps unwittingly, subscribed to the mythology of the helplessness of the handicapped and the "mentally ill." In one way or another, the social welfare model, labelling theory, and the dramaturgical model of the actor are tacitly infused with commonsense assumptions of the deviant actor as individualistic, passive, and powerless. The sociology of deviance must revise its conceptions to account for active attempts on the part of those labelled as deviant to mold their own identities....

STRATAGEMS FOR IDENTITY MANAGEMENT

So far I have spoken as though identity politics were the only, or the prevailing, response to handicap or stigma. Political activism is, however, only one of an array of possible stratagems for the management of a somewhat problematic identity. It is theoretically worthwhile to contrast political activism with these other responses in order to delineate its essential features.

These stratagems can, I believe, be contrasted with respect to two central dimensions: the individual's conception of self and his/her relationship to prevailing societal values. To begin with, the handicapped and those labelled as "mentally ill" must develop some posture *vis-à-vis* certain salient cultural values which portray them in a less than favorable light. As Davis points out in his study of polio children and their families, the handicapped person must contend with the fact that

> he is at a disadvantage with respect to several important values emphasized in our society: e.g., physical attractiveness; wholeness and symmetry of body parts; and various physiognomic attributes felt to be prerequisite for a pleasant and engaging personality [15].

The former mental patient, while usually free from the obtrusiveness of an immediately visible stigma, is also said to violate some of the sacred principles of our society: the canons of rationality, self-determination, and full responsibility for the consequences of one's actions. No matter what the particulars of the stigma, the individual must ultimately, consciously or unwittingly, accept or reject the societal values which his/her very ontology contradicts. Moreover, the stigmatized person invariably adopts a stratagem which carries profound implications for his/her identity or conception of self. By combining these two dimensions—stance toward societal values and self-concept—it is possible to develop a typology of four[2] modal responses to stigma, represented schematically below:

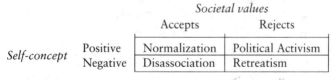

Stratagems for Stigma
Management

Societal values

		Accepts	Rejects
Self-concept	Positive	Normalization	Political Activism
	Negative	Disassociation	Retreatism

The terms "normalization" and "disassociation" were drawn from Davis's study of polio children and their families. In the first stratagem, *normalization,* the individual is firmly committed to cultural conceptions of normalcy and endorses commonly-held assumptions about the "ideal" person. But while accepting these societal values and cognizant that (s)he fails to measure up to them, the individual makes a concerted effort to minimize, rationalize, explain away, and downplay the stigma attached to his/her differentness. The typical existential stance of the normalizer is that (s)he is "superficially different but basically the same as everyone else," or that ultimately "differences don't really matter." Generally, the normal-izer attempts, insofar as possible, to participate in the round of activities available to "normals" and to aspire to "normal" attainments. As Davis indicates, the societal "idealization of the normal, healthy, and physically attractive," and the "democratic fiction" that differences wither away in the face of a fundamental equality of human beings, make normalization the favored response [15]. There is another societal factor which often impels the disabled toward normalization: the ever-present American myth of success. Our culture abounds with symbolic inducements to overcome even the weightiest of obstacles. F.D.R. and Helen Keller may be said to be the Horatio Algers of the handicapped, reminders that, given hard work, diligence, and individual effort, the courageous disabled can reach the loftiest pinnacles of achievement.

Normalization carries a certain undeniable advantage: the individual is able to maintain a relatively sanguine and confident attitude toward the self. Yet the normalizer purchases this positive self-conception at a certain price. First, interactions with "normals" are necessarily strained, for an obvious disability inevitably tends to obtrude upon the social situation. In their gambits to "disavow their deviance," normalizers must continually manage and contend with the inescapable tension of an interaction which is fragile, problematic, and easily subject to "slips" and disruptions [17].

Secondly, normalization is premised on a number of contradictory beliefs, and hence the normalizer is fated to experience a certain degree of "cognitive dissonance." Most obvious of these contradictions is the gap between the "democratic fiction"—the "You-can't-tell-a-book-by-its-cover" ideology—and the actual obsession with ascriptive attributes which plagues our culture. Then there is the discrepancy between the canons of civility—the norms of polite society which proffer a superficial acceptance to the handicapped—and the actual emotional displays conveyed non-verbally by "normals" in social intercourse. This gap between what Goffman [16] terms the "expressions given" and the "expressions given off" renders the existential state of the normalizer one of profound *distrust* and suspicion of a rejection that may lurk beneath the façade of civility. Finally, there is the economic gap between the myth of success and individual achievement propagated by rehabilitative ideology and the harsh realities of economic discrimination against the handicapped and former mental patients. The list of gaps between myth and reality could be multiplied indefinitely, but the point is that the normalizer's valiant attempts to preserve a positive self-image are undoubtedly punctuated by moments of anguish, despair, and internal turmoil.

The next two responses—disassociation and retreatism—require little explanation and entail for the disabled person a less than felicitous conception of self. In *disassociation*, the individual remains attached to the values of the wider society and aware that (s)he is disqualified according to them. Unable to accept the harsh fact of their disqualification and unwilling to aspire to acceptance by "normals," those who disassociate live with an identity that is tainted and tarnished. This negative self-conception leads them to avoid contacts with "normals," perhaps in an effort to spare themselves the pain of impending rejection. Self-exclusion, resentment, and anger toward "normals"—these are the emotional concomitants of the disassociative response [15].

In the third response, *retreatism* (a term borrowed from Merton), the self-image of the individual is profoundly negative, and (s)he neither accepts societal values nor aspires to "normal" attainments. The profound despair of retreatists lead them to withdraw from the world of "normals" to a world of private hopes and fears. These are the people who have "given up"— found in mental hospitals, flophouses, welfare hotels, and other margins of "civilization."

Political activism has recently come to represent a viable collective alternative to the previous individualistic responses.[3] Like the normalizer, the activist seeks to attain a favorable conception of self, often asserting a claim to superiority over "normals." But unlike the normalizer, the activist relinquishes any claim to an acceptance which (s)he views as artificial and consciously repudiates prevailing societal values. The new activist demands institutional equality rather than friendship. Because of this separatist stance on the part of the activist, (s)he may be apt to experience less internal turmoil than is the normalizer. Although some emotional conflicts undoubtedly ensue whenever the allure of "acceptance" and the strain of militancy beckon the activist to return to a normalizing response, political activism is a response which is less conflictual and less fraught with dissonance than is normalization. Paul Hunt, a disabled writer, provides perhaps the most eloquent statement of the activist's repudiation of societal values and exaltation of self:

> What I *am* rejecting is society's tendency to set up rigid standards of what is right and proper and to force the individual into a mould....
>
> For the disabled person with a fair intelligence or other gifts, perhaps the greatest temptation is to use them just to escape from his disabledness, to buy a place in the sun, a share in the illusory normal world where all is light and pleasure and happiness. Naturally we want to get away from and forget the sickness, depression, pain, loneliness, and poverty of which we probably see more than our share. But if we deny our special relation to the dark in this way, we shall have ceased to recognize the most important asset of disabled people in our society—the uncomfortable subversive position from which we act as a living reproach to any scale of values that puts attributes or possessions before the person [7]....

THE STRATAGEMS OF IDENTITY POLITICS

Political activism, as contrasted with other responses to disability, seeks, in repudiating societal values, to elevate the self-concept of its participants. In this section I will explore in greater detail just how these two aspects of identity social movements—repudiation and self-elevation—are accomplished. In so doing, I am relying largely on the published statements of articulate disabled activists, especially those generated by the 1975 Conference on Human Rights and Psychiatric Oppression. While such pronouncements cannot be construed as "representative" of the breadth and scope of identity politics, and while they are biased toward the "official," such official ideologies do reveal basic themes of identity politics. And ideology, after all, is one medium through which selves are created.

Most activists endeavor to dispel stigma by viewing their deviation in nonmedical terms. The politicized mental patient groups adhere to some notion of *societal etiology*. The cause of mental disorder is to be sought not in individual pathology, but rather in perceived political, economic, or social repression. The Mental Patients' Liberation Front, a Boston-based activist group, provides perhaps the most militant illustration of this tenet, when it states its goal to be "to transform the classist, racist, and sexist society, with its oppressive power relations, that caused our pain and incarceration." Project Release, an organization based in New York City, is concerned with the problem of recidivism, or the "revolving door," in which patients are released, only to return quickly to the confines of the mental hospital. But Project Release explains an otherwise conventional problem for the psychiatric profession by reference to a socio-economic model: its leaders state that their "ideology is that recidivism is primarily caused by *socio-economic conditions* and not by 'mental illness' "[18].

Another group attending the conference runs a halfway house based on Laingian principles, which emphasizes the creative aspects of madness and expressly condemns the use of psychotropic drugs. Its leaders expressed another variant of this theme:

> The "system" is set up to keep many people struggling for a living, for a place in society, for a feeling of self worth. People in emotional crises are experiencing their pain for legitimate reasons. The pressures of living in the world today are many and can severely tax anyone's emotional stability. It is a myth that "emotional breakdown" is due to an individual's weakness or inadequacies, a myth perpetrated by existing "mental health" facilities and other social and economic power structures [18].

In this framework, those who suffer "crises" (and this term is substituted for "mental illness") are neither weak nor emotionally unstable. Rather, their crises are viewed as legitimate and reasonable responses to the travails of an oppressive civilization. In providing a rationale for suffering, the Laingian ideology legitimates mental patients' experience and, in so doing, allows them to sustain viable conceptions of self. This same group adds an additional nuance, echoed by other activist groups:

> In traditional psychiatric settings, people's expressions of emotional distress are usually labelled as "mental illness," and are invalidated rather than listened to with respect. The patients are cut off from their feelings by mind-numbing psychotropic drugs, and by their environment.... We will help people to find their own solutions to problems, rather than having solutions imposed by psychiatric authorities [18].

This blame of and disdain for "psychiatric authorities" and professionals is a salient theme found in the ideological pronouncements of most patient activist groups. Psychoactive drugs and shock treatments in particular, and enforced medical interventions in general, are viewed as infringements upon patients' integrity and dignity. The Network Against Psychiatric Assault, an organization in San Francisco claiming more than 100 members, has successfully halted enforced shock treatments at Langley-Porter Neuropsychiatric Institute, and has agitated, with some degree of success, for broader legislative restrictions on enforced treatments. Similar lawsuits and demonstrations are being carried out in other states. This struggle against institutions and professionals on the part of activist groups indicates that the rehabilitative model has been supplanted by an ideology of overt conflict.

Physically disabled activists, unlike mental patients, cannot fault "society" for their disability. Yet even here we find a variant on the theme of societal culpability: disabled activists blame society for the stigmatization of a mere difference. Paul Hunt, a muscular dystrophy victim, faults contemporary society for its mindless obsession with achievement, its fetishism of commodities and conformity, and its use of ascriptive attributes and material possessions as the salient yardstick of personal worth [7]. In creating such a portrait of the world around him, Hunt safeguards his own sense of integrity and the validity of the experience of disability.

Hunt's writings, with their religious overtones, begin to define the parameters of a "pedagogy of the oppressed" [19]. He not only legitimates the experience of disability but equates disability with revolution against the constraints of rigid normative standards. The handicapped, by their very *being,* reproach materialism and petty conformity, standing as a reminder to all of their own tragedy and finitude. The disabled, then, play a symbolic missionary role. Former patients who adhere to Laingian ideology also celebrate their own condition and equate madness with revolutionary experience:

> Our basic philosophy is that "breakdown" or extreme emotional crisis, with suitable conditions of emotional and physical support, can be a constructive and growth-producing experience; "breakdown" is potentially "breakthrough" [18].

In identifying handicap with subversion and madness with revolution, the activists conceive themselves as playing an *active* role in transforming the social order. Hence the tendency of the disabled and former patients to "elevate" their status by identifying themselves with more politicized and active minority groups and revolutionaries:

> Our constant experience of this pressure towards unthinking conformity in some way relates us to other obvious deviants and outcasts like the Jew in a gentile world, the Negro in a white world, homosexuals, the mentally handicapped; and also the more voluntary rebels in every sphere—artists, philosophers, prophets, who are essentially subversive elements in society. This is an area where disabled people can play an important role [7].

One can only marvel at the power of these stratagems of self-affirmation. Madness emerges not as affliction, but as creative rebellion, and the disabled emerge not as passive victims, but as prophets, visionaries, and revolutionaries.

Language, too, is of paramount importance. The older self-help groups and many professionals sought to replace the usual names for disabilities with more delicate labels, such as "hard of hearing" [18]. Some disabled activists have attempted, usually unsuccessfully, to find substitute terms which remove the pejorative connotations of the words "handicapped" and "disabled." (And this is testimony to the power of language in structuring experience.) But the most militant proudly and self-consciously flaunt the most degrading terms: "cripple," "inmate," "madness," and "proud paranoids" are found in their published statements. This stratagem—*de-euphemization*—demonstrates a subtle mastery of the language game of "normals." Like Richard Wright before them, who created a linguistic revolution when he coined the term "black power," these activists use the very terms which directly assault the "liberal toleration" of "normal" outsiders. Their words, then, are at once an affront to "normals," a signal of conflict and battle, a repudiation of the illusory acceptance implicit in the euphemism, and a testimony to the intrinsic viability of their own experience.

Societal etiology, identification of deviation with revolution, and de-euphemization—these are the stratagems by which the politicized disabled seek to reformulate their condition and to redefine their situation. Identity politics, then, is a sort of phenomenological warfare, a struggle over the social meanings attached to attributes rather than an attempt to assimilate these attributes to the dominant meaning structure.

CONCLUDING REMARKS

Throughout, I have used the concept of identity politics to describe the incipient political activism of the disabled and former mental patients. The new political activists attempt to create an identity for themselves and to propagate this newly-created sense of self to "normals." This is accomplished in two ways. First, the *actions* of the disabled, their militancy and their reliance on social protest, demonstrate that they are independent, rational beings, capable of self-determination and political action. These actions *symbolically* assault the prevailing commonsense (and sociological) imagery of passivity and victimization. Secondly, unlike other responses to stigma and disability, political activism creates an *ideology* which repudiates societal values and normative standards and, in so doing, creates a viable self-conception for participants.

The political activism of the handicapped and former mental patients has far-reaching significance for the professionals who work with them and the sociologists why study them. Many rehabilitative tenets, appropriate to an era when normalization was the favored and modal response to disability, no longer seem applicable to those whose aspirations transcend an often illusory social acceptance by "normals." The identity politics of the disabled and "mentally ill" also challenges the sociologies of deviance, stigma, and disability to create new conceptions of the deviant actor, which embrace concerted political action which resists, rather than subscribes to, societal imputations.

As other identity social movements, such as the Radical Feminist Movement and the Gray Panthers, create new images of sex roles and aging, we can anticipate that the sociologists who study them will re-examine their own assumptions in the light of new historical circumstances.

Notes

1. By this I mean that the labelling theorists have actually altered the negotiated model of interaction first proposed in earlier symbolic interactionist formulations.

2. Davis and Goffman discuss a fifth stratagem, passing, in which the individual accepts the normal standard yet attempts to conceal his/her condition. This response, while available to the former mental patient, is, of course, impossible for the person with a visible handicap.

3. Political activism may, however, be seen as the collective form of a more diffuse strategy of redefinition, reconstitution, and value transcendence. It is possible to respond to stigma in this fashion without belonging to a larger social movement. However, only with the development of larger social movements is such a response viewed as a viable alternative for a significant number of persons.

References

1. Horowitz I. and Liebowitz M. Social deviance and political marginality. *Soc. Probl.* 281–296, 280, 282. 1968.
2. *Washington Post.* April 7, 1977.
3. *Los Angeles Times.* April 6, 1977.
4. Deutsch A. *The Mentally Ill in America.* Doubleday. New York. 1937.
5. Gusfield J. R. *Symbolic Crusade.* p. 179. University of Illinois Press. Urbana. 1963.
6. Ritter B. The rise of the handicapped. *New West* 29, 55, 54. 1976.
7. Hunt P. A critical condition. In *Stigma: The Experience of Disability* (Edited by Hunt P.). pp. 129–130, 151, 159, 151, 144–199. Chapman. London. 1966.
8. Becker H. S. *Outsiders: Studies in the Sociology of Deviance.* p. 7, 17. Free Press. New York. 1963.
9. Davis N. *Sociological Constructions of Deviance Perspectives: Issues in the Field.* Brown. New York. 1975.
10. Mankoff M. Societal reaction and career deviance: a critical analysis. *Sociol. Q.* 12, 205–217. 1971.
11. Akers R. Problems in the sociology of deviance: social definitions and behavior. *Soc. Forces* 455–465. 1976.
12. Goffman E. *Asylums: Essays on the Social Situation of Patients and Other Inmates.* Doubleday. Garden City. 1961.
13. Scheff T. *Being Mentally Ill. A Sociological Theory.* Aldine. Chicago. 1968.
14. Goffman E. *Stigma: Notes on the Management of Spoiled Identity.* pp. 116–24. 1963.

15. Davis F. The family of the polio child: some problems of identity. In *Illness, Interaction and the Self* (Edited by Davis F.). p. 105, 107. Wadsworth. Belmont. 1972.
16. Goffman E. *The Preservation of Self in Everyday Life.* p. 2. Doubleday. Garden City. 1959.
17. Davis F. Deviance disavowal: the management of strained interaction by the visibly handicapped. In *Illness, Interaction and the Self* (Edited by Davis F.). pp. 133–149. Wadsworth. Belmont. 1972.
18. Conference on Human Rights and Psychiatric Oppression. *Newsletter* 1974.
19. Freire P. *The Pedagogy of the Oppressed.* Herder & Herder. New York. 1970.

42 / Return to Sender: Reintegrative Stigma-Management Strategies of Ex-Psychiatric Patients

NANCY J. HERMAN

Although scholars have addressed the exit phase of deviant careers (cf. Adler and Adler 1983; Faupel 1991; Frazier 1976; Glassner et al. 1983; Harris 1973; Inciardi 1978; Irwin 1970; Luckenbill and Best 1981; Meisenhelder 1977; and Ray 1961), the issue of reintegrating deviants into society has received little sociological attention. So too has little attention been given to the wide array of factors affecting role exit and reintegration....

Despite the preponderance of sociological research on the mentally ill, there is a dearth of ethnographically-based studies dealing with the post-hospital lives of ex-psychiatric patients. Such studies, as they do exist, deal largely with chronic ex-patients living in halfway houses or boarding homes, or involved in specific aftercare treatment programs (Cheadle et al. 1978; Estroff 1981; Lamb and Goertzel, 1977; Reynolds and Farberow 1977). Little systematic attention has been given to ex-patients' perceptions of mental illness as a stigmatizable/stigmatizing attribute,[1] the numerous problems they face on the outside, the ways such persons manage discreditable information about themselves in the context of social interaction with others, and the consequences of employing these strategies for altering their deviant identities and social reintegration. In this paper I address these deficits in the sociological literature by presenting ethnographic evidence from a study of 146 non-chronic,[2] ex-psychiatric patients. First, I begin with a discussion of the setting and methods used in this study. Second, I illustrate how ex-patients came to perceive their attribute as potentially stigmatizing. Third, I analyze the five strategies these persons developed and employed in their "management work." Finally, I address the implications of adopting such stratagems for identity transformation and social reintegration. In this paper I hope to contribute to the existing literature on stigma, deviant career exit, management work, and the reintegration of deviants.

SETTING AND METHODS

My interest in mental illness and psychiatric patients has been a long-standing one. My father was employed as an occupational therapist for twenty-five years at a large psychiatric institution in a metropolitan city in Ontario, Canada. Throughout my childhood and adolescent years, I made frequent trips to the institution, interacting with many of the patients on the "admission" and "back" wards, in the hospital canteen, in the occupational therapy workshop, and on the grounds. Moreover, during those years, my father often brought a number of his patients into our home (those, in particular, whose families had abandoned them or who did not have any relatives) to spend Easter, Thanksgiving, and Christmas holidays with our family.

My childhood interest in mental patients sparked my initial involvement in this topic, and I began to study mental patients in 1980 as a graduate student at McMaster University. Having a father who was highly esteemed by the institutional gatekeepers greatly facilitated my access....I spent eight months studying the institutionalization of psychiatric patients ethnographically (Herman 1981). After completing this study on the pre- and in-patient phases of the patients' careers, I became interested in learning about the post-patient phase of their careers. As a result of the movement toward deinstitutionalization, chronic patients, once institutionalized for periods of years, were being released into the community. Moreover, newly diagnosed patients were being hospitalized for brief periods and shortly released. I became interested in examining the post-hospital social worlds and experiences of these ex-psychiatric clients.

I began a four-year research project on this topic in January 1981 (see Herman 1986). In contrast to my earlier study on institutionalized mental patients, where I encountered numerous problems with institutional gatekeepers, this time I encountered relatively few such problems. Rather than dealing with the same provincial institution to obtain a list of discharged patients, I contacted the Director of Psychiatric Services and Professor of Psychiatry at the Medical School affiliated with my university. After hearing about my research proposal, he granted his support for the project and served as my sponsor to the Ethics Committee of the hospital. Approximately one month later, I was given access to a listing of discharged (chronic[3] and non-chronic) ex-psychiatric patients who had been released from the psychiatric wards of seven general hospitals and from two psychiatric institutions in the Southern Ontario area between 1975 and including 1981. In order to protect the identities of those ex-patients not wishing to participate in my study, and to avoid litigation against the hospital for violating rights of confidentiality, I agreed to only be given access to the names of those individuals who agreed to participate. A stratified random sample of 300 ex-patients was formed from the overall discharge list. Upon drawing this sample, the hospitals sent out a letter to each potential subject on my behalf, outlining the general nature of the study, my identity, and my affiliation. Two weeks later, hospital officials made follow-up telephone calls asking potential subjects if they were willing to participate in the study. I was subsequently given a list containing the names of 285 willing participants, 146 non-chronic and 139 chronic ex-patients.[4]

I initially conducted informal interviews with each of the ex-patients in coffee shops, in their homes, in malls, or at their places of work. The interviews lasted from three to five and one-half hours. These interviews not only provided me with a wealth of information about the social worlds of ex-patients, but many subjects invited me to subsequently attend and participate with them in various social settings, including self-help group meetings, activist group meetings and protest marches, and therapy sessions. In addition, I frequently met ex-patients where they worked during coffee and lunch breaks and was able to observe them interacting with co-workers. I ate lunches and dinners in their homes (as they did in mine) and watched them interacting with family members, friends, and neighbors. Each Wednesday afternoon, I met a group of six ex-patients at a local doughnut shop where they would discuss the problems they were facing "on the outside" and collectively search for possible remedies.

PERCEPTIONS OF MENTAL ILLNESS AS STIGMA

In his classic work *Stigma*, Goffman (1963:4) distinguishes between stigmata that are "discrediting" and those that are "discreditable"; the former refer to attributes that are immediately apparent to others, such as obesity, physical abnormalities, and blindness; the latter refer to attributes that are not visible or readily apparent to others, such as being a secret homosexual or ex-prisoner. Mental illness is conceptualized, for the most part, as a discreditable or potentially stigmatizing attribute in that it is not readily apparent to others. It is equally important to note, however, that for some ex-psychiatric patients, mental illness is a deeply discrediting attribute. Many ex-patients, especially chronic ones, were rendered discredited by inappropriate patterns of social interaction and the side effects of medication, which took the forms of twitching, swaying, jerking, and other bizarre mannerisms (see Herman 1986).[5] When ex-patients made voluntary disclosures of personal information about their psychiatric histories or when other people somehow became aware of their histories, ex-patients were categorized in negative terms, as representing some sort of personal failure to "measure up" to the rest of society. Tom, age 45, summed it up for most of the ex-patients:

> Having been diagnosed as a psychiatric patient with psychotic tendencies is the worst thing that has ever happened to me. It's shitty to be mentally ill; it's not something to be proud of. It makes you realize just how different you are from

everybody else—they're normal and you're not. Things are easy for them; things are hard for you. Life's a ball for them; life's a bitch for you! I'm like a mental cripple! I'm a failure at life!...

MENTAL ILLNESS AND STRATEGIES OF INFORMATION MANAGEMENT

Some studies on the discreditable (Edgerton 1967; Humphreys 1972; Ponse 1976) have suggested that individuals either disclose their attribute to others *or* make attempts to actively conceal such information about their selves. Other studies (Bell and Weinberg 1978; Miall 1986; Schneider and Conrad 1980; Veevers 1980) have suggested that being a "secret deviant" is far more complex than either choosing to disclose or not disclose one's "failing." These studies suggest that individuals *selectively* conceal such information about themselves at certain times, in certain situations, and with certain individuals and freely disclose the same information at other times, in other situations, and with other individuals. Concealment and disclosure, then, are contingent upon a "complex interaction of one's learned perceptions of the stigma [of their attribute], actual 'test' experiences with others before/or after disclosure, and the nature of the particular relationship involved" (Schneider and Conrad 1980:39).

The complex reality of how individuals selectively conceal and disclose information was evident in the case of non-chronic ex-psychiatric patients. Examination of their post-hospital worlds revealed not only that many ex-patients faced economic hardships, had problems coping in the community, and experienced adverse side effects from their "meds"[6] but also that their perception of mental illness as a potentially stigmatizing attribute presented severe problems in their lives. Many lived their lives in states of emotional turmoil, afraid and frustrated—deciding who to tell or not tell, when to tell and when not to tell, and how to tell. Joan, a 56-year-old waitress, aptly summed it up for most non-chronics:

> It's a very difficult thing. It's not easy to distinguish the good ones from the bad ones.... You've gotta figure out who you can tell about your illness and who you better not tell. It is a tremendous stress and strain that you have to live with 24 hours a day!

Ex-psychiatric patients learned how, with whom, and under which circumstances to disclose or conceal their discreditable aspects of self, largely through a process of trial and error, committing numerous *faux pas* along the way. Frank, a 60-year-old factory worker, spoke of the number of mistakes he made in his "management work":

> I was released over two years now. And since then, I've developed an ulcer trying to figure out how to deal with my "sickness"—that is, how or whether others could handle it or not. I screwed up things a few times when I told a couple

of guys on the bowling team. I made a mistake and thought that they were my buddies and would accept it.

In fact, even if no *faux pas* were committed, there was no guarantee that others would accept preferred meanings and definitions of self. As Charlie, a 29-year-old graduate student, hospitalized on three occasions, remarked:

> I'm not a stupid person. I learned how to handle effectively the negative aspects of my sickness—I mean how others view it. I've been doing OK now since my discharge, but still, each time I'm entering a new situation, I get anxious; I'm not always a hundred percent sure of whether to tell or not to—especially in the case of dating relationships. Even if you've had success in telling certain types of people, there's always the chance—and it happens more than you think, that people will just not "buy" what you're trying so desperately to "sell" them.

Nearly 80 percent of the non-chronics in this study engaged in some form of information control about their illnesses and past hospitalizations. Specifically, the stratagems adopted and employed by the ex-patients, resembling those observed in other deviant groups (cf. Davis 1961; Hewitt and Stokes 1975; Levitin 1975; Miall 1986; Schneider and Conrad 1980), included (1) selective concealment, (2) therapeutic disclosure, (3) preventive disclosure, and (4) political activism—stratagems adopted by ex-patients in their effort to lessen or avoid the stigma potential of mental illness, elevate self-esteem, renegotiate societal conceptions of mental illness as a discreditable attribute, and alter deviant identities.

Selective Concealment

Selective concealment can be defined as the selective withholding or disclosure of information about self perceived as discreditable in cases where secrecy is the major stratagem for handling information about an attribute. Especially during the period directly following their psychiatric treatment, the majority of non-chronics had a marked desire to conceal such information about their selves from all others. Decisions about disclosure and concealment were made on the basis of their perceptions of others—that is, whether they were "safe others" or "risky others." So too were decisions based on prior, negative experiences with "certain types" of others. Speaking of her classification of others into "trustworthy" and "untrustworthy" others, Dawina, a 46-year-old secretary, institutionalized on seven occasions, said:

> It's like this. There are two types of people out there, "trustworthy" ones—the people who will be understanding and supportive—and "untrustworthy" ones. Out of all of my friends and relations and even the people I work with at the company, I only decided to tell my friend Sue.

Moreover, there was a hierarchical pattern of selective disclosure based upon the individual's perceived degree of closeness and the ex-patient's revealing his or her discreditable attribute. In general, such information was most frequently revealed to family members, followed by close friends, and then acquaintances, a pattern also reflected in the literature on epileptics (Schneider and Conrad 1980) and involuntary childless women (Miall 1986). As Sarah, a 36-year-old mother of two, put it:

> When I was discharged, I didn't automatically hide from everyone the fact that I was hospitalized for a nervous breakdown again. But I didn't go and tell everyone either. I phoned and told my relatives in "Logenport," and I confided in two of my close, good friends here in town.

Further, selective disclosures to normal others were frequently made to test reactions. Similar to Schneider and Conrad's (1980) epileptics, the ex-patients continued to disclose mental illness contingent upon responses they had received to previous disclosures. Rudy, a 39-year-old man hospitalized on ten occasions, stated:

> You learn through trial and error. When I was let out back in 1976, I was still naive, you know. I decided to tell a few people. Boy, was that a mistake. They acted as if I had AIDS. Nobody wanted anything further to do with me.... Since then, I've pretty much dummied up and not told anyone!

In those cases where concealment was the dominant strategy of information management, ex-patients usually disclosed only to one or two individuals. As Simon, a 25-year-old ex-patient, aptly expressed:

> I decided from the moment that my treatment ended, I would tell as few people as possible about my stay in the psychiatric hospital. I figured that it would be for the best to "keep it under a lid" for the most part. So, to this day, I've only confided in my friend Paul and a neighbor who had a similar illness a while back.

The employment of concealment as a stratagem of information management took the following forms: avoidance of selected "normals," redirection of conversations, withdrawal, the use of disidentifiers, and the avoidance of stigma symbols. Speaking on his efforts to redirect conversations, Mark, a 34-year-old non-chronic, explained:

> Look, you've got to remain on your toes at all times. More often than not, somebody brings up the topic about my past and starts probing around. Sometimes these people won't let up....I use the tactic where I change the subject, answer their question with a question....I try to manipulate the conversation so it works out in my favor.

For still others, concealment of their discreditable attribute was achieved through withdrawal. Over two-thirds of the ex-patients in this study engaged in withdrawal as a form of concealment, especially during the early months following discharge. Speaking of his use of this technique, Harry, a college junior, remarked:

> Sometimes when I'm at a party or some type of gathering with a number of people, I just remain pretty reticent. I don't participate too much in the conversations....

I'm really unsure how much to tell other people. For the most part, I just keep pretty quiet and remain a wallflower. People may think I'm shy or stuck-up, but I'd rather deal with that than with the consequences of others finding out that I'm a mental patient.

A third technique, employed by over one-third of the ex-patients to conceal their discreditable aspects from others, involved the use of disiden-tifiers (Goffman 1963:44). That is, ex-patients utilized misleading physical or verbal symbols in an effort to prevent normal others from discovering their "failing." Similar to homosexuals (Carrier 1976; Delph 1978), unwed parents (Christensen 1953; Pfuhl 1978), and lesbians (Ponse 1976), who frequently made use of disidentifiers in their management work, non-chronic ex-patients also employed such techniques. Specifically, disidentifiers took the form of making jokes about psychiatric patients while in the presence of "normal" others and participating in protests *against* the integration of ex-patients into the community. Mike, a 26-year-old ex-patient, recently released after three hospitalizations, remarked (with some remorse) on his use of this tactic:

They wanted to use this house down the street for a group home for discharged patients. All the neighbors on the street were up in arms over it. It didn't upset me personally, but the neighbors made up this petition, and to protect myself, I not only signed it, but I also went door-to-door convincing other neighbors to sign it and "keep those mentals out".... I felt sort of bad afterwards, but what else could I do?

In a similar vein, Morgan, a 49-year-old history professor, explained how his joke-telling aided in the concealment of his attribute:

I conceal this information about myself—my psychiatric past—by frequently telling jokes about mental patients to my colleagues in the elevator, and sometimes even my lectures, and in everyday conversation. It's really a great ploy to use. People may think the jokes are in bad taste, but at the very least, it helps me to keep secret my illness.

A final form of concealing information on the part of ex-patients was through the avoidance of stigma symbols (cf. Goffman 1963:43)—signs that would bring into the forefront or disclose their discreditable attribute. It is interesting to note that the data presented here on non-chronics and their avoidance of stigma symbols supports observations made of other deviant groups, for example, transsexuals (Bogdan 1974; Kando 1973) and unwed fathers (Pfuhl 1978).... Among the 146 ex-patients studied, over two-thirds avoided contact with such stigma symbols as other ex-mental patients with whom they had become friends while institutionalized and self-help groups for ex-patients. So, too, did they avoid frequenting drop-in centers, attending dances and bingo games for ex-patients, and, in general, placing themselves where other "patients and ex-patients hung out." For still others, avoid-ance of stigma symbols entailed not attending post-hospital therapy sessions.

Margarette, a stocky, middle-aged woman of German descent, explained her avoidance of post-discharge therapy sessions in the following manner:

> After I was released, my psychiatrist asked that I make appointments and see him every two weeks for follow-up maintenance treatments. But I never did go because I didn't want someone to see me going into the psychiatric department of "Meadowbrook Hospital" and sitting in the waiting room of the "Nut Wing." Two of my nosy neighbors are employed at that hospital, and I just couldn't take the chance of them seeing me there one day.

In sum, as a strategy of information management, selective concealment of their attribute and past hospitalizations was done to protect themselves from the perceived negative consequences that might result from the revelation of their illness—an "offensive tactical maneuver" through which ex-patients attempted (although often unsuccessfully) to mitigate the stigma potential of mental illness on their daily lives. Notably, employing concealment as a strategy of information management was a *temporal* process. The majority of ex-patients employed this strategy primarily during the first eight months following their discharge. During this time, in particular, they expressed feelings of anxiety, fear, and trepidation. As time passed, however, ex-patients began to test reactions. They encountered both positive and negative responses from certain "normals," and their strong initial desires for secrecy were replaced by alternative strategies.

Therapeutic Disclosures

Therapeutic disclosure can be defined as the selective disclosure of a discreditable attribute to certain "trusted," "empathetic" supportive others in an effort to renegotiate personal perceptions of the stigma of "failing." ... Thirty-six percent of the ex-patients felt that discussing their mental illnesses and past hospitalizations, getting it off their chests in a cathartic fashion, functioned to alleviate much of the burden of their loads. Attesting to the cathartic function disclosing served, Vincent, a 29-year-old ex-patient, remarked:

> Finally, letting it all out, after so many secrets, lies, it was so therapeutic for me. Keeping something like this all bottled up inside is self-destructive. When I came clean, this great burden was lifted from me!

Therapeutic disclosure was most often carried out with family members, close friends, and with other ex-psychiatric patients—individuals "sharing the same fate." Ida, age 52, discussing the circumstances surrounding her disclosure to a neighbor who had also been hospitalized in a psychiatric facility at one time, said:

> At first, I was apprehensive to talk about it. But keeping it inside of you all bottled up is no good either. One day, I walked down the street to a neighbor of mine and she invited me in to have tea. I knew what had happened to her years ago (her deceased husband confided in my husband). I let out all my anxieties and fears

to her that afternoon....I told her everything and she was so sympathetic....She knew exactly what I was going through. Once I let it all out, I felt so much better.

Even in cases where ex-patients disclosed to individuals who turned out to be unsympathetic and unsupportive, some considered this therapeutic:

> When I came out of hiding and told people about my sickness, not everyone embraced me. A lot of people are shocked and just tense up. Some just stare....A few never call you after that time or make up excuses not to meet with you....But I don't care, because overall, telling made me feel better.

Just as therapeutic disclosure functioned to relieve ex-patients' anxieties and frustrations, it also allowed for the renegotiation of personal perceptions of mental illness as a discreditable attribute. Speaking of the manner by which she came to redefine mental illness in her own mind as a less stigmatizing attribute, Edith explained:

> When I finally opened up and started talking about it, it really wasn't so bad after all. My Uncle John was very supportive and helped me to put my mind at rest, to realize that having mental illness isn't so bad; it's not like having cancer. He told me that thousands of people go into the hospital each year for psychiatric treatment and probably every third person I meet has had treatment....After much talking I no longer think of myself as less human, but more normally.... Having mental illness isn't the blight I thought it was.

In short, then, ex-patients employed therapeutic disclosure in order to relieve feelings of frustration and anxiety, to elevate their self-esteem, and to renegotiate (in their own minds) personal perceptions of mental illness as stigmatizing.

Preventive Disclosure

Preventive disclosure can be described as the selective disclosure to "normals" of a discreditable attribute in an effort to influence others' actions or perceptions about the ex-patient or about mental illness in general (cf. Miall 1986; Schneider and Conrad 1980). Preventive disclosure of their mental illness and past hospitalizations occurred in situations where ex-patients anticipated future rejection by "normal" others. In order to minimize the pain of subsequent rejection, 34 percent of the sample decided that the best strategy to employ with certain people was preventive disclosure *early* in their relationships. As Hector, a 40-year-old janitor, said:

> I figured out that, for me, it is best to inform people right off the bat about my mental illness. Why? Because you don't waste a lot of time developing relationships and then are rejected later. That hurts too much. Tell them early and if they can't deal with it, and run away, you don't get hurt as much!

Preventive disclosure, then, represented a way ex-patients attempted to prevent a drop in their status at a later date, or a way of testing acquaintances in an effort to establish friendship boundaries.

Just as non-chronics used preventive disclosure to avoid future stigma and rejection, so too did they employ this strategy to influence normals' attitudes about themselves and about mental illness in general. Specifically, ex-patients used the following devices: (1) medical disclaimers (cf. Hewitt and Stokes 1975; Miall 1986; Schneider and Conrad 1980); (2) deception/coaching (cf. Goffman 1963; Miall 1986; Schneider and Conrad 1980); (3) education (cf. Schneider and Conrad 1980); and (4) normalization (cf. Cogswell 1967; Davis 1961, 1963; Levitin 1975; McCaghy 1968; Scott 1969).

Medical Disclaimers. Fifty-two percent of the ex-patients frequently used medical disclaimers in their management work—"blameless, beyond-my-control medical interpretation(s)" developed in order to "reduce the risk that more morally disreputable interpretations might be applied by naive others" discovering their failing (Schneider and Conrad 1980:41). Such interpretations were often used by ex-patients to evoke sympathy from others and to ensure that they would be treated in a charitable manner. As Dick, an unemployed laborer, put it:

> When I tell people about my hospitalization in a psychiatric hospital, I immediately emphasize that the problem isn't anything I did, it's a biological one. I didn't ask to get sick; it was just plain biology; or my genes that fucked me up. I try to tell people in a nice way so that they see mental illness just like other diseases—you know, cancer or the mumps. It's not my parents' fault or my own.... I just tell them, "Don't blame me, blame my genes!"

In a similar vein, Anna, a 29-year-old waitress, explained her use of medical disclaimers:

> Talking about it is quite tricky. When I tell them about it, I'm careful to emphasize that the three times I was admitted, was due to a biochemical imbalance—something that millions of people get. I couldn't do anything to help myself—I ate properly, didn't drink or screw around. It's not something I deserved. When you give people the facts and do it in a clinical fashion, you can sway many of them to sympathize with you.

Further, eleven ex-patients revealed their mental illness and past hospitalizations as a side effect of another medical problem or disease, such as childbirth, stroke, or heart disease, thereby legitimizing what otherwise might be considered a potentially stigmatizing condition. As Rebecca, age 36, confessed:

> I have had heart problems since birth. I was a very sick baby. I've had four operations since that time and I've been on all kinds of medications. The stress of dealing with such an illness led to my depression and subsequent breakdowns.... When my friends hear about mental illness in this light, they are very empathetic.

While Sue spoke of her successes in influencing others' perceptions about her attribute and mental illness in general, Lenny lamented about his failure with the same strategy:

Life's not easy for ex-nuts, you know. I tried telling two of my drinking buddies about my schizophrenia problem one night at the bar. I thought if I told 'em that it's a "disease" like having a heart problem that they would understand and pat me on the butt and say it didn't matter to them and that I was OK. Shit, it didn't work out like I planned; they flipped out on me. Sid couldn't handle it at all and just let out of there in a hurry; Jack stayed around me for about twenty minutes and then made some excuse and left.

In sum, through the use of medical disclaimers, ex-patients hoped to elevate their self-esteem and to renegotiate personal perceptions of mental illness as a non-stigmatizing attribute.

Deception/Coaching. Deception differed from strategies of concealment in that with the former, ex-patients readily disclosed their illness and past hospitalizations but explicitly distorted the conditions or circumstances surrounding it. Similar to Miall's (1986) involuntary childless women and Schneider and Conrad's (1980) epileptics, about one-third of the ex-patients employed deceptive practices developed with the assistance of coaches. Coaches included parents, close friends, spouses, and other ex-patients sharing the same stigma. Coaches actively provided ex-patients with practical suggestions on how to disclose their attribute in the least stigmatizing manner and present themselves in a favorable light. Maureen, age 32, explained of her "coaching sessions" with relatives:

My parents and grandma really helped me out in terms of what I should say or tell others. They were so afraid I'd be hurt that they advised me what to tell my school mates, the manager at Wooldo where I got hired. We had numerous practice exercises where we'd role-play and I'd rehearse what I would say to others.... After a while I became quite convincing.

Moreover, it is interesting to note that about one quarter of the ex-patients employed deceptive practices together with medical disclaimers. As Benjamin, age 62, aptly expressed:

To survive in this cruel, cold world, you've got to be sneaky. I mean, that you've got to try to win people over to your side. Whoever you decide to tell about your illness, you've got to make it clear that you had nothing to do with getting sick; nobody can place blame on anyone.... And you've got to color the truth about how you ended up in the hospital by telling heart-sob stories to get people sympathetic to you. You never tell them the whole truth or they'll shun you like the plague!

Education. A third form of preventive disclosure used by ex-patients to influence others' perceptions of them and their ideas about mental illness was education.... Twenty-eight percent of the ex-patients revealed their attribute in an effort to educate others. Marge, age 39, speaking on her efforts to educate friends and neighbors, said:

I have this urge inside of me to teach people out there, to let them know that they've been misinformed about mental illness and mental patients. We're not the way the media has portrayed us. That's why people are afraid of us. I feel very strongly that someone has to tell people the truth...give them the facts....And when they hear it, they're amazed sometimes and begin to treat me without apprehension....Each time I make a breakthrough, I think more highly of myself too.

Ex-patients did not automatically attempt to educate everyone they encountered but, rather, based on subjective typification of normals, made value judgments about whom to "educate." Brenda, speaking on this matter, explained:

You just can't go ahead and tell everyone. You ponder who it is, what are the circumstances, and whether you think that they can be educated about it. There are some people that these efforts would be fatal and fruitless. Others however, you deem as a potential. And these are the people you work with.

While education proved successful for some ex-patients in their management activities with certain individuals, others found it less successful. Jim, recalling one disastrous experience with a former poker buddy, said:

I really thought he would learn something from my discussion of the facts. I really misjudged Fred. I thought him to be an open-minded kind of guy but perhaps just naive, so I sat him down one afternoon and made him my personal "mission." I laid out my past and then talked to him about all the kinds of mental illnesses that are out there. He reacted terrible. All his biases came out, and he told me that all those people should be locked up and the key thrown away—that they were a danger to society. He was probably thinking the same thing about me too!

Following Goffman (1963:101), medical disclaimers, deception/coaching, and education are forms of "disclosure etiquette"—they are formulas for revealing a stigmatizing attribute "in a matter of fact way, supporting the assumption that those present are above such concerns while preventing them from trapping themselves into showing that they are not."

Normalization. A final form of preventive disclosure employed by ex-psychiatric patients to manage stigma was normalization. This concept is drawn from Davis's (1963) study on children with polio and is akin to deviance disavowal (cf. Davis 1961). Normalization is a strategy individuals use to deny that their behavior or attribute is deviant. It "seeks to render normal and morally acceptable that which has heretofore been regarded as abnormal and immoral" (Pfuhl 1986:163). Similar to observations made on pedophiles (McCaghy 1968), the obese (Millman 1980), the visibly handicapped (Levitin 1975), and paraplegics (Cogswell 1967), about one quarter of the ex-psychiatric patients I studied also employed this same strategy. Such persons were firmly committed to societal conceptions of normalcy and were aware that according to these standards, they were disqualified—they would never "measure up." Yet ex-patients made active attempts at rationalizing and downplaying the stigma attached to their failing. So, for example, they participated in a full round of normal activities and aspired to normal attainments. They participated in amateur theater groups, played competitive sports such as hockey and tennis, enrolled in college, and the like. Ex-patients whose stigma could be considered "discreditable," that is, not readily or visibly apparent to others, would disclose such information for preventive reasons, thereby rendering them "discredited" in the eyes of others. They would then attempt to negotiate with normals for preferred images, attitudes, roles, and non-deviant conceptions of self and definitions of mental illness as less stigmatizing. Discussing his utilization of this technique, "Weird Old Larry," age 59, said:

The third time I got out [of the hospital], I tried to fit right in. I told some of my buddies and a couple of others about my sickness. It was easier to get it out in the open. But what I tried to show 'em was that I could do the same things they could, some of them, even better. I beat them at pool, at darts; I could outdrink them, I was holding down two jobs—one at the gas station and at K-mart. I tried to show them I was normal. I was cured! The key to success is being up-front and making them believe you're just as normal as them.... You can really change how they see and treat you.

If successfully carried out, this avowal normalized relations between ex-patients and others.

This is not to imply, however, that the strategy of normalization worked for all patients in all situations. Similar to Millman's (1980:78) overweight females who were accepted in certain roles but treated as deviant in others, many ex-patients expressed similar problems. Frederick, speaking on this problem with respect to co-workers, said:

It's really tragic, you know. When I told the other people at work that I was a manic-depressive but was treated and released, I emphasized that I was completely normal in every way...but they only accepted me normally part of the time, like when we were in the office....But they never really accepted me as their friend, as one of "the boys"; and they never invited me over to dinner with their wife and family—they still saw me as an ex-crazy, not as an equal to be worthy being invited to dinner, or playing with their kids.

It is interesting to note that just as ex-patients whose attribute was discreditable employed the strategy of normalization, so, too, did other ex-patients with discrediting attributes (conditions *visibly apparent* or *known* to others) employ this same technique. Explaining how medication side effects rendered him discredited and how he attempted to reduce the stigma of mental illness through normalization, Ross said:

Taking all that dope the shrinks dish out makes my hands tremble. Look at my shaking legs too. I never used to have these twitches in my face either, but that's just the side effects, a bonus you get. It really fucks things up though. If I wanted to hide my illness, I couldn't; everyone just looks at me and knows....So, what I do is to try to get people's attention and get them to see my positive side—that I can be quite normal, you know. I emphasize all the things that I can do!

In short, by presenting themselves as normals, ex-patients hoped to elicit positive responses from others whose reactions were deemed to be important. From a social-psychological perspective, others accepted and reinforced a non-deviant image of self through this process of negotiation, allowing ex-patients to achieve more positive, non-deviant identities.

In many cases, ex-psychiatric patients progressed from one strategy to another as they managed information about themselves. Specifically, they moved from a strategy of initial selective concealment to disclosure for therapeutic and preventive reasons. According to the ex-patients, such a progression was linked to their increased adjustment to their attribute as well as the result of positive responses from others to the revelation of their mental illness.

Political Activism

Just as ex-psychiatric patients developed and employed a number of individualized forms of information management to deal with the stigma potential of mental illness, enhance self-images, and alter deviant identities, they also employed one collective management strategy[7] to achieve the same ends, namely, joining and participating in ex-mental patient activist groups (cf. Anspach, 1979). Such groups, with their goal of self-affirmation, represent what Kitsuse (1980:9) terms "tertiary deviation—referring to the deviant's confirmation, assessment, and rejection of the negative identity embedded in secondary deviation, and the transformation of that identity into a positive and viable self-conception."

Political activism served a three-fold function for ex-patients: (1) it repudiated standards of normalcy (standards to which they couldn't measure up) and the deviant labels placed upon these individuals; (2) it provided them with a new, positive, non-deviant identity, enhanced their self-respect, and afforded them a new sense of purpose; and (3) it served to propagate this new, positive image of ex-mental patient to individuals, groups, and organizations in society. The payoff from political activism, was, then, personal as well as social.

Similar to such activist groups as the Gay Liberation Front, the Disabled in Action, the Gray Panthers, or the Radical Feminist Movement, ex-mental patient activists rejected prevailing societal values of normalcy through participation in their groups. They repudiated the deviant identities, roles, and statuses placed on them. Moreover, these individuals flatly rejected the stigma associated with their identities. Steve, a 51-year-old electrician, aptly summed it up for most ex-patient activists:

> The whole way society had conceived of right and wrong, normal and abnormal is all wrong. They somehow have made us believe that to be mentally ill is to be *ashamed* of something; that these people are to be feared, that they are to blame for their sickness. Well I don't accept this vein anymore.

Upon repudiating prevailing cultural values and deviant identities, ex-patient activists collectively redefined themselves in a more positive, non-deviant light according to their *own* newly constructed set of standards. Speaking of her embracing a new non-deviant identity, Susan, age 39, who recently returned to teaching school, said:

> I no longer agree to accept what society says is normal and what is not. It's been so unfair to psychiatric patients. Who are they to say, just because we don't conform, that we're rejects of humanity.... The labels they've given us are degrading and make us feel sick.... [The labels] have a negative connotation to them.... So, we've gotten together and liberated ourselves. We've thrown away the old labels and negative images of self-worth, and we give ourselves new labels and images of self-worth—as human beings who should be treated with decency and respect.

In contrast to other ex-patients who employed various individual management strategies to deal with what they perceived to be their *own* problems—personal failings—ex-patient activists saw their problems not as personal failings or potentially stigmatizing attributes but as *societal* problems. To the extent that ex-patients viewed their situations in this manner, it allowed them to develop more positive self-images. Speaking of this process as one of "stigma conversion," Humphreys (1972:142) writes:

> In converting his stigma, the oppressed person does not merely exchange his social marginality for political marginality.... Rather, he emerges from a stigmatized cocoon as a transformed creature, one characterized by the spreading of political wings. At some point in the process, the politicized "deviant" gains a new identity, an heroic self-image as crusader in a political cause.

Sally, a neophyte activist, placed the "blame" on society for her deviant self-image:

> It's not any of our faults that we ended up the way we did. I felt guilty for a long time.... I crouched away feeling that I had something that made me "different" from everyone else, a pock on my life.... But I learned at the activist meetings that none of it was my fault. It was all society's fault—they're the one who can't deal with anything that is different. Now I realize that having mental illness is nothing to be ashamed of; it's nothing to hide. I'm now proud of who...and what I am!

Just as political activism, as contrasted with other adaptive responses to stigma, sought, in repudiating the dominant value system, to provide ex-patients with positive, non-deviant statuses, so too, did it attempt to propagate this new positive, normal image of ex-psychiatric patients to others in society. Thus, through such activities as rallies, demonstrations, protest marches, attendance at conferences on human rights for patients, lobbyist activities directed toward politicians and the medical profession, and the production of newsletters, ex-patient activists sought to promote social change. Specifically, they sought to counter or remove the stigma associated with their "differentness" and present society with an image of former psychiatric patients as "human beings" capable of self-determination and political action. Abe, the president of the activist group, aptly summed up the aim of political activism during a speech to selected political figures, media personnel, and "upstanding" citizens:

> Simply put, we're tired of being pushed around. We reject everything society says about us, because it's just not accurate. We reject the type of treatment we get...both in the hospital...and out. We don't like the meaning of the words [people] use to describe us—"mentals" and "nuts." We see ourselves differently, just as good and worthy as everybody out there. In our newsletter, we're trying to get across the idea that we're not the stereotypical mental patient you see in the movies. We're real people who want to be treated equally under the Charter of Rights. We're not sitting back now, we're fighting back!

In sum, then, through participation in political activist groups, many ex-patients internalized an ideology that repudiated societal values and conventional standards of normalcy, rejected their deviant identities and statuses, adopted more positive, non-deviant identities, and attempted to alter society's stereotypical perceptions about mental patients and mental illness in general....

Notes

1. The stigmatized status of individuals and the information management strategies they employ have been well-documented for other groups such as the retarded (Edgerton 1967), epileptics (Schneider and Conrad 1980), secret homosexuals (Humphreys 1975), involuntary childless women (Miall 1986), swingers (Bartell 1971), and lesbians (Ponse 1976), among others.

2. Chronicity, for the purposes of this study, was defined *not* in diagnostic terms, that is, "chronic schizophrenic"; rather, it was defined in terms of duration, continuity, and frequency of hospitalizations. Specifically, the term "non-chronic" refers to those individuals hospitalized for periods of less than two years, those institutionalized on a discontinuous basis, those hospitalized on fewer than five occasions, or those treated in psychiatric wards of general hospitals.

3. The term "chronic" ex-psychiatric patient refers to those institutionalized in psychiatric hospitals for periods of two years or more, institutionalized on a continual basis, or hospitalized on five or more occasions.

4. The decision to stratify the sample by chronicity was based upon my interests and prior fieldwork activities. My earlier study (Herman 1981) indicated that when we speak of "deinstitutionalized" or "discharged" patients, we cannot merely assume that they are one homogeneous grouping of individuals with like characteristics, and similar post-hospital social situations, experiences, and perceptions of reality. Rather, prior research led me to believe that there might be distinct subgroups of individuals with varying perceptions of reality and experiences (see Herman 1986).

5. In Estroff's (1981) ethnography on chronic ex-mental patients, she points out the catch-22 situation in which they find themselves. Ex-patients need to take their medications regularly in order to remain on the outside. Ironically, however, in an effort to become more like others, they take "meds" that make them "different." The various side effects reinforce their deviant identities.

6. See Herman (1986) for a detailed discussion of such other post-hospital problems.

7. Following Lyman's (1970) typology of deviant voluntary associations, ex-mental patient political activist groups represent an "instrumental-alienative" type of association. It is interesting to note that chronic ex-patients also employed one collective form of stigma management; specifically, they formed and participated in deviant subcultures (see Herman 1987).

References

Adler, Patricia A. 1992. "The 'post' phase of deviant careers: Reintegrating drug traffickers." *Deviant Behavior* 13:103–126.

Adler, Patricia A., and Peter Adler. 1983. Shifts and oscillations in deviant careers: The case of upper-level drug dealers and smugglers. *Social Problems* 31:195–207.

Anspach, Renee. 1979. From stigma to identity politics: Political activism among the physically disabled and former mental patients. *Social Science and Medicine* 13A:765–773.

Bartell, Gilbert D. 1971. *Group Sex: A Scientist's Eyewitness Report on the American Way of Swinging*. New York: Wyden.

Bell, Alan, and Martin S. Weinberg. 1978. *Homosexualities: A Study of Diversity among Men and Women*. New York: Simon and Schuster.

Bogdan, Robert. 1974. *Being Different: The Autobiography of Jane Fry*. New York: Wiley.

Carrier, J. M. 1976. Family attitudes and Mexican male homosexuality. *Urban Life* 50:359–375.

Cheadle, A. J., H. Freeman, and J. Korer. [1978.] Chronic schizophrenic patients in the community. *British Journal of Psychiatry* 132:221–227.

Christensen, Harold T. 1953. Studies in child spacing: Premarital pregnancy as measured by the spacing of the first birth from marriage. *American Sociological Review* 18:53–59.

Cogswell, B. 1967. Rehabilitation of the paraplegic: Processes of socialization. *Sociological Inquiry* 37:11–26.

Davis, Fred. 1961. Deviance disavowal: The management of strained interaction by the visibly handicapped. *Social Problems* 9:120–132.

———. 1963. *Passage through Crisis: Polio Victims and Their Families*. Indianapolis: Bobbs-Merrill.

Delph, E. 1978. *The Silent Community: Public Homosexual Encounters*. Beverly Hills, CA: Sage.

Edgerton, Robert. 1967. *The Cloak of Competence: Stigma in the Lives of the Mentally Retarded*. Berkeley: University of California Press.

Estroff, Sue E. 1981. *Making It Crazy: An Ethnography of Psychiatric Clients in an American Community*. Berkeley: University of California Press.

Faupel, Charles E. 1991. *Shooting Dope: Career Patterns of Hard-Core Heroin Users*. Gainesville: University of Florida Press.

Frazier, Charles. 1976. *Theoretical Approaches to Deviance*. Columbus, OH: Merrill.

Glassner, Barry, Margret Ksander, Bruce Berg, and Bruce D. Johnson. 1983. A note on the deterrent effect of juvenile vs. adult jurisdiction. *Social Problems* 31:219–221.

Goffman, Erving. 1961. *Asylums*. New York: Doubleday.

———. 1963. *Stigma*. Englewood Cliffs, NJ: Prentice Hall.

Harris, Mervyn. 1973. *The Dilly Boys*. Rockville, MD: New Perspectives.

Herman, Nancy J. 1981. *The Making of a Mental Patient: An Ethnographic Study of the Processes and Consequences of Institutionalization upon Self-Images and Identities*. Unpublished master's thesis, McMaster University, Hamilton, Ontario.

———. 1986. *Crazies in the Community: An Ethnographic Study of Ex-Psychiatric Clients in Canadian Society—Stigma, Management Strategies and Identity Trans-*

formation. Unpublished Ph.D. dissertation, McMaster University, Hamilton, Ontario.

————. 1987. "Mixed nutters" and "looney tuners": The emergence, development, nature, and functions of two informal, deviant subcultures of chronic, ex-psychiatric patients. *Deviant Behavior* 8:235–258.

Hewitt, J., and R. Stokes. 1975. Disclaimers. *American Sociological Review* 40:1–11.

Humphreys, Laud. 1972. *Out of the Closets: The Sociology of Homosexual Liberation.* Englewood Cliffs, NJ: Prentice Hall.

————. 1975. *Tearoom Trade.* New York: Aldine de Gruyter.

Inciardi, James. 1975. *Careers in Crime.* Chicago: Rand McNally.

Irwin, John. 1970. *The Felon.* Englewood Cliffs, NJ: Prentice Hall.

Kando, T. 1973. *Sex Change: The Achievement of Gender Identity among Feminized Transsexuals.* Springfield, IL: Charles C. Thomas.

Kitsuse, John. 1980. Presidential address. *Society for the Study of Social Problems* 9:1–13.

Lamb, J., and V. Goertzel. 1977. The long-term patient in the era of community treatment. *Archives of General Psychiatry* 34:679–682.

Levitin, T. 1975. Deviants as active participants in the labelling process: The case of the visibly handicapped. *Social Problems* 22:548–557.

Luckenbill, David F., and Joel Best. 1981. Careers in deviance and respectability: The analogy's limitations. *Social Problems* 29:197–206.

Lyman, Stanford M. 1970. *The Asian in the West.* Reno and Las Vegas, NV: Western Studies Center, Desert Research Institute.

McCaghy, Charles H. 1968. Drinking and deviance disavowal: The case of child molesters. *Social Problems* 16:43–49.

Meisenhelder, Thomas. 1977. An exploratory study of exiting from criminal careers. *Criminology* 15:319–334.

Miall, Charlene E. 1986. The stigma of involuntary childlessness. *Social Problems* 33(4):268–282.

Millman, Marcia. 1980. *Such a Pretty Face.* New York: Norton.

Pfuhl, Erdwin H., Jr. 1978. The unwed father: A "non-deviant" rule breaker. *Sociological Quarterly* 19(Winter):113–128.

Ponse, Barbara. 1976. Secrecy in the lesbian world. *Urban Life* 5:313–338.

Ray, Marsh. 1961. The cycle of abstinence and relapse among heroin addicts. *Social Problems* 9:132–140.

Reynolds, David K., and Norman Farberow. 1977. *Endangered Hope: Experiences in Psychiatric Aftercare Facilities.* Berkeley: University of California Press.

Schneider, J., and P. Conrad. 1980. In the closet with illness: Epilepsy, stigma potential and information control. *Social Problems* 28(1):32–44.

Scott, Robert. 1969. The socialization of blind children. In *Handbook of Socialization Theory and Research,* edited by D. Goslin. Chicago: Rand McNally.

Veevers, Jean. 1980. *Childless by Choice.* Toronto: Butterworths.

43 / The Professional Ex-: An Alternative for Exiting the Deviant Career

J. DAVID BROWN

This study explores the careers of professional ex-s, persons who have exited their deviant careers by replacing them with occupations in professional counseling. During their transformation professional ex-s utilize vestiges of their deviant identity to legitimate their past deviance and generate new careers as counselors.

Recent surveys document that approximately 72% of the professional counselors working in the over 10,000 U.S. substance abuse treatment centers are former substance abusers (NAADAC 1986; Sobell and Sobell 1987). This attests to the significance of the professional ex- phenomenon. Though not all ex-deviants become professional ex-s, such data clearly suggest that the majority of substance abuse counselors are professional ex-s.[1]

Since the inception of the notion of deviant career by Goffman (1961) and Becker (1963), research has identified, differentiated, and explicated the characteristics of specific deviant career stages (e.g., Adler and Adler 1983; Luckenbill and Best 1981; Meisenhelder 1977; Miller 1986; Shover 1983). The literature devoted to exiting deviance primarily addresses the process whereby individuals abandon their deviant behaviors, ideologies, and identities and replace them with more conventional lifestyles and identities (Irwin 1970; Lofland 1969; Meisenhelder 1977; Shover 1983). While some studies emphasize the role of authorities or associations of ex-deviants in this change (e.g., Livingston 1974; Lofland 1969; Volkman and Cressey 1963), others suggest that exiting deviance is a natural process contingent upon age-related, structural, and social psychological variables (Frazier 1976; Inciardi 1975; Irwin 1970; Meisenhelder 1977; Petersilia 1980; Shover 1983).

Although exiting deviance has been variously conceptualized, to date no one has considered that it might include adoption of a legitimate career premised upon an identity that embraces one's deviant history. Professional ex-s exemplify this mode of exiting deviance.

Ebaugh's (1988) model of role exit provides an initial framework for examining this alternative mode of exiting the deviant career. Her model

633

suggests that former roles are never abandoned but, instead, carry over into new roles. I elaborate her position and contend that one's deviant identity is not an obstacle that must be abandoned prior to exiting or adopting a more conventional lifestyle. To the contrary, one's lingering deviant identity facilitates rather than inhibits the exiting process.

How I gathered data pertinent to exiting, my relationship to these data, and how my personal experiences with exiting deviance organize this article, follow. I then present a four stage model that outlines the basic contours of the professional ex- phenomenon. Finally I suggest how the professional ex- phenomenon represents an alternative interpretation of exiting deviance that generalizes to other forms of deviance.

METHODS

Data for this research consists of introspective and qualitative material.

Introspective Data

My introspections distill 20 years of experience with substance abuse/alcoholism, social control agents/agencies, and professional counselor training. I spent 13 years becoming a deviant drinker and entered substance abuse treatment in 1979. For 5 years (1981–1986), I was a primary therapist and family interventionist for a local private residential treatment facility.

"Systematic sociological introspection" (Ellis 1987, 1990), "auto-ethnography" (Hayano 1979), and "opportunistic research" (Reimer 1977) accessed the introspective data. Each group status—abuser, patient, therapist—indicates the "complete membership role" (Adler and Adler 1987) that combines unique circumstances with personal expertise to enhance research. The four stage model of exiting described later is, in part, informed by reexamination of the written artifacts of my therapeutic/recovery experiences (e.g., alco-biography, moral inventory, daily inventory journal) and professional counselor training (e.g., term paper, internship journal).

Qualitative Data

Qualitative data were collected over a six month period of intensive interviews with 35 counselor ex-s employed in a variety of community, state, and private institutions that treat individuals with drug, alcohol, and/or eating disorder problems.[2]

These professional ex-s worked in diverse occupations prior to becoming substance abuse counselors. A partial list includes employment as accountants, managers, salespersons, nurses, educators, and business owners. Although they claimed to enter the counseling profession within two years of discharge from therapy, their decision to become counselors usually came within one year. On the average they had been counselors for four and one half years. Except one professional ex- who previously counseled learning disabled children, all claimed they had not seriously considered a counseling career before entering therapy.

THE EXIT PROCESS

Ebaugh (1988) contends that the experience of being an "ex" of one kind or another is common to most people in modern society. Emphasizing the sociological and psychological continuity of the ex- phenomenon she states, "[I]t implies that interaction is based not only on current role definitions but, more important, past identities that somehow linger on and define how people see and present themselves in their present identities" (p. xiii). Ebaugh defines the role exit as the "process of disengagement from a role that is central to one's self-identity and the reestablishment of an identity in a new role that takes into account one's ex-role" (p. 1).

Becoming a professional ex- is the outcome of a four stage process through which ex-s capitalize on the experience and vestiges of their deviant career in order to establish a new identity and role in a respectable organization. This process comprises emulation of one's therapist, the call to a counseling career, status-set realignment, and credentialization.

Stage One: Emulation of One's Therapist

The emotional and symbolic identification of these ex-s with their therapists during treatment, combined with the deep personal meanings they imputed to these relationships, was a compelling factor in their decisions to become counselors. Denzin (1987, pp. 61–62) identifies the therapeutic relationship's significance thus: "Through a process of identification and surrender (which may be altruistic), the alcoholic may merge her ego and her self in the experiences and the identity of the counselor. The group leader ... is the group ego ideal, for he or she is a successful recovering alcoholic.... An emotional bond is thus formed with the group counselor...."

Professional ex-s not only developed this emotional bond but additionally aspired to have the emotions and meanings once projected toward their therapists ascribed to them. An eating disorders counselor discussed her relationship with her therapist and her desire to be viewed in a similar way with these words:

> My counselor taught me the ability to care about myself and other people. Before I met her I was literally insane. She was the one who showed me that I wasn't crazy. Now, I want to be the person who says, "No, you're not crazy!" I am the one, now, who is helping them to get free from the ignorance that has shrouded eating disorders.

Counselors enacted a powerfully charismatic role in professional ex-s' therapeutic transformation. Their "laying on of verbal hands" provided initial comfort and relief from the ravaging symptoms of disease. They came to represent what ex-s must do both spiritually and professionally for themselves. Substance abuse therapy symbolized the "sacred" quest for divine grace rather than the mere pursuit of mundane, worldly, or "profane" outcomes like abstinence or modification of substance use/abuse behaviors; counselors embodied the sacred outcome.

Professional ex-s claimed that their therapists were the most significant change agent in their transformation. "I am here today because there was one very influential counselor in my life who helped me to get sober. I owe it all to God and to him," one alcoholism counselor expressed. A heroin addiction counselor stated, "The best thing that ever happened in my life was meeting Sally [her counselor]. She literally saved my life. If it wasn't for her I'd still probably be out there shootin' up or else be in prison or dead."

Subjects' recognition and identification of a leader's charismatic authority, as Weber (1968) notes, is decisive in validating that charisma and developing absolute trust and devotion. The special virtues and powers professional ex-s perceived in their counselors subsequently shaped their loyalty and devotion to the career.

Within the therapeutic relationship, professional ex-s perform a priestly function through which a cultural tradition passes from one generation to the next. While knowledge and wisdom pass downward (from professional ex- to patient), careers build upward (from patient to professional ex-). As the bearers of the cultural legacy of therapy, professional ex-s teach patients definitions of the situation they learned as patients. Indeed, part of the professional ex- mystique resides in once having been a patient (Bissell 1982). In this regard,

> My counselor established her legitimacy with me the moment she disclosed the fact that she, too, was an alcoholic. She wasn't just telling me what to do, she was living her own advice. By the example she set, I felt hopeful that I could recover. As I reflect upon those experiences I cannot think of one patient ever asking me about where I received my professional training. At the same time, I cannot begin to count the numerous times that my patients have asked me if I was "recovering."

Similar to religious converts' salvation through a profoundly redemptive religious experience, professional ex-s' deep career commitment derives from a transforming therapeutic resocialization. As the previous examples suggest, salvation not only relates to a changed universe of discourse; it is also identified "with one's personal therapist."[3]

At this stage, professional ex-s trust in and devote themselves to their counselors' proselytizations as a promissory note for the future. The promise is redemption and salvation from the ever-present potential for self-destruction or relapse that looms in their mental horizon. An eating disorders counselor shared her insights in this way:

> I wouldn't have gotten so involved in eating disorders counseling if I had felt certain that my eating disorder was taken care of. I see myself in constant recovery. If I was so self assured that I would never have the problem again there would

probably be less of an emphasis on being involved in the field but I have found that helping others, as I was once helped, really helps me.

The substance abuse treatment center transforms from a mere "clinic" occupied by secularly credentialed professionals into a moral community of single believers. As Durkheim (1915) suggests, however, beliefs require rites and practices in order to sustain adherents' mental and emotional states.

Stage Two: The Call to a Counseling Career

At this juncture, professional ex-s begin to turn the moral corner on their deviance. Behaviors previously declared morally reprehensible are increasingly understood within a new universe of discourse as symptoms of a much larger disease complex. This recognition represents one preliminary step toward grace. In order to emulate their therapist, however, professional ex-s realize they must dedicate themselves to an identity and lifestyle that ensure their own symptoms' permanent remission. One alcoholism counselor illustrated this point by stating:

> I can't have my life, my health, my family, my job, my friends, or anything, unless I take daily necessary steps to ensure my continued recovery. My program of recovery has to come first. Before I can go out there and help my patients I need to always make sure that my own house is in order.

As this suggests, a new world-view premised upon accepting the contingencies of one's illness while maintaining a constant vigilance over potentially recurring symptoms replaces deviant moral and social meanings. Professional ex-s' recognition of the need for constant vigilance is internalized as their moral mission from which their spiritual duty (a counseling career) follows as a natural next step.

Although professional ex-s no longer engage in substance abuse behaviors, they do not totally abandon deviant beliefs or identity. "Lest we become complacent and forget from whence we came," as one alcoholism counselor indicated the significance of remembering and embracing the past.

Professional ex-s' identification with their deviant past undergirds their professional, experiential, and moral differentiation from other professional colleagues. A heroin addiction counselor recounted how he still identified himself as an addict and deviant:

> My perspective and my affinity to my clients, particularly the harder core criminals, is far better than the professor and other doctors that I deal with here in my job. We're different and we really don't see things the same way at all. Our acceptance and understanding of these people's diseases, if you will, is much different. They haven't experienced it. They don't know these people at all. It takes more than knowing about something to be effective. I've been there and, in many respects, I will always be there.

In this way, other counselors' medical, psychiatric, or therapeutic skills are construed as part of the ordinary mundane world. As the quotation indicates, professional ex-s intentionally use their experiential past and therapeutic transformations to legitimate their entrance into and authority in counseling careers.

Professional ex-s embrace their deviant history and identity as an invaluable, therapeutic resource and feel compelled to continually reaffirm its validity in an institutional environment. Certainly, participating in "12 Step Programs"[4] without becoming counselors could help others but professional ex-s' call requires greater immersion than they provide. An alcoholism counselor reflected upon this need thus:

> For me, it was no longer sufficient to only participate "anonymously" in A.A. I wanted to surround myself with other spiritual and professional pilgrims devoted to receiving and imparting wisdom.

Towards patients, professional ex-s project a saintly aura and exemplify an "ideal recovery." Internalization of self-images previously ascribed to their therapist and now reaffirmed through an emotional and moral commitment to the counseling profession facilitate this ideation. Invariably, professional ex-s' counseling careers are in institutions professing treatment ideologies identical to what they were taught as patients. Becoming a professional ex-symbolizes a value elevated to a directing goal, whose pursuit predisposes them to interpret all ensuing experience in terms of relevance to it.

Stage Three: Status-Set Realignment

Professional ex-s' deep personal identification with their therapist provides an ego ideal to be emulated with regard to both recovery and career. They immerse themselves in what literally constitutes a "professional recovery career" that provides an institutional location to reciprocate their counselors' gift, immerse themselves in a new universe of discourse, and effectively lead novitiates to salvation. "I wouldn't be here today if it wasn't for all of the help I received in therapy. This is my way of paying some of those people back by helping those still in need," one alcoholism counselor related this.

Professional ex-s' identities assume a "master status" (Hughes 1945) that differs in one fundamental respect from others' experiencing therapeutic resocialization. Specifically, their transformed identities not only become the "most salient" in their "role identity hierarchy" (Stryker and Serpe 1982), but affect all other roles in their "status-sets" (Merton 1938). One alcoholism counselor reflected upon it this way:

> Maintaining a continued program of recovery is the most important thing in my life. Everything else is secondary. I've stopped socializing with my old friends who drink and have developed new recovering friends. I interact differently with my family. I used to work a lot of overtime but I told my old boss that overtime jeopardized my program. I finally began to realize that the job just didn't have anything to do with what I was really about. I felt alienated. Although I had been thinking about becoming a counselor ever since I went through treatment, I finally decided to pursue it.

Role alignment is facilitated by an alternative identity that redefines obligations associated with other, less significant, role identities. In the previous example, the strains of expectations associated with a former occupation fostered a role alignment consistent with a new self-image. This phenomenon closely resembles what Snow and Machalek (1983, p. 276) refer to as "embracement of a master role" that "is not merely a mask that is taken off or put on according to the situation.... Rather, it is central to nearly all situations...." An eating disorders counselor stated the need to align her career with her self-image, "I hid in my former profession, interacting little with people. As a counselor, I am personally maturing and taking responsibility rather than letting a company take care of me. I have a sense of purpose in this job that I never had before."

Financial remuneration is not a major consideration in the decision to become a professional ex-. The pure type of call, Weber (1968, p. 52) notes, "disdains and repudiates economic exploitation of the gifts of grace as a source of income...." Most professional ex-s earned more money in their previous jobs. For instance, one heroin addiction counselor stated:

> When I first got out of treatment, my wife and I started an accounting business. In our first year we cleared nearly sixty thousand dollars. The money was great and the business showed promise but something was missing. I missed being around other addicts and I knew I wanted to do more with my life along the lines of helping out people like me.

An additional factor contributing to professional ex-s' abandonment of their previous occupation is their recognition that a counseling career could resolve lingering self-doubts about their ability to remain abstinent. In this respect becoming a professional ex- allows "staying current" with their own recovery needs while continually reaffirming the severity of their illness. An eating disorders counselor explained:

> I'm constantly in the process of repeating insights that I've had to my patients. I hear myself saying, to them, what I need to believe for myself. Being a therapist helps me to keep current with my own recovery. I feel that I am much less vulnerable to my disease in this environment. It's a way that I can keep myself honest. Always being around others with similar issues prevents me from ignoring my own addiction clues.

This example illustrates professional ex-s' use of their profession to secure self-compliance during times of self-doubt. While parroting the virtues of the program facilitates recognition that they, too, suffer from a disease, the professional ex- role, unlike their previous occupations, enables them to continue therapy indirectly.

Finally, the status the broader community ascribes to the professional ex- role encourages professional ex-s' abandonment of previous roles. Association with an institutional environment and an occupational role gives the professional ex- a new sense of place in the surrounding community, within which form new self-concepts and self-esteem, both in the immediate situation and in a broader temporal framework.

The internal validation of professional ex-s' new identity resides in their ability to successfully anticipate the behaviors and actions of relevant others. Additionally, they secure validation by other members of the professional ex- community in a manner atypical for other recovering individuals. Affirmation by this reference community symbolizes validation by one's personal therapist and the therapeutic institution, as a heroin addiction counselor succinctly stated:

> Becoming a counselor was a way to demonstrate my loyalty and devotion to helping others and myself. My successes in recovery, including being a counselor, would be seen by patients and those who helped me get sober. It was a return to treatment, for sure, but the major difference was that this time I returned victorious rather than defeated.

External validation, on the other hand, comes when others outside the therapeutic community accord legitimacy to the professional ex- role. In this regard, a heroin addiction counselor said:

> I remember talking to this guy while I was standing in line for a movie. He asked me what I did for a living and I told him that I was a drug abuse counselor. He started asking me all these questions about the drug problem and what I thought the answers were. When we finally got up to the door of the theater he patted me on the back and said, "You're doing a wonderful job. Keep up the good work. I really admire you for what you're trying to do." It really felt good to have a stranger praise me.

Professional ex-s' counseling role informs the performance of all other roles, compelling them to abandon previous work they increasingly view as mundane and polluting. The next section demonstrates how this master role organizes the meanings associated with their professional counselor training.

Stage Four: Credentialization

One characteristic typically distinguishing the professions from other occupations is specialized knowledge acquired at institutions of higher learning (Larson 1977; Parsons 1959; Ritzer and Walczak 1986, 1988). Although mastering esoteric knowledge and professional responsibilities in a therapeutic relationship serve as gatekeepers for entering the counseling profession, the moral and emotional essence of being a professional ex- involves much more.

Professional ex-s see themselves as their patients' champions. "Knowing what it's like" and the subsequent education and skills acquired in training legitimate claims to the "entitlements of their stigma" (Gusfield 1982), including professional status. Their monopoly of an abstruse body of knowledge and skill is realized through their emotionally lived history of shame and guilt as well as the hope and redemption secured through therapeutic transformation. Professional ex-s associate higher learning with their experiential history of deviance and the emotional context of therapy.

Higher learning symbolizes rediscovery of a moral sense of worth and sacredness rather than credential acquisition. This distinction was clarified by an alcoholism counselor:

> Anymore, you need to have a degree before anybody will hire you. I entered counseling with a bachelors but I eventually received my MSW about two years ago. I think the greatest benefit in having the formal training is that I have been able to more effectively utilize my personal alcoholism experiences with my patients. I feel that I have a gift to offer my patients which doesn't come from the classroom. It comes from being an alcoholic myself.

These entitlements allow professional ex-s to capitalize on their deviant identity in two ways: the existential and phenomenological dimensions of their lived experience of "having made their way from the darkness into the light" provide their experiential and professional *legitimacy* among patients, the community, and other professionals, as well as occupational *income*. "Where else could I go and put bulimic and alcoholic on my resume and get hired?" one counselor put it.

Professional ex-s generally eschew meta-perspective interpretations of the system in which they work. They desire a counseling method congruent with their fundamental universe of discourse and seek, primarily, to perpetuate this system (Peele 1989; Room 1972, 1976). The words of one educator at a local counselor training institute are germane:

> These people [professional ex-s]...are very fragile when they get here. Usually, they have only been in recovery for about a year. Anyone who challenges what they learned in therapy, or in their program of recovery [i.e., A.A., Narcotics Anonymous, Overeaters Anonymous]...is viewed as a threat. Although we try to change some of that while they're here with us, I still see my role here as one of an extended therapist rather than an educator.

Information challenging their beliefs about how they, and their patients, should enact the rites associated with recovery is condemned (Davies 1963; Pattison 1987; Roizen 1977). They view intellectual challenges to the disease concept as attacks on their personal program of recovery. In a Durkheimian sense, such challenges "profane" that which they hold "sacred."

Within the walls of these monasteries professional ex-s emulate their predecessors as one generation of healers passes on to the next an age old message of salvation. Although each new generation presents the path to enlightenment in somewhat different, contemporary terms, it is already well lit for those "becoming a professional ex-."

DISCUSSION

Focusing on their lived experiences and accounts, this study sketches the central contours of professional ex-s' distinctive exit process. More generally, it also endeavors to contribute to the existing literature on deviant careers.

An identity that embraces their deviant history and identity undergirds the professional ex-s' careers. This exiting mode is the outcome of a four stage process enabling professional ex-s to capitalize on their deviant history. They do not "put it all behind them" in exchange for conventional lifestyles, values, beliefs, and identities. Rather, they use vestiges of their deviant biography as an explicit occupational strategy.

My research augments Ebaugh's (1988) outline of principles underlying role exit in three ways. First, her discussion suggests that people are unaware of these guiding principles. While this holds for many, professional ex-s' intentional rather than unintentional embracement of their deviant identity is the step by which they adopt a new role in the counseling profession. Second, Ebaugh states that significant others' negative reactions inhibit or interrupt exit. Among professional ex-s, however, such reactions are a crucial precursor to their exit mode. Finally, Ebaugh sees role exit as a voluntary, individually initiated process, enhanced by "seeking alternatives" through which to explore other roles. Professional ex-s, by contrast, are compelled into therapy. They do not look for this particular role. Rather, their alternatives are prescribed through their resocialization into a new identity.

Organizations in American society increasingly utilize professional ex-s in their social control efforts. For example, the state of Colorado uses prisoners to counsel delinquent youth. A preliminary, two year, follow-up study suggests that these prisoner-counselors show only 13% recidivism (Shiller 1988) and a substantial number want to return to college or enter careers as guidance counselors, probation officers, youth educators, or law enforcement consultants. Similarly, a local effort directed toward curbing gang violence, the Open Door Youth Gang Program, was developed by a professional ex- and uses former gang members as counselors, educators, and community relations personnel.

Further examination of the modes through which charismatic, albeit licensed and certified, groups generate professional ex- statuses is warranted. Although the examples just described differ from the professional ex-s examined earlier in this research in terms of therapeutic or "medicalized" resocialization, their similarities are even more striking. Central to them all is that a redemptive community provides a reference group whose moral and social standards are internalized. Professional ex- statuses are generated as individuals intentionally integrate and embrace rather than abandon their deviant biographies as a specific occupational strategy.

Notes

1. Most individuals in substance abuse therapy do not become professional ex-s. Rather, they traverse a variety of paths not articulated here including (1) dropping out of treatment, (2) completing treatment but returning to substance use and/or abuse, and (3) remaining abstinent after treatment but feeling no compulsion to enter the counseling profession. Future research will explore the differences among persons by mode of exit. Here, however, analysis and description focus exclusively on individuals committed to the professional ex- role.

2. I conducted most interviews at the subject's work environment, face-to-face. One interview was with a focus group of 10 professional ex-s (Morgan 1988). Two interviews were in my office, one at my home, and one at a subject's home. I interviewed each individual one time for approximately one hour. Interviews were semi-structured, with open-end questions designed to elicit responses related to feelings, thoughts, perceptions, reflections, and meanings concerning subjects' past deviance, factors facilitating their exit from deviance, and their counseling career.

3. I contend that significantly more professional ex-s pursue their careers due to therapeutic resocialization than to achieving sobriety/recovery exclusively through the 12 Step Program (e.g., A.A.). It is too early, however, to preclude that some may enter substance abuse counseling careers lacking any personal therapy. My experiences and my interviews with other professional ex-s suggest that very few professional ex-s enter the profession directly through their contacts with the 12 Step Program. The program's moral precepts—that "sobriety is a gift from God" that must be "given freely to others in order to assure that one may keep the gift"—would appear to discourage rather than encourage substance abuse counseling careers. Financial remuneration for assisting fellow substance abusers directly violates these precepts. Further, professional ex-s are commonly disparaged in A.A. circles as "two hatters" (cf. Denzin 1987). They are, therefore, not a positive reference group for individuals recovering exclusively through the 12 Step Program. Sober 12 Step members are more inclined to emulate their "sponsors" than pursue careers with no experiential referents or direct relevance to their recovery. Further data collection and analysis will examine these differences. Extant data, however, strongly indicate that therapeutic resocialization and a professional role model provide the crucial link between deviant and substance abuse counseling careers.

4. "12 Step Program" refers to a variety of self-help groups (e.g., A.A., Narcotics Anonymous, Overeaters Anonymous) patterning their recovery model upon the original 12 Steps and 12 Traditions of A.A.

References

Adler, Patricia, and Peter Adler. 1983. "Shifts and Oscillations in Deviant Careers: The Case of Upper-Level Drug Dealers and Smugglers." *Social Problems* 31: 195–207.

———. 1987. *Membership Roles in Field Research.* Newbury Park, CA: Sage.

Becker, Howard. 1963. *Outsiders: Studies in the Sociology of Deviance.* New York: Free Press.

Best, Joel, and David F. Luckenbill. 1982. *Organizing Deviance.* Englewood Cliffs, NJ: Prentice Hall.

Bissell, LeClair. 1982. "Recovered Alcoholism Counselors." Pp. 810–817 in *Encyclopedic Handbook of Alcoholism,* edited by E. Mansell Pattison and Edward Kaufman. New York: Gardner.

Davies, D. L. 1963. "Normal Drinking in Recovered Alcoholic Addicts" (comments by various correspondents). *Quarterly Journal of Studies on Alcohol* 24: 109–121, 321–332.

Denzin, Norman. 1987. *The Recovering Alcoholic.* Beverly Hills: Sage.

Durkheim, Emile. 1915. *The Elementary Forms of the Religious Life.* New York: Free Press.

Ebaugh, Helen Rose Fuchs. 1988. *Becoming an Ex: The Process of Role Exit.* Chicago: University of Chicago Press.

Ellis, Carolyn. 1987. "Systematic Sociological Introspection and the Study of Emotions." Paper presented to the annual meetings of the American Sociological Association, Chicago.

———. 1990. "Sociological Introspection and Emotional Experience." *Symbolic Interaction* 13(2): Forthcoming.

Frazier, Charles. 1976. *Theoretical Approaches to Deviance.* Columbus: Charles Merrill.

Glassner, Barry, Margret Ksander, Bruce Berg, and Bruce D. Johnson. 1983. "A Note on the Deterrent Effect of Juvenile vs. Adult Jurisdiction." *Social Problems* 31: 219–221.

Goffman, Erving. 1961. *Asylums*. Garden City, NY: Anchor.

Gusfield, Joseph. 1982. "Deviance in the Welfare State: The Alcoholism Profession and the Entitlements of Stigma." *Research in Social Problems and Public Policy* 2: 1–20.

Hayano, David. 1979. "Auto-Ethnography: Paradigms, Problems and Prospects." *Human Organization* 38: 99–104.

Hughes, Everett. 1945. "Dilemmas and Contradictions of Status." *American Journal of Sociology* L: 353–359.

Inciardi, James. 1975. *Careers in Crime*. Chicago: Rand McNally.

Irwin, John. 1970. *The Felon*. Englewood Cliffs: Prentice Hall.

Larson, Magali. 1977. *The Rise of Professionalism*. Berkeley: University of California Press.

Livingston, Jay. 1974. *Compulsive Gamblers*. New York: Harper and Row.

Lofland, John. 1969. *Deviance and Identity*. Englewood Cliffs: Prentice Hall.

Luckenbill, David F., and Joel Best. 1981. "Careers in Deviance and Respectability: The Analogy's Limitations." *Social Problems* 29: 197–206.

Meisenhelder, Thomas. 1977. "An Exploratory Study of Exiting from Criminal Careers." *Criminology* 15: 319–334.

Merton, Robert. 1938. *Social Theory and Social Structure*. Glencoe: Free Press.

Miller, Gale. 1986. "Conflict in Deviant Occupations." Pp. 373–401 in *Working: Conflict and Change,* 3rd ed., edited by George Ritzer and David Walczak. Englewood Cliffs: Prentice Hall.

Morgan, David L. 1988. *Focus Groups as Qualitative Research*. Beverly Hills: Sage.

NAADAC. 1986. *Development of Model Professional Standards for Counselor Credentialing*. National Association of Alcoholism and Drug Abuse Counselors. Dubuque: Kendall/Hunt.

Parsons, Talcott. 1959. "Some Problems Confronting Sociology as a Profession." *American Sociological Review* 24: 547–559.

Pattison, E. Mansell. 1987. "Whither Goals in the Treatment of Alcoholism." *Drugs and Society* 2/3: 153–171.

Peele, Stanton. 1989. *The Diseasing of America: Addiction Treatment Out of Control*. Toronto: Lexington.

Petersilia, Joan. 1980. "Criminal Career Research: A Review of Recent Evidence." Pp. 321–379 in *Crime and Justice: An Annual Review of Research,* vol. 2, edited by Norval Morris and Michael Tonry. Chicago: University of Chicago Press.

Reimer, Jeffrey. 1977. "Varieties of Opportunistic Research." *Urban Life* 5: 467–477.

Ritzer, George, and David Walczak. 1986. *Working: Conflict and Change*. 3rd ed. Englewood Cliffs: Prentice Hall.

———. 1988. "Rationalization and the Deprofessionalization of Physicians." *Social Forces* 67: 1–22.

Roizen, Ron. 1977. "Comment on the Rand Report." *Quarterly Journal of Studies on Alcohol* 38: 170–178.

Room, Robin. 1972. "Drinking and Disease: Comment on the Alcoholist's Addiction." *Quarterly Journal of Studies on Alcohol* 33: 1049–1059.

———. 1976. "Drunkenness and the Law: Comment on the Uniform Alcoholism Intoxication Treatment Act." *Quarterly Journal of Studies on Alcohol* 37: 113–144.

Shiller, Gene. 1988. "A Preliminary Report on SHAPE-UP." Paper presented to the Colorado District Attorneys Council, Denver.

Shover, Neil. 1983. "The Later Stages of Ordinary Property Offenders' Careers." *Social Problems* 31: 208–218.

Snow, David, and Richard Machalek. 1983. "The Convert as a Social Type." Pp. 259–289 in *Sociological Theory 1983*, edited by Randall Collins. San Francisco: Jossey-Bass.

Sobell, Mark B., and Linda C. Sobell. 1987. "Conceptual Issues Regarding Goals in the Treatment of Alcohol Problems." *Drugs and Alcohol* 2/3: 1–37.

Stryker, Sheldon, and Richard Serpe. 1982. "Commitment, Identity Salience, and Role Behavior: Theory and Research Example." Pp. 199–218 in *Personality, Roles, and Social Behavior,* edited by William Ickes and Eric S. Knowles. New York: Springer-Verlag.

Volkman, Rita, and Donald Cressey. 1963. "Differential Association and the Rehabilitation of Drug Addicts." *American Journal of Sociology* 69: 129–142.

Weber, Max. 1968. *On Charisma and Institution Building*. Edited by S. N. Eisenstadt. Chicago: University of Chicago Press.

44 / Rehabilitating Social Systems and Institutions

DELOS H. KELLY

One fact that should be apparent now is that as long as failure, criminal, and deviant values and traditions exist, we will obtain outcomes commensurate with these phenomena. Correlatively, getting tough on crime and delinquency, for example, will not begin to get the job done, primarily because...those normative structures, conditions, and environments that guarantee the continued production of perceived deviation will remain virtually unchanged. Predictably, then, individuals will become exposed to and recruited out to play the role of the school failure, the young criminal, and the deviant. And some willing or unwilling recruits will...participate at times or drop out, while others will become regular members. These are some of the inescapable and basic facts the practitioners must begin to come to grips with. Unfortunately,...the efforts of these individuals (as well as the legislators, the policy makers, the professionals, and others) often do nothing more than to help perpetuate a medical-clinical-individualistic model of change and treatment. Thus, instead of looking within society to explain deviation, they look within the individual. Thereafter, the individual is taught how to cope or perhaps even feel good about himself or herself. And for some, a strategy of this type may work. For most, however, the efforts not only fail but the individuals experience a relapse; this is certainly understandable and most predictable.

THE CLINICAL MODEL REVISITED, OR BLAMING THE INDIVIDUAL

What the practitioners and others do not seem to recognize is that behavior viewed as criminal or deviant to them may be perceived as being acceptable and *normal* to the individual. In fact,...nonconformity is often the demanded response on the part of a group member. It may be recalled, for example, that Miller's (1958) gang boys received positive sanctions and rewards when they acted in accordance with the "focal concerns" (e.g., fighting and getting into trouble). Moreover, failure to conform, Miller (1958) claimed, would have probably resulted in exclusion from the gang.

Similarly, Reiss' (1961), Cohen's (1955), and Hargreaves' (1967) delinquent males were expected to live up to the values and normative systems they were immersed in. The same held for the nudists, prostitutes, mental patients, and the like. Observations such as these contain an underlying message: Efforts at change focused exclusively upon the individual are usually doomed from the start, mainly because the policy makers and the practitioners fail to recognize that most individuals are actually responding normally to their own *immediate* world. Thus, and even though people are removed, treated, or incarcerated, they do, upon their return, become a part of that environment once again. Quite clearly, Weinberg's (1966) nudists, Bryan's (1965) prostitutes, Scheff's (1964) mental patients, and Wallace's (1965) skid rowers may leave; however, they must, upon their return, conform to the existing normative structure.[1] In a very real sense, the labeled deviants, criminals, delinquents, failures, and others become caught between two worlds: the conforming and the nonconforming; this dilemma creates some obvious problems for individuals so situated. If, for example, an actor elects to go straight, he or she runs the risk of being defined as a deviant and perhaps even rejected by his or her peers. On the other hand, conformity to group norms and values may produce further contact with social control agencies. What this often means is that the individual must weight the costs and benefits that may ensue by virtue of involvement with one culture as opposed to another. Ray's (1961) research on abstinence and relapse cycles among heroin addicts offers an excellent illustration of how these processes frequently operate.

Ray (1961:133) notes initially that the social world of addiction, like any other world (e.g., the world of nudism or prostitution), can be characterized by its organizational and cultural elements (e.g., its argot or language, market, pricing system). Not only this but commitment to the addict world provides the member with a major status and associated identity. Addiction, however, often means that the addict will come to assume or exhibit other secondary status features. For example, as the habit grows, most efforts will be oriented toward obtaining drugs. Thus one may become careless about his or her appearance and cleanliness, and this frequently means that non-addicts will begin to label the addict as a "bum," "degenerate," or lacking "will power." Of significance here, at least as far as the potential for change is concerned, is Ray's (1961:134) observation that even though the addict is *aware* that he or she is being judged in terms of these secondary characteristics or definitions and may, therefore, try to *reject* or shed the labels, it is virtually impossible to do so, primarily because most interactions and institutional experiences operate in such a manner as to ratify the labels or definitions that have been applied to the addict. In fact, incarceration in correctional and mental facilities plays a most important role in the ratification process, particularly in view of the fact that contacts with non-addicts and their values often produce significant changes in one's identity or view of self. Ray (1961:133) comments on how the inmate and others may react to institutionalization:

> The addict's incarceration in correctional institutions has specific meanings which he finds reflected in the attitudes toward him by members of non-addict society and by his fellow addicts. Additionally, as his habit grows and the demands for drugs get beyond any legitimate means of supply, his own activities in satisfying his increased craving give him direct experiential evidence of the criminal aspects of self. These meanings of self as a criminal become internalized as he begins to apply criminal argot to his activities and institutional experiences....

In effect, the inmate often accepts the criminal label and begins to act accordingly (i.e., becomes a career criminal); this same type of situation exists relative to the mental institution. However, instead of promoting the ideology that the client is criminal, the operating assumption is that the addict is psychologically inadequate or deficient. Thus, attempts are made to treat the individual's mind, usually through the use of some kind of counseling or group therapy. Contacts with psychiatric or psychological personnel produce another effect: They remind the addict that the institution and its staff view him or her as being mentally ill. In the words of one addict (Ray, 1961:134):

> When I got down to the hospital, I was interviewed by different doctors and one of them told me, "you now have one mark against you as crazy for having been down here." I hadn't known it was a crazy house. You know regular people [non-addicts] think this too.

And like the criminal, the addict may eventually accept the identity that is being imputed to him or her. Acceptance of this new status, as well as its associated labels, does reduce the odds that a cure can be effected, primarily because the addict becomes further entrenched within the addict and other (perceived) deviant cultures (e.g., the inmate).

Even though the overall prognosis for change is certainly poor, some addicts will experience a cure (i.e., remain free of drugs). The most likely candidates are drawn from the ranks of those addicts who, for some reason (e.g., incarceration), begin to question their addict identity, as well as the values of the drug world. Ray (1961:134) has stated this most succinctly:

> An episode of cure begins in the *private thoughts* of the addict rather than in his overt behavior. These deliberations develop as a result of experience in specific situations of interaction with *important others* that cause the addict to experience social stress, to develop some feeling of alienation from or dissatisfaction with his present identity, and to call it into question and examine it in all of its implications and ramifications. In these situations the *addict engages in private self-debate* in which he juxtaposes the values and social relationships which have become immediate and concrete through his addiction with those that are sometimes only half remembered or only imperfectly perceived. [Italics mine.]

Such questioning or self-debate may begin because of some kind of institutional contact (e.g., confinement in a hospital or correctional facility). It may also occur as a result of what Ray (1961:135) has termed a "socially disjunctive experience" with other addicts (e.g., an addict may be sent to buy drugs but never returns). More typically, however, the analysis of self or introspection emerges by virtue of some type of interaction or experience with a non-addict and/or the non-addict world; these provide the major catalytic elements for change (Ray, 1961:135).

Once withdrawal has been completed and a decision has been made to abstain (i.e., to structure an abstainer identity), the former addict is confronted immediately with some serious identity and self-image problems. During this initial period, Ray (1961:136) maintains that the individual becomes locked in a "running struggle" with problems of social identity. He or she is not sure of self; however, certain expectations are held about the future and its possibilities. Thus, the early stages of a cure are often characterized by substantial ambivalence; this is produced by the abstainer's efforts to find out where he or she stands relative to the addict and non-addict groups. Such ambivalence or lingering uncertainty may, according to Ray (1961:136), manifest itself through the type of pronouns used in discussions of addicts and their world (e.g., the use of "we" and "they" to refer to non-addicts as opposed to addicts), as well as in terms of how the attempted abstainer speaks of self (e.g., he or she may preface a statement with "When I was an addict.... ").

Whether a former addict will continue to remain abstinent is, however, problematic. And critical to the success of any cure appears to be the role played by significant others (e.g., family members, spouses, friends, etc.). As Ray (1961:136) puts it: " ... Above all, he appears to desire ratification by significant others of his newly developing identity, and in his interactions during an episode of abstinence he expects to secure it." Stated somewhat differently, if others are generally supportive and caring, the chances are much greater that an abstainer identity can be built and perhaps maintained. Probably most important to the successful completion of this process are the reactions of one's immediate family members. If, as a result of perceived positive changes on the part of the individual (e.g., obtaining and keeping a job, improving appearance, professing an allegiance to non-addict values), the family's attitudes undergo modification, the probability of a long-term cure appears more likely (Ray, 1961:136). At this point Ray (1961:137) stresses the fact that attitudinal changes, whether they occur on the part of the abstainer or the family, are usually not enough to produce a cure. Rather, professed commitment to the non-addict life style and its values "must be grounded in action." In other words, the abstainer must, in his or her interactions with the non-addicts, be allowed to actually occupy and play out the role of the non-addict; this not only helps to strengthen one's image as an abstainer but it also provides an opportunity whereby the non-addict values and perspectives can be learned and shared. Failure to satisfy this latter condition, it can be noted, increases the likelihood of a relapse. And a relapse is most apt to occur when the expectations held of self and others are not met. As Ray (1961:137) puts it:

> The tendency toward relapse develops out of the meanings of the abstainer's experiences in social situations when he develops an image of himself as socially different from non-addicts, and relapse occurs when he redefines himself as an addict. When his social expectations and the expectations of others with whom he interacts are not met, social stress develops and he is required to re-examine the meaningfulness of his experience in non-addict society and in so doing question his identity as an abstainer. This type of experience promotes a mental realignment with addict values and standards. . . .

Ray (1961:137) notes that relapse or re-addiction is most likely to occur during the initial period following physical withdrawal; this is the time in which the addict becomes actively engaged in the "running struggle" or battle with identity problems (i.e., he or she engages in a great deal of self-debate). Coupled with this is the fact that the addict identity, values, life style, and experiences are still most immediate, while these same elements of the non-addict world are often unclear or hazy. A situation such as this (i.e., pressing identity problems, familiarity with the addict world, and a corresponding unfamiliarity with the non-addict society), however, places the individual in an especially vulnerable position and, predictably, many former addicts or attempted abstainers will, as a result of pressure by other addicts, relapse. The possibility of this occurring appears noticeably great when the social expectations and reactions of addicts are such that the individual finds it virtually impossible to identify with or even act out any significant non-addict roles. Other addicts may, according to Ray (1961:137), dislike any attempt at presenting a "square" image of self, and they may begin to view the individual as being peculiar or strange. Thus, the perceived "deviant" will be pressured to conform.

Ray (1961:138) makes an important point to the effect that relapse is not necessarily due to one's associations. Rather, it is a function of how the individual evaluates self relative to the social situations he or she encounters. For example, some abstainers will have contacts with former addicts and still maintain their abstainer identity, while others will redefine themselves as addicts and move back into the fold. Similarly, some ex-addicts will associate with non-addicts and stay abstinent, while others will reject the abstainer role and then reassume the addict role. Predicting which outcome is most likely is difficult; however, if the abstainer is pressured by other addicts to conform and if, further, he or she is not allowed to assume a non-addict status, the probability of relapse is high. The same applies to associations with non-addicts. In fact, unsatisfactory experiences with non-addicts often contribute heavily to a lack of cure, and particularly those interactional situations and associated exchanges which operate in such a manner as to keep the individual locked into his or her addict role (Ray, 1961:138). Stated more simply, the abstainer may try to move from an addict to a non-addict status, and correspondingly, he or she expects others to accept, as well as ratify, the attempted status change. And when this acceptance is not forthcoming (e.g., significant others may continue to refer to the individual in terms of his or her prior addict identity and status), questions about one's identity and status begin to emerge. Ray (1961:138–139) offers the comments of an addict who experienced this type of treatment:

> My relatives were always saying things to me like "Have you really quit using that drug now?" and things like that. And I knew that they were doing a lot of talking behind my back because when I came around they would stop talking but I overheard them. It used to burn my ass.

A person such as this would probably be an excellent candidate for relapse. Relapse itself entails movement back into the addict world. It also involves some resocializing of the individual. In the words of Ray (1961:139):

> [Reentry] requires a recommitment to the norms of addiction and limits the degree to which he may relate to non-addict groups in terms of the latter's values and standards. It demands participation in the old ways of organizing conduct and experiences and, as a consequence, the readoption of the secondary status characteristics of addiction. He again shows a lack of concern about his personal appearance and grooming. Illicit activities are again engaged in to get money for drugs, and as a result the possibility of more firmly establishing the criminal aspect of his identity becomes a reality.

Thus, complete resocialization not only demands a recommitment to the values of the addict world but it also requires a redefinition of self as an addict.

What may not be recognized from research such as the preceding is that a medical-clinical-individualistic model of change is very much in evidence. Understandably, then, if a change in personal and public identity, attitudes, or behavior is to occur, it must come from within the individual. It is he or she who must make the move. And even if, because of some socially disjunctive experience or personal crisis, a person begins to question or redefine his or her present deviant identities, he or she must attempt to operate in two worlds: the conforming and the nonconforming; this produces some obvious difficulties relative to any attempt to structure and maintain a non-deviant personal and public identity. Not only will deviant peers often pressure the "deviant" to conform to their values and associated normative system, but similar requests or demands will be made by selected non-deviants. In fact, the responses of, as well as interactions with, generalized (e.g., hospital and correctional staff) and significant (e.g., family) others are an especially important ingredient in the success or failure of any attempted cure or rehabilitation. Are these others willing to alter their perceptions of the deviant (i.e., begin to view him or her as non-deviant or conformist)?

Equally critical, is the labeled or perceived deviant allowed to actually occupy and act out the role of a non-deviant, or is he or she kept effectively locked into a deviant status? In most cases, the evidence on these matters exhibits a mistakenly clear pattern: Not only are people unwilling to modify their views and expectations of those deviants and/or ex-deviants who are trying to restructure their complement of identities, but the "straights" also fail to provide any realistic opportunities whereby the perceived "misfits" can learn, or perhaps even relearn, the conventional, non-deviant roles; this unwillingness or reluctance to change can be used to highlight the most basic flaw of virtually all treatment and change programs. Specifically, environments, values, and normative systems remain unchanged. What this means with respect to theory and practice is that the legislators, law enforcement personnel, practitioners, therapists, and others either generally neglect or else ignore those factors, conditions, and influences responsible for producing deviant outcomes and, instead, concentrate on the actor. And, predictably, failure becomes defined in *individual* terms and not in *structural-organizational* terms. Obviously, blaming the individual is a much easier task than blaming the system.

REHABILITATING SOCIAL SYSTEMS AND INSTITUTIONS

Unfortunately, blaming the individual does nothing more than protect the real culprits. If . . . a student is designated as a potential failure or delinquent and placed in a non-academic or delinquent career line, that pupil will, in more cases than not, live up to such expectations. Yet, instead of charging the educators and their system with malfeasance, we indict the academic failure or "misfit" and build a case against him or her. And not only will the student be convicted, so to speak, but the guilty parties escape prosecution and conviction.

What people at all levels must begin to recognize, however, is that failure, alienation, delinquency, misconduct, dropout, and so on are guaranteed products of the school. Another way of saying this is that the educational system's underlying organizational structure is geared to produce these outcomes and others. . . . Thus, and most predictably, students will be assigned to deviant career lines and they will, once socialized, exhibit attitudes and behaviors commensurate with their status; this, as I have stressed, also applies to any other social system an actor may become a part of (e.g., the nudist or skid row culture). The point that must be emphasized at this stage is, therefore, basic, yet most fundamental: If school failure, youth crime, and deviance are to be reduced significantly, then the organizational structure of the educational system must be attacked and altered radically. Eliminating deviant career lines (e.g., low ability groups or tracks) would be an important and necessary first step. Changing the *content* of some of the values of the school's existing subcultures or social systems would constitute another.

If, for example, the anti-academic values of Hargreaves' (1967) delinquent subculture were replaced with those of the academic, the patterns of school failure, misconduct, and petty delinquency would look much different. In fact, not only would there be a sharp reduction in outcomes such as these, but an educational environment with a *common* set of academic values would have been created. Altering the value structure in this manner would, however, require other basic changes. Most dramatically, educators, school administrators, and others would be required to question the presumed validity of the success-fail philosophy that guides their interactions with students. Stated more simply, instituting a common set of values would eliminate the need for deviant career lines and this strategy would, in turn, require the development of a new working ideology—one that is based upon *the presumption of ability*. Translating this official perspective (i.e., the belief that *all* children and students possess ability and can perform) into action would not be easy, nor necessarily successful, primarily because changes would be required at all levels, regardless of whether focus is given to educators, parents, or others. In effect, we are dealing with a problem with deep societal roots.

Even though the existing theory and evidence actually call for a total revamping or restructuring of society, the probability of this occurring in either the short- or long-run is, admittedly, most remote. Nor should one expect much to happen within the educational system. Not only is the success-fail philosophy embedded deeply within the organizational structure of the school, but the educators, the administrators, and the students have been indoctrinated with this ideology. Most parents, as I argued, have also been socialized to believe in the current educational philosophy (i.e., they follow the belief that some students have ability, while others have little or none). Thus, parents, like the educators, must be a part of any plan to change the present situation.

Given the prospects for change, then it becomes an easy task to advance the argument that nothing can be done about those conditions responsible for producing *careers* of failure, youth crime, and deviance. And most do, in fact, argue along these lines. Such reasoning is, however, faulty and, even more basic, it fails to address the cold, hard facts. In this respect, the evidence is crystal clear: Institutions, by virtue of the way they are structured and intersect with each other, are geared to produce our failures, our delinquents, and our young criminals. The most graphic representation of this would have to be my analysis of how the educational system builds, maintains, and perpetuates a variety of deviant careers and identities— careers and identities that are often reinforced, strengthened, and solidified by a range of social control agencies and their agents. What evidence of this type points to, once again, is the need for structural-organizational change.

If change is to come about, then I believe that it must begin with the educational system. Not only is this one of our basic institutions but most children spend at least ten years or more within the system; they also spend many hours each day in school. The same does not exist with respect to many families or the community. Thus, the school probably represents the most stable environment in which to impact; this should not be taken to mean that the family units or peer networks should be ignored. On the contrary, they must be involved. Ideally, changes in the structure and process of schooling should emanate out to these elements.

Although most educators find very little wrong with the way they go about educating students, I have argued that they and their organization actually help to create many of the problems they would like to get rid of. And the basic problem is structural in nature. Stated most bluntly, the educators, parents, and others have bought the script, along with all of its value-laden stereotypes. The script must be rewritten. Hence, my initial call for the introduction of an educational philosophy predicated upon the presumption of ability—a theory of the office or working ideology that would, as I pointed out, eliminate the need for such sorting machines as ability groups, tracks, and streams; this, in turn, would require the elimination of the diagnostic stereotypes that characterize the *deviant* or non-academic career lines. In a sense, the school and its agents must begin to make it extremely difficult for the student to fail.

A new ideology and its corresponding diagnostic stereotypes call for some obvious desocialization and resocialization of present, as well as future, educators; this could be accomplished through a variety of methods. For example, teachers and other educational personnel would be required to attend seminars or workshops where they could be educated in terms of how the school, by virtue of its action or inaction, can help in the production of deviant careers and identities. Also, future educators of all types would not receive their credentials or even be allowed to teach until they had completed a set of mandatory courses dealing with basic issues, concepts, and processes . . . (e.g., courses which sensitize them to the way in which conflicting perspectives, such as the clinical versus the social system, affect the identifying and processing of clients; how and why career lines and subcultures may originate; how teachers can perpetuate academic stereotypes; how teachers may initiate status degradation ceremonies; how teachers may destroy a student's identity and self-image, and so on).

Additional strategies could be provided (e.g., implementing a range of institutional sanctions that would be used to deal with those who fail to comply with the new working ideology); however, what needs to be stressed at this stage is that parents, peers, and others must also be desocialized and resocialized accordingly. Obviously, and as with respect to the educational arena, the probability of producing noticeable change is low. Still, the logic and evidence point to such a need.

One of the basic problems with most families is that they have placed too much faith in the educational system and its agents. The guiding assumption is that, somehow, the educators really know what is best for their children; this, I contend, is not only a fallacious view but actually does nothing more than to give free rein to the educators. Thus, and predictably, it should not be surprising to find them operating on the basis of stereotypic notions about ability—the very same stereotypes that are, as we have seen, used to select out students for placement in deviant career lines. The responses on the part of the parents and the educators are certainly understandable, particularly in view of the fact that both have, as a result of their formal and informal socializing experiences, been indoctrinated with the success-fail philosophy. A major outcome of this socialization is that parents, peers, students, and others are taught not to question the educational decision makers. . . . In effect, whenever a parent questioned a decision, he or she was "cooled out" by the counselor.

Parents, like the educators and all others, should be resocialized. And as a start, they must become aware and begin to question and challenge the presumed validity of the success-fail philosophy, as well as each and every decision that is rendered on the behalf of their children. Parents must also begin to recognize that they can have a direct say in terms of how their children are handled by the educational decision makers. The same applies with respect to students; they, too, must begin to heighten their "consciousness" and become aware of what is actually happening at the hands of the educators. As an illustration, and in the area of career decisions, options must be presented to all—options, I might add, that are not only available for all to achieve but options that are actually attainable. For example, pupils must be apprised of what it takes to become a doctor, lawyer, professor, dentist, and the like, and they must be encouraged to pursue options such as these if they so choose; this strategy would not produce a glut of professionals. Some students, once the requirements and the nature of the occupations are spelled out, will elect to follow other career routes. The point that must be emphasized, however, is that career options must be *genuine* options and the choice factor must be *real*. And to be effective, information relative to careers and the right of choice must be presented at the earliest possible stage. Waiting until the junior or senior year is often too late, and this is especially so for those who have been processed as non-college material. The educational and occupational prospects of these students have already been damaged seriously; this does not mean that these individuals should be written-off. Quite the contrary, they, too, like the educators and the parents, could be retrained and resocialized. Admittedly, the task would be onerous, primarily because we would be required to undo what has taken many years to produce. Another way of saying this is that it takes a great deal of time and effort to produce a *good* non-college-bound product, failure, dropout, delinquent, criminal, and so on. Hence, we should not expect any instant cures or miracles.

SOME FINAL COMMENTS

Yet . . . this is exactly what the people are looking for. Thus, demands are being made continually for more laws, longer sentences, more cells, and the like—demands that are predicated firmly upon the belief that if we really crack down on crime, this will solve the problem. Unfortunately, the call for the use of "quick-fix" or "band-aid" solutions or measures will not begin to get the job done. As an illustration, we can incarcerate more people for longer periods of time; however, this will only aggravate the situation, primarily because we will have an even greater number of individuals operating under the brunt of stigmatizing labels—labels that will certainly mitigate against the probability that one will elect to go straight; this, it may be recalled, was one of the basic messages offered by Ray's research. In effect, addicts found it very difficult to structure and maintain an abstainer identity, both in the personal and public sense. Not only did they experience difficulty with the other addicts but non-addicts continued to respond to them as addicts. Equally important, the attempted abstainer was not allowed to assume nor act out the non-addict role. And predictably, most relapsed and moved back into the addict world. The same situation holds for the rest of society's deviants or ex-deviants; they, too, may try to build a non-deviant personal and public identity, and a few will actually succeed in doing so. All, however, will soon learn that society does not look too kindly upon its deviators, and they will also come to realize that structures, environments, and traditions are relatively unchanging. And, as I have argued rather repeatedly, if change is to occur, it must come from within the individual. It is he or she who must be rehabilitated.

Probably the most curious, as well as perplexing, feature of such a position or argument concerns the failure of the proponents to recognize the fact that most behavior, however defined, emerges out of a group or social psychological context; this holds regardless of whether we are focusing on the family, the peer group, the gang, the skid row culture, the nudist society, or the homosexual subculture. Thus, an ideology such as the preceding (i.e., promoting the notion of individual failure, pathology, or deficiency) must be viewed as being eminently uninformed, unsubstantiated, and most unscientific. It also contains some potentially damaging, as well as dangerous, features. For example, when we get down to the point of actually doing something about failure, crime, or deviance, we stop being sociologists or social scientists and become psychiatrists, psychologists, or some other type of clinician. Henceforth, we neglect the value and normative systems of which one is or has been implicated in—the very same structures that have given definition and shape to the person's behavior, identities, and self-image—and go to work on the mind; this is a most unfortunate and unproductive strategy, and it becomes especially so when considered in the light of the logic, theory, and evidence pointing to the need for rehabilitating some social systems and institutions. The best illustrations in support of this need, at least as found in this book, would have to be the evidence indicating how the *disadvantaged* or *powerless* (broadly defined) are frequently perceived and responded to by our schools, our mental institutions, our police departments, our courts, and our parole units. It is not a pretty sight.

Promoting the ideology of individual failure or deficiency is associated with other, equally subtle and pernicious, effects. Most prominently, focusing in on the individual deflects our attention away from the real problems. If, for example, people buy the arguments—and many certainly do—that school failure is an individual problem, that gang behavior is a function of a disturbed psyche, or that homosexuality and prostitution are manifestations of some type of genetic or biological abnormality, then the search for the actual causes or origins of these behaviors stops; this, too, is an unfortunate state of affairs. In effect, and as I have also argued, blaming the individual is and continues to be a very handy and effective political smokescreen. If, for example, the politicians, educators, and law enforcement officials can blame the individual, then they do not have to deal with the basic fact that the schools can, by virtue of the way they dispense education, contribute very heavily to the production of careers in failure, dropout, crime, deviance, and so on; nor do they have to deal with the fact that gang activity, when analyzed in terms of the normative systems that produce and demand such behavior, is often viewed as normal behavior by its members. This should not be taken to mean that violence should be tolerated. It should not. What these statements do mean is that we *have* some good evidence available to us. Being able to develop and implement programs on the basis of this information is where the difficulty comes in. How many politicians, for example, are willing to indict the educational or law enforcement system? Concomitantly, how many would be willing to provide the necessary funds for the restructuring of the educational system, as well as for the retraining of educational personnel, parents, and others? Quite obviously, none, if they are concerned with enhancing their political careers, would dare to venture into these areas; these are politically hot issues. Yet, and as I have illustrated, changes are needed—changes that could, in fact, be made. And changes that would make a difference.

Finally, failure to address the structural-organizational sources of crime, delinquency, and deviance only gives further credence to a clinical-medical model of explanation; this, too, is associated with some detrimental consequences. Most significantly, it not only allows for the continued perpetuation of myths about the nature and extent of social deviance but, in a related sense, it also provides the basis upon which many irresponsible statements are made. Like my comments relative to the school, there is, however, a way out. As a start, people should not be allowed to make statements about crime until they have studied it thoroughly and begin to know something about it; this holds for the politicians, the social scientists, the practitioners, and others. As an illustration, campaigning on the basis of a "lock them up" or "get tough on crime" plank will certainly produce the votes; however, such a platform, even if translated into policy, will not make a substantial dent in crime. Crime, whatever its variety, is, as I have demonstrated, more complex than this. And the basic flaw with an ideology or mentality such as this is that it is much too simplistic and clinical in nature. It also, as I have stressed rather repeatedly, fails to incorporate a direct and systematic concern for those factors, conditions, and environments that have actually given shape to the behavior or behaviors under scrutiny. Structures thus remain intact....

Note

1. For a more complete discussion of the works mentioned thus far, see Chapter 5 in D. H. Kelly, *Creating School Failure, Youth Crime, and Deviance*. Los Angeles: Trident Shop, 1982.

Reference

Bryan, J. H. (1965) "Apprenticeships in prostitution." *Social Problems* 12:287–297.

Cohen, A.K. (1955) *Delinquent Boys*. New York: Free Press.

Hargreaves, D. (1967) *Social Relations in a Secondary School*. New York: Humanities Press.

Miller W. B. (1958) "Lower class culture as a generating milieu of gang delinquency." *The Journal of Social Issues* 14:5–19.

Ray, M. B. (1961) "The cycle of abstinence and relapse among heroin addicts." *Social Problems* 9:132–140.

Reiss, A. J., Jr. (1961) "The social integration of queers and peers." *Social Problems* 9:102–120

Scheff, T. J. (1964) "The societal reaction to deviance: Ascriptive elements in the psychiatric screening of mental patients in a midwestern state." *Social Problems* 11:401–413.

Wallace, S. E. (1965) *Skid Row as a Way of Life*. Totowa, N. J.: Bedminster.

Weinberg, M. S. (1966) "Becoming a nudist." *Psychiatry* 29:15–24.

Acknowledgments *(cont'd)*

J. Mark Watson, "Outlaw Motorcyclists: An Outgrowth of Lower Class Cultural Concerns," reprinted from *Deviant Behavior* (1980), vol. 2, no. 1, pp. 31–48, Taylor & Francis, Inc. Washington, D.C., 20005. Reproduced by permission. All rights reserved.

Gresham M. Sykes and David Matza, "Techniques of Neutralization: A Theory of Delinquency," reprinted from *American Sociological Review*, vol. 22, 1957, pp. 666–670.

Diana Scully and Joseph Marolla, "Convicted Rapists' Vocabulary of Motive: Excuses and Justifications," Copyright © 1984 by the Society for the Study of Social Problems. Reprinted from *Social Problems*, vol. 31, no. 5, June 1984, pp. 530–544 by permission of the University of California Press Journals.

Robert K. Merton, "Social Structure and Anomie," reprinted from *American Sociological Review*, vol. 3, 1938, pp. 672–682.

John M. Hagedorn, "Homeboys, Dope Fiends, Legits, and New Jacks," reprinted by permission of The American Society of Criminology from *Criminology*, vol. 32, no. 2, May 1994, pp. 197–219.

Jeffrey H. Reiman, "A Radical Perspective on Crime," reprinted with the permission of Simon & Schuster from the Macmillan College Division title *The Rich Get Richer and the Poor Get Prison*, by Jeffrey H. Reiman. Copyright © 1970 by Jeffrey H. Reiman.

William J. Chambliss, "A Sociological Analysis of the Law of Vagrancy," Copyright © 1964 by the Society for the Study of Social Problems. Reprinted from *Social Problems*, vol. 12, no. 1, Summer 1964, pp. 67–77, by permission of the University of California Press Journals.

Travis Hirschi, "A Control Theory of Delinquency," pp. 16–26. Copyright © 1969 by The Regents of the University of California. Reprinted by permission of the author.

Neal Shover and David Honaker, "The Socially Bounded Decision Making of Persistent Property Offenders," reprinted from *Howard Journal*, vol. 31 (1992), pp. 276–293. Reprinted by permission of the Howard League.

Howard S. Becker, "Career Deviance," reprinted by permission of The Free Press, a Division of Simon & Schuster. From *Outsiders*, by Howard S. Becker. Copyright © 1963 by The Free Press.

Penelope A. McLorg and Diane E. Taub, "Anorexia Nervosa and Bulimia: The Development of Deviant Identities," reprinted from *Deviant Behavior* (1992), vol. 13, no. 3, pp. 291–311, Taylor & Francis, Inc. Washington, D.C., 20005. Reproduced by permission. All rights reserved.

Erving Goffman, "Information Control and Personal Identity: The Discredited and the Discreditable," reprinted by permission of Prentice Hall, a Division of Simon & Schuster. From *Stigma* (1962) pp. 41–48. Copyright © 1995 assigned to Prentice Hall, a Trade Division of Simon & Schuster, Inc.

Patricia A. Adler and Peter Adler, "Tinydopers: A Case Study of Deviant Socialization," reprinted from *Symbolic Interaction*, vol. 1, no. 2 (Spring, 1978), pp. 90–105, by permission.

Joseph W. Schneider and Peter Conrad, "In the Closet with Illness: Epilepsy, Stigma Potential and Information Control," Copyright © 1980 by the Society for the Study of Social Problems. Reprinted from *Social Problems*, vol. 22, no. 1, October 1980, pp. 32–44 by permission of the University of California Press Journals.

Joan K. Jackson, "The Adjustment of the Family to the Crisis of Alcoholism," reprinted from the *Quarterly Journal of Studies in Alcohol*, vol. 15, pp. 562–586, 1954, by permission of the Center for Alcohol Studies, P.O. Box 969, Piscataway, New Jersey, 08854.

Kathleen J. Ferraro and John M. Johnson, "How Women Experience Battering: The Process of Victimization," Copyright © 1983 by the Society for the Study of Social Problems. Reprinted from *Social Problems*, vol. 39, no. 3, February 1983, pp. 325–335, by permission of the University of California Press Journals.

Delos H. Kelly, "Bureaucratic Slots and Client Processing," from *Creating School Failure, Youth Crime, and Deviance*, by Delos H. Kelly, Los Angeles: Trident Shop, 1982. Copyright © by Delos H. Kelly.

Jennifer Hunt and Peter K. Manning, "The Social Context of Police Lying," reprinted from *Symbolic Interaction*, vol. 14, no. 1, pp. 51–70 (Spring, 1991). reprinted by permission of JAI Press.

Elijah Anderson, "The Police and the Black Male," pp. 190–206, from *Streetwise*, by Elijah Anderson. Reprinted by permission of the University of Chicago Press (1990).

Leslie Margolin, "Deviance on Record: Techniques for Labeling Child Abusers in Official Documents," Copyright © 1992 by the Society for the Study of Social Problems. Reprinted from *Social Problems*, vol. 39, no. 1, February 1992, pp. 58–70, by permission of the University of California Press Journals.